Germany FOR DUMMIES®

1ST EDITION

by Donald Olson

WILEY

Wiley Publishing, Inc.

Germany For Dummies® 1st Edition

Published by
Wiley Publishing, Inc.
909 Third Avenue
New York, NY 10022
www.wiley.com

Copyright © 2003 by Wiley Publishing, Inc., Indianapolis, Indiana

Published simultaneously in Canada

For general information on our other products and services or to obtain technical support, please contact our Customer Care Department within the U.S. at 800-762-2974, outside the U.S. at 317-572-3993, or fax 317-572-4002.

Wiley also publishes its books in a variety of electronic formats. Some content that appears in print may not be available in electronic books.

Library of Congress Cataloging-in-Publication Data:

Library of Congress Control Number: 2003101849

ISBN: 0-7645-5478-6

ISSN: 1541-6429

Manufactured in the United States of America

10 9 8 7 6 5 4 3 2 1

About the Author

Novelist, playwright, and travel writer, **Donald Olson** is the author of *London For Dummies* and *England For Dummies,* which won the Lowell Thomas Travel Writing Award for Best Guidebook in 2002. He has contributed travel stories to the *New York Times,* National Geographic Books, and many other national publications, and has written guidebooks to Berlin, Italy, Oregon, and the Pacific Northwest. His plays have been seen in Europe and the United States. Bantam London published his novel *The Confessions of Aubrey Beardsley.* Kensington Books will publish his latest novel, *My Three Husbands,* in 2003 under the pen name Swan Adamson.

FOR DUMMIES®

The fun and easy way™ to travel!

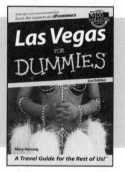

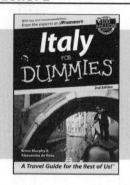
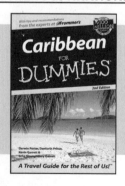
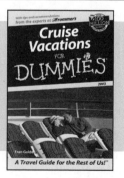

Maps at a Glance

Table of Contents

Part IV: Munich and Southern Germany 215

Chapter 14: Munich: Capital of Gemütlichkeit 217

Chapter 15: Bavaria: The German Alps and Fairy-Tale Castles 253

Introduction

. . . .

So you're going to Germany. *Wunderbar!* But what parts of Deutschland (Germany) do you want to visit? Because of this country's many offerings, answering this question isn't easy. But don't worry. I can help you make the right choices for your vacation.

Situated in the very heart of Europe, Germany stretches from the Alps in the south to Denmark and the Baltic and North seas in the north. France bounds Germany to the southwest, with Luxembourg, Belgium, and the Netherlands to the west and the Czech Republic and Poland to the east. Because of these shared borders, a certain amount of cultural and culinary cross-pollination has occurred within Germany, making the various regions very different from one another. For example, you find plenty of French cuisine in the southwest and an emphasis on seafood in the far north. The sober brick architecture that predominates in the far north gives way to exuberant baroque churches and palaces in the south.

Dramatic regional differences also exist in the landscape. The sunny southwest is where you find the Bodensee, one of the largest lakes in Europe, and the forested hills of the scenic Schwarzwald (Black Forest). In the west, every crag in the Rhine Valley seems to have its own romantic legend — or carefully tended vineyard. Drive or take the train a couple of hours east and you're in the Bavarian Alps, where the peaks are tipped with snow until May. In the far north, the location of the country's great ports, you find a flat maritime landscape.

Germany isn't a huge country — on a superfast train you can buzz from Berlin in the north to Munich in the south in about eight hours — but sightseeing possibilities pack the terrain.

So what cities or regions or specific attractions do you want to see? Berlin, the exciting new capital of a newly reunified republic? Elegant, fun-loving Munich, the city where most Germans would live if they could? The great port city of Hamburg? The romantic university town of Heidelberg? Are there specific landscapes you want to see, such as the Bavarian Alps or the Rhine Valley? What castles and cathedrals would you like to visit? The fairy-tale castles built by King Ludwig of Bavaria are not just images on travel posters. They are real places with amazing stories attached to them. And how about other historic sites? Do you want to visit Weimar, where Goethe lived, or Leipzig, where Bach conducted? Do you want to stroll down Frankfurt's Zeil, the busiest shopping street in Germany? Are you interested in seeing eastern Germany now that the border is open between east and west? The eastern city of Dresden, after all, is one of the great art cities of Europe.

Germany has an embarrassment of riches. In this book, I help you choose from among its many highlights to create the best trip for you. Together we can plan a *wunderschöne Reise* (wonderful journey).

About This Book

This is a selective guidebook to Germany. From an enormous list of possibilities, I chose only what I consider to be the best and most essential places for first-time visitors. If you're new to this part of the world, this guidebook is for you.

I exclude places that other, more exhaustive guidebooks routinely include. So much is really worth seeing in Germany that you don't need to waste your time with the second-rate, the overrated, or the boring. And, you can bypass places that are difficult to reach or of interest only to a scholar.

Use *Germany For Dummies* as a reference guide. You can, of course, start at the first page and read all the way through to the end. But, if you've already been to Germany and know the basics of international travel, you can flip to the specific part you need or hone in on one specific chapter.

Please be advised that travel information is subject to change at any time — and this is especially true of prices. I therefore suggest that you write or call ahead for confirmation when making your travel plans. The authors, editors, and publisher cannot be held responsible for the experiences of readers while traveling. Your safety is important to us, however, so we encourage you to stay alert and be aware of your surroundings.

Conventions Used in This Book

I recently tried to extract some information from a guidebook and felt that I needed training in hieroglyphics to interpret all the different symbols. I'm happy to report that the user-friendly *Germany For Dummies* is not like that. The use of symbols and abbreviations is kept to a minimum.

Credit card abbreviations include AE (American Express), DC (Diners Club), MC (MasterCard), and V (Visa).

I also include some general pricing information to help you as you decide where to unpack your bags or dine on the local cuisine. In addition to giving you exact prices, I employ a system of dollar signs ($) to show a range of costs for one night in a hotel (double room, year-round) or a meal at a restaurant (appetizer, entree, and dessert). Check out the following table to decipher the dollar signs:

Cost	Hotel	Restaurant
$	$125 and under	$20 or under
$$	$126 to $175	$21 to $30
$$$	$176 to $225	$31 to $40
$$$$	$226 and up	$41 and up

Prices in this guide for hotels, restaurants, attractions, and services are given only in euros (€), the currency that replaced the deutsche mark in 2002. Prices are not translated into dollars because as of press time the euro had achieved parity with the dollar. That makes a trip to Germany even easier for you. You no longer have to calculate prices in deutsche marks. The price in euros is basically the same as in dollars.

I first give the name of a sight in German, followed by an English translation. If you don't speak or read German, the words look daunting, I know. But if you take this book with you, and are looking for a directional sign, the German name is the one that you'll need to know.

Foolish Assumptions

I made some assumptions about you, *lieber Leser* (dear reader), including:

- ✔ When it comes to Germany, you may be a beginner but you're definitely not a *Dumkopf*. You want advice and answers, but you don't want to be talked down to.

- ✔ You've never been to Germany and want to learn more about this country, starting with the basics. Or, perhaps, you've been to Germany and now want to explore further.

- ✔ You're not looking for a book that provides all the information available about Germany or that lists every hotel, restaurant, or attraction available to you. Instead, you're looking for a book that focuses on the places that will give you the best or most unique experience in Germany.

If you fit any of these criteria, then *Germany For Dummies* gives you the information you're looking for!

How This Book Is Organized

The book is broken down into seven parts. The first two parts deal with trip planning and organization. They provide information, advice, and suggestions that can help you map out a wonderful holiday. The other parts of the book are devoted to Berlin, Munich, and different regions of the country. All of the parts can be read independently, so if you want to zero in on a specific city or area — Hamburg, say, or the Bavarian Alps — you can turn right to that part.

Part 1: Getting Started

This first part introduces Germany and gives you some excellent reasons for going there. This overview gives you the big picture. The individual chapters help you decide when to visit and what to see, give you sound advice on planning a realistic budget, tell you about German food and beer, and provide special tips for Germany-bound travelers who may have special needs or interests: families, travelers with disabilities, gay and lesbian travelers, and Jewish travelers.

Part 11: Ironing Out the Details

This part helps take some of the wrinkles out of the trip-planning stage. I talk about your options for airlines and airfares, how package tours can save you bucks, and what kinds of guided tours are available. This part helps you to decide what form of transportation (train, rental car) to use to get around the country and explains what kind of accommodation you can expect for your money. Pretrip loose ends, from passports to booking hotel rooms, are also dealt with.

Part 111: Berlin and Eastern Germany

All you need to know about Germany's capital and most exciting city is contained in this part. Along with providing a basic orientation, I point out the best hotels and restaurants and the top attractions to the east and west and all around this remarkable city, including the palace of Sanssouci in Potsdam. In this part, I also visit the great eastern German cities of Dresden, Leipzig, and Weimar. Difficult to visit during the Communist years, these remarkable showcases of art and culture are now "open for business." From Dresden, I tell you how to take a boat trip into a scenic region called Saxon Switzerland. I also include a description of the memorial at Buchenwald concentration camp near Weimar and an overview of touring options in the Thuringian Forest.

Part 1V: Munich and Southern Germany

Munich, Germany's "secret capital" and most popular big city, gets a big chapter of its own. I provide information on how to get there, how to get around, and what to see, plus a selection of great hotels and special restaurants. I also include an easy trip to Nymphenburg Palace and the moving memorial at Dachau. From Munich, the next chapter heads south to the Bavarian Alps and the fairy-tale castles (Neuschwanstein, Linderhof, and Hohenschwangau) associated with King Ludwig of

Bavaria. If you want to rent a car, I include an overview of the Deutsche Alpenstrasse (German Alpine Road), one of the most beautiful drives in Europe, and introduce you to three Bavarian towns: Garmisch-Partenkirchen, Füssen, and Oberammergau. The last chapter visits the Schwarzwald (Black Forest) and the Bodensee (Lake Constance), scenic hotspots in Germany's sunny southwestern corner.

Part V: Western Germany

In this part, I tell you all about the lively Rhineside city of Cologne, founded by the Romans 2,000 years ago, with its world-famous cathedral and array of first-class museums. I also provide information on side trips, including boat trips down the mighty Rhine, with its castles and vineyards, and the picturesque Mosel River. Frankfurt, with the busiest international airport in Germany, gets a chapter of its own. You find plenty to see and enjoy in "Mainhattan," as Frankfurt is known, from designer skyscrapers and great museums to distinctive apple-wine taverns. Rounding out my coverage of western Germany are two important cities: Heidelberg, with the oldest university in Germany and the brooding ruins of a mighty castle, and Nuremberg, one of Germany's most attractive cities.

Part VI: Northern Germany

Northern Germany has a personality uniquely its own. Bordering on the North Sea and the Baltic Sea, this maritime world is where you find Hamburg, Germany's largest port city. I hit the highlights, from the mighty harbor to the lurid Reeperbahn (where *un*coverage might better describe the sights). Lübeck, once capital of the powerful Hanseatic League, is a nearby picturesque city of Gothic church spires and ancient brick buildings.

Part VII: The Part of Tens

The Part of Tens allows me to focus a little more attention on extra-special places and sights I want you to know about. My "tens" include lessons on the German language, ten great hotels, and ten outstanding museums.

You also find two other elements near the back of this book. I include an appendix with an A to Z list of fast facts, like how the telephone system works and what numbers to call in an emergency. You also find a list of toll-free telephone numbers and Web sites for airlines, car-rental agencies, and hotel chains serving Germany, as well as resources for locating additional information on specific cities or areas. All of this is followed by a few helpful worksheets to help make your trip planning easier.

Icons Used in This Book

In the margins, you find five different icons, little pictures that point out helpful trip-planning details or items that are just for fun.

Bargain Alert is my favorite icon, and I suspect it may be yours, too. I'm not cheap, but I love to save money. You see this icon every time I tell you about something that can save you money.

This icon points out tidbits about German personalities and places of special interest.

I'm not an alarmist, so you won't find too many of these icons. If you do see one, I want you to be aware of something such as a scam that could cost you money or a hazardous situation.

Traveling with children? Keep your eyes peeled for this icon, which points out hotels, restaurants, or attractions that welcome children or that kids actually enjoy.

The Tip icon highlights useful bits of information that can save you time or enhance your travel experience. A Tip alerts you to something that you may not otherwise consider or even know about.

Where to Go from Here

To Germany, of course. How you want to use this guide is up to you. You can start at the beginning and read the book straight through to the end. Or you can start anywhere in between and extract information as you want or need it. I hope you'll think of me as your guide or companion on this journey to Germany, which is sure to be *wunderbar*.

Part I
Getting Started

The 5th Wave   By Rich Tennant

"...and remember, no more German tongue twisters until you know the language better."

In this part . . .

Where to begin? This part gives you the advice and information you need to start planning your trip to Germany. **Chapter 1** is a brief overview that introduces you to the best Germany has to offer and sketches the main events in Germany's long and tumultuous history. **Chapter 2** offers more specific information to help you plan when and where you'd like to go. In **Chapter 3,** I suggest four possible itineraries for visitors who want to sample a wide range of sights. In **Chapter 4,** I get into the nitty-gritty of *Geld* — that is, money — so you have at least an approximate idea of what things cost. And finally, in **Chapter 5,** I offer specific advice and tips for visitors with special needs and interests: families traveling with children, senior travelers, gay and lesbian travelers, and Jewish travelers.

Chapter 1

Discovering the Best of Germany

- -

In This Chapter

▶ Experiencing the greatest cities

▶ Exploring romantic landscapes, castles, and palaces

▶ Discovering German arts and culture

▶ Eating and drinking German-style

▶ Shopping in outdoor markets and indoor emporiums

- -

*G*ermany holds a special fascination for travelers. This land of contrasting moods appeals to visitors for many different reasons. Perhaps you, like millions of others, have German ancestors. You grew up hearing a few words of German, or eating German food, and now you want to see for yourself what the country of your forebears is like. Or perhaps you have an image of Germany in your mind — a castle on a hilltop, a palace in a landscaped garden, or a giant beer hall with an oom-pah-pah band — and you want to check it out for yourself. As many different reasons exist for wanting to visit Germany as there are tourists who arrive daily, by the thousands, at the airports in Berlin, Munich, and Frankfurt.

This chapter introduces you to some of the things that make traveling in Germany such a fascinating experience. I present a broad overview so you can begin to identify those aspects of Germany that interest you most. Consider this a rundown of the best Germany has to offer.

Touring Germany's Cities

When it comes to size and tourist interest, Berlin and Munich are the two biggies. But Germany has scores of smaller or lesser-known cities to lure visitors.

Checking out brilliant Berlin

If you ask me, **Berlin** (Chapters 11 and 12) is the most exciting city in Europe. With its endlessly dramatic history and cache of cultural and artistic riches, Berlin has always had a major-league buzz. But since 1989, when the Wall separating East and West Germany came down, Germany's largest city has become something of an international superstar. Once again, Berlin is Germany's capital, the lightning rod between the newly unified East and West. More happens in Berlin than in any other city in Germany. The amount of new building is staggering, and the restoration of historic museums and monuments is nothing less than amazing. The pulse of Berlin is felt throughout Europe, and when you're walking down Berlin's two most famous avenues, the Kurfürstendamm or Unter den Linden, you may feel it, too.

Marveling at magnificent Munich

Germany has two capitals. Berlin, the country's official capital, is a northern city with a heady and exciting urban grittiness. **Munich** (Chapter 14), the "unofficial" capital, is a southern German city where the urban pleasures are as soft and sweet as *Schlagsahne* (whipped cream) on a rich slab of cake, or as exuberant as an oom-pah-pah band in a giant beer hall during Oktoberfest. The capital of Bavaria is sensuous, sophisticated, and fun-loving. Munich is far more beautiful than Berlin, with a splendid array of baroque and neoclassical churches, palaces, and monuments. Munich rivals Berlin in the category of cultural offerings, and its magic snares the hearts of millions of visitors each year.

Discovering other urban greats

Cities like **Hamburg** (Chapter 20) with its great port; **Cologne** (Chapter 17) with its Romanesque churches, Roman remains, and Rhine setting; and **Frankfurt** (Chapter 18) with its bevy of skyscrapers, yield plenty of pleasant surprises. Romantic **Heidelberg** and medieval **Nuremberg** have much to offer as well (all in Chapter 19). In all of these cities you find first-class museums, historic sights, fine hotels and restaurants, and up-to-the-minute European glamour. And now that the country is reunited, you have an opportunity to visit the great cities in eastern Germany, too. Historic treasures and a fresh infusion of energy and optimism make **Dresden** and **Leipzig** (both Chapter 13) so appealing.

Roaming Romantic Landscapes

Whether you travel by train, boat, or car, Germany offers a remarkably diverse landscape with scenic highlights. Cruises down the **River Rhine** (Chapter 17) take you past castle-crowned crags and legendary sights such as Lorelei rock. Sophisticated health spas and recreational activities abound in the forest-clad mountains of the **Schwarzwald** (Chapter 16). Part of Germany's sunny southwestern border is an enormous lake, the **Bodensee** (Chapter 16), where semi-tropical gardens flourish and life has an almost Italian languor. Perhaps the most dramatic of all German landscapes is the **Bavarian Alps** (Chapter 15), where snow-clad peaks tower above the chalets of alpine villages.

From Dresden you can easily explore a scenic region called **Saxon Switzerland** (Chapter 13), where rocky cliffs rise dramatically above the Elbe River. And you don't have to be a wine-lover to appreciate the beauty found in the great wine-growing regions of the **Rhine** and **Mosel valleys** or along the **Deutsche Weinstrasse (German Wine Road)** west of Heidelberg (all in Chapter 17). Vineyards add to the attractiveness of these memorable landscapes, where you also find medieval towns, castle ruins, and ancient churches.

Marveling at Castles and Palaces

For many visitors, the quintessential image associated with Germany is a castle on a hilltop. Indeed, you do see castles scattered throughout the country. Ruined castles dot the landscape of the **Rhine** (Chapter 17) and enhance its romantic appeal. Enormous castle ruins crown **Heidelberg** and **Nuremberg** (both in Chapter 19). But for sheer opulence, nothing can compare to the fairy-tale castles built in the 19th century by Ludwig II of Bavaria. **Linderhof** and **Neuschwanstein** (Chapter 15), which are preserved almost exactly as they were in Ludwig's lifetime, are the most visited attractions in Germany.

Germany is also rich in palaces. **Charlottenburg Palace** in Berlin (Chapter 12) is home to several museums as well as staterooms that can be visited on guided tours. Even more remarkable (in part because it suffered almost no damage during World War II) is **Sanssouci** (Chapter 12), Frederick the Great's 18th-century rococo palace in Potsdam, just outside of Berlin. **Nymphenburg Palace** on the outskirts of Munich is another king-sized showplace, as is the enormous **Residenz** right in the heart of the city (both Chapter 14). With their precious paintings and porcelains and furniture, these stately homes reveal aspects of German life and the monarchy that lasted up until 1918.

Enjoying Awesome Arts and Culture

When you visit Germany you can enjoy a year-round feast of arts and culture. World-class museums exhibiting painting collections that span every artistic era in Germany and Europe fill cities like Berlin, Munich, Cologne, and Frankfurt. Works by Old Masters abound, and so do museums devoted entirely to classical Greek and Roman sculpture and modern and contemporary international art. You find museums for every taste and interest, from the **Mercedes-Benz Museum** (Chapter 23) in Stuttgart to the science-and-technology-oriented **Deutsches Museum** (Chapter 14) in Munich and the charming **Spielzeugmuseum** (Toy Museum; Chapter 19) in Nuremberg. The **Pergamon Museum** (Chapter 12) in eastern Berlin's historic **Museumsinsel** (Museum Island) is the repository of fabulous archeological treasures, and the same city's **Ägyptisches Museum** (Egyptian Museum) displays the world-famous bust of the ancient Egyptian queen Nerfertiti.

For lovers of classical music and opera, Germany is a gold mine. **Berlin** alone is home to three major symphony orchestras and three opera companies. A trip to **Leipzig** (Chapter 13) can include a concert by the world-renowned Gewandhaus Orchestra; a visit to **Dresden** (Chapter 13) can be made even more memorable by an evening at the famed Semper Opera. German churches throughout the country regularly offer organ and choral concerts, and concert halls are home to symphonic and chamber concerts and recitals.

You find no lack of pop performances, either. Major rock stars and entertainers regularly tour Germany. And, for those who know a bit of the language or want to experience something unique, German cabarets and variety shows are still a time-honored part of popular culture. The country of Goethe and Schiller pays special attention to theater — every city of any size has a playhouse where actors perform the classics and contemporary dramas.

Feasting on German Food

German cooking tends to be hearty and filling, with many regional variations and specialties. Seasonal specialties include *Spargel* (white asparagus) in May and June, *Matjes* (white herring) in June and July, *Erdbeeren* (strawberries) in spring, *Forelle* (trout) in the summer, and *Reh* (venison) in the fall. In the country as a whole, you can taste about 150 different types of sausage; Berlin, Munich, and Nuremberg all have their special kinds. When it comes to baked goods — bread and pastries — Germany has more variety than any country in the world. You can choose among 300 different types of bread and about 1,200 varieties of biscuits and cakes.

Ratskellers, traditional cellar restaurants beneath a city's *Rathaus* (Town Hall), always serve good and fairly inexpensive traditional food and wine. Restaurants that serve French, Italian, and an international roster of cuisines fill Germany's larger cities. And although not kind to the waistline, the German tradition of afternoon *Kaffee und Kuchen* (coffee and cake) is always something to look forward to. Look out for regional specialties, too: **Lübeck** (Chapter 20), for example, is the capital of *marzipan* (almond paste), and **Nuremberg** (Chapter 19) is famous for its *Lebkuchen* (spice cakes). German wines, mostly from grapes grown in the scenic Rhine and Mosel valleys (Chapter 17), provide excellent accompaniments to any meal. And German beers are

Sampling German beer

Germans have long been among the world's top beer drinkers, quaffing enough foamy brew to rank in the top five of the annual liters-per-person ranking. *Bier* (pronounced *beer*) remains a vital part of the culture, so much so that the right to drink beer is written into some labor contracts, and a beer with lunch in the factory cafeteria is taken for granted. The traditional *Biergarten* (beer garden) with tables set outdoors under trees or trellises is still very popular, especially in southern Germany. A *Bräuhaus* (*broy*-house) serves its own brew along with local food. You can also order beer at a cafe, a restaurant, or any bar.

When you're ordering *ein Bier* (*ine* beer, meaning "a beer") in Germany, you have many choices. The range of beer varieties includes **Altbier, Bockbier, Export, Kölsch, Lager, Malzbier, Märzbier, Pils, Vollbier,** and **Weizenbier.** The ratio of ingredients, brewing temperature and technique, alcoholic content, aging time, color, and taste all contribute to a German beer's unique qualities. A German law adopted in 1516 dictates that German beer may contain no ingredients other than hops, malt (barley), yeast, and water.

Dark and sweet Malzbier (*malltz*-beer; malt beer) contains hardly any alcohol. Vollbier (*foal*-beer, the standard stock beer) has 4% alcohol, Export has 5%, and Bockbier has 6%. Pils, or Pilsener, beers are light and contain more hops. Weizenbier (*vie*-tsen-beer), made from wheat, is a Bavarian white beer. Märzbier (*maertz*-beer), or "March beer," is dark and strong. The most popular beer in Germany is Pils (Pilsner), followed by Export. **Alkoholfreies Bier** (al-ko-hole-*fry*-iss, meaning nonalcoholic) has grown in popularity in Germany; but "lite" beers have never really caught on.

To order a beer, decide whether you want a **dunkles Bier** (dark beer, brewed with darkly roasted malt fermented for a long period of time) or a **helles Bier** (light beer, brewed from malt dried and baked by the local brewery). You ask for *ein Grosses* (ine *grow*-ses, meaning large) or *ein Kleines* (ine *kly*-nis, meaning small), and tell the waiter or tavernkeeper whether you want *ein Bier vom Fass* (fum fahss, meaning draft beer) or in a *Flasche* (*flah*-shuh, meaning bottle).

Germany has few national beer brands, so the brand of beer offered generally depends on where you are in the country. When in doubt, always order the local brew on draft. In Cologne, for instance, try the light and delicious Kölsch (coalsh). In Berlin you can order a special Berliner Weisse (*vie*-suh), a wheat beer flavored with raspberry or woodruff syrup. The beer is always served cold, but not too cold, in an appropriate beer glass or mug, with a long-lasting head of white foam. A proper draft beer, according to the Germans, can't be poured in less than seven minutes to achieve the proper head.

legendary. Each city has its favorites, brewed right in the area. To help you with your gastronomic interests, I talk about regional foods and wines and beers in the "Where to dine" sections of this guidebook. You also find a primer of German food and dining terms on the Cheat Sheet in the front of this book. *Guten Appetit!*

Shopping for Local Treasures

Shopping is an activity some people do well and others detest. For those who love to shop, Germany offers a retail-minded paradise. In this sophisticated shopping country, you find the latest fashions and newest design trends. All large German cities have their primary shopping streets, such as the **Ku-Damm** in Berlin (Chapter 12) and the **Zeil** in Frankfurt (Chapter 18). But part of the fun is exploring off-the-beaten-path areas, where you can find anything from a store with kitsch from the 1920s to a candy shop selling chocolate-covered marzipan. Germany is famous for its porcelain, especially hand-painted Meissen and pure-white Hochst.

Most German cities have lively **market squares** where vendors sell fresh produce, cheese, meats, fish, herbs, baked goods, honey, sausages, or plants. Even if you don't buy anything, these outdoor markets are great fun to explore. The **Viktualienmarkt** (Food Market) in Munich is a wonderful place where you can easily hang out all day. You also find weekly **flea markets** (a *Flohmarkt* or a *Trödelmarkt* in German), where old clothes, medals, housewares, postcards, books, and just about anything else you can name shows up. Shopping becomes a kind of magical experience during the Christmas season, when cities throughout Germany set up month-long **Christmas markets.** While choirs sing and musicians play, you can drink hot spiced wine and browse the bright stalls for hand-made ornaments, baked goodies, and regional handicrafts.

Remembering the Nazi-Era Past

As the saying goes, those who don't learn from the past are doomed to repeat it. Germany's Nazi-era past and the enormity of the crimes committed during World War II are facts that can't be glossed over or overlooked. You can visit Germany today and entirely avoid any and all reminders of that gruesome chapter of German history. But for those who want or need to remember World War II, and perhaps try to come to terms with its horrors, Germany is full of memorials. The most wrenching are the memorials at the concentration camps **Buchenwald** (Chapter 13), near the eastern German town of Weimar, and **Dachau** (Chapter 14), northwest of Munich. **Berlin** (Chapter 12) is particularly rich in memorials that commemorate the hundreds of thousands of Jews, gays, gypsies (*Sinta,* in German), and other groups that were murdered by the National Socialists between 1933 and 1945. In Berlin, you find walking tours that take visitors past Nazi-era buildings, and exhibits that interpret Nazi methods. Germany's Jewish past is the subject of Berlin's remarkable new **Jüdisches Museum** (Jewish Museum), the most comprehensive of its kind. In Berlin, you also find preserved segments of the **Wall,** visceral reminders of Germany's more recent past as a country divided between conflicting ideologies.

Chapter 2

Deciding When and Where to Go

In This Chapter

▶ Exploring Germany's main points of interest

▶ Getting a grip on the seasons: tourism and weather

▶ Flipping through the country's calendar of events

When do you want to visit Germany, and what do you want to see? In this chapter, I help you to narrow your focus so you can start your trip planning in earnest. This chapter points out the highlights of each region and gives you the lowdown on the weather so you can determine the best destinations and the time of year for your visit. You also find a calendar of events so you can time your trip to coincide with, or avoid, special festivals and happenings.

Everywhere You Want to Be: What This Book Covers and Why

Germany For Dummies, 1st Edition, is a selective guidebook, geared to first-time travelers who want to know more about Germany's leading sights. I don't cover every state, region, and city in Deutschland, only the essential highlights. My aim in this book is to introduce you to the best cities, historic towns, special sights, and scenic regions that Germany has to offer. To help figure out which regions to visit during your trip, check out the following thumbnail sketches. For locations, see "The Regions in Brief" map in this chapter.

Discovering Berlin and Eastern Germany

When I say new, I mean newly new, because Berlin was the capital of the old German Reich for 70 years. Divided into two cities — one capitalist,

The Regions in Brief

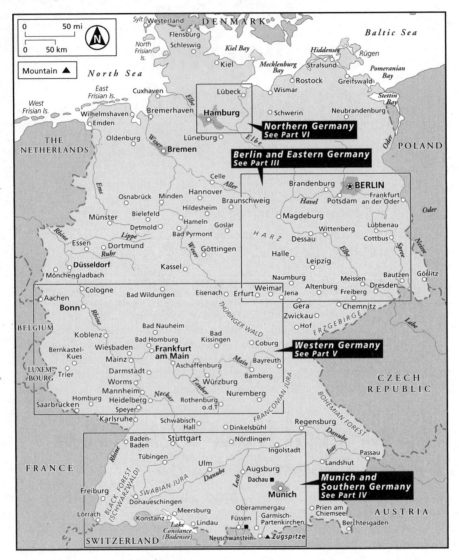

one Communist — after the war, Berlin has stitched itself back together and become one of the most fascinating cities in the world. Does the *Berliner Luft* (Berlin air) account for Berlin's endless and ongoing fizz of excitement, as some people claim? This is where it's all happening in Germany right now. The top sights include the **Brandenburg Gate, Charlottenburg Palace** with its bevy of important museums inside and nearby, the **Gemäldegalerie (Painting Gallery)** in the Kulturforum area, the new buildings of **Potsdamer Platz,** the **Pergamon Museum** and the other museums on **Museumsinsel (Museum Island)** in eastern Berlin, the beautiful **Gendarmenmarkt** square, the revitalized **Friedrichstrasse** area and **Unter den Linden** avenue, and the **Reichstag** building with its fabulous new glass dome. An easy day trip from Berlin is Frederick the Great's charming, 18th-century **Sanssouci Palace** in Potsdam.

Now that Germany is reunited, you have an opportunity to visit sections of eastern Germany that were inaccessible, or at least difficult to visit, under the Communist regime of the German Democratic Republic (GDR). **Dresden,** on the Elbe River and only two hours from Berlin by train, has treasures beyond measure in the **Zwinger Palace** and the **Albertinum** museum. **Leipzig** has been less interested in restoring its past than in looking toward the future. This big city does big business, and plenty of it. The peaceful revolution of 1989 began in Leipzig, and the city seems to be working overtime to shake off the GDR legacy: The **Museum in der Runden Ecke** is devoted to the role the Stasi, East Germany's secret police, played in the lives of citizens, and the new **Zeitgeschichtliches Museum (Contemporary History Museum)** chronicles the history and artifacts of the GDR years. In addition, the **Bach House** is of interest to music lovers.

Weimar is in a category of its own. This small, quiet town, little damaged in the war, was the home of Germany's greatest writer, the poet and dramatist Johann Wolfgang von Goethe (1749–1832), and the playwright Friedrich Schiller (1759–1805). The homes of these two literary giants are Weimar's most popular tourist attractions. The small **Bauhaus Museum** exhibits paintings, textiles, pottery, furniture, and drawings from the Bauhaus school, which began here in 1919. A visit to the **Buchenwald Memorial** just outside of Weimar can be an intense and profoundly moving experience.

Marveling at Munich and Southern Germany

Southern Germany is worlds apart from the north. Bavaria, Germany's largest and most prosperous *Land* (state), is a place seemingly tailor-made for tourists. **Munich,** the capital, is Germany's most beautiful city. Cultured and elegant, this city has an upscale chic found nowhere else in the country. It's also boisterous, even raucous: Millions pour into the city during **Oktoberfest,** and Munich is renowned for its giant **beer halls** and **beer gardens.** Ranking right up there with the offerings of Berlin are Munich's museums: the **Alte Pinakothek** (for Old Masters), the **Neue Pinakothek** (for 19th-century German and European art), and the brand-new **Pinakothek Moderne Kunst** (for major 20th-century artists like Picasso, Matisse, and Giacometti). The city's most popular museum is the **Deutsches Museum,** the largest science and technology museum in the world. In the center of town sits an enormous palace, the **Residenz,** used by the rulers of Bavaria from the 14th century up to 1918. You also find lovely **churches** with sober Gothic and exuberant baroque interiors. Munich's musical life is the envy of many cities, with year-round opera, symphony, and concerts of all kinds.

Just south of Munich you find the scenic glories of the **Bavarian Alps. Garmisch-Partenkirchen** is a small mountain resort town close to the **Zugspitze,** Germany's highest peak, accessible by cable car. This alpine region, where cowbells clang in the meadows and classic alpine chalets nestle in picturesque valleys, is the location of Germany's most famous castles: **Linderhof** and **Neuschwanstein,** dream castles created by King Ludwig II of Bavaria. The lovely historic town of **Füssen** makes a good base for visiting the castles, and for reaching **Oberammergau,** famous for its wood carvers and for the Passion Play performed there every ten years — a tradition dating back to the 17th century.

Southern Germany also includes the **Bodensee** (also called **Lake Constance**). Germany's largest lake, the Bodensee sits in a sun-filled basin with a view of the Alps to the south; semitropical gardens flourish on **Mainau,** an island in the lake, and vineyards and fruit trees grow around its shoreline. **Lindau,** an island-city connected to the mainland by a causeway, is the best spot to stay.

Southern Germany also includes the famous **Schwarzwald,** or **Black Forest,** an area of great natural beauty. Tucked into a forest valley, the lively and lovely city of **Freiburg** is a delight to explore. From there you can explore the surrounding forest or hunt for a cuckoo clock, one of the traditional industries of the Black Forest. Further north is the city of **Baden-Baden,** with its famous mineral baths and glamorous casino.

Winging through Western Germany

Western Germany is a densely populated area with an ancient history and wonderful cities that feature vibrant personalities all their own. **Frankfurt,** the most modern-looking and technologically sophisticated city in Germany, is probably the best-known metropolis, in part because it's the point of entry for most visitors flying into Germany from outside Europe. Frankfurt is the banking capital of Germany and the European Union. Among its cultural offerings are several important museums.

Köln, or **Cologne** (as it's known in English), occupying a prime spot on the Rhine River, comes as a wonderful surprise to many visitors. This lively, sophisticated, good-natured town offers more than enough to keep you busy for a couple of days. The city's chief glory is its awe-inspiring **Dom (Cathedral),** the largest Gothic structure north of the Alps. Cologne was an important Roman town, a period that is wonderfully interpreted in the **Romisch-Germanisches Museum (Roman-Germanic Museum).** In contrast, Cologne is also the contemporary art capital of Germany. Chief among its many outstanding museums is the **Wallraf-Richartz Museum,** one of Germany's best for art from the Middle Ages to the 19th century, and the **Museum Ludwig,** one of the top modern-art museums in Europe.

Heidelberg is for many people the quintessential romantic German town. Sitting on the Neckar River amidst green hills, Heidelberg has an enormous ruined castle that looks down on its picturesque **Altstadt (Old Town).** Perfect for strolling and relaxing, this town is easy to savor.

This part of western Germany is one of Europe's top wine-producing areas. If you're a wine fan, consider renting a car and driving the **Deutsche Weinstrasse (German Wine Road),** which starts west of Heidelberg. River cruises, which originate in Cologne, Heidelberg, and many other cities in the area, can take you through the **Rhine and Mosel valleys,** where neatly clipped vineyards soak up the sun on the steep hillsides. You can also visit many wine towns by train.

Nürnberg, or **Nuremberg** (as it's known in English), is one of the most interesting and prettiest cities in western Germany. Little more than a pile of smoldering rubble at the end of World War II, Nuremberg was rebuilt in a style that evokes the medieval era when it was one of the most important cities in Germany. Nuremberg has as many romantic corners as Heidelberg, and some very worthwhile museums. The country's largest museum of art and culture, the **Germanisches Nationalmuseum (German National Museum),** displays the entire spectrum of German craftsmanship and fine arts from prehistoric to modern times, and the delightful **Spielzeugmuseum (Toy Museum)** shows off a collection of toys spanning half a millennium. Nuremberg's **Christmas Market** is the oldest in Germany.

Rothenburg ob der Tauber is Germany's most intact medieval city. Surrounded by thick walls, and still entered through ancient city gates, Rothenburg gives you a remarkable sense of a past era.

Exploring Northern Germany

Northern Germany is different from southern Germany. Architecturally, the north's sober red-brick Gothic churches and buildings lack the ornate baroque decorations found in the Catholic south. The very solidity of these northern cities makes them attractive, as does their seafaring history as Hanseatic ports in an important medieval trade network (called the Hanseatic League) that stretched from England to Russia. The climate, influenced by the North Sea and the Baltic, is often wet or misty, but that maritime atmosphere is part of the overall appeal.

Hamburg is the largest city in northern Germany. Its **harbor,** one of the biggest in the world, is a major tourist attraction, as are the breezy **Alster lakes** in the center of the city. **Sightseeing boats** that take you into the harbor and canals, or across the lakes, operate year-round. You can also explore beautiful 19th-century neighborhoods, such as **Altona,** now a lively area with restaurants, cafes, and bars, and the **Hamburger Kunsthalle (Fine Arts Museum),** which contains an outstanding, multifaceted collection.

Lübeck, further north, has so many medieval brick buildings that UNESCO designated it a World Heritage Site. As capital of the Hanseatic

League, Lübeck was one of the richest cities in northern Europe. In the **Altstadt,** you see examples of its 900-year-old history everywhere you turn, from the Gothic **Rathaus (Town Hall)** and the **Heiligen-Geist-Hospital,** a 15th-century almshouse, to the Gothic church spires that still dominate the skyline.

The Secret of the Seasons

How do you decide what time of year to travel to Germany? This section presents the pros and cons of each season, so you can choose the best time for your visit.

Traveling during high and low seasons

Roughly speaking, the high season for travel in Germany is from Easter to the end of September with another peak in December. The country is most crowded during the months of May and June. July and August may be less expensive because that's when Germans take off on their own holidays, and many hotels consequently offer lower summer rates. October and November and January through March are the low seasons.

During your trip you probably want to visit Berlin or Munich, destinations on almost every German itinerary. The capital of Germany and the capital of Bavaria are popular destinations year-round, and they tend to be more expensive than the rest of Germany (Munich is probably the most expensive city in Germany). Because of their popularity, and because they host giant trade shows and conventions in addition to attracting tourists, booking a hotel room before you arrive is wise.

In general, crowds and prices tend to rise during big **trade fairs.** Nearly all large German cities have a *Messe,* or convention/fairgrounds, with a year-round schedule of major trade shows in all industries. These trade fairs can put a real squeeze on hotel rooms.

In the winter months, generally from October through March, you find that museums, castles, and tourist offices have shorter hours and may be closed certain days of the week. Hours and opening days are increased during the period from Easter to the end of September. Most castles and palaces can be visited daily, year-round, but from April through September the lines for major attractions, like Neuschwanstein and Linderhof castles in Bavaria, or the Reichstag dome in Berlin, may be more than two hours long. Long-distance train schedules don't change much between winter and summer, and Germany's excellent public transportation systems in its cities run smoothly year-round.

Watching those unpredictable skies

Before I write about the weather in Germany, I feel I should add a disclaimer. As in many parts of the world, the weather in Germany has become less predictable than in the past. In northern Germany, for instance, some locals claim that they now receive less snow and more rain than in decades past. In southern Germany, some report a hotter and drier climate. So, although I can give you a very broad overview of general weather patterns in Germany, be prepared for variations.

Overall, Germany has a predominantly mild, temperate climate. Average summer temperatures range from 72°F to 80°F (20°C–30°C). The average winter temperature hovers around 32°F (0°C). That said, keep in mind that the climate is constantly affected by colliding continental and maritime air masses from the Baltic and North seas, resulting in plenty of unpredictable weather, especially in the north. For average temperatures and rainfalls, see Table 2-1 for Berlin in the north and Table 2-2 for Frankfurt in the south.

Table 2-1 Berlin's Average Daytime Temperature and Rainfall

	Jan	Feb	Mar	Apr	May	June	July	Aug	Sept	Oct	Nov	Dec
Temp °F	30	32	40	48	53	60	64	62	56	49	40	34
Temp °C	-1	0	4	9	12	16	18	17	13	9	4	1
Rainfall (in.)	2.2	1.6	1.2	1.6	2.3	2.9	3.2	2.7	2.2	1.6	2.4	1.9

Table 2-2 Frankfurt's Average Daytime Temperature and Rainfall

	Jan	Feb	Mar	Apr	May	June	July	Aug	Sept	Oct	Nov	Dec
Temp °F	34	36	42	49	57	63	66	66	58	50	41	35
Temp °C	1	2	6	9	14	17	19	19	14	10	5	2
Rainfall (in.)	6.5	5.1	5.6	5.7	5.9	5.5	5.0	5.1	4.2	4.8	6.5	6

If your trip includes northern Germany, consider visiting in April and May, the months that are least cloudy. Even with clear skies, though, the weather up north can remain, shall we say, *invigorating*. In the interior of Germany the least gray months are usually June and September.

Blossoming in spring

Spring comes earliest in the south and in the Rhine Valley. The *Föhn*, a dry south wind from the Alps, heralds the approach of spring around the giant Bodensee (Lake Constance) and in the river valleys of the Black Forest and throughout southwestern Germany.

Highlights of the season include:

✔ The warmth of the springtime sun coaxes out the new vines in Germany's Rhineland wine country.

✔ Blossoms appear on the fruit trees grown around the Bodensee and the Rhine.

✔ In towns around Bodensee, such as Lindau, an early spring means that tables are set up in sunny squares and life begins to move outdoors.

✔ The carefully tended parks and gardens in German cities show off their first spring flowers.

✔ May and June is *Spargel* (white asparagus) season throughout Germany; you find asparagus specialties on menus everywhere.

But keep in mind these springtime pitfalls:

✔ Cold, rainy weather can last well into early summer in Berlin and other northern cities.

✔ The snow in the Alps usually melts by April, leaving May as an "in-between" off-month: The winter sports have ended and the summer hiking and recreation season hasn't yet begun. The weather in the Alps tends to be soggy and foggy at this time.

✔ During school holidays, especially around Easter, major attractions in cities throughout Germany tend to be more crowded.

Shining (and raining) in summer

From April through September, you can generally count on warm, mild weather in southern Germany. However, around Cologne, even as far north as Berlin, mid- and late-summer days can become hot, humid, and thundery. This can also be the case in Dresden, Leipzig, and the landlocked eastern portion of the country. Summer weather in the Bavarian Alps is extremely variable and changes according to altitude, local winds, and the orientation of individual valleys to the sun. Summer in the north comes later and remains variable because of maritime influences from the North and Baltic seas.

Some summer perks to consider:

✔ Prices for hotels are often lower in July and August.

✔ Warm summer nights stay light much longer, until 10 p.m. or sometimes later.

✔ Outdoor musical performances and street fairs take place in many cities and regions.

✔ Lakes in the Alps, the Black Forest, and Berlin, become more inviting as warm weather settles in.

✔ Many attractions are open longer hours.

✔ You can dine alfresco in most German cities.

But keep in mind:

✔ Airfares tend to be higher in the summer months.

✔ In traffic-jammed cities like Berlin, Munich, and Frankfurt, gasoline and diesel exhaust can create air pollution on hot, windless days.

✔ Heat and humidity can make for sticky sightseeing throughout central and southern Germany.

✔ Air-conditioning is not common in Germany; hotels and concert halls can be broiling.

✔ Getting into top attractions like Neuschwanstein and Linderhof castles can take two hours or more.

Glowing in autumn

Fall is one of the best times to visit Germany. Autumn days are beautiful in the scenic regions of south, central, and eastern Germany. The deciduous trees in the Black Forest and the Thuringian Forest and along the Rhine, Neckar, and other river valleys turn golden as the days grow shorter. After the grapes are harvested, the vines turn yellow. Indian summer, or what the Germans call *Altweibersommer* (old women's summer), frequently makes a welcome appearance during October and November. In the north, autumn is likely to be rainy and blustery, heralding gray, wet winters.

A few advantages of autumn are:

✔ Summer crowds have thinned out by the end of September.

✔ Airfares usually drop.

✔ Germany's cultural calendar of opera, symphony, and other events swings into high gear.

✔ Scenic areas like the Black Forest, the Bavarian Alps, and the Rhineland glow with autumn tints.

✔ The smell of new wine fills the old streets of wine-growing towns.

✔ Towns in wine-growing areas celebrate with wine festivals.

This season has only one real drawback:

■ ✔ Autumn may be gray and rainy, especially in the north.

Welcoming in winter

Snow can fall anywhere in Germany, lending a special air to Christmas markets. But with winter temperatures hovering right around freezing, snow doesn't stay on the ground for long, and often turns into sleet. This story is different in the Bavarian Alps and the Black Forest, where the winter weather is colder and snow adds to the beauty of the mountain and forest landscapes. Both the Alps and the Black Forest are known for their fine skiing and winter sports. Overall, this season is becoming an increasingly popular time to visit Germany.

Winter can be wonderful because:

✔ In December, cities throughout the country set up magical outdoor Christmas markets where you find tree ornaments, handcrafted goods, and baked delights.

✔ When the snow starts to fall in the Alps and the Black Forest, skiiers head for the slopes and cross-country trails.

✔ In the weeks before Lent, Cologne and Munich celebrate with citywide carnivals *(Fasching)*.

But winter has its downside:

✔ Brrr. The cold can be raw, numbing, and seemingly endless, especially in the north.

✔ Daylight drops dramatically: Darkness falls as early as 3:30 or 4 p.m.

✔ Although you'll be comfortable in your hotel, Germans tend to under- rather than overheat their spaces.

✔ Almost everything shuts down on December 25 and 26 and New Year's Day.

Germany's Calendar of Events

Germany hums year-round with festivals and special events of all kinds. The dates below were accurate in 2002 but may change from year to year. Verifying dates beforehand with the German National Tourist Board is a good idea. Check their Web site (www.germany-tourism.de), or call or write to them for a free calendar of events. See the Appendix for the tourist board's contact addresses and phone numbers.

Many museums and attractions close during the following **public holidays:** January 1 (New Year's Day), Easter (Good Friday and Easter Monday), May 1 (Labor Day), Ascension Day (ten days before Pentecost/Whitsunday, the seventh Sunday after Easter), Whitmonday (day after Pentecost/Whitsunday), October 3 (Day of German Unity), November 17 (Day of Prayer and Repentance), and December 25 to 26 (Christmas). In addition, the following holidays are observed in some German states: January 6 (Epiphany), Corpus Christi (ten days after Pentecost), August 15 (Assumption), and November 1 (All Saints' Day).

January

New Year's Day International Ski Jumping, in Garmisch-Partenkirchen, is one of Europe's major winter sporting events. For more information, contact Tourist Information, Richard-Strauss-Platz 2, 82467 Garmisch-Partenkirchen (☎ 08821/180-700; Internet: www.garmisch-partenkirchen.de). January 1.

February

The well-respected **Berlin International Film Festival** lasts for one week and showcases the work of international film directors as well as the latest German films. Tickets can be purchased at any box office. Contact the **Internationale Filmfestspiele Berlin,** Potsdamer Strasse 5, 10786 Berlin (☎ 030/25920; Internet: www.berlinale.de). February 6 to 17.

Fasching (Carnival) festivals take place in Catholic cities throughout Germany, reaching their peak on the Tuesday (Mardi Gras) before Ash Wednesday. Celebrations in Cologne and Munich are particularly famous. For information, contact **Fremdenverkehrsamt München,** Sendlinger Strasse 1, 80331 München (☎ 089/233-0300; Internet: www.muenchen-tourist.de), or **Köln Tourismus Office,** Unter Fettenhennen 19, 50667 Köln (☎ 0221/9433; Internet: www.koeln.de). A week in February.

April

Frühlingsfest (Spring Festival), a big Frankish folk festival in Nuremberg, features folk music, jazz concerts, and events for the whole family. For more information contact **Schaustellerverband Nürnberg** (☎ 0911/468-600; Internet: www.volksfest-nuernberg.de). April 19 to May 4.

May

Hamburg Summer is a summer-long series of cultural events, including concerts, plays, festivals, and special exhibitions. For information, contact **Tourismus-Zentrale Hamburg,** Steinstrasse 7, 20095 Hamburg (☎ 040/3005-1201; Internet: www.hamburg.de). May through July.

By drinking a huge tankard of wine (an event called **Der Meistertrunk**) during the **Historisches Festspiel (Historic Festival),** Rothenburg ob der Tauber celebrates the story of how a brave citizen saved the town from destruction. Events take place twice a year. For information, contact **Tourist Information,** Marktplatz, 91541 Rothenburg o.d. Tauber (☎ 09861/40492; Internet: www.rothenburg.de). May 17 to 20, September 6 to 8.

The renowned **Bachfest (Bach Festival)** in Leipzig features performances of Bach's work in the famous Thomaskirche, where he was choirmaster, and in other churches and concert halls. For more information, contact the **Tourist Information** office, Richard-Wagner-Strasse 1, 04109 Leipzig (☎ 0341/913-7333; Internet: www.bach-leipzig.de). May 23 to June 1.

On special Saturday nights during **Rhein im Feuerzauber (Rhine in Flames),** various towns along the Rhine (between Bonn and Linz, Koblenz and Braubach, Bingen and Rüdesheim, and St. Goar and St. Goarshausen) illuminate their castles and set off fireworks. The best vantage point is from a riverboat on the Rhine. For details, contact the **German National Tourist Office** (see the Appendix for its address and phone number). May through September.

June

Fireworks enliven the sky in the romantic university city of Heidelberg during the **Floodlighting of the Castle.** For more information, contact **Heidelberg Tourist-Information,** Pavillon am Hauptbahnhof (☎ 06221/19433; Internet: www.heidelberg.de). June 5, July 10, and September 4.

Berlin and Cologne have the largest **Gay Pride** festivals, featuring parades, performances, and street fairs. For events in Berlin, log on to www.berlin.gay-web.de or contact **Berlin Tourist Information** (☎ 0190/016-316). For events in Cologne, log on to www.koeln.gay-web.de or contact **Köln Tourismus Office,** Unter Fettenhennen 19, 50667 Köln (☎ 0221/9433). Berlin, last weekend in June. Cologne, first weekend in June.

During the **Schleswig-Holstein Music Festival,** one of the best music festivals in Germany, classical concerts take place in venues in and around the lovely old city of Lübeck. For more information, contact the **Schleswig-Holstein Music Festival** (☎ 0800/7463-2002; Internet: www.shmf.de). June through August.

Enjoy vintages from the surrounding Black Forest area during Freiburg im Breisgau's **Public Wine Tasting.** Events take place in the Münsterplatz surrounding Freiburg's magnificent cathedral. For information, contact

Freiburg Tourist Information, Rotteckring 14, 79098 Freiburg im Breisgau (☎ 0761/388-1880; Internet: www.freiburg.de). Last weekend in June.

July

One of Europe's major opera events, the **Richard Wagner Festival** in Bayreuth, takes place in the composer's famous Festspielhaus (opera house). Unfortunately, opera tickets must be booked *years* in advance. For information, contact Festival Administration, **Bayreuther Festspiele,** Am Festspiele, 95445 Bayreuth (☎ 0921/78780; Internet: www.festspiele.de). Late July to late August.

August

During **Weinkost (Food and Wine Fair)** in Freiburg im Breisgau, local residents and visitors enjoy the first vintages from grapes grown in the Black Forest district and regional food specialties. For information, contact **Freiburg Tourist Information,** Rotteckring 14, 79098 Freiburg im Breisgau (☎ 0761/388-1880; Internet: www.freiburg.de). Mid-August.

The **Traditional Rüdesheim Wine Festival,** in Rüdesheim am Rhein, is held in the Rhine village most famous for red wines. For information, contact the **Rüdesheim Tourist Bureau,** Giesenheimer Strasse 22, 65385 Rüdesheim am Rhein (☎ 06722/19433). August 16 to 19.

Arts and pleasure abound during Hamburg's **Alstervergnügen (Alster Pleasures).** Events, which take place around Binnenalster lake, include food stalls, fireworks, and shows. For information contact **Tourismus-Zentrale,** Steinstrasse 7, 20095 Hamburg (☎ 040/3005-1201; Internet: www.hamburg.de). August 29 to September 1.

September

Munich's **Oktoberfest,** Germany's most famous festival, happens mostly in September, not October. Millions show up, and visitors pack hotels. (Always reserve hotel rooms well in advance.) Most activities occur at Theresienwiese, where local breweries sponsor gigantic tents that can hold up to 6,000 beer drinkers. Contact the **Fremdenverkehrsamt München,** Sendlinger Strasse 1, 80331 München (☎ 089/233-0300; Internet: www.muenchen-tourist.de) for particulars. Mid-September to the first Sunday in October.

One of the high points on the cultural calendar of Germany, the **Berliner Festwochen (Berlin Festival)** brings an international roster of performing artists to Berlin for opera, symphony, and theatrical presentations. Contact **Berlin Tourist Information** (☎ 0190/016-316; Internet: www.berlin.de). September 1 to October 11.

Nuremberg's lovely Old Town becomes the scene of performances, music, and fun during **Nürnberger Altstadtfest (Old Town Festival).** For information, contact Nuremberg's **Tourismus-Zentrale,** Frauentorgraben 3, 90443 Nürnberg (☎ **0911/23360;** Internet: www. Nuremberg.de or www.altstadtfest.de). September 23 to 29.

November

The annual **Jazz-Fest Berlin,** staged at the Philharmonie, attracts some of the world's finest jazz artists. Contact **Berlin Tourist Information** (☎ **0190/016-316;** Internet: www.berlin.de) for information. November 1 to 4.

Hamburger Dom (also called Winter Dom), an annual amusement fair at Hamburg's Heiligengeistfeld, is the biggest public event in northern Germany. For information, contact **Tourismus-Zentrale Hamburg,** Steinstrasse 7, 20095 Hamburg (☎ **040/3005-1201;** Internet: www. hamburg.de). November 9 to December 9.

December

Christmas Markets, generally called a *Weihnachtsmarkt* (*Weihnachten* is Christmas) or a *Christkindlmarkt* (literally, "Christ Child Market"), take place in town squares throughout Germany. You find them in Cologne, Dresden, Frankfurt, Leipzig, Munich, Nuremberg, and Rothenburg ob der Tauber, among other cities. Contact the individual tourist offices of each city, or the German National Tourist Board, for details (see the Appendix for contact information). Late November or early December until Christmas.

Chapter 3

Presenting Five Great Itineraries

In This Chapter

▶ Seeing Germany's top attractions in one or two weeks

▶ Discovering the best of the great outdoors

▶ Planning trips for wine aficionados

*P*utting together a good itinerary is one of the hardest parts of any trip. If you haven't been to a place before, how do you know what's worth seeing and what isn't? So in this chapter, I lay out some suggested travel itineraries for those with limited time or special interests. (See Chapter 1 for some preliminary information on what the country offers.)

You can reach all of the destinations in this chapter by train or public transportation. However, some of these itineraries are more enjoyable if you have a car. For details on getting around the country, see Chapter 7.

Just the Highlights: Germany in One Week

Everyone's tastes are different, so generalizing about what constitutes the greatest sights in Germany is difficult. This seven-day itinerary, beginning in Munich and ending in Berlin, shows you the contrasts between southern Germany and northern Germany, and introduces you to the country's two greatest cities. I include two of Ludwig's castles and a brief stop in Cologne, on the Rhine. For more information on the sights that I mention, refer to Chapter 14 for Munich, Chapter 15 for the Alps and its castles, Chapter 17 for Cologne, and Chapter 12 for Berlin.

Spend **Day 1** in marvelous **Munich.** Shake out your plane-cramped legs by taking to the streets for some general exploring. Head first for **Marienplatz,** the city's main square. Attractions surround this square, which teems with life. You can go up to the top of the **Rathaus** tower for a bird's-eye view, watch the **Glockenspiel,** and visit the nearby **Frauenkirche,** Munich's largest church. Then walk over to the adjacent **Viktualienmarkt,** one of the greatest food markets of Europe. Browse around and find a place for lunch from among the dozens of possibilities in the area. Afterwards, make your way to the **Asamkirche** for a glimpse of the baroque decoration for which southern Germany is famous. In the afternoon, choose a museum to visit. If you're an art lover, you may want to see the priceless collection of Old Masters at the **Alte Pinakotheke.** If you are interested in science and technology, make your way to the famous **Deutsches Museum.** If you're in the mood for oom-pah-pah, have dinner at the fun-loving **Hofbräuhaus.** Munich is one of Germany's top cultural capitals, so you may want to end your evening at a concert or the opera.

Start **Day 2** in a palace. You need the entire morning to wander through the enormous **Residenz** in central Munich. Or make an easy excursion to beautiful **Schloss Nymphenburg,** which you can reach by streetcar. If you choose Nymphenburg, allow some extra time to wander through the gardens. Be sure, also, to visit the collection of carriages, which includes the bizarrely ornate sleighs and coaches used by King Ludwig of Bavaria, creator of Linderhof and Neuschwanstein castles. Have lunch near Marienplatz. In the afternoon, choose another museum to visit. Three possibilities are the **Neue Pinakothek,** a showcase for 19th-century German and European art; the brand-new **Pinakothek Moderne Kunst,** which displays an international collection of 20th-century masterpieces; and the **Bayerisches Nationalmuseum,** the location for Bavaria's greatest historic and artistic treasures. At some point, fit in a stroll in the bucolic **Englisher Garten,** Munich's largest and prettiest park. You can bring a picnic or order a meal at the park's famous beer garden.

On **Day 3,** head to the Bavarian Alps, just south of Munich. If you rent a car you can easily explore the sights along the **Deutsche Alpenstrasse (German Alpine Road),** a 300-mile scenic road. But you can also take a train to **Garmisch-Partenkirchen,** an alpine resort famed for its winter sports and summer hiking. From Garmisch you can ascend the **Zugspitze,** Germany's highest peak, for a spectacular view of the Alps. Special cog railways and cable cars can take you up and bring you back down. From Garmisch, the trip is only 40 minutes by train or car to **Oberammergau,** the closest town to Linderhof castle. Wander through this small Bavarian town famous for its woodcarvers, whose wares you may want to purchase. If you're without wheels, take a bus from Oberammergau to **Schloss Linderhof,** Ludwig II's French-inspired castle. Spend the night in Garmisch, Oberammergau, or Füssen.

On **Day 4,** make your way to **Füssen,** the town closest to Neuschwanstein and Hohenschwangau castles. Make Neuschwanstein your top priority; as Germany's most popular tourist attraction, this castle quickly fills up with tourists as the day wears on. By train from Oberammergau, the trip takes a little over an hour. If you're without a car, you can easily get a bus from Füssen for the 4-mile trip to the castle. Tours of Ludwig's fairy-tale castle take about one hour. You can dine near the parking area below Neuschwanstein. Then, if you're still in a "royal" mood, visit adjacent **Hohenschwangau** castle, Ludwig's childhood home. Spend the night in Füssen, and be sure to take time to stroll around the lovely historic district of town. If you're driving, you can make an easy excursion to the **Wieskirche (Church in the Meadow),** a beautiful baroque masterpiece located just a few miles north of Füssen. If the legend of Ludwig still has you intrigued, you can spend an evening at "Ludwig II: Longing for Paradise," a long-running musical about his life.

If you have your car for a two-day rental, you may be able to return the vehicle in Füssen, or you can drive back to Munich and return it there. From either city, hop on the train and make your way to **Köln (Cologne)** for **Day 5.** (By fast train, the trip from Cologne takes about 5½ hours; the fastest train from Füssen takes about 7 hours.) You'll see Cologne's greatest sight — the enormous Gothic **Dom** (cathedral) — as you step out of the train station. Enjoy the afternoon in this lively Rhine-side city by visiting the cathedral and one or two of its many fine museums: the **Römisch-Germanisches Museum (Roman-Germanic Museum),** dedicated to the Romans who made Cologne one of their strategic forts nearly 2,000 years ago; the **Wallraf-Richartz Museum,** displaying Old and Modern Masters; and **Museum Ludwig,** entirely devoted to 20th-century and contemporary art. You can also take a sightseeing **boat ride** along the Rhine. Stay overnight in Cologne and have dinner at one of the city's famous beer halls (be sure to sample Kölsch, Cologne's delicious beer). The city has an excellent music scene, too, so you may want to see an opera or attend a concert.

On the morning of **Day 6,** take one of the sleek, superfast trains to **Berlin,** Germany's capital and largest city with about 3½ million residents. The trip from Cologne is under 4½ hours. Huge, sophisticated Berlin has endless things to do. Settle into your hotel and then take one of the sightseeing **bus tours** of the city — otherwise you'll only see a fraction of this enormous metropolis. After your tour, make your way over to **Potsdamer Platz,** the new quarter under construction (much has been finished) where the Berlin Wall once stood. From Potsdamer Platz, you can walk to the **Brandenburg Gate,** the symbol of the city, and the **Reichstag,** the country's parliamentary headquarters. Take the elevator up to the new dome on top of the Reichstag — the dome is open late, so come back later if the line is long. Then walk east down **Unter den Linden** to **Museumsinsel (Museum Island),** a group of four museums on an island in the Spree River. You want to see the **Pergamon Museum** with its fantastic collection of antiquities. Berlin is famed for its nightlife, so when darkness falls you may want to attend an opera, a concert, or a cabaret.

Hopefully your flight home departs sometime in the afternoon on **Day 7.** Take advantage of the morning by going over to the **Ägyptisches**

Museum (Egyptian Museum) to see the world-famous bust of Egyptian queen Nerfertiti. Then stroll down the Ku-Damm, western Berlin's renowned boulevard, before making your way to the airport.

On the plane, you may wonder about the things you didn't see. And, yes, you're right: You didn't have enough time to see everything, but at least you got a good glimpse. Now you have to decide what you'll see when you come back next time.

East Side/West Side: Germany in Two Weeks

What a treat — two weeks to take in the sights. You don't have to rush around quite as much as on a one-week trip, but you still have a lot of ground to cover. This suggested itinerary makes a clockwise circuit of Germany. For detailed information on the cities and sights I mention, refer to Chapter 12 for Berlin and Potsdam Chapter 13 for Dresden, Leipzig, and Weimar; Chapter 14 for Munich; Chapter 15 for the Alps and its castles; Chapter 16 for the Black Forest and the Bodensee; and Chapter 19 for Heidelberg and Nuremberg.

Berlin, Germany's capital and largest city, is the starting point on **Day 1** for your two-week tour of Deutschland. Berlin is an enormous city, so start the morning by taking one of the sightseeing **bus tours.** Devote your afternoon to exploring eastern Berlin, the most historic part of the city. Start at **Potsdamer Platz,** to see "new" Berlin (this area is all new since the Wall came down), then head over to the **Reichstag,** the German Parliament building, and take the elevator up to the new dome for a view of the city. You can have lunch up there, or grab a snack on the street. Afterwards, walk to the **Brandenburg Gate** and head east down **Unter den Linden,** the most famous boulevard in this part of the city. Eastern Berlin has numerous attractions: make sure you stop at the **Gendarmenmarkt,** a beautiful neoclassical square, and wander into the **Nikolaiviertel (Nicholas' Quarter),** before you head up to the **Museumsinsel (Museum Island)** to visit the **Pergamon Museum.** From Museumsinsel, you can walk to **Friedrichstrasse,** the upscale shopping street, or take the S-Bahn to **Hackescher Markt,** a pre–World War I quarter that now features several smart cafes and shops.

Spend **Day 2** on the western side of the city. If you want to learn more about Berlin itself, start at the multimedia show **The Story of Berlin,** which traces the city's history. Otherwise, head over to the Charlottenburg neighborhood for a tour of **Schloss (Palace) Charlottenburg** and a stroll through the palace gardens. Several museums are in and around the palace; the most famous is the **Ägyptisches Museum (Egyptian Museum),** which displays the stunning bust of Egyptian Queen Nerfertiti. Head back to the **Kurfürstendamm** (known as Ku-Damm), the most famous boulevard in western Berlin, for lunch or to find a café for *Kaffee und Kuchen* (coffee and cake). Stop by the **Kaiser-Wilhelm-Gedächtniskirche (Kaiser Wilhelm Memorial Church),** left as a colossal ruin after the devastation of World War II, then spend a while strolling in the **Tiergarten,** Berlin's most famous park. Have something fun lined up for the evening: Berlin has three opera houses, three major symphony orchestras, cabarets, variety shows, and, of course, countless bars and clubs.

Spend the morning of **Day 3** at **Schloss Sanssouci** in **Potsdam,** an easy trip from Berlin by S-Bahn. You want to give yourself at least three hours for this excursion, which includes a tour of Frederick the Great's rococo palace and a walk through the landscaped grounds. You can eat near the palace or back in Berlin. (You find lots of cafes and restaurants around Savignyplatz in Berlin.) In the afternoon, visit one of Berlin's great museums, such as the **Gemäldegalerie (Painting Gallery)** or the new **Jüdisches Museum (Jewish Museum).** Plenty of entertainment options exist for the evening.

On **Day 4,** you see a different side of Germany (literally) in the eastern cities of the former German Democratic Republic (GDR) ruled by the Communists until 1990. **Dresden,** on the Elbe River about two hours south of Berlin by train, is one of the great art cities of Germany. In Dresden you want to focus your attention on the **Albertinum,** a vast collection of treasures accrued by Saxon rulers, and the **Zwinger,** a restored royal palace that is home to four museums, the most important being the **Gemäldegalerie Alte Meister (Old Masters Gallery).** Dresden's restored historic center is fairly small and easily walkable. Make it a point to see the **Frauenkirche (Church of Our Lady),** which is being painstakingly restored after destruction in the war; parts of it were retrieved from the Elbe river. One of Dresden's most famous buildings is the **Semper Opera House;** if you're an opera lover, you won't want to miss seeing a performance there. Spend the night in Dresden.

From Dresden on **Day 5,** you may want to take an excursion boat along the Elbe into the area known as **Saxon Switzerland.** From April through September, 3- to 4½-hour trips take place daily. Otherwise (or afterwards), hop on a train for **Leipzig,** only an hour away. Leipzig is a busy, bustling city with a long musical tradition. Johann Sebastian Bach was the choirmaster of the famous **Thomaskirche (St. Thomas Church),** where he is buried, and the **Bach-Museum** is dedicated to his life and works. If you love symphonic music, be sure to reserve a seat to hear the world-famous Gewandhaus Orchestra.

Leipzig is where the peaceful revolution that ultimately toppled the GDR began. The city has two unusual museums that shed light on the GDR era: The **Museum in der Runden Ecke** documents the methods of the dreaded Stasi, East Germany's secret police, and the **Zeitgeschichtliches Forum Leipzig (Contemporary History Forum)** examines all aspects of life in the GDR from 1945 to 1989. By 2003 the **Museum der Bildenden Künste (Museum of Fine Arts)** is scheduled to move into a brand-new building close to **Marktplatz,** the town's liveliest square. Enjoy a dinner of regional food in the famous **Auerbachs Keller,** a vaulted underground restaurant.

From Leipzig, fast trains take less than an hour to reach **Weimar,** your destination for **Day 6.** This small, pretty city, filled with leafy parks and neoclassical buildings, is one of Germany's literary meccas. Johann Wolfgang von Goethe and his friend, the great German dramatist Friedrich Schiller, lived here. **Goethes Wohnhaus (Goethe's House),** portions of which have been left much as they were in his lifetime, is the town's most visited site. Weimar was one of Germany's great centers of art and culture during the late 18th and early 19th centuries. Visit the scene of Duchess Anna Amalia's glittering salons in the **Wittumspalais,** a "city palace" near Goethe's house, and at **Schloss Belvedere,** 2 miles south. In the early 20th century, the Bauhaus School of Art and Design operated in Weimar; today, you can visit the small **Bauhaus Museum.** Weimar has its dark side, too. Not far from the city center, on the site of a Nazi-era concentration camp, is the **Gedenkstätte Buchenwald (Buchenwald Memorial).** Stay overnight in Weimar, or take the train to Munich, the next stop on this itinerary; the journey takes about 5 hours.

Your destination for **Day 7** is delightful **Munich,** Germany's "secret capital." With only two days, you have to make some decisions about what to see. Start your explorations at **Marienplatz,** the city's main square, and then head over to the adjacent **Viktualienmarkt** to wander through this wonderland of an outdoor market. Choose a museum you'd especially like to visit: most visitors make the **Alte Pinakothek (Old Masters Gallery)** their top priority, but the **Deutsches Museum,** devoted to science and industry, is one of the most popular museums in the country. Stay overnight in Munich. You have innumerable ways to spend the evening in this cultural mecca: opera, symphony, pop concerts, theater, beer halls, beer gardens, and clubs.

Start **Day 8** with a self-guided tour of the **Residenz,** Munich's gigantic "in town" palace. You need at least two hours to visit the entire complex. After lunch near Marienplatz, take in another museum. Then, if the afternoon is fine, stroll in the lovely **Englisher Garten** and stop for a drink or a meal at the park's famous beer garden. At night, sample one of the city's many entertainment options. Stay overnight in Munich.

On **Day 9,** you might want to consider renting a car for the next four days, but doing so is not essential. By car or train, from Munich make your way to **Füssen,** 4 miles from the most famous tourist attraction in all of Germany: Ludwig II's **Neuschwanstein** castle. Give yourself some leeway with time because the crowds can be dense. You can also visit neighboring **Hohenschwangau** castle, where Ludwig spent his childhood. If you have a car, visit the nearby **Wieskirche (Church in the Meadow),** a world-famous baroque masterpiece. If you're without a car, stay overnight in Füssen or return to Munich. But first, enjoy a stroll through Füssen's lovely historic quarter. If you have a car, you can continue on to Lindau, exploring the Bavarian Alps along the **Deutsche Alpenstrasse (German**

Alpine Road). Some small Bavarian village with a cozy *Gasthaus* (guesthouse) may catch your fancy.

From Munich or Füssen, the trip to **Lindau** for **Day 10** is about three hours by train. Even if you're driving from Füssen, travel time is about the same. Germany's sunny southwestern corner comes as a surprise to many visitors. Here you find the **Bodensee,** or Lake Constance, the country's largest lake and one of the largest bodies of water in Europe. Spend the day strolling in the sun (hopefully), sitting under an umbrella at a cafe, swimming, or taking a boat ride on the lake to the garden island of **Mainau.** Lindau's sunny charms are reminiscent of Italy. You don't have to race around sightseeing, as the area has no important museums; just take it easy.

You've no doubt heard about the **Schwarzwald,** or **Black Forest,** your destination on **Day 11.** This scenic area of forested hills, valleys, and mountains in the southwestern corner of Germany is famed for its health resorts, its hiking and recreational sports facilities, and its cuckoo clocks. Take your pick of cities to stay in. The charming and lively university town of **Freiburg** is about three hours by train from Lindau. In Freiburg you can happily spend a few hours strolling through old streets lined by *Bächle* (little streams). Freiburg's lovely **Münster (cathedral)** and its surrounding square constitute the main sights in town. This wine town has vineyards nearby and yearly wine festivals. **Baden-Baden,** about 1½ hours further north by train, is one of Germany's premier spa towns. This upscale, resort-oriented town offers fine hotels and restaurants, lots of expensive shops, and a famous **casino.** If you opt for Baden-Baden, be sure to "take the waters" at **Friedrichsbad,** a 125-year-old mineral-bath establishment; the experience takes about 3½ hours.

On **Day 12,** make your way to **Heidelberg,** which is less than an hour by train from Baden-Baden or 2½ to 3 hours from Freiburg. Everyone seems to love this ancient university town on the Neckar River. The **Altstadt (Old Town)** is where you want to stay, and where you want to wander. Hike or take the funicular train up the hillside to famed **Heidelberg castle** for a stunning view of the town and the river valley. The castle is mostly in ruins, but you can take a tour of some restored rooms. Then take a relaxing **boat ride** down the Neckar. Stop in at the **Kurpfälzisches Museum (Museum of the Palatinate)** for a look at Tilman Riemenschneider's powerfully carved altarpiece. The museum's restaurant is one of the nicest places to dine in Heidelberg, especially on a warm evening when your table is in the courtyard near the fountain.

On **Day 13,** hop on the *Bahn* (train) in Heidelberg and in 3½ to 4 hours, you'll be in **Nürnberg** (or **Nuremberg,** as its known in English), one of the most attractive towns in Germany. As in many German cities, the entire **Altstadt** is a pedestrian zone. You find squares with lovely fountains, a picturesque area alongside the Pegnitz River, the **Kaiserburg (castle),** and two fine Gothic churches, **St.-Lorenz-Kirche** and **St. Sebaldus-Kirche,** to explore. Give yourself at least two hours to visit the marvelous **Germanisches Nationalmuseum (German National Museum),** which covers the entire spectrum of German fine arts from its prehistoric beginnings to the present day. And then, if you're in the mood, stop at the **Spielzeugmuseum (Toy Museum)** for a glimpse of the toys for which this city has long been famous.

On **Day 14,** head back to **Berlin,** where your tour began, to catch your flight home. The train ride from Nuremberg is about 5½ hours. (Alternatively, you can fly home from Frankfurt, a little over two hours by train from Nuremberg, or from Munich, under two hours from Nuremberg.) Sit back and enjoy the scenery. If you have time in any of these cities before your flight departs, just wander around without an itinerary. Find a cafe to sit and people-watch while you plan your next trip to Germany.

Fresh Air: Germany for Lovers of the Outdoors

Yes, museums are great, but you'd rather be *draussen* (outside) in the *frischer Luft* (fresh air). So pack a good pair of hiking boots, a swimsuit, and any other outdoor gear you may need, and book your flight. Being outdoors is easy in Germany. If you want to be active, you can find opportunities for hiking, biking, swimming, skiing — just about every sport you can think of. If you want less-strenuous activities, there are plenty of cable cars and river excursions where you can soak up the scenery. Every town and city has parks and biking paths. In the following weeklong itinerary, I keep you outside in southern and western Germany. The itinerary begins and ends in Munich, or you can fly into Munich and out of Frankfurt. For more information on the attractions listed below, see Chapter 14 for Munich, Chapter 15 for the Bavarian Alps, and Chapter 16 for the Black Forest and the Bodensee.

Spend **Day 1** in **Munich.** Of course, other visitors may head to this great city's museums, but you prefer to explore *outside* on foot. The entire inner city is a car-free pedestrian zone where you can stroll to your heart's content. You find plenty of outdoor cafes around **Marienplatz,** the city's main square, and right next to Marienplatz is the **Viktualienmarkt,** the best outdoor market in Germany. The formal **Hofgarten** (court gardens) behind the **Residenz** (Munich's in-city palace) is lovely, but the queen (or king) of Munich outdoor spaces is the **Englisher Garten (English Garden),** one of the largest and most beautiful city parks in Europe, and the oldest public park in the world, established in 1789. You can wander for hours along the tree-shaded walks, dance in the meadows, or sit in the famous beer garden.

Yes, yes, you'll get around to that museum *eventually*. But on **Day 2, Schloss Nymphenburg** is on the top of your list. The Schloss (palace) is a breeze to get to (it's right in the city on the streetcar line), and 500-acre

Nymphenburg Park is grand and inviting, with formal, French-style gardens behind the palace and an English-style park with quiet meadows, forested paths, and some intriguing buildings, including an 18th-century swimming pool and a baroque hunting lodge.

On **Day 3,** you can rent a car or take the train to **Garmisch-Partenkirchen** in the Bavarian Alps south of Munich. Here you're going to ascend the **Zugspitze,** Germany's highest peak (9,720 feet/2,960 m). A cog railway and a cable car take you up and bring you back. The view from the summit is — what else? — *spectacular.* If you're a dedicated hiker, the area around Garmisch-Partenkirchen is magnificent hiking country. Most hikes take an energetic four to five hours, but some of them are shorter and easy enough for children. Stay overnight in Garmisch (good skiing and ice-skating are available all winter).

Drive or take the train to **Füssen** on **Day 4,** and then drive or take a bus to **Neuschwanstein,** "Mad" Ludwig's fairy-tale castle. Germany's most-visited tourist attraction perches on a rocky spur that requires a good uphill hike to reach. (You can also reach the castle by horse-drawn cab or bus.) The forested hills all around Neuschwanstein and neighboring **Hohenschwangau** castle are full of excellent hiking paths. Stay overnight in Füssen and explore the charming old town on foot.

Bodensee (Lake Constance) is your destination for **Day 5.** By car or train make your way to **Lindau,** a sunny flower-filled resort town that sits on its own small island in the Bodensee. You can see the Alps south across the vast expanse of the lake. This is Germany's sunniest corner, and the lake is clean enough for swimming. You can bike along the shore or relax on an excursion boat ride to the island of **Mainau,** a plant-lover's paradise. Spend the night in Lindau.

Drive or train north to **Freiburg,** your headquarters in the **Schwarzwald,** or Black Forest, on **Day 6.** If you're traveling by train, I suggest that you rent a car, just for one day. From Freiburg you can make an easy 90-mile (145 km) circuit through a scenic part of the Schwarzwald, with stops for short hikes and cable-car rides to the top of the **Belchen,** a famous mile-high peak with spectacular views of the Rhine plain, and to the 4,750-foot (1,450-meter) summit of a peak called **Seebuck.** On this drive, you can stop at two Black Forest lakes, the **Schluchsee** and **Titisee.**

The week is up and you have yet to visit a museum! On **Day 7** make your way back to Frankfurt or Munich for the trip home. You look swell in those new *Lederhosen* and your green Tyrolean hat.

Prosit! Germany for Wine Lovers

When you raise a glass of wine in Germany, the toast is often a simple *"Prosit!"* (pronounced *prohst*). This itinerary takes you to the wine regions in western Germany. The trip begins and ends in Frankfurt. You may want to incorporate this four-day itinerary into a longer trip. For more information, see Chapter 16 for the Black Forest and the Bodensee and Chapter 17 for Cologne and sights along the Rhine.

From Frankfurt airport, you can hop on a train on **Day 1** and be in **Freiburg** in about two hours. Or you may want to rent a car in Frankfurt for the duration of the trip. Freiburg, a lively university town in the Black Forest, is surrounded by 1,600 acres of vineyards, more than any other city in Germany. On the last weekend in June, the city celebrates with a four-day wine festival that includes public tastings. *Weinkost* is another wine-tasting event in mid-August. Most of the grapes grow on the warm lower slopes of the nearby **Kaiserstühl (Emperor's Throne),** a volcanic massif. The young, light Silvaner wine is an ideal accompaniment to *Spargel* (white asparagus) in May. For a great meal with regional wines, dine at **Zum Roten Bären,** the oldest inn in Freiburg.

Head to Cologne on the River Rhine for **Day 2.** The train trip from Freiburg takes about four hours. Residents and visitors alike celebrate Cologne's special beer, *Kölsch,* as much as its wine. From Cologne, by car or boat, you can explore the neighboring wine country. In the **Rheingau wine district,** a 27-mile (45-km) stretch of the Rhine between the towns of **Biebrich** and **Bingen,** wine has been produced since Roman times. Those who know about such things consider Rheingau Rieslings to be among the best white wines made anywhere. You can drive through this area on a day trip from Cologne. Or you can take a Rhine cruise between Koblenz and Mainz, a scenic wine-growing region.

The **Mosel Valley,** southwest of Cologne, is another scenic wine-growing region and your destination on **Day 3.** The valley follows the course of the Mosel River for more than 100 miles (160 km) between **Trier** and **Koblenz.** Beautiful scenery and fine wines make this a prime area for leisurely exploration. The easiest way to enjoy a cruise down the Mosel River is to take a train to Koblenz. Between late April and the third week in October, cruises depart daily from Koblenz to **Cochem,** a picturesque wine village surrounded by vineyards and a popular spot for wine tastings and festivals. **Mosel-Wein-Woche (Mosel Wine Week),** held the first week in June, celebrates the region's wines with tasting booths and a street fair; **Weinfest** takes place the last weekend of August. The half-timbered **Alte Thorschenke** in Cochem, both a hotel and a wine restaurant, is one of the oldest and best-known establishments along the Mosel.

From Cochem, or Cologne, or Freiburg, make your way back to **Frankfurt** on **Day 4.** If you have a few more days, you can continue your tasting tour of Germany. Wherever you go, look for the local *Weinstube,* a convivial spot to sample Germany's many fine vintages.

Chapter 4

Planning Your Budget

. . . .

In This Chapter

▶ Planning a realistic budget for your trip

▶ Pricing things in Germany

▶ Uncovering hidden expenses

▶ Considering money-saving tips

. . . .

So, you want to go to Germany. You're excited and eager to pack. But can you really afford the trip? At this point, a financial reality check is in order. This chapter is all about *Geld* (pronounced *gelt*, meaning money). You may have heard that Germany is an expensive country — but just how expensive? What does a hotel cost in Munich? How much does a train ticket cost for travel from Berlin down to Bavaria, for instance? And how much is a meal in a nice restaurant after you get there? This chapter points you toward all the answers.

You may think a trip to Germany is prohibitively expensive because of the transatlantic flight. But you can often find bargain airfares to Frankfurt and Munich (the two German airports with direct international flights), and in some cases those flights are cheaper than what you'd pay to fly within the States. Adding everything up, your trip to Germany — even if you visit Munich and/or Berlin, the two most expensive German cities — can actually cost less than a trip to New York, San Francisco, or Los Angeles. And you get an experience that's rich in history and priceless in atmosphere.

After the events of September 11, 2001, tourism throughout Europe took a nose dive. Americans remained hesitant about flying. The German National Tourist Board and regional tourist boards throughout Germany offered plenty of special promotions to get visitors back to Germany — and many of these deals are still available. Keep your eyes open and you may nab an amazing deal.

Adding Up the Elements

You can easily budget for your Germany trip, but holding down costs while you're there may be another matter. Use the worksheets at the back of this book to get an approximate idea of what you'll spend throughout your trip. A good way to get a handle on all costs is to keep a tally from the moment you leave home. Walk yourself mentally through the trip, and see the following sections or the destination chapters in this book for prices:

- ✔ Begin with transportation to your nearest airport. Add flight costs and the price of getting from your destination airport to your hotel.

- ✔ Add the hotel rate for every night of your trip.

- ✔ Factor in a daily allotment for meals and snacks, but exclude the cost of breakfast if this meal is included in your hotel rate.

- ✔ Add admission prices to museums and castles, the opera or concerts, and any other attractions or entertainment expenses.

- ✔ If you're touring a city, figure in costs for public transportation (you really don't want to drive in Munich or Berlin, and every city in Germany has a great public transportation system).

- ✔ If you're traveling to a couple of destinations within Germany, add the cost of taking the train or renting a car.

- ✔ Determine what you'd like to spend on souvenirs and add the figure to your running total.

- ✔ Finally, add the cost of getting to the airport for your return flight and of traveling from your local airport back home.

After you've done all that, tack on another 15% to 20% for good measure.

Budgeting for your biggest expense: Lodging

The biggest bite from your budget comes from the cost of your hotel(s) or other accommodation. And that cost is going to be higher in Munich or Berlin than anywhere else in Germany. Fortunately, because you'll need to book rooms in these cities well in advance, you'll know this expense up front. Nearly all hotels throughout Germany (except for five-star luxury hotels) include a buffet breakfast as part of the room rate, so you save a few euros there.

Euro equivalent to U.S. dollar

Throughout this book, I give prices for restaurants, hotels, attractions, and services in euros rather than U.S. dollars. Why? Because the euro (€) has achieved near parity with the U.S. dollar — one euro equals one dollar. Every time you see €, think $.

As a general rule, you can always find a good hotel in Germany for under €150 a night, sometimes even under €100 a night. But because rates vary from hotel to hotel depending on their government-appointed category (one-star, two-star, and so on), giving a reliable average can't really be done. For the recommendations in this guide, however, the rate at an inexpensive hotel in Munich or Berlin, the major cities, is *generally* under €125, a moderate hotel runs from €126 to €175, and an expensive hotel costs from €176 to €225. After that, you hit the high end of €226 plus. As you can see, these prices — even for the most expensive cities in Germany — are not exorbitant. See Chapter 8 for information on what to expect in each price range and for a discussion of your lodging options and how to get the best rate.

Outside of Munich and Berlin, hotel rates are lower, generally from €80 to €125 per double room per night, and include *Frühstück* (pronounced *froo*-shtook, meaning breakfast). (Overall, prices are lower for everything once you leave Munich or Berlin.) But you still find plenty of opportunities to drop a king's ransom for a hotel, especially in some of the truly elegant five-star properties. Make sure to ask about special deals wherever you stay. Many hotels in the Bavarian countryside, for instance, offer bed, breakfast, lunch, and a full dinner at bargain prices. Throughout the country, hotels offer special price breaks for weekends (*Wochenende*) and during the summer (generally July and August). In some cases, the price drops so dramatically that you can stay in a double room in a five-star luxury hotel for under €175 per night.

Traveling by train: Transportation

You won't need to rent a car in any German city because the public transportation is so good. That saves you a bundle. You can also tour throughout the whole of Germany by train, without ever renting a car. Keep in mind, though, that in some areas, such as Bavaria and the Black Forest, having a car makes exploration of the countryside much easier.

Berlin, Munich, Frankfurt, Hamburg, and Cologne all have subway systems called the *U-Bahn* (short for *Untergrundbahn,* or "underground train"). U-Bahns are fast, convenient, and easy to use. The same cities also have light-rail or above-ground trains called the *S-Bahn,* and a system of trams or streetcars and buses. Special reduced-price transportation passes good for a full day (*Tageskarten*) or longer on all forms of public transportation make getting around German cities fairly inexpensive. Many larger cities have special passes that include public transportation and free or reduced-price admission to various attractions. I mention money-saving cards in the city sections of this guide whenever such cards are available and worthwhile.

In the smaller towns and cities of Germany, you can walk almost everywhere because the city centers are so compact and close to the train stations. The historic inner-city area in German cities is nearly always called the *Altstadt* (Old Town). If you don't want to walk, you can hop on a bus or tram, as the locals do. If you're traveling by train and want to see some of Germany's great castles, such as Neuschwanstein in Bavaria, you may need to take a local bus or taxi from the nearest town (Füssen, for Neuschwanstein) to the castle.

If you're going to travel around Germany by train, you can save money by buying a **German Railpass** before you leave home. I talk more about these cost-cutting train passes, and the popular **Eurailpass,** in Chapter 7. You can order them through a travel agent or by calling **Rail Europe** at ☎ **888-382-7245** in the United States or 800-361-7245 in Canada, or by going online at www.raileurope.com.

Eating cheaply or splurging: Restaurants

The food in Germany is often characterized as heavy. This may be true, but German food is also *ganz schmackhaftig* (very tasty). Although easy to find, and generally reasonably priced, traditional food is not the only cuisine you find in this country. In recent years large cities like Berlin and Munich have emerged as international food capitals. You find wonderful restaurants in the rest of the country, too, although smaller towns offer fewer cuisine options. Of course, eating at the top restaurants, no matter where you are, is going to cost you. However, in nearly every town and village throughout Germany, you can find a *Ratskeller* (restaurant beneath a town hall), a beer hall, a *Weinstube* (restaurant where wine is the primary beverage served), or some other kind of nonfancy restaurant where you can dine cheaply and well — and where you can enjoy your meal along with the locals. In addition, many of the best restaurants in Berlin, Munich, and elsewhere offer special fixed-price meals that can be real bargains.

As with hotels, food is more expensive in the big cities like Berlin and Munich. If you eat lunch and dinner at moderately priced restaurants in Berlin, you can expect to pay between €35 to €50 per person per day for meals, not including beer or wine (assuming that your hotel rate includes breakfast). Outside of Berlin or Munich, unless you splurge on really high-priced restaurants, your daily food cost is about €25 to €40. In the countryside, you find that many hotels offer *voll pension,* that is, bed, breakfast, lunch, and dinner along with your room. In most cases this adds up to considerable savings.

If you eat breakfast at a cafe instead of your hotel and are content with coffee and a roll at a stand-up counter, expect to pay about €3 to €5 anywhere in the country. But remember, a big buffet breakfast is nearly always included in your hotel cost. Oddly enough, only in luxury hotels do you have to pay extra for breakfast — usually €20 to €22 — but usually the buffet breakfast is fabulous. Afternoon *Kaffee und Kuchen* (coffee and cake) sets you back about €5 or €6 anywhere in Germany.

Paying as you go: Sightseeing

Your budget for admission fees depends, of course, on what you want to see. But why skimp when it comes to sightseeing? After all, the attractions are what you came all this way to see. Fortunately, sightseeing in Germany is fairly inexpensive. Finding a museum that costs more than €6 is rare. And some of the top sights — such as the Reichstag in Berlin or the Frauenkirche and Englisher Garten in Munich — are free. Admission to Neuschwanstein, the Bavarian castle that is Germany's top attraction, costs only €7. In addition, if you're a senior or a student, you can often get a reduced-price admission.

Strolling down Berlin's great avenues, Kurfürstendamm or Unter den Linden, or viewing the Brandenburg Gate, is *kostenlos* (free). In fact, exploring by foot in almost any German town is a good way to soak up the local culture free of charge.

As a general rule, expect to pay between €2 to €4 for admission to museums and local attractions outside of the big cities. In some locations, the top attraction is a cable car that can whisk you to the top of a famous peak for a spectacular view. The most expensive ride is to the top of the Zugspitze, Germany's highest mountain, and back again; the cost for adults is €31. Most cable cars cost much less, generally around €5 for a round trip. Sightseeing boat excursions are typically between €7 and €15, depending on the duration of the trip.

Kaffee und Kuchen at twice the price

Prices for some items in Germany have risen dramatically since the country switched its currency from deutsche marks (DM) to euros (€) in 2002. In fact, there have been widespread accusations that price-gouging occurred during the euro conversion. How did it happen? During the conversion, the euro amount was to be half the DM amount. In other words, a cup of coffee that cost 3 DM (about $1.50) should have cost, after conversion, €1.50. But some vendors made the exchange rate 1:1, so the price for their coffee became €3 ($3). In other words, with some less expensive items, prices actually doubled. As you may expect, a government committee is looking into the matter.

Controlling costs: Shopping and nightlife

Shopping and entertainment are the most flexible parts of your budget. You don't have to buy anything at all, and you can hit the sack right after dinner instead of going to a concert or dancing at a club. You know what you want. Flip through the shopping and nightlife options of each destination chapter. If anything strikes you as something you can't do without, budget accordingly. (Keep in mind that a small beer sets you back about €2.50, a glass of good German wine about €5, and an opera ticket in either Berlin or Munich anywhere from €10 to €80.) Berlin, especially, is a late-night city, so you may want to check out the club scene while you're there; cover charges are rarely more than €5, but drinks other than beer can be pricey.

Tables 3-1 and 3-2 give you an idea of what things typically cost in Berlin and the rest of the country.

Table 3-1 What Things Cost in Berlin	
Item	**Cost in Euros***
Transportation from airport to Central Berlin	
From Tegel by bus	€2.10
From Tegel by taxi	€18
One-way U-Bahn (subway) fare within Central Berlin	€2.10
Tageskarte (one-day) public transportation pass for two zones	€6.10
Double room without breakfast at Adlon Hotel ($$$$)	€310–€375
Double room with breakfast at Brandenburger Hof ($$$)	€240–€280
Double room with breakfast at Sorat Art'otel ($$)	€145–€245
Double room with breakfast at Arco Hotel ($)	€75–€102
Dinner for one excluding wine at Die Quadriga ($$$$)	€55
Dinner for one excluding wine at Marjellchen ($$–$$$)	€30
Meal for one excluding wine at La Riva ($$)	€22
Cafe meal for one at Café Silberstein ($)	€8
Sausage at stand-up snack stand ($)	€2.50
Kaffee und Kuchen at a cafe or stand-up coffee shop	€4–€8
Large glass of beer at a cafe, bar, or tavern	€3.50

Item	Cost in Euros*
Adult/child admission to the Gemäldegalerie (Painting Gallery)	€6/€3
Adult/child admission to The Story of Berlin	€9.30/€3.50
Adult/child admission to the Pergamon Museum	€6/€3
Adult/child admission to Charlottenburg Palace	€8/€5
Opera ticket	€10–€90
Theatre program	€2

*Item cost in euros (€) = Item cost in U.S. $

Table 3-2	What Things Cost outside Berlin
Item	**Cost in Euros***
First-class/second-class one-way train ticket Berlin–Dresden	€49/€36
First-class/second-class one-way train ticket Berlin–Munich	€161/€110
Double room with breakfast at Der Kleine Prinz, Baden-Baden ($$)	€15–€250
Double room with breakfast at Röten Bären, Freiburg ($$)	€133–€148
Double room with breakfast at Hotel-Garni Brugger, Lindau ($)	€79–€87
Double room without breakfast at Kempinkski Vier Jahreszeiten, Munich ($$$$)	€285–€335
Fixed-price dinner for one excluding wine at Der Kleine Prinz, Baden-Baden ($$$)	€52–€70
Lunch for one excluding beer at Café Schinkelwache, Dresden ($)	€10
Fixed-price dinner for one excluding wine at Zum Röten Bären, Freiburg ($$$)	€30–€40
Dinner for one including one glass of beer at Hofbräuhaus, Munich ($)	€20
Adult/child admission to Neuschwanstein Castle, Bavaria	€7/€6
All ages admission to Zwinger Palace (all museums), Dresden	€6.10
Adult/child admission to Alte Pinakothek (Old Masters Gallery), Munich	€4.60/€3
Adult/child admission to Deutsches Museum (Science and Industry), Munich	€6/€2.50
Opera ticket, Semper Opera House, Dresden	€10–€80

(continued)

Table 3-2 (continued)

Item	Cost in Euros*
Complete bath and massage treatment at Friedrichsbad, Baden-Baden	€29
Average losses at gambling tables, Baden-Baden	€5,000
Tank of unleaded gas, economy car	€60

Item cost in euros (€) = Item cost in U.S. $

Keeping a Lid on Hidden Expenses

Let me introduce you to Germany's version of a sales tax, called the *Mehrwertsteuer,* or **value-added tax** (VAT). Brace yourself: The tax amounts to 16%. This hefty percentage is already figured into the total price of consumer goods and hotel and restaurant bills. (The general hotel and restaurant prices in this book include VAT.) This tax isn't a hidden expense, and you really can't avoid paying it — unless you plan to do some heavy-duty shopping.

If you're not a resident of the European Union, you can get a VAT refund on purchases made in Germany (this doesn't include hotel and restaurant bills). See Chapter 9 for details.

As a general rule, Germany isn't a country where you must tip excessively, unless, of course, you're staying in an expensive hotel with porters who carry your bags (€1 per bag carried) and doormen who'll hail you a cab (€1 per successful hail). Otherwise, service charges are included in the bill. In restaurants, if the service has been very good, you can add 5% to 10% to your bill, or round up to the next euro.

The telephone in your hotel is convenient, but I recommend that you avoid using it if you're on a budget. A local call that costs €.20 at a phone booth may cost you €1 or more from your hotel phone. If you plan to make a number of calls during your trip, get a phone card (see the Appendix for details) and use a phone outside the hotel.

Cutting Costs for Bargain Hunters

Throughout this book, Bargain Alert icons highlight money-saving tips and/or great deals. Here are some additional cost-cutting strategies:

✔ **Go in the off-season.** If you can travel at off-season times (October and November or January to March), you'll find hotel prices can be as much as 20% less than during peak months. The same is true for July and August, which are peak travel months for Germans and often a time of lower hotel prices.

✔ **Travel on off days of the week.** Generalizing about airfares is difficult because the entire industry has changed in the past year. In general, airfares vary depending on the day of the week and even the hour you fly. If you can travel on a Tuesday, Wednesday, or Thursday, you may find cheaper flights to Frankfurt, Munich, or Berlin. When you inquire about airfares, ask if you can obtain a cheaper rate by flying on a specific day.

✔ **Try a package tour.** For popular destinations like Frankfurt and Munich, you can book airfare, hotel, ground transportation, and even some sightseeing by making just one call to a travel agent, airline, or packager — and you'll pay a lot less than if you tried to put the trip together yourself (see Chapter 6).

✔ **Always ask for discount rates.** Membership in AAA, frequent-flyer plans, trade unions, AARP, or other groups may qualify you for discounts on plane tickets, hotel rooms, car rentals, and guided tours booked before you go. Attractions within Germany usually offer a lower admission rate for seniors, children, and students with ID.

✔ **Ask if your kids can stay in your room with you.** A room with two double beds usually doesn't cost any more than one with a queen-size bed. And many hotels won't charge you the additional person rate if that person is pint-sized and related to you. Even if you have to pay a few extra euros for a rollaway bed, you save alot by not taking two rooms.

✔ **Ask about weekend, midweek, and off-season special offers.** To encourage year-round tourism, many hotels in Germany offer special price breaks on weekends or mid-week off-season. Sometimes these are offered as romantic getaway packages and include dinner and a glass of wine. Surfing the Web is the best way to find out about special packages at specific hotels. (See Chapter 8 for some recommended Web sites).

✔ **Try expensive restaurants at lunch instead of dinner.** At most top restaurants in Berlin and Munich, prices at lunch are lower than those at dinner, and the menu often includes many of the dinnertime specialties. Also, wherever you travel in Germany, look for the fixed-price menus.

✔ **Travel second-class.** A first-class train ticket generally costs about one-third more than a standard second-class ticket.

✔ **Know the advantages and disadvantages of buying a rail pass before you leave home.** The amount of money you save with a rail pass depends on how often you use it and how far you go. If you are headquartering in one city and making side trips to nearby towns, buying your local train tickets in Germany is cheaper.

✔ **Walk a lot.** That's what the Germans do. Most German cities are compact and eminently walkable. They have a historic Altstadt (Old Town), which contains most of the attractions and is within walking distance of the train station. A good pair of walking shoes can save you money on taxis and other local transportation. As a bonus, you get to know the city and its inhabitants more intimately, and you can explore at a slower pace.

✔ **Skip the souvenirs.** Your photographs and memories will make the best mementos of your trip. If you're worried about your budget, do without the T-shirts, key chains, beer steins, cuckoo clocks, Bavarian hats, and the trinkets sold at major tourist attractions.

Chapter 5

Planning Ahead for Special Needs or Interests

● ●

In This Chapter

▶ Traveling with your kids

▶ Discovering discounts and special tours for seniors

▶ Locating wheelchair-accessible attractions

▶ Finding lesbigay communities and special events

▶ Learning about Germany's Jewish history

● ●

Many of today's travelers have special interests or needs. Parents may want to take their children along with them on trips. Seniors may like to take advantage of discounts or tours designed especially for them. People with disabilities may need to ensure that sites on their itineraries offer wheelchair access. Gays and lesbians may want to know about welcoming places and events. Jewish visitors may want to visit Holocaust memorials and worship in a synagogue. In response to these needs, this chapter offers advice and resources.

Bringing the Brood: Advice for Families

Traveling with *Kinder* (pronounced *kin*-der, meaning children), from toddlers to teens, is a challenge — no doubt about it. Family travel can put a strain on the budget and influence your choices of activities and hotels. But in the end, isn't sharing your experiences as a *Familie* (pronounced fa-*mee*-leah, meaning family) great?

Look for the Kid Friendly icon as you flip through this book. I use it to highlight hotels, restaurants, and attractions that are particularly family-friendly. Zeroing in on these places can help you plan your trip more quickly and easily.

In addition, the following resources can help with your planning:

- ✔ **Family Travel Forum** (☎ 212/665-6124; Internet: www. familytravelforum.com) offers a call-in and on-line service for subscribers. You can order a subscription ($48 per year) by writing FTF, 891 Amsterdam Ave., New York, NY 10025, or call to request its free information packet.

- ✔ **Family Travel Network** (Internet: www.familytravelnetwork. com) offers travel tips and reviews of family-friendly destinations, vacation deals, and thoughtful features such as "What to Do When Your Kids Are Afraid to Travel."

- ✔ **Travel with Your Children** (Internet: www.travelwithyourkids. com) is a comprehensive site offering sound advice for traveling families.

Admission prices for attractions throughout Germany are reduced for children ages 6 to 15. Under-6s almost always get in for free. If you're traveling with one or two children 5 to 15, always check to see whether the attraction offers a money-saving **family ticket,** which considerably reduces the admission price for a group of two adults and two children. The same is true for public transportation: Low-priced family or group tickets are usually available.

Your kids will be more interested in their trip if they know about the attractions that they're seeing. Budgeting some extra money for guided sightseeing tours with English-language commentary is a good idea. These tours are available in Germany's larger cities and at top attractions.

Locating family-friendly businesses

Most German hotels will happily accommodate your family if you reserve your rooms in advance and make the staff aware that you're traveling with kids. The establishment may bring in an extra cot or let you share a larger room; these types of arrangements are common. Smaller *pensions* (pronounced pen-see-*own,* meaning a room rented in a home or apartment and always including breakfast) may present problems such as cramped rooms and shared toilet facilities. Ask questions before you reserve.

Berlin, Munich, and other mid-sized German cities have American-style fast-food places, including **Burger King** and **McDonald's.** You won't find these food chains in smaller villages and towns, however. Younger teens traveling in Berlin and Munich may want to check out the **Hard Rock Cafe** in those cities. In larger cities, you can keep costs down by eating at low-key, local restaurants.

The best of the *Wurst*

Your time in Germany may be a good opportunity to introduce your kids to some dishes that they've never tried. Germany's ever-present *Wurst* (pronounced *voorst*, and meaning sausage) is 100% meat with no filler. For something more familiar, kids can choose from a selection of cereals at most buffet breakfasts in hotels; however, the selection may not include as many presweetened varieties as in the United States.

Expensive, high-toned restaurants in Germany are not particularly welcoming toward young children. The menus aren't geared to the tastes of U.S. youngsters, and the staff can be less than welcoming to children who are not well-behaved. In fact, in Germany you don't see many families dining in expensive restaurants even if the place welcomes kids.

Planning your trip together

Your children may become more excited about their trip to Germany if they know some of the special sights and events in store for them. Before you leave, sit down with your kids and make a plan. Go over the sights and activities in this book and let your children list a few of the things that they'd like to experience, in order of preference. Make a similar list of your own. Older children may want to do some research on the Internet. Together, plot out a day-by-day schedule that meets everyone's needs.

When considering museums, bear in mind that most German museums do not translate their signage and texts into English. Therefore, a trip to a museum may try the patience of those children who can't understand what they're reading.

You can spur your kids' interest (and your own) by buying a German language tape or checking one out from the library. In the evening, everyone can spend an hour together, listening to the tape, and familiarizing themselves with the sounds of the German language and learning at least a few words.

You can generate excitement about the trip by letting your younger children read *Grimm's Fairy Tales*. Incite your kids' curiosity about "awesome" historic sites such as **Neuschwanstein castle** (the original fairy-tale castle) by reading the information in this book and by going online. Two attractions to consider with older children are Munich's **Deutsches Museum (Museum of Science and Industry),** a repository of "neat old stuff" and gadgets galore, and Stuttgart's **Mercedes-Benz Museum,** with its century's worth of vintage cars. Older children may also enjoy anticipating a boat trip down the Rhine or a trip on a city's U-Bahn (pronounced *oo*-bahn, and meaning subway). All kids will no doubt be curious about touring Germany by train.

Enjoying the outdoors with your kids

If your kids enjoy adventure- and outdoor-related travel, Germany offers special scenic regions that are full of outdoor attractions. The **Bavarian Alps** (see Chapter 15) provide gorgeous outdoor scenery with hiking and skiing opportunities as well as mob-scene mega-attractions like Ludwig's fairy-tale castles. The **Schwarzwald** (Black Forest; see Chapter 16) is a famed outdoor recreation area, with intriguing cities like the university town of Freiburg and the glamorous health spa Baden-Baden (where the whole family can "take the waters"). In Bavaria and the Black Forest, you find cable cars and mountain-climbing funiculars that whisk you up to breathtaking panoramas. Keep the **Bodensee, or Lake Constance** (see Chapter 16), in mind, too. Besides being in an unusually warm and sunny area, this enormous lake is clean enough for swimming.

Picnicking may be just the ticket for enjoying the outdoors *and* a cheap family meal. Pick up supplies at an outdoor market, bakery, or grocery store, and head to **Englisher Garten** in Munich, **Tiergarten** in Berlin, or to just about any palace or castle park in the rest of Germany.

Traveling on planes and trains

Flying time to Frankfurt from New York is about 7½ hours and from Seattle, about 9 hours. Air time from Australia may be 25 hours. This is a lot of time for kids to sit still and be quiet. Although they can spend some of the journey time watching a movie (or two), come prepared with extra diversions: games, puzzles, books — whatever you know will keep your kids entertained. Request a special kids' menu at least a day in advance. If your child needs baby food, bring your own and ask a flight attendant to warm it. Dealing with jet lag can be hard on adults but even harder on small children. Don't schedule too much for your first day in Germany. Get everyone comfortably settled before diving into an itinerary.

Passing through beautiful countryside on a sleek, ultramodern ICE (InterCity Express) train is a pleasure the whole family can enjoy. Plus, taking the train is far more fun, and usually far less expensive, than renting a car, something you don't need to do in Germany anyway. For information on traveling by train through Germany, including money-saving rail passes, see Chapter 7.

Hiring a baby-sitter in Germany

What you really need is an exciting evening at the opera and a romantic late dinner with a glass of fine German wine. But you can't take Junior along on this special evening. What are your options? Ask your hotel staff if they can recommend a local baby-sitting service. Most of the hotels marked with a Kid Friendly icon in this book can help arrange baby-sitting.

Going Gray: Suggestions for Seniors

Germany won't present any problems for you if you're a senior who gets around easily. If not, when you plan your trip be aware that not all hotels — particularly smaller, less expensive pensions and guest-houses — have elevators. The staircases in some places are a test for *anyone* with luggage. When you reserve a hotel, ask whether or not you'll have access to an elevator or a *Fahrstuhl* (*far*-shtool), as they're called in Germany.

Although large German cities can be crowded, people are generally polite and courteous. And you don't need to be overly concerned about crime. Yes, crime does occur (mostly in bigger cities), but if you follow common-sense precautions, you're unlikely to encounter trouble. (Car break-ins are one of the biggest problems. You can avoid this issue by traveling by train, the best way to tour Germany.)

Being a senior may entitle you to some terrific travel bargains, such as lower prices for German Rail passes and reduced admission at museums and other attractions. Always ask, even if the reduction isn't posted. Carrying ID with proof of age can pay off in all these situations. *Note:* In Germany, you may find that some discounts are available only to German or EU (European Union) residents.

These sources can provide information on discounts and other benefits for seniors.

✔ **AARP** (formlerly known as the American Association of Retired Persons; 601 E St. NW, Washington, DC 20049; ☎ **800/424-3410**; Internet: www.aarp.org), offers member discounts on car rentals and hotels. With a $12.50 annual membership (anyone over 50 can join), AARP offers members a wide range of benefits, including discounts on U.S. Airways flights to Munich from several U.S. cities; discounts on cruise ships that sail on the Rhine, Mosel, Danube, and Elbe rivers (via the Web site www.eWaterways.com); and discounts on escorted tours from Globus and Cosmos, major tour operators offering trips to Germany.

✔ **Elderhostel** (75 Federal St., Boston, MA 02110-1941; ☎ 877/426-8056; Internet: www.elderhostel.org) offers people 55 and over a variety of university-based education programs in Berlin and throughout Germany. These courses are value-packed, hassle-free ways to learn while traveling. The price includes airfare, accommodations, meals, tuition, tips, and insurance. And you'll be glad to know that there are no grades. Popular Germany offerings have included "Opera in Berlin" and "Bavaria to Bauhaus."

✔ **Grand Circle Travel** (347 Congress St., Boston, MA 02210; ☎ 800/221-2610 or 617/350-7500; Internet: www.gct.com) offers package deals for the 50-plus market, mostly of the tour-bus variety, with free trips thrown in for those who organize groups of ten or more.

Most of the major U.S. domestic airlines, including American, United, and Continental, offer discount programs for senior travelers — be sure to ask whenever you book a flight.

Accessing Germany: Information for People with Disabilities

The German word for "disabled" is *behindert* (bee-*hin*-dert). A disability needn't stop anybody from traveling because more options and resources are available than ever before. In fact, Germany is one of the more advanced countries in Europe when it comes to accessibility for disabled travelers.

When talking with a travel agent, be sure to discuss the means of travel that will accommodate your physical needs (train, plane, bus tour groups, and so on). Also address special accommodations or services you may require (transportation within the airport, help with a wheelchair, and special seating or meals) and the type of special assistance you can expect from your transportation company, hotel, tour group, and so on.

Locating resources

The German National Tourist Office's Web site, www.visits-to-germany.com, with its section on travel for the disabled, is a good place to begin researching your trip. Another good resource is **Freewheeling's** www.freewheeling.net, an online German/English magazine dedicated to independent travel for those with handicaps. **Half the Planet**, www.halftheplanet.com, is an excellent, well-designed Web site promoting all aspects of barrier-free living, including travel.

Here are some other helpful resources in the United States.

- **The Moss Rehab Hospital** (☎ 215/456-9603; Internet: www. mossresourcenet.org) provides friendly, helpful phone assistance through its **Travel Information Service.**

- **The Society for Accessible Travel and Hospitality** (☎ 212/447-7284; Fax: 212-725-8253; Internet: www.sath.org) offers a wealth of travel resources for all types of disabilities and informed recommendations on destinations, access guides, travel agents, tour operators, vehicle rentals, and companion services. Annual membership costs $45 for adults; $30 for seniors and students.

- **Mobility International USA** (☎ 541/343-1284; Internet: www. miusa.org) publishes *A World of Options,* a 658-page book of resources that covers everything from biking trips to scuba outfitters, and a newsletter, *Over the Rainbow.* Annual membership is $35.

- **The American Foundation for the Blind** (☎ 800/232-5463; Internet: www.afb.org) provides information on traveling with Seeing Eye dogs.

British travelers with disabilities may want to contact **RADAR** (Royal Association for Disability and Rehabilitation), Unit 12, City Forum, 250 City Rd., London EC1V 8AF (☎ **020/7250-3222;** Fax: 020/7250-0212), which publishes vacation "fact packs," containing information on trip planning, travel insurance, specialized accommodations, and transportation abroad.

If you can read German, you may want to use one of these resources.

- *Handicapped-Reisen in Deutschland* (Handicapped Travel in Germany) by Yvo Escales is an excellent all-round resource, listing wheelchair-accessible hotels, resorts, and youth hostels and providing detailed information on disabled travel through the country. The publication costs €19.50 (including postage) and can be ordered from the publisher, **Fremdenverkehrsmarketing GmbH,** Postfach 1547, 53005 Bonn, Germany (☎ **0228/616-135;** Fax: 0228/622-500). You can find more information about this and other books in German for the disabled at www.morbus-pompe.de/html/literatur.html.

- **Nationale Koordinationsstelle Tourismus für Alle** (NatKo; national Tourism Coordination Agency for All People), Kötherhofstrasse 4, 55116 Mainz; ☎ **06131/250-410;** Fax: 0631/214-848; Internet: www.natko.de) is the central organization in the country for all inquiries concerning barrier-free travel. On the Web site, under "Wer hilft" (Who is helping?), you can find special offers and a list of German tour operators offering special tours and travel opportunities.

✔ The Web site **You-Too** (www.you-too.net) has information on the accessibility of public buildings throughout Germany, accessible accommodations, and accessible activities.

Several organizations offer tours designed to meet the needs of travelers with disabilities. Some tour operators with trips to Germany include:

✔ **Accessible Journeys** (☎ **800/TINGLES** or 610/521-0339; Internet: www.disabilitytravel.com)

✔ **S E Unlimited Travel** (☎ **800 552-9798** in the U.S. and Canada, or 605 366-0202; Fax: 605 334-0000; Internet: www.seunlimitedtravel.com)

✔ **TravelAbility** (☎ **0870/241-6127** in the United Kingdom; Fax: 01452/729-853; Internet: www.atlholidays.com)

Touring in a Rollstuhl (wheelchair)

Traveling in a wheelchair (called a *Rollstuhl,* pronounced *roll*-shtool) presents unique challenges. Being spontaneous is more difficult, for one thing, because you have to be aware of potential barrier problems. For many wheelchair-bound travelers, an escorted tour is a necessity. But others want the adventures of being on their own. Thanks to its comprehensive accessibility, Germany offers both options.

The international airports in Munich and Frankfurt are wheelchair accessible.

Deutsche Bahn (German Rail) offers transportation service for the disabled. Some 385 stations throughout the country have lifting aids or mobile ramps. You can reserve your seat in advance and obtain information about traveling with a disability by calling the special **Deutsche Bahn number for disabled travelers, ☎ 01805/512-512.** You can also find information (in German only) for disabled travelers on their Web site, www.bahn.de (click on "Service" and "Mobilitätseingeschränkte").

Not all U-Bahn (subway) stations have wheelchair access. However, in larger cities, public buses are generally wheelchair accessible.

A disabled badge or car sticker does *not* entitle a disabled driver to unrestricted parking. A handicapped-ID is required. You must obtain this from the local tourist information office.

Many hotels in Berlin, Munich, and the rest of Germany (more in the western part than the east) have rooms for the disabled (these tend to be in larger, more modern hotels). Most of the older and less expensive pensions and guesthouses don't have elevators, or they may not be wide enough for a wheelchair. Ask about this issue before you reserve, or use one of the travel agencies that specialize in travel for people with disabilities (see "Locating resources," earlier in this section).

Although not all restaurants provide wheelchair ramps, most restaurants are happy to accommodate people with disabilities.

A fair number of the top sights in the country are wheelchair accessible, although calling ahead to make arrangements and to get directions to special entrances and/or elevators is always a good idea. Larger theaters and performing-arts venues are often wheelchair accessible, too (again, call first). Also keep in mind that although Germany's streets and sidewalks are generally kept in good repair, you won't find many modern curb cuts. In historic areas, you have to deal with cobblestones.

If you're interested in gliding down the Rhine and Mosel rivers, looking at vineyards and castles, the **Köln-Düsseldorfer (KD) line** has wheelchair-accessible boats (see Chapter 17 for more on KD and Rhine journeys).

Stepping Out: Advice for Gays and Lesbians

Germany is one of the most "developed" countries in the world when it comes to gay pride, gay culture, and gay tourism. If you are *schwul* (pronounced *shwool*, and meaning gay) or *lesbisch* (pronounced *lez*-bish, meaning lesbian), you'll find a lot to do in Deutschland. Berlin, Munich, Hamburg, Frankfurt, and Cologne all have large gay communities, but gay life flourishes outside the cities, too. Throughout the country, in small towns and large, you find a network of gay or gay-friendly restaurants, cafes, stores, bar, dance clubs, and community centers.

Gay and lesbian couples qualify for family tickets on public transportation in many Germany cities. With most family, or *Gruppen* (group) tickets, all that matters is that two (or more) individuals travel together.

Pride and politics

Perhaps some of the openness of gay life in Germany today has to do with the murderous anti-homosexual policies of the Nazis — between 1933 and 1945, untold thousands of homosexuals were arrested and sent to their deaths in labor camps. That may explain why German gays and lesbians today are so politically active and determined not to tolerate discrimination. At Europride 2002, the huge Europe-wide Gay Pride celebration that was held in Cologne (the location of the event changes yearly), the featured speaker was the German Foreign Minister, Joschka Fischer.

Celebrating Gay Pride in Germany

Every summer parades and special events celebrate Gay Pride. Lesbigay travelers may want to time their visits to coincide with these big festivals.

- ✔ **Berlin** holds its annual **Gay & Lesbian Street Festival** in mid-June, celebrates its **Christopher Street Day and Parade** around the third weekend in June, and holds its famous **Love Parade** in mid-July. You find information on the Web at www.berlin.de.

- ✔ **Munich** celebrates **Christopher Street Day** in mid-July.

- ✔ **Hamburg** celebrates with a **Gay Pride Parade and Festival** around June 8 to 10.

- ✔ **Cologne's Christopher Street Weekend** is usually the first weekend in June.

- ✔ **Frankfurt's Christopher Street Weekend** takes place around the third weekend in July.

Finding gay-friendly travel agents and tour operators

If you want to keep your hard-earned travel money pink, you can use a gay travel service. The **International Gay and Lesbian Travel Association (IGLTA)** maintains a worldwide network of gay and lesbian travel-agent professionals who can help you plan your trip. For information on the nearest IGLTA travel agent, contact **IGLTA** (☎ **800/ 448-8550;** Internet: www.IGLTA.org).

One company (with two names) that offers gay-friendly travel packages is **Going Your Way Tours** and **Winelovertours.com** (☎ **860/447-1845;** Internet: www.winelovertours.com). However, Germany seems to fall below the radar screen of most gay tour operators (too bad, since Berlin is such a great destination for gay tours). The following tour operators deal in one way or another with gay *European* travel packages but do not (yet) offer special tours to just Germany:

- ✔ **Above and Beyond Tours** (☎ **800/397-2681;** Fax: 760/325-1702; Internet: www.abovebeyondtours.com)

- ✔ **Alyson Adventures** (☎ **800/825-9766;** Internet: www. alysonadventures.com)

- ✔ **David's Trips and Tours** (☎ **888/723-0699;** Fax: 949/723-0666; Internet: www.davidtours.com)

You may have more luck with these Germany-based gay tour operators.

- **Hellkamp Reisen,** Hellkamp 17, Hamburg 20255, Germany (☎ 040/4019-6186; Fax: 040/491-9100; Internet: www.gaytravel. de), offers tours to Bavaria and the northern island of Sylt.

- **Teddy Travel,** Mathiasstrasse 4–6, Cologne 50676, Germany (☎ 0221/234-967; Fax: 0221/241-774; Internet: www.teddy-travel. de) sometimes has special opera offerings.

Researching German lesbigay life on the Web

The following are just a few of the Web sites you may want to check out as you begin to plan your trip to Germany.

Beloved Berlin — lesbigayest of all German cities

You find plenty of gay life in all large German cities, but Berlin is something special. Statistics claim that out of a population of 3.5 million, 300,000 gays and lesbians call Berlin home! The openness of the city, starting at the turn of the 20th century and lasting up to the Nazi era, made Berlin a travel destination for gays and lesbians. More happens in Berlin for the gay and lesbian traveler than in any other city in Germany.

Gay life goes on all over Berlin, but gay bars and cafes abound in three main areas. In western Berlin, the oldest gay neighborhood extends from **Nollendorfplatz** to **Wittenbergplatz. Kreuzberg,** long known for its healthy mix of alternative lifestyles, is pretty homo-geneous as well. In eastern Berlin, the new gay beehive is **Prenzlauer Berg,** especially on and around Schönhauser Allee.

A great way to acquaint yourself with Berlin's incredible gay past is by taking the **gay sightseeing tour** called "Von der Kaiserzeit zum Nationalsozialismus" ("From the Kaisers to the Nazis"). From April to October, the tour departs from Lutherkirche Dennewitzplatz (U-/S-Bahn: Yorkstrasse) at 3 p.m. on Saturday and Sunday and lasts about 90 minutes. Call **Movin' Queer Berlin,** Liegnitzer Strasse 5 (☎ 030/ 618-6955) for current price information and to verify times. **Frauen-Touren Unterwegs (Women's Tours),** Potsdamer Strasse 139 (☎ 030/215-1022), offers tours with gender-specific themes like "Women in the Middle Ages" and "Jewish Women"; you can request lesbian themes as well. If you don't speak any German, check to make sure that an English-speaking guide is available.

Mann-o-Meter, the gay community center at Bülowstrasse 106 (☎ 030/216-8008), has free information on what's going on in this gayest of German cities and an English-speaking staff. See Chapter 12 in this guide for lesbigay places to visit in Berlin.

✔ www.pinkpassport.com. This site is a destination service provider for international gay travelers. You can select a city in Germany and find out pertinent travel-related information.

✔ www.stadt.gay-web.de. One of the best all-purpose gay sites for lesbigay travelers planning a trip to Germany, this site allows you to access a lesbigay guide for each city you want to visit. (By the way, *Stadt* means "city.")

✔ Try the following Web sites for information on specific cities: www.berlin.gay-web.de; www.munich.gay-web.de; www.hamburg.gay-web.de; www.frankfurt.gay-web.de; and www.koeln.gay-web.de or www.gaykoeln.com.

I provide extensive coverage of gay Berlin in *Frommer's Gay & Lesbian Europe* (Wiley, 2002), available at most bookstores.

Remembering the Past: Resources for Jewish Travelers in Germany

In this guidebook, I can't even begin to scratch the surface of this huge and sensitive issue. Jewish life in Germany dates back hundreds of years. Throughout the centuries, Jews from all levels of society contributed to German culture. Large Jewish communities flourished in cities throughout Germany until the Nazi era, when systematic persecution, banishment, seizure of property and assets, and extermination policies created horrors that are almost beyond comprehension. Today, with a number of around 70,000, Germany's Jewish population is the third largest in Western Europe and one of the few that's actually growing, in large part because many Jewish people from the former Soviet Union are choosing to live in Germany.

Special and very emotional issues confront Jewish visitors to Germany. The Germany you visit today is a democratic federal republic sensitive to the past. Several places are dedicated to remembering the Jewish experience in this country. One of the most remarkable is the new **Jüdisches Museum (Jewish Museum)** in Berlin (see Chapter 12). Another is the Holocaust memorial, the largest in Europe, soon to be completed in Berlin between the Brandenburg Gate and Potsdamer Platz. Throughout the country, synagogues have been restored, and memorials erected. The most moving memorials are at **Dachau** (see Chapter 14), near Munich, and **Buchenwald** (see Chapter 13), near Weimar.

For assistance in planning your itinerary, contact the German National Tourist Office (see the Appendix for the address and phone number) and request a copy of *Germany for the Jewish Traveler.* This free booklet presents an overview of Jewish history and lists recommended places to go and what to see.

Part II
Ironing Out the Details

The 5th Wave   By Rich Tennant

ACHTUNG!

"It says, children are forbidden from running, touching objects or appearing bored during the tour of the castle."

In this part . . .

This part helps you with the practical details of planning your trip to Germany. In **Chapter 6,** I go over the transportation options for getting you to Germany, including information on travel agents, guided and package tours, and how to choose the best airline and get the best fare. In **Chapter 7,** I tell you about traveling through Germany by train, car, plane, and boat. In **Chapter 8,** I discuss all the various accommodation options, outlining the kinds of hotels and guesthouses that you'll find, explaining what hotel rack rates are, and offering suggestions for landing a room if you arrive without a reservation. Every day on your trip, you'll deal with euros, Germany's currency, so **Chapter 9** is all about money: whether to use traveler's checks, credit cards, cash, or ATMs and how to exchange your money. I load **Chapter 10** with information about getting a passport; buying travel and medical insurance; reserving in advance for shows; sightseeing, and restaurants; and even what to pack (or not) for your trip.

Chapter 6

Getting to Germany

· ·

· ·

*Y*ou always wanted to take a trip to Berlin, a city you've been curious about for years, and maybe spend a few days traveling around Germany. But now you are overwhelmed trying to make all the necessary decisions. Do you need a travel agent? Do you want to travel with a tour group and have all the decisions made for you, or do you want to strike out on your own? How do you find the best airfares to Germany? This chapter helps find the answers, so you can really start planning your trip to Deutschland.

Consulting a Travel Agent

A travel agent can help you find a bargain airfare, hotel room, or rental car. The best travel agents can tell you how much time to budget for a destination, find you a cheap flight that doesn't require you to change planes in strange airports, get you a better hotel room for about the same price, and even give recommendations on restaurants.

The best way to find a good travel agent is by word of mouth. Check with family members, neighbors, or friends. Make sure that you select an agent who knows Germany.

Travel agents work on commission. The good news is that *you* don't pay the commission; accommodations, tour companies, and airlines do — at least for now, that is. The bad news is that you may run into unscrupulous travel agents who will try to persuade you to book the vacations that bring them the highest commissions.

Some airlines and resorts have begun limiting or eliminating travel-agent commissions altogether. If more airlines and companies throughout the industry lower commissions, travel agents may have to start charging customers for their services.

To make sure that your travel agent meets your needs, find out all you can about the destinations in Germany that you want to visit (you've already made a sound decision by buying this book). Pick out some hotels and attractions that appeal to you. If you have access to the Internet, check prices on the Web in advance so you can look out for your own interests. Then take your guidebook and Web information to a travel agent and ask him or her to make the arrangements for you.

Because an agent has access to more resources than even the most complete Web travel site, he or she can often get you a better price than you can get by yourself. And an agent can issue your tickets and vouchers on the spot. If the agent can't get you into the hotel of your choice, ask for an alternative recommendation; then, look for an objective review in your guidebook. Remember, too, that a travel agent can take care of German Rail and Eurailpasses, airport-to-city transfers, sightseeing tours, and admission to castles and other historic sites throughout Germany.

Considering Escorted Tours

When you travel, do you like to let a bus driver worry about maneuvering through the traffic and locating the destination — while you sit in comfort and listen to a tour guide describe the sights? Or do you prefer heading out on foot and following your intuition, even if you don't catch all the highlights? Do you plan each day's events, or would you rather improvise? The answers to these questions determine whether you should choose a guided tour or travel on your own. Many travelers to Germany who don't speak German feel more comfortable with an escorted tour.

Some people love escorted tours, which are formally defined as groups brought together by an agency for purposes of travel. Participants pay one fee that covers transportation, hotels, admission fees, commentaries, and sometimes airfare. Tour guides take care of all the details, thereby freeing up travelers from spending lots of time getting from one place to the next. Escorted tours can take you to the maximum number of sights in the minimum amount of time with the least amount of hassle. Plus, most of the tour guides are wonderfully knowledgeable about the country and its sights so you probably get more information in less time than you could gather on your own.

Some people want total freedom and spontaneity when they travel. They prefer to explore a destination on their own time and at their own pace. They don't mind trying to communicate in another language, losing their way to a museum, or finding that a recommended restaurant has disappeared — they'll happily find another spot to eat. If you fit into this category, an escorted tour probably isn't for you.

If you plan to join an escorted tour, ask a few important questions before signing up.

✔ **What is the cancellation policy?** How late can you cancel if you can't go? Do you get a refund if you cancel? Do you get a refund if the operator cancels?

✔ **How jampacked is the schedule?** Does the tour schedule try to fit 25 hours into a 24-hour day, or does it give you ample time to relax or shop? If getting up at 7 a.m. every day and not returning to your hotel until 6 or 7 p.m. sounds like a grind, certain escorted tours may not be for you.

✔ **How big is the group?** The smaller the group, the less time you spend waiting for people to get on and off the bus. Tour operators may be evasive about this because they may not know the exact size of the group until everybody has made their reservations, but they should be able to give you a rough estimate.

✔ **Does the tour require a minimum group size?** Some tour operators require a minimum group size and may cancel the tour if they don't book enough people. If a quota exists, find out what it is and how close they are to reaching it. Again, tour operators may be evasive in their answers, but the information may help you select a tour that's sure to take place.

✔ **What exactly is included?** Don't assume anything. You may be required to get yourself to and from the airports at your own expense. A box lunch may be included in an excursion, but drinks may be extra. Beer may be included but not wine. How much flexibility does the tour offer? Can you opt out of certain activities, or does the bus leave once a day, with no exceptions? Are all your meals planned in advance? Can you choose your entree at dinner or does everybody get the same chicken cutlet?

If you're taking an escorted tour, I recommend that you purchase travel insurance, especially if the tour operator asks you to pay up front. But don't buy insurance from the tour company! If they don't fulfill their obligation to provide you with the vacation you've paid for, they probably won't fulfill their insurance obligations either. Get travel insurance through an independent agency (see Chapter 10).

Tour operators in the United States

Several companies offer escorted tours to Berlin, Munich, and destinations in the rest of Germany (or that include Germany in a Europe-wide tour). Many escorted-tour companies cater to special interests, such as castles on the Rhine for history buffs, while others are more general. A good travel agent can help you find a tour that suits your particular interests. The following companies offer various escorted tours to Germany:

- **Brendan Tours** (☎ 800/421-8446; Internet: www.brendantours. com) offers escorted tour packages and customized group tours to Germany.

- **Contiki Holidays** (Internet: www.contiki.com) provides escorted tours for 18 to 35 year olds and has offices in the United States, Canada, Australia, and the United Kingdom. Their 12-day European Horizon tour (from $789 per person double occupancy without airfare) visits the Rhine Valley and Munich, and their 11-day, 8-country European Magic tour (from $779 per person double occupancy without airfare) stops in Munich.

- **Destination Europe Resources** (☎ 800/782-2424; Internet: www.der.com) offers independent and excorted tours.

- **Globus** (Internet: www.globusjourneys.com) offers Leisurely Germany, an 11-day tour that includes Munich and Neuschwanstein castle, Leipzig, Weimar, Dresden, and Berlin; prices start at $1,389.

- **Maupintour** (Internet: www.maupintour.com) has a 15-day Discover Germany tour that includes highlights in Berlin, Dresden, Nuremberg, Munich, the Bavarian Alps, the Black Forest, and Frankfurt; prices start at $3,995, double occupancy, not including airfare. Other tours go to Berlin, Munich, and Bavaria (to see Ludwig's castles).

- **Travel Impressions/American Express Vacations** (☎ 800/ 284-0022; Internet: www.travelimpressions.com) sells independent air/land packages and first-class escorted bus tours.

Tour operators in Canada and Australia

This section includes just a few of the Canadian and Australian tour operators that offer tours to Germany. (See also Contiki Holidays in the previous section.) Call or check the Web sites for tour offerings from:

- **Horizon Holidays,** Toronto (☎ 416/585-9911; Internet: www. horizon-holidays.com)

- **The Pavlik Travel Group Ltd.,** Vancouver (☎ 604/929-0275; Internet: www.pavliktravel.com)

- ✔ **Nordic Travel** (☎ 02/9968-1783; E-mail: nordic@loom.net.au)

- ✔ **Tours Chanteclerc,** Montreal (☎ 514/398-9393; Internet: www.tourschanteclerc.com)

Tour operators in Germany

You can also plan your tour through a tour operator based in Germany. This section includes a brief list of German tour operators who provide individual tours in Germany with English-speaking guides. You or your travel agent can contact them for more information.

- ✔ **Alpha Travel Consultants** (☎ 030/7890-6800; Internet: www.alpha-travel.de) offers tailor-made special-interest tours and city packages.

- ✔ **Becker's Travel** (☎ 069/609-860; Internet: www.beckers-travel.de) provides individual travel planning for senior citizens, including special-interest tours and city packages.

- ✔ **European Travel and Events** (☎ 030/284-9360; Internet: www.european-travel.de) offers special-interest tours and city and town packages.

- ✔ **Kruegl Travel Germany** (☎ 089/812-9031; Internet: www.kruegl.de) offers spa and health resort tours and study tours.

Benefiting from Package Tours

Package tours are different from escorted tours. Package tours are only a way of buying your airfare and accommodations at the same time. And for popular destinations, such as Germany, they can really be the smart way to go because with a package tour you can save a *ton* of money.

A package tour to Germany that includes airfare, hotel, and transportation to and from the airport almost always costs less than if you arranged the tour on your own. That's because package tours are sold in bulk to tour operators, who resell them to the public. Each destination usually has one or two packagers that offer better deals than the rest because they buy in even greater volume.

Package-tour costs — and the packages themselves — vary greatly. Prices vary according to departure city, the quality of the hotels, and extras, such as car rental and optional tours. Timing is as important as other options in determining price. Adjusting your travel dates by a week (or even a day) can yield substantial savings. Shop around and ask plenty of questions before you book your trip. The time you spend doing research will be worth the bucks you save.

Finding package tours

Information about package tours is available from a variety of sources.

- ✔ **Liberty Travel** (☎ **888/271-1584;** Internet: www.libertytravel.com), one of the biggest packagers in the northeastern United States, offers reasonably priced packages. Liberty has packages to just about every country *surrounding* Germany, but not Germany itself. If you're planning a Europe-wide trip, one of these packages (with add-on days for time in Germany) could be a good deal.

- ✔ Look in the travel section of your **local Sunday newspaper** for advertisements. One reliable packager that you may see is **American Express Vacations** (☎ **800/346-3607;** Internet: http://travel.americanexpress.com/travel).

- ✔ Check the ads in the back of **national travel magazines,** such as *Arthur Frommer's Budget Travel, Travel & Leisure, National Geographic Traveler,* and *Condé Nast Traveler.*

- ✔ At www.vacationpackager.com you can plug in your destination and interests and the site suggests companies that you can contact on your own or through a travel agent.

Locating airline and hotel packages

The airlines are a good source of money-saving air/hotel packages for places like London and Paris. Unfortunately, not many airlines provide packages to Germany. In my research for this book, I found only three airlines that offered packages to Germany from the United States in 2002.

- ✔ **American Airlines Vacations** (☎ **800/321-2121;** Internet: www.aavacations.com) offered an air/hotel package to Frankfurt. The hotel portion, double occupancy, ranged from $42 to $100 per night per person. Sightseeing add-ons were not available.

- ✔ **Northwest Airlines World Vacations** (☎ **800/800-1504;** Internet: www.nwaworldvacations.com) had air/hotel packages to Frankfurt, Munich, and Berlin, and an array of sightseeing and transportation add-ons, including Frankfurt and Munich city tours, a half-day tour of Heidelberg, a day tour of the Rhine, a day-long Black Forest tour, a day tour of Rothenburg ob der Tauber, and a day tour of Neuschwanstein and Linderhof castles. You can also rent a car or buy a Eurailpass for train travel.

- ✔ **United Vacations** (☎ **800/800-1504;** Internet: www.unitedvacations.com) had air/hotel packages to Berlin, Munich, Frankfurt, and Heidelberg. Add-ons included a Munich city tour, a day-long Rhine tour from Frankfurt, and a day-tour of Neuschwanstein and Linderhof castles.

Airline packages don't include airport taxes and surcharges, which typically amount to about $80.

The biggest hotel chains may offer packages or special rates on sightseeing options. The following hotel groups have properties in Germany and occasionally offer packages:

- ✔ **Best Western International** (☎ **800/528-1234** in the U.S. or 0181/221-2588 in Germany; Internet: www.bestwestern.com)

- ✔ **Hilton Hotels** (☎ **800/HILTONS;** Internet: www.hilton.com)

- ✔ **Hyatt Hotels & Resorts** (☎ **800/228-9000;** Internet: www.hyatt.com)

- ✔ **Inter-Continental Hotels & Resorts** (☎ **888/567-8725;** Internet: www.interconti.com)

- ✔ **Kempinski Hotels & Resorts** (☎ **800/426-3135;** Internet: www.kempinski.com)

- ✔ **Le Meridien Hotels & Resorts** (☎ **800/225-5843** in the U.S. or 069/238-5430 in Germany; Internet: www.meridien.com)

- ✔ **Radisson Hotels International** (☎ **800/333-3333** in the U.S. or 0611/990-080 in Germany; Internet: www.radissonsas.com)

- ✔ **Sheraton Hotels & Resorts** (☎ **800/325-3535;** Internet: www.sheraton.com)

- ✔ **Steigenberger Hotels & Resorts** (☎ **800/223-5652** in the U.S. and Canada or 800/7779-6753 in Germany; Internet: www.steigenberger.de)

If you already know where you want to stay, call the hotel and ask whether special packages are available.

Making Your Own Arrangements

Are you a totally independent traveler? Maybe you're a control freak and can't stand the idea of even one single detail being out of your hands. Or perhaps you're into spontaneity and hate having anything prearranged except for what's absolutely essential (like, say, your flight). Or perhaps you just like to be on your own. Whatever your reason, I'm happy to supply some basic transportation data for those who want to make their own travel arrangements.

Finding out who flies where

In Germany, an airport is called a *Flughafen* (*floog*-haf-en). Germany has several airports, but direct flights from the United States only fly into

Frankfurt, Munich, and Düsseldorf. You can also fly to Berlin, Cologne, and other cities in Germany, but if you're coming from the United States, these routes require a change of planes — usually in Frankfurt, Amsterdam, Copenhagen, Paris, or London. For a list of the main international carriers with direct flights into Germany from the United States, Canada, the United Kingdom, and Australia, see the Appendix.

Flying into Frankfurt

Frankfurt airport, called **Flughafen Frankfurt Main,** is Germany's main international hub. **Lufthansa,** Germany's national carrier (now partnered with United Airlines and Air Canada), has direct flights to Frankfurt from New York JFK, Newark, Toronto, and Vancouver, B.C.; Lufthansa also offers flights from Atlanta, Boston, Chicago, Dallas/Fort Worth, Detroit, Houston, Los Angeles, Miami, Philadelphia, San Francisco, and Washington, D.C. **American Airlines** has nonstop service to Frankfurt from Dallas/Fort Worth, Chicago, and Miami. **Delta Air Lines** has daily nonstops from Newark and Atlanta. **Northwest Airlines** (partnered with KLM) flies nonstop to Frankfurt from Boston, Chicago, Minneapolis/ St. Paul, and Washington, D.C. **United Airlines** offers nonstop service to Frankfurt from Chicago and Washington, D.C. From the U.K., **British Airways** flies direct to Frankfurt from London. From Australia, **Qantas** flies to Frankfurt from Melbourne and Sydney.

Frankfurt is a very large airport, but the signage is good, so you can find your way around fairly easily. Flights to other cities in Germany from Frankfurt rarely take more than 1½ hours. The two airport terminals are linked by a people-mover system (called Sky Line). Inside the terminals you find banks with currency exchange windows, privately operated currency exchanges, and ATMs.

From Frankfurt you can easily get to sights in the Rhine Valley, or to any major German city, via train. The airport has its own train station, so you can fly in, hop on a train, and be off to your first destination. The long-distance **AIRail Terminal** links the airport to cities throughout Germany and neighboring countries. Regional and local trains operate from the **Regional Station** directly below **Terminal 1.** You can easily catch a train to Frankfurt's Hauptbahnhof (main railway station), a ten-minute journey that costs €4.85. A taxi ride into Frankfurt costs about €25. For more information on the Frankfurt airport, see Chapter 18.

Flying into other German airports

Here's a brief rundown of other major airports in Germany and some of the airlines that fly into them. In each city section of this guide, I give you more-specific information on how to get into the city from the airport.

- ✓ **Munich: Franz Josef Strauss International Airport,** located 18 miles (29 km) northeast of the city center, is Germany's second-largest airport. Opened in 1992, this airport is among the most modern and efficient in the world (completely accessible for the disabled). **Lufthansa** flies nonstop to Munich from Newark, JFK,

Boston, Chicago, and San Francisco; **Delta** flies nonstop from Atlanta; and **British Airways** flies nonstop from London. A commuter train connects the airport with the Hauptbahnhof (main railroad station) in downtown Munich; the fare for the 40-minute trip is €8, or you can take the **Lufthansa Airport Bus,** which takes about 40 minutes and costs €9. A taxi into the center costs about €70 and can take more than an hour. Munich is one of Germany's great cities, as well as the jumping-off point for trips into the Bavarian Alps and to Neuschwanstein, Linderhof, and Hohenschwangau castles. See Chapter 14 for more on flying into Munich.

✔ **Berlin:** Berlin has three airports, but you will probably fly into **Tegel** or **Schönefeld,** both of which are quite small and have easy public transportation into central Berlin. See Chapter 11 for a complete description of all of Berlin's airports. As Germany's capital, Berlin is a major business and tourist destination. From Berlin you can easily reach other cities in eastern Germany by train, especially Dresden, Leipzig, and Weimar (all in Chapter 13), and you're also close to Hamburg and the northern Hanseatic cities (Chapter 20).

✔ **Cologne: Konrad-Adenauer-Flughafen Köln/Bonn** is 9 miles (14 km) southeast of the city. **British Airways** has several nonstops a day. **British Midland** flies direct to Cologne from the United Kingdom. There are direct flights from most major European cities. The bus from the airport to the Cologne Hauptbahnhof (main train station) takes 20 minutes and costs €4.70; a taxi to the city center costs about €25. Cologne, or Köln as it's called in German, sits on the Rhine and is a leading cultural capital of Germany. Excursion boats leave from Cologne for trips on the Rhine and other German rivers (see Chapter 17). This is a good spot to land if you are going to tour Germany's Rhineland wine country.

✔ **Düsseldorf:** I do not cover Düsseldorf in this guidebook. The closest city that I cover is Cologne (Chapter 17). You can use the airport in Düsseldorf as an alternative to Cologne. From Düsseldorf reaching the Rhine Valley is easy. **Lufthansa** and **Continental** offer direct flights from Newark. **Aer Lingus** flies nonstop from Dublin. **British Midland** has flights from London.

✔ **Hamburg: Flughafen Hamburg-Fuhlsbüttel** is located 5 miles (8 km) north of the city center. There are direct flights to Hamburg from most major European cities. **Delta** offers service from Atlanta via Paris. The Airport Express bus is the easiest way to reach the city's Hauptbahnhof (main train station); the journey takes about 25 minutes and costs €4.35. A taxi from the airport to the city costs about €17 and takes about 30 minutes. Hamburg is a tourist destination in and of itself, but you may want to fly into Hamburg if you're interested in exploring northern Germany (Chapter 20).

Getting the best airfare

Airfares are capitalism at its purest. All the passengers in the same cabin on an airplane rarely pay the same fare; they pay what the market will bear. Business travelers pay the premium rate — known as the *full fare* — if they want the flexibility to buy their tickets at the last minute, to change their itineraries at a moment's notice, or to get home before the weekend. Leisure passengers pay the least — usually a fraction of the full fare — if they can book their tickets long in advance, don't mind staying over Saturday night, or are willing to travel on a Tuesday, Wednesday, or Thursday.

Airlines often lower the prices on their most popular routes, such as those to Frankfurt and Munich. These lower fares have advance-purchase requirements and date-of-travel restrictions, but you can't beat the price — usually no more than $600 for a transatlantic flight to Frankfurt from the East Coast (the price may be even less if you aggressively shop around on the Internet). Watch for these sales as you're planning your vacation, and if you find them, grab them. The sales tend to take place in seasons of low travel volume. Sales are almost never available around the peak months of April through September, and December. But with the airline industry today you never know what deals you may find, or when they'll become available.

Airfares during Germany's peak season (Easter through September, and December) are generally higher than those during the off-season (October and November and January through March).

Surfing the Web for the best airfare

Another way to find the cheapest fare is to search the Internet. The number of virtual travel agents on the Internet has increased exponentially in recent years.

The list of sites below is selective, not comprehensive. Some sites may have evolved or disappeared by the time you read this.

- ✔ **Travelocity** (incorporates Preview Travel; www.travelocity.com; www.previewtravel.com; www.frommers.travelocity.com) is Frommer's online travel planning/booking partner. It uses the SABRE system to offer reservations and tickets for more than 400 airlines, plus reservations and purchase capabilities for more than 45,000 hotels and 50 car-rental companies. An exclusive feature is its Low Fare Search Engine, which automatically searches for the three lowest-priced itineraries based on your criteria. Travelocity's Destination Guide includes updated information on some 260 destinations worldwide — supplied by Frommer's.

- ✔ **Orbitz** (www.orbitz.com) is a popular site launched by United, Delta, Northwest, American, and Continental Airlines. With this site, you're granted access to the largest data bank of low rates, airline tickets, rental cars, hotels, vacation packages, and other travel products. You get, among other offerings, available fares from more than 450 airlines.

✔ **Priceline** (www.priceline.com) lets you "name your price" for airline tickets, hotel rooms, and rental cars. For airline tickets, you can't say what time you want to fly—you have to accept any flight between 6 a.m. and 10 p.m. on the dates you've selected, and you may have to make one or more stopovers. Tickets are nonrefundable, and no frequent-flyer miles are awarded.

Last-minute specials, such as weekend deals or Internet-only fares, are offered by airlines to fill empty seats. The airlines announce most of these specials on Tuesday or Wednesday. Tickets, which must be purchased online, are only valid for travel that weekend, but some can be booked weeks or months in advance. Sign up for weekly e-mail alerts at airline Web sites (see the Appendix for listings) or check mega-sites that compile comprehensive lists of last-minute specials, such as **Smarter Living** (www.smarterliving.com) or **WebFlyer** (www.webflyer.com).

Using consolidators to cut ticket cost

Consolidators, also known as bucket shops, are good places to find low fares. Consolidators buy seats in bulk and resell them at prices that undercut the airlines' discounted rates. Be aware that tickets bought this way are usually nonrefundable or carry stiff cancellation penalties (as much as 75% of the ticket price). *Important*: Before you pay, ask the consolidator for a confirmation number, and then call the airline to confirm your seat. Be prepared to book your ticket through a different consolidator if the airline can't confirm your reservation.

Traveling by train

Germany is extremely well connected by train to the rest of Europe. Perhaps you're flying into Paris and from there going on to Berlin or Heidelberg as part of your European dream vacation. Have no fear. You can reach all major German cities by train with ease. Trains are very much a part of the German (and European) travel ethic. **EuroCity** (EC) trains connect Germany with neighboring countries, and sleek, high-speed **Thalys** trains link Cologne and Düsseldorf with Paris and Brussels. When you are traveling between countries, border formalities such as passport checks are generally taken care of on board the train. Major cities, such as Berlin and Hamburg, have more than one station, but you almost always find one main or central inner-city station called a *Hauptbahnhof* (*howpt*-bahn-hof). In every city section of this guide, I tell you how to get into the city center from the train station, which is usually conveniently located.

In Chapter 7, I discuss traveling around Germany by train and the various rail passes that can cut down transportation costs. For more information on trains in Europe, contact **Rail Europe** (☎ 888/382-RAIL in the U.S., 800/361-RAIL in Canada; Internet: www.raileurope.com). Their Web site provides useful trip-planning information on train schedules and travel times, promotional offers, and fares and rail pass prices. By the way, German trains *do* run on time.

Driving into Germany

I personally don't recommend driving in Europe because taking the train is so much easier, and usually far cheaper. But perhaps you're driving all around Europe, and Germany is on your itinerary. You've rented a car in Barcelona, and you want to drive all the way to Berlin.

Germany, which lies in the center of Europe, has an excellent road network. The fastest main roads, called *Autobahns* (*otto*-bahns), connect the main cities and feed into a Europe-wide road system. You find 24-hour gas stations, service stations, and restaurants along the Autobahns. Nowadays, since Germany is part of the larger European Union, border crossings usually don't require much more than showing your passport. Get a good road atlas if you're going to drive into Germany, and be prepared to spend extra time looking for parking. You can't park anywhere in most of the historic city centers because they are pedestrian-only zones. You can usually find clearly marked parking lots outside the city centers. Find out about available parking from your hotel. See Chapter 7 for more on driving in Germany.

Arriving by boat

Germany's northern coast lies along the North Sea and the Baltic Sea. International ferry services are available from the United Kingdom, Denmark, Norway, Sweden, Finland, Poland, Russia, Latvia, and Estonia. **DFDS Seaways** (☎ 800/533-3755 ext. 114 (in the U.S. and Canada); Internet: www.seaeurope.com) provides ferry service from Harwich, England, to Hamburg; the journey takes 20 hours. You can sail from Helsinki across the Baltic to Rostock in northern Germany on **Silja Lines;** for information in the United States, contact **Norwegian Coastal Voyage,** 405 Park Ave., New York, NY 10022 (☎ 800/323-7436 or 212/319-1300; Internet: www.coastalvoyage.com).

Chapter 7

Getting around Germany

● ●

In This Chapter

▶ Traveling through Germany by train

▶ Touring the sites by car

▶ Cruising the rivers of Germany

▶ Flying from city to city

● ●

*I*n comparison to the United States, Australia, or Canada, Germany is a fairly small country. With the area added by reunification, Germany (137,735 square miles/356,734 square kilometers) is smaller than the state of Montana (but with more than 80 million people). By fast train or car, you can get from Berlin, in the north, to Munich, in the south, in about seven or eight hours. Many historic towns and castles in Germany are manageable day trips from larger cities.

If you want to get a feel for the country, consider exploring at least a portion of Germany that has nothing to do with huge urban Berlin or Munich. When you get out of the cities and into the countryside, where you can sip wine in a small Rhineland village or explore a scenic region like Bavaria, the atmospheric charms of Germany are most strongly felt. You'll notice fascinating differences in culture, customs, food, and language as you travel from one part of Germany to another.

Weighing the Options: Train or Car?

Because of Germany's *comparatively* small size and easy-access train and road networks, the country is a snap to explore. From Berlin you can reach Dresden or Leipzig in about two hours. The train trip between Hamburg and Lübeck is under an hour. From Munich, the trip to Garmisch-Partenkirchen in the Bavarian Alps is only an hour by car and under 90 minutes by train. The cities in western Germany — Cologne, Heidelberg, Nuremberg — are usually no more than two or three hours apart by car or train.

So should you rent a car or take the train? In almost all cases, I recommend train travel for its convenience and speed. However, having a car in scenic areas, such as the Bavarian Alps and the Black Forest, does allow you to explore the countryside more easily.

Taking the Train: The Easy Way to Go

When Germans travel around their country, they take the train (called an *Eisenbahn,* pronounced *eye*-sen-bawn, or a *Zug,* pronounced zoog). I do too. I recommend traveling by train over all other forms of transportation — especially if you're a first-time visitor to Germany. Traveling by train is fast, fun, and convenient.

If you need any kind of train-related information while you're in Germany — from timetables to fares and special services — call **Deutsche Bahn (German Rail)** at ☎ **01805/996-633.** Someone who speaks English will be available to help you.

Following basic training

The railway system in Germany is operated by **Deutsche Bahn** (DB; German Rail; Internet: www.bahn.de). Throughout Germany, long-distance and local train timetables are coordinated to minimize waiting for connections. And, yes, German trains almost always run on time.

Train types

The federally owned and operated Deutsche Bahn has been steadily modernizing and upgrading its trains while integrating two different systems (Deutsche Bundesbahn in western Germany and Deutsche Reichsbahn in eastern Germany) into one. You may be surprised at the bright-red, high-tech look of the newest trains. What follows is a rundown of the trains that you find within Germany.

- **InterCity (IC)** passenger trains offer express service between all major German cities at intervals of one or two hours. IC trains have adjustable cushioned seats, individual reading lights, and telephone service. Dining cars (*Speisewagen,* pronounced *shpy*-zuh-vahg-en) and cafe or bistro cars (for lighter snacks) are on all trains. On IC trains, you can choose whether to sit in a compartment with six seats or in an open saloon coach.

- **InterCity Express (ICE)** trains, which connect major cities on heavily traveled routes, are among the fastest in Europe, reaching speeds of 165 mph (265 kmph). ICE trains run from Hamburg to Munich; from Frankfurt to Munich; and from Berlin to Munich. Each train makes stops at cities along the way. ICE significantly reduces travel time, allowing passengers to cross the entire country in a few hours. ICE trains have telephones, a restaurant, and a very high standard of comfort in both first and second class.

✔ The **CityNightLine (CNL)** is one of the most comfortable night trains in Europe. This train operates between Berlin and Zürich (stopping at Frankfurt, Baden-Baden, and Freiburg, among other towns), Berlin and Dresden, Hamburg and Zürich, and Dortmund and Vienna. The CNL offers four different categories. Sleeping accommodations in Deluxe include compartments with a shower and toilet, key cards, phones for wake-up service, and a panoramic window with blinds. Comfort Single or Double gives you a single or double-bed compartment with washing facilities. Economy provides a four-bed compartment with washing facilities (you can book this class as a single or double). The *Ruhesessel* ("sleeper chairs") category offers open saloon seating with reclining seats. The CNL includes a restaurant and cafe car. Advance reservations are mandatory for all sleeping accommodations. Eurail and GermanRail pass holders are accepted on this train but have to pay for the seat or sleeper reservation.

✔ **DB Nachtzug (Night Train)** service is available between many cities in Germany and continues on to Amsterdam, Brussels, Paris, Prague, and Copenhagen. The night trains have comfortable *couchettes* (basic sleeping compartments) and some more deluxe sleeping compartments with showers.

✔ For shorter local trips, usually within a suburban area around a large town, **S-Bahn (urban light-rail)** trains are used. For some out-of-the-way places, you may need to transfer to a **RegionalBahn (RB)** to reach your destination. **RegionalExpress (RE)** trains link rural areas to the long-distance rail network.

An announcement is made before the train arrives at each station. Station stops are short, so have your luggage in hand and be ready to disembark when the train comes to a halt. In new high-speed trains, you find a well-marked button that opens the door automatically. In other trains, you may need to open the door by pulling up on a handle.

Ticket classes

German trains have a two-tiered ticket system: first class (*Erste Klasse*) and second class (*Zweite Klasse*). First-class tickets cost about one-third more than second class. The first-class cars have roomier seats, fewer passengers, and a more luxurious feel. But you can travel quite comfortably in second class. You may appreciate the difference on long-distance journeys — from Berlin to Munich, say, when you're in the train for seven hours or more.

First-class service on InterCity Express (ICE) trains includes a higher standard of personal service (you can order beverages and snacks that are brought to your seat). First- and second-class passengers otherwise use the same dining cars and cafe cars for buying sandwiches and drinks. On some trains, an employee comes through both first- and second-class cars with a food and beverage trolley. Local and commuter trains don't have food service.

Auto trains

If you want to avoid long-distance driving but need a car after you arrive at your destination, you can take yourself and your car on a car-sleeper **Auto Train.** Although less common, daytime automobile trains also operate.

Heading to the Hauptbahnhof

A German city's *Hauptbahnhof* (pronounced *howpt*-bahn-hof), or main train station, is rarely more than a few minutes' walk from the historic town center and all the main attractions. The station is always a main link in the city's public transportation system, so you can continue your local explorations by subway, light rail, tram, or bus from there.

German train stations in major cities offer all kinds of services, including currency exchange, food and beverage, newsstands, and usually a tourist information office. Hotels are always close at hand. If you are arriving in a city for sightseeing only, and not spending the night, you can check your luggage (*Gepäck,* pronounced geh-*peck*) at a luggage checkroom. At larger stations, porters (recognized by their red or blue uniforms) can transport your luggage, or you can use self-service luggage trolleys available for €1. You can also take advantage of a luggage-forwarding service in which a courier picks up your bags and delivers them to your hotel or next destination.

 In many German train stations, you can take an elevator to the track level. But in others, you must climb stairs, which sometimes have a ramp for luggage trolleys and baby carriages. If you are loaded down with several large, heavy bags, getting to your track without help may be difficult. (This is another way of saying: Don't overpack.)

Getting off on the right track

Once in the station, you need to find the right track (*Gleis,* pronounced *glice*) for your departing train. In large cities, prominently placed departure and arrival boards list train numbers, arrival or departure times, final destinations, and track numbers. This information is also posted as a printed schedule in the station.

 The German (and Europe-wide) train system works on a **24-hour clock.** Midnight is always listed as 0:00 hours and noon is 12:00. Therefore, train times can be 13:00 (1 p.m.), 14:00 (2 p.m.), 15:00 (3 p.m.), and so on, up to 23:59 (11:59 p.m.). If your train leaves at 4:20 p.m., the time on the schedule will read 16:20.

Trains can be very long, so you want to be near the appropriate area for boarding when the train pulls into the station. After you've made your way to the right track, you see diagrams posted on the platform that show the layout of the train. The diagram displays the location of first-class, second-class, and restaurant cars. Each car, or *Wagen*

(pronounced *vah*-ghen), is numbered. The Wagen numbers correspond to numbers on the platform, usually 1 to 6. If you have a reserved seat, your ticket lists the Wagen number. Check the diagram and then make your way to the appropriate area of the platform before the train arrives. If you have a Eurailpass and are risking a journey without a seat reservation, make your way to the platform areas where the first- or second-class cars will stop.

Reserving your seat

When traveling for any distance in Germany, reserving your seat in advance, even if you have a Eurailpass or German Railpass, is always a good idea. Otherwise, the only free seat you find may be in the smoking area or out in the hallway (I speak from experience).

You can make a seat (*Platz*, pronounced plotz) reservation and buy train tickets (*Fahrkarten*, pronounced *far*-karten) at any train station. In larger stations, look for the *Reisezentrum* (travel center). In smaller stations, make your booking at the ticket counter. The staff in larger stations usually speak English, and they can answer any questions you have. If you have a German Railpass or a Eurailpass (see the next section), the seat reservation costs about €3. You're issued a ticket that lists the *Wagen* (car) number and the *Platz* (seat) number.

Saving time and euros with rail passes

Rail passes are tickets that allow you to travel for a certain number of days without buying a ticket for each leg of your journey. They help you save time (ticket lines can be long) and, usually, money. Most rail passes must be purchased before you leave home; they can't be purchased after you arrive in Germany or the rest of Europe.

Before you buy a rail pass, do a little research to find out if it's going to save you money. At Rail Europe's Web site, www.raileurope.com, you can click on "Fares and Schedules" and get an estimated cost (in U.S. or Canadian dollars) of fares between destinations within Germany.

Travel agents throughout the United States and Canada sell all the rail passes described later in this section, but the biggest supplier is **Rail Europe** (☎ **888/382-RAIL** in the U.S., or 800/361-RAIL in Canada; Internet: www.raileurope.com), which allows you to order online.

Many different rail passes are available in the United Kingdom for travel in Germany and continental Europe. You can check out passes and prices at Rail Europe's U.K. Web site: www.raileurope.co.uk. Or stop in at the **International Rail Centre,** Victoria Station, London SWIV 1JY (☎ **0990/848848** in the U.K., or 020/7834-2345). Some of the most popular passes, including Inter-Rail and Euro Youth, are only available to travelers under 26 years of age; these allow unlimited second-class travel through most European countries.

German railpasses: For Deutschland only

The **German Railpass** allows for four to ten nonconsecutive days of travel in one month within Germany. To give you an idea of the prices: A four-day pass costs $260 first class or $180 second class; a seven-day pass costs $392 first class, $270 second class; a ten-day pass costs $458 first class, $316 second class.

A **German Rail Youth Pass** is valid only for persons under 26 years of age and available only in second class (for four to ten days of travel in one month). Sample prices: $142 for four days, $180 for seven days, $216 for ten days in one month.

An even bigger bargain is the **German Rail Twinpass,** for two adults (they do not have to be married and can be of the same sex) traveling together in first or second class. The second pass represents a 50% savings over single prices. Sample prices *per person:* $195 for four days first class or $135 for second class; $269 for seven days first class or $186 second class; $344 for ten days first class or $237 second class.

German Railpasses for kids ages 4 to 11 are half the adult price. Children under 4 travel free.

A German Railpass also entitles the bearer to free or discounted travel on selected bus routes operated by Deutsche Touring/Europabus, including destinations not serviced by trains, and free travel on **KD German Line steamers** (day trips only) along the Rhine, Main, and Mosel rivers.

German Railpasses are most conveniently available from **Rail Europe** (☎ 888/382-RAIL in the U.S., or 800/361-RAIL in Canada); you can purchase the passes online at www.raileurope.com. Rail Europe can also arrange cost-effective "Rail and Drive" packages that combine a certain number of days on the train with a certain number of days in a rental car. For instance, you can ride the train from Frankfurt to Munich, spend three days exploring the city, and then rent a car for a two-day excursion into the Bavarian Alps to see Ludwig's castles.

Eurailpass: For travel throughout Europe

The **Eurailpass** is one of Europe's best bargains. With a Eurailpass you can enjoy unlimited first-class rail travel in 17 countries, including Germany. Passes are for periods as short as 15 days or as long as 3 months. These passes are for *consecutive* days of travel.

Eurailpasses can be bought and used by non-European residents only. Buy your Eurailpass before you leave home, from a travel agent or from **Rail Europe** (☎ 888/382-RAIL in the U.S., or 800/361-RAIL in Canada; Internet: www.raileurope.com). The Eurailpass costs $572 for 15 days, $740 for 21 days, $918 for 1 month, $1,298 for 2 months, and $1,606 for 3 months. Children ages 4 to 11 are charged half the adult fare; children under 4 travel free providing they don't occupy a seat.

If you're under 26, you can purchase a **Eurailpass Youth,** entitling you to unlimited second-class travel for $401 for 15 days, $518 for 21 days, $644 for 1 month, $910 for 2 months, and $1,126 for 3 months.

Seat reservations are required on some trains. The night trains have *couchettes* (sleeping cars), which cost extra. Eurailpass holders are entitled to considerable reductions on certain buses and ferries as well.

Other Eurailpasses: For those who want to save euros

Eurail offers many different passes, all variations on a theme (saving money).

✔ The **Eurailpass Saver** is valid for two to five persons traveling together and offers an approximate 15% reduction on the standard price to each passenger. Saver Passes are available for first class only.

✔ A **Eurail Selectpass** is worth considering if you are going visit a limited number of countries. A Selectpass allows travelers to select three, four, or five countries linked by rail or ferry out of the 17 countries covered by Eurailpass. This is a *flexipass,* meaning that travel days need not be consecutive; you can buy passes for five, six, eight, or ten days within a two-month period. Passes are valid in first class only. Prices for a Eurail Selectpass begin at $356 per person for five days within three countries.

✔ The **Eurail Selectpass Saver** is valid for two to five persons traveling together and offers an approximate 15% savings to each passenger. Prices start at $304 for five days in two months within three countries.

✔ The **Eurail Selectpass Youth** is for unlimited second-class travel in a selection of 17 countries, including Germany. You must be under 26 years old. The pass offers about a 30% savings. Prices begin at $249 for five days within two months within three countries.

Touring by Car: Autobahns, Tankstellen, and Benzin

I'm a *Zug* (train) nut. To me, nothing is more pleasant than sitting in a train and watching the countryside roll by. However, Germany has scenic regions — the Bavarian Alps, the Bodensee, and the Black Forest, for example — where even I succumb to car rental in order to explore the countryside.

If you're going to tour Germany by car, you may want to pick up a copy of *Frommer's Germany's Best-Loved Driving Tours* (Wiley, 2002).

Renting a car in Germany

Renting a car is fairly easy in Germany. Drivers from the United States, Canada, Australia, and other non–European Union countries must have a valid driver's license, but no other special license is required. I recommend that you make all the arrangements *before* you leave home. You can pick up your car at most airports and major train stations, or at an office within German cities. You can often rent a car in one German city and return the vehicle in another city for no additional charge.

There are some advantages to **prepaying rentals** in dollars before leaving the United States. You get an easy-to-understand net price (which you have to prepay at least 14 days before departure by credit card), the rental process is more streamlined, and you can avoid unpleasant surprises caused by sudden unfavorable changes in currency exchange rates. Remember, however, that if you opt to prepay and your plans change, you have to go through some rather complicated paperwork (and, in some cases, have to pay a penalty of around $25) for changing or canceling a prepaid contract. Whenever you rent, keep in mind that you may get a better rate if you reserve the car at least seven days in advance.

Several **international car-rental firms** rent cars in Germany. See the Appendix for a list of names and contact information. You can rent a car before you go from all of these companies.

You can also rent a car through **Rail Europe** (☎ **888/382-RAIL** in the U.S., or 800/361-RAIL in Canada; Internet: www.raileurope.com) at the same time you book your German Railpass or Eurailpass (see "Saving time and euros with rail passes," earlier in this chapter). They also offer a **German Rail 'n Drive** option that gives you two days of unlimited train travel (first or second class) and two days of Hertz car rental within one month. You can purchase extra days for both train travel and car rental. Prices start at $232 for first class, $202 for second class.

If you rent a car in Germany, I recommend that you purchase all the optional insurance coverage. A ***Collision-Damage Waiver*** (**CDW**) is an optional insurance policy that can be purchased when you sign a rental agreement. For an extra fee, the rental agency agrees to eliminate all but a small percentage of your financial responsibility for collision damage in case of an accident. If you don't have a CDW and have an accident, you'll pay for all damages up to the cost of actually replacing the vehicle. Some credit cards (especially gold cards) cover the CDW, so call your company to check on these benefits before you spend the extra money on additional insurance. Credit-card companies do *not* cover liability if you injure yourself, another passenger, or someone else, so if your own car insurance doesn't cover you abroad, consider taking out ***Personal Accident Insurance*** (**PAI**) for extra liability coverage.

Taking the roads less traveled

The **Autobahn** (pronounced *otto*-bahn) forms Germany's main long-distance highway network. Emergency telephones are located every 2 km (about 1¼ miles); the point of the black triangle on posts alongside the road indicates the direction of the nearest one. In theory, the Autobahn does not have a speed limit (in the left, fast lane), but many drivers going too fast report that they have been stopped by the police and fined on the spot. So exercise reasonable caution. A German driver on the Autobahn can be like one possessed, so you may prefer the slower, right lane. The government recommends an Autobahn speed limit of 130 kmph (80 mph).

The **Bundesstrassen** (state roads) vary in quality from region to region. The roads in the major touring areas of the Rhine Valley, the Black Forest, and the Bavarian Alps are smoothly paved and kept in good repair. In eastern Germany, some secondary and local roads are not in good shape.

Michelin publishes the best regional **maps,** available at all major bookstores throughout Germany. Hallweg also produces good road maps. However, in general, finding your way by looking for directional signs rather than highway number signs is easier. Germany's **road signs** are standard international signs. See Table 7-1 for a few important words that you should know.

Table 7-1	German Road Signs
German	*English Translation*
Anfang	Start, or beginning
Ausfahrt	Exit
Baustelle	Building site, or roadworks
Einbahnstrasse	One-way street
Ende	End
Einfahrt	Entrance
Gefahr	Danger
Rechts einbiegen	Turn right
Links einbiegen	Turn left
Verengte Fahrbahn	Road narrows
Vorsicht	Attention! Look out!

Following the rules of the road

If you're going to drive in Germany, you need to know a few general facts.

✔ In Germany, signs show distances and speed limits in **kilometers** (km) and **kilometers per hour** (kmph). A kilometer is 0.62 of a mile, and a mile is 1.62 kilometers.

✔ Unless posted differently, **speed limits** are:

- 50 kmph (30 mph) in towns
- 100 kmph (60 mph) on regular highways
- 130 kmph (78 mph) on Autobahns

✔ On Autobahns, the **left lane** is the fast lane. And I mean fast. Do not drive in this lane unless you are passing another car.

✔ You can **pass** other vehicles **on the left** only. German motorists will generally flash their lights if they want you to move over so they can pass.

✔ The law requires that all passengers wear **seat belts.** Children under 12 must sit on booster seats in the back so that regular seat belts can be used safely. Children under 4 must ride in a car seat.

✔ You must use **low-beam headlights** at night and during fog, heavy rain, and snow falls.

✔ **Parking** in the center of most big towns is difficult, expensive, or just plain impossible because most historic town centers are for pedestrians only. Look for parking lots and parking garages outside the center. They are always identified by a large P; in some larger cities, signs on the way into town indicate how much space is available in various lots or parking garages. Most parking lots use an automated ticket system. You insert coins (or credit cards) to purchase a certain amount of time.

✔ You must stop for pedestrians in **crosswalks.** They have the right of way.

✔ **Driving while introxicated** and drinking while driving are very serious offenses in Germany. If you've had more than a glass of wine or beer, don't risk driving.

Handling a roadside emergency

The major automobile club in Germany is **Allgemeiner Deutscher Automobile Club (ADAC),** Am Westpark 8, 81373 München (☎ 089/ 76760). If you have a breakdown on the Autobahn, you can call ADAC from an emergency phone. On the Autobahn, you find emergency phones every 2 km (about 1¼ miles); the point of the black triangle on posts alongside the road indicates the direction of the nearest phone.

If you don't belong to an auto club, call ADAC's breakdown service at ☎ **01802/222-222.** In English, ask for "road service assistance" (*Strassenwachthilfe*). Emergency assistance is free, but you pay for parts or materials.

Fill 'er up, bitte (please)

Gasoline, called *Benzin* (pronounced ben-*seen*) is readily available throughout Germany, and gas stations, called *Tankstelle* (pronounced *tonk*-shtel-leh) appear frequently along the Autobahns. The cheapest gasoline is at stations marked SB-TANKEN (*Selbstbedienung,* or self-service). But remember that gas is always much more expensive than in the United States. A liter (about a fourth of a gallon) of regular unleaded gas costs about €1.10 (in 2002). Filling up the tank of a medium-size car costs about €60.

The self-service process is basically the same as that of the United States. You fill your tank and pay inside at the counter. The types of gasoline are: *Normal Bleifrei* (regular unleaded), *Super Bleifrei* (super unleaded), *Super Plus Bleifrei* (supreme unleaded), and diesel.

Sailing through Germany: River Cruises

Germany's major river is the **Rhine,** which flows through the heart of Europe from the Alps to the North Sea. Over the centuries, more castles were built in the Rhine Valley than in any other valley in the world. This area has great appeal to visitors. The **Main** flows from the Danube, past Frankfurt, and enters the Rhine at the city of Mainz. The **Elbe,** which begins in the Czech Republic, cuts through Germany's eastern border in a beautiful area called Saxon Switzerland, flows past the great art city of Dresden, and continues northeastward; situated on tributaries of the Elbe are Berlin and Hamburg.

Viking KD River Cruises and Peter Deilman EuropAmerica Cruises offer several cruises along these three great waterways. Itineraries range from 2 to 20 nights, mostly between April and October but with some in December and over New Year's Day. If you are looking for an unusual and relaxing way to see Germany, you may want to consider this option. For more information, contact **Viking KD River Cruises of Europe,** represented in North America by JFO Cruise Service, 2500 Westchester Ave., Purchase, NY 10577 (☎ **800/346-6525;** Internet: www.rivercruises.com), or **Peter Deilman EuropAmerica Cruises** (☎ **800/348-8287;** Internet: www.deilmann-cruises.com).

In the city and regional chapters of this guidebook, I tell you about river excursions along the Mosel and Neckar rivers, and local sightseeing cruises in Berlin, Cologne, Dresden, Frankfurt, and Heidelberg.

Flying around Germany: A Good Idea?

Flying from city to city within Germany makes sense if you're traveling from, say, Hamburg or Berlin in the north to Munich in the south, or from Cologne in the west to Leipzig in the east. A trip that would take seven or eight hours by train or car takes about an hour by plane. The downside is that you won't see the countryside.

Flying doesn't make much sense if you're traveling short distances between cities that are connected by high-speed trains. The train from Frankfurt to Stuttgart, for example, takes 1 hour and 20 minutes. You can fly this route, but when you factor in time spent getting to the airport, going through security, waiting for your departure, and then getting into the city after your plane lands . . . you could already be there, in the city center, by train.

In the city sections of this guidebook, I tell you whether the airport is near the city. You can reach any German airport by public transportation or taxi. The airports are efficient and well run. But planes, unlike trains, don't always arrive or depart on time, so you may end up tapping your toes.

Lufthansa (☎ **800/645-3880** in the U.S. and Canada, 9639-6499 in Australia, 01803/803-803 in Germany; Internet: www.lufthansa-usa.com or www.lufthansa.de) offers the most extensive and frequent flights within the country, but other European carriers are increasing their German domestic routes.

Chapter 8

Booking Your Room

● ●

● ●

Making hotel arrangements in advance of your trip has its advantages. Having a reservation gives you the security of knowing where you'll rest your weary head in a strange town. Because you've already spoken to the hotel, you also know how much your accommodations will cost. And, booking ahead saves you valuable time that can be spent sightseeing instead of trudging around looking for a place to stay.

In Germany, booking ahead is essential in large cities like Berlin and Munich — especially if you're going to be in Munich during Oktoberfest, which is actually held in September, but that's another story. Throughout the year, both Berlin and Munich host large trade fairs and special events when rooms are scarce. From April through September and again in December, the period that constitutes *high season,* hotels in the inexpensive-to-moderate range are always the first to be snapped up, but space can be tight everywhere, at any time of year, if a major trade show or convention is happening in the city.

Booking ahead isn't as important in the rest of Germany, but I still recommend doing so — particularly if you're going to be spending a Friday or Saturday night in a major tourist spot like Dresden or Füssen, near Ludwig's castles. Hotels in popular tourist areas, such as the Black Forest, the Rhine and Mosel valleys, and the Bodensee (Lake Constance), also fill up during high season. During *off-season,* especially in the middle of winter, you won't have a problem booking a room on the spot, wherever you are. In a small village, finding a room may be as simple as spotting a sign in a house window that reads *Zimmer frei* (room available).

You find **tourist information centers,** which can help you find a room, in all German cities and towns, in or near the main train station. Charges for this service vary. Some places charge nothing, others charge a small fixed fee (usually no more than €3), and others charge 10% of the first night's hotel rate, but you get that back at the hotel, so the service ends up costing nothing. Most tourist information centers also have a free directory of local accommodations.

Finding the Place That's Right for You

Germany has very high standards for hotels and inns. You find all types of lodging, from luxury Old World palaces and super-high-tech showoffs to small hotels, cozy inns, chain hotels, rustic guesthouses, vacation villas, and simple rooms in private homes and apartments. You won't find a speck of *Schmutz* (dirt) in any of them. Hotel associations, regional tourist associations, and local tourist boards control standards in all categories of accommodation. Even the smallest *pension* (bed-and-breakfast, or B&B) must open its doors for inspection in order to list and rent rooms. That said, standards for some smaller hotels in eastern Germany — the old Communist GDR — are not yet on a par with those in western Germany. And, unlike in the United States, Germany is full of small and medium-size hotels, many family-owned and -operated. You'll be glad to know that German hotels in every category are reasonably priced.

Breakfast (*Frühstück*) is always included in the price of a room, except at very high-end luxury hotels. In a pension, breakfast may be coffee, a roll with butter and jam, an egg, and some cold cuts. At hotels, depending on the size and degree of luxury, breakfast may be a self-serve buffet with juice, cereal, yogurt, fruit, pastries, fresh bread, eggs, cold cuts, and smoked fish or pickled herring. Coffee or tea is brought to your table.

In Germany, state agencies and tourist boards rate hotels according to a **star system.** The system is not used to recommend hotels but simply to categorize them according to their amenities. A one-star hotel is very basic and inexpensive. A five-star hotel is a luxury property with an on-site spa or pool and a rate at the top end of the price spectrum. I don't use that system in this book except when I refer to a hotel as having "five-star luxury." But, you will encounter this star system if you book your hotel in Germany.

Smoke-free rooms and **smoke-free floors** are finally catching on in Germany. You're most likely to find them in mid-range to high-end hotels. But remember that Europeans in general are not as committed to smoke-free environments as Americans are. The term for "no smoking" is *nicht rauchen* (nicked *rauh*-kin).

In all accommodation types in Germany, you find a **Decke** (*deck*-uh) on the bed. If two beds are joined to make a double, you find a Decke on each side. A Decke is what Americans call a "comforter" or "duvet." This light, feather-filled covering, which is buttoned within a sheet and takes the place of blankets, keeps you toasty.

In Germany, you have several different kinds of hotels and accommodations from which to choose. In the following sections, I describe each type, beginning with the most expensive.

Luxury hotels

You know upon entering the lobby if a hotel is in this category. Public spaces in luxury hotels are sophisticated and elegant. The staff is unusually welcoming and the service, impeccable. Porters are available to take your luggage up to your room (tip €1 per bag). The rooms themselves are spacious and beautifully furnished with amenities, such as a minibar, a couple of phones, cable and satellite TV, and bathrobes. Bathrooms are large and well equipped with magnifying mirrors, tubs (often with whirlpools) and showers, and high-quality toiletries. Your bed is turned down at night, 24-hour room service is available, and the property has an on-site health club, usually with a sauna and pool. The hotel has at least two fine gourmet restaurants, which are often the best restaurants in town. What you don't get is a free breakfast. Charges for the (no doubt fabulous) breakfast buffet are anywhere from €18 to €22. Some brand-name hotel chains — Hyatt, Kempinski, Le Meridien, and Steigenberger, in particular — have properties in this luxury category. Expect to pay €175 and up, but also look for special weekend rates on the hotels' Web sites.

Chain hotels

Holiday Inn, Radisson SAS, Sheraton, Best Western, Ramada — names you probably know — all have hotels in Germany. German, European, and international chains include Accor, InterCity Hotels (always near train stations), Inter-Continental, Mövenpick, Park Plaza/art'otel, Ringhotels, Swissôtel, Travel Charme, and Treff Hotels. For the most part, chain hotels offer brand-name familiarity and dependable service. They also tend to be newish, enormous, and somewhat anonymous. Tour packagers and convention planners often house their groups in chain hotels. The rooms are smaller and have a more standardized decor than rooms in luxury hotels. Amenities include a minibar, telephone, and cable TV. Bathrooms are smaller and less glamorous than in a luxury property, too. Room service is available, and the hotel usually has an on-site pool or health club with sauna. You generally find different room categories, some with breakfast included. Prices vary greatly for chain-name hotels, depending on time of year and the presence of trade shows or conventions. In general, expect to pay anywhere from €110 to €175 (more in Berlin or Munich). Shopping around on the Web may net you some big savings.

Smaller independent hotels

Many small- and medium-size hotels in Germany are family owned and operated. Some of these independent properties, like Der Kleine Prinz in Baden-Baden, are luxury hotels with a unique charm and ambience. Others, like Hotel Jedermann in Munich or Garni-Hotel Brugger in Lindau, are much more basic, offering comfortable rooms without much personality but at hard-to-beat prices. If the hotel is in the luxury category, you find the kinds of amenities mentioned earlier in this chapter. If not, you find at least a telephone and cable TV. Rates at small and medium-size properties always include a buffet breakfast. Prices for a small luxury hotel tend to be €150 and up; for less-fancy independents, prices range from €85 to €175.

Garni, a word sometimes attached to a hotel's name, means that breakfast is the only meal that the hotel serves.

Guesthouses

A guesthouse, called a *Gasthaus* (*gahst*-house) or a *Gasthof* (*gahst*-hofe), is basically an inn with a restaurant that serves breakfast, lunch, and dinner to hotel guests and outside patrons. You're more likely to find guesthouses in small towns, medium-size cities, or in the country than in large cities. The ambience tends to be rustic and cozy, and many of the properties are older. The restaurant occupies the main or first floor, and the upper floors, usually no more than three total, have just a few rooms. Most guesthouses don't have an elevator. Some rooms have small private bathrooms with showers or bathtubs; other rooms have sinks but share bathrooms and showers in the hallway. The rooms themselves are often charming — what you'd typically expect in an Old World inn. You probably won't find a telephone in your room or too many amenities, but your rate will include breakfast. The inn may also offer a special rate for dinner or lunch and dinner. The Feriengasthof Helmer (*Ferien* means vacation) in Schwangau is an example of this kind of accommodation. Rates are typically from €55 to €110.

Pensions

The pension (pronounced pen-see-*own*) has long been the backbone of budget travel in Germany. A pension is the same as a B&B: a room in a private home or apartment, with breakfast included in the price. Some half a million beds are available in private homes across the country, often advertised with the simple sign, *Zimmer frei* (room available). You may luck out and find a place with a private bathroom, or you may have to share the bathroom. In some cases, you can use the kitchen as well. Amenities vary from place to place, so you may or may not have a TV, but you generally won't have a phone. In smaller towns, rooms start around €30 per person per night; prices are higher in large cities.

Note: Most pensions do not accept credit cards (cash only). Pension Niebuhr in Berlin is a good big-city pension.

Vacation villas

When they're not using them for their own holidays, Germans often rent out their vacation homes or apartments to visitors. These places are called *Ferienwohnungen* (fair-ee-en-voe-nung-en) or *Ferienapartments* (fair-ee-en-a-part-ments). You may find them advertised in travel magazines, or you can ask local tourist offices or your travel agent for details on what's available in a specific region. Each property is different, as are the arrangements regarding bed linens and so on. Rates vary, too, but the cost is generally lower the longer your stay.

Health spas and resorts

Health is taken seriously in Germany. What do you say when someone sneezes? *Gesundheit!,* which means "health!" The country has some 330 officially registered spas and health resorts where the amenities include modern facilities to treat a wide variety of ailments or to pamper your body with special treatments like hot mud or seaweed. These properties usually have recreational facilities on the premises or nearby, and entertainment as well. You find most spas and resorts in Bavaria and the Black Forest. Germans generally go to spas and resorts as part of a *Kur* (cure) package that includes room and board, doctors' fees, and various treatments. Costs vary considerably, depending on the hotel and the treatment.

Beating the Rack Rate

The maximum rate that a hotel charges for a type of room is the *rack rate.* If you walk in off the street and ask for a room for the night, the hotel may charge you this top rate. Be aware that you don't always have to pay the rack rate! Hardly anybody does. Just ask for a cheaper or discounted rate. The result is often favorable when savvy travelers make this request at larger or some medium-size hotels. However, prices aren't negotiable at smaller hotels, pensions, and guesthouses. Some of these properties do offer special rates for longer stays, however, or if you're there in the off-season (October and November and from January through March).

Before you make your hotel reservation, call a hotel's **U.S. toll-free number** or check its **Web site,** if such options exist. Quoted rates vary so widely that checking these sources can save you a bundle, especially because Web sites often contain last-minute or special offers. (For more on booking a hotel online, see the next section, "Surfing the Web for Hotel Deals.")

A **travel agent** may be able to negotiate a better room rate for you than you can get by yourself. (The hotel gives the agent a discount in exchange for steering his or her business toward that hotel.) For more on working with a travel agent, see Chapter 6.

For more tips on how to get the best room rate, see Chapter 4.

Surfing the Web for Hotel Deals

Although the major travel booking sites (Frommers, Travelocity, Expedia, and Orbitz; see Chapter 6 for details) offer hotel booking, you may be better off using a site devoted primarily to lodging. You can often find properties not listed with more general online travel agencies. Some lodging sites specialize in a particular type of accommodation, such as B&Bs, which you won't find on the more mainstream booking services. Others, such as TravelWeb in the following list, offer weekend deals on major chain properties, which cater to business travelers and have more empty rooms on weekends. The following list includes sites that allow you to make online reservations at hotels through Germany:

- ✔ **Hotel Reservations Network** (www.180096hotel.com) lists bargain rates at hotels in the United States and international cities, including Berlin, Frankfurt, and Munich. Because the site prebooks blocks of rooms, HRN sometimes has rooms at hotels that are "sold out." Call its toll-free number (☎ **800/96-HOTEL**) if you want more options than the Web site lists online.

- ✔ **Ihr Hotel** (www.ihrhotel-online.de) is a site you may want to use if you can read German. Ihr Hotel (meaning "your hotel") features independent hotels in northern Europe, including Germany, that are a good value for your money.

- ✔ **InnSite** (www.innsite.com) provides B&B listings for inns in dozens of countries around the globe, including Germany. You can find a B&B in Berlin or the Black Forest, look at images of the rooms, check prices and availability, and then e-mail the innkeeper if you have questions. This extensive directory includes listings only if the innkeeper has written one (getting on the list is free).

- ✔ **Landidyll** (www.landidyll.de), another good site if you can read German, focuses on family hotels all over Germany that are managed according to ecological principles and have gastronomic flair.

- ✔ **SRS-WorldhotDels** (www.srs-worldhotels.com) has about 400 hotels worldwide, including first-class and resort hotels throughout Germany. You can check for special discounted and weekend rates at many great German hotels.

✔ **TravelWeb** (`www.travelweb.com`) lists more than 16,000 hotels worldwide, including Germany, and focuses on chains such as Hyatt and Hilton. You can book almost 90% of these online. Its Click-It Weekends, updated each Monday, offers weekend deals at many leading chains.

Reserving the Best Room

After you know where you're staying, asking a few more questions can help you land the best-possible room.

✔ Ask about staying in a corner room. They're usually larger, quieter, and brighter, and may cost a bit more.

✔ If your urban hotel is a high-rise, request a room on a high floor. Being farther away from the street means your room may be quieter. Plus, a higher room may give you the added bonus of a better view.

✔ Ask if the hotel is renovating. If the answer is yes, request a room away from the renovation work, and make sure you ask again when you check in.

✔ If you have any physical impairments, be sure to ask if the hotel has a *Fahrstuhl* (*far*-shtool; elevator). Many small and older hotels throughout Germany do not have elevators. If the hotel lacks a lift, ask if a ground-floor room is available.

✔ Inquire about the location of restaurants, bars, and meeting facilities, which can be noisy.

✔ If you aren't happy with your room when you arrive, return to the front desk right away. If another room is available, the staff should be able to accommodate within reason.

If you need a room where you can smoke, be sure to request one when you reserve. If you can't bear the lingering smell of smoke, tell everyone who handles your reservation that you need a smoke-free room. Mid-size and larger hotels in Germany usually have nonsmoking rooms.

Paying for Your Room

Hotels almost never consider a room reservation confirmed until they receive partial or full payment (this policy varies from hotel to hotel). You can almost always confirm your reservations immediately with a credit card; otherwise, you must mail in your payment (generally using an International Money Order, available at most banks). Before booking, always ask about the cancellation policy—if your plans change, you don't want to pay for a room you didn't use. At some hotels you can get your money back if you cancel a room with 24 hours' notice; in others, you must notify the hotel five or more days in advance. After you've booked the room, request a written confirmation by fax, e-mail, or mail and be sure to take the document along on your trip.

Smaller pensions, and smaller hotels in eastern Germany, do not generally accept credit cards. If you're going to ramble through the Thuringian Forest or Bavarian Alps and choose small pensions as they strike your fancy, make sure you have enough cash (in euros).

Sorry, you can't escape that annoying 16% *Mehrwertsteuer* (value-added tax, or VAT). In Germany, the quoted room rate for a hotel always includes all local taxes and service charges. (Unfortunately, VAT refunds for travelers who live outside the European Union are only for store purchases and not for VAT paid at hotels and restaurants.)

Arriving without a Reservation

If your trip to Germany includes a stay in Munich or Berlin, I want to remind you again: *Reserve your room in advance.* However, if you do arrive without a reservation, your first and best option is the **tourist information center** located in or near all main train stations of major cities. The center can help you find a decent room within your price range for a small fee or for no fee at all. They don't recommend hotels, but all of the hotels they list have been inspected and meet certain criteria. If you're at a German **airport,** another good option is to use the on-site hotel-booking service (charges for these services vary).

You can also **call hotels directly.** But you may encounter difficulties if you contact smaller hotels or pensions where the owner does not speak English. Usually, however, someone at the hotel understands enough English so that you can make your needs known. For a guide to some of the German terms you may need, see Chapter 21. (The registration staff at most medium-size, large, and luxury hotels speak English.)

In many small towns, you can find a modest pension in a house or apartment by looking for a sign that reads *Zimmer frei* (room available).

Chapter 9

Managing Your Money

● ●

In This Chapter

▶ Introducing the euro

▶ Deciding whether to bring cash, traveler's checks, or credit cards

▶ Changing your dollars into euros

▶ Dealing with theft and loss

▶ Paying and recouping German sales tax

● ●

Money makes the world go around, but dealing with an unfamiliar currency can make your head spin. Travelers to foreign destinations, especially first-time travelers, often have big money worries. They don't worry so much about having enough money as they do about the difference between money in their home countries and money abroad. What are the conversion rates? Where can they change one currency into another for the best rate? Are traveler's checks better than credit cards or ATM cards? Travelers have a long list of money matters to consider.

You can't avoid these questions because you'll spend money every day of your trip. But the new euro currency used in Germany and throughout the European Union is a snap to understand (and spend). In this chapter, I explain the basic money matters you'll run into.

Knowing Your Euros

In January 2002, Germany's unit of currency changed from the deutsche mark to the *euro* (€). One euro is divided into *100 cents*. Coins come in denominations of 1¢, 2¢, 5¢, 10¢, 20¢, 50¢, €1, and €2. Notes are available in €5, €10, €20, €50, €100, €200, and €500 denominations. As with any unfamiliar currency, euros take a bit of getting used to. The coins have different sizes, shapes, and weights according to value. Each bank-note denomination has its own color.

 For American travelers, using the euro couldn't be easier. The euro has achieved parity with the U.S. $, so the exchange rate is €1 for $1. In this book, I list prices for German goods and services in euros only.

Choosing Traveler's Checks, ATMs, Credit Cards, or Cash

In Germany, you pay for things in euros, meaning you have to convert your own currency into euros. When it comes to getting cash in Germany, should you bring traveler's checks or use ATMs? What about paying with credit cards? In this section, I talk about what you may need to know so you can decide.

Toting traveler's checks: Safer than cash

Today, *traveler's checks* are something of an anachronism from the days before credit cards and ATMs. These days, you don't really need traveler's checks in Germany because every city has 24-hour ATMs linked to an international network that most likely includes your bank at home (see the next section on using ATMs). Still, if you want the security of traveler's checks and don't mind the hassle of showing your passport every time you want to cash one, you can get them at almost any bank before you leave home.

Traveler's checks are issued from your home bank in your local currency. You generally pay a 1% commission fee to buy the checks. After you arrive in Germany, you need to convert them to euros, which means paying another fee.

The good thing about carrying traveler's checks instead of cash is that you can get a refund if your checks are lost or stolen. Be certain that you keep the checks separate from the official receipt that you receive for buying them, and write down each check number as you cash it. You need this record for any refund.

Never pay for hotels, meals, or purchases with traveler's checks denominated in any currency other than euros. You get a bad exchange rate if you try to use traveler's checks as cash.

Using ATMs: How did we live without them?

In less than ten years, ATMs (called a *Geldautomat* in Germany) have revolutionized the money side of travel. You can fly to Germany with as little as $20 in your pocket and use your bank card to withdraw the cash you need, in euros, on arrival. ATMs offer a fast and easy way to exchange money at the bank's bulk exchange rate, which is better than any rate you can get on the street. If you withdraw only as much cash as you need every couple of days, you won't feel the insecurity of carrying around a huge wad of bills.

If you plan to use ATMs, make certain you have a four-digit *PIN* (personal identification number) *before* you arrive. Contact your bank or credit-card company to find out if your PIN is suitable for use in Germany. Keep in mind that many European ATMs won't allow you to withdraw money from savings accounts, so be sure to transfer any funds you may need to your checking account before leaving home.

Many German banks impose a fee of 50¢ to $3 every time you use an ATM. Your own bank may also charge you a fee for using ATMs from other banks. Obviously, you need to think twice about the amount you're withdrawing in order to avoid unnecessary trips to the ATM.

In German cities, you can easily find 24-hour ATMs in airports, train stations, and outside banks. You can get cash 24 hours a day using your bank card or an international credit card (American Express, Diners Club, MasterCard, and Visa). *Cirrus* (☎ **800/424-7787**; Internet: www.mastercard.com) and *Plus* (☎ **800/843-7587**; Internet: www.visa.com) are the most popular networks; check the back of your ATM card to see to which network your bank belongs. The toll-free numbers and Web sites above give you locations of ATMs where you can withdraw money in Germany.

Paying with plastic: Classy and convenient

Credit cards are invaluable when traveling — they're a safe way to carry money and provide a convenient record of all your travel expenses. American Express, Diners Club, MasterCard, and Visa are widely accepted throughout Germany. A Eurocard or Access sign displayed at an establishment means that it accepts MasterCard.

Credit-card purchases are translated from euros to dollars and show up on your monthly statement, so keeping track of expenditures is easy.

You can also use credit cards to get cash advances at any bank or from ATMs, although you start paying interest on the advance the moment you receive the cash. (You won't receive frequent-flyer miles on an airline credit card, either.)

In smaller towns and villages in Germany, you may have trouble paying for low-price pensions (B&Bs) and restaurants with credit cards. Many pensions with one to three guest rooms operate on a cash-only basis, as do some small restaurants.

Bringing cash: Always appropriate

Germany has no exchange controls, so you can bring as much cash and as many traveler's checks into the country as you wish. Some folks like to change a small amount (say $100) of currency into euros before leaving home. (You can often exchange your dollars in airports that offer international flights to Germany.) This small emergency fund is always enough to cover transportation from the airport to the hotel.

Nowadays, though, waiting until you arrive in Frankfurt, Munich, or Berlin before changing money may be simpler. The currency-exchange windows at most German airports will almost certainly be open when your flight arrives, or you can use one of the ATMs.

Exchanging Your Currency

The *exchange rate,* which fluctuates daily, is the rate you get when you use your own currency to buy euros. In general, **$1 = €1.** I use this *approximate* exchange rate for prices in this book. (I round the figures to the nearest euro.) When you are about to leave on your trip, check with your bank or look in the newspaper to find out the current rate.

Changing money or traveler's checks is a simple and straightforward operation. Just remember that every time you make an exchange, you need to show your passport and pay a fee. You can easily change cash or traveler's checks by using a currency-exchange service called a **Geldwechsel** or **bureau de change.** These services are available in several locations: German airports, any branch of a major bank, all major rail stations, post offices countrywide, some Tourist Information offices, and American Express offices. Currency-exchange windows in airports and rail stations are generally open daily from 6 a.m. to 10 p.m.

Almost every major bank in Germany has a foreign-currency window where you can exchange traveler's checks or cash. Weekday hours for banks are generally from 8:30 a.m. to 1 p.m. and from 2:30 p.m. to 4 p.m. (Thursdays to 5:30 p.m.). All banks are closed on Saturday, Sunday, and public holidays, but many branches have 24-hour banking lobbies with ATMs and/or ATMs on the street outside.

Reputable German banks and bureaux de change exchange money at a competitive rate but charge a commission (typically 1–3% of the total transaction). Some currency-exchange services now guarantee you the same exchange rate when you return unspent euros for dollars (remember to keep your receipt if you want to use this service).

All German bureaux de change and other money-changing establishments are required to clearly display exchange rates and full details of any fees and rates of commission. Rates must be displayed near the entrance to the premises. Rates and fees fluctuate from place to place, so shopping around sometimes pays.

 You can avoid paying a second commission fee by using **American Express** traveler's checks and cashing them at an American Express office. American Express has offices in Berlin, Cologne, Dresden, Frankfurt am Main, Hamburg, Heidelberg, Leipzig, Munich, and Nuremberg, among other cities. You find addresses for American Express offices throughout Germany at www.americanexpress.com.

 Citibank customers using ATMs at German branches of Citibank don't pay additional withdrawal fees. You find Citibank branches in Berlin, Cologne, Frankfurt, Hamburg, Leipzig, and Munich. For addresses of Citibanks in Germany, go online to www.citibank.com.

Handling Loss or Theft

Oh no! You reach for your money and find that it's missing. Or you've fallen afoul of a thief. German cities are very safe, but crime happens. If you follow four basic rules, you can minimize the risk of a crime happening to you:

✔ Keep your wallet or purse out of sight, but *not* in your back pocket or in your backpack.

✔ Never leave your purse, briefcase, backpack, or coat unattended in any public place.

✔ Ladies: Don't hang your purse over the back of your chair in crowded or outdoor cafes or restaurants.

✔ Don't flash your money or credit cards around.

In the unlikely event that your wallet or purse is stolen, you need to cancel all your credit cards. Almost every credit card company has an emergency toll-free number you can call for this purpose. The company will cancel the card number immediately, and may also be able to wire you a cash advance; in many places, you can get an emergency replacement card in a day or two. If your credit card gets lost or stolen while you're in Germany, call the following numbers immediately:

✔ **American Express** ☎ **954/503-8850** (collect)

✔ **Diners Club** ☎ **702/797-5532** (collect)

✔ **MasterCard** ☎ **0800/819-1040** (toll-free)

✔ **Visa** ☎ **0800/811-8440** (toll-free) or 417/581-9994 (collect)

Write down the number of all your credit cards and keep the paper somewhere other than in your wallet or purse. If your card is lost or stolen, you can then access the card number immediately.

If you carry traveler's checks, be sure to keep a record of their serial numbers, and keep the record separate from the checks. Write down the numbers of the checks as you cash them. If the checks are stolen, you need to report exactly which checks are gone in order to get them replaced. The check issuer will tell you where to pick up the new checks.

If your purse or wallet is gone, the police (*Polizei,* pronounced po-litz-eye) aren't likely to recover it for you. However, after you cancel your credit cards, call to inform the police (☎ 110 anywhere in Germany). You may need the police report number for insurance purposes later.

Talking Taxes and the VAT

No discussion of money matters in Germany would be complete without a reference to the *Mehrwertsteuer* or value-added tax (VAT), Germany's version of a sales tax. This 16% tax is added to the total price of all consumer goods (the price tag already includes it) as well as hotel and restaurant bills. If you're not a resident of the European Union, you can get a portion of your VAT refunded on large purchases made in Germany but not the VAT paid at hotels and restaurants.

To receive a refund, shop at stores displaying a **Tax-Free Shopping** sign. Most stores have a minimum amount that you must spend in order to qualify for the refund. When you make a qualifying purchase, you'll receive a **tax-free voucher,** which must be completed by the store and have a copy of your sales receipt attached to it.

Before you check your luggage upon your departure from Germany, have the voucher stamped by German customs to confirm that the goods have been exported. Then, redeem the voucher for cash (euros or dollars) at a **Europe Tax-Free Shopping** window, located at all major airports, border crossings, ferry ports, and railroad stations.

Chapter 10

Tying Up the Loose Ends

*B*efore you depart for Germany to sip beer in Munich, or visit the Pergamon Museum in Berlin, or explore mad Ludwig's castles in Bavaria, you have some loose ends to tie up. Do you have an up-to-date passport? Have you taken steps to meet your health needs while you're on your trip? Have you made reservations for the Berlin restaurant you have to try, and do you have tickets for the opera you just can't miss? Do you know what to pack for a trip to Germany? This chapter helps you wrap up these and other last-minute details.

Dealing with Passports

A valid passport is the only legal form of identification accepted around the world. You can't cross an international border without it. Getting a passport is easy, but the process takes some time.

Applying for a U.S. passport

If you're applying for a first-time passport, follow these steps:

1. Complete a **passport application** in person at a U.S. passport office; a federal, state, or probate court; or a major post office. To find your regional passport office, either check the **U.S. State Department** Web site, http://travel.state.gov, or call the **National Passport Information Center** (☎ 900/225-5674); the fee is 55¢ per minute for automated information and $1.50 per minute for operator-assisted calls.

2. Present a **certified birth certificate** as proof of citizenship. (Bringing along your driver's license, state or military ID, or social security card is also a good idea.)

3. Submit **two identical passport-sized photos,** measuring 2-x-2 inches in size. You often find businesses that take these photos near a passport office. *Note:* You can't use a strip from a photo-vending machine because the pictures aren't identical.

4. Pay a **fee.** For people 16 and over, a passport is valid for ten years and costs $85. For those 15 and under, a passport is valid for five years and costs $70.

Allow plenty of time before your trip to apply for a passport; processing normally takes three weeks but can take longer during busy periods (especially spring).

If you have a passport in your current name that was issued within the past 15 years (and you were over age 16 when it was issued), you can renew the passport by mail for $55. Whether you're applying in person or by mail, you can download passport applications from the U.S. State Department Web site at http://travel.state.gov. For general information, call the **National Passport Agency** (☎ **202/647-0518**).

American Passport Express (☎ **800/841-6778;** Internet: www.americanpassport.com) can process your first-time passport application in five to eight business days for $145, plus a $60 service fee; for renewals, the cost is $115 plus a $60 service fee. If you need the passport in three to five business days, the service fee is $100, and for a $150 service fee you can receive your passport in 24 hours.

Applying for other passports

The following list offers more information for citizens of Australia, Canada, New Zealand, and the United Kingdom.

✔ **Australians** can visit a local post office or passport office, call the **Australia State Passport Office** (☎ **131-232** toll-free from Australia), or log on to www.passports.gov.au for details on how and where to apply. Passports cost A$136 for adults and A$68 for those under 18.

✔ **Canadians** can pick up applications at passport offices throughout Canada, at post offices, or from the central **Passport Office, Department of Foreign Affairs and International Trade,** Ottawa, Ont. K1A 0G3 (☎ **800/567-6868;** Internet: www.dfaitmaeci.gc.ca/passport). Passports are valid for five years and cost $60. Applications must be accompanied by two identical passport-sized photographs and proof of Canadian citizenship. Processing takes five to ten days if you apply in person, or about three weeks by mail.

✔ **New Zealanders** can pick up a passport application at any travel agency or Link Centre. For information, contact the **Passport Office,** Department of Internal Affairs, P.O. Box 10-526, Wellington (☎ **0800/225-050;** Internet: www.passports.govt.nz). Passports are NZ$80 for adults and NZ$40 for those under 16.

✔ **United Kingdom** residents, as a member of the European Union, need only an identity card, not a passport, to travel to other EU countries, such as Germany. However, if you already possess a passport, carrying the document with you is a good idea.

Understanding passport rules

If you're a citizen of the United States, Australia, or Canada, you must have a valid passport to enter Germany.

You need to show your passport at the Customs and Immigration area when you arrive at a German airport, or when you cross a border into Germany. After your passport is stamped, you can remain in Germany as a tourist for up to three months.

Keep your passport with you at all times. You only need to give your passport to airline reservation clerks (who must check the document if you're on an international flight), customs and immigrations officials at the airport, and at the bank or currency exchange when you're converting traveler's checks or foreign currency. A hotel clerk may also ask to see your passport upon check in. If you don't need your passport for exchanging currency while traveling, ask whether the hotel has a safe where you can keep it locked up.

Dealing with a (gulp) lost passport

If you lose your passport in Germany, you'll need to take steps to replace it *immediately.* First notify the police. Then contact your consulate or high commission office, all of which are located in Berlin (see the Appendix for addresses). If you're in Berlin, bring all available forms of personal ID to the respective office, and the staff can get started on generating a new passport for you.

Having a photocopy of your passport can be helpful if you lose the original document while traveling. Make the copy before you leave home and keep the paper in a safe place.

Considering Visas and Health Certificates

No visa is required if you're going to stay in Germany for less than three months. The U.S. Department of State's Bureau of Consular Affairs operates a phone line for current visa information: ☎ **202/663-1225** (Mon–Fri 8:30 a.m.–4 p.m.). Or you can check its Web site at www. travel.state.gov.

Likewise, you don't need an International Certificate of Vaccination to enter Germany, as you would if traveling to Southeast Asia or parts of Africa.

Deciding Insurance Needs

Three kinds of travel insurance are available: trip-cancellation insurance, medical insurance, and lost-luggage insurance. Here is my advice on all three.

- ✔ **Trip-cancellation insurance** is a good idea if you signed up for an escorted tour and paid a large portion of your vacation expenses up front (for information on escorted tours, see Chapter 6). Trip-cancellation insurance covers three emergencies — if a death or sickness prevents you from traveling, if a tour operator or airline goes out of business, or if some kind of disaster prevents you from getting to your destination.

- ✔ Buying **medical insurance** for your trip doesn't make sense for most travelers. Your existing health insurance should cover you if you get sick while on vacation (although if you belong to an HMO, check to see whether you're fully covered while in Germany).

- ✔ **Lost-luggage insurance** is not necessary for most travelers. Your homeowner's or renter's insurance should cover stolen luggage if you have off-premises theft coverage. Check your existing policies before you buy any additional coverage. If an airline loses your luggage, the airline is responsible for paying $2,500 per bag on domestic flights (including U.S. portions of international trips) and $635 per bag (maximum of two bags) on international flights. If you plan to carry anything more valuable than that, keep it in your carry-on bag.

Some credit cards (American Express and certain gold and platinum Visas and MasterCards, for example) offer automatic flight insurance against death or dismemberment in case of an airplane crash if you charged the cost of your ticket.

If you're interested in purchasing travel insurance, try one of the following companies:

- ✔ **Access America** (☎ **800/284-8300;** Internet: www.accessamerica.com)
- ✔ **Travel Guard International** (☎ **800/826-1300;** Internet: www.travelguard.com)
- ✔ **Travel Insured International** (☎ **800/243-3174;** Internet: www.travelinsured.com)
- ✔ **Travelex Insurance Services** (☎ **800/228-9792;** Internet: www.travelex-insurance.com)

 Don't pay for more insurance than you need. For example, if you need only trip-cancellation insurance, don't buy coverage for lost or stolen property. Trip-cancellation insurance costs about 6% to 8% of the total value of your vacation.

Taking Care of Your Health

Getting sick will ruin your vacation, so I *strongly* advise against it (of course, last time I checked, the bugs weren't listening to me any more than they probably listen to you).

 If you have health insurance, be sure to carry your insurance card in your wallet. Most U.S. health insurance plans and HMOs cover at least part of the out-of-country hospital visits and procedures if insurees become ill or are injured while out of the country. Most require that you pay the bills up front at the time of care, issuing a refund after you return and file all the paperwork. For information on purchasing additional medical insurance for your trip, see the previous section.

Talk to your doctor before leaving on a trip if you have a serious and/or chronic illness. For conditions such as epilepsy, diabetes, or heart problems, wear a **Medic Alert Identification Tag** (☎ **800/825-3785;** Internet: www.medicalert.org), which immediately alerts doctors to your condition and gives them access to your records through Medic Alert's 24-hour hotline.

 Before leaving home, you can obtain a directory of German doctors who speak English from the **International Association of Medical Assistance to Travelers** (IAMAT; Internet: www.iamat.org). Its address in the United States is 417 Center St., Lewiston, NY 14092 (☎ **716/754-4883**); in Canada, 40 Regal Rd., Guelph, Ontario N1K 1B5 (☎ **519/836-0102**); and in New Zealand, P.O. Box 5049, Christchurch 5 (no phone).

Bring all your medications with you, as well as prescriptions for more (in generic, not brand-name, form) if you worry that you'll run out. A **pharmacy** in Germany is called an *Apotheke* (pronounced ah-po-*tay*-kuh). Pharmacies are open regular shopping hours, and they take turns staying open all night and on weekends. If you have an emergency and need a prescription filled after hours or on weekends, go to any pharmacy. There will be a notice in the window giving the address and telephone number of the closest on-duty pharmacy.

If you fall ill while traveling, ask the concierge or hotelkeeper to recommend a local doctor. (*Arzt,* pronounced *artst,* is the German word for a medical doctor.) At night and on weekends you can call the **Ärtzlicher Notdienst** (Medical Emergency Service) listed in the telephone directory. In a life-threatening situation, dial ☎ **110** (free call anywhere in Germany), the number for general emergencies. The word for hospital is *Krankenhaus* (pronounced *kronk*-in-house).

Getting Reservations and Tickets Before You Leave Home

You're going to Germany, your time is limited, and you don't want to miss an opera performance at the Semper Opera House in Dresden or a concert by the acclaimed Berlin Philharmonic Orchestra — what do you do? Just make your reservations or buy your tickets in advance.

Your finest table, please: Dinner reservations

For dinner reservations, call the restaurant directly from home (all my restaurant listings include phone numbers). But keep in mind the time change (Germany operates on central European time, which is six hours later than eastern standard time and nine hours later than pacific standard time; when it's noon in New York, it's 6 p.m. in Berlin). You can also ask your hotel concierge to make the reservation for you after you arrive.

Two on the aisle: Theater tickets

Seeing an opera or symphony concert in Berlin, Munich, Cologne, Dresden, Hamburg, Frankfurt, or Leipzig is a must for many visitors. Germany's many opera houses and symphony orchestras are among the world's greatest. The theater scene is outstanding, but, of course, most productions are in German. American musicals such as *The Lion King* (currently playing a long run in Hamburg) and plays originally written in English are translated into German for German audiences.

Ten things to do before you leave home

For peace of mind on your trip, make sure that you take care of some housekeeping details before you leave. Although most are fairly obvious, they are easy to overlook in the excitement of getting ready for a trip.

✔ Pay any bills that will come due while you're away.

✔ Get someone to look after your pets (or kennel them) and water the plants.

✔ Put a hold on your mail and newspaper deliveries.

✔ Empty/defrost your refrigerator.

✔ Put several lights in the house on timers (dining room at dinner time, TV room during prime time, and so on).

✔ Lock all windows and doors (don't forget the basement and garage).

✔ Reconfirm your airline seat reservation.

✔ Call the airline to double-check that your flight is on time.

✔ Use public transportation or arrange for a friend or taxi to take you to the airport. (This approach is cheaper and better than leaving your car in the airport's long-term parking garage.)

✔ Get to the airport at least two hours before your flight.

✔ Sit back on the plane, take a deep breath, and tell yourself: "I'm on my way to Germany!" *Auf Wiedersehen!* I hope you have a great time.

Your chances of getting a seat for any opera, orchestra performance, play, or musical are good if you go directly to the theater box office (*Kasse,* pronounced *kah*-suh). The box office at most venues is open daily and also one hour before the performance. In most cities you can buy tickets for all major venues at the **Tourist Information office.** If you're looking forward to a specific concert or opera, and missing the show would spoil your trip, book your seat in advance. You can sometimes do this on the Web. I list major performing arts venues in every city chapter of this book. If the venue has a Web site, I give the address. If not, I also a give the phone number so you can call the box office directly. You can often order tickets for specific venues at a city's official Web site (see the Appendix for these addresses). For the top music venues throughout the country, see the music lovers' itinerary in Chapter 3.

In the know: What's playing and where

Before you depart on your trip, you can find out what's happening in each city by doing some online research. I list each city's tourism Web site in the destination chapters of this book. City Web sites are sometimes available in English versions and always have a schedule of what's going on in that city. On the sites, click onto "Tourist Information," "Kultur und Unterhaltung" (Culture and Entertainment), or "Bühne" (stages). You may also find links to online ticket outlets or to specific venues.

After you arrive in Germany, head to the local Tourist Information office to obtain a schedule of events and to buy tickets.

Packing It Up and Taking It on the Road

If you ask me, packing is a spiritual exercise that teaches you a great deal about yourself and your basic needs. Packing is about lightening your load.

Before you start packing, think realistically about what you need for the length of time you'll be gone. And think practically. A sauce stain makes a white silk dress or dress shirt unwearable (I hope). In general, plan to dress in *layers*. Pack *nonwhite* clothing. And unless you're going to Germany in the height of summer, consider that the temperature will probably be between *40 and 60 degrees Fahrenheit*. In the summer, except in the north, the weather can be hot and muggy. German hotels, restaurants, and performing arts venues tend not to have air conditioning. In the winter, thermostats are generally not turned up as high as in the United States. Northern Germany during winter is often rainy, misty, foggy, and generally damp.

Deciding what to bring

To start packing, compile everything that you think you'll need on your trip. Then get rid of half of it. You don't want to injure yourself as a result of lugging half your house around with you. If you're staying in a pension (B&B) without an elevator, lugging a heavy load of suitcases up and down narrow stairways can be a pain in the gluteus max.

Some essentials for your trip include

- Comfortable walking shoes
- A pair of jeans or khakis
- Bermuda shorts if visiting in summer
- A waterproof jacket or coat; select outerwear that's lined and has a hood if visiting in late fall or winter
- A versatile sweater (gray or dark colored); make this a heavy sweater if visiting in late fall or winter

Keeping in step with the Germans

Germany is the land of Birkenstocks, sandals worn with white socks, and "Dr. Scholl's," a sandal with a shaped wooden bottom and an adjustable strap above the toes (both men and women wear them). Having healthy, comfortable feet is important in this nation of walkers.

- ✔ A couple wrinkle-free shirts or blouses
- ✔ Something to sleep in, if you don't sleep au naturel (even if the room is chilly you'll be toasty under the feather comforter, or *Decke,* found on every bed)
- ✔ A collapsible umbrella (or *Regenschirm* as the Germans call it)
- ✔ Gloves, a hat, and a scarf if visiting in late fall or winter

The Germans, especially young Germans, are as casual as Americans when it comes to dress. You won't find many restaurants that require a jacket and tie for men, but in a fine restaurant you'll feel like a hick if you're wearing blue jeans and running shoes. Similarly, you don't *have* to dress up for the opera or to go to a concert — but you'll notice that most patrons do dress up because "going out" in Germany is considered a special event, and you always promenade during the intermissions.

Dressing like a native

Berlin, Munich, and Frankfurt — like Paris, Milan, and New York — are fashion-conscious cities. This doesn't mean that you *must* be fashionable, only that you *can* be, and that if you *are,* other fashionable people will probably notice you. If you plan to eat in any upscale restaurants, you should consider a "smart but casual" look. And keep in mind that black is always in fashion.

Smart-but-casual men need to bring along a pair of dressy but comfortable trousers and a sports jacket (or a suit if you like), a shirt and tie (or dressy sweater), and semidressy shoes. Smart-but-casual women can wear a dress, a skirt and blouse, a suit with skirt and jacket, or a pantsuit.

Traveling with a carry-on bag

In the wake of the September 11, 2001, terrorist attacks, the Transportation Security Administration (TSA), the government agency that now handles all aspects of airport security, devised new restrictions for carry-on baggage not only to expedite the screening process but also to prevent potential weapons from passing through airport security. Passengers are now limited to bringing just **one carry-on bag** and one personal item onto the aircraft (previous regulations allowed two carry-on bags and one personal item, like a briefcase or a purse). For more information, go to the TSA's Web site, www.tsa.gov. Regarding items that are permitted in your carry-on bag, the TSA gives the following guidelines:

- ✔ **Not permitted:** Knives and box cutters, corkscrews, straight razors, metal scissors, golf clubs, baseball bats, pool cues, hockey sticks, ski poles, and ice picks

- ✔ **Permitted:** Nail clippers, nail files, tweezers, eyelash curlers, safety razors (including disposable razors), syringes (with documented proof of medical need), walking canes, and umbrellas (must be inspected first).

Your airline may have additional restrictions on items you can and can't carry on board. Call ahead to avoid problems.

You may be asked to turn on your laptop computer or any other kind of electric or electronic gadget you want to carry on board. Make sure that these items are working in advance.

So what are a few good items to have with you? Your carry-on should contain a book (this one, of course), any medications you use, any breakable items that you don't want to put in your suitcase, a snack in case you don't like the airline food, your vital documents (such as return tickets and passport), and items, such as a toothbrush, toothpaste, and moisturizer, to help you stay clean and refreshed during the long flight.

Leaving electronics at home

When I'm on an exciting trip, the last thing I want is to tune myself *out* of what is going on around me. I want to enjoy the sights and atmosphere. People today think that they need to haul along every new electronic toy or gadget wherever they go. Trust me, doing so won't add anything to your trip — it'll detract from it. Even the mobile phone that's glued to your ear at home can be turned off and left behind.

If you think that you won't enjoy your trip without a few electrical gadgets, here's what you need to know if you're coming from North America: You can't plug an appliance from the United States or Canada into a German outlet without frying your appliance and/or blowing a fuse. North American current runs 110V; the standard voltage throughout Germany is 220V. You need an electric-current converter or transformer to bring the voltage down. Two-pronged North American plugs won't fit into the two-pronged, round, German wall sockets, so you also need an adaptor plug if you use North American appliances in Germany. Plug adapters and converters are available at most travel, luggage, electronics, and hardware stores. Some plug adapters are also current converters. Most contemporary laptop computers automatically sense the current and adapt accordingly (check the manual, bottom of the machine, or manufacturer first to make sure that you don't destroy your data and/or equipment).

The standard voltages and wall plugs in Australia, New Zealand, and the United Kingdom are also different from those in Germany. If you're coming from one of these countries, you'll need to bring an electric-current converter and a plug adaptor with you.

Travel-size versions of hair dryers, irons, shavers, and so on are dual voltage, which means that they have built-in converters (usually you have to turn a switch to go back and forth). If you insist on lugging your own hair dryer or electric shaver to Germany, make sure that the item has dual voltage or that you carry along a converter and a plug adapter. To avoid voltage issues, use a straight-edge razor for shaving, unless you have a battery-operated electric shaver. However, many upscale hotels have a special plug for low-wattage shavers *and shavers only.*

Getting comfortable on the plane

What follows are a few tips to ensure that your flight is as comfortable as possible.

- ✔ Wear comfortable, low-heeled shoes and dress in loose-fitting layers that you can remove as the cabin temperature fluctuates. Don't underdress: Airline cabins can be chilly, and blankets may be unavailable. Wear breathable, natural fabrics instead of synthetics.

- ✔ Hydrate before, during, and after your flight to combat the lack of humidity in airplane cabins — which can be as dry as the Sahara Desert. Bring a bottle of water on board.

- ✔ Preorder a special meal. The airlines' vegetarian and kosher meals are usually fresher than standard plane fare. Or bring your own meal in a brown bag.

- ✔ Get up and walk around whenever you can or perform stretching exercises in your seat to keep your blood flowing.

- ✔ Bring a toothbrush and moisturizer to stay fresh.

- ✔ If you're flying with kids, don't forget a deck of cards, toys, extra bottles, pacifiers, diapers, and chewing gum to help them relieve ear pressure buildup during ascent and descent. Let each child pack his or her own backpack with favorite toys.

- ✔ If you're flying with a cold or chronic sinus problems, use a decongestant ten minutes before ascent and descent, to minimize pressure buildup in the inner ear.

Arriving in Germany

If you're flying directly to Germany from Australia, Canada, New Zealand, the United Kingdom, or the United States, you'll land in Frankfurt, Munich, or Düsseldorf and immediately proceed to **Immigration and Customs.** If you're landing elsewhere — in Amsterdam or Paris, say — you'll pass through Immigration and Customs in that city.

The procedure is straightforward and rarely takes longer than half an hour. All the passengers on your flight will be directed to Immigration and Customs, where you'll see one line for residents of the European Union (EU) and another for non-EU residents. You'll show your passport to the official, and he or she stamps one of the pages and waves you on. You may be asked a couple of questions, such as where you'll be staying or how long you plan to remain in Germany.

Next, you'll enter the baggage-claim area. You'll need to claim your baggage and take it through customs even if you are continuing on to another flight within Germany. Again, you'll find two lines: One line is for "Goods to Declare," and the other line is "Nothing to Declare." The signs are in German and English. You pass through the appropriate door and into the terminal. As you're passing through "Nothing to Declare," a customs official may ask you to open your bag for inspection. This is usually nothing more than a spot-check.

Goods brought into Germany are tax-free up to a value of €175. Maximum duty-free quantities that you can bring into Germany are as follows:

✔ **Tobacco products:** 200 cigarettes or 100 cigarillos or 50 cigars or 250 grams of tobacco

✔ **Alcohol:** 1 liter of alcohol 22 proof or higher, or 2 liters of alcohol less than 22 proof, or 2 liters of sparkling or fortified wine and 2 liters of still wine

✔ **Coffee:** 17.5 ounces (500 grams) of coffee or 7 ounces (200 grams) of freeze-dried coffee

✔ **Perfume:** 1.75 ounces (50 grams) of perfume

Part III
Berlin and Eastern Germany

The 5th Wave   By Rich Tennant

In this part . . .

History has left its mark throughout eastern Germany, and nowhere more so than in **Berlin,** the country's "new" capital. I devote two chapters to Berlin. **Chapter 11** fills you in on all the Berlin basics: getting there, getting around, and finding the best hotels and restaurants. I devote **Chapter 12** to exploring the largest and most exciting city in Germany. Since reunification in 1990, eastern Germany has been in the midst of a major building and rebuilding boom. In **Chapter 13,** I introduce you to the best places to visit in this newly opened region: **Dresden,** with its superb museums, historic panache, and location on the Elbe river; **Leipzig,** a busy business city where the "peaceful revolution" began; and **Weimar,** city of Goethe and one of Germany's cultural jewels. In Chapter 13, I also tell you about visiting the **Thuringian Forest** and taking a boat trip into the scenic region known as **Saxon Switzerland.**

Chapter 11

Settling into Berlin

● ●

In This Chapter

▶ Arriving in Berlin

▶ Getting from the airport into the city

▶ Orienting yourself to the neighborhoods

▶ Getting around by subway, train, and bus

▶ Choosing your hotel

▶ Picking a good restaurant

▶ Finding a cafe or brewpub

● ●

*U*ntil 1989, every time I visited West Berlin, I'd make a trip over to Communist East Berlin. The visit was fascinating but not exactly fun. First, you had to face hostile-looking guards with machine guns at Friedrichstrasse station. And then you had to get your passport stamped and obtain a day visa, which required you to exchange valuable West *marks* (the currency at the time) for worthless East marks. Going out into East Berlin was like entering a Third World country. Shoddy-looking Soviet-bloc buildings and lifeless memorials to Communist heroes lined the streets. The food was lousy, and the people seemed grimly determined to make your stay as unpleasant as possible. You weren't supposed to talk to anyone, and taking photographs was strictly *verboten* (forbidden).

Those were the days when West Berlin was a walled island of capitalism in the Communist sea of the *Deutsche Demokratische Republik* (German Democratic Republic, or GDR). A social system was in place that "protected" East Germans from cradle to grave. But life in the GDR was hardly an idyllic workers' paradise. Spies and informers riddled the system, and corruption was rampant at the top levels of government.

Now all that's gone. Reunited Berlin is once again Germany's political and cultural capital. The Wall and border crossing are no more, and the decrepit and grimy buildings in the historic, eastern part of the city are being restored and cleaned. But, Berliners need at least another generation to bring down the Wall that still exists in their heads. Not everyone in the former East Berlin was overjoyed with the introduction of a capitalist economy. Watching politicians and business people from the West take over *their* city has been difficult for original residents. The division between "Westies" and "Osties" is no longer a concrete wall, but a separation still exists.

But when all is said and done, *"Berlin bleibt doch Berlin,"* an old song lyric meaning "Berlin always remains Berlin," still holds true. This city has seen it all — Prussian power, artistic brilliance, endless political upheaval, and Nazi terror — and survived to tell the tale. By the end of World War II, much of Berlin had been reduced to smoldering rubble. The city was then divided up into American, British, and Russian sectors. Later, during the Berlin Airlift of 1948, food and supplies had to be flown in because the Soviets blockaded the city. The Wall went up in 1961, and for almost 30 years the city was split in two.

Deutschland was reunited over a decade ago when the Wall came down. Berlin is once again the capital of the Federal Republic of Germany. The incredible cultural resources that were divvied up between the two sides of the city are now accessible to everyone. At Potsdamer Platz, where designer skyscrapers and a new shopping and government quarter have replaced the grim Wall, you can see this fascinating city grow and reinvent itself. And if you tire of the urban scene, lakes and forests are minutes away by public transportation.

Berlin is, for my money, the most exciting city in Europe. You feel a sense of immediacy here because everything is happening at once — past, present, and future meet and meld all over the place. You can dive into Berlin on many levels, even if you don't speak German. Your experience can be as sophisticated, cultured, or raunchy as you want it to be.

Berlin has a kind of inexhaustible energy, a fizz and a flair and a drive that you find nowhere else in Germany. The Berliners, perhaps because they've seen so much, both triumph and tragedy, have always been a breed apart. Their cosmopolitan live-and-let-live attitude, laced with sharp-edged humor and sarcastic irreverence, gives the city an added bite. When you're in Berlin, you see a city in transition, part of the reason why a visit here is so intriguing. But, even as the city reinvents itself yet again, *"Berlin bleibt doch Berlin."*

Getting There

As the capital and largest city in Germany, Berlin is very accessible. You can arrive by plane, train, or car. Upon arrival, you'll have to pass through immigration and customs; for details, see Chapter 10.

By plane

There are currently no direct flights to Berlin from anywhere in the United States. If you fly from the United States, you have to change planes in Frankfurt or another European city, depending on what airline you use. Berlin has three airports, all with easy public transportation connections to the city at standard public fares.

Arriving at Berlin-Tegel

Tegel (TXL) airport (☎ **01805/000-186**), Berlin's main and most convenient airport, is on the outskirts of central Berlin in Reinickedorf. The facility was recently revamped to make it more passenger-friendly. Inside the terminal, you find currency-exchange windows and a small branch of the **Tourist Information Center** (no phone; open daily 5:30 a.m.–10 p.m.) where you can pick up free city transit maps and general-interest brochures and buy a bus ticket into town.

To get into central Berlin from Tegel, you can take a bus or taxi. Buses arrive outside the airport terminal, where you also find the taxi stand. On the bus, buy your ticket from the driver in euro coins (no bills). For information on public transportation, see "Getting around Berlin," later in this chapter. Four buses run from the airport into central Berlin.

- ✔ **JetExpress Bus TXL** runs about every 10 minutes between the airport and Potsdamer Platz, Friedrichstrasse, and Unter den Linden in Mitte, the "new" center of Berlin. Tickets cost €3.10. A *Tageskarte* (day ticket), good for the rest of the day, costs €8.10.

- ✔ **Bus X9** connects to Jakob-Kaiser-Platz *U-Bahn* (underground train) station. From there you can change to the subway and reach any destination. You pay the regular two-zone fare of €2.10. (See "Getting around Berlin," later in this chapter, for zone information.)

- ✔ **Buses X9** and **109** both go to Bahnhof Zoologischer Garten (Zoo Station), the central train station in the western part of the city near Kurfürstendamm. The fare is the standard two-zone fare for public transporation: €2.10. The X9 is an express bus and takes about 20 minutes to reach Zoo Station. Bus 109, which travels down Kurfürstendamm, takes about 30 minutes. At the train station, you can connect to the U-Bahn or the *S-Bahn* (elevated train). Berlin's main Tourist Information Center is at the nearby Europa Center (see "Where to Find Information After You Arrive," later in this chapter).

A **taxi** ride to central Berlin (east or west) costs about €18 and takes about 20 minutes.

A tale of three airports

Tempelhof, built in the 1920s, was Berlin's main airport during the Third Reich. The airport was also the base for the Berlin Airlift in 1948, when U.S. and other Allied forces brought food and supplies to the city during the Soviet blockade. During the Cold War, the U.S.–built **Tegel** airport served West Berlin, while another airport, **Schönefeld,** served travelers to the city's Communist, eastern sector.

A massive $4 billion expansion of Schönefeld airport is now underway. When the project is completed, a few years from now, Berlin's other two airports will close. All air traffic will then be consolidated into a single hub called Berlin Brandenburg International Airport.

Arriving at Berlin-Schönefeld

Schönefeld (SXF) (☎ **01805/000-186**), located about 15 miles (24 km) southeast of the city, is the old East Berlin airport, now mostly used for European charter flights. The easiest way to get into town from this airport is by **Airport Express,** an S-Bahn that leaves Flughafen Berlin-Schönefeld station about every 20 minutes for central Berlin, stopping at Alexanderplatz and Fredrichstrasse in Berlin Mitte (eastern Berlin), and Bahnhof Zoo (about a 30-minute journey) in the western center of Berlin. The S-Bahn station is a 10-minute walk from the airport terminal, or you can take **Bus 171,** a shuttle service that runs from the airport to the S-Bahn station and the **Rudow U-Bahn station.** From the U-Bahn station, you can take the U7 subway to Bahnhof Zoo in about 50 minutes. Bus, U-Bahn, or S-Bahn fare is €2.10.

A **taxi** ride to the Alexanderplatz area in Mitte takes about 45 to 60 minutes and costs about €40. Taxis wait outside the terminal.

By train

You can reach Berlin by train from everywhere in Europe. Three main train stations currently handle all long-distance trains. The railway stations are connected to public transport, such as buses, subways, and elevated trains.

By 2005, all high-speed Europe-wide trains will arrive at or depart from one central station, **Lehrter Bahnhof.** When that happens, for the first time in its history Berlin will have one train station that dominates all others. Until then, three main stations continue to operate: Bahnhof Zoologischer Garten (Zoo Station), Ostbahnhof (East Station), and Bahnhof Lichtenberg.

For 24-hour train information, call **Bundesbahn-Reiseauskunft** (German Train Information) at ☎ **01805/996-633;** ask for an English-speaking operator.

Arriving at Bahnhof Zoologischer Garten (Zoo Station)

Usually called **Bahnhof Zoo** (Zoo Station; Hardenbergplatz 11, ☎ **01805/ 996-633**), this busy station is centrally located close to Kurfürstendamm, the main artery in western Berlin. Zoo station is the point of arrival from western destinations including Hamburg and Amsterdam. In addition to long-distance trains, U-Bahn and S-Bahn trains converge at this station. Inside the station, the train travel office **Reisezentrum Bahnhof Zoo** (☎ **030/19419**) is open daily from 6 a.m. to 11 p.m. to handle train tickets and information. At the **BVG-Pavilion** outside the station, you can buy tickets and special passes for buses, underground trains (U-Bahn), and elevated trains (S-Bahn); the pavilion is open daily from 6 a.m. to 10 p.m.

Arriving at Ostbahnhof (East Station)

Ostbahnhof (☎ **01805/996-633**), in the eastern neighborhood of Friedrichshain, is currently Berlin's second main station. Trains entering and departing Berlin for destinations in Bavaria and eastern Germany usually stop here and at Zoo Station. Unless you're staying in the eastern section of Berlin, you probably won't use Ostbahnhof. The U5 U-Bahn line connects the station to Alexanderplatz and Zoo Station.

Arriving at Bahnhof Lichtenberg

Some trains from eastern European destinations arrive at **Bahnhof Lichtenberg,** Weitlinger Strasse 22 (☎ **01805/996-633**), in eastern Berlin. You may arrive at Lichtenberg if you're coming from a destination such as Prague or Budapest. The station is on the U5 U-Bahn line, which runs to Alexanderplatz and Zoo Station.

By car

Four *Autobahn* (freeway) routes enter Berlin from western Germany; three enter from the east. The drive from Frankfurt or Munich takes about eight hours, depending on traffic. Once you're in Berlin, however, a car is a nuisance. In fact, you'll want to keep the car parked at your hotel or in a garage. Unless you know this huge city well, getting around by public transportation is far easier than by car. See "Driving a car" later in this chapter for general driving tips in the city.

Finding Information After You Arrive

At a **Tourist Info Center,** you can find information or book a hotel room (for a fee of €3). You can also buy the Welcome Card (see "Transportation basics," later in this chapter), the SchauLUST museum pass (described in Chapter 12), or bus and subway tickets. Berlin has three walk-in locations.

✔ The main office in western Berlin is in the **Europa-Center,** Budapester Strasse 45, close to Bahnhof Zoo (U-/S-Bahn: Zoologischer Garten). The office is open Monday through Saturday from 8:30 a.m. to 8:30 p.m., Sunday from 10 a.m. to 6:30 p.m.

✔ The eastern Berlin branch is in the south wing of the **Brandenburg Gate** (U-/S-Bahn: Potsdamer Platz or Unter den Linden). The office is open daily from 9:30 a.m. to 6 p.m.

✔ Another eastern Berlin branch is located under the **Fernsehturm** (Television Tower) at Alexanderplatz. This center is open daily from 9:30 a.m. to 8 p.m.

The three Tourist Info Centers operate one **information line** (☎ **0190/016-316**), which costs €.40 to €1.15 per minute. You can book hotels by calling ☎ **030/250-025,** which is just the cost of a local call.

Smaller information offices, called **Info Points,** are in the main hall of **Tegel Airport** (open daily 5 a.m.–10:30 p.m.) and on the ground floor of **KaDeWe department store,** Tauentzienstrasse 21 (U-Bahn: Kurfürstendamm; open Mon–Fri 9:30 a.m.–8 p.m., Sat 9 a.m.–4 p.m.).

Orienting Yourself in Berlin

Covering some 60 square miles, Berlin is one of the world's largest cities. For first-time visitors, getting a handle on this sprawling, complex metropolis can be difficult. Even though the Wall has been down since 1989, the first and simplest way to understand Berlin is still to think in terms of the old political boundaries of "West" and "East." (See the "Berlin Neighborhoods" map in this chapter.)

Introducing western Berlin

From 1961 to 1989, West Berlin was an island of capitalism in Communist East Germany. West Berlin was richer, showier, and wilder than its drab eastern counterpart. You'll probably still want to find a hotel in western Berlin, although several luxury hotels now exist in the eastern part of the city. The city's main attractions are spread almost evenly across the whole city.

West Berlin's glitziest artery was — and remains — the 2½-mile- (4 km-) long boulevard known as **Kurfürstendamm,** or **Ku-Damm** for short.

The train station **Bahnhof Zoologischer Garten,** or **Bahnhof Zoo** for short, near the Ku-Damm, is the major transportation hub on the western side of the city and a good landmark for orienting yourself. The zoo itself is part of the **Tiergarten,** a beautiful park stretching east and ending at the cultural center known as the **Kulturforum,** near Potsdamer Platz.

Charlottenburg

This is the wealthiest and most commercialized district of western Berlin. The famous **Ku-Damm** runs through this district. Along this wide boulevard, you find the best concentration of hotels, restaurants, theaters, cafes, nightclubs, shops, and department stores. The 22-story **Europa Center,** a shopping center and entertainment complex, rises just across the plaza from the **Kaiser-Wilhelm-Gedächtnis Kirche** (Memorial Church) near Ku-Damm and Zoo Station. Charlottenburg's regal center-piece is **Schloss Charlottenburg** (Charlottenburg Palace), with its lovely gardens and nearby museums: the **Ägyptisches** (Egyptian) **Museum,** the **Bröham Museum,** and the **Bergruen Sammlung** (Collection). Charlotten-burg is also the home of the **Deutsche Oper Berlin** (German Opera House), one of Berlin's three opera houses. Upscale shops, restaurants, and cafes fill the neighborhood around **Savignyplatz,** a tree-lined square a short walk north of Kurfürstendamm. Charlottenburg, which has plenty of hotels and *pensions* (B&Bs), makes a convenient base for visitors.

Dahlem

Now the university district, Dahlem was originally established as an independent village to the southwest of Berlin's center. Up until reunification, Dahlem was the site of western Berlin's major museums; however, most of them have now moved closer into the city. This neigh-borhood is no longer a convenient place to stay, but you may want to come here to visit the **Die Brücke Museum.**

Kreuzberg

Filled with 19th-century tenement buildings (called *Hinterhof,* because they have an interior courtyard) constructed for the workers of a rapidly industrializing Prussia, Kreuzberg has traditionally been the poorest and most crowded of western Berlin's districts. Today, about 35% of its population is composed of *Gastarbeiter* ("guest workers," most of whom worked in the service industry) from Turkey, the former Yugo-slavia, and Greece, many of whom have now lived here for 30 years or more. Starting in the 1960s and 1970s, the district became home to the city's artistic countercultural scene. Although gentrification is taking place, the neighborhood remains funky around the edges, with lots of bars and clubs. Kreuzberg is where you find the new **Jüdisches** (Jewish) **Museum** and the small museum called **Haus am Checkpoint Charlie,** dedicated to the history of divided Berlin. The area is more residential than hotel-oriented.

Berlin Neighborhoods

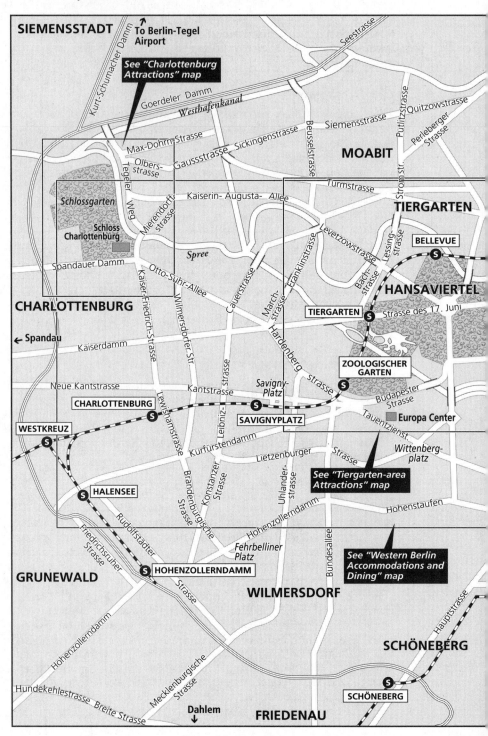

SIEMENSSTADT

To Berlin-Tegel Airport

See "Charlottenburg Attractions" map

Kurt-Schumacher Damm

Goerdeler Damm

Westhafenkanal

Seestrasse

Quitzowstrasse

Putlitzstrasse

Perleberger Strasse

Siemensstrasse

MOABIT

Max-Dohrn-Strasse

Olbers-strasse

Gaussstrasse

Sickingenstrasse

Beusselstrasse

Tegeler Weg

Mierendorff-strasse

Kaiserin- Augusta- Allee

Turmstrasse

Strom-str.

TIERGARTEN

Schlossgarten

Schloss Charlottenburg

Spree

Levetzowstrasse

Lessing-strasse

BELLEVUE

Franklinstrasse

Bach-strasse

HANSAVIERTEL

Spandauer Damm

Otto-Suhr-Allee

Cauerstrasse

March-strasse

TIERGARTEN

Strasse des 17. Juni

CHARLOTTENBURG

← Spandau

Kaiser-Friedrich-Strasse

Kaiserdamm

Wilmersdorfer-Str.

Hardenberg strasse

ZOOLOGISCHER GARTEN

Neue Kantstrasse

Kantstrasse

Leibniz-strasse

Savigny-Platz

Budapester Strasse

Tauentzienstr.

Europa Center

CHARLOTTENBURG

Lewishamstrasse

SAVIGNYPLATZ

Wittenberg-platz

WESTKREUZ

Kurfürstendamm

Brandenburgische Strasse

Konstanzer Strasse

Lietzenburger

Strasse

Uhlander-strasse

See "Tiergarten-area Attractions" map

HALENSEE

Hohenzollerndamm

Hohenstaufen

Friedrichsruher Strasse

Rudolfstädter

Fehrbelliner Platz

Bundesallee

See "Western Berlin Accommodations and Dining" map

GRUNEWALD

HOHENZOLLERNDAMM

Strasse

WILMERSDORF

Hauptstrasse

SCHÖNEBERG

Hohenzollerndamm

Hundekehlestrasse Breite Strasse

Mecklenburgische Strasse

Dahlem ↓

FRIEDENAU

SCHÖNEBERG

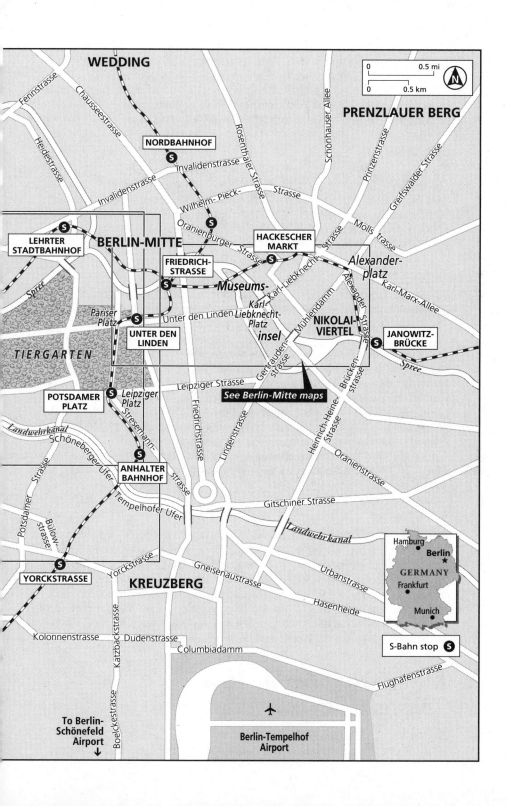

WEDDING

0   0.5 mi
0   0.5 km

N

PRENZLAUER BERG

Fennstrasse
Chausseestrasse
Heidestrasse

NORDBAHNHOF
S
Invalidenstrasse

Rosenthaler Strasse
Schönhauser Allee
Prinzenstrasse
Greifswalder Strasse

Invalidenstrasse
Wilhelm- Pieck-
Strasse

LEHRTER
STADTBAHNHOF
S
BERLIN-MITTE
FRIEDRICH-
STRASSE
Oranienburger Strasse
S
HACKESCHER
MARKT
S
Molls trasse

Alexander-
platz

Spree

Museums-
Karl-
Liebknecht-
Platz

Pariser
Platz
S
Unter den Linden
insel

Karl-Liebknecht- Strasse
Alexander- strasse
Karl-Marx-Allee

UNTER DEN
LINDEN

NIKOLAI-
VIERTEL

JANOWITZ-
BRÜCKE
S

TIERGARTEN

Mühlendamm
Gertrauden- strasse
Brücken- strasse
Spree

POTSDAMER
PLATZ
S
Leipziger
Platz
Stresemann-
strasse

Leipziger Strasse
Lindenstrasse
Friedrichstrasse

See Berlin-Mitte maps

Heinrich-Heine- Strasse

Landwehrkanal
Schöneberger Ufer

ANHALTER
BAHNHOF
S

Oranienstrasse

Potsdamer- Strasse
Bülow- strasse

Tempelhofer Ufer
Gitschiner Strasse
Landwehrkanal

Hamburg
Berlin ★
GERMANY
Frankfurt
Munich

YORCKSTRASSE
S
Yorckstrasse
KREUZBERG
Gneisenaustrasse
Urbanstrasse
Hasenheide

S-Bahn stop S

Kolonnenstrasse
Katzbackstrasse
Dudenstrasse
Columbiadamm

Flughafenstrasse

To Berlin-
Schönefeld
Airport
↓

Boelckestrasse

✈

Berlin-Tempelhof
Airport

Schöneberg

Like Kreuzberg, Schöneberg developed in the 19th century as an independent suburb for workers. After World War II, the area was rebuilt as a middle-class neighborhood. The borough is centrally located, close to the Ku-Damm, with good U-Bahn connections and many hotels and pensions. Berlin's densest concentration of gay bars and clubs is in Schöneberg between Nollendorfplatz and Victoria-Luise-Platz.

Spandau

Set near the junction of the Spree and Havel Rivers, about 6 miles (10 km) northwest of the city center, Spandau was a medieval town that became the site of **Zitadelle Spandau,** a still-standing fortress. Although the town merged with Berlin in 1920, its *Altstadt* (old city) is still intact. You probably won't visit Spandau unless you have extra days for exploring.

Tiergarten

The name Tiergarten means "Animal Garden," and it refers both to western Berlin's massive urban park and a business-residential district of the same name. The Tiergarten park, originally intended as a backdrop to the grand avenues laid out by the German kaisers, contains the **Berlin Zoo** in its southwest corner. The **Hansaviertel** (Hansa Quarter), occupying the northwest section of Tiergarten, contains a series of residential buildings designed in the late 1950s by different architects, including Le Corbusier, Walter Gropius, and Alvar Aalto. The Tiergarten neighborhood also contains the **Kulturforum,** home of the **Philharmonie** (Philharmonic Hall), the famed **Gemäldegalerie** (Painting Gallery), the **Neue Nationalgalerie** (New National Gallery), and other museums. This is also where you find the **Brandenburg Gate** and the **Reichstag** (Parliament) building. Tiergarten is one of the best areas in Berlin for hotels and restaurants.

Wilmersdorf

The huge park called the **Grünewald** (*groo*-nuh-vald) takes up the western portion of this borough. This 15-square-mile lake-filled forest begins just beyond the western edge of the Kurfürstendamm and is Berlin's largest uninterrupted wooded area. **Wannsee** is the most popular lake for swimming and boating. Closer in, towards the Ku-Damm, Wilmersdorf is a quiet residential neighborhood filled with an excellent assortment of hotels and pensions and plenty of low-key restaurants and cafes. All in all, Wilmersdorf is a very pleasant borough in which to stay.

Introducing Berlin-Mitte (eastern Berlin)

Berlin-Mitte, also called **Stadtmitte** (City Center) or just plain **Mitte** (Center), is the new name of the central section of former East Berlin.

Before the war and the division of the city, this area was, in fact, the center of Berlin. The oldest and most historic part of Berlin, Berlin-Mitte has numerous attractions. I recommend that you give this fascinating area at least a full day of your time. Most of the hotels in Mitte contain five-star luxury. If you have the means, or can get a good deal on a hotel room, consider staying here.

Berlin-Mitte symbolically begins at **Potsdamer Platz** and the **Brandenburg Gate,** on the east side of Tiergarten park. Both areas formerly stood behind the Berlin Wall and are now full of new buildings and on-going construction. The grand boulevard called **Unter den Linden,** which starts at the Brandenburg Gate and extends east, is lined with 18th- and 19th-century palaces and monuments. The **Staatsoper Unter den Linden** is the main opera house in eastern Berlin. (The **Komische Oper,** Berlin's third opera house, is also in Berlin-Mitte.) The beautiful neoclassical square called **Gendarmenmarkt,** just off Unter den Linden, is where you find the magnificently restored early 19th-century Schauspielhaus (theater), now called **Konzerthaus am Gendarmenmarkt** and used for concerts. At the eastern end of Unter den Linden, you find the marvelous **Museumsinsel** (Museum Island), site of four major museums.

Friedrichstrasse, which intersects Unter den Linden, is working hard to restore its prewar glamour and reputation as Berlin's pre-eminent shopping street. Luxury boutiques and department stores crowd the street. U-Bahn and S-Bahn lines converge at **Friedrichstrasse train station,** the transportation hub of Berlin-Mitte.

Alexanderplatz, a square named for Russian Czar Alexander I, was the center of activity in the Soviet era. Surrounded by dreary buildings from that time, the square is still pretty grim, although the opening of small markets is bringing new life. The 1,100-foot (335-meter) **Fernsehturm** (TV tower) on Alexanderplatz is the second-highest structure in Europe and has an observation platform.

The **Nikolaiviertel** (Nicholas Quarter), just south of Alexanderplatz along the Spree River, is a charming area restored to look as it did in Berlin's medieval and baroque eras. Period taverns and riverside restaurants make this quarter ideal for a leisurely and picturesque stroll.

Prenzlauer Berg, northeast of Mitte, is an up-and-coming neighborhood in eastern Berlin. Except to check out the ongoing gentrification, short-term travelers find little of interest. Gay and lesbian visitors may want to explore Prenzlauer Berg's burgeoning gay cafe and club scene.

Getting around Berlin

Berlin is a huge city, and some of its attractions are miles apart. Even dedicated walkers won't be able to cover the city entirely on foot. Luckily, Berlin has a comprehensive public transportation system. The following sections describe the various options you have for getting from place to place.

Going public: U-Bahn, S-Bahn, bus, and Strassenbahn

Berlin's excellent public transportation system makes getting around fast, convenient, safe, and relatively inexpensive. The system consists of the **U-Bahn** (underground train), the **S-Bahn** (surface or elevated train), and **buses,** plus **ferries** on the lakes and a few *Strassenbahnen* (streetcars) that still operate in eastern Berlin only. This well-integrated public transport system is run by BVG, Berlin's Transport Authority. Reunification necessitated an overhaul of the system, including several new stations and rail connections linking former East and West stations.

Transportation basics

You can **buy your ticket** at any U-Bahn station (at windows or machines, which have English translations) or from a bus driver. The ticket machines can be identified by the words "Fahrscheine/Tickets." You can also buy tickets and passes (and receive a free transportation map) at the **BVG-Pavillion** on Hardenbergplatz, directly outside Zoo Station; the office is open daily from 6 a.m. to 10 p.m. The same ticket can be used on any form of public transport.

The fare is based on **three zones** (A, B, and C). One ticket allows you to change from U-Bahn, to S-Bahn, and to the bus during a two-hour period. All of your sightseeing will be in zones A and B. Zone C extends far beyond the city's borders.

A regular *Normaltarif* or *Einzelfahrscheine* (one-way fare), good for two hours in zones A/B or B/C, is €2.10. For all three zones, the fare is €2.40.

For short hops (three consecutive U- or S-Bahn stops or six stops on a bus or streetcar), you can get a *Kurzstrecke* (short-stretch) ticket for €1.20.

When purchasing tickets for public transportation, you also have three money-saving options.

> ✔ A **Tageskarte** (day ticket) is an economical way to travel around Berlin on public transportation for one day. The ticket is good on all forms of transportation from validation until 3 a.m. the follow- ing day and costs €6.10 for two zones and €6.30 for three zones. (For details on validating your ticket, see the last paragraph in this section.)

✔ If you're in Berlin for three days, consider the **WelcomeCard,** which costs €18 and is good for all public transportation in Berlin and Potsdam for 72 hours. The ticket is valid for one adult and up to three children from 6 to 14 years of age. With the WelcomeCard, you also get price reductions of up to 50% at many tourist attractions in Berlin.

✔ The **7-Tage-Karte** (seven-day ticket) is great if you're going to be in Berlin for a week. This card costs €22 for zones A/B, €23 for zones B/C, or €28 for all three zones.

The entire transportation system runs on an honor system — you won't find turnstiles or ticket collectors. You must **validate your ticket** by sticking it into one of the red validation boxes on all U-Bahn and S-Bahn platforms or inside buses and streetcars. Long-term tickets are validated only once, before your first trip. Ticket inspectors may suddenly appear to check everyone's ticket. If yours hasn't been validated, you're guilty of *schwarzfahren* (black travel) and fined €50 on the spot.

U-Bahn (underground train)

The subway in Berlin is called the U-Bahn. Ten lines crisscross the city in all directions and extend to the far reaches of Brandenburg. A large U in a blue box identifies each station, and the routes are clearly marked in all stations and in the trains. Service is fast and efficient, but after midnight only two lines, U9 and U2, run on a limited schedule; they intersect at Bahnhof Zoo. In each car, you find a map of the stops, which are announced. For general **U-Bahn information,** call ☎ **030/19449** (daily 6 a.m.–11 p.m.).

S-Bahn (elevated train)

The venerable elevated train system in Berlin is called the S-Bahn. Thirteen lines cover most of central Berlin. A large S in a green circle identifies each station. S-Bahn and U-Bahn stations sometimes overlap, so you can change from one to the other. Service is basically nonexistent after midnight. Bahnhof Zoo has an **S-Bahn customer-service center** (☎ **030/2971-9843**) open Monday through Friday from 6 a.m. to 9 p.m., Saturday and Sunday from 7 a.m. to 9 p.m. Each car contains a map of the stops, which are announced.

The S-Bahn is particularly handy if you're going from Bahnhof Zoo east to the Friedrichstrasse/Unter den Linden area or southwest to Grünewald and the lakes.

Bus

Riding atop one of Berlin's double-decker buses (single-deckers also operate) is a fun way to see the city. A green H (for *Haltstelle,* or stop) in a yellow circle identifies each stop. Regular service begins about 5 a.m. and ends about midnight. Night buses (designated with an "N") leave every half an hour, going west and east, from Bahnhof Zoo and Bahnhof Hackescher Markt (near Alexanderplatz in eastern Berlin).

One of the best and cheapest sightseeing routes is on **Bus 100,** which leaves from Bahnhof Zoo and travels through the Tiergarten, passing Bellevue Palace (the Berlin residence of the German president), the Reichstag, and the Victory Column all the way to the Brandenburg Gate, Unter den Linden, Museum Island, and Alexanderplatz.

Strassenbahn (streetcar)

Streetcars, called **Strassenbahnen,** run in eastern Berlin only. Because you can get practically everywhere on the U-Bahn or S-Bahn, you probably won't be using the streetcar. Ticket prices are the same as for the U-Bahn, S-Bahn, and buses.

Taking a taxi

Thousands of ivory-colored taxis cruise Berlin's main streets. Hailing one during the day is easier than at night. Cabs can be expensive, though, if you're going any distance. The fare starts at €2.10 and costs €1.05 per kilometer (.6 mile).

One option that helps cut down on the cost of taxi rides is the *Kurz-strecke* (*kurtz*-stre-kuh), which means "short-distance ride." For €2.50, the driver takes you 2 kilometers (1.2 miles). You have to hail the cab on the street and inform the driver you want a Kurzstrecke *before* the meter starts. To order a taxi, call ☎ 210-101. Tip taxi drivers by rounding up to the nearest euro.

Driving a car

I don't recommend renting *ein Auto* in Berlin. Local drivers tend to be aggressive, and the street system itself can be fiendishly difficult to navigate. The public transport system gets you everywhere you want at a fraction of the cost. If you're out very late, you can grab a cab to get back to your hotel. The only time a car may come in useful is if you want to explore the surrounding countryside. The offices for **Hertz** (Budapester Strasse 37, ☎ 030/262-1053) and **Avis** (Budapester Strasse 43, ☎ 030/230-9370) are close to Bahnhof Zoo.

If you drive in town, be aware that the right lanes in inner-city areas are often reserved for buses, taxis, and bicycles *only*. When making a right turn, you must give way to any vehicle (including bikes) in that lane. Some right-hand lanes are reserved for buses at stated times and otherwise can be used by cars.

In Berlin and throughout Germany cars can park on the right side of the road only. In most inner-city areas you must obtain a parking ticket at one of the street-side ticket machines to display on your dashboard; one hour costs around €.50 (.50¢). The police quickly tow cars that violate these laws. If that happens, you can go to any police station to find out where your car is. The whole process costs more than

€150 — and a great deal of time. Parking garages are more expensive than street parking but save you the potential hassle of getting towed.

Staying in Style

Finding a hotel room in Berlin is easy, unless a big trade fair or soccer match is happening in town. And, prices are generally lower than in other major European cities. (You can find a good hotel in Berlin for under €150 a night.) I do, however, strongly recommend that you reserve your room before you arrive.

Except in the most expensive luxury hotels, **breakfast** (*Frühstück,* pronounced *froo*-shtook) is almost always included in the room rate. Breakfast typically consists of rolls (*Brötchen*), butter and jam, cheese, and cold cuts. Larger hotels often have buffets that include fresh fruit, yogurt, and cereal. The staff speak English at all the hotels on this list.

If you arrive in Berlin without a hotel room, you can go to the main **Tourist Information Center** in the Europa Center, close to Bahnhof Zoo (entrance on Budapester Strasse; U-/S-Bahn: Zoologischer Garten). For €3, the center's staff will find you a room. The office is open Monday through Saturday from 8:30 a.m. to 8:30 p.m., Sunday 10 a.m. to 6:30 p.m. You can also book hotels by calling ☎ **030/250-025.**

For locations of the hotels in this chapter, see the maps "Western Berlin Accommodations and Dining" and "Berlin-Mitte Accommodations and Dining."

The top hotels

For details on two of the city's best hotels, **Sorat Art'otel Berlin** ($$–$$$$) and **Hotel Brandenburger Hof** ($$$$), see Chapter 22.

Alsterhof Ringhotel Berlin
$–$$$ Wilmersdorf

Location — just a few minutes walk from Bahnhof Zoo and the Ku-Damm — is this hotel's greatest asset. If you're in Berlin on business and need a full-service hotel in a central location, this place fits the bill. The 195 rooms are comfortable and quiet, and have lots of extra amenities (trouser press, safe, minibar, hair dryer), although they aren't particularly stylish. You find a pool and sauna on the sixth floor. The breakfast buffet costs €15.

Augsburger Strasse 5, 10789 Berlin. ☎ ***030/212-420.*** *Fax: 030/218-3949. Internet:* www.alsterhof.com. *U-Bahn: Kurfürstendamm (then a 5-minute walk east across Joachimstaler Platz and east on Augsburger Strasse). Rack rates: €74–€200 double. AE, DC, MC, V.*

Western Berlin Accommodations and Dining

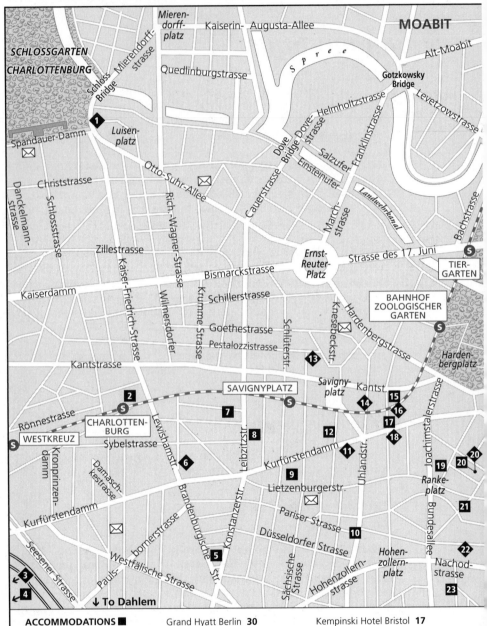

ACCOMMODATIONS ■

Alsterhof Ringhotel Berlin **25**

Ambassador Berlin **28**

Arco Hotel **24**

Artemisia **5**

Bleibtreu Hotel **9**

Grand Hotel Esplanade **29**

Grand Hyatt Berlin **30**

Hecker's Hotel **12**

Hotel Art Nouveau **8**

Hotel Brandenburger Hof **20**

Hotel Charlottenburger Hof **2**

Hotel Domus **10**

Hotel Wilmersdorf **21**

Kempinski Hotel Bristol **17**

Pension München **23**

Pension Niebuhr **7**

Pension Nürnberger Eck **26**

The Ritz-Carlton Schlosshotel **4**

Savoy Hotel **15**

Sorat Art'otel Berlin **19**

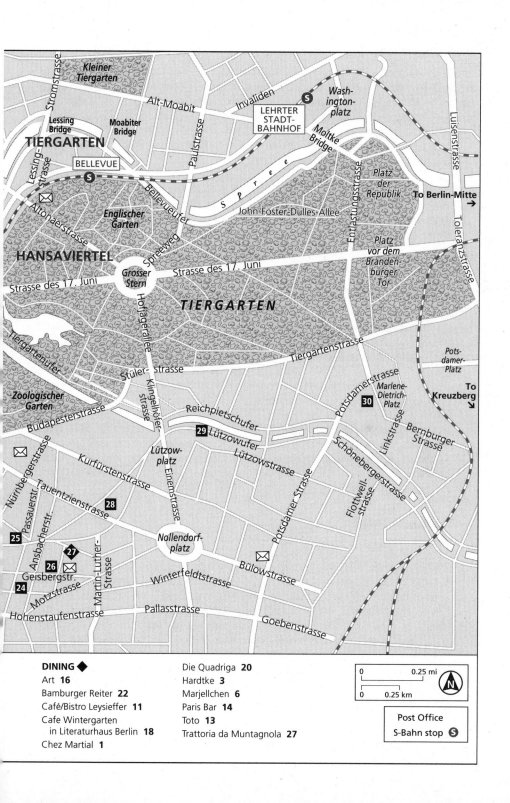

DINING ◆

Art **16**

Bamburger Reiter **22**

Café/Bistro Leysieffer **11**

Cafe Wintergarten
in Literaturhaus Berlin **18**

Chez Martial **1**

Die Quadriga **20**

Hardtke **3**

Marjellchen **6**

Paris Bar **14**

Toto **13**

Trattoria da Muntagnola **27**

0		0.25 mi
0		0.25 km

Post Office ✉

S-Bahn stop Ⓢ

Arco Hotel

$ Schöneberg

This small, gay-friendly hotel is housed in a four-story turn-of-the-century building on a quiet street near the Ku-Damm. Most of the 21, fairly large rooms have high windows and modern furniture. Private bathrooms, all with showers, are on the small side. One of the nicest features is the airy breakfast room, which looks out on a courtyard garden (you can eat outside in warm weather). The English-speaking staff is friendly and helpful. One potential drawback: no elevator.

*Geisbergstrasse 30, 10777 Berlin. ☎ **030/218-8065**. Fax: 030/2147-5178. Internet: www.arco-hotel.de. U-Bahn: Wittenbergplatz (then a 5-minute walk south on Ansbacher Strasse and west on Geisbergstrasse). Rack rates: €75–€102 double. Rates include breakfast. AE, DC, MC, V.*

Artemisia

$ Charlottenburg

Located on the top floors of a large apartment building, Artemisia is an excellent hotel for women only. The rooms are large, light, and free of frou-frou but still have a warm ambience heightened by splashes of color. Ten of the 12 rooms have toilets and small showers. You can save money by renting one of the two rooms that share a toilet and shower. A private roof terrace with wonderful views over Berlin becomes a gathering spot on warm afternoons and evenings.

*Brandenburgischestrasse 18, 10707 Berlin. ☎ **030/873-8905**. Fax: 030/861-8653. Internet: www.frauenhotel-berlin.de. U-Bahn: Blissestrasse (then a 3-minute walk northwest on Brandenburgischestrasse). Rack rates: €89–€104 double with bathroom, €69 double without bathroom. Rate includes breakfast. AE, DC, MC, V.*

Bleibtreu Hotel

$$–$$$ Charlottenburg

If you're looking for chic, contemporary luxury combined with state-of-the-art technology, this 60-room hotel is *the* place for you. The rooms aren't particularly large but are beautifully designed and furnished. The furniture coverings are hypoallergenic, and no chemicals of any kind are used for cleaning. The stylish bathrooms have sinks of carved stone. Other features include remote–control-operated lights, wireless phones, fax machines in every suite, and electric awnings over street-facing windows. The hotel has a "Wellness Center" where you can take a pore-cleansing sauna. Restaurant 31, near the small lobby, lays out a healthy breakfast buffet (an extra €14).

Berlin-Mitte Accommodations and Dining

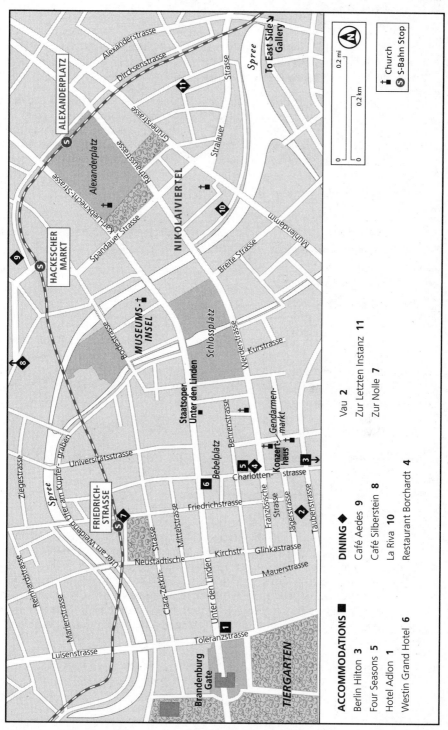

ACCOMMODATIONS ■

Berlin Hilton **3**
Four Seasons **5**
Hotel Adlon **1**
Westin Grand Hotel **6**

DINING ◆

Café Aedes **9**
Café Silberstein **8**
La Riva **10**
Restaurant Borchardt **4**

Vau **2**
Zur Letzten Instanz **11**
Zur Nolle **7**

✝ Church
Ⓢ S-Bahn Stop

0.2 mi
0.2 km

Bleibtreustrasse 31, 10707 Berlin. ☎ ***030/884-740.*** *Fax: 030/8847-4444. Internet:* www.bleibtreu.com. *S-Bahn: Savignyplatz (then a 5-minute walk south on Bleibtreustrasse). Rack rates: €185–€235 double. AE, DC, MC, V.*

Grand Hyatt Berlin

$$$–$$$$ Tiergarten

The Grand Hyatt Berlin, right smack-dab in the center of all the action in the new Potsdamer Platz area, is one of the coolest places to stay. This big hotel, built in 1998 with 342 rooms, is sleek and glamorous throughout. Rooms are large and have beautiful wood finishes and wonderful bathrooms set up with Japanese-style soaking tubs. Restaurants include Vox, for Eurasian cuisine and sushi; Tizian, for Italian food; and Bistro Dietrich, for casual cafe-style food. The staff can arrange baby-sitting.

Marlene-Dietrich-Platz 2, 10785 Berlin. ☎ ***030/2553-1234.*** *Fax: 030/2553-1235. Internet:* www.berlin.hyatt.com. *U-Bahn: Potsdamer Platz (then a 5-minute walk west to Marlene-Dietrich-Platz). Rack rates: €190–€310 double. AE, DC, MC, V.*

Hotel Adlon

$$$$ Mitte

The old Adlon, across from the Brandenburg Gate, was the most famous and glamorous hotel in prewar Berlin. The new Adlon, built on part of the original site and completed in 1997, attempts to recapture the Art Deco glory of the original. Everything about this property is five-star deluxe. The 337 rooms are sumptuously decorated and have huge bathrooms with double sinks. Service is top-notch, and baby-sitting can be arranged.

Unter den Linden 77, 10117 Berlin. ☎ ***800/426-3135*** *U.S. or 030/22610. Fax: 030/2261-2222. Internet:* www.hotel-adlon.de. *U-/S-Bahn: Unter den Linden (the hotel is right outside the station). Rack rates: €310–€375 double. AE, DC, MC, V.*

Hotel Charlottenburger Hof

$–$$ Charlottenburg

Located across from the Charlottenburg S-Bahn station, this is one of the best and brightest budget hotels in Berlin. This inexpensive property is unusually well decorated for its price range and offers several amenities, such as in-room safes, hair dryers, and laundry facilities. Primary colors of blue, yellow, red, and white brighten some of the 45 contemporary-style rooms, a few of which have balconies. Rooms and bathrooms, which have showers, are fairly small. You're given a voucher for breakfast at the Café Voltaire downstairs.

Stuttgarter Platz 14, 10627 Berlin. ☎ ***030/329-070.*** *Fax: 030/332-3723. Internet:* www.charlottenburger-hof.de. *S-Bahn: Charlottenburg (the hotel is north of the station). Rack rates: €75–€150 double. Rate includes breakfast. AE, MC, V.*

The big splurge

If you're looking for top-of-the-line luxury, here are a few more $$$$ suggestions:

✔ **Berlin Hilton,** Mohrenstrasse 30, 10117 Berlin. ☎ **800/445-8667** in the U.S. and Canada, or 030/20230. Fax: 030/2023-4269. Internet: www.hilton.com. U-Bahn: Stadtmitte.

✔ **Four Seasons,** Charlottenstrasse 49, 10117 Berlin. ☎ **800/332-3442** in the U.S., or 030/203-38. Fax: 030/2033-6166. Internet: www.fourseasons.com. U-Bahn: Unter den Linden.

✔ **Grand Hotel Esplanade,** Lützowufer 15, 10785 Berlin. ☎ **030/254-780.** Fax: 030/265-1171. Internet: www.esplanade.de. U-Bahn: Zoologischer Garten.

✔ **The Ritz-Carlton Schlosshotel,** Brahmsstrasse 10, 14193 Berlin-Grünewald. ☎ **030/895-840.** Fax: 030/8958-4801. Internet: www.ritzcarlton.com. S-Bahn: Grünewald.

Hotel Domus

$ **Wilmersdorf**

Set in an unusually pretty section of Wilmersdorf, down the street from St. Ludwig's Church and within walking distance of the Ku-Damm, this modern 73-room hotel has a calm, appealing simplicity. The spacious rooms are carpeted, quiet (thanks to soundproof windows), and tastefully decorated with high-quality contemporary furniture (lots of light-colored wood). Rooms face the inner courtyard or the street. The bathrooms are unusually large and have either a shower or a tub. Breakfast is served in a lovely dining room.

Uhlandstrasse 49, 10719 Berlin. ☎ _**030/880-3440.** Fax: 030/8803-4444. Internet:_ www.hotel-domus-berlin.de. _U-Bahn: Spichernstrasse (then a 5-minute walk west on Hohenzollerndamm and north on Uhlandstrasse). Rack rates: €115–€130 double. Rate includes breakfast. AE, DC, MC, V._

Kempinski Hotel Bristol

$$$$ **Charlottenburg**

One of Berlin's most famous luxury hotels, the 301-room Kempinski is right in the thick of things on the Ku-Damm. This place posseses high-toned classic styling. Every room is unique, but the general color scheme favors dark blues and greens enlivened by lustrous wood finishes. The bathrooms are large and have double sinks. The public rooms are predictably grand, with amenities such as a business center, a fitness center, a pool, and 24-hour room service. The staff can also arrange baby-sitting. The only thing you don't get is breakfast, but if you can afford to stay here, that probably doesn't matter.

Kurfürstendamm 27, 10719 Berlin. ☎ *800/426-3135 in the U.S. or 030/884-340. Fax: 030/883-6075. Internet:* www.kempinski-bristol.de. *U-Bahn: Kurfürstendamm (then a 2-minute walk west on Kurfürstendamm). Rack rates: €235–€312 double. AE, DC, MC, V.*

Pension Niebuhr

$ Charlottenburg

This pleasant, gay-friendly pension in Charlottenburg is one of the best deals in Berlin. The 12 rooms, all on the second floor of a turn-of-the-century apartment building (no elevator), have a fresh, modest flair. The furnishings and color schemes are bright and cheerful. Three street-facing rooms have balconies; the rooms facing the courtyard *(Hinterhof)* can be a bit dark, but they're very quiet. One bonus: Breakfast is brought up to your room.

Niebuhrstrasse 74, 10629 Berlin. ☎ *030/324-9595. Fax: 030/881-4707. Internet:* www.pension-niebuhr.de. *S-Bahn: Savignyplatz (then a 5-minute walk west on Niebuhrstrasse). Rack rates: €90 double with bathroom, €65 double without bathroom. Rate includes breakfast. AE, MC, V.*

Pension Nürnberger Eck

$ Charlottenburg

If you're seeking an atmospheric old-fashioned pension, try this one on the second floor of a building near the Europa Center. High-ceilinged rooms with heavy doors open off a long, dark hallway. Although the eight rooms are stylistically something of a mish-mash, with patterned wallpaper, Oriental rugs, and big pieces of furniture, the pension does convey an Old Berlin charm. The bathrooms are a decent size, and the breakfast room is pleasant.

Nürnberger Strasse 24a, 10789 Berlin. ☎ *030/235-1780. Fax: 030/2351-7899. U-Bahn: Wittenbergplatz (then a 5-minute walk west on Tauentzienstrasse and south on Nürnberger Strasse). Rack rates: €87–€92 double. Rates include breakfast. MC, V.*

Savoy Hotel

$$$–$$$$ Charlottenburg

The quietly elegant Savoy, which opened in 1930, has hosted more than a few celebrities over the years. You can't beat the location just a skip from the Ku-Damm. The lobby is a luxe version of neoclassical styling. All 125 rooms are individually decorated and provide spacious and comfortable accommodation, with unusually large bathrooms. Public areas include a fitness room with a sauna and solarium.

Fasanenstrasse 9–10, 10623 Berlin. ☎ *800/223-5652 U.S. or 030/311-030. Fax: 030/3110-3333. Internet:* www.savoy-hotels.com. *U-Bahn: Zoologischer Garten (then a 5-minute walk west on Kantstrasse and north on Fasanenstrasse). Rack rates: €186–€236 double. AE, DC, MC, V.*

Westin Grand Hotel

$$$$ Mitte

Ironically, one of the last buildings erected in Communist East Berlin was this luxury hotel. If you're interested in paying top dollar for the experience of staying in the newly chic Friedrichstrasse area, the 358-room Grand is, well, grand. The finishes throughout are beautiful, and the overall ambience, enhanced by dramatic staircases, chandeliers, and a glass-domed ceiling, tries to recapture the luxurious Grand Hotel era. You find restaurants, bars, and every amenity you can imagine, including 24-hour room service, a fitness center, and a pool.

Friedrichstrasse 158–164, 10117 Berlin. ☎ *800/937-8461 U.S. or 030/20270. Fax: 030/2027-3362. Internet:* www.westin-grand.com. *U-/S-Bahn: Stadtmitte (then a 3-minute walk north on Friedrichstrasse). Rack rates: €240–€365 double. AE, DC, MC, V.*

Runner-up hotels

Ambassador Berlin

$$ Schöneberg   Kids love the swimming pool in this well-maintained family-friendly hotel. *Bayreutherstrasse 42–43, 10787 Berlin.* ☎ *030/219-020. Fax: 030/2190-2380. Internet:* www.ambassador-berlin.de. *U-Bahn: Wittenbergplatz.*

Hecker's Hotel

$$–$$$ Charlottenburg   The streamlined rooms in this small, trendy hotel may look a bit sterile to some, but the place is conveniently located and impeccably maintained. *Grolmanstrasse 35, 10623 Berlin.* ☎ *030/88900. Fax: 030/889-0260. Internet:* www.heckershotel.com. *S-Bahn: Savignyplatz.*

Hotel Art Nouveau

$ Charlottenburg   This small, atmospheric hotel is on the fourth-floor of an Art Nouveau apartment house. *Leibnizstrasse 59, 10629 Berlin.* ☎ *030/327-7440. Fax: 030/327-7440. Internet:* www.hotelartnouveau.de. *S-Bahn: Savignyplatz.*

Hotel Wilmersdorf

$ Wilmsersdorf   This no-fuss pension is large, clean, and comfortable, and offers a buffet breakfast overlooking the rooftops of Berlin. *Schaperstrasse 36, 10719 Berlin.* ☎ *030/2177-07476. Fax: 030/217-7077. U-Bahn: Spichernstrasse.*

Pension München

$ Wilmersdorf You find simple, modern decor and lots of nice touches in this third-floor pension. *Günzelstrasse 62, 10717 Berlin.* ☎ *030/857-9120. Fax: 030/8579-1222. Internet:* www.hotel-pension-muenchen-in-berlin.de. *U-Bahn: Günzelstrasse.*

Dining Out

Berlin offers every kind of international cuisine. The local culinary tradition is fairly basic and very filling. Typical Berlin dishes include grilled or pickled herring with onions, fried potatoes, and bacon; pickled or roast pork *(Schweinefleisch)* or pork knuckles *(Eisbein)* with red cabbage and dumplings; meatballs *(Buletten)* with boiled potatoes; and pea soup *(Erbsensuppe)*. A plate with various cold meats is called a *Schlachteplatte* (*schlock*-tuh-plat-tuh). Game like venison, duck, and wild boar appears seasonally; carp and trout are often available. Fancier restaurants often serve what's called *neue Deutsche Küche* (New German Cuisine), which uses the old standbys as a starting point but dolls them up with unusual ingredients and international touches.

Restaurant and cafe bills include the service charge and value-added tax (VAT), but rounding out the total bill with an extra amount is standard practice. If the bill is €6.30, for example, round the total up to €7. If the service and the meal have been very good, add an additional 10% for a tip.

Scattered all over town are vendors selling Berlin's classic fast-food snacks: *Currywurst* (sausage with a glob of "curry" sauce) or fried Bratwurst. Grabbing a Wurst or eating at the stand-up counters of the fast-food snack shops (look for signs that read IMBISS or SCHNELL-IMBISS) are a good way to save time and money.

You can always get an inexpensive meal (soup, sandwiches, and lighter dishes) at one of Berlin's plentiful cafes. And speaking of cafes: Don't forget that in Germany, afternoon *Kaffee und Kuchen* (coffee and cake) is a time-honored tradition. I list some good cafe choices at the end of this chapter.

For a few recommended brewpubs, places to enjoy a casual meal with a freshly drawn beer, see Chapter 12.

For locations of the restaurants in this chapter, see the maps "Western Berlin Accommodations and Dining" and "Berlin-Mitte Accommodations and Dining."

The top restaurants

Art

$ **Charlottenburg GERMAN/INTERNATIONAL**

Restaurant, bar, and cafe rolled into one, Art is tucked beneath the S-Bahn track at Fasanenstrasse. Come to this great, gay-friendly place for an English breakfast (bacon, eggs, and beans). For lunch, try a bowl of potato soup with sausage or one of the many salads. Dinner choices include homemade pasta, duck with red-wine sauce, fish, and a vegetarian tofu schnitzel. The staff is friendly and outdoor seating is available in good weather.

Fasanenstrasse 81A. ☎ 030/313-2625. U-Bahn: Zoologischer Garten (then a 5-minute walk west on Hardenberg Strasse and south on Fasanenstrasse). Reservations recommended for dinner. Main courses: €10–€17. AE, DC, MC, V. Open: Summer Mon–Fri 11 a.m.–2 a.m., Sat–Sun 10 a.m.–2 a.m.; winter Sat–Sun 12:30 p.m.–2 a.m.

Bamburger Reiter

$$$$ **Schöneberg AUSTRIAN**

Housed in a 100-year-old wine tavern at the corner of Regensburger Strasse and Bamburger Strasse, Bamburger Reiter is small (maximum 35 diners) and rustic, with parquet floors, flowers, and lots of antiques. For many years, this was a temple of *neue Deutsche Küche* (New German Cuisine), but the place now serves mostly Austrian dishes. The menu changes monthly and may include cream of mushroom soup, roast quail, *wiener schnitzel* (breaded veal cutlets), marinated boiled beef with chive cream, or smoked-fish pie. The restaurant has a leafy outdoor arbor for summertime dining.

Regensburgerstrasse 7. ☎ 030/218-4282. U-Bahn: Spichernstrasse (then a 10-minute walk east on Regensburgerstrasse). Reservations required. Main courses: €22–€39; 5- or 7-course fixed-price menu €85–€100. No credit cards. Open: Tues–Sat 5:30–11:30 p.m.

Chez Martial

$$ **Charlottenburg FRENCH**

Top-quality products and good cooking have helped establish Chez Martial as one of Berlin's most popular French restaurants. Every dish is freshly prepared, so be ready to wait (while savoring a bottle of good French wine). If the weather is fine, try to get a table outside. The menu changes daily and offers about 15 main courses. The menu includes fresh Atlantic fish, poultry, lamb, beef, and couscous. The fish soup, cooked in a broth of fish and shellfish that's whipped into a foam, is wonderful. For dessert, try the pumpernickel mousse.

Otto-Suhr-Allee 144. ☎ *030/341-1033. U-Bahn: Richard-Wagner-Platz (then a 5-minute walk north on Richard-Wagner-Strasse and west on Otto-Suhr-Allee). Reservations required. Main courses: €15–€17. MC, V. Open: Tues–Sun 6–11:30 p.m.*

Die Quadriga
$$$$ Wilmersdorf FRENCH

Die Quadriga, the one-star Michelin restaurant in the beautiful Brandenburger Hof hotel, offers a truly memorable dining experience, but you need to reserve well in advance because the elegant restaurant seats only 28 diners. Everything is of the finest quality. Dishes are classically French and seasonally fresh. The wonderful wine list includes several wines available by the half-bottle or by the carafe.

In Hotel Brandenburger Hof, Eislebener Strasse 14. ☎ *030/214-050. U-Bahn: Kurfürstendamm (then a 2-minute walk south on Eislebener Strasse). Reservations required. Main courses: €24–€34. AE, D, MC, V. Open: Mon–Fri 7–11 p.m. Closed July 17–Aug 20.*

Hardtke
$ Wilmersdorf BERLINER

Hardtke, out near the Grünewald forest park, has been around for what seems like forever, and its continued success stems from the fact that the restaurant serves vast portions of good, traditional Berlin fare. The specialties include liverwurst on sauerkraut with potatoes, thick pea soup, and pig's knuckles. The best beer to wash down this food is Pilsner Urquell (*Pils*-ner *Ur*-kwell).

Hubertusalle 48. ☎ *30/892-5848. S-Bahn: Halensee (then a 10-minute walk south on Hubertusallee; or bus 110). Reservations required. Main courses: €8–€16. V. Open: Daily 11 a.m. to midnight.*

La Riva
$$ Mitte ITALIAN/SEAFOOD

One of the prettiest buildings in the restored Nikolaiviertel (Nicholas Quarter), just south of Alexanderplatz, is the Ephraim-Palais, a richly ornamented 1765 mansion. Part of the building is a museum, while another section contains this Italian-influenced restaurant, which sits right next to the Spree River. You'll want a table outside if the weather is fine. And you'll probably want to order fish, since that's what they do best. Choices include salmon with white-wine sauce; swordfish with fresh tomatoes, onions, and basil; and grilled or baked crayfish. Pasta is made fresh daily, and the good pizzas are kid-pleasing. The restaurant also has a well-stocked wine cellar.

Spreeufer 2. ☎ *030/242-5183. U-Bahn: Klosterstrasse (then a 5-minute walk south-west on Mühlendamm to Spreeufer, the pedestrian street along the river). Reservations recommended. Main courses: €12–€18. AE, MC, V. Open: Daily 11 a.m. to midnight.*

Marjellchen

$$–$$$ Charlottenburg EAST PRUSSIAN

Old East Prussian recipes prepared by the owner's grandmother inspired the dishes that are served at this popular restaurant. For an appetizer, try homemade aspic, smoked Pomeranian goose, or fried chicken legs. Other starters include *Beetenbartsch,* a delicious red-beet soup with beef strips and sour cream, and a delicious potato soup with shrimps and bacon. Main courses are something of an adventure: stewed pickled beef with green dumplings and stewed cabbage, smoked ham in cream sauce, pork kidneys in sweet-and-sour cream sauce, or roast of elk with chanterelle mushrooms. You find also vegetarian dishes, such as broccoli soufflé.

Mommsenstrasse 9. ☎ *030/883-2676. U-Bahn: Uhlandstrasse (then a 3-minute walk west on Mommsenstrasse). Reservations recommended. Main courses: €11–€23. AE, DC, MC, V. Open: Mon–Sat 5 p.m. to midnight.*

Paris Bar

$$–$$$ FRENCH/AUSTRIAN/MEDITERRANEAN

Around since the end of the last war, the Paris Bar, between Savignyplatz and the Memorial Church, is a Berlin institution. In the last couple of years, the restaurant has expanded its French bistro menu to include more upscale Austrian and Mediterranean-inspired dishes. Main courses change often. You may find asparagus with hollandaise sauce, ham, and new potatoes; risotto with porcini mushrooms; wiener schnitzel; fresh fish; or grilled foie gras.

Kantstrasse 152. ☎ *030/313-8052. U-Bahn: Zoologischer Garten (then a 5-minute walk west on Kantstrasse). Reservations recommended. Main courses: €16–€31. No credit cards. Open: Daily 6 p.m.–1 a.m.*

Restaurant Borchardt

$$–$$$ Mitte FRENCH/INTERNATIONAL

You can recognize Borchardt, directly across from the Gendarmenmarkt, by its blood-colored awning and red sandstone facade. Inside, the restaurant is large, spare, and elegant, with marble, gilding, and a bit of French attitude. If you like it rich, go for the foie gras fillet with caramelized onions. Menu offerings typically include baked tuna fish with Asian vegetables, glazed duck breast, saddle of veal with lemon butter, and suckling pig. The best bet for lunch is one of the fixed-price specials.

Französische Strasse 47. ☎ *030/2038-87110. U-Bahn: Französische Strasse (then a 3-minute walk east on Französische Strasse). Reservations recommended. Main courses: €15–€26; lunch specials €12. AE, V. Open: Daily 11:30 a.m. to midnight.*

Toto
$ **Charlottenburg   ITALIAN**

This is a good place to sit outside on a warm Berlin afternoon and have a good, inexpensive lunch. The restaurant's interior, with wooden tables and benches, is nothing fancy. But the Italian chef knows his stuff. You can get a good plate of spaghetti or a good salad. The bean soup is filling. Fresh fish, available every Tuesday and Friday (market days), includes grilled salmon with butter and lemon and grilled crayfish cooked in olive oil. The menu includes a nice selection of Italian wines and aperitifs. The casual atmosphere makes Toto a good place to bring kids.

Bleibtreustrasse 55. ☎ *030/312-5449. S-Bahn: Savignyplatz (then a 5-minute walk south on Bleibtreustrasse). Main courses: €7.50–€20. Open: Daily noon to 2 a.m.*

Trattoria da Muntagnola
$ **Wilmersdorf   ITALIAN**

This popular Italian place is casually rustic, with braids of garlic hanging from the beamed ceiling. The menu is huge and the cooking is reliable, not remarkable; however, the menu has several items that kids generally like. Some of the pastas are made on the premises. The lasagna is worth trying. All kinds of meat dishes and some good seafood (calamari and scampi grilled or cooked with radicchio and rosemary in white-wine sauce) round out the menu. The pizzas are good, too, particularly the Pizza della Mamma with bacon and Parma ham. *Note:* The restaurant can be a bit smoky.

Fuggerstrasse 27. ☎ *030/211-6642. U-Bahn: Nollendorfplatz (then a 5-minute walk west on Motzstrasse, north on Luther Strasse, and west on Fuggerstrasse). Reservations recommended. Main courses: €4.50–€20. AE, DC, MC, V. Open: Daily 6 p.m. to midnight.*

Vau
$$$$ **Mitte   INTERNATIONAL**

This sleek and unabashedly upscale gastronomic showcase, opened near the Gendarmenmarkt in early 1997, has earned a Michelin star for its refined cooking. Vau is a very dress-up kind of place for a superfancy lunch or dinner with impeccable service. The menu choices are deftly prepared and can be surprisingly unfussy: *carpaccio* (thinly sliced beef) with *langoustines* (a small, spiny lobster), potato soufflé with caviar, classic wiener schnitzel and *coq au vin* (chicken in wine sauce), and many fish choices. In this long, rather narrow room with an arched ceiling, everything is very precise, very modern, and very beautiful.

Jägerstrasse 54–55. ☎ *030/202-9730. U-Bahn: Stadtmitte (then a 5-minute walk east across Gendarmenmarkt). Reservations essential. Main courses: €22–€38; lunch main courses €10; fixed-price dinner €75–€100. AE, DC, MC, V. Open: Mon–Sat noon to 2:30 p.m. and 7–10:30 p.m.*

Zur Letzten Instanz
$–$$ Mitte   BERLINER

The former East Berlin now has several trendy new restaurants, but I still recommend this place, which happens to be Berlin's oldest restaurant, dating from 1525. The restaurant occupies two floors of a much-restored baroque building in the Nikolaiviertel (Nicholas Quarter), and the menu is as traditional and atmospheric as can be. Main courses include Old Berlin staples like grilled herring, meatballs, and braised lamb knuckles with green beans and dumplings. For dessert, try the chocolate-covered pancakes filled with blueberries, vanilla ice cream, and whipped cream.

Waisenstrasse 14–16. ☎ *030/242-5528. U-Bahn: Klosterstrasse (then a 3-minute walk south on Waisenstrasse). Main courses: €9–€13. AE, DC, MC, V. Open: Mon–Sat noon to 1 a.m., Sun noon to 11 p.m.*

Zur Nolle
$ Mitte   GERMAN

A hundred years ago, Zur Nolle was a busy working-class beer hall. The place closed in 1968 (GDR years) but reopened in 1993, as a sign of post-reunification nostalgia for a bit of Old Berlin. The menu is unpretentious and the portions hearty. Try the jacket potatoes with herring, yogurt, apple, or onion fillings. Vegetarian offerings include vegetable lasagna and roasted broccoli with cheese served on pasta. For old time's sake, I recommend the homemade *Bulette* (meatballs), which come with a variety of sauces, spices, and additions (fried egg, bacon, onions, or mushrooms), or the roast Bratwurst. Wash everything down with a cold, foamy *Bier von Fass* (beer from the tap).

Beneath the arches of Friedrichstrasse S-Bahn station (S-Bahnbogen 30). ☎ *030/208-2655. U-/S-Bahn: Friedrichstrasse (then a 1-minute walk east along the street below the tracks). Main courses: €6.50–€10. AE, DC, MC, V. Open: Mon–Sat 11:30 a.m. to midnight, Sun 11:30 a.m.–6 p.m.*

The best cafes

Berlin is a city filled with cafes. These are places to go for breakfast, a cup of coffee and a piece of *Kuchen* (cake), or a light meal or snack.

The cafes are also bars, so you can get a beer or a glass of wine as well. Bleibtreustrasse (U-Bahn: Savignyplatz), between Savignyplatz and the Ku-Damm, is particularly rich in cafes.

- ✔ **Café Aedes,** Rosenthaler Strasse 40–41 (☎ 030/285-8278; U-Bahn: Weinmeisterstrasse), is trendy, convivial, and very hip. The menu usually has dishes like tortellini with cheese sauce, soups, and vegetarian salads. Meals range from €7 to €9. The cafe is open daily from 10 a.m. to midnight.

- ✔ **Café/Bistro Leysieffer,** Kurfürstendamm 218 (☎ 030/885-7480; U-Bahn: Kurfürstendamm), has a pastry and candy shop at street level; upstairs, you find an old-fashioned cafe with a balcony overlooking the busy Ku-Damm. This is a good place to have an elegant breakfast or light lunch. Meals range from €10 to €16. The cafe is open daily from 10 a.m. to 7 p.m.

- ✔ **Café Silberstein,** Oranienburger Strasse 27 (☎ 030/281-2095; S-Bahn: Oranienburger Tor), is one of the best places to see the "new" eastern Berlin in all its up-to-the-nanosecond trendiness. The cafe is housed in a long, tall, narrow room with original 1920s wall paintings and modern furniture. On the menu, you find sushi, salads, miso soup with noodles, and an all-day breakfast. A meal costs around €6.50. The cafe is open Monday to Friday from 10 a.m. to 4 a.m., Saturday and Sunday from 10 a.m. to 5 a.m.

- ✔ **Cafe Wintergarten in Literaturhaus Berlin,** Fasanenstrasse 23 (☎ 030/882-5414; U-Bahn: Hohenzollernplatz), occupies two modern-looking rooms in a 19th-century villa one block south of the Ku-Damm. The menu includes pastas, soups, salads, and vegetarian curries. Main courses range from €6.50 to €18. The cafe is open daily from 9:30 a.m. to 1 a.m.

Chapter 12

Exploring Berlin

● ●

In This Chapter

▶ Visiting Berlin's top attractions

▶ Choosing a tour that's right for you

▶ Finding the hot shopping spots

▶ Discovering Berlin's performing arts and nightlife

▶ Taking a side trip to Potsdam and Sanssouci Palace

● ●

Berlin overflows with sightseeing options and diversions. In fact, you'd need a month to see everything. (But don't worry. I can help you hit the highlights in one to three days.) Berlin is particularly rich in museums, although you also find picturesque parks and lakes, famous avenues, and historic architecture. Plus, thanks to rebuilding in Potsdamer Platz and portions of eastern Berlin, this city has more new buildings than any other city in the world.

Berlin is a huge metropolis, so planning your visit is essential. First, arm yourself with a good map; I recommend the detailed Falk map, available at most newsstands. Second, choose a geographical area or cluster of attractions you want to see. When you're ready to go, take the U-Bahn or S-Bahn to the area you selected. After seeing the top sights, spend some time exploring the neighborhood.

I recommend that you allot at least one full day to the former East Berlin, now called **Mitte (Center),** the oldest part of the city. For a change of pace in western Berlin, wander through the Tiergarten or the Grünewald or spend an afternoon at the lakes.

For locations, see the maps "Tiergarten-Area Attractions," "Charlotten-burg Attractions," and "Berlin-Mitte Attractions," all in this chapter.

Sightseeing in Berlin

Where do you begin? Do want to spend all your time in Berlin's fabulous museums? Saunter and shop your way down famous avenues like Unter den Linden or the Ku-Damm? See historic buildings like the Reichstag?

Check out the "new" Berlin at Potsdamer Platz? You have to make some decisions because the possibilities for sightseeing in Berlin are almost endless. The places described in this section are my roster of the most important Berlin attractions. I first give the name of the attraction in German, as you see it on a local map or street sign, and then I translate the name into English. (Some names require no translation.) For locations, see the "Tiergarten-Area Attractions," "Charlottenburg Attractions," and "Berlin-Mitte Attractions" maps in this chapter.

Remember: Nearly all Berlin museums are **closed on Monday** throughout the year. They are also closed on January 1; December 24, 25, and 31; and the Tuesday after Easter.

Touring by neighborhood

You can save a lot of time by clustering your museum and other sightseeing visits geographically. The main museum areas in Berlin are as follows:

- ✔ **Charlottenburg:** Across from **Charlottenburg Palace** are three museums worth visiting: The **Ägyptisches Museum** (with the famous bust of Nerfertiti), the **Sammlung Bergruen** (with Picassos), and the **Bröhan Museum** (with Art Nouveau and Art Deco furniture). Charlottenburg Palace also has museums, which you can visit before or after a guided palace tour, as well as historic buildings in the palace gardens.

- ✔ **Tiergarten:** In or near the Tiergarten, Berlin's great city park, you find the the **Bauhaus-Archiv,** the **Hamburger Bahnhof Museum für Gegenwart** (with contemporary art), and the **Reichstag** (House of Parliament). On the eastern edge of the Tiergarten, close to Potsdamer Platz, is a group of buildings known as the **Kulturforum** (Culture Forum), home to the **Gemäldegalerie** (Painting Gallery)**,** the **Neue Nationalgalerie** (with 20th-century art), and the **Kunstgewerbe** (with applied and decorative arts). The Kulturforum area is within walking distance of **Potsdamer Platz,** the newest area of Berlin, where you find the new **Filmmuseum Berlin.**

- ✔ **Museum Island (Museumsinsel):** Museum Island in eastern Berlin has four of the city's oldest museums. They include the **Altes Museum** (with Greek and Roman antiquities), the **Alte Nationalgalerie** (with 19th-century art), the **Pergamon Museum** (with the Pergamon altar and Middle Eastern antiquities), and the **Bode Museum,** which is closed until 2005. In this same vicinity, you can visit the **Brandenburg Gate; Unter den Linden,** a grand **boulevard; Gendarmenmarkt,** a baroque square; and the **Nikolaiviertel** (Nicholas Quarter), a restored historic neighborhood.

Saving money with a museum pass

SchauLUST Museen Berlin is a money-saving three-day museum pass that gets you into 50 top Berlin museums and collections for €10 adults, €5 seniors and children. The pass gains you admittance into all the museums described in the next section, "Discovering the top attractions from A to Z." You can purchase the SchauLUST museum pass at the three Berlin Tourist Info Centers (Europa Center, Brandenburg Gate, Television Tower; for addresses, see Chapter 11).

An admission ticket purchased at any one of the state museums is good for the rest of the day at any of the other state museums operated by **Staatliche Museen Preussischer Kulturbesitz.** Included within this group are museums on Museum Island in Berlin Mitte, in the Kulturforum, and at Charlottenburg Palace.

Discovering the top attractions from A to Z

Ägyptisches Museum (Egyptian Museum)
Charlottenburg

The greatest treasure of the Egyptian Museum is the famous and fabulous **bust of Queen Nefertiti,** dating from around 1350 B.C. The piece occupies a small room of its own and is worth a trip to the museum. Other collection highlights include the small, expressive head of Queen Tiy, the world-famous head of a priest in green stone, and the monumental Kalabasha Gateway, built by Emperor Augustus around 30 B.C. If you're interested in Egyptian antiquities, you'll find enough here to make you linger for at least an hour.

Schlossstrasse 70. ☎ 030/2090-5555. U-Bahn: Sophie-Charlotte-Platz (then a 5-minute walk north on Schlossstrasse). Admission: €6 adults, €3 children; free admission 1st Sun of each month. Open: Tues–Sun 10 a.m.–6 p.m.

Alte Nationalgalerie (Old National Gallery)
Museum Island, Mitte

Behind the Altes Museum is the Alte Nationalgalerie, which looks like a Corinthian temple and contains a collection of 19th-century painting and sculpture. The gallery displays paintings and sculpture from the end of the 18th to the beginning of the 20th century, including works by van Gogh, Manet, Monet, Renoir, and Cézanne. Give yourself at least an hour just for the highlights of this rich collection. A free audio tour in English is available.

Tiergarten-Area Attractions

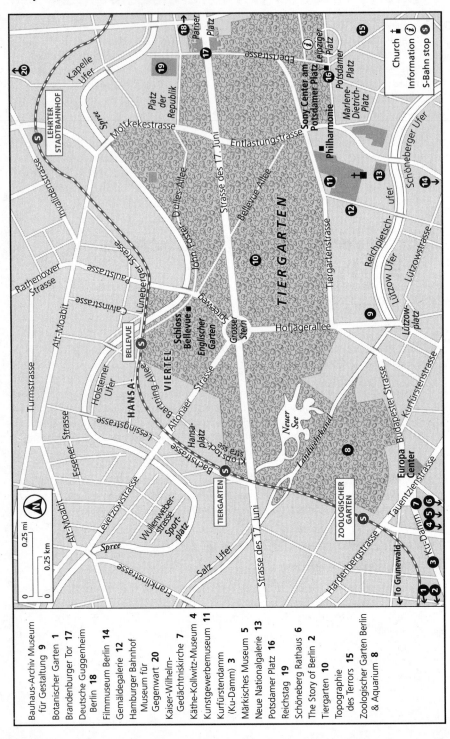

Bauhaus-Archiv Museum für Gestaltung 9
Botanischer Garten 1
Brandenburger Tor 17
Deutsche Guggenheim Berlin 18
Filmmuseum Berlin 14
Gemäldegalerie 12
Hamburger Bahnhof Museum für Gegenwart 20
Kaiser-Wilhelm-Gedächtniskirche 7
Käthe-Kollwitz-Museum 4
Kunstgewerbemuseum 11
Kurfürstendamm (Ku-Damm) 3
Märkisches Museum 5
Neue Nationalgalerie 13
Potsdamer Platz 16
Reichstag 19
Schöneberg Rathaus 6
The Story of Berlin 2
Tiergarten 10
Topographie des Terrors 15
Zoologischer Garten Berlin & Aquarium 8

Charlottenburg Attractions

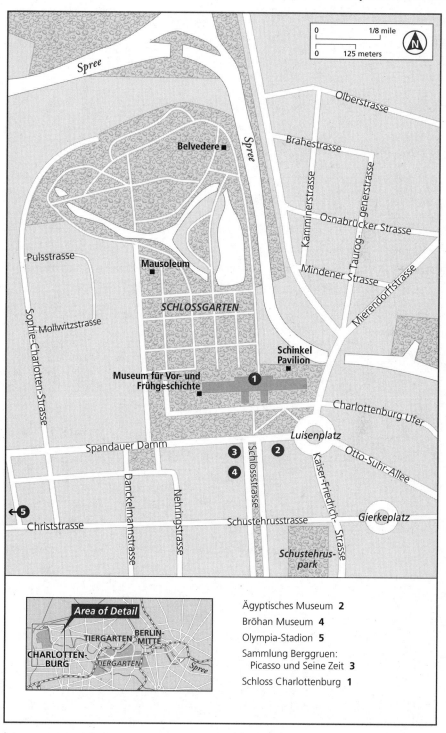

0	1/8 mile
0	125 meters

Spree

Olberstrasse

Brahestrasse

Kamminerstrasse

Tauro̶g̶-generstrasse

Osnabrücker Strasse

Mindener Strasse

Mierendorffstrasse

Belvedere ■

Spree

Pulsstrasse

Mausoleum ■

SCHLOSSGARTEN

Sophie-Charlotten-Strasse

Mollwitzstrasse

Schinkel Pavilion

Museum für Vor- und Frühgeschichte

❶

Charlottenburg Ufer

Luisenplatz

Spandauer Damm

❸

Schlossstrasse

❷

Otto-Suhr-Allee

❹

Kaiser-Friedrich-Strasse

Danckelmannstrasse

Nehringstrasse

←❺

Christstrasse

Schustehrusstrasse

Gierkeplatz

Schustehrus-park

Area of Detail

TIERGARTEN

BERLIN-MITTE

CHARLOTTEN-BURG

TIERGARTEN

Spree

Ägyptisches Museum **2**

Bröhan Museum **4**

Olympia-Stadion **5**

Sammlung Berggruen: Picasso und Seine Zeit **3**

Schloss Charlottenburg **1**

Berlin-Mitte Attractions

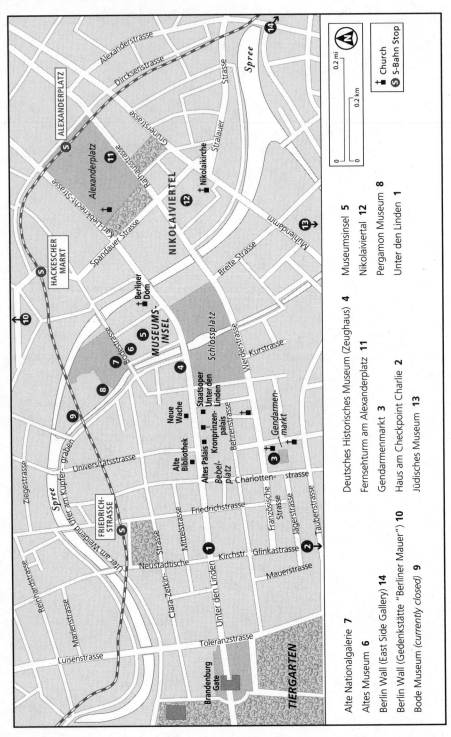

Alte Nationalgalerie **7**

Altes Museum **6**

Berlin Wall (East Side Gallery) **14**

Berlin Wall (Gedenkstätte "Berliner Mauer") **10**

Bode Museum *(currently closed)* **9**

Deutsches Historisches Museum (Zeughaus) **4**

Fernsehturm am Alexanderplatz **11**

Gendarmenmarkt **3**

Haus am Checkpoint Charlie **2**

Jüdisches Museum **13**

Museumsinsel **5**

Nikolaiviertel **12**

Pergamon Museum **8**

Unter den Linden **1**

Bodestrasse. ☎ *030/2090-5555. U-/S-Bahn: Friedrichstrasse (then a 5-minute walk east on Georgenstrasse to Museum Island). Admission: €6 adults, €3 children; free admission 1st Sun of each month. Open: Tues–Sun 10 a.m.–6 p.m.*

Altes Museum (Antiquities Museum)
Museum Island, Mitte

In 1822, Berlin's greatest architect, Karl Friedrich Schinkel, designed this building, which resembles a Greek temple. The museum's **Antikensammlung** (Antiquities Collection), on the main floor, reopened in 1998 and mostly consists of Etruscan, Greek, and Roman pottery, carved ivory, glassware, jewelry, and wood and stone sarcophagi. You can also see a rare portrait of Cleopatra (from Alexandria). Allow yourself at least an hour.

Bodestrasse 1–3. ☎ *030/2090-5555. U-/S-Bahn: Friedrichstrasse (then a 5-minute walk east on Georgenstrasse to Museum Island). Admission: €6 adults, €3 children. Open: Tues–Sun 10 a.m.–6 p.m. (Thurs until 10 p.m.).*

Berlin Wall
Mitte

The Wall is no more, but the fragments that remain are grimly essential pieces of Berlin's history. By 1990, most of the concrete barrier that divided this city into two political entities had been razed. Only two portions of the Wall (*Mauer* in German, pronounced *Mao*-er) are left.

The **East Side Gallery** is a half-mile-long section on Mühlenstrasse on the banks of the Spree River in the former East Berlin. An international group of artists painted murals on this section in 1990.

The other remaining section of the Wall, known as the **Gedenkstätte "Berliner Mauer" (Berlin Wall Memorial)** lies between Bernauer Strasse and Invalidenstrasse. The 230-foot-long memorial consists of two walls that include fragments of the original wall (much of which was bulldozed away or carried off by souvenir hunters). The memorial is mostly made of mirrorlike stainless steel and has slits that allow visitors to peer through it. A plaque reads "In memory of the division of the city from 13 August 1961 to 9 November 1989."

East Side Gallery: Mühlenstrasse along the Spree River; U-/S-Bahn: Warschauer Strasse. Gedenkstätte "Berliner Mauer": between Bernauer Strasse and Invalidenstrasse; U-Bahn: Bernauer Strasse.

Brandenburger Tor (Brandenburg Gate)
Mitte

If you watched the televised fall of the Communist German Democratic Republic (GDR) in 1989, you saw this historic monument, one of Berlin's most potent symbols, in every news clip. When the Wall came down, hundreds of thousands of East Germans walked freely through the gate into West Berlin for the first time since 1961. A neoclassical triumphal arch completed in 1791, the gate is crowned by the famous **Quadriga,** a four-horse copper chariot drawn by the goddess Victoria. The revolutionary events of 1848 and 1918, such as those in 1989, saw the gate used as a symbolic gathering place. In the Room of Silence, built into one of the guardhouses, visitors still gather to meditate and reflect on Germany's past.

Pariser Platz. U-/S-Bahn: Unter den Linden (you see the gate to the west). Admission: Free. Open: Room of Silence daily 11 a.m.–6 p.m.

Gemäldegalerie (Painting Gallery)
Kulturforum, Tiergarten

The Gemäldegalerie moved to the Kulturforum complex in 1998. The gallery houses Berlin's greatest collection of European painting, with an emphasis on medieval German and Dutch art and 16th-century Italian and 17th-century Dutch painting. Several Italian masterpieces are on display including Raphael's *Virgin and Child with the Infant St. John* and Bronzino's *Portrait of Ugolino Martelli.* The gallery contains one of the world's largest collections of Rembrandts.

Matthäiskirchplatz. ☎ 030/2090-5555. U-/S-Bahn: Potsdamer Platz (then a 5-minute walk west on Potsdamer Strasse and Margaretenstrasse). Admission: €6 adults, €3 children; free on 1st Sun of the month. Open: Tues–Sun 10 a.m.–6 p.m.

Gendarmenmarkt
Mitte

Twin churches inspired by Rome's Piazza del Popolo flank this monumentally graceful baroque square — one of the most beautiful architectural ensembles in Berlin. Looking at the square today, it's hard to imagine that by the end of World War II the Gendarmenmarkt had been reduced to a pile of smoldering rubble and remained in ruins until 1977, when East Berlin finally began its reconstruction. The square was named for the Gens d'Armes regiment, which had its guardhouse and stables here from 1738 to 1782.

The centerpiece of the square is Friedrich Schinkel's beautiful neoclassical **Schauspielhaus,** or theater (now also called the Konzerthaus, or Concert House), completed in 1821. On the north side of the square is the **Französicher Dom** (French Cathedral; ☎ 030/229-1760; open daily 9 a.m.–7 p.m.), built for the influx of French Huguenots (Protestants) who settled in Berlin after being forced to flee Catholic France in 1685. Facing this church like a mirror image on the south side is the **Deutscher Dom** (German Cathedral; ☎ 030/202-2690; open Tues–Sun 10 a.m.–6 p.m.). Surrounding the square is a bevy of chic new restaurants.

U-Bahn: Französische Strasse (then a 2-minute walk east on Taubenstrasse).

Hamburger Bahnhof Museum für Gegenwart (Museum of Contemporary Art)
Tiergarten

This showcase of contemporary art opened in 1996 in the 19th-century Hamburger Bahnhof, the oldest train station in Berlin. The building still retains traces of its former use, including the high roof designed for steam engines. The modern art on display includes everything from Andy Warhol's now legendary *Mao* to an audio-visual Joseph Beuys archive. You also find a major collection of Cy Twombly's work, and major works by Robert Rauschenberg and Roy Lichtenstein, as well as changing exhibitions. You can see everything in about an hour.

Invalidenstrasse 50–51. ☎ *030/2090-5555. S-Bahn: Lehrter Stadtbahnhof (then a 3-minute walk northeast on Invalidenstrasse). Admission: €6 adults, €3 children. Open: Tues–Sun 10 a.m.–6 p.m. (Thurs until 10 p.m.).*

Haus am Checkpoint Charlie (Checkpoint Charlie Museum)
Kreuzberg

If you're interested in the history of the Berlin Wall, this small museum in Kreuzberg is well worth an hour of your time. Located near what was once Checkpoint Charlie, the most frequently used traffic crossing into East Berlin, the museum documents the Wall's history from its construction in 1961 to its fall in 1989–1990. The photographs, newspaper clippings, and attempted escape devices (chairlifts, false passports, hot-air balloons, even a minisub) used by East Germans may give you a new take on the meaning of freedom.

Friedrichstrasse 44. ☎ *030/253-7250. U-Bahn: Kochstrasse (then a 5-minute walk north on Friedrichstrasse). Admission: €6 adults, €3 children and students. Open: Daily 9 a.m.–10 p.m.*

Jüdisches Museum (Jewish Museum)
Kreuzberg

The newest and most talked about museum in Berlin is located in Kreuzberg, just south of Berlin Mitte. Designed by American architect Daniel Libeskind, the building is shaped like a stretched-out Star of David and houses Europe's largest Jewish museum. Items on display include ceremonial objects, portraits of prominent Jewish figures (men and women), historical objects, works of Jewish artists, documents, photos, and memorabilia. You follow a chronological pathway occasionally interrupted by deliberately disorienting memorial spaces. This is a museum with a lot to see. I recommend that you give yourself at least three hours.

Lindenstrasse 9–14. ☎ *030/2599-3300. U-Bahn: Hallesches Tor (then a 5-minute walk east on Gitschiner Strasse and north on Lindenstrasse). Admission: €5 adults, €2.50 children, €10 family ticket (2 adults, 2 children). Open: Daily 10 a.m.–8 p.m. Closed on Jewish holy days.*

Kaiser-Wilhelm-Gedächtniskirche (Emperor William Memorial Church)

Charlottenburg

One of Berlin's most famous landmarks, the Gedächtniskirche (Memorial Church) is a ponderous neo-Romanesque structure from the late 19th century. Built to commemorate the 1871 establishment of the German Empire, the church was later blasted by a bomb in World War II. The ruined shell was preserved as a symbol of the ravages of war. You probably won't want to spend more than a few minutes inside. The small modern church beside the Gedächtniskirche is an octagonal hall designed by Egon Eierman in 1961. Free organ concerts take place there every Saturday, year-round, at 6 p.m.

Kurfürstendamm at Breitscheidplatz. ☎ *030/218-5023. U-/S-Bahn: Zoologischer Garten (then a 5-minute walk south on Budapester Strasse). Admission: Free. Open: Memorial church Mon–Sat 10 a.m.–4 p.m.; new church daily 9 a.m.–7 p.m.*

Kurfürstendamm

Tiergarten

The famous boulevard known as the "Ku-Damm" is western Berlin's answer to Paris's Champs-Elysées. For years the Ku-Damm hogged all the city's glamour because dreary East Berlin had nothing to rival it. Today's busy commercial artery began as nothing more than a humble log road, built in 1542 for the Prince-Electors (Kurfürsten) to reach their hunting lodge in the Grünewald more easily. From the turn of the century until World War II, the Ku-Damm was the most brilliant, lively, and elegant street in this part of Berlin, filled with legendary cafes and renowned for its nightlife. The street is still a good place to shop, stroll, sit, and people-watch.

U-Bahn: Kurfürstendamm (you on are the Ku-Damm when you exit the station).

Neue Nationalgalerie (New National Gallery)

Kulturforum, Tiergarten

The only "old" structure in the aggressively modern Kulturforum complex is the New National Gallery, designed in 1968 by famed German architect Ludwig Mies van der Rohe. The museum, an enormous expanse of glass windows and simple symmetry, contains a small but impressive collection of international 20th-century painting and sculpture, including works by de Chirico, Dalí, Miró, Mark Rothko, and Frank Stella. Of special interest are the paintings by early- to mid-20th-century German artists Max Beckmann, Max Ernst, and Otto Dix, and two bitter and brilliant oils by George Grosz that capture the decadent despair of the Weimar years in the 1920s.

Potsdamer Strasse 50. ☎ *030/2090-5555. U-/S-Bahn: Potsdamer Platz (then a 5-minute walk south on Potsdamer Strasse). Admission: €6 adults, €3 children and students. Open: Tues–Sun 10 a.m.–6 p.m. (Thurs until 10 p.m.).*

Pergamon Museum
Museum Island, Mitte

Of all the museums on Museum Island, the renowned Pergamon Museum is the one must-see. And what you must see is the **Pergamon Altar,** considered one of the Seven Wonders of the ancient world and still holding its own today. Part of the enormous Temple of Zeus and Athena, dating from 180 to 160 B.C., the altar was discovered in 1876 in western Turkey. The altar now rests in the central hall of the Department of Greek and Roman Antiquities, housed in the north and east wings of the museum. Another showpiece is the ornate two-storied Market Gate of Miletus, a Roman building facade from the time of Emperor Marcus Aurelius (around A.D. 165).

The **Near East Museum** in the museum's south wing contains one of the largest collections anywhere of antiquities from ancient Babylonia, Persia, and Assyria.

Am Kupfergraben. ☎ *030/2090-5555. U-/S-Bahn: Friedrichstrasse (then a 5-minute walk east on Georgenstrasse to the Museum Island). Admission: €6 adults, €3 children; free admission 1st Sun of each month. Open: Tues–Sun 10 a.m.–6 p.m. (Thurs until 10 p.m.).*

Potsdamer Platz
Tiergarten

Before the war, Potsdamer Platz was the busiest spot in Berlin. In 1961, the square was cut off from the Western sector by the Wall and became an ugly strip of mined no man's land. After reunification, corporations like Sony and Mercedes-Benz rushed in and bought the entire area. Today Potsdamer Platz is a brand-new, supermodern showcase of corporate glitz, government offices, upscale housing, and entertainment. To experience the area, stroll along The Potsdamer Platz Arcades, where 140 stores, restaurants, and cafes invite you to shop and relax. One of the most visited attractions is the **Sony Center am Potsdamer Platz** (☎ 030/ 2094-5400), which has two movie theaters and a viewing area that lets you look out over the Philharmonie, the Kulturforum, and the Tiergarten. Around newly created **Marlene-Dietrich-Platz,** you find the Berlin IMAX-Theater, the Stella Musical-Theater, the Grand Hyatt Hotel, the Madison City Suites, the Berlin Casino, and the Cine-Max cinema center.

U-Bahn: Potsdamer Platz (you are on Potsdamer Platz as you exit the station).

Reichstag (House of Parliament)
Tiergarten

The Reichstag is the seat of the reunified German Parliament. Built in a pompous High Renaissance style between 1884 and 1894, the building was partially destroyed by a fire in 1933 that was probably set by the

Museumsinsel (Museum Island): Art by decree

Four museums on an island in the River Spree form the oldest museum complex in Berlin. The buildings, some dating back to the early and mid-19th century, were constructed after Frederick William III issued a decree stipulating that the privately owned artworks of the royal family should be made accessible to the public. The museums were the main attractions in old East Berlin. After reunification, a complicated process of restoring the buildings and reuniting various collections from the East and West began. The domed neo-baroque **Bode Museum** at the far northern end of the island will be closed until 2005, so I don't include it in this guide, but you can visit the other three museums on Museum Island: the Altes Museum, the Alte Nationalgalerie, and the Pergamon Museum.

Nazis, who, blaming the fire on the Communists, used the incident as an opportunity to seize power. Allied bombs destroyed part of the Reichstag in World War II. Today, a new glass dome designed by British architect Sir Norman Foster crowns the building. After a security check, you take an elevator up to the dome, where a sweeping vista of Berlin opens out before you. The dome also has an outdoor observation area and a rooftop restaurant with so-so food (reservations ☎ **030/226-2990**). I recommend that you arrive as early as possible; otherwise, you may have to stand in line for up to three hours before getting in.

Platz der Republik. ☎ *030/2273-2131. U-/S-Bahn: Friedrichstrasse (then a 5-minute walk west along the Reichstagufer, the street that follows the river). Admission: Free. Open: Dome daily 8 a.m.–10 p.m.*

Schloss Charlottenburg (Charlottenburg Palace)
Charlottenburg

The oldest section of this lovely, yellow baroque palace was built in 1695 as a breezy summer abode for Sophie Charlotte, the wife of Friedrich I. Its present form dates from 1790. Much of the palace was destroyed in World War II and painstakingly reconstructed.

You can see the palace only on a tour, and to take that tour you have to don huge felt slippers (so you're effectively polishing the wood floors as you slide around after the guide). The tour is given only in German (you can buy an English-language guide at the ticket counter) and includes the **historical rooms,** the living quarters of Friedrich I and Sophie Charlotte; the eye-catching **porcelain room;** and the **royal chapel.** With a combined ticket you can additionally visit, on your own, the **Galerie der Romantik,** with its fine collection of paintings from the neoclassical, Romantic, and Biedermeier periods, and the beautifully landscaped **Schlossgarten** (palace gardens). In the Schlossgarten, you find the charming **Schinkel**

Pavilion, an Italianate summer house designed by Karl Friedrich Schinkel, the leading architect of the day, in 1825. At the far end of the Schlossgarten, close to the Spree River, is the **Belvedere.** This former royal teahouse contains exquisite Berlin porcelain, much of it from the 1700s. To see the palace and museums, you need at least four to five hours.

The **Museum für Vor- und Frühgeschichte** (Museum of Prehistory and Early History), in the New Wing, displays the famous Schliemann collection of antiquities from Troy. You must pay a separate admission of €6 adults, €3 children for this museum, which is open from Tuesday through Sunday from 10 a.m. to 6 p.m.

Luisenplatz. ☎ 0331/969-4202. U-Bahn: Sophie-Charlotte-Platz (then a 5-minute walk north on Schlossstrasse). Admission: Combination ticket for historical rooms, Galerie der Romantik, and Schlossgarten €8 adults, €5 children under 14. Open: Palace and museums Tues–Fri 9 a.m.–5 p.m.; Sat–Sun 10 a.m.–5 p.m. (last tour at 4 p.m.).

Tiergarten

Tiergarten

The popular Tiergarten (literally, "animal garden") covers almost 1 square mile (2.5 km) and is the most popular green space in central Berlin. Tiergarten is also the name of Berlin's smallest neighborhood. With its lawns, canals, leafy trees, and more than 14 miles (23 km) of meandering paths, the Tiergarten park is a great place to stroll and relax. The Tiergarten was originally laid out by Peter Josef Lenné, one of the great landscape architects of the early 19th century, as a private park for the electors of Prussia. The park was devastated during and just after World War II, when desperate citizens chopped down the trees for fuel. Beginning in 1955, trees were replanted and walkways, ponds, and flower beds restored to their original patterns. The Berlin Zoo (described below) occupies the park's southwestern corner. In the northwestern corner, you find the Hansaviertel (Hansa Quarter), a residential area where architects were invited to build projects in the 1950s, and pretty **Schloss (Palace) Bellevue** (S-Bahn: Bellevue), residence of Germany's president. If you just want to stroll, give yourself a couple of hours.

The **Siegessäule** (Victory Column), a golden goddess of victory perched high atop a red-granite pedestal, is the most famous of the Tiergarten's many monuments. The column stands in the center of the Strasse des 17 Juni, a wide boulevard that bisects the Tiergarten and is the western extension of Unter den Linden. The column's 157-foot- (48-meter-) high observation platform, reached by climbing up a 290-step spiral staircase, is open daily from 9:30 a.m. to 6:30 p.m. Admission is €1 for adults, free for children under 12.

Bounded on the west by Bahnhof Zoo and the Europa Center, on the east by Berlin Mitte, the Brandenburg Gate, and Potsdamer Platz. U-Bahn: Zoologischer Garten or Hansaplatz. S-Bahn: Tiergarten or Bellevue. Bus: 100.

Unter den Linden
Mitte

Laid out in 1647 and extending about three-quarters of a mile east from the Brandenburg Gate, Unter den Linden is one of Berlin's most famous and historically significant streets. The name, which means "under the lindens," came from the linden trees that were originally planted along the street. This is the oldest and royalest boulevard in central Berlin, with several monumental buildings from the 18th and 19th centuries.

Friedrich Schinkel's 1818 **Neue Wache** (New Watch) served as headquarters for the King's Guard and now contains the Tomb of the Unknown Soldier and the Tomb of the Unknown Resistance Fighter. The **Zeughaus** (Armory), Berlin's largest baroque building and the first (1706) major building to be constructed on Unter den Linden, will eventually house the Deutsches Museum. The giant **Berliner Dom** (Berlin Cathedral; Lustgarten; open daily 9 a.m. to 8 p.m.) squats at the end of Unter den Linden.

U-/S-Bahn: Unter den Linden (you are on the avenue as you exit the station).

Zoologischer Garten Berlin & Aquarium (Berlin Zoo-Aquarium)
Tiergarten

Founded in 1844, Germany's oldest and Europe's largest zoo occupies almost the entire southwest corner of the Tiergarten. More than 13,000 animals live here, many of them in open habitats. The most popular residents are the giant pandas. The zoo also has a modern aviary, with more than 550 species of birds. The aquarium is home to more than 9,000 fish, reptiles, amphibians, insects, and other creatures. The "hippoquarium" is a new attraction. With kids in tow you can easily spend half a day in the zoo and aquarium.

Hardenbergplatz 8. ☎ 030/254-010. U-/S-Bahn: Zoologischer Garten (the entrance is a 3-minute walk east on Budapester Strasse). Admission: Zoo €7 adults, €6 children; aquarium €7 adults, €6 children; combined ticket €12 adults, €10 children. Open: Zoo Apr–Oct daily 9 a.m.–6:30 p.m.; Nov–Mar daily 9 a.m.–5 p.m.; aquarium year-round daily 9 a.m.–6 p.m.

Finding more cool things to see and do

Berlin offers *viel mehr* (much more) to see than the places described in the "Discovering the top attractions from A to Z " section of this chapter. That section describes the essential A-list sights that almost everyone who visits Berlin wants to see. If you have more time, you can pick and choose from the following attractions to round out your visit (and don't forget to check out the side trip to Potsdam and Sanssouci Palace that I describe separately at the end of this chapter).

✔ The **Bauhaus–Archiv Museum für Gestaltung** (Bauhaus Design Museum), Klingelhöferstrasse 14 (☎ 030/254-0020; U-Bahn: Nollendorfplatz, is a museum dedicated to the Bauhaus school, which sought to combine art, design, and technology. The Bauhaus was founded in 1919 at Weimar, moved to Dessau, and finally settled in Berlin, before the Nazis forced the school to disband in 1933. The museum, completed in 1979, is one of the last works of the great Berlin-born architect Walter Gropius. English-language texts describing the exhibits are available. You need at least an hour to peruse the exhibits. The museum, near the Tiergarten, is open Wednesday through Monday from 10 a.m. to 5 p.m. Admission is €4 adults, €2 children under 12.

✔ Berlin's **Botanischer Garten** (Botanical Garden), Königin-Luise-Strasse 6–8 (☎ 030/8385-0111; S-Bahn: Botanischer Garten; U-Bahn: Rathaus Steglitz, is located near the Dahlem Museums, on the outskirts of Berlin. The huge garden contains vast collections of European and exotic plants. The Palm House is one of the largest in the world. You also find an extensive arboretum amd several special collections, including a garden for blind visitors and another with water plants. A small botanical museum, more of interest to dedicated gardeners than the general public, is also on the premises. Give yourself an hour or so to stroll through the garden itself. Admission is €4 for adults, €2 for children, free for children under 6. The garden is open daily April through August from 9 a.m. to 8 p.m.; September through March the garden opens at 9 a.m. and closes at dusk. The museum (admission €1) is open daily 10 a.m. to 6 p.m.

✔ The **Bröhan Museum,** Schlossstrasse 1A (☎ 030/3269-0600; U-Bahn: Sophie-Charlotte-Platz), privately operated and generally overlooked by visitors, houses one of the world's finest collections of *Jugendstil* (Art Nouveau) and Art Deco furniture, painting, sculpture, glass, silverware, and crafts, all from 1889 to 1939. A must-see is the **Suite Emile-Jacques Ruhlman,** a completely decorated set of rooms from a luxurious private residence of the 1920s and 1930s. The museum is small enough so that you can see everything in an hour. Admission is €4.10; free for children 11 and under. Hours are Tuesday through Sunday 10 a.m. to 6 p.m.

✔ The **Deutsche Guggenheim Berlin,** Unter den Linden 13–15 (☎ 030/202-0930; U-Bahn: Stadtmitte), is a state-of-the-art museum in the newly restored Berlin office of Deutsche Bank at the intersection of Unter den Linden and Charlottenstrasse. The museum is devoted to modern and contemporary art. Throughout the year, the Guggenheim Foundation presents changing exhibitions in a ground-floor exhibition space, and displays newly commissioned works created specifically for the space. You can usually see the artwork in under an hour. Admission is €4.10 adults, €2.56 children. It's open daily from 11 a.m. to 8 p.m.

✔ Housed in the former Zeughaus (Arsenal), the **Deutsches Historisches Museum** (German History Museum), Unter den Linden 2 (☎ 030/203-040; S-Bahn: Hackescher Markt), is a big, new museum scheduled to open in 2003. From the Neanderthals to the Nazis, the whole saga of German history will be presented. The collection will include extensive posters and documents of the history of the workers' movement as well as display military artifacts from the Zeughaus collection. Opening hours and admission prices were unavailable at press time.

✔ The **Fernsehturm am Alexanderplatz** (Television Tower), Panoramastrasse 1a, Alexanderplatz (☎ 030/242-3333; U-/S-Bahn: Alexanderplatz), is a weird-looking television tower built by the Communists back in the 1960s. Berliners call it "the onion" because of its shape. An elevator whisks you up to the top for a stunning panorama. You find a revolving restaurant up there, too. The tower is open daily March through October from 9 a.m. to 1 a.m., and daily November through February from 10 a.m. to midnight. The elevator to the top costs €6 for adults and €2.50 for children.

✔ The new **Filmmuseum Berlin,** Sony Center in Potsdamer Platz (☎ 030/300-9030; U-/S-Bahn: Potsdamer Platz), appeals to anyone who has an interest in German film, or film in general. One wing is devoted to the legendary Marlene Dietrich, a native Berliner who catapulted to international fame in 1930 in Josef von Sternberg's *Der Blaue Engel (The Blue Angel)* and went on to become Germany's only major star in Hollywood. The fascinating Marlene memorabilia includes photos, costumes, props, letters, and documents. You need at least an hour here. Admission is €6 for adults, and €4 for students, children, and senior citizens. The museum is open Tuesday through Sunday from 10 a.m. to 6 p.m. (Thurs until 8 p.m.).

✔ The **Grünewald** (S-Bahn: Grünewald), a 15-square-mile forest that begins just beyond the western edge of the Kurfürstendamm, is Berlin's largest uninterrupted wooded area. From Heerstrasse, the forest stretches some 6 miles (9.7 km) south to the popular **Wannsee** lake. Havelchausee, the forest's western border, winds past several picturesque bays and beaches along the Havel River, while the eastern border is roughly marked off by four lakes: **Schlachtensee, Krumme Lanke, Grünewaldsee,** and **Schildhorn.** Loaded with wooded paths and sandy beaches, the Grünewald ("green forest") is a good place to get away from the urban jungle, although on weekends you have plenty of company.

✔ The **Käthe-Kollwitz-Museum,** Fasanenstrasse 24 (☎ 030/882-5210; U-Bahn: Uhlandstrasse), is devoted to the powerful works of Berlin-born artist Käthe Kollwitz (1867–1945). The first woman ever elected to the Prussian Academy of the Arts, Kollwitz resigned her position in 1933 to protest Hitler's rise to power. The Nazis later banned her works. Many of Kollwitz's works express the sorrow, loss, and deprivations of wartime and have a stark, grieving quality. The lower floors of the museum display woodcuts and lithographs; the upper floors contain sculptures. Admission is €5 for adults, €3 for children and students. The museum is open Wednesday through Monday from 11 a.m. to 6 p.m.

✔ **Kunstgewerbemuseum** (Arts and Crafts Museum), Matthäiskirchplatz, Kulturforum (☎ **030/2090-5555;** U-/S-Bahn: Potsdamer Platz), opposite the Philharmonie in the Kulturforum, displays applied arts and crafts from the Middle Ages through the 20th century. The Guelph Treasure, its most dazzling exhibit, is a collection of medieval church articles in gold and silver. The basement rooms display contemporary design from the German Bauhaus school to American Charles Eames and the Memphis design group. You also find a nice cafeteria, open from 10 a.m. to 4:30 p.m. Admission is €2 for adults, €1 for children. The museum is open Tuesday through Sunday from 10 a.m. to 6 p.m.

✔ The **Märkisches Museum,** Am Köllnischen Park 5 (☎ **030/308-660;** U-Bahn: Märkisches Museum), is a large, often overlooked museum on the banks of the Spree in Berlin Mitte. The cultural history of Berlin and its environs is displayed in 42 rooms. Some rooms contain collections of artifacts discovered in regional excavations, everything from Bronze Age finds to Slav silver. Other sections explore theater, literature, and the arts in Berlin and Brandenburg, and you find a fun collection of mechanical musical instruments that can be played. The museum is open Tuesday to Sunday from 10 a.m. to 6 p.m. Admission is €4.10 for adults and €2.05 for children; free admission on Wednesday.

✔ **Nikolaiviertel** (Nicholas Quarter; U-Bahn: Klosterstrasse), not far from the Gendarmenmarkt in Berlin Mitte, is a historic riverside quarter restored to resemble its medieval and baroque heyday (with a few modern design touches). Reconstructed palaces, period taverns, and old churches make this quarter ideal for a leisurely and picturesque ramble along the Spree River, down narrow streets illuminated by gas lanterns. Named for Berlin's oldest church, the **Nikolaikirche** (Church of St. Nicholas; Nikolaikirchplatz; ☎ **030/ 2472-4529;** open Tues–Sun 10 a.m.–6 p.m.), the quarter was the last major reconstruction project of the German Democratic Party that ruled former East Germany; the church was restored in time for the city's 750th anniversary in 1987.

✔ **Sammlung Bergruen: Picasso und Seine Zeit** (Bergruen Collection: Picasso and His Times), Schlossstrasse 1 (☎ **030/ 2090-5555;** U-Bahn: Sophie-Charlotte-Platz), located across from the Egyptian Museum in Charlottenburg, is a small museum that showcases several important paintings by Picasso and some playful works by Paul Klee. You can see the collection in about half an hour. Admission is €4.10 for adults, and €2.05 for students and children. The museum is open Tuesday through Sunday from 10 a.m. to 6 p.m.

✔ **Schöneberg Rathaus** (Schöneberg City Hall), John-F.-Kennedy-Platz (☎ **030/75600;** U-Bahn: Rathaus Schöneberg), the former political and administrative center of West Berlin, is of special interest to Americans. John F. Kennedy delivered his memorable "Ich bin ein Berliner" speech here on June 26, 1963, at the height of Cold War tensions between East and West. A replica of the Liberty Bell is rung every day at noon. A gift from the American people in 1950, the Freedom Bell symbolized U.S. support for the West Berliners during the Cold War. The building has little to see inside. Admission is free. The building is open daily from 10 a.m. to 6 p.m.

✔ **The Story of Berlin,** Ku'damm-Karree, Kurfürstendamm 207–208 (☎ **030/8872-0100;** U-Bahn: Uhlandstrasse), is an enjoyable multi-media museum that uses films, photos, sounds, and colorful displays to tell about eight centuries of life in Berlin. Beginning with the city's founding in 1237, the themed exhibits chronicle all the major historical events, including the reign of Frederick the Great, the Industrial Revolution, the Golden 1920s, World War II and its aftermath, divided Berlin during the Cold War, and the fall of the Wall. At the end of the tour, a guide takes you down to visit an underground nuclear bomb shelter built in the 1970s. Allow at least two hours to see everything. This is a good overall introduction to Berlin that teens may enjoy. Admission is €9.30 for adults, €3.50 for children 6 to 14, and €21 for families (2 adults, 2 children). The museum is open daily from 10 a.m. to 8 p.m. (last admission 6 p.m.).

✔ **Topographie des Terrors** (Topography of Terror), Niederkirchnerstrasse 8 (☎ **030/2548-6703;** U-/S-Bahn: Potsdamer Platz), located in what was once part of the Nazi SS and Gestapo headquarters, is an exhibit detailing how the Nazis came to power and the crimes against humanity they committed under the leadership of *der Führer,* Adolf Hitler. The exhibit is open daily from 10 a.m. to 6 p.m. (until 8 p.m. May–Sept). Admission is free.

Seeing Berlin by Guided Tour

Taking a guided sightseeing tour *(Stadtrundfahrt)* can help you to see parts of this huge city that you may otherwise miss. You can tour Germany's capital with an experienced guide by bus, on foot, or by boat.

Bus tours

Severin+Kühn, Kurfürstendamm 216 (☎ **030/880-4190;** U-Bahn: Kurfürstendamm), offers a two-hour "12-Stops City Tour" that departs daily every half-hour from 10 a.m. to 4 p.m. (Nov–March until 3 p.m.). Tickets cost €16 per person. The tour passes 12 important stops in Berlin, including the Europa Center, the Brandenburg Gate, and Potsdamer Platz. You can get on and off the bus at any point during the hour. The same company's three-hour "Big Berlin Tour" departs at 10 a.m. and 2 p.m. daily, costs €19.95 per person, and covers more sites. All tours include a guide who delivers commentaries in German and English, making them accessible and enjoyable for kids as well as adults. From May through September, Severin+Kühn also conducts an interesting tour of Potsdam, site of Sanssouci Palace, former residence of Frederick the Great (see "Day-tripping to Potsdam and Sanssouci Palace," later in this chapter). The price is €33.20 per person. Departures are Tuesday through Sunday at 10 a.m.; from April through October, Severin+Kühn operates additional Saturday and Sunday tours at 2:15 p.m.

Although you don't get a guide, the cheapest bus tour of Berlin is **public bus 100,** which leaves from Bahnhof Zoo and passes most of the major sites in western and eastern Berlin. You can catch the bus in front of Bahnhof Zoologischer Garten (Zoo Station).

Walking tours

For an excellent introduction to Berlin and its history, try one of the walking tours offered by **Berlin Walks** (☎ **030/301-9194;** Internet: www.berlinwalks.com). "Discover Berlin" is a three-hour introductory tour that takes you past the New Synagogue, the Reichstag, and the Brandenburg Gate, among other major sites. This walk starts daily at 10 a.m. and 2:30 p.m. (in winter at 10 a.m. only). "Infamous Third Reich Sites" focuses on the sites of major Nazi buildings in central Berlin, such as Goebbels's Propaganda Ministry and Hitler's New Reichschancellery; this tour starts at 10 a.m. on Saturday, Sunday, Tuesday, Wednesday, and Thursday. "Jewish Life in Berlin" takes you through the prewar Jewish community; sights include the Old Cemetery and the former Boys' School. The tour starts at 10 a.m. Monday and Friday. You don't need advance reservations for any of the tours. You meet the guide, who wears a Berlin Walks badge, outside the main entrance to Bahnhof Zoologischer Garten (Zoo Station), at the top of the taxi stand. Tours last from 2½ to 3 hours and cost €10 for adults, €7.50 for those under 26, free for children under 14.

Boat tours

A boat tour is the most unusual way to see portions of Berlin. Local waterways include the Spree and Havel rivers — ranging in size from narrow channels to large lakes — as well as many canals created in the 19th century. **Stern- und Kreisschiffahrt,** Pushkinallee 60–70 (☎ **030/ 536-3600**), the city's best-known boat operator, offers boat trips from April through October. Be aware, though, that all of its tours are given only in German — a fact that doesn't prevent most kids from enjoying the boat ride. "Historische Stadtfahrt" (Historic City Journey) takes you along the Spree, the river that helped build Berlin. Two-, three-, and four-hour tours depart at 10 a.m. and 2 p.m. from Jannowitzbrücke in Berlin-Mitte. These trips offer good views of the Reichstag, the Pergamon Museum, the Königliche Bibliothek (Royal Library), and the

Gay and lesbian Berlin

Berlin has a century-old gay and lesbian history, and the city remains a mecca for international gay and lesbian travelers. The city's gay information center is **Mann-o-Meter**, Bülowstrasse 106 (☎ **030/216-8008**; U-Bahn: Nollendorfplatz). The center is open Monday through Friday from 5 to 10 p.m., and Saturday and Sunday from 4 to 10 p.m. Another good source for information is **Prinz Eisenherz**, Bleibtreustrasse 52 (☎ **030/313-9936**; S-Bahn: Savignyplatz), one of the world's oldest gay and lesbian bookstores. The store stocks a vast array of new and rare fiction, nonfiction, art books, and magazines in German, English, and other languages. The staff is extremely knowledgeable and helpful.

Berlin is the only city in the world with a gay museum. The **Schwules Museum** (Gay Museum), Mehringdamm 61 (☎ **030/693-1172**; U-Bahn: Mehringdamm), is a large gallery-like space with changing exhibitions on gay life in Germany and around the world. The museum is open Wednesday through Monday from 2 to 6 p.m., Saturday until 5 p.m. Admission is €5.

Traditionally, lesbian and gay life has centered around **Nollendorfplatz** (U-Bahn: Nollendorfplatz), the so-called Pink (or Gay) Village. A **memorial plaque** mounted on the outside south wall of the Nollendorfplatz subway station, in the heart of what has been for decades the gay heart of Berlin, reads: *Totgeschlagen-Totgeschiegen. Den Homosexuellen Opfern des National Socialismus* ("Killed and Forgotten. The homosexual victims of National Socialism."). The plaque serves as a poignant reminder that the Nazis exterminated thousands of homosexuals in addition to millions of Jews, Gypsies, and other political victims.

In mid-June, Nollendorfplaz is the site of the **Lesbisch-Schwules Stadtfest** (Lesbian–Gay Street Fair). The **Christopher Street Day** parade is an even larger city-wide gay event held the last week in June; up to 500,000 people congregate for this Gay Pride festival.

The gay scene is more international in the area around **Nollendorfplatz,** which has had gay bars since the 1920s. **Kreuzberg** is another hot gay borough with a big selection of bars. In the eastern part of the city, **Prenzlauer Berg** has become the new gay area. For my recommended gay and lesbian nightspots, see "Checking out the dance clubs and bars," later in this chapter.

monumental heart of the former East Berlin. A one-hour tour costs €7.15 per person; two-hour tours cost €9.20; four-hour tours cost €14.30. The same company offers other boat tours from Schlossbrücke near Charlottenburg Palace.

Following an Itinerary

Every visitor to Berlin faces one problem: how to see as much as possible in a limited amount of time. What do you see if you have only one, two, or three days at your disposal? The itineraries in this section are commonsense, limited-time suggestions that include the top Berlin sights. For descriptions of each stop, see " Discovering the top attractions from A to Z," earlier in this chapter, unless noted otherwise.

If you have one day in Berlin

Start early. First visit the **Reichstag,** where the new dome provides a marvelous view out over the city. From there you can walk to the **Brandenburg Gate,** symbol of Berlin, then walk down **Unter den Linden,** exploring the nearby **Gendarmenmarkt** and paying a brief visit to the **Pergamon Museum** to see the Pergamon Altar. Return to Potsdamer Platz to see the newest section of Berlin, and then go on to **Schloss Charlottenburg** (Charlottenburg Palace) for a palace tour. Afterward, stop in at the **Ägyptisches Museum** (Egyptian Museum) for a look at the celebrated bust of Queen Nefertiti. In the evening, walk along the Kurfürstendamm and dine in a local restaurant.

If you have two days in Berlin

On the second day, visit the **Gemäldegalerie** (Painting Gallery) in the Kulturforum and the nearby **Neue Nationalgalerie,** where you can have lunch. Afterward, head over to the **Jüdisches Museum** in Freuzberg or **The Story of Berlin** multimedia show (see "Finding more cool things to see and do," earlier in this chapter). In the evening, enjoy an opera, a concert, or a cabaret/variety show.

If you have three days in Berlin

Spend half of the day in **Potsdam,** visiting **Sanssouci Palace** and grounds (see "Day-tripping to Potsdam and Sanssouci Palace," later in this chapter). In the afternoon, stop in at **Haus am Checkpoint Charlie,** with its Cold War museum, and end with a stroll through the **Tiergarten.**

Shopping for Local Treasures

You can buy just about anything you want in Berlin, a great shopping city. But keep in mind that you'll pay less for goods made in Germany and the European Union than for goods imported to Germany from the United States. German porcelain, china, and cutlery, for example, are prized for their quality, and their prices are lower here than in the United States.

Most stores in Berlin are open Monday through Friday from 9 or 10 a.m. to 6 or 6:30 p.m. Many stay open late on Thursday evenings, often to 8:30 p.m. Saturday hours are usually 9 or 10 a.m. to 2 p.m.

Don't expect a lot of "deals" in Berlin, except on the sales racks in the department stores. For the two major *Trödelmarkts* (flea markets), see the sidebar, "Berlin flea markets."

Shopping in western Berlin

Throughout the decades when the Wall divided Berlin, the only decent shopping was in western Berlin, which remains the best place for all-purpose, all-around shopping.

Neighborhoods and malls

The main shopping boulevard in the western part of Berlin is the famous **Ku-Damm,** short for Kurfürstendamm (U-Bahn: Kurfürstendamm). Quality stores, as well as stores carrying cheap souvenirs and T-shirts, line the street. The specialty stores on the side streets around the Ku-Damm, especially between **Breitscheidplatz** and **Olivaer Platz,** are good shopping grounds.

Another good shopping street in western Berlin, close to Ku-Damm, is **Tauentzienstrasse** (U-/S-Bahn: Zoologischer Garten) and its intersecting streets: **Marburger Strasse, Ranke Strasse,** and **Nürnberger Strasse.** This area offers a wide array of stores, many specializing in German fashions for women. Stores here are often cheaper than on the fancier Ku-Damm. Berlin's first shopping mall, the **Europa Center** (☎ 030/348-0088), is on Tauentzienstrasse (U-/S-Bahn: Zoologischer Garten); here you find around 75 shops, as well as restaurants and cafes.

The **Uhland-Passage,** at Uhlandstrasse 170 (U-Bahn: Uhlandstrasse), has some of the best boutiques and big-name stores in Berlin. Shoppers interested in quality at any price should head to **Kempinski Plaza,** Uhlandstrasse 181–183 (U-Bahn: Uhlandstrasse), home to some of the most exclusive boutiques in the city, including haute-couture women's clothing. You find trendier boutiques along **Bleibtreustrasse.**

The new **Potsdamer Platz Arkaden** (U-/S-Bahn: Potsdamer Platz), one of the most comprehensive shopping malls in Berlin, contains about 100 shops, with more being added all the time, scattered over three levels. Some of the stores offer cost-cutting clothing and housewares.

Department stores

Kaufhaus des Westens (called KaDeWe [ka-day-vay] for short), Tauentzien 21 (☎ 030/21210; U-Bahn: Zoologischer Garten), is a huge department store, known for its six floors of upscale merchandise and sixth-floor food department. **Wertheim,** Kurfürstendamm 231 (☎ 030/880-030; U-Bahn: Kurfürstendamm), is good for travel aids and general basics: perfumes, clothing for the entire family, jewelry, electrical devices, household goods, photography supplies, and souvenirs. Wertheim has a large restaurant with a view over half the city.

Berlin flea markets

A flea market in Germany is called a *Trödelmarkt* or a *Flohmarkt.* **Antik & Flohmarkt** (**☎ 030/208-2645;** U-/S-Bahn: Friedrichstrasse), a daily flea market from 9 a.m. to 4 p.m. in the Friedrichstrasse S-Bahn station, has some 60 vendors selling all manner of bric-a-brac, including brassware and World War II mementos. The **Berliner Trödelmarkt** (**☎ 030/2655-0096;** S-Bahn: Tiergarten), adjacent to the Tiergarten S-Bahn station near the corner of the Bachstrasse and Strasse des 17 Juni, is the favorite weekend shopping spot for countless Berliners, who come to find pieces of kitsch, nostalgia, sort-of-antiques, and used clothing. The market is held every Saturday and Sunday from 10 a.m. to 5 p.m.

Fashion

Bleibgrün, Bleibtreustrasse 30 (**☎ 030/885-0080;** S-Bahn: Savignyplatz), a small, fashionable women's clothing store with a helpful staff, sells Paul Smith, Marithé François Girbaud, and a handful of other fashionable trendsetters. **Bogner Zenker-Berlin,** Kurfürstendamm 45 (**☎ 030/ 881-1000;** S-Bahn: Savignyplatz), is a long-established shop for women's clothing made in Germany, Austria, and Italy. **Chapeaux Hutmode Berlin,** Bleibtreustrasse 51 (**☎ 030/312-0913;** S-Bahn: Savignyplatz), is a couture hatmaker inspired by vintage fashion magazines and glamorous movies from the 1930s. **Modenhaus Horn,** Kurfürstendamm 213 (**☎ 030/881-4055;** U-Bahn: Kurfürstendamm), sells whatever is *au courant* for chic Berlin women. **Treykorn,** Savignyplatz 13 Passage (**☎ 030/312-4275;** S-Bahn: Savignyplatz), carries the most avant-garde jewelry in Berlin, showcasing more than three dozen of the boldest jewelry artisans in the city.

Perfumes

Harry Lehmann, Kantstrasse 106 (**☎ 030/324-3582;** U-Bahn: Wilmersdorferstrasse), is a wonderfully old-fashioned parfumerie where most of the scents come from old family recipes, distilled from flowers, grasses, and leaves. The prices are amazingly reasonable for the quality of the perfumes.

Porcelain and china

Königliche Porzellan-Manufaktur (KPM; Royal Porcelain Factory), Kurfürstendamm 27 in Kempinski Hotel Bristol (**☎ 030/8867-2110;** U-Bahn: Kurfürstendamm), sells porcelain pieces hand-painted and hand-decorated with patterns based on traditional 18th- and 19th-century KPM designs. **Meissener Porzellan,** Kurfürstendamm 26A (**☎ 030/8868-3530;** U-Bahn Kurfürstendamm), one of the most famous porcelain manufacturers in Europe, offers an array of Meissen dinner plates, sculptures, and chandeliers. **Rosenthal,** Kurfürstendamm 226 (**☎ 030/885-6340;** U-Bahn: Kurfürstendamm), is the place to go for contemporary Rosenthal porcelain and china from Bavaria.

Shopping in eastern Berlin

The eastern part of the city has undergone major changes in the retail sector since reunification a decade ago. The main street, **Friedrich-strasse** (U-/S-Bahn: Friedrichstrasse), now offers some of Berlin's most elegant shopping, with upmarket boutiques selling everything from women's fashions to Meissen porcelain. The largest shopping mall in eastern Berlin, offering a little bit of everything, is at the **Berliner Markthalle,** at the corner of Rosa-Luxemburg-Strasse and Karl-Liebknecht-Strasse (U-/S-Bahn: Alexanderplatz).

For more shopping in the eastern part, see this chapter's sidebar, "Berlin's newest old shopping neighborhood: Scheuneviertel."

Discovering Nightlife in Berlin

You find more going on in Berlin than in any other city in Germany. The performing arts scene is jammed with opera, dance, classical-music concerts, and theater performances every night of the week. Berlin's nightlife is legendary, with hundreds of bars, clubs, and cabarets appealing to every taste.

Finding out what's happening

Check the listings in *Zitty* (Internet: www.zitty.de) or *Berlin Programm,* available at all newsstands, for the latest schedules of what's going on where. An excellent online source is www.berlin.de; click "What's On" to access a complete list of events in any category for the specific dates of your visit.

Getting tickets

You can buy tickets at the venue's box office (the box office is called a *Kasse,* pronounced *kah*-suh). Tickets can usually be purchased right up to curtain time. Alternatively, you can buy tickets from ticket agencies, which charge a commission. **Theater Konzertkasse,** Kurfürstendamm 16 (☎ **030/852-4080;** U-Bahn: Kurfürstendamm), is one of the most centrally located agencies.

For some of the larger opera, ballet, and classical-music venues, you can buy tickets online. If the venue does not have its own Web site, you may be able to order tickets online at www.berlin.de.

Unsold tickets for over 100 venues, including opera, classical concerts, and cabarets, are available for up to 50% off at **Hekticket,** with outlets at Hardenbergstrasse 29 (☎ **030/230-9930;** U-Bahn: Zoologischer Garter)

Berlin's newest old shopping neighborhood: Scheuneviertel

The newest shopping, arts, and happening-neighborhood area is eastern Berlin's Scheuneviertel, or "barn district" (S-Bahn: Hackescher Markt), named for the hay barns that once stood here. The area later became Berlin's Jewish quarter, and, amazingly, some of its oldest buildings survived the World War II bombing raids that reduced most of Berlin to rubble. A grand pre–World War I shopping arcade with interconnected courtyards (*Hinterhöfe)* occupies most of the block formed by Oranienburger Strasse, Rosenthaler Strasse, Grosse Hamburger Strasse, and Sophienstrasse. The spaces within the courtyards have now been turned into a series of galleries, studios, and theaters. Cutting-edge shops line the streets around the arcade.

---

and Liebknechtstrasse 12, Alexanderplatz (☎ **030/230-9930**; U-Bahn: Alexanderplatz); both are open Monday through Friday only from 10 a.m. to 6 p.m.

Raising the curtain on performing arts and music

Good news for culture vultures: With three major symphony orchestras, three opera houses, ballet companies, and dozens of theaters and cabarets, you won't be lacking for things to do. The newest trend is to start performances as early as 6 p.m., so everyone can get home at a reasonable hour. Whenever possible, I include Web sites in this section so you can check performances and schedules before you arrive in Berlin.

Opera and ballet

In Charlottenburg, the **Deutsche Oper Berlin,** Bismarckstrasse 35 (☎ **030/341-0249** recorded information or 030/343-8401; Internet: www.deutscheoperberlin.de; U-Bahn: Deutsche Oper), is the 1950s-era opera house that served the former West Berlin. You can see both opera and ballet here; some tickets bought on the day of performance are 25% off. The box office is open Monday through Saturday from 11 a.m. up to time of performance, and on Sunday from 10 a.m. to 2 p.m. You can also buy tickets online. Ticket prices range from €15 to €77.

The **Staatsoper Unter den Linden,** Unter den Linden 7 (☎ **030/2035-4555**; Internet: www.staatsoper-berlin.org; U-Bahn: Unter den Linden), is housed in a historic building in Berlin-Mitte. The programs feature opera and ballet performances. The box office is open Monday through Friday from 10 a.m. to 8 p.m., and Saturday and Sunday from 2 to 8 p.m. You can buy tickets online. Tickets range from about €9 to €73.

Berlin's **Komische Oper,** Behrenstrasse 55–57 (☎ 030/479-7400; Internet: www.komische-oper-berlin.de; U-/S-Bahn: Unter den Linden), is a famous and well-respected East Berlin house with a unique artistic identity, but performances don't include internationally known stars, and every opera is sung in German. The box office is open Monday through Saturday from 11 a.m. to 7 p.m., and Sunday from 1 p.m. to time of performance. Prices ranges from about €26 to €67. Tickets bought on the day of performance are about 40% off.

Symphony orchestras and classical music

In the Kulturforum complex, the renowned **Berlin Philharmonic Orchestra** plays in the acoustically outstanding **Philharmonie,** Matthäikirchstrasse 1 (box office ☎ 030/2548-8126; Internet: www.berlin-philharmonic.com; U-Bahn: Potsdamer Platz). Chamber music concerts are given at the adjoining **Kammermusiksaal.** The box office is open Monday through Friday from 3 to 6 p.m., Saturday and Sunday from 11 a.m. to 2 p.m., and one hour before performances. Ticket prices range from about €7 for standing room to €105. You can order tickets by e-mail (kartenbuero@@berlin-philharmonic.com).

The historic Schauspielhaus in the former East Berlin has undergone a stunning transformation and is now the **Konzerthaus am Gendarmenmarkt,** Gendarmenmarkt (☎ 030/203-090; S-Bahn: Unter den Linden). The **Berlin Symphony Orchestra** and other orchestras and classical music groups perform in this glittering, pitch-perfect hall. Different ticket prices apply for each event. A ticket for the Berlin Symphony Orchestra is generally about €8 to €30. You can buy tickets at the Konzerthaus box office.

The city's third major orchestra, the **Berlin Symphony,** performs at both the Philharmonie and the Konzerthaus am Gendarmenmarkt. Tickets are available at the box offices of both venues.

Theater

Berlin's theater scene is outstanding but, of course, most of the plays are performed in German. The Web site www.berlin.de has a useful listing of plays and films in English.

The **Berliner Grundtheater** (☎ 030/7800-1497; Internet: www.thebgt.de) performs English-language plays in different venues around the city. If you don't speak the language but want to experience German theater, I recommend going to see a production by the famous **Berliner Ensemble,** Bertolt-Brecht-Platz 1 (☎ 030/2840-8108; Internet: www.berliner-ensemble.de; U-Bahn: Friedrichstrasse). Playwright Bertolt Brecht formed this group with his wife, Helene Weigel, and many theater fans enjoy seeing Brecht's plays performed in "his" theater. The box office is open Monday through Friday from 8 a.m. to 6 p.m., and Saturday and Sunday from 11 a.m. to 6 p.m. and one hour before performances. Ticket prices range from about €5 to €30.

Cabarets and variety shows

Berlin has long been famous for its cabarets and variety shows. Cabarets are nightclubs or theaters where you can sit at a table, order a drink, and watch a floor show full of comic patter (usually satirizing the political and social scene), and usually featuring variety acts. Variety shows offer more of the same, but take place in theaters. Spending an evening in a Berlin cabaret or at a variety show can be enjoyable even if you don't speak a word of German.

Chez Nous Travestie-Theater, Marburgerstrasse 14 (☎ 030/213-1810; U-Bahn: Wittenbergplatz), is a famous little cabaret where all the performers are in drag and most of the audience is heterosexual. Believing that these glamorous ladies are really gentlemen is sometimes difficult. Shows are nightly at 8:30 and 11 p.m. Cover is €30.

Die Stachelschweine (The Porcupine), Europa Center, Tauentzienstrasse and Budapester Strasse (☎ 030/261-4795; U-Bahn: Kurfürstendamm), is a cabaret that's been poking fun at the German and American political scenes for many years now. Part of the performance usually involves a selection of popular songs. Shows take place Tuesday through Friday at 7:30 p.m. and Saturday at 6 p.m. and 9:15 p.m. The cover charge is €13 to €22. This cabaret is closed in July.

Friedrichstadt-Palast, Friedrichstrasse 107 (☎ 030/2326-2326; U-/S-Bahn: Friedrichstrasse), in Mitte, is a big theater that features variety acts from around the world. Shows and showtimes vary, but most nights (except Monday, when the theater's closed) the performances begin at 8 p.m. with 4 p.m. matinees on Saturday and Sunday. Ticket prices range from €33 to €50.

Wintergarten Variété, Potsdamer Strasse 96 (☎ 030/2308-8230; U-Bahn: Kurfürstenstrasse), is the largest and most nostalgic Berlin cabaret, with a nightly variety show featuring magicians, clowns, jugglers, acrobats, and live music. The most expensive seats are on stage level; balconies have conventional theater seats (but drinks are sold there, too). Shows begin at 8 p.m. Monday through Friday, and Saturday at 6 and 10 p.m. Cover is about €38 to €51.

Checking out the dance clubs and bars

If you're into nightlife, you can find something to do all over the city. This section includes just a few of the bars and dance clubs in Berlin.

Bars and clubs don't generally get going until midnight. Many bars now have an open-ended closing policy. An empty club may choose to close at 2 a.m., but a packed club could stay open until 6 a.m. Please keep in mind that new bars open and bars close all the time. This section includes places that are likely to be around for years to come.

Dance clubs

Big Eden, Kurfürstendamm 202 (☎ 030/882-6120; U-Bahn Uhland-strasse), which has been around for three decades, holds 1,000 dancers on its huge dance floor. DJs play the latest international hits with impressive light effects and sound equipment. Cover, which includes one drink, is €7 to €9, depending on the night. The club is open Sunday through Thursday from 9 p.m. to 5 a.m., Friday and Saturday until 6 a.m.

Chip, Berlin Hilton, Mohrenstrasse 30 (☎ 030/20230; U-Bahn: Stadtmitte), is a glossy and popular dance club with a great lighting system, video clips, and fog machine. Club hours are Wednesday through Saturday from 10 p.m. to 4 a.m. Cover is €5.50.

Far Out, Kurfürstendamm 156 (☎ 030/3200-0717; U-Bahn: Adenauer-platz), is a large, industrial-looking late-night disco that plays mostly high-energy retro rock for a crowd that includes lots of students. The club is open Tuesday through Sunday from 10 p.m. to 4 a.m. The cover ranges from €3 to €8 depending on the night.

Metropole, Nollendorfplatz 5 (☎ 030/217-3680; U-Bahn: Nollendorf-platz), housed in an old theater with an Egyptian temple interior, draws a young 20-something crowd. Cover is €10 to €15.50. The club is open Friday and Saturday nights from 9:30 p.m. to 5 a.m.

SO36, Oranienstrasse 190 (☎ 030/6140-1306; U-Bahn: Prinzenstrasse), in trendy Kreuzberg, has two very large rooms, a stage for floor shows, and highly danceable music; the crowd is a hip mixture of gay and straight. The club is open most nights from 10:30 p.m. to 4 a.m.; call first to verify. Cover is usually about €5.

Live music

A Trane, Pestalozzistrasse 105 (☎ 030/313-2550; U-Bahn: Savigny-platz), is a small, smoky jazz club featuring musicians from around the world. The club is open Monday through Thursday from 8 p.m. to 4 a.m., Friday and Saturday from 9 p.m. to 4a.m. Cover is €8 to €13, depending on the night and who's playing.

Knaack-Klub, Greifswalderstrasse 224 (☎ 030/442-7060; U-Bahn: Alexanderplatz), in happening Prenzlauer Berg, is a four-story club with live rock shows four nights a week featuring German and interna-tional touring bands. Show days vary, so call first. You always find dancing on Wednesday, Friday, and Saturday nights. Hours are Monday to Friday 10 p.m. to 4 a.m., Saturday and Sunday until 7 a.m. Cover is €3 to €8, depending on the band.

Quasimodo, Kantstrasse 12A (☎ 030/312-8086; U-Bahn: Zoologischer Garten), is Berlin's top jazz club, where you encounter many different styles of music, including rock and Latin jazz. The club is open Tuesday through Saturday from 9 p.m. to 2 a.m. Admission is free on Tuesday and Wednesday when local musicians perform, otherwise €13.

Wild at Heart, Wienerstrasse 20 (☎ **030/611-7010;** U-Bahn: Görlitzer Bahnhof), is dedicated to hard-core punk, rock, and rockabilly, with bands from Germany and elsewhere playing Wednesday through Saturday nights. The club is open Monday through Friday from 8 p.m. to 4 a.m., Saturday and Sunday from 8 p.m. to 10 a.m. Admission is about €4 for concerts, otherwise free.

Popular bars

Later is better if you want to go out bar-hopping and see what's happening in Berlin. Expect to pay at least €6 for a straightforward drink, more for anything exotic, less for a glass of beer. The following bars are currently popular. These places tend to be fashion-conscious, so you may feel out of place if you show up in blue jeans and sneakers.

Bar am Lützowplatz, Lützowplatz 7 (☎ **030/262-6807;** U-Bahn: Nollendorfplatz), one of the longest and narrowest bars in Berlin, is hip and fun. The bar is open daily from 3 p.m. until 4 a.m.

Harry's New York Bar, Lützowufer 15 in Grand Hotel Esplanade (☎ **030/2547-8821;** U-Bahn: Nollendorfplatz), with minimalist decor, pop art, and photographs of American presidents, has a menu listing almost 200 drinks, as well as a limited selection of food. Harry's is open daily from noon to 2 a.m.

Lore Berlin, Neue Schönhauser Strasse 20 (☎ **030/2804-5134;** U-Bahn: Rosenthaler Platz), features cutting-edge design, great dance music, and an intriguing mix of people hanging around a long and narrow bar with theatrical lighting that makes almost everyone look attractive. Lore Berlin is open nightly until 3 a.m.

Reingold, 11 Novalistrasse (☎ **030/2838-7676;** U-Bahn: Friedrichstrasse), is chic and elegant, geared toward a very late-night glamour crowd. The place is open nightly until 4 a.m.

Times Bar, Savoy Hotel, Fasanenstrasse 9 (☎ **030/311-030;** U-/S-Bahn: Zoologischer Garten), quiet, cozy, and intimate, is reminiscent of a wood-paneled private club in London. This is not a late-night-scene bar, but a place where you can relax in a big leather chair and read *The Times* of London. Times Bar is open daily from 11 a.m. to 2 a.m.

Neighborhood bars: Kneipes and Lokals

Do you want to find a casual, unpretentious spot for a plain old glass of *Bier vom Fass* (beer on tap)? What you need is a *Kneipe* (ka-*nigh*-puh), a cozy place similar to a neighborhood pub in the United Kingdom. A small bar like this is sometimes called a *Lokal* (low-*call*). Many Berliners have a favorite Kneipe where they stop in after work or later in the evening for a

Sampling fresh beer at brewpubs

The first *Bierhaus* (brewpub, or microbrewery) in Berlin, **Gasthaus Luisenbräu**, Luisenplatz 1 (☎ **030/341-9388**; U-Bahn: Richard-Wagner-Platz), opened in 1987 across the street from Charlottenburg Palace. The house beer is a pale, blond, unfiltered, top-fermented beer. You can order beer in a smallish 6-ounce (0.2-liter) glass (€1.60) or in an 11-ounce (0.4-liter) serving (€3.20). The smoky interior of this brewpub is comfortably Old Berlin, even though the building is relatively new. You can order hearty portions of German food (meat, sauerkraut, dumplings, and salads) to accompany your beer. The brewpub is open Sunday to Thursday from 10 a.m. to 12:30 a.m., Friday and Saturday 10 a.m. to 2 a.m.

Gasthaus Georgenbräu, Spreeufer 4 (☎ **030/242-4244**; U-Bahn: Klostergasse), a new brewpub in the Nikolaiviertel beside the River Spree, is named after the statue of St. George right outside. You can choose between beers brewed on-premises; the *helles* (light) is top-fermented, blonde, and unfiltered. The *dunkles* (dark), also unfiltered and top- fermented, has a darkish amber color, a yeasty aroma, and a nice balance of hop bitterness and malt flavor. A small glass of beer is €1.55, a large glass is €3.05. You can also order plates of hearty German food; main courses go for €8.50 to €11.50. The Gasthof is open daily from 10 a.m. to midnight.

beer and a chat with their friends. Brewpubs are also good places to sample beer, and they offer meals as well. See this chapter's sidebar "Sampling fresh beer at brewpubs."

There are hundreds of Kneipes and Lokals in Berlin. A famous one is **Gaststätte Hoeck,** Wilmersdorferstrasse 149 (☎ **030/341-8174**; U-Bahn: Bismarckstrasse). Dating from 1892, Gaststätte Hoeck is the oldest Kneipe in Charlottenburg and still has its original wood panels with inlaid glass on the walls. The bar can be loud, smoky, and raucous. Bartenders pour more than a dozen kinds of beer, as well as wine by the glass. Hours are 8 a.m. to midnight. Traditional food is served in an adjacent room Monday through Saturday from 11 a.m. to 10:30 p.m.; main courses run from €5.50 to €12.85.

Day-tripping to Potsdam and Sanssouci Palace

Frederick the Great's **Schloss Sanssouci** (Sanssouci Palace) in Potsdam is the architectural signature of one of Germany's most dominating personalities. Allow yourself at least half a day to visit this remarkable palace and its beautiful grounds. Potsdam, 15 miles (24 km) southwest of Berlin, a former garrison town on the Havel River, is now the capital of the state of Brandenburg. The town celebrated its 1,000th anniversary in 1993, and has some historic sites, but make Sanssouci Palace your top priority. (See the "Potsdam" map in this chapter.)

Getting there

To get to Sanssouci, you must first get to Potsdam. The trip couldn't be easier: From Berlin, **S-Bahn** line **S7** stops at the **Potsdam Hauptbahnhof** station. Hop on **bus no. 695** in front of the station and ride nine stops to the Schloss Sanssouci stop. The bus fare is €1.40. Cross the road, turn left, and you'll almost immediately come to a flight of stairs leading up to the palace. If you don't want to hassle with anything, you can take one of the **Potsdam–Sanssouci bus tours** offered by the sightseeing bus companies on Ku-Damm (see "Bus tours" earlier in this chapter); the cost is generally around €30 for a half-day fast-track tour.

Finding tourist information

Maps, brochures, and inexpensive guidebooks for both the town and the palace are available at the Potsdam **Tourist Information** office in the Hauptbahnhof (☎ 0331/270-9051), open daily from 9 a.m. to 8 p.m. You find another tourist office at Friedrich-Ebert-Strasse 5 (☎ 0331/ 275-580), open Monday through Friday from 9 a.m. to 6 p.m. (Apr–Oct until 7 p.m.) and on Saturday and Sunday from 10 a.m. to 2 p.m. (in summer, Sat until 6 p.m. and Sun until 4 p.m.)

Discovering the top attractions

Potsdam didn't gain true importance until the "Great Elector" Friedrich Wilhelm (1620–1688) chose the lovely, leafy, lakey area to be his second seat of residence outside Berlin. From then on, Potsdam was a Hohenzollern hangout. To escape the rigors of Berlin court life, Friedrich II (called Frederick the Great; 1712–1786) built in Potsdam a "small" country palace where he could retire "sans souci" (without a care) and indulge his passions for music, poetry, and philosophy.

Schloss (Palace) **Sanssouci** (☎ 0331/969-4202) is open Tuesday through Sunday from 9 a.m. to 5 p.m. (Nov–Mar to 4 p.m.). You can see the palace only on a guided tour costing €8 for adults, and €5 for children and students. Your tour time is printed on your ticket. Before setting off on the tour you're required to don huge felt slippers so you don't scuff the floors. The tour is given only in German, but information sheets in English are available from the guide. You must ask for them.

A timed-entry system is in effect at Sanssouci. Your ticket tells you what time you can enter the palace to begin your guided tour. If you don't arrive early, you may have to wait for a much later tour. Waits in the summer months can be up to three hours long.

Potsdam

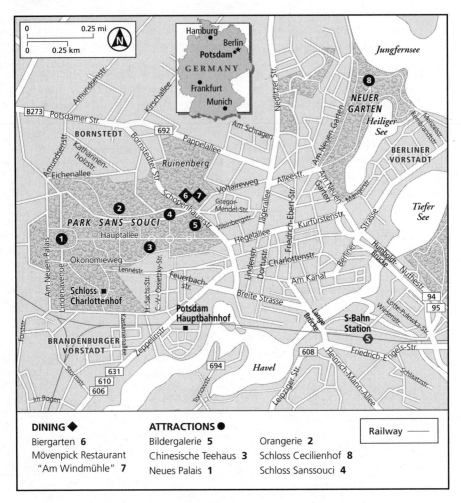

DINING ◆	ATTRACTIONS ●	
Biergarten **6**	Bildergalerie **5**	Orangerie **2**
Mövenpick Restaurant	Chinesische Teehaus **3**	Schloss Cecilienhof **8**
"Am Windmühle" **7**	Neues Palais **1**	Schloss Sanssouci **4**
	Railway ———	

One of the greatest and most beautiful examples of European rococo, Sanssouci was built between 1745 and 1747 as Frederick's summer-house. Here he could let his wig down, discuss weighty matters with French philosopher Voltaire, and make music with composer Carl Philip Emanuel Bach. In short, Sanssouci was a summer resort for an enlightened monarch. All kinds of rococo treasures fill the palace, which you see on a tour that lasts about 45 minutes.

Either before or after your tour, spend some time wandering through the magnificent landscaped **gardens** with their bevy of historic buildings. Fred the Great created the original design for the grounds, and his planning is still evident in the restored vineyard terraces and the area immediately around the palace. All the buildings listed here are sign-posted so you won't get lost on the grounds.

- The **Bildergalerie** (Picture Gallery; ☎ 0331/969-4181), on the eastern side of the palace grounds, was completed in 1763 and displays a collection of works from the Italian Renaissance and baroque eras. The gallery is open Tuesday through Sunday from 9 a.m. to 5 p.m. (Nov–Mar until 4 p.m.). Admission is €2.

- The **Chinesische Teehaus** (Chinese Teahouse) is a little gem of a rococo building resembling a pagoda. Ornamental "Oriental" buildings like this were all the rage in 18th-century Europe. The privileged classes would retire here to drink a new beverage called tea. This building is not open to the public.

- The **Neues Palais** (New Palace; ☎ 0331/969-4255), the largest building in Sanssouci park, was completed in 1769 and used by the Hohenzollern royal family. Inside you see rococo rooms filled with paintings and antiques. The palace is open Saturday through Thursday from 9 a.m. to 5 p.m. (Nov–Mar until 4 p.m.). Admission is €4.

- The mid-19th-century **Orangerie** (☎ 0331/969-4280), west of the palace, contains copies of paintings by Raphael and features ornately decorated salons. The Orangerie is open mid-May to mid-October, 10 a.m. to 5 p.m. (closed Thurs). Admission is €3.

- Built to look like an English country manor, **Schloss Cecilienhof** (Cecilienhof Palace; ☎ 0331/969-4200) was a royal residence from 1917 until 1945. At the end of World War II, the palace was used as headquarters for the Potsdam Conference attended by the heads of the Allied powers, including U.S. President Harry Truman, British Prime Minister Winston Churchill, and Russian dictator Joseph Stalin. Now the palace serves as a hotel and conference center. On a guided tour, you can visit the private rooms used by Crown Prince Wilhelm and Princess Cecelie. More interesting are the rooms used for the Potsdam Conference. The palace is open Tuesday through Sunday from 9 a.m. to 5 p.m. (Nov–Mar until 4 p.m.). Admission for the guided tour is €8.

Dining at Sanssouci

From May through September, you can grab a quick, inexpensive bite at the **Biergarten** kiosk (no phone; open May–Sept daily 10 a.m. to 5 p.m.) across the road behind Sanssouci Palace. The food is basic *Wursts* (sausages) with *Kartoffelsalat* (potato salad). You can eat for under €4 and sit at outdoor tables. In the adjacent Pavillon, you find the fancier **Mövenpick Restaurant "Am Windmühle,"** where you can order a complete meal (open year-round daily 10 a.m. to 6 p.m.).

Fast Facts: Berlin

American Express

American Express has two main offices: Bayreutherstrasse 37–38 (☎ 030/214-9830; U-Bahn: Wittenbergplatz), open Monday through Friday 9 a.m. to 7 p.m. and Saturday 10 a.m. to 1 p.m.; and Friedrichstrasse 172 (☎ 030/201-7400; U-bahn: Friedrichstrasse), open Monday through Friday 9 a.m. to 7 p.m and Saturday 10 a.m. to 2 p.m.

ATMs

You find ATM machines all over Berlin. Two convenient bank branches with 24-hour ATM service are Deutsche Bank at Wittenbergplatz (U-Bahn: Wittenbergplatz) and Dresdner Bank at Kurfürstendamm 237 (U-Bahn: Kurfürstendamm).

Business Hours

Most banks are open Monday through Friday 9 a.m. to 1 or 3 p.m. Most other businesses and stores are open Monday through Friday 9 or 10 a.m. to 6 or 6:30 p.m. and Saturday 9 a.m. to 2 p.m. On *langer Samstag* (longer Saturday), the first Saturday of the month, shops stay open until 4 or 6 p.m. Some stores stay open late on Thursday (usually until 8:30 p.m.). Stores are not open on Sunday.

Country Code and City Code

The city code for Berlin is **30**. Use 30 if you're calling Berlin from outside Germany. If you're within Germany but not in Berlin, use 030. If you're calling within Berlin, leave off the city code and dial only the regular phone number. Berlin phone numbers may have from five to eight digits. See also "Telephone" later in this list and the Appendix.

Currency Exchange

The currency exchange office in Bahnhof Zoo is open Monday through Saturday from 8 a.m. to 9 p.m. and on Sunday from 10 a.m. to 6 p.m. You can also exchange money at American Express (see the beginning of this list for addresses).

Dentists and Doctors

The Berlin tourist office in the Europa Center (U-Bahn: Wittenbergplatz) keeps a list of English-speaking dentists and doctors in Berlin. For an emergency doctor, call ☎ 030/304-505 (24 hours); for an emergency dentist, call ☎ 030/8900-4333.

Embassies and Consulates

See the Appendix for the addresses of the Australian, Canadian, Irish, South African, U.K., and U.S. embassies and consulates.

Emergencies

To call the police, dial ☎ **110**. To report a fire or to summon an ambulance, dial ☎ **112**.

Hospitals

Hotel employees are familiar with the locations of the nearest hospital emergency room. In an emergency, call ☎ 112 for an ambulance.

Information

The main Tourist Info Center in western Berlin is in the Europa Center, Budapester Strasse 45, close to Bahnhof Zoo (U-/S-Bahn: Zoologischer Garten). The eastern Berlin branch is in the south wing of the Brandenburg Gate (U-/S-Bahn: Potsdamer Platz or Unter den Linden). Another eastern Berlin branch is located under the Fernsehturm (Television Tower) at Alexanderplatz. For the hours of each office, see Chapter 11. The three offices operate one information line (☎ 0190/016-316), which costs €.40 to €1.15 per minute.

Internet Access

Berlin's largest internet cafe is Website, Joachimstaler Strasse 41 (☎ 030/886-79630; U-/S-Bahn: Zoologischer Garten), offering 30 terminals that rent for €4 per hour. Another convenient cybercafe is Cyberbar KaDeWe, Tauentzienstrasse 21 (☎ 030/2121-2175; U-Bahn: Wittenbergplatz).

Maps

The most detailed Berlin map with a complete street index is the fold-out Falk plan, available at most newsstands.

Newspapers/Magazines

Newsstands carry *Zitty* and *Berlin-Programm*, which list events around the city. See also the Appendix.

Pharmacies

If you need a pharmacy (*Apotheke*, pronounced ah-po-*tay*-kuh) at night, go to the nearest one and look for a sign in the window giving the address of the nearest pharmacy with nighttime hours (such postings are required by law). For a centrally located pharmacy, go to Europa–Apotheke, Tauentzienstrasse 9–12 (☎ 030/261-4142; U-Bahn: Wittenbergplatz), located near the Europa Center. In Mitte, a few steps from Unter den Linden, is the Dorotheenstadtische Apotheke, Friedrichstrasse 154 (☎ 030/204-4817; U-Bahn: Friedrichstrasse).

Police

To call the police, dial ☎ **110.**

Post Office

The main post office at Joachimstaler Strasse 7 (☎ 030/8870-8611; U-/S-Bahn: Zoologischer Garten) is open Monday through Saturday from 8 a.m. to midnight, Sunday and holidays from 10 a.m. to midnight. Regular post-office hours are Monday through Friday 8 a.m. to 6 p.m., Saturday 8 a.m. until noon.

Restrooms

You find public facilities throughout Berlin and at all train terminals.

Safety

One unfortunate side effect of reunification has been an increase in muggings, hate crimes, and car break-ins. But Berlin is still safer than most large American cities. As in any large metropolis, use common sense and caution when you're in a crowded public area. Single women should avoid the dimly lit streets in Kreuzberg at night.

Taxes

See the Appendix for details.

Taxis

You can hail a taxi along Berlin's major streets. Taxis with illuminated roof signs are available. The meter starts at €2.10. A €1 supplement is added if you call a cab to a specific address by phone. Within the city center, each kilometer costs between €1.10 to €1.25, depending on the time of day. Call a cab by dialing ☎ 030/210-101, 030/261-026, or 030/69022.

Telephones

Finding a telephone in Berlin that operates with coins is now rare; most accept only Telefonkarte (telephone cards), which you can purchase in €6 and €25 denominations at any post office. Some phones now accept Visa cards as well. To make an international call, use a call box marked *Inlands und Auslandsgespräche*. Most have instructions in English. You can also make long-distance calls from post offices.

Transit Assistance

The Transit Authority (BVG) provides U-Bahn information (☎ 030/19449) and S-Bahn information (☎ 030/2971-9843) daily from 6 a.m. to 11 p.m. The same hours apply to the BVG information kiosk outside Bahnhof Zoo, where you can buy tickets and obtain a free transit map.

Weather

You can check the weather online before you go at www.zitty.de.

Web Sites

The best overall Web sites for tourist information on Berlin are www.berlin.de and www.berlin-tourism.de. At both sites, you find information in English on events, nightlife, shopping, restaurants, and more.

Chapter 13

Dresden, Leipzig, and Weimar: Jewels of the East

• •

In This Chapter

▶ Visiting Dresden and its famous museums

▶ Discovering old and new Leipzig

▶ Enjoying the beautiful town of Weimar

▶ Remembering the past at Buchenwald

Saxony and **Thuringia** (Thüringen in German) are two side-by-side *Länder* (states) in eastern Germany that are well worth visiting. (See the "Saxony and Thuringia" map in this chapter.) The cities of **Dresden** and **Leipzig,** with their outstanding museums, historic buildings, and musical heritage, are the largest cities in Saxony. **Weimar,** associated with Goethe (Germany's greatest writer, author of *Faust*) and the German Enlightenment of the late 18th and early 19th centuries, is the cultural jewel in Thuringia's crown.

Both states are rich in sightseeing possibilities. In Saxony, the mighty Elbe River flows through an area near Dresden known as **Saxon Switzerland,** famed for its river scenery and rock formations. Thuringia is considered the "green heart" of Germany because the **Thüringer Wald** (Thuringian Forest) covers much of its southern portion. Narrow, winding roads lead through spruce-covered hills to unspoiled villages that waft you back to the Middle Ages.

Dresden: Florence on the Elbe

Dresden, located 123 miles (198 km) south of Berlin and 69 miles (111 km) southeast of Leipzig, was once known as "Florence on the Elbe" because of its many beautiful buildings. (See the "Dresden" map in this chapter.) Dresden was celebrated throughout Europe for its architecture and art treasures. Since the late 15th century, when the ruling Wettin dynasty decided to make the city its capital, Dresden had been the most important city in Saxony. Under the rule of Elector Augustus the Strong — the pre-eminent personality in the town's history — Dresden flourished as the cultural center of Saxony.

Saxony and Thuringia

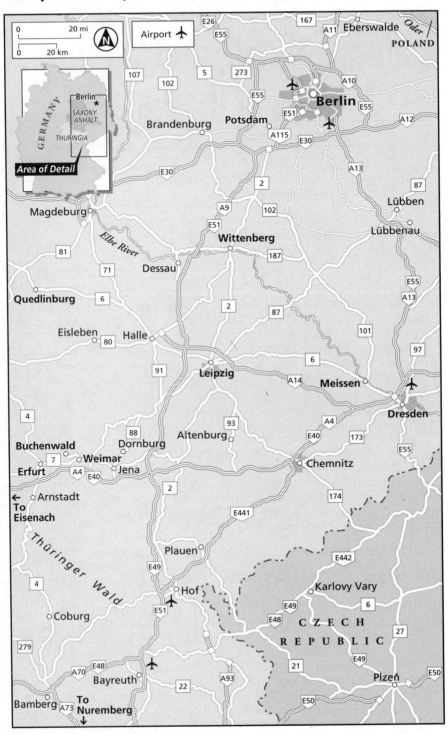

0   20 mi
0   20 km

Airport ✈

GERMANY

Berlin ★
SAXONY-
ANHALT

THURINGIA

Area of Detail

E26
167
A11 Eberswalde
E55
POLAND
Oder

107
5
273
A10
102
E55
✈
Berlin
E51
E55
Potsdam
✈
A12
Brandenburg
A115
E30
A13

Magdeburg
E30
2
87
Lübben
A9
102
E51
Wittenberg
Lübbenau
Elbe River
81
71
Dessau
187
E55
Quedlinburg
6
2
A13
87
Eisleben
80 Halle
101
97
91
6
Leipzig
A14 **Meissen**
4
93
Altenburg
A4 ✈
173
Dresden
88
Dornburg
E40
E55
Buchenwald
7 **Weimar**
Chemnitz
Erfurt A4 E40 Jena
2
174
Arnstadt
To
Eisenach
E441

Thüringer Wald
Plauen
E442
E49
4
Karlovy Vary
Hof
E49
6
E51 ✈
E48
C Z E C H
Coburg
R E P U B L I C
27
279
A70 E48 ✈
21
E49
Bamberg A73 Bayreuth
22 A93
Plzeň E50
To
Nuremberg
E50

Dresden

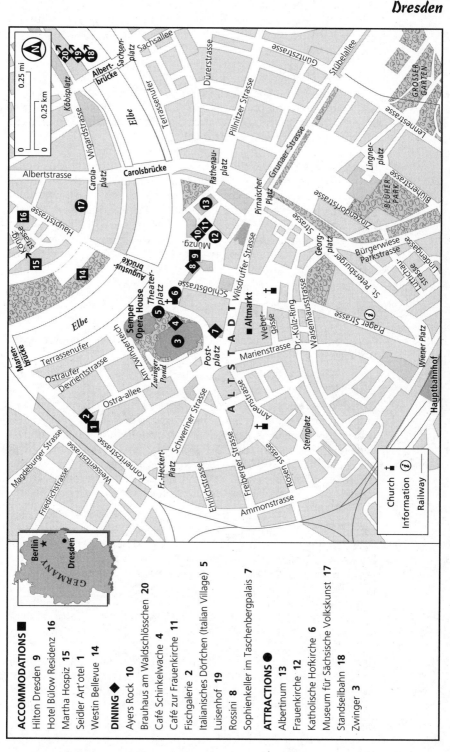

ACCOMMODATIONS ■
Hilton Dresden **9**
Hotel Bülow Residenz **16**
Martha Hospiz **15**
Seidler Art'otel **1**
Westin Bellevue **14**

DINING ◆
Ayers Rock **10**
Brauhaus am Waldschlösschen **20**
Café Schinkelwache **4**
Café zur Frauenkirche **11**
Fischgalerie **2**
Italianisches Dörfchen (Italian Village) **5**
Luisenhof **19**
Rossini **8**
Sophienkeller im Taschenbergpalais **7**

ATTRACTIONS ●
Albertinum **13**
Frauenkirche **12**
Katholische Hofkirche **6**
Museum für Sächsische Volkskunst **17**
Standseilbahn **18**
Zwinger **3**

Then came the night of February 13, 1945, when Allied firebombs destroyed three-quarters of Dresden's *Altstadt,* the beautiful old core of the city. Historic buildings have been rebuilt, but the work has taken decades.

After reunification, Dresden emerged as the top contender for tourists in the former East Germany. Decades of neglect under the Communists had taken their toll on the city's grandest buildings, but Dresden is now in the midst of a dramatic restoration. Many visitors come just to visit the museums in the Zwinger Palace.

In August 2002, Eastern Europe was hit by its worst floods in a hundred years. The Elbe River in Dresden rose to record levels, submerging part of the famed Semper Opera House and forcing the evacuation of art treasures from the Zwinger Palace. As of press time clean-up efforts were well underway. If you plan to visit Dresden in 2003, contact the German National Tourist Office to find out if the sights you want to see are open; you'll find up-to-date information at their Web site, www.germany-tourism.de.

Getting there

Getting to Dresden is easy. This major city has an airport, frequent train service, and a good road network.

By plane

Dresden-Klotsche airport lies 5½ miles (9 km) north of the city center. Lufthansa and other international carriers provide regularly scheduled service between Dresden and cities throughout Germany and Europe. For flight information, call ☎ **0351/881-3360.** A shuttle bus, **Airport-City-Liner** (☎ **0351/251-8243**), runs from the airport to the city center. The trip takes 20 minutes and costs €4.10. You can buy your ticket on the bus. A **taxi** from the airport to the center of Dresden costs about €16.

By train

Dresden has two main rail stations. All long-distance trains pull into the **Hauptbahnhof** (main train station)**,** on Wiener Platz on the south side of the Elbe. The station is within easy walking distance of the Altstadt (Old Town), where you find nearly all of Dresden's major attractions. **Dresden-Neustadt,** the station on the north side of the river, at Schlesischer Park, is used more for regional trains, although some trains stop at both stations.

Getting to Dresden by train from anywhere in Germany or Europe is easy. More than a dozen trains make the trip daily from Berlin (trip time: 2–2½ hours) and Frankfurt (trip time: 7–8 hours). For rail information and schedules, call ☎ **1805/996-633.**

By car

The **A13** Autobahn connects Dresden to Berlin. The **A4** comes in from Leipzig and Bavaria (eventually the A4 will connect Dresden to Prague). The highways run along the west side of the city. Four exits (Altstadt, Neustadt, Hellerau, and Wilder Mann) lead into the center. Trying to find a parking spot in the center of Dresden is not easy. I recommend that you park on the outskirts and travel to the city center by bus or tram.

Finding information

At the **Information-Center,** Prager Strasse (☎ **0351/491-920** information line), near the main train station, you can book a hotel room and purchase a map of Dresden and information booklets in English. You can also buy theater, opera, or concert tickets. The center is open Monday through Friday from 10 a.m. to 7 p.m., Saturday and Sunday from 9 a.m. to 4 p.m. The same services are available at the Information Center located in the **Schinkelwache** (Old City Guard House), at Theaterplatz square. The hours are Monday through Friday 10 a.m. to 8 p.m., Saturday and Sunday 10 a.m. to 4 p.m.

The **Dresden-Card** is good for 48 hours on all trams, busses, and ferries in Dresden, plus admission to all of the top museums, including those in the Zwinger and the Albertinum. You get reduced prices for other museums in the Dresden area and on city tours and boat tours. The cost is €16. You can buy the Dresden Card at any of the tourist information centers.

Orienting yourself

The Elbe River divides Dresden more or less in half. On the south side, between the main train station (Hauptbahnhof) and the river, you find all the major cultural attractions. These include the art museums, churches in the **Altmarkt** (Old Market) and **Neumarkt** (New Market) squares, the Zwinger Palace museums, and the Semper Opera House. **Prager Strasse,** a wide pedestrian street lined with shops, hotels, and restaurants, is the main thoroughfare (and site of the main tourist information office).

On the north side of the river is **Dresden-Neustadt.** Pretty, pink-and-gold, 19th-century houses reconstructed to hold shops, apartments, and restaurants line **Hauptstrasse,** its main street. Germany's reunification triggered a real estate and reconstruction boom in this picturesque neighborhood of art galleries, boutiques, and cafes.

Getting around Dresden

If you plan to visit only the historic center of Dresden, you can easily get around on foot. The **Dresdner Verkehrsbetriebe (DVB; ☎ 0351/ 857-1011** 24-hour service line), the city's transport authority, maintains an extensive system of **bus** and **tram** lines within the city and far out into the suburbs. Service is limited after midnight, but the major lines continue to operate every hour.

The city is divided into fare zones; unless you're visiting the outskirts of Dresden, you only need a two-zone ticket. Purchase your tickets and a transportation map from the vending machines (marked "Fahrkarten") outside the train stations, or at DVB service centers inside the Hauptbahnhof or at Postplatz; both are open Monday through Friday from 7 a.m. to 7 p.m., and Saturday and Sunday from 8 a.m. to 6 p.m. A single ticket for the bus or tram costs €.90 within the inner city, €1.50 for a one-hour ride anywhere in Zone 1. A one-day *Tageskarte* (day pass) costs €4. A *Familientageskarte* (family day ticket) good for two adults and up to four children in two zones costs €9. Validate your ticket (by stamping the ticket in a machine) upon entering the bus or tram.

Seeing Dresden by guided tour

Stadtrundfahrt Dresden, Königstrasse 6 (☎ **0351/899-5650**), offers a daily 90-minute Super Dresden Tour *(Grosse Stadtrundfahrt),* a guided prerecorded (in English) bus tour that leaves from Schlossplatz, adjacent to the Augustusbrücke (Augustus Bridge), and includes a visit to the Zwinger. From April through October buses leave every half-hour from 9:30 a.m. to 5 p.m.; from November to March they leave every hour starting at 10 a.m. You can hop on or off the bus at any of 19 points along the way. The price is €17 for adults, free for children 14 and under. The same company offers a one-hour Historical City Tour *(Historischer Stadtrundgang),* a walk through the city's historic center. This tour departs from Theaterplatz daily at 10:30 a.m. and costs €10. Buy your tickets on the bus.

Sächsische Dampfschiffahrt (☎ 0351/866-090) offers 90-minute boat trips along the Elbe daily from May into October at 11 a.m., 1 p.m., 3 p.m., and 5 p.m. An English-speaking guide accompanies the 1 and 3 p.m. tours from Thursday through Sunday. The paddle-steamers depart from the Terrassenufer quay below the Brühlsche Terrasse (embankment) along the south bank of the river and travel upstream to Loschwitz and back again. The cost is €10 for adults, €5 for children 6 to 14. Buy your tickets at the kiosk on the quay.

Staying in Dresden

Since reunification and the amazing increase in tourism, Dresden's hotel prices have soared, as has the demand for rooms. If you want to stay here, book your room ahead of time.

Hilton Dresden

$$–$$$ **Altstadt**

This new 333-room hotel across from the Frauenkirche is one of the best in eastern Germany. Rooms are mid-size and somewhat short on style but well-maintained. Bathrooms have shower-tub combinations. You find a pool, fitness club, and sauna on the premises, and the staff can arrange baby-sitting. Breakfast is an addition €17.

An der Frauenkirche 5, 01067 Dresden. ☎ *800/445-8667 in the U.S. and Canada, or 0351/8642-777. Fax: 0351/864-2725. Internet:* www.hilton.com. *Tram: 4 or 8 to Theaterplatz. Rack rates: €165–€200 double. AE, DC, MC, V.*

Hotel Bülow Residenz

$$–$$$ **Neustadt**

One of the finest restorations in Neustadt, on the north bank of the Elbe River, this small luxury hotel is housed in a building that dates from 1730. Each of the 30 spacious rooms is laid out differently and furnished with modern designer and reproduction Biedermeier pieces. The large marble-tiled bathrooms have shower-tub combinations. The hotel's elegant Caroussel Restaurant serves nouvelle-style regional Saxon and international cuisine (main courses from €21–€35). The staff is unusually friendly and helpful. Baby-sitting can be arranged. Breakfast is an additional €15.

Rähnitzgasse 19, 01097 Dresden. ☎ *0351/80030. Fax: 0351/800-3100. Internet:* www.buelow-residenz.de. *Tram: 4 or 9 to Palaisplatz. Rack rates: €170–€210 double. AE, DC, MC, V.*

Martha Hospiz

$ **Neustadt**

This simple but comfortable four-story hotel is a 15-minute walk from the heart of Dresden's Altstadt. The 50 rooms have a simple, modern decor and are well maintained. Bathrooms, each with a shower, are on the small side.

Nieritzstrasse 11, 01097 Dresden. ☎ *0351/81760. Fax: 0351/817-6222. Internet:* www.marthahospiz-dresden.de. *Tram: 4 or 9 to Palaisplatz. Rack rates: €97–€118 double. Rates include buffet breakfast. AE, MC, V.*

Seidler Art'otel

$ Altstadt

The six floors of this dramatic postmodern hotel, located a bit out of the center of the Altstadt, are the "artiest" of any hotel in Dresden. The 174 stylish bedrooms are good-size and comfortably chic without being pretentious. Double rooms have bathrooms with stainless-steel sinks and a shower. You find a small gym and sauna on the premises. The hotel opened in 1995.

Ostra-Allee 33, 01067 Dresden. ☎ *0351/49220. Fax: 0351/492-2777. Internet:* www. artotel.de. *Tram: 11 to Haus der Presse. Rack rates: €108–€150 double. Rates include buffet breakfast. AE, DC, MC, V.*

Westin Bellevue

$–$$$$ Neustadt

The 339-room Westin Bellevue is located near the most attractive part of the Elbe River, and many of the rooms have lovely river and Altstadt views. The rooms are large if not spacious, well appointed, and comfortable. The bathrooms have shower units or shower/tub combinations. You find an on-site pool and health club, and the staff can arrange babysitting. A green, grassy, riverside park stretches behind the hotel; you can walk across the river to the Altstadt in 10 minutes. Children under 18 stay for free in their parents' room.

Grosse Meissner Strasse 15, 01097 Dresden. ☎ *800/937-8461 in the U.S. and Canada, or 0351/805-1733. Fax: 0351/805-1749. Internet:* www.westin.com. *Tram: 9 from the Hauptbahnhof stops in front of the hotel at Neustädter Markt. Rack rates: €122–€250 double. AE, DC, MC, V.*

Dining in Dresden

Dresden is bursting with new restaurants of every kind. For a sample of the city's culinary offerings, wander down Münzgasse, the narrow lane that runs north from the Frauenkirche to the river.

Ayers Rock

$–$$ Altstadt   AUSTRALIAN

This likable Australian restaurant with outdoor tables is famous for its cocktails but also serves German and Aussie beer on tap. Menu items include kangaroo rump steak, grilled lamb cutlets, ostrich steak, grilled salmon, and salads. As the night wears on, the bar area becomes a crowded singles scene.

Münzgasse 8. ☎ *0351/490-1188. Tram 4 or 8 to Theaterplatz. Main courses: €8–€15. AE, DC, MC, V. Open: Daily 10 a.m.–2 a.m.*

Brauhaus am Waldschlösschen

$ Neustadt GERMAN

Some 250 diners can fit into the dining rooms in this newly built replica of an old-fashioned beer hall, and another 800 can be accommodated within the sprawling beer garden (open Apr–Oct). The menu features heaping plates of traditional favorites such as roast pork shank, sautéed fish with parsley and onions, *schnitzels* (breaded veal cutlets), soups, *Wursts* (sausages), and roasts. Waldschlösschen beer is brewed on the premises. On Saturday and Sunday afternoons, you can eat and drink to the sounds of an oompah band.

Am Brauhaus 8B, Neustadt (3 miles/5 km northeast of city center). ☎ *0351/811-990. Reservations required. Tram: 11 to Brauhaus am Waldschlösschen. Main courses: €7–€14. AE, DC, MC, V. Open: Daily 11 a.m.–1 a.m.*

Café Schinkelwache

$ Altstadt CONTINENTAL

This sandstone structure in the center of Theaterplatz was built in 1832 by architect Karl Friedrich Schinkel to house soldiers and guards. In 1995, the building was rebuilt and reconfigured into an intimate cafe with outdoor tables on the terrace (you find a Tourist Information center around the other side). Menu selections include pastries, meal-size salads, soups, crepes with mushrooms and chicken, and veal stew. You can also sit and enjoy wine, beer, or coffee.

Sophienstrasse am Theaterplatz. Tram: 1, 2, 4, 7, 8, 11, 12, 14, or 17. ☎ *0351/490-3909. Tram: 4 or 8 to Theaterplatz. Pastries: €2–€5; main courses: €6.50–€11.50. AE, MC, V. Open: Daily 10 a.m. to midnight.*

Café zur Frauenkirche

$–$$ Altstadt GERMAN/INTERNATIONAL

This streetside corner cafe, located directly across from the Frauenkirche, is a good place to sit outside and eat or have a drink. The menu typically has dishes such as grilled lamb cutlet with asparagus and sauce Bearnaise; pastas such as fusilli with ham, leek, tomato, and melted cheese or rigatoni with chicken breast; and pork goulash with cabbage and dumplings. For dessert try the homemade *Quarkkeutchen,* a baked dumpling filled with cheese and raisins.

An der Frauenkirche 5. ☎ *0351/498-9836. Tram: 4 or 8 to Theaterplatz. Main courses: €5.50–€8. AE, MC, V. Open: Daily 10 a.m.–2 a.m.*

Fischgalerie

$$–$$$ Altstadt SEAFOOD

The interior of Dresden's best fish restaurant is a sophisticated affair with an open-view kitchen, dramatic lighting, minimalist design, and a blue-black color scheme. The menu changes every week. Fresh seafood dishes may include salmon with champagne sauce, scampi and white fish served with tomato-flavored *spaghettini,* or bouillabaisse with North Sea fish. Fresh oysters from Brittany, or marinated herring served with black bread, are good appetizers. Fresh sushi is available on Wednesday and Friday nights.

Maxstrasse 2. ☎ 0351/490-3506. Reservations recommended. Tram: 11 to Haus der Presse. Main courses: €14–€22.50. AE, MC, V. Open: Tues–Fri noon to 3 p.m., Tues–Sat 6–11 p.m.

Italianisches Dörfchen (Italian Village)
$$ Altstadt ITALIAN/INTERNATIONAL

This quartet of restaurants in a neoclassical building, erected on the site of a cluster of cottages ("the Italian Village"), once housed Italian work-ers. Each of the four restaurants has a different theme. The **Bierkeller** (beer hall) with a painted ceiling serves traditional dishes such as Sauerbraten (pot- or oven-roasted marinated beef), as does the formal, red-walled **Weinzimmer** (wine room). **Bellotto,** an upscale Italian eatery on the top floor with an outdoor balcony overlooking Theaterplatz, serves dishes such as risotto with artichokes and radicchio and veal scaloppini. The **Café,** a graceful-looking room whose windows overlook the river, is a good place for *Kaffee und Kuchen* (coffee and cake).

Theaterplatz. ☎ 0351/498-160. Tram: 4 or 8 to Theaterplatz. Pastries: €4–6.50; main courses: €10–€18. AE, DC, MC, V. Open: Daily 10 a.m. to midnight.

Rossini
$$$ Altstadt ITALIAN

Rossini offers fine Italian cuisine in a stylish, dress-up setting, one floor above the lobby of the Dresden Hilton. Menu items may include home-made gnocchi with asparagus and Parma ham in cream sauce; filet of perch; *carpaccio* of swordfish (thin slices of raw swordfish) marinated in marsala vinaigrette; Sicilian-style fish soup, or risotto with spring veg-etables. For dessert try the *cassata* (tart) made with ricotta cheese and candied fruit or a *granita* (sorbet) of oranges and lemons floating on white wine.

An der Frauenkirche 5 (in the Dresden Hilton). ☎ 0351/864-2855. Tram: 4 or 8 to Theaterplatz. Main courses: €19–€24.50. AE, DC, MC, V. Open: Daily noon to 3 p.m. and 6–11:30 p.m.

Sophienkeller im Taschenbergpalais
$$ Altstadt GERMAN

The food in this famous cellar restaurant is a modern approximation of a medieval feast. Flickering candles set beneath vaulted ceilings provide suitable atmosphere, as do the waitresses in their traditional German

Dinner with a view

For a fun, easy, and memorable dining experience, take one of Dresden's old funiculars up to the top of a hill in the suburb of Loschwitz and dine in a pleasant restaurant overlooking the city. First, take Tram 8 to Schillerplatz and walk across the bridge. On the other side, at Trachtenbergerstrasse 40, you'll see the **Standseilbahn,** a funicular that began operation in 1895. The funicular runs from 6 a.m. to 9 p.m. and costs €3 round-trip. Take the funicular to the top, a residential area called Weisser Hirsch. Across the street from the station is **Luisenhof,** Bergbahnstrasse 8 (☎ **0351/ 214-9960),** a restaurant with an outdoor terrace offering wonderful panoramic views of the Elbe River and Dresden in the distance. The German/Saxon menu features traditional dishes such as potato soup with sausages, and Sauerbraten with cabbage and dumplings. Main courses go for €7.50 to €16.50. The service can be slow, but relax with a glass of beer or wine and enjoy the view of Dresden's spires. The restaurant is open Monday through Saturday from 11 a.m. to 1 a.m., Sunday from 10 a.m. to midnight (brunch from 10 a.m.–2 p.m.). The restaurant accepts MasterCard and Visa.

dresses, called *dirndls*. You can order dishes such as grilled rabbit with thyme or trout fried in butter. Or you may want to try the famous house specialty, "August's Hunting Trophy": roasted medallions of venison, wild boar, and juniper sauce, served with asparagus and roast potatoes. The restaurant has a menu in English to help you make up your mind.

Taschenberg 3. ☎ *0351/497-260. Reservations recommended. Tram: 4 or 8 to Theaterplatz. Main courses: €10–€16. AE, DC, MC, V. Open: Daily 11 a.m.–1 a.m.*

Exploring Dresden

The amount of restoration work going on throughout Dresden is tremendous. Despite the rebuilding, you still encounter war-time ruins as you walk through the relatively compact **Altstadt,** the historic center where you find Dresden's major attractions.

The **Neustadt** quarter on the north bank of the Elbe is also an area you may want to visit. Although you won't find the museum attractions of the Altstadt here, the Neustadt quarter has Germany's largest concentration of houses from the Gründerzeit (Biedermeier) period.

Albertinum

Altstadt

Between 1884 and 1887, the Saxon king Albert converted this former royal arsenal into a home for his vast collection of art and precious jewelry. Today the Albertinum is one of Germany's greatest art galleries.

Displayed in the extraordinary **Grünes Gewölbe** (Green Vaults) is a dazzling collection of 16th- to 18th-century treasures, including rococo chests, ivory carvings, gold jewelry, bronze statuettes, intricately designed mirrors, and priceless porcelain. You want to save at least an hour for this treasure-trove.

The **Gemäldegalerie Neue Meister** (New Masters Gallery), taking up two floors, is a rich collection of 19th- and 20th-century art. The collection concentrates on German art, starting with moody works by Caspar David Friedrich, the great German Romantic artist, and going up to the brilliant works of Dresden-born Otto Dix (1891–1969), a brilliant painter who ran afoul of the Nazis. Allot at least an hour for this section of the museum.

Brühl Terrace. ☎ 0351/491-4619. Tram: 3, 7, or 8 to Rathenau Platz. Admission: €4.50 adults, €2.50 children and students. Open: Fri–Wed 10 a.m.–6 p.m. Closed 2 weeks in Jan.

Frauenkirche (Church of Our Lady)
Altstadt

Built between 1726 and 1743, the Frauenkirche on the southeast side of Neumarkt (New Market Square) was the most important Protestant church in Germany and had one of the most famous domes in Europe. After the war, the East German government let the charred ruin remain as a memorial. Since 1993, however, a major restoration project has been underway, and today the Frauenkirche is the biggest rebuilding job in Germany. As of press time, the church was entirely covered with scaffolding and expected to reopen sometime in 2005. The area around the Frauenkirche is full of cafes.

Neumarkt. Tram: 4 or 8 to Theaterplatz.

Katholische Hofkirche (Catholic Court Church)
Altstadt

The restored Hofkirche, also known as the Cathedral of St. Trinitas, is the largest church in Saxony. Built by the son of Augustus the Strong, Frederick Augustus II (ruled 1733–1763), the church was constructed in a lavish Italian baroque style with a curving facade and 282-foot (86-meter) bell tower decorated with statues of saints and apostles. Inside, you can see the crypt with the tombs of 49 kings and princes of Saxony. You need about 15 minutes to look around.

Schlossplatz. ☎ 0351/495-1133. Tram: 4 or 8 to Theaterplatz. Admission: Free. Open: Mon–Fri 9 a.m.–4:30 p.m., Sat 10 a.m.–4 p.m., Sun noon to 4 p.m.

Museum für Sächsische Volkskunst (Museum of Saxon Arts and Crafts)
Neustadt

The oldest Renaissance building in Dresden, the 16th-century Jägerhof (Hunters Court) houses this fine collection of regional folk art. What you see are everyday objects used by the common folk — a far cry from the gem-encrusted treasures in the Albertinum. On display are pieces of painted furniture, handwoven baskets, pottery, tableware, and folk costumes. Also shown are toys, carvings, and Christmas decorations from the nearby Erzgebirge region.

Jägerhof, Kopckestrasse 1. ☎ 0351/803-0817. Tram: 3, 5, 7, 8, or 51 to Carolaplatz. Admission: €1.50 adults, €1 seniors and children. Open: Tues–Sun 10 a.m.–6 p.m.

Zwinger
Altstadt

Augustus the Strong, elector of Saxony and king of Poland, built this magnificent baroque palace in 1719. He wanted the Zwinger to be his Versailles and a place where he could show off his incredible art collections. The architect, M. D. Pöppelmann (1662–1736), designed a series of galleries and domed pavilions to enclose a large rectangular courtyard with formal gardens, fountains, and promenades. The semicircular **Wallpavilion** at the west end and the adjacent **Nymphenbad** (Bath of Nymphs), with its graceful fountains and mythological figures, are notable buildings that rely on the exuberant sculptures of the Bavarian artist Balthasar Permoser (1651–1732). On the northeast side is the **Semper Gallery,** a Renaissance-style two-story pavilion linked by one-story galleries; Gottfried Semper added the pavilion in 1846. Today, this entire complex of buildings contains a stunning collection of museums.

The hours are the same for the four museums in the Zwinger complex, but separate admission prices apply. A **Tageskarte** (day ticket) gets you into all four museums, plus the Museum für Sächsische Volkskunst (see the listing earlier in this section), for €6.10 adults, €4 children and senior citizens.

The most important museum is the **Gemäldegalerie Alte Meister** (Old Masters Gallery) in the Semper Gallery (entrance at Theaterplatz 1; admission €3.50 adults, €2 children and senior citizens). This gallery, one of the best in the world, has as its showpiece Raphael's *Sistine Madonna.* The collection also includes Flemish, Dutch, and German paintings by van Dyck, Vermeer, Dürer, Rubens, and Rembrandt. In Galleries two through four, you find a series of detailed townscapes of Dresden painted by Canaletto in the mid-18th century. Canaletto's views of Dresden are so true to life that they were used as reference works during the post–World War II reconstruction of the city. Allow at least two hours for unhurried browsing.

Your ticket for the Gemäldegalerie Alte Meister also gets you into the **Rüstkammer** (Armory), a separate section of the Semper Gallery. Here you can see a small but superlative collection of armor and weapons from the 15th to 18th centuries. Give yourself about 15 minutes to wander through. Admission to the Armory is €1.50 for adults, €1 for children and senior citizens; the entrance is directly across from the entrance to the Gemäldegalerie Alte Meister.

The **Porzellansammlung** (Porcelain Collection), with its entrance in the Glockenspiel (carillon) Pavillon, displays Japanese, Chinese, and Meissen porcelain from the 18th and 19th centuries. The "giant animal room" on the second floor has a collection of 18th-century Meissen animals. Depending on your interest, you can see everything in under half an hour. Admission is €1.50 adults, €1 children and seniors. This collection is closed on Thursday.

On the west side of the Zwinger, to the left of the Wallpavillon, you find the **Mathematische-Physikalischer Salon** (Salon of Mathematics and Physics), with all manner of clocks and scientific instruments of the 16th to 19th centuries. Again, depending on your interest level, you can spend 15 minutes or an hour. Admission is €1.50 for adults, €1 for children and senior citizens.

Theaterplatz 1. ☎ 0351/491-4622. Tram: 2, 4, or 8 to Postplatz. Admission: See above text for individual museum admissions and a combined ticket. Open: Tues–Sun 10 a.m.–6 p.m; Porzellansammlung closed Thurs.

Shopping in Dresden

Dresden's main shopping streets are **Prager Strasse,** where you find department stores, **Wilsdruffer Strasse,** and **Altmarkt.** More-exclusive shops reside in Neustadt on the north side of the river on **Königstrasse** and **Hauptstrasse.**

In Neustadt, you find many high-quality antiques dealers lining both sides of a lane called **Am Goldenen Reiter,** accessible via Hauptstrasse 17–19 (Tram: 9).

A **Trödelmarkt** (flea market) is held on Saturdays from 9 a.m. to 3 p.m. beneath the Albertbrücke (bridge) (Tram: 1, 4).

The best shops

Weihnachtsland am Zwinger, Kleine Brüdergasse 5 (☎ 0351/862-1230; Tram: 4 or 8), in the Altstadt, is the best-stocked and most interesting gift shop in Dresden, selling handmade Christmas, New Year's, and Easter ornaments from the nearby Erzgebirge region.

The oldest manufacturer of porcelain in Dresden is **Wehsener Porzellan,** 3 miles (5 km) southeast of the center at Donaustrasse 72

(☎ 0351/470-7340; Tram: 13; bus: 72 or 76). Its hand-painted objects are the most charming and interesting in Dresden. Anything you buy can be shipped. You can also take a free tour of the studios and factory.

The famous Christmas market

Dresden's **Weihnachtsmarkt** (also called the **Striezelmarkt**) is the oldest Christmas market in Germany. This December event, which began in 1434, is held in the Altmarkt and features handmade regional crafts and gift items and homemade foods. Look for wood carvings from the Erzgebirge mountains, indigo printed cloth and pottery from Lusatia, gingerbread from Pulsnitz, filigree lace from Plauen, Advent stars from Hermhut, and blown-glass tree decorations from Lauscha.

Discovering nightlife in Dresden

Dresden is the cultural center of Saxony, so a variety of nightlife options are always available. Depending on your tastes, you can find classical concerts, rock shows, discos, or just a good place to drink.

Tickets for classical concerts, dance, and opera are available from the **Tourist Information Centers** on Prager Strasse and Theaterplatz.

Opera and classical concerts

The **Semperoper** (Semper Opera House), Theaterplatz 2 (☎ 0351/491-1705; tram: 4, or 8), is one of the world's great opera houses. Several operas by Richard Wagner and Richard Strauss had their premieres in this house, which was built in the mid-19th century and twice rebuilt after that. If you're an opera buff, seeing a performance by the resident company, the **Sächsisches Oper** (Saxon Opera), could be a highlight of your trip. The opera and ballet season lasts from September to mid-July. Ticket prices range from €8 to €62.

The **Dresden Philharmonic** performs at the **Kulturpalast,** in the Altmarkt (☎ 0351/48660; tram: 3 or 5). Tickets cost €10 to €23. Summer concerts take place in the courtyards of the Zwinger.

The main stage for classical theater in the city is the **Schauspielhaus,** Postplatz (☎ 0351/491-350; tram: 1, 2, 4, or 7), where actors perform (in German) dramas by Goethe, Schiller, and Shakespeare. Tickets are €10 to €22. The theater is closed during August.

Bars and clubs

Café Hieronymous, Louisenstrasse 10 (☎ 0351/801-1739; tram: 7 or 8), a small, low-key bar without intrusive music, is open daily from 7 p.m. to 2 a.m. **Die 100,** Alaunstrasse 100 (☎ 0351/801-3957; tram: 7, 8, or 11), is a trendy drinking place set in a cellar and popular with students and artists; open daily from 5 p.m. to 3 a.m.

Sailing through Saxon Switzerland

If you have the time, I recommend that you take a boat trip along the Elbe River. The **Sächsische Dampfschiffahrtsgesellschaft** (Saxon Excursion Boat Company; ☎ 0351/866-090) runs several trips on historic paddle-wheelers and modern boats through a scenic region known as **Sächsiches Schweiz** (Saxon Switzerland), where you see giant rocks, deep gorges, and sheer sandstone cliffs. Other routes travel to Meissen and through Bohemia. Elbe cruises leave from the dock below Brühl Terrace, the esplanade that runs along the south bank of the river. From May into October daily excursions depart for the Saxon Switzerland route. The round-trip cost is €17 per person. The trips take from 3 to 4½ hours. Food and drink are for sale on board. You can check out all the Elbe excursions, in English, online at www.saechsische-dampfschiffahrt.de.

The upstairs cafe at **Planwirtschaft,** Louisenstrasse 20 (☎ **0351/801-3187; tram: 7 or 8**), is open from 9 a.m. to 1 a.m.; the downstairs bar stays open until 3 a.m. on weekends. It doesn't look like much, but **Raskolnikoff,** Böhmische Strasse 34 (☎ **0351/804-5706; tram: 3, 5, 7, 8, or 11**), is a hip dive with sand-covered floors. The place is open Monday to Friday from 11 a.m to 2 a.m.; Saturday and Sunday from 10 a.m. to 2 a.m.

A dance club with room for everyone is **DownTown and Groove Station,** Katherinenstrasse 11–13 (☎ **0351/802-8801; tram: 7 or 8**). Monday is gay and lesbian night, and on Sunday you find dinner and dancing. The club is open daily from 9 p.m. until the last person leaves. Cover is €4.

Leipzig: City of Heroes

Historic Leipzig, located at the confluence of the Weisse Elster and Pleisse rivers, is called a *Heldenstadt,* or "city of heroes," for its role in toppling the former Communist government of East Germany. Visiting Leipzig is worth the trip to see a proud East German city of today, postreunification, shaking off years of Communist rule. (See the "Leipzig" map in this chapter.)

With a population of about 450,000 people, Leipzig is only a little smaller than Dresden. Leipzig has long been a major cultural and commercial force in Saxony, a center of publishing, and home to a famous university with some 20,000 students. For centuries, trade fairs have played an important role in the city's life. Leipzig is also a city with many great musical traditions, including the famed Gewandhaus Orchestra. Johann Sebastian Bach is closely associated with Leipzig, Mozart and Mendelssohn performed here, and Richard Wagner was born in Leipzig in 1813.

Leipzig

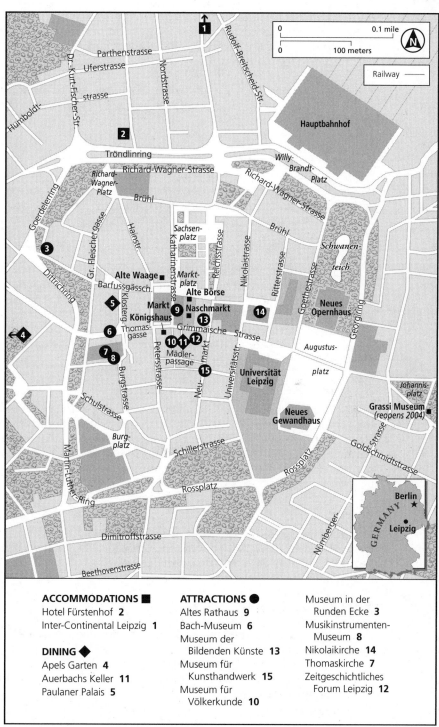

ACCOMMODATIONS ■
Hotel Fürstenhof **2**
Inter-Continental Leipzig **1**

DINING ◆
Apels Garten **4**
Auerbachs Keller **11**
Paulaner Palais **5**

ATTRACTIONS ●
Altes Rathaus **9**
Bach-Museum **6**
Museum der
  Bildenden Künste **13**
Museum für
  Kunsthandwerk **15**
Museum für
  Völkerkunde **10**

Museum in der
  Runden Ecke **3**
Musikinstrumenten-
  Museum **8**
Nikolaikirche **14**
Thomaskirche **7**
Zeitgeschichtliches
  Forum Leipzig **12**

Leipzig was heavily bombed by British and American forces in 1943, and much of the city is rebuilt or being rebuilt. You still find some narrow streets and houses dating back to the 16th and 17th centuries, as well as some *Jugendstil* (Art Nouveau) buildings and arcades from the early 20th century. Today, its skyscrapers and glitzy nightlife give Leipzig a cosmopolitan flair that's unique for this region.

You can easily visit Leipzig as a day trip from Dresden, 68 miles (111 km) to the northwest, or you may want to spend the night in this lively Saxon metropolis.

Getting there

Leipzig has all the transportation options of a major city: airport, train station, and a good road network. You can easily get there from anywhere in Germany.

By plane

Several airlines link Leipzig to major German cities such as Munich and Frankfurt, and to other European destinations. **Leipzig-Halle International Airport** (☎ 0341/224-1156) lies 7 miles (11 km) northwest of the city center. A **bus** runs between the airport and the Leipzig Hauptbahnhof (main train station) every 30 minutes from 4:30 a.m. to 8 p.m.; trip time is about 40 minutes. The fare is €8. The 25- to 30-minute **taxi** ride to the city center costs about €30.

By train

The **Leipzig Hauptbahnhof** (main train station), Willy-Brandt-Platz, is the largest on the Continent. Trains arrive daily from Berlin (trip time: about 2½ hours), Dresden (about 1½–2 hours), and Frankfurt (5 hours). For information and schedules, call ☎ 1805/996-633. The recently restored Hauptbahnhof is one of the most happening places in Leipzig, a new commercial flash point for cafes, shops, and restaurants.

By car

Leipzig is connected to the **A9** (Berlin–Munich) and the **A14** (Halle–Dresden) Autobahns. A number of federal highways (B2, B6, B87, B95, B181, B184) pass by or skirt Leipzig.

Finding information

Pick up a city map at the **Tourist-Information** office, Richard-Wagner-Strasse 1 (☎ 0341/710-4260; Internet: www.leipzig.de), open Monday through Saturday from 9 a.m. to 7 p.m., Sunday 9 a.m. to 2 p.m. You can also book a hotel room here, purchase tickets for concerts, or buy the Leipzig Card.

The **Leipzig Card** is good for transportation within the city and offers special reductions at museums, some restaurants, and performances of musical and theatre events. A one-day Leipzig Card costs €5.90, a three-day card costs €11.50, and a three-day Family Ticket good for two adults and up to three children costs €19.

Attending musical events

Leipzig's famous **Bachfest** (Bach Festival) takes place in May and features performances of Bach's work in the famous Thomaskirche and in other churches and concert halls (see this chapter's sidebar "Bach in Leipzig"). In early June, the city stages its official **Street Music Festival,** when musicians play in the main square, the parks, and other outdoor stages. The **Leipziger Stadtfest** (City Fair), held the second week in June, turns Sachsenplatz and Grimaische Strasse near the university into one big carnival. In late June, Leipzig hosts **Leipziger Jazztage** (Jazz Days), with performances in venues throughout the city. The tourist office has details of all these events.

Getting around Leipzig

If you arrive by train for a day trip, you can easily walk from the train station to all the attractions in the Altstadt (Old Town). **LVB (☎ 0341/ 19449)**, the public transit authority, runs the city's tram, S-Bahn (surface trains), and bus network. Fares are based on zones. An *Einzelfahrkarte* (single ticket) in "Zone Leipzig" costs €1.30. You can purchase tickets from automated machines at the stops.

Staying in Leipzig

Twice a year, usually the first week in September and the second week in March, Leipzig is the site of huge trade fairs that bring in tens of thousands of visitors. If you travel to Leipzig during those periods, booking your room in advance is essential.

Hotel Fürstenhof
$$$–$$$$ **City Center**

Housed in a historic 18th-century building, this hotel has 92 rooms redecorated to reflect the original neoclassical styling. The rejuvenated bathrooms are nicely done and have a combination tub and shower. An on-site health club has a pool and a sauna.

Tröndlinring 8, 04105 Leipzig. ☎ 800/426-3135 in the U.S. or 0341/14-00. Fax: 0341/ 140-3700. Internet: www.arabellasheraton.com. *Tram: 15. Rack rates: €200–€266 double. AE, DC, MC, V.*

Inter-Continental Leipzig

$$–$$$ City Center

One of the city's tallest buildings, and one of its finest modern hotels, the 27-story Inter-Continental reflects the Leipzig of today. The 447 rooms are comfortably furnished and have good-size bathrooms with shower-tub combinations. This full-service hotel contains a health club, pool, and sauna, and has room service. The restaurant **Brühl** serves traditional German food, while **Yamato** is one of the best places in Leipzig for Japanese food. The hotel is a convenient five-minute walk from the train station, and within easy walking distance of all the sights in the Altstadt.

Gerberstrasse 15, 04105 Leipzig. ☎ *800/327-0200 in the U.S. and Canada, or 0341/ 9880. Fax: 0341/988-1229. Internet:* www.hotel-interconti-leipzig.de. *Tram: 4 or 6. Rack rates: €150–€180 double. Special weekend rates. AE, DC, MC, V.*

Dining in Leipzig

Apels Garten

$–$$ GERMAN/SAXON

This restaurant, in a quiet Leipzig neighborhood close to the Altstadt, is known for its home-style German food. Specialties include Saxon potato soup with Wurst, roast duck with arugula, and pork steaks. Although more robust than refined, the cuisine is good. The decor is nostalgically old-fashioned. You can dine out on the porch in warm weather. The restaurant is named after one of the old pleasure gardens that used to adorn Leipzig.

Kolonnadenstrasse 2. ☎ *0341/960-7777. Reservations recommended. Tram: 4, 6, 8, 10, 11, or 13. Main courses: €7.50–€16. AE, MC, V. Open: Mon–Sat 11:30 a.m. to midnight, Sun 10 a.m.–3:30 p.m.*

Auerbachs Keller

$–$$ SAXON/INTERNATIONAL

A group of sculpted bronze characters from Goethe's play *Faust* adorns the staircase leading down to this famous medieval cellar restaurant where Goethe had Faust debate Mephistopheles. Guests have a choice of the Historic Rooms (dinner only) or the Big Room (lunch and dinner), with its painted ceiling. The menu features regional cuisine of Saxony, such as *warmes Bratenneckchen* (roasted pork on brown bread with a pepper dip), along with a selection of international dishes. Kids enjoy the underground atmosphere and can usually find something on the menu to their liking.

Mädlerpassage, Grimmaischestrasse 2–4. ☎ *0341/216-100. Reservations recommended for dinner in Historic Rooms. Tram: 4 or 6. Main courses: €8–€19; fixed-price menu €33–€61. AE, MC, V. Open: Historic Rooms Mon–Sat 6 p.m. to midnight; Big Room daily 11:30 a.m. to midnight.*

Paulaner Palais
$ GERMAN/BAVARIAN/AUSTRIAN

This large, popular restaurant, housed in an 18th-century rococo building, has a restaurant and a more casual pub section, each offering the same menu. The summer courtyard within the building is the nicest place to dine. The menu emphasizes boiled meats such as *Tafelspitz* (beef) with heavy sauces, but you can also get Saxon Sauerbraten, *Weisswurst* (steamed pork sausage) from Munich, or *Rostbratwurst* (roasted sausages) from Nuremberg. The only beer they serve is the Munich-brewed Paulaner Bier.

Klostergasse 3–5. ☎ *0341/211-3115. Reservations recommended. Tram: 4 or 6. Main courses: €8–€12.50. AE, DC, MC, V. Open: Daily 11 a.m. to midnight.*

Exploring Leipzig

Bombing in 1943 destroyed about one-quarter of Leipzig. The city has placed more of an emphasis on constructing the new than on restoring the old. Most of both the old and the new Leipzig that has appeal for visitors is concentrated in the **Zentrum** (City Center), a small, easily walked area south of the Hauptbahnhof (main train station).

Remnants of old Leipzig have been reconstructed around the **Markt,** the city's best-known square. On the east side of the square is the long, gabled, Renaissance **Altes Rathaus.** Reconstructed on the north side of the square is the step-gabled Renaissance **Alte Waage** (Old Weighing House). Across from this house, on the south side of the square, is the **Königshaus** (King's House), once used by the rulers of Saxony as a royal guesthouse (Peter the Great of Russia and Napoleon also stayed there). In the neighboring **Naschmarkt,** behind a statue of Goethe as a student, stands the yellow and white **Alte Börse** (Old Produce Exchange), with curving stairs and stucco garlands above the windows; completed in 1687, the Alte Börse was the first baroque building in Leipzig. To the south of Marktplatz is the **Mädlerpassage,** a famous arcade of shops and restaurants, home of Auerbachs Keller (see "Dining in Leipzig," earlier in this chapter). A short walk leads to the pastel baroque houses along **Katharinenstrasse** and the **Brühl.** Just east of the Marktplatz is the 12th-century **Nikolaikirche** (St. Nicholas Church), where demonstrators for democracy gathered in 1989. To the west rises the high-pitched roof of the 1,000-year-old **Thomaskirche** (St. Thomas Church), where Bach served as choirmaster for 27 years. The **Universität Leipzig** (Leipzig University) occupies the area south of Grimmaisch-Strasse.

Augustus-Platz, to the east of the Nikolaikirche and the university, serves as the cultural heart of modern Leipzig. The immense and not very attractive new opera house occupies the north side of the square; the **Neues Gewandhaus** concert hall stands on the south.

Bach in Leipzig

The composer Johann Sebastian Bach (1685–1750) is Leipzig's most famous citizen. He came to Leipzig at the age of 38 to be choirmaster and director of the Thomaskirche's boys' choir and director of music at Leipzig University, and stayed for the rest of his life. In Leipzig, Bach wrote more than 200 cantatas, the *Passion According to St. Matthew,* and the Mass in B-minor. Bach was the father of no fewer than 17 children (4 by his first wife; 13 with his second). Three of his sons, Carl Philipp Emanuel, Johann Christian, and Wilhelm Friedemann, also became composers. Every May, Leipzig celebrates Bach's musical legacy with the famous **Bachfest** (☎ **0341/913-7333**; Internet: www.bach-leipzig.de), during which Bach's works are performed in the Thomaskirche and other venues around town.

Altes Rathaus (Old Town Hall)

Leipzig's impressive Renaissance town hall was carefully reconstructed after being badly damaged by Allied bombs in World War II. The building houses the **Stadtgeschichtliches der Stadt Leipzig** (City History Museum), which chronicles Leipzig's cultural and political past. General visitors find little of compelling interest, but if you're a music lover, you may want to check out the room devoted to Felix Mendelssohn-Bartholdy, composer and conductor of the Leipzig Gewandhaus orchestra from 1835 to 1847.

Markt 1. ☎ *0341/965-130. Tram: 4 or 6. Admission: €2.50 adults, €2 seniors and students. Open: Tues–Sun 10 a.m.–6 p.m.*

Bach-Museum

This reconstructed house standing in the shadow of the Thomaskirche was once the home of the Bose family, friends of J. S. Bach's. The house now contains the largest Bach archive in Germany. Many mementos of the composer, including scores and letters, are on display. You can see everything in this small museum in about half an hour; if you love Bach, you'll be tempted to linger. An excellent audio guide in English is included in the price of admission.

Thomaskirchhof 16. ☎ *0341/964-4133. Tram: 21. Admission: €3 adults, €2 children, €6 family ticket. Open: Daily 10 a.m.–3 p.m. Tours: Guided tours at 11 a.m. and 3 p.m.*

Grassi Museum

Completed in 1929, the Grassi Museum, on Johannis-Platz just east of the Zentrum, houses Leipzig's important arts and crafts, ethnography, and musical instruments collections. The building complex is an interesting combination of Expressionist and Art Deco styles. A restoration project that will transform the museum complex over the coming years is currently underway. The locations for the three collections listed here are temporary until the museum reopens in 2004.

- ✔ The **Museum für Kunsthandwerk** (Arts and Crafts Museum), Neumarkt 20 (☎ **0341/213-3719**), has a wonderful array of handmade objects from the Middle Ages up to the early 20th century. You find beautiful examples of furniture, porcelain, and glassware. Look for the extremely rare, jointed doll dating from 1526. Admission is €2.50 for adults, €2 seniors and students. The museum is open Tuesday through Sunday from 10 a.m. to 6 p.m., Wednesday until 8 p.m.

- ✔ The **Museum für Völkerkunde** (Museum of Ethnography), Mädlerpassage, Grimmaische Strasse 2–4 (☎ **0341/268-9568**) displays highlights from the permanent collection of cultural artifacts relating to the peoples of the world. Admission is €2 adults, €1 seniors and children. The museum is open Tuesday through Friday from 10 a.m. to 5:30 p.m., Saturday and Sunday from 10 a.m. to 5 p.m.

- ✔ The **Musikinstrumenten-Museum** (Musical Instruments Museum), Thomaskirchhof 20 (☎ **0341/214-2125**), considered one of the best of its kind in the world, exhibits Italian, German, and French musical instruments of the 16th to the 19th centuries. Admission is €3 for adults, €1 seniors and children. The museum is open Tuesday through Sunday from 11 a.m. to 5 p.m.

Museum der Bildenden Künste (Museum of Fine Arts)

In 2004, this collection, — one of Germany's most important art collections with some 2,500 paintings and sculptures including works by Dürer, Rubens, Rembrandt, Rodin, and van Eyck — is scheduled to move to a new museum on Sachsenplatz. The new Museum der Bildenden Künste will be a 112-foot (34-meter) glass cube. In the meantime, you find the collection in a not very inspiring building on Grimmaische Strasse. Highlights include 16th-century portraits by Lucas Cranach the Elder, a work by Rogier van der Weyden, *The Resurrection of Lazarus* by Tintoretto, and German paintings from the 19th and 20th centuries. The sculpture collection contains works by Rodin, Balthasar Permoser (who worked on the Zwinger in Dresden), and Berthel Thorvaldsen. Give yourself at least an hour, preferably two.

Grimmaische Strasse 1–7. ☎ 0341/216-990. Tram: 2, 3, 4, 6, or 11. Admission: €2.50 adults, €1 seniors and children. Open: Tues and Thurs–Sun 10 a.m.–6 p.m., Wed 1–9:30 p.m.

Museum in der Runden Ecke (Stasi Museum)

This museum, one of Leipzig's newest, is chillingly fascinating. The building was once the headquarters of the dreaded Stasi (short for *Staatssicherheit,* or "state security"), the East German Ministry for State

Security. An exhibition called "The Power and Banality of the East German Secret Police" documents the meticulous and paranoid methods by which Stasi agents monitored every exchange of information in East Germany, confiscating private letters and listening in on phone conversations. On the nights of December 4 and 5, 1989, local citizens took a giant step toward toppling the government of East Germany when they seized this building. You can easily spend an hour here.

Dittrichring 24. ☎ *0341/961-2443. Tram: 1, 2, 4, 6, 15, 17, 21, or 24. Admission: Free. Open: Daily 10 a.m.–6 p.m.*

Nikolaikirche (St. Nicholas Church)

The present church was built in the 16th century and has a white, neo-classical interior. In 1989, on this site, a group of 10,000 demonstrators gathered with candles and began the peaceful revolution that toppled the GDR, East Germany's Communist government. The movement started as a prayer group in the Nikolaikirche in 1982.

Nikolaikirchhof. ☎ *0341/960-5270. Tram: 4, 6, 15, or 20. Admission: Free. Open: Daily 8 a.m.–5 p.m.*

Thomaskirche (St. Thomas Church)

Leipzig's most famous resident, Johann Sebastian Bach, was choirmaster in this church from 1723 until his death 27 years later. His body was moved here in 1950 on the 200th anniversary of his death and reburied in front of the altar. Bach wrote his great cantatas for the Thomanerchor, the church's famous boys' choir, first organized in the 13th century. Both Mozart and Mendelssohn performed in the Thomaskirche as well, and Richard Wagner was christened here in 1813. The church was built on the site of a 13th-century monastery and was heavily restored after World War II and again after reunification. Its high-pitched roof dates from 1496. When it's not touring, the choir presents concerts every Sunday morning and Friday evening.

Thomaskirchhof 18 (just off Marktplatz). ☎ *0341/960-2855. Tram: 4, 6, 8, 10, 11, or 13. Admission: Free. Open: Daily 9 a.m.–6 p.m.*

Zeitgeschichtliches Forum Leipzig (Contemporary History Forum)

I recommend that anyone traveling to Leipzig visit this free multimedia exhibition, which opened in 2002. Described as a place of "living remembrance," the exhibit may help you to better understand contemporary German history, what life was like in Communist East Germany, and the events that triggered the fall of the GDR. Set up chronologically, the exhibit uses photos, documents, newsreels, audio, and memorabilia to guide you through the tumultuous last half century in eastern Germany. Give yourself at least an hour.

Grimmaische Strasse 6. ☎ *0341/22200. Tram: 2, 4, 6, or 8. Admission: Free. Open: Tues–Fri 9 a.m.–6 p.m., Sat–Sun 10 a.m.–6 p.m.*

Shopping in Leipzig

Exploring the handsomely restored Art Nouveau **Arkaden** (arcades) that thread through the historic core of Leipzig is fun. **Mädlerpassage** is Leipzig's finest arcade, lined with chic, sophisticated, expensive boutiques.

The **Naschmarkt,** open Monday through Saturday, is a lively, centrally located outdoor market that sells vegetables, plants, cheeses, meats, and a bit of everything.

Leipzig's **Hauptbahnhof** (Central Station) was recently transformed into a giant shopping mall, with about 140 shops and cafes that open between 6:30 and 9 a.m. and close at 10 p.m. on weekdays and 4 p.m. on Saturday.

Held daily in December in front of the Altes Rathaus, **Leipzig's Weihnachtsmarkt** (Christmas Market) is a tradition dating back to 1767. Stalls (open daily 10 a.m.–8 p.m.) sell a variety of craft items and Christmas food and drink. Special organ concerts and performances of Bach's Christmas Oratorio and Handel's Messiah also take place.

Discovering nightlife in Leipzig

Leipzig's active nightlife offers something for everyone, from opera and classical concerts to late-night bars and discos. The area around the Markt is full of bars, cafes, and other entertainment options. For a sampling of lively cafes, walk down **Barfüssergässchen,** just south of the Altes Rathaus.

The **Neues Gewandhaus,** Augustusplatz (☎ 0341/127-0280; tram: 4, 5, 12, 13, or 15), a concert hall built in 1981, is the home of the world-famous **Gewandhaus Orchestra.** Founded in 1781, the orchestra premiered works by Beethoven, Felix Mendelssohn, Franz Schubert, and Johannes Brahms. Ticket prices range from €10 to €37.

The **Leipzieger Oper** is one of Germany's most acclaimed opera companies. Its home is the **Opernhaus,** Augustusplatz 8 (☎ 0341/126-1261; tram: 4, 5, 12, 13, or 15), opposite the Neues Gewandhaus (see the preceding paragraph). Ticket prices for opera and ballet range from €9 to €31.

Leipzig's main theater, the **Schauspielhaus,** Bosestrasse 1 (☎ 0341/ 12680; tram 1, 2, 4, 6, 15, 17, 21, or 24), is home to several arts companies that stage a mix of theatrical and musical productions in German. Ticket prices range from €10 to €26.

Mephisto Bar, Mädlerpassage (☎ **0341/216-100;** tram: 4 or 6), which honors Goethe and the *Faust* legend, is the hippest bar and cafe in Leipzig, great for people-watching. Live music takes place Thursday through Saturday, beginning around 8 p.m.

Weimar: Capital of the Enlightenment

Beautiful Weimar (*Vi*-mar), a 1,000-year-old town on the edge of the Thuringian Forest, is one of Germany's greatest cultural shrines. Some of the country's most revered painters, writers, and composers made their home in this small Thuringian town on the River Ilm, or spent portions of their creative lives here. Goethe, considered Germany's greatest literary genius (he wrote the play *Faust*), lived and worked in Weimar for 50 years. Weimar is also famous in the history of Germany because the German national assembly met here in 1919 to draw up the constitution for the ill-fated "Weimar Republic," Germany's first democratic government after World War I. The town is well known to architecture buffs because the first Bauhaus School of Art and Design was founded here in 1919. During World War II, the Nazis established the concentration camp Buchenwald on the outskirts of this city that had once been a center of the German Enlightenment.

Weimar is a joy to explore, in part because its old winding streets are sprinkled with the homes (now museums) of famous figures. Unlike Dresden and Leipzig, Weimar was not completely destroyed by bombs in World War II. Enough of old Weimar remains to give you a good sense of what the town was like when Goethe lived there.

Weimar is an easy day trip from Leipzig or Dresden. Because Weimar offers plenty to see, you may want to spend the night.

Getting there

Weimar lies 162 miles (262 km) southwest of Berlin, 74 miles (118 km) southwest of Leipzig, and 134 miles (215 km) miles southwest of Dresden. You find good **train** connections to Weimar's **Hauptbahnhof** (main train station) from throughout Germany. Fast InterCityExpress (ICE) trains run from Frankfurt, Leipzig, and Dresden, and Weimar is a stop on the InterRegio express train between Frankfurt and Berlin. For rail information and schedules, call ☎ **1805/996-633.**

By **car,** you can reach Weimar via the **A4** Autobahn linking Frankfurt and Dresden, or the **A9** Autobahn between Berlin and Munich, turning off at Hermsdorfer Kreuz for Weimar.

Weimar

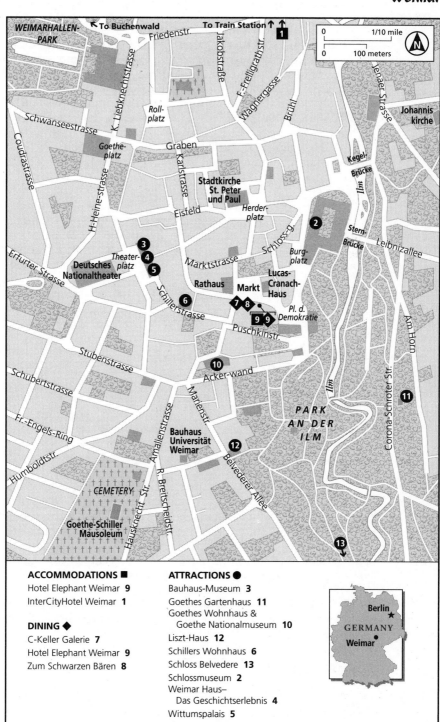

ACCOMMODATIONS ■
Hotel Elephant Weimar **9**
InterCityHotel Weimar **1**

DINING ◆
C-Keller Galerie **7**
Hotel Elephant Weimar **9**
Zum Schwarzen Bären **8**

ATTRACTIONS ●
Bauhaus-Museum **3**
Goethes Gartenhaus **11**
Goethes Wohnhaus &
   Goethe Nationalmuseum **10**
Liszt-Haus **12**
Schillers Wohnhaus **6**
Schloss Belvedere **13**
Schlossmuseum **2**
Weimar Haus–
   Das Geschichtserlebnis **4**
Wittumspalais **5**

Finding information and taking a tour

Weimar has two tourist information centers where you can pick up a map and brochures, book guided tours, buy tickets for cultural events, and get a hotel room. If you're arriving by train, the most convenient center is the **Tourist-Information am Hauptbahnhof** (☎ 03643/240-045;** Internet: www.weimar.de), located in the main train station, open daily from 10 a.m. to 8 p.m. **Tourist-Information am Markt,** Markt 10 (☎ **03643/24000**), in the town's central marketplace, is open April to October, Monday to Friday from 9:30 a.m. to 6 p.m., Saturday from 9:30 a.m. to 4 p.m., and Sunday from 9:30 a.m. to 3 p.m.; November through March, Monday through Friday from 10 a.m. to 6 p.m., Saturday and Sunday from 10 a.m. to 4 p.m. *Takt,* the local entertainment listings magazine, is available free at both centers.

The tourist office offers a two-hour **walking tour** of Weimar daily at 10 a.m. and 2 p.m. The meeting point is the Tourist-Information office at Markt 10. Tours are in German only. The price is €6 for adults, €4 for students, children under 14 free. Buy tickets at either of the tourist offices.

The **Weimar Card,** available at the tourist offices, costs €10 and is good for three days. The card allows you to ride on all buses and trams and gets you into the Goethe-Nationalmuseum and several other castles and museums. The card also gives you a 50% reduction on the walking tours listed in the previous paragraph.

Staying in Weimar

Hotel Elephant Weimar
$$$–$$$$ City Center

The Hotel Elephant is Weimar's most famous hotel, with a past guest roster that includes Bach, Tolstoy, even Adolf Hitler. The elegant late-17th-century facade, fronting Weimar's picturesque marketplace, hides a stylishly contemporary interior. The 99 rooms come in different sizes but are furnished basically the same, with pearwood furniture and Art Deco styling. Bathrooms are large; most have a tub and shower combination. The staff can arrange baby-sitting. Breakfast costs an addition €18.

Am Markt 19, 99423 Weimar. ☎ *03643/802-631. Fax: 03643/802-655. Internet:* www. arabellasheraton.com. *Bus: 10, 11, or 71. Rack rates: €205–€245 double. AE, DC, MC, V.*

InterCityHotel Weimar
$ City Center

This good, convenient, moderately priced hotel sits right across the street from the train station. InterCityHotels is an always reliable German chain. The 134 rooms are not large or luxurious, but they are fully equipped, comfortable, and very well maintained. Bathrooms are small and have showers only. The staff is friendly, and the buffet breakfast is good. One nice perk: The hotel gives you a free bus pass.

Carl-August-Allee 17, 99423 Weimar. ☎ *03643/2340. Fax: 03643/234-444. Internet:* www.intercityhotel.de. *Rack rates: €100–€112. Rates include buffet breakfast. MC, V.*

Dining in Weimar

Hotel Elephant Weimar
$$–$$$ GERMAN/INTERNATIONAL

Weimar's oldest hotel has two restaurants. **Anna Amalia** is modern and airy, a dress-up sort of place with beautifully set tables, a garden terrace, and good service. Its German and French dishes, among the best in the region, make use of local produce and ingredients. Main courses include fish and meat dishes, as well as a fine rack of lamb, veal filet, and entrecôte (a boned rib steak) with red-wine sauce.

Down one flight of steps is the historic **Elephantenkeller** (Elephant Cellar), a place for more-casual dining in a rustic atmosphere. In October, when Weimar's famous *Zwiebelmarkt* (onion market) is held (a tradition dating back to 1653), this restaurant serves specialty onion salads. Otherwise, try local specialties such as "scrap soup" (with vegetable strips, *Knackwurst* (a highly seasoned sausage), and croutons), sweet-and-sour Thuringian pot roast with dumplings, or Thuringian-style grilled Bratwurst on sauerkraut with pureed peas.

Am Markt 19. ☎ *03643/802-639. Reservations recommended. Bus: 10, 11, or 71. Main courses: Anna Amalia €15–€22; Elephantenkeller €3.50–€16. AE, DC, MC, V. Open: Anna Amalia daily 6:30–10:30 p.m.; Elephantenkeller Mon–Sat noon to 3 a.m. and 6 p.m. to midnight, Sun 12:30–3 p.m.*

Zum Schwarzen Bären
$ THURINGIAN

Located next door to the Hotel Elephant, this is the oldest restaurant in Weimar. There's nothing fancy about it, but you can get a good, hefty meal for a reasonable cost. Dishes include potato soup with sausage, rumpsteak, schnitzel with potatoes, and pork medallions with gorgonzola sauce.

Markt 20. ☎ *03643/853-847. Bus: 10, 11, or 71. Main courses: €6.50–€14.50. MC, V. Open: Daily 11a.m. to midnight.*

A cafe for *Kaffee, Kuchen,* and *Kunst* (art)

C-Keller Galerie, Markt 21 (☎ 03643/502-755), combines an art gallery with a cafe that serves beer, wine, tea, and light meals. The art gallery, which sells works by local, national, and European artists, is open daily from noon to midnight. Meals range from €4 to €9.

Exploring Weimar

Weimar enjoys a scenic location on the Ilm River, set against the backdrop of the Ettersberg and Vogtland hills. The **Altstadt** (Old City), with its large park, has many historic sights, all of which you can easily see on foot. **Markt,** the town's main square, remains the lively heart of the old city. Surrounding the Altstadt is the newer Weimar, with broad, tree-lined boulevards and many 19th-century buildings.

Bauhaus-Museum

The focus of this museum is the Bauhaus movement, which was founded in Weimar in 1919 and sought to unify arts and crafts within the context of architecture. The collection of Bauhaus memorabilia includes rugs, architectural drawings, furniture, tea sets, and toys collected by the school's director, the architect Walter Gropius. One room showcases the work of Henry van de Velde, an important architect-designer of Art Nouveau. The museum is fairly compact, so you can see everything in about half an hour.

Theaterplatz. ☎ 03643/564-161. Bus: 1, 2, 3, 5, 6, or 7. Admission: €3 adults, €2 seniors and students. Open: Apr–Oct Tues–Sun 10 a.m.–6 p.m., Nov–Mar 10 a.m.–4:30 p.m.

Goethes Gartenhaus (Goethe's Garden House)

This simple stone cottage with a high-pitched roof, located in the bucolic park on the Ilm River, was Goethe's first residence when he came to Weimar in 1775 as a guest of Duke Karl August. Throughout his life, Goethe used the house as a summer retreat. The structure was built as a garden house in the 16th century, enlarged in the 17th century, and reconstructed in 1996 according to the plans of 1820. You can see the interior, which has a few pieces of period furniture, in less than 15 minutes.

Im Park an der Ilm. ☎ 03643/545-375. Bus: 1, 10, or 12. Admission: €2.50 adults, €1 students and children. Open: Apr–Oct Wed–Mon 9 a.m.–6 p.m.; Oct–Mar 10 a.m.–4 p.m.

Goethes Wohnhaus (Goethe House) & Goethe Nationalmuseum

The large baroque house where Goethe lived from 1782 to 1832 is Weimar's most popular attraction. When Goethe returned from Italy, overflowing with enthusiasm for all things Italian, he replaced the baroque staircase with broad stairs in the style of the Italian Renaissance, filled the house with casts of ancient busts and statues, and designed special cabinets to display his Italian majolica plates. Believing that colors affect mood, Goethe had his dining room painted a sunny yellow, his study a soothing green, and his reception room a calming blue. The house has 14 rooms, some of them pretty much as Goethe and his wife, Christiane, left them. Goethe died in his sparsely furnished bedchamber on March 22, 1832, when he was 82 years old. You need about a half an hour to see everything, longer if you're a Goethe fan; an audio guide in English is available. The house is part of the adjoined Goethe National Museum, but the museum requires a separate admission. In the musuem, you find more Goethe memorabilia.

Frauenplan 1. ☎ *03643/545-320. Bus: 1, 2, 5, 6, or 8. Admission: House €6 adults, €4.50 students and seniors; museum €2.50. Open: House and museum Tues–Sun April–Oct 9 a.m.–6 p.m., Nov–Mar 9 a.m.–4 p.m. Tours (in German): Tues and Fri at 1 p.m., €2.*

Liszt-Haus

Franz Liszt, the Hungarian composer and most famous pianist of the 19th century, spent the last period of his life in this house located at the west entrance of Park an der Ilm. Liszt gathered young musicians around him in the high-ceilinged, handsomely furnished rooms. Displayed in the red-carpeted salon are one of Liszt's pianos and the portable clavichord he used to exercise his fingers while he was travelling. Letters and other personal and musical mementos are also on view.

Goethe and the court of Weimar

In 1775, Johann Wolfgang von Goethe (1749–1832)) was invited to the duchy of Weimar by the teenaged Duke Karl August. Goethe's fame rested on the novel *The Sorrows of Young Werther,* which had become a sensation throughout Europe for its depiction of a suffering, suicidal artist. Duke Karl, Goethe's patron, wanted to surround himself with clever, entertaining people. His mother, Duchess Anna Amalia, set the tone for the salons, which were referred to as the "Court of the Muses." Thanks to Goethe and his friends, particularly the playwright Friedrich Schiller, the little duchy of Weimar gained renown as a center of the German Enlightenment *(Aufklärung),* which brought a new, classically inspired rationalism to German art and literature. In Weimar, Goethe wrote the play *Faust,* the work for which he is most famous.

Marienstrasse 17. ☎ *03643/545-388. Bus: 1, 10, or 12. Admission: €2 adults, €1.50 students and children under 12. Open: Tues–Sun Apr–Oct 9 a.m.–1 p.m. and 2–6 p.m.; Nov–Mar 10 a.m.–1:00 p.m. and 2–4p.m.*

Schillers Wohnhaus (Schiller House)

After his friend Goethe, Friedrich von Schiller (1759–1805) is the greatest name in German literature. He lived with his family in this house, located just up the street from Goethe's house, from 1802 to 1805. The house is furnished as it would have been in Schiller's day. In the attic rooms Schiller wrote his last works, including *Wilhelm Tell (William Tell)*. You can wander through the entire house in about 15 minutes.

Schillerstrasse 12. ☎ *03643/545-350. Bus: 1, 2, 3, 5, 6, 7, or 8. Admission: €3.50 adults, €2.50 seniors, €1 students. Open: Wed–Mon Apr–Oct 9 a.m.–6 p.m.; Nov–Mar 9 a.m.–4 p.m. Tours (in German): Mon 1 p.m., €2.*

Schloss Belvedere (Belvedere Palace)

A pretty, baroque chateau located 2 miles (3 km) south of Weimar, Belvedere Palace was a favorite retreat of Duchess Anna Amalia and her son's "enlightened" Weimar court. The orangerie displays a collection of historical coaches. Inside the chateau, you find a collection of decorative art from the rococo period. The English-style park was laid out between 1814 and 1840. You can visit both in about two hours.

Belvederer Allee. ☎ *03643/546-162. Bus: 12. Admission: €3 adults, €2 children. Open: Apr–Oct Tues–Sun 10 a.m.–6 p.m.*

Schlossmuseum (Castle Museum)

This neoclassical structure, begun in 1789 and completed in 1803, replaced the royal castle that burned down in 1774. The museum has a series of galleries dedicated to Schiller, Goethe, and other famous names associated with Weimar. Of more general interest are the painting galleries containing important works by Lucas Cranach the Elder (including a portrait of Martin Luther), Flemish and Italian paintings, and Expressionist paintings by Max Beckmann and Max Lieberman. Give yourself about 45 minutes to wander through the galleries.

Burgplatz 4. ☎ *03643/546-160. Bus: 1, 5, 6, 8, or 10. Admission: €3 adults, €1.50 children. Open: Tues–Sun Apr–Oct 10 a.m.–6 p.m.; Nov–Mar 10 a.m.–4:30 p.m.*

Weimar Haus–Das Geschichtserlebnis (Weimar House–The Weimar Story)

This overpriced multimedia attraction provides a good introduction to Weimar's history. Wax figures created by artists who worked for London's Madame Tussaud, theater sets, and videotaped projections help tell Weimar's story from the earliest settlers in 3,000 B.C. through the time of

Goethe, Schiller, Luther, and Napoleon. The tour lasts about 30 minutes; audio guides in English are available.

Schillerstrasse 16–18. ☎ *03643/901-890. Bus: 1, 2, 3, 4, 5. or 6. Admission: € 12.80 adults, € 10.80 seniors, students, and children. Open: Daily, winter 10 a.m.–6 p.m., summer 10 a.m.–8 p.m.*

Wittumspalais

A short walk along Schillerstrasse from the Schiller House leads to the elegant Wittumspalais (*vit*-ooms-pa-*lay*), or "Widow's Palace." Completed in 1767, this was the residence of the widowed Dowager Duchess Anna Amalia, who presided over a "Court of the Muses," where artists, poets, doctors, and philosophers met to discuss issues of science, thought, and art. The house, devoted to mementos of the German Enlightenment, has an extensive collection of paintings, silhouettes (all the rage back then), and costumes.

Theaterplatz. ☎ *03643/545-377. Bus: 1, 2, 3, 4, 5. or 6. Admission: €3 adults, € 1 students and children. Open: Tues–Sun Apr–Oct 9 a.m.–6 p.m., Nov–Mar 10 a.m.–4 p.m.*

Exploring the Thuringian Forest

Weimar sits in the northeastern corner of the Thüringer Wald, long extolled by nature lovers for its scenic beauty. Within the forest, spruce-clad mountains rise to about 3,225 feet (985 meters), old castles crown the tops of hills, and dozens of picturesque medieval villages dot the narrow, winding roads. **Erfurt,** 14 miles (22 km) west of Weimar, is the oldest town in the region and the capital of Thuringia. Just south of Erfurt is picturesque **Arnstadt,** once the home of Johann Sebastian Bach. **Ilmenau,** a lively university town south of Arnstadt, is the starting point of a popular hiking trail known as *Auf Goethes Spuren* (In Goethe's Footsteps), which leads to places associated with the great poet. If you want to explore this picturesque area by car, a 68-mile (110-km) scenic road called the **Thuringer Hochstrasse** (Thuringian High Road) runs from Eisenach to Ilmenau.

Shopping in Weimar

A visit to Weimar's antiques stores offers a chance to buy porcelain, silver, crystal, and furniture that survived the devastation of World War II. The most interesting shops include **Antikitäten am Palais,** Schillerstrasse 22 (☎ 03643/59625), and its immediate neighbor, **Kaiser Antikitäten,** Schillerstrasse 22 (same phone). Also appealing are **Antikitäten am Schloss,** Obereschlossgasse 2 (☎ 03643/512-993); **Goethe-Antiquariat,** Kaufenstrasse 7 (☎ 03643/402-567), selling books only; and **Thiersch Antikitäten,** Bräuhausgasse 15 (☎ 03643/402-540).

Discovering nightlife in Weimar

Weimar's main performance venue is the **Deutsches Nationaltheater** (German National Theater), Theaterplatz (☎ **03643/755-334**), where Franz Liszt and Richard Strauss once conducted. (This is also the building where in 1919 the National Congress passed the new democratic constitution that was the basis for the short-lived Weimar Republic.) You can buy tickets for opera, dance, and concerts at the tourist information centers or the theater box office; prices range from €8 to €21.

Weimar's bars and outdoor cafes are good places to drink and talk into the night. You find a good selection to choose from along **Schillerstrasse** and around **Theaterplatz**.

Buchenwald: Remembering the past

About 6 miles (10 km) from Weimar, one of the great cities of German art and culture, in a beech woods *(Buchenwald)* where Goethe and Schiller once walked, the Nazis set up one of their nightmare concentration camps. Bus no. 6 from Weimar's main train station makes the trip northwest of town to **Gedenkstätte Buchenwald** (Buchenwald Memorial; ☎ **03643/4300**), the site of the camp. The Nazis confined about a quarter of a million Jews, Slavs, Gypsies, homosexuals, political prisoners, prisoners of war, and others in this work camp from 1937 until the camp's liberation by the U.S. Army in 1945. At least 56,000 people died at Buchenwald, and many thousands of others were sent from here to death camps in the east. Later, Soviet occupation forces also used the site as an internment camp. Between 1945 and 1951, the Soviets sent thousands of prisoners here to die. A memorial with a cluster of "larger than life" people, representing victims of fascism, honors the people from 32 nations who lost their lives at Buchenwald. The museum reflects both the Soviet and the Nazi past of the camp. You can visit Buchenwald May through September, Tuesday to Sunday from 9:45 a.m. to 6 p.m.; October through April, Tuesday to Sunday from 8:45 a.m. to 5 p.m. Admission is free. To reach the memorial, take bus no. 6 marked "Buchenwald."

Part IV

Munich and Southern Germany

"I think we should arrange to be there for the 'Sauerbraten–Bratwurst–Sauerkraut Week,' and then shoot over to the 'Antacid–Breathmint–Festival.'"

In this part . . .

Southern Germany is very different from other regions in Germany, as you discover in this part. I devote **Chapter 14** entirely to **Munich,** the beautiful capital of Bavaria. You find everything you need to know about Germany's "secret capital": how to get there and get around, how to find a fine hotel or restaurant, and what to see. I describe picturesque towns and must-see attractions in the **Bavarian Alps** south of Munich in **Chapter 15,** which includes information about visiting **Neuschwanstein** and **Linderhof,** two of the dramatic fairy-tale castles built by Ludwig II. I also tell you about driving through the Bavarian Alps on the scenic **Deutsche Alpenstrasse** (German Alpine Road). In **Chapter 16,** I highlight lovely Lake Constance, known as the **Bodensee** in Germany, and the **Schwarzwald,** or Black Forest, one of the most scenically delightful areas in all of Deutschland, home to the cities of **Freiburg** and **Baden-Baden.**

Chapter 14

Munich: Capital of Gemütlichkeit

Munich (München, pronounced *Mewn*-shin, in German), the capital of Bavaria, is a town that likes to celebrate. Walk through the *Altstadt* (Old Town) on a warm, sunny day or a balmy night and you see people sitting outside, in every square, drinking, eating, and enjoying life. **Oktoberfest,** which draws some 7 million revelers, starts in late September and lasts for 16 days. Before Lent, from January through February, the city goes into party mode again and celebrates **Fasching** (Carnival), a whirl of colorful parades, masked balls, and revelry. Throughout the year, people gather in the giant beer halls and beer gardens to quaff liters of beer, listen to the oom-pah-pah bands, and have a good time.

Oom-pah-pah aside, Munich is also a rich, elegant, sophisticated city, with an unparalleled array of artistic and cultural treasures. World-class museums, palaces, concert halls, and theaters are part and parcel of life in the Bavarian capital. The city is all about prosperity and good-natured *Gemütlichkeit,* one of those hard-to-translate words that means something like cozy and/or good-natured. Think of *Gemütlichkeit* as a kind of cozy charm, and you'll get the picture.

If you believe the polls, Munich is the Germans' first choice as a desirable place to live. Many Germans — especially the 1.5 million people who live in Munich — think of the city as Germany's secret capital. Munich offers so much to visitors that I recommend you give yourself at least three days here.

> # The little monk of Munich
>
> In the ninth century, a small village located near a Benedictine abbey on the river Isar called itself Mönch, German for "monk." Since that time, Munich's coat of arms has included a figure of the *Münchner Kindl,* or "little monk."

Getting There

As one of Germany's major cities, Munich has no lack of transportation options. Like Frankfurt, Munich has an international airport, so you can fly there directly from the United States. The city is easily accessible from anywhere within Germany or Europe.

By plane

Munich's Franz Josef Strauss International Airport (☎ 089/9752-1313 flight information; Internet: www.munich-airport.com) is located 18 miles (29 km) northeast of the city center. Opened in 1992, the airport is among the most modern and efficient in the world. The S-8 S-Bahn (☎ 089/4142-4344) train connects the airport with the *Hauptbahnhof* (main railroad station) in downtown Munich. Trains leave from the S-Bahn platform beneath the airport every 20 minutes between 4:45 a.m. (5:45 a.m. on Saturday and Sunday) and 12:15 a.m. The fare for the 40-minute trip is €8 adults, €.90 children. The Lufthansa Airport Bus (☎ 089/323-040) also runs between the airport and the main train station in Munich every 20 minutes from 5:10 a.m. to 7:50 p.m. The trip takes about 40 minutes and costs €9 for adults, €4.50 for children. A taxi to the city center costs about €70 and can take more than an hour if traffic is heavy.

By train

You can easily reach Munich by train from any city in Germany or Europe. Daily trains arrive from Frankfurt (trip time: 3¾ hours) and Berlin (trip time: 8 hours). Munich's **Hauptbahnhof,** on Bahnhofplatz near the city center, is one of Europe's largest train stations, with a hotel, restaurants, shopping, and banking facilities. You find a train information office on the mezzanine level, open daily from 7 a.m. to 8 p.m.; you can also call **Deutsche Bahn** (German Rail; ☎ 01805/996-633 for train information and schedules; an English speaker will be available to help you). Connected to the rail station are the city's extensive **S-Bahn** rapid-transit system and the **U-Bahn** (subway) system.

By car

I do not recommend driving in Munich. Most of downtown is a pedestrian-only area, wonderful if you're a walker, a nightmare if you're a driver. Traffic jams are frequent, and parking spaces are elusive and costly. If you plan on making excursions into the countryside, renting a car in the city center instead of trekking out to the airport is more convenient. Car-rental companies with windows at the main train station include **Avis** (☎ 089/1260-000), **Hertz** (☎ 089/1295-001), and **Sixt Autovermietung** (☎ 089/550-2447).

Finding Information After You Arrive

The tourist office, **Fremdenverkehrsamt München** (☎ 089/233-0300; Internet: www.muenchen-tourist.de), operates a **Tourist Information center** (☎ 089/2333-0257) in the main train station (Bahnhofplatz 2, adjacent to the DER Reisebüro/German Rail Travel Office). You can pick up a map of Munich, obtain information on cultural events, and book a hotel room. The center is open Monday through Saturday from 9 a.m. to 8 p.m. and Sunday from 10 a.m. to 6 p.m. You find another branch of the tourist office in the city center at Marienplatz in the **Neues Rathaus** (New Town Hall; ☎ 089/2333-0272); hours are Monday through Friday from 10 a.m. to 8 p.m., Saturday from 10 a.m. to 4 p.m.

Orienting Yourself in Munich

The **Altstadt,** or Old Town, is an oval-shaped pedestrian-only district on the west bank of the Isar River. (See the "Munich Neighborhoods" map in this chapter.) Munich's **Hauptbahnhof** (main train station) lies just west of the Altstadt. **Marienplatz,** the Altstadt's most important square, is where you find several important churches, the **Residenz** (former royal palace), the **National Theater,** and the **Viktualienmarkt,** a wonderfully lively outdoor market. Between Marienplatz and the Nationaltheater is the **Platzl** quarter, famed for its nightlife, restaurants, and the landmark **Hofbräuhaus,** the most famous beer hall in the world.

Odeonsplatz, to the north of Marienplatz, is Munich's most beautiful square. Running west from Odeonsplatz is Briennerstrasse, a wide shopping avenue that leads to **Königsplatz** (King's Square). Flanking this large square, in an area known as the **Museum Quarter**, are three neoclassical buildings constructed by Ludwig I and housing Munich's antiquities: the **Propyläen,** the **Glyptothek,** and the **Antikensammlungen.** Another triad of world-famous art museums — the **Alte Pinakothek** (Old Masters Gallery), the **Neue Pinakothek** (New Masters Gallery), and the brand-new in 2002 **Pinakothek Moderne Kunst** (Gallery of Modern Art) — also lie in the Museum Quarter, just northeast of Königsplatz.

Munich Neighborhoods

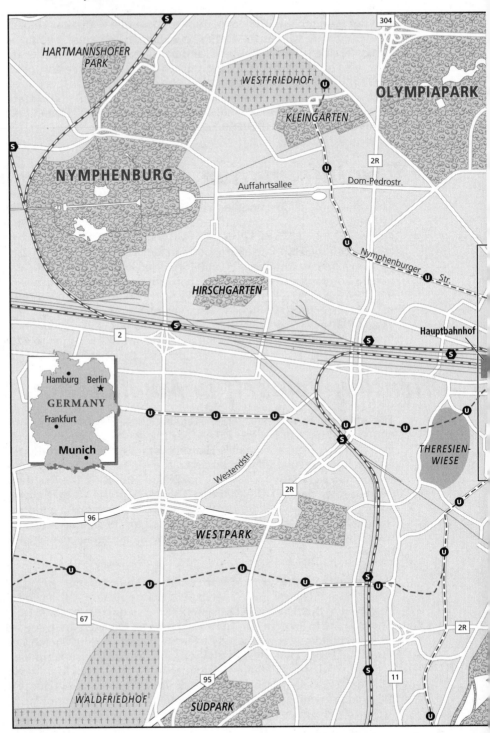

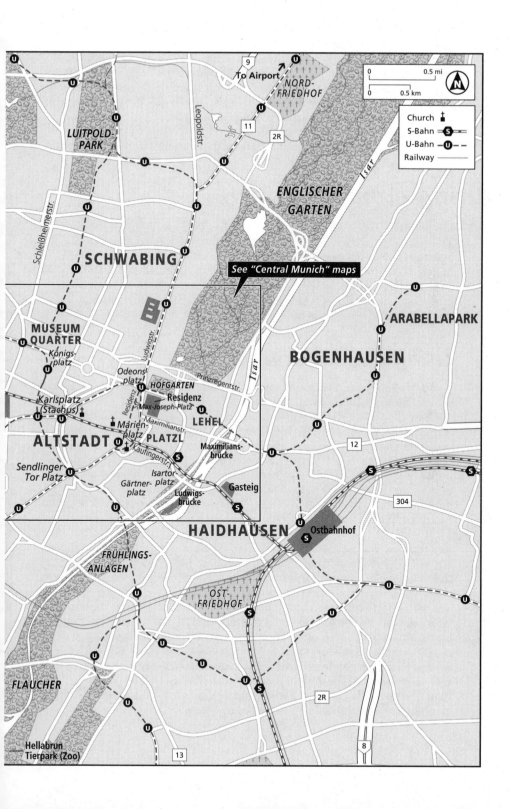

See "Central Munich" maps

Ludwigstrasse connects the Altstadt with **Schwabing,** a former artists' quarter located north of the Altstadt and known for its cafes, restaurants, and nightlife. **Olympiapark,** site of the 1972 Olympics, is northwest of Schwabing. The sprawling park known as the **Englischer Garten** is located east of Schwabing. East of the Isar River lie **Bogenhausen** and **Haidhausen,** leafy neighborhoods just outside the city center where you find some hotels and restaurants. **Theresienwiese,** site of the annual Oktoberfest, and **Schloss Nymphenburg** (Nymphenburg Palace), one of Germany's most beautiful palaces, are both located west of the Altstadt.

Getting around Munich

Munich is a large city, only slightly smaller than Berlin or Hamburg. The best way to explore is by walking and using the excellent public transportation system. Subways (U-Bahn), trams (Strassenbahn), buses, and light-rail lines (S-Bahn) make getting anywhere in the city easy. In the Altstadt, you can walk to all the attractions — in fact you have to, because the Altstadt is a car-free zone. For information, call the public transportation authority, **MVV,** at ☎ **089/4142-4344.**

Using public transportation

You'll probably use the underground **U-Bahn** (subway) and the aboveground **Strassenbahn** (tram) systems most frequently. The same ticket entitles you to ride U-Bahn, S-Bahn, trams, and buses. Purchase tickets from vending machines marked *Fahrkarten* in U-Bahn and S-Bahn stations; the machines display instructions in English. You can also buy tickets in the tram or from a bus driver. Tickets must then be **validated** in the machines found on platforms and in buses and trams; stick your ticket into the machine, which stamps it with the date and time. A validated tickets is valid for two hours. You can transfer as often as you like to any public transportation as long as you travel in the same direction.

Munich has four concentric fare zones. Most, if not all, of your sightseeing will take place in Zone 1, which includes the city center. A **single ticket** (*Einzelfahrkarte*) for adults and children in Zone 1 costs €2.

The **München Welcome Card** lets you ride all public transportation and offers discounts of up to 50% off on major tourist attractions and city tours. You buy the Welcome Card at the tourist office. A **Tageskarte** (day ticket) good for a day of travel within the city limits costs €5.50 for adults, €1.70 for children 6 to 14. A **3-Tageskarte** (3-day ticket) costs €11. A **Partner 3-Tageskarte,** good for up to five people traveling together, costs €17.50. You can buy these cards from the ticket vending machines or at station ticket windows.

Catching a cab

Taxis are cream-colored, plentiful, and expensive. You can get a taxi at one of the stands located all over the city, or you can hail a cab on the street if its rooftop light is illuminated. Taxi fares begin at €2.50; each additional kilometer costs €1.20. Call ☎ **089/21610** for a radio-dispatched taxi.

Staying in Style

Hotels in Munich are more expensive than elsewhere in Germany, and rooms can be scarce, particularly during Oktoberfest or when trade fairs are in town. I strongly recommend that you book your Munich hotel room well in advance. On the precept that anyone can find an expensive hotel in Munich, I weighted my choices more toward those in the low to moderate range in central Munich.

The **Fremdenverkehrsamt** (tourist office) in the main train station (see "Finding Information After You Arrive," earlier in this chapter) can book a room for you and give you a map with instructions for reaching it. The service is free, but the office collects a 10% deposit of the total value of the room; the hotel then deducts this amount from your hotel. For direct access to the hotel booking department, call ☎ **089/2333-0123.**

For locations, see the "Central Munich Accommodations and Dining" map in this chapter.

The top hotels

See also the listing for the outstanding **Kempinski Hotel Vier Jahreszeiten München** ($$$$) in Chapter 22.

Advokat Hotel
$$–$$$ Altstadt

You don't find frills or frou-frou in this streamlined 50-room hotel in a 1930s apartment building. Advokat Hotel is strictly minimalist in approach and has an understated elegance. The rooms are medium-size, with clean, simple furnishings. Each room comes with a compact bathroom, most with tub and shower.

Baaderstrasse 1, 80469 München. ☎ *089/216-310. Fax: 089/216-3190. Internet:* www. hotel-advokat.de. *S-Bahn: Isartor (then a 5-minute walk south on Zweibrücken Strasse and west on Baaderstrasse). Rack rates: €165–€185 double. Rates include breakfast. MC, V.*

Central Munich Accommodations and Dining

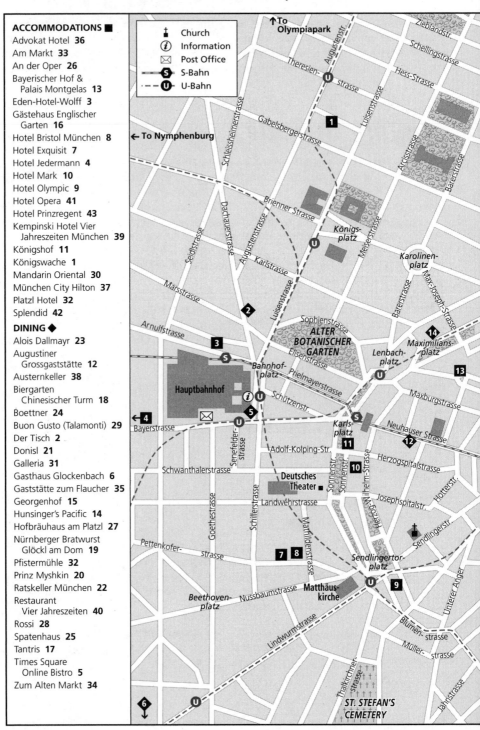

ACCOMMODATIONS ■
Advokat Hotel **36**
Am Markt **33**
An der Oper **26**
Bayerischer Hof &
    Palais Montgelas **13**
Eden-Hotel-Wolff **3**
Gästehaus Englischer
    Garten **16**
Hotel Bristol München **8**
Hotel Exquisit **7**
Hotel Jedermann **4**
Hotel Mark **10**
Hotel Olympic **9**
Hotel Opera **41**
Hotel Prinzregent **43**
Kempinski Hotel Vier
    Jahreszeiten München **39**
Königshof **11**
Königswache **1**
Mandarin Oriental **30**
München City Hilton **37**
Platzl Hotel **32**
Splendid **42**

DINING ◆
Alois Dallmayr **23**
Augustiner
    Grossgaststätte **12**
Austernkeller **38**
Biergarten
    Chinesischer Turm **18**
Boettner **24**
Buon Gusto (Talamonti) **29**
Der Tisch **2**
Donisl **21**
Galleria **31**
Gasthaus Glockenbach **6**
Gaststätte zum Flaucher **35**
Georgenhof **15**
Hunsinger's Pacific **14**
Hofbräuhaus am Platzl **27**
Nürnberger Bratwurst
    Glöckl am Dom **19**
Pfistermühle **32**
Prinz Myshkin **20**
Ratskeller München **22**
Restaurant
    Vier Jahreszeiten **40**
Rossi **28**
Spatenhaus **25**
Tantris **17**
Times Square
    Online Bistro **5**
Zum Alten Markt **34**

Legend:
✝ Church
ⓘ Information
✉ Post Office
Ⓢ S-Bahn
Ⓤ U-Bahn

↑To Olympiapark

← To Nymphenburg

Hauptbahnhof

ALTER BOTANISCHER GARTEN

Deutsches Theater

Matthäus-kirche

ST. STEFAN'S CEMETERY

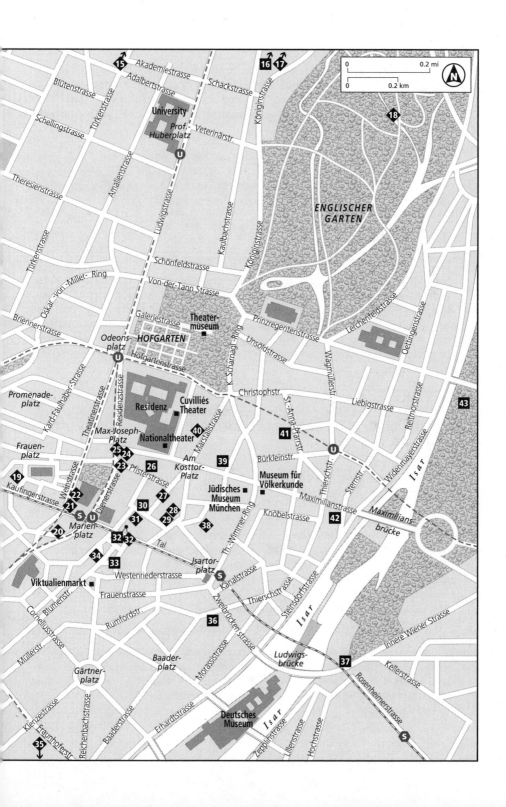

An der Oper

$$ Altstadt

This five-story hotel, dating from 1969, is wonderfully situated for sight-seeing and shopping in the Altstadt. The decor is basic modern without being particularly distinguished. The 68 rooms are on the small side but have double-glazed windows and a small sitting area. The bathrooms are small, too, and come with a shower.

Falkenturmstrasse 11 (just off Maximilianstrasse, near Marienplatz), 80331 München. ☎ *089/290-0270. Fax: 089/2900-2729. Tram: 19 to Nationaltheater stop (then a 5-minute walk south on Sparkassen Strasse and east on Falkenturmstrasse). Rack rates: €144–€174 double. Rates include buffet breakfast. AE, MC, V.*

Eden-Hotel-Wolff

$$–$$$$ Near train station

From the outside this large hotel in the vicinity of the train station looks a bit austere, but the interior has a warm, traditional look with chandeliers and wood paneling. Most of the 211 rooms are fairly large, and all are nicely furnished in a variety of styles. Bathrooms are larger than average, with tub and shower. For those with sensitive skin, some units are hypoallergenic. One child under age 6 is allowed to stay free in the parents' room.

Arnulfstrasse 4–8, 80335 München. ☎ *089/551-150. Fax: 089/5511-5555. Internet: www.ehw.de. U-/S-Bahn: Hauptbahnhof (the hotel is opposite the north side of the train station). Rack rates: €169–€282 double. Rates include buffet breakfast. AE, DC, MC, V.*

Gästehaus Englischer Garten

$ Schwabing

This 25-room guesthouse near the Englischer Garten is quiet, charming, and an excellent value. The rooms are small to medium in size and decorated with a homey mixture of antiques, old-fashioned beds, and Oriental rugs. The bathrooms are small, with showers only. You can save a few euros by renting one of the six rooms that share bathrooms. In an annex across the street are 15 small apartments, each with a bathroom and a kitchenette. Breakfast costs an extra €9; on nice mornings, you can eat outside in the back garden.

Liebergesellstrasse 8, 80802 München-Schwabing. ☎ *089/383-9410. Fax: 089/3839-4133. U-Bahn: Münchener Freiheit (then a 10-minute walk east on Haimhäuserstrasse to Erninger Platz and east on Liebergesellstrasse). Rack rates: €60–€82 double without bathroom; €68–€95 double with bathroom. AE, MC, V.*

Hotel Bristol München
$$–$$$$ **Altstadt**

Built around 1960, this boxy-looking hotel is a congenial, convenient place to stay in central Munich. The 57 rooms are pretty small, but each has a little balcony. Furnishings are comfortable but nondescript. Bathrooms are compact and have showers. For a quieter room, request one that faces the courtyard.

Pettenkoferstrasse 2, 80336 München. ☎ *089/548-2220. Fax: 089/591-451. Internet:* www.bristol-muc.com. *U-Bahn: Sendlinger Tor (then a 5-minute walk west on Pettenkoferstrasse). Rack rates: €130–€249 double. Rates include breakfast. AE, MC, V.*

Hotel Exquisit
$–$$ **Altstadt**

This small, appealing hotel built in 1988 in the same vicinity as the Hotel Bristol München (see the preceding listing) is located on a quiet residential street in the heart of Munich. The 50 rooms are large and comfortably furnished. About half of them overlook a pretty garden. The small bathrooms contain tiled showers. The staff is unusually pleasant. The hotel is attached to the famous Augustiner beer hall and restaurant (see the next section, "Dining Out").

Pettenkoferstrasse 4, 80336 München. ☎ *089/551-9900. Fax: 089/5519-9499. Internet:* www.augustiner-restaurant.com. *U-Bahn: Sendlinger Tor (then a 3-minute walk west on Pettenkoferstrasse). Rack rates: €112–€174 double. Rates include breakfast. AE, DC, MC, V.*

Hotel Jedermann
$–$$ **Near train station**

Jedermann means "everyman," and that translates here into affordable, family-friendly prices (as well as cribs and cots, adjoining rooms, and babysitting). This pleasant, family-run hotel offers a central location and 55 comfortable rooms, most with roomy, shower-only bathrooms. Fourteen newly redecorated rooms have air conditioning; you can check your e-mail on the computer in the lobby. The hotel serves a generous breakfast buffet.

Bayerstrasse 95, 80335 München. ☎ *089/543-240. Fax: 089/5432-4111. Internet:* www.hotel-jedermann.de. *U-/S-Bahn: Hauptbahnhof (then a 10-minute walk west on Bayerstrasse from south exit) or Tram 19 to Herman-Lingg-Strasse (the stop across from the hotel). Rack rates: €49–€74 double without bathroom; €67–€149 double with bathroom. Rates include buffet breakfast. MC, V.*

Hotel Olympic

$–$$ **Altstadt**

Built as a private villa around 1900, this hotel has a high-ceilinged lobby and a large wood-paneled breakfast room that retain much of their original Victorian detailing. The 38 rooms, however, are white, minimalist, and modern. Most of the midsize bathrooms come with shower only. The hotel is popular with gay travelers because of its location near several gay bars and cafes.

Hans Sachs Strasse 4, 80469 München. ☎ **089/231-890.** *Fax: 089/2318-9199. Internet:* www.hotel-olympic.de. *U-Bahn: Sendlinger Tor, then Tram 18 or 20 east to Hans Sachs Strasse. Rack rates: €118–€134 double. Rates include breakfast. AE, DC, MC, V.*

Hotel Opera

$$$ **Altstadt**

A turn-of-the-century Italianate building with a courtyard and garden houses this small, elegant, boutique hotel. The 25 distinctively decorated rooms have country antiques or a postmodern look. Some of the rooms have small balconies. Rooms in the rear on the third and fourth floors are quieter but also smaller than those facing the street. The bathrooms have a tub and shower. The hotel is a short walk from chic Maximilianstrasse and several major attractions.

St.-Anna-Strasse 10, 80538 München. ☎ **089/225-533.** *Fax: 089/2104-0977. Internet:* www.hotelopera.de. *U-Bahn: Lehel (then a 5-minute walk north on St.-Anna-Strasse). Rack rates: €185–€210 double. Rates include breakfast. AE, MC, V.*

Hotel Prinzregent

$$$–$$$$ **Bogenhausen**

This quiet hotel on the east bank of the Isar has a lobby, dining area, and 64 rooms that are tastefully decorated in a Bavarian-chalet style with lots of wood paneling and carved wooden furniture. The rooms are fairly large and have good bathrooms. The level of service is exceptional. The hotel is a 10-minute walk from Maximilianstrasse and the center of the city.

Ismaninger Strasse 42–44, 81675 Munich. ☎ **089/416-050.** *Fax: 089/4160-5466. Internet:* www.hotel-prinzeregent.de. *U-Bahn: Prinzregenten-Platz (then a 5-minute walk west on Prinz Regenten Strasse and south on Ismaninger Strasse). Rack rates: €200–€215 double. Rates include buffet breakfast. AE, MC, V.*

Mandarin Oriental

$$$$ **Altstadt**

The sophisticated, superclassy Mandarin Oriental, located in the historic heart of Munich, occupies an ornate 19th-century building that was turned into a hotel in 1990. Biedermeier-era (early 19th-century) furnishings, fine prints and engravings, and big marble-tiled bathrooms with tub/shower combinations outfit the 73 rooms and suites. Most of the rooms have terraces with panoramic views of the city. The hotel has a heated rooftop swimming pool. The staff at this full-service hotel will arrange babysitting.

Neuturmstrasse 1, 80331 München. ☎ *089/290-980. Fax: 089/222-539. Internet:* www. mandarinoriental.com. *Tram: 19 to Nationaltheater (then a 3-minute walk south on Neuturmstrasse). Rack rates: €312–€385 double. AE, DC, MC, V.*

Platzl Hotel
$$–$$$$ Altstadt

Owned by the Ayinger brewery, this reconstructed "medieval" hotel is located across from the Hofbräuhaus, Munich's famous beer hall. If you're looking for a gulp of old-fashioned Bavarian ambience, this is one of the best choices in Munich. The 167 rooms tend to be small, but they're paneled in chestnut and alderwood and furnished with 19th-century reproduction antiques. Each comes with a compact tiled bathroom, most with a tub and shower combination. The rooftop terrace provides a view of Munich's steeples and spires.

Sparkassenstrasse 10, 80331 München. ☎ *089/237-030. Fax: 089/2370-3800. Internet:* www.platzl.de. *U-Bahn: Marienplatz (then a 5-minute walk north on Sparkassenstrasse). Rack rates: €168–€238 double. Rates include buffet breakfast. AE, DC, MC, V.*

Splendid
$–$$ Altstadt

In this attractive Old World hotel, antiques, Oriental rugs, and chandeliers decorate the public areas. Most of the 36, Bavarian baroque–style rooms have bathrooms with a combination tub and shower. Breakfast costs an additional €10. In the morning, you can eat in your room or outside on a patio.

Maximilianstrasse 54, 80538 München. ☎ *089/296-606. Fax: 089/291-3176. U-Bahn: Lehel (then a 5-minute walk south on Pfarrstrasse and west on Maximilianstrasse). Rack rates: €44–€102 double without bathroom; €124–€164 double with bathroom. AE, DC, DISC, MC, V.*

Runner-up hotels

Am Markt
$–$$ Altstadt   This popular budget hotel centrally located in the Altstadt has small, neat rooms, many of which share bathrooms. *Heiliggeiststrasse 6, 80331 München.* ☎ *089/225-014. Fax: 089/224-017. No credit cards. U-/S-Bahn: Marienplatz.*

Bayerischer Hof & Palais Montgelas

$$$$ **Altstadt** This full-service luxury hotel has individually decorated rooms with large bathrooms, plus a health club with pool and sauna. The staff can arrange baby-sitting. *Promenadeplatz 2–6, 80333 Munich.* ☎ *800/ 223-6800 in the U.S. or 089/21200. Fax: 089/212-0906. Internet:* www.bayerischer hof.de. *Tram: 19.*

Hotel Mark

$–$$ **Near the train station** Although not fancy, this 90-room hotel is convenient, well-maintained, and moderately priced. *Senefelderstrasse 12, 80336 München.* ☎ *089/559-820. Fax: 089/5598-2333. Internet:* www.heh.de. *U-/S- Bahn: Hauptbahnhof.*

Königshof

$$$$ **Altstadt** This famous hotel boasts a Michelin-starred restaurant and has lushly decorated rooms with marble bathrooms. *Karlsplatz 25, 80335 Munich.* ☎ *089/551-360. Fax: 089/5513-6113. U-/S-Bahn: Karlsplatz/Stachus.*

Königswache

$–$$ **Near Altstadt** This 1960s-era hotel features modern, comfortable rooms with compact tiled bathrooms. *Steinheilstrasse 7, 80333 München.* ☎ *089/542-7570. Fax: 089/523-2114. U-Bahn: Theresienstrasse.*

München City Hilton

$$$ **Haidhausen** An excellent choice for business travelers and families with children, the München City Hilton lies on the east bank of the river and features well-designed rooms with nice bathrooms. *Rosenheimerstrasse 15, 81667 München.* ☎ *800/455-8667 in the U.S. and Canada or 089/48-040. Fax: 089/4804-4804. Internet:* www.hilton.com. *S-Bahn: Rosenheimer Platz.*

Dining Out

Munich is a city that loves to eat, and eat big. Homemade dumplings are a specialty, as are all kinds of sausages and *Leberkäse,* a large loaf of sausage eaten with freshly baked pretzels and mustard. *Schweinbraten,* a braised loin of pork served with potato dumplings and rich brown gravy, is Bavaria's answer to the north's *Sauerbraten* (pot- or oven-roasted marinated beef). Filling the city are all kinds of fine restaurants, small cafes and bistros, and beer halls that serve food.

If you want a refreshing nonalcoholic drink, served everywhere, ask for *Apfelsaftschorle* (*ap*-fell-saft-shor-luh), apple juice mixed with sparkling water.

If a restaurant bill says *Bedienung,* which means that a service charge has already been added, round up the total to the nearest euro. If service is not included, round up the total to the nearest euro and add another euro. The server takes the tip when you pay the bill; don't leave the tip on the table.

The top restaurants

Alois Dallmayr
$$–$$$ Altstadt   DELICATESSEN/CONTINENTAL

In business for almost 250 years, Alois Dallmayr is the most famous delicatessen in Germany. Downstairs you can buy fine food products; upstairs you can order a tempting array of dishes, including herring, sausages, smoked fish, and soups in the dining room. A crowd always fills the restaurant at lunchtime.

Dienerstrasse 14–15. ☎ *089/213-5100. U-/S-Bahn: Marienplatz (then a 2-minute walk north on Dienerstrasse). Main courses: €12–€34; fixed-price menus €28–€40. AE, DC, MC, V. Open: Mon–Wed 9:30 a.m.–7 p.m.; Thurs–Fri 9:30 a.m.– 8 p.m.; Sat 9 a.m.–4 p.m.*

Augustiner Grossgastätte
$$ Altstadt   BAVARIAN/GERMAN

Located on Munich's main pedestrians-only shopping street, this famous beer hall/restaurant has cavernous rooms and a genuinely *gemütlich* atmosphere. Specialties include dumpling soup and roast duck with red cabbage. The house beer, Augustiner Brau, comes from one of Munich's oldest breweries, which owns the restaurant.

Neuhauser Strasse 27. ☎ *089/2318-3257. U-Bahn: Karlsplatz/Stachus (then a 5-minute walk east on Neuhauser Strasse). Main courses: €10–€18. MC, V. Open: Daily 9 a.m. to midnight.*

Austernkeller
$$$ Altstadt   SEAFOOD

At this "oyster cellar," you find the largest selection of oysters in town, served raw or in dishes such as oysters Rockefeller. The shellfish platter with fresh oysters, mussels, clams, scampi, and sea snails is a delicious way to start your meal. Menu offerings include fresh fish, as well as time-honored favorites such as lobster thermidor and shrimp grilled in the shell.

Stollbergstrasse 11. ☎ *089/298-787. U-Bahn: Isartor (then a 5-minute walk north on Herrnstrasse and northeast on Stollbergstrasse. Reservations required. Main courses: €18–€30. AE, DC, MC, V. Open: Daily 5–11:30 p.m.*

Boettner

$$$$ Altstadt INTERNATIONAL

When this century-old restaurant moved to its new location, in a 16th-century building in the heart of Munich, it brought its wood-paneled interior with it. The cooking is light and refined, with a French influence, but several traditional Bavarian dishes are also on the menu. Special offerings include lamb, beef filet, lobster stew in a cream sauce, and dishes with white truffles. The desserts are sumptuous.

Pfisterstrasse 9. ☎ 089/221-210. U-Bahn: Marienplatz (then a 5-minute walk north on Sparkassen Strasse and east on Pfisterstrasse). Reservations required. Main courses: €25–€35; fixed-price lunch €31, fixed-price dinner €71. AE, DC, MC, V. Open: Mon–Sat 11:30 a.m.–3 p.m. and 6–10 p.m.

Buon Gusto (Talamonti)

$$ Altstadt TUSCAN/ITALIAN

This highly regarded Italian restaurant has two dining areas — a simple bistro overlooking an open kitchen and a more formal dining room — with the same menu items and prices. Try the *Tris di pasta* (three pastas with vegetables), pasta with truffles, spaghetti carbonara, ravioli stuffed with mushrooms and herbs, or the roasted lamb with potatoes. The various *risottos* (rice dishes) are especially good.

Hochbrückenstrasse 3. ☎ 089/296-383. U-/S-Bahn: Marienplatz (then a 5-minute walk east on Tal and northeast on Hochbrückenstrasse). Reservations recommended. Main courses: €8.50–€20. AE, DC, MC, V. Open: Mon–Sat 11 a.m. to midnight.

Der Tisch

$$$ North of train station INTERNATIONAL

"The Table" is one of the best and most fashionable bistros in Munich, with a small, 36-seat dining room. The eclectic menu changes daily and concentrates on market-fresh ingredients. The eggplant mousse with tomato vinaigrette and the tuna flavored with tomato sauce, olives, and capers make good starters. Seasonal main courses include fish and venison dishes.

Maxvorstadt, Nymphenburger Strasse 1. ☎ 089/557-154. U-Bahn: Stiglmeier Platz (then a 2-minute walk west on Nymphenburger Strasse). Reservations required. Main courses: €14–€26. AE, DC, MC, V. Open: Mon–Fri 11:30 a.m.–3 p.m. and 6 p.m. to midnight.

Donisl

$ Altstadt BAVARIAN/INTERNATIONAL

Munich's oldest beer hall dates from 1715 and provides diners and drinkers with a relaxed, comfortable atmosphere. In summer you can dine in the garden area out front. The standard menu offers traditional Bavarian food as well as weekly specials. *Weisswürste,* the little white sausages famous in Munich, have long been a specialty. The beers come from Munich's Hacker-Pschorr Brewery. Serenading the diners are a zither player at noon and an accordion player in the evening.

Weinstrasse 1. ☎ *089/220-184. U-/S-Bahn: Marienplatz (then 1-minute walk north on Weinstrasse). Reservations recommended. Main courses: €7. AE, DC, MC, V. Open: Daily 9 a.m. to midnight.*

Galleria

$$–$$$ **Altstadt   ITALIAN**

The roster of dishes at this appealing Italian restaurant changes season-ally, but you may find main courses such as veal liver with asparagus and orzo, poached fish with fresh vegetables in fennel sauce, beefsteak with roast potatoes, herb-flavored risotto with chunks of lobster and braised radicchio, or roasted soft-shell crabs.

Ledererstrasse 2. ☎ *089/297-995. U-/S-Bahn: Marienplatz (then a 3-minute walk north on Sparkassenstrasse to Ledererstrasse). Reservations recommended. Main courses: €19–€23; fixed-price dinner €46–€56. AE, DC, MC, V. Open: Mon–Sat noon to 3 p.m. and 6:30–11 p.m. Closed Aug 10–30.*

Gasthaus Glockenbach

$$$$ **South of train station   INTERNATIONAL**

This elegant but unpretentious restaurant serves imaginative nouvelle French-German-Bavarian cuisine and has earned a Michelin star. The menu offerings change with the seasons and typically include venison and pheasant in autumn and lamb and veal dishes in spring. The vegetables come from local farms. Wines are mostly from Italy, France, and Austria.

Kapuzinerstrasse 29. ☎ *089/534-043. U-Bahn: Goetheplatz (then a 10-minute walk south on Lindwurm and east on Kapuzinerstrasse to the corner of Maistrasse). Reservations recommended. Main courses: €23–€30; fixed-price menus €28 lunch, €92 dinner. AE, MC, V. Open: Tues–Sat noon to 2 p.m. and 7–10 p.m. Closed 1 week at Christmas.*

Georgenhof

$$ **Schwabing   GERMAN/INTERNATIONAL**

This pleasant Schwabing eatery has a comfortably rustic interior with a wood-fired grill, but if the weather is nice, sit outside under the chestnut trees. The menu reflects seasonal specialties (*Spargel* (asparagus) in May and June) and regional favorites. Bavarian game dishes include *Rehpfeffer* (venison) with egg *spätzle* (German pasta) or tagliatelle with venison ragout. Grilled meats such as lamb and steak are popular. For dessert, try the simple but delicious Bavarian cream with strawberries.

Fredrichstrasse 1. ☎ 089/3884-9890. U-Bahn: Universität (then a 10-minute walk west on Schelling Strasse and north on Turkenstrasse to the corner of Friedrichstrasse and Georgenstrasse). Main courses: €11–€21. MC, V. Open: Daily noon to midnight.

Hunsinger's Pacific

$–$$ Altstadt   CONTINENTAL/ASIAN

This restaurant offers good food at reasonable prices. The menu emphasizes fresh fish prepared according to classic French cooking techniques but using spices from Malaysia (coconut milk), Japan (wasabi), Thailand (lemongrass), and India (curry). The tuna carpaccio with sliced plum, fresh ginger, and lime is a delicious starter. Main courses include bouillabaisse with aïoli (a fish soup with a spicy mayonnaise), cold melon soup, fried monkfish, and turbot in chili and ginger sauce.

Maximiliansplatz 5. ☎ 089/5502-9741. U-/S-Bahn: Karlsplatz/Stachus (then a 10-minute walk northeast on Oskar-von-Miller Strasse to the entrance on Max-Joseph-Strasse). Main courses: €19–€27; fixed-price 2-course lunch €12. AE, MC, V. Open: Mon–Fri noon to 2:30 p.m.; daily 6–10:30 p.m. Closed Sun May–Sept.

Hofbräuhaus am Platzl

$$ Altstadt   GERMAN

A boisterous atmosphere prevails in Munich's huge and world-famous beer hall. In the *Schwemme* (tap room) on the ground floor, you sit on benches at bare wood tables as a brass band plays; a big courtyard is on this level, too. Upstairs are a number of smaller, quieter dining rooms. The beer is Hofbrau, which is served by the "mass," equal to about a quart. The food is heavy and hearty with a menu that includes *Weisswürste* and several other sausages, *Schweinsbraten* (roasted pork), *Spanferkel* (roast suckling pig), and stuffed cabbage rolls. Everything on the menu is translated into English.

Am Platzl 9. ☎ 089/290-1360. U-/S-Bahn: Marienplatz (then a 5-minute walk north on Sparkassenstrasse and east on Bräuhausstrasse). Main courses: €6–€14. No credit cards. Open: Daily 9 a.m. to midnight.

Nürnberger Bratwurst Glöckl am Dom

$ Altstadt   BAVARIAN

A short walk from Marienplatz, across from the cathedral *(Dom)*, this is the coziest and friendliest of Munich's local restaurants. You sit in carved wooden chairs at shared tables. *Nürnberger Schweinwurstl mit Kraut* (pork sausages with cabbage, a specialty from Nuremberg) is the dish to try. Hot dogs will never taste the same again after your kid has tried one of these delectable little sausages.

Frauenplatz 9. ☎ *089/295-264. U-/S-Bahn: Marienplatz (then a 5-minute walk west on Sporerstrasse to Frauenplatz beside the Frauenkirche). Main courses: €8–€16. No credit cards. Open: Daily 10 a.m.–1 a.m.*

Pfistermühle

$$ Altstadt BAVARIAN

This old-fashioned, vine-covered restaurant housed in a converted mill serves hearty portions of traditional Bavarian food in a series of charmingly decorated dining rooms or at outdoor tables. Come for roast meats served with fresh vegetables, fresh trout accompanied by chive-flecked sour cream and a potato pancake, or the fish platter served with ragout and noodles. For dessert try vanilla custard with fresh berry sauce. Toast the end of your Bavarian meal with a glass of wild-cherry schnapps.

In the Platzl Hotel, Pfistermühle 4. ☎ *089/2370-3865. U-Bahn: Marienplatz (then a 5-minute walk north on Sparkassenstrasse and east on Pfisterstrasse). Reservations recommended. Main courses: €15.50–€20. AE, DC, MC, V. Open: Mon–Sat 11:30 a.m. to midnight.*

Prinz Myshkin

$ Altstadt VEGETARIAN

If sausages and meat dishes are getting to you, you may want to try this popular vegetarian restaurant near Marienplatz. The menu includes freshly made salads, macrobiotic dishes, Indian and Thai vegetarian entrees, and vegetarian *involtini* (stuffed rollups). The casseroles, soups, and pizzas are generally excellent.

Hackenstrasse 2. ☎ *089/265-596. U-/S-Bahn: Marienplatz (then a 10-minute walk southwest on Rindermarkt and Oberanger and north on Sack Strasse to Hackenstrasse). Reservations recommended. Main courses: €9–€16. AE, MC, V. Open: Daily 11 a.m.–1 a.m.*

Ratskeller München

$–$$ Altstadt BAVARIAN

A *Ratskeller* is a cellar restaurant in a *Rathaus* (town hall), where you find good, inexpensive food and wine. Munich's Ratskeller has a dark, woody interior with carved wooden chairs and tables and painted ceilings. The menu showcases regional dishes but also includes some vegetarian choices.

Marienplatz 8, in the Rathaus. ☎ *089/219-9890. U-/S-Bahn: Marienplatz (the Rathaus is on the square). Main courses: €10–€22. AE, MC, V. Open: Daily 10 a.m. to midnight.*

Restaurant Vier Jahreszeiten

$$$$ Altstadt FRENCH/INTERNATIONAL

The service is extremely polished at this refined hotel restaurant, and the food is prepared along classic French lines with an Asian twist. The menu changes every month or so, but appetizers are likely to include mushroom soufflé served with artichoke-cream sauce, freshly made vegetable soup, and basil-crusted turbot. Main courses worth trying include breast of chicken with scampi, flavored with a ginger sauce, and roast medallions of venison with cherry-pepper sauce. For dessert, choose from selections like tangerine soufflé served with vanilla sauce.

Maximilianstrasse 17, in the Kempinski Hotel Vier Jahreszeiten München. ☎ 089/21250. Tram: 19 to Nationaltheater (the hotel is across the street). Reservations required. Main courses: €18–€34; 3-course fixed-price menu €40. AE, DC, MC, V. Open: Daily noon to 1:30 a.m.

Rossi

$$ Altstadt ITALIAN

With its columns, red-tiled floor, and white walls with wood-paneled ceiling, this well-liked Italian restaurant across from the famous Hofbräuhaus is an inviting place to dine. The simply prepared pastas (*Teigwaren* in German) are always good. Try spaghetti *alle pomodoro* (with tomatoes) or *penne ai formaggi* (with cheese). You can also get a good pizza, veal piccata with lemon sauce, or grilled steak *(Rindfilet).*

Bräuhausstrasse 6. ☎ 089/227-735. U-/S-Bahn: Isartor (then a 5-minute walk west on Tal and northeast on Hochbrücken to Bräuhausstrasse). Main courses: €6–€18. AE, MC, V. Open: Mon–Fri noon to 3 p.m. and 6 p.m. to midnight, Sat 6 p.m. to midnight.

Spatenhaus

$$ Altstadt BAVARIAN/INTERNATIONAL

This well-known beer restaurant with big windows overlooking the opera house serves hearty portions of typical Bavarian food at reasonable prices. The *Bayerische Teller* (Bavarian Plate) comes loaded with various meats, including pork and sausages. Wash down your meal with the restaurant's own beer, Spaten-Franziskaner-Bier.

Residenzstrasse 12. ☎ 089/290-7060. U-Bahn: Marienplatz (then a 10-minute walk north on Diener Strasse and Residenzstrasse). Reservations recommended. Main courses: €14–€24. AE, MC, V. Open: Daily 9:30 a.m.–12:30 a.m.

Tantris

$$$$ Schwabing FRENCH/GERMAN/INTERNATIONAL

A famed culinary mecca since 1972, this Michelin-starred restaurant has an interior that is supposed to be very chic but in reality looks like an airport lounge. The choice of dishes is limited and changes often. You might begin with a terrine of smoked fish served with green cucumber sauce, followed by roast duck on mustard-seed sauce, or perhaps lobster medallions on black noodles.

Johann-Fichte-Strasse 7, Schwabing. ☎ *089/361-9590. U-Bahn: Dietlindenstrasse (then a 10-minute walk west on Potsdamer Strasse, north on Leopold Strasse, and east on Johan-Fichte-Strasse). Reservations required. Fixed-price lunch €80; fixed-price dinners €102–€115. AE, DC, MC, V. Open: Tues–Sat noon to 3 p.m. and 6:30 p.m.–1 a.m. Closed public holidays and annual holidays in Jan and May.*

Times Square Online Bistro

$ Train station   CONTINENTAL/SNACKS

A bank of online computers, which you can rent for €2.50 per quarter hour, takes up one side of this bright, high-ceilinged, technobistro in the main train station. The bistro also has a section for noncomputerized dining, where you can order simple but tasty dishes such as pork cutlets, baked camembert, tagliatelle, and spinach strudel. The food is well prepared, and the fresh salads are especially good.

Bayerstrasse 10 A, in the main train station. ☎ *089/550-8800. U-/S-Bahn: Hauptbahnhof. Breakfasts €4–€10; main courses €7–€14. AE, DC, MC, V. Open: Sun–Thurs 6 a.m.–1 a.m; Fri–Sat 6 a.m. to midnight.*

Zum Alten Markt

$$ Altstadt   BAVARIAN/INTERNATIONAL

This snug, friendly eatery is located on a tiny square just off the Viktualienmarkt, Munich's big outdoor produce market. In summer, tables are set up outside. You might begin with homemade cream of carrot soup or black-truffle tortellini in cream sauce. The chef makes a great *Tafelspitz* (boiled beef). You can also order classic dishes such as roast duck with apple sauce or roast suckling pig.

Dreifaltigkeitsplatz 3. ☎ *089/299-995. U-/S-Bahn: Marienplatz (then a 5-minute walk south to Dreifaltifkeitsplatz on the east side of the Viktualienmarkt). Main courses: €12–€20. No credit cards. Open: Mon–Sat 11 a.m.–10:30 p.m.*

The best beer gardens

Munich is famed for its beer gardens *(Biergartens),* where you can sit outdoors, quaff Munich's famous brews, and order hearty Bavarian food at reasonable prices. For a glass or mug of beer expect to pay between €3 and €6, depending on its size. A simple meal generally costs around €10. Salty pretzels and large white radishes *(Radl)* are traditional accompaniments to the beer. Oompah bands sometimes add to the jovial atmosphere. The food, drink, and atmosphere are much the same in the two places that I recommend.

- ✔ **Biergarten Chinesischer Turm,** Englischer Garten 3 (☎ 089/383-8720; U-Bahn: Giselastrasse), one of Munich's largest and most popular beer gardens, is located in the Englischer Garten at the foot of the *Chinesischer Turm* (Chinese Tower), an easy-to-find landmark. This beer garden is open daily from May to October from 11 a.m. to 1 a.m.

- ✔ **Gaststätte zum Flaucher,** Isarauen 8 (☎ 089/723-2677; bus: 52), near the zoo, has tables set in a tree-shaded garden overlooking the Isar river. This beer garden is open daily from May to October from 10 a.m. to midnight; November to April, it's open Friday, Saturday, and Sunday from 10 a.m. to 9 p.m.

For two of the best beer halls in Munich, see the listings under "The top restaurants," earlier in this chapter, for the **Hofbräuhaus** and **Augustiner Grossgastätte.**

Sightseeing in Munich

Munich is one of the great sightseeing cities in Germany. You can discover several world-class museums with exhaustive collections, many fine churches and historic buildings, and lovely parks and gardens. Visitors on limited schedules have to make some difficult decisions.

For locations, see the "Central Munich Attractions" map in this chapter.

Discovering the top attractions from A to Z

Alte Pinakothek (Old Masters Gallery)
Museum Quarter

Pinakothek means "painting gallery," and the nearly 800 paintings on display in this enormous building represent the greatest European artists of the 14th through the 18th centuries. The museum is so immense that you could easily spend several days exploring the two floors of exhibits. To make the most of your time here, pick up a museum guide at the information desk, decide which paintings you particularly want to see, and then spend at least two to three hours.

A free audio tour in English is available in the lobby. When you see a painting you want to know more about, punch the corresponding number into your audio guide to hear a full commentary.

Two other major art museums, the Neue Pinakothek and the new Pinakothek der Moderne (both described later in this section), cluster around the Alte Pinakothek.

Barer Strasse 27. ☎ *089/2380-5216. Tram: 27 to Pinakothek (the museum entrance on Theresienstrasse is across the street). Admission: €4.60 adults, €3 students, free for children 14 and under; free admission on Sun. Open: Tues–Sun 10 a.m.–5 p.m. (Thurs until 10 p.m.).*

Bayerisches Nationalmuseum (Bavarian National Museum)
East of Altstadt

This museum contains three vast floors of sculpture, painting, folk art, ceramics, furniture, and textiles, as well as clocks and scientific instruments. The objects on view are among Bavaria's greatest historic and artistic treasures.

A major highlight is the **Riemenschneider Room,** which contains works in wood by the great sculptor Tilman Riemenschneider (1460–1531). The museum also contains a famous collection of Christmas Nativity cribs from Bavaria, Tyrol, and southern Italy. Give yourself at least an hour just to cover the highlights.

Prinzregentenstrasse 3. ☎ *089/211-2401. U-Bahn: Lehel (then a 10-minute walk north on Wagmüllerstrasse and east on Prinzregentenstrasse). Admission: €3 adults, €2 students and seniors, free for children under 15; free admission on Sun. Open: Tues–Sun 9:30 a.m.–5 p.m.*

Deutsches Museum (German Museum of Science and Technology)
Museumsinsel

Located on the Museumsinsel, an island in the Isar River, this is the largest science and technology museum in the world and one of the most popular attractions in Germany. Its huge collection of scientific and technological treasures includes the first electric locomotive (1879), the first electric generator (called a *dynamo;* 1866), the first automobile (1886), the first diesel engine (1897), and the laboratory bench at which the atom was first split (1938). This hands-on, kid-friendly museum has interactive exhibits and an English-speaking staff to answer questions and demonstrate glass blowing, papermaking, and how steam engines, pumps, and historical musical instruments work.

The **Automobile** department in the basement is noteworthy, with a collection of luxury Daimler, Opel, and Bugatti vehicles. In the **Aeronautics** section, you see a biplane flown by the Wright brothers in 1908, the first airliner (1919), and an assortment of military aircraft. Spending half a day here is easy.

Museumsinsel 1. ☎ *089/21791. Tram: 18 to Deutsches Museum (the tram stops outside the museum). Admission: €6 adults, €2.50 students and children 6–16. Open: Daily 9 a.m.–5 p.m. Closed major holidays.*

Central Munich Attractions

Alte Pinakothek **5**
Antikensammlungen **7**
Asamkirche **9**
Bayerisches
Nationalmuseum **18**
Deutsches Museum **10**
Englischer Garten **19**
Frauenkirche **15**
Glockenspiel **14**
Glyptothek **6**
Marienplatz **14**
Michaelskirche **8**
Münchner
Stadtmuseum **12**
Neue Pinakothek **3**
Olympiapark **1**
Olympiaturm **1**
Pinakothek der Moderne **4**
Peterskirche **13**
Residenz **17**
Schloss Nymphenburg **2**
Theatinerkirche **16**
Viktualienmarkt **11**

NYMPHENBURG
Amalienburg **24**
Badenburg Pavilion **20**
Magdalenenklause **23**
Marstallmuseum **25**
Pagodenburg **22**
Porzellan-Manufaktur-
Nymphenburg **28**
Porzellansammlung **26**
Schloss **27**
Schlosspark **21**

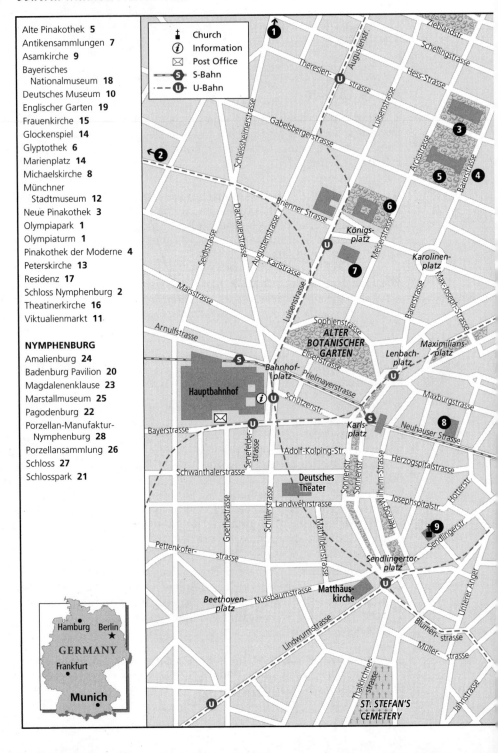

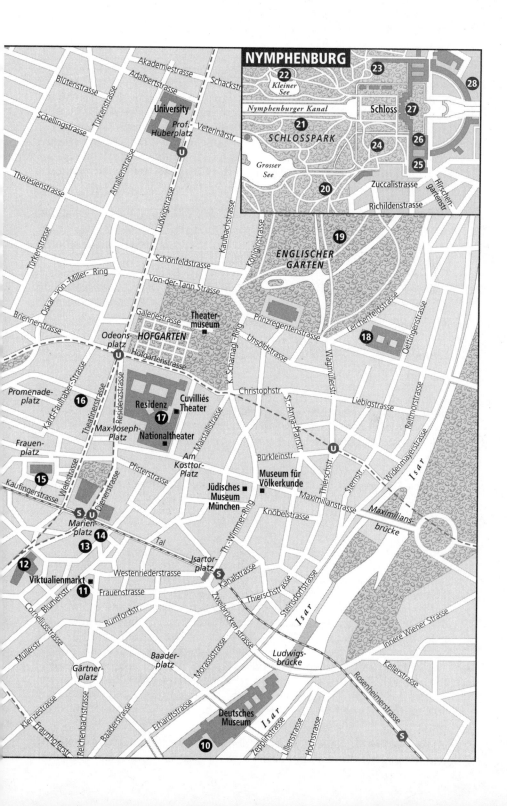

Englisher Garten (English Garden)
Northwest of Altstadt

Munich's famous city park is one of the largest (922 acres) and most beautiful city parks in Europe. Established in 1789, the Englisher Garten is also the oldest public park in the world. You can wander for hours along the tree-shaded walks, streams, and lake, and admire the view of Munich's Altstadt from the round, hilltop temple called the **Monopteros,** constructed in the 19th century. The banks of the Eisbach, the stream that runs through the park, are popular nude-sunbathing spots. A giant beer garden occupies the plaza near the **Chinesischer Turm** (Chinese Tower).

The park is a lovely place to have a picnic. You can pick up expensive picnic goodies at **Alois Dallmayr** (see "Dining Out," earlier in this chapter), or less-expensive fare from **Hertie,** the department store across from the Hauptbahnhof.

Bounded on the south by Von-der-Tann Strasse and Prinzregentenstrasse, on the west by Königinstrasse, on the east by Lerchenfeldstrasse. U-Bahn: Odeonsplatz (then a 10-minute walk northeast through the Hofgarten to the park).

Frauenkirche (Cathedral of Our Lady)
Altstadt

Munich's largest church, completed in the late 15th century, was a pile of smoldering rubble at the end of World War II. Only its landmark twin onion-domed towers from 1525 remained standing. The rebuilt church is strikingly simple and dignified, and the view from the tower is spectacular.

Frauenplatz 12. ☎ *089/290-0820. U-/S-Bahn: Marienplatz (then a 5-minute walk west on Sporerstrasse to the church). Admission: Church free; tower €3 adults, €1.50 students. Open: Church Sat–Thurs 7 a.m.–7 p.m.; Fri 7 a.m.–6 p.m.; tower Apr–Oct daily 10 a.m.–5 p.m.*

Marienplatz
Altstadt

This large pedestrian-only square in the heart of the Altstadt is also the old heart of Munich. Chances are you'll return here again and again, since many of the city's attractions are clustered in the vicinity. On the north side of Marienplatz is the **Neues Rathaus** (New City Hall), built in 19th-century Gothic style and famous for its Glockenspiel (see the sidebar "Watching the Glockenspiel," in this chapter). You can take an elevator to the top of the Rathaus's tower for a good view of the city center. The tower is open Monday to Friday from 9 a.m. to 7 p.m., Saturday and Sunday from 10 a.m. to 7 p.m. Admission is €1.50 for adults, €.75 for children 6 to 18.

To the right of the Neues Rathaus stands the **Altes Rathaus** (Old City Hall), with its plain, 15th-century Gothic tower. Inside is the **Spielzeugmuseum**

Watching the Glockenspiel

The best show on Marienplatz takes place at 11 a.m. and 9 p.m. daily (also at noon and 5 p.m. during the holiday seasons) when the 43-bell *Glockenspiel* (carillon) on the 280-foot central spire of the Neues Rathaus (New Town Hall) goes through its paces. Brightly painted mechanical figures re-enact two famous events from Munich's history: the knights' tournament during the 1586 wedding feast of Wilhelm V and Renate of Lorraine, and, one level below, the *Schäfflertanz* (Coopers' Dance), first performed in 1683 to express gratitude for the end of the plague.

(☎ 089/294-001), a historical toy collection, open daily from 10 a.m. to 5:30 p.m. Admission is €2.50 for adults, €.50 for children, and €5 for a family.

In the center of the Altstadt. U-/S-Bahn: Marienplatz.

Münchner Stadtmuseum (Munich City Museum)
Altstadt

This museum chronicles Munich's history and the everyday lives of its residents. The museum's one must-see exhibit is the **Moorish Dancers** *(Moriskentanzer):* ten carved and brightly painted 15th-century wooden figures. The second-floor photo museum traces the early history of the camera back to 1839. Children love the third-floor collection of marionettes and hand puppets from around the world and the gallery of fairground art, which includes the oldest-known carousel horses, dating from 1820. You find a cafeteria in the museum's main courtyard.

St.-Jakobs-Platz 1. ☎ *089/2332-2370. U-/S-Bahn: Marienplatz (then a 5-minute walk south on Rindermarkt and Oberanger). Admission: €2.50 adults, €1.30 students and children 6–15; free on Sun. Open: Tues–Sun 10 a.m.–6 p.m.*

Neue Pinakothek
Museum Quarter

Housed in a postmodern building from 1981, this museum is a showcase for 19th-century German and European art, starting right around 1800. Not quite as daunting as the Alte Pinakothek, this museum still contains plenty to see. Artists whose works are on view include Thomas Gainsborough, Joshua Reynolds, William Turner, Francesco Goya, Caspar David Friedrich, Vincent van Gogh, and Paul Gauguin, among many others. A tour of the highlights takes a couple of hours.

Barer Strasse 27 (across Theresienstrasse from the Alte Pinakothek). ☎ *089/ 2380-5195. Tram: 27 to Pinakothek (the museum entrance on Theresienstrasse is across the street). Admission: €5 adults, €3.50 students and seniors; free admission on Sun. Open: Weds–Mon 10 a.m.–5 p.m. (Thurs until 10 p.m.).*

Pinakothek der Moderne (Gallery of Modern Art, Architecture, Design)
Museum Quarter

Munich's newest museum, the Pinakothek der Moderne, opened in September 2002. You find four collections housed inside. The most important is the **Staatsgalerie moderner Kunst** (Gallery of Modern Art), displaying major 20th-century classics by internationally known artists including Matisse, Picasso, Juan Gris, Kandinsky, Kirchner, Max Ernst, Giacometti, and others. The other collections include the **Neue Sammlung** (Craft and Design Collection), the **Museum of Architecture,** and the **Graphische Sammlung** (Graphics Collection).

Barer Strasse 40. ☎ *089/2380-5360. Tram: 27 to Pinakothek (the museums are across the street). Admission: €5 adults, €2.50 for students 10–18, free for children under 10. Open: Tues–Sun 10 a.m.–5 p.m.*

Peterskirche (St. Peter's Church)
Altstadt

The belltower of this 13th-century Gothic church, remodeled during the baroque era, is known locally as Old Pete. You get a splendid view from the top, but you have to climb (and climb and climb) 306 steps to see it. The interior of the church contains baroque-era sculptures, frescoes, and a bizarre relic in the second chapel on the left: the gem-studded skeleton of St. Mundita, who stares at you with two false eyes in her skull.

Rindermarkt 1. ☎ *089/260-4828. U-/S-Bahn: Marienplatz (then a 2-minute walk south on Rindermarkt). Admission: Church free; tower €1.50 adults, €.75 students. Open: Apr–Oct daily 8 a.m.–7 p.m.; Nov–Mar daily 8 a.m.–6 p.m.*

Residenz (Royal Palace)
Altstadt

This magnificent building was the official residence of the Wittelsbach family, the rulers of Bavaria, from 1385 to 1918. Added to and rebuilt over the centuries, the palace is a compendium of various architectural styles, including German and Florentine Renaissance, and Palladian. Artisans painstakenly restored the Rezidenz, which was almost totally destroyed in World War II. The must-sees are the **Residenz Museum,** with arts and furnishings displayed in some 130 rooms; the **Schatzkammer** (Treasury), with three centuries' worth of accumulated treasures; and the **Altes Residenztheater,** a stunning rococo theater. You enter both the Residenz Museum and the Schatzkammer from Max-Joseph-Platz on the south side of the palace. On the north side of the palace is the Italianate **Hofgarten** (Court Garden), laid out between 1613 and 1617.

Max-Joseph-Platz 3. ☎ *089/290-671. Tram: 19 to Nationaltheater (the palace is on the same square as the theater) or U-Bahn: Odeonsplatz (the palace is southeast across the square). Admission: Residenz Museum and Schatzkammer each €4 adults, €3 students and seniors; theater €1.50 adults, €1 students, free for children 15 and under. Combined ticket for Residenz Museum, Schatzkammer, and theater €7 adults, €6 students and children. Open: Residenz Museum and Schatzkammer Apr 1–Oct 15 daily 9 a.m.–6 p.m. (Thurs until 8 p.m.), Oct 16–Mar 30 daily 10 a.m.– 4 p.m. Guided tours (in German): Daily at 10 a.m. and 12:30 p.m.*

Schloss Nymphenburg (Nymphenburg Palace)
Nymphenburg

Schloss Nymphenburg, the Wittelsbachs's summer residence, is one of the most sophisticated and beautiful palaces in Europe. The palace was begun in 1664 and took more than 150 years to complete. In 1702, Elector Max Emanuel decided to enlarge the original Italianate villa by adding four large pavilions connected by arcaded passageways. From central Munich, you can easily reach the palace by tram in about 20 minutes. You need at least half a day to explore the buildings and grounds.

Inside, you come first to the **Great Hall,** decorated in a vibrant splash of rococo colors and stuccowork. In the south pavilion, you find Ludwig I's famous **Gallery of Beauties** with paintings by J. Stieler (1827–1850). The beauties include Schöne Münchnerin (Lovely Munich Girl) and a portrait of Lola Montez, the raven-haired dancer whose affair with Ludwig caused a scandal.

To the south of the palace buildings, in the rectangular block of low structures that once housed the court stables, is the **Marstallmuseum,** where you find a dazzling collection of ornate, gilded coaches and sleighs, including those used by Ludwig II. The **Porzellansammlung** (Porcelain Collection; entrance across from the Marstallmuseum) contains superb pieces of 18th-century porcelain, including miniature porcelain copies of masterpieces in the Alte Pinakothek.

A factory on the grounds of Schloss Nymphenburg still produces the famous Nymphenburg porcelain. **Porzellan-Manufaktur-Nymphenburg,** Nördliches Schlossrondell 8 (☎ **089/179-1970**), has a sales room and exhibition center open Monday through Friday from 8:30 a.m. to 5 p.m.

A canal runs through 500-acre **Schlosspark,** stretching all the way to the so-called grand cascade at the far end of the formal, French-style gardens. In the English-style park, full of quiet meadows and forested paths, you find the **Badenburg Pavilion,** with an 18th-century swimming pool; the **Pagodenburg,** decorated in the Chinese style that was all the rage in the 18th century; and the **Magdalenenklause** (Hermitage), meant to be a retreat for prayer and solitude. Prettiest of all the buildings in the park is **Amalienburg,** built in 1734 as a hunting lodge for Electress Amalia; the interior salons are a riot of flamboyant colors, swirling stuccowork, and wall paintings.

Schloss Nymphenburg 1, 5 miles (8 km) northwest of the city center. Tram: 12, 16, or 17 to Romanplatz (then a 10-minute walk west to the palace entrance). ☎ *089/ 179-080. Admission: Palace grounds free; admission to all attractions €7.50 adults, €6.50 seniors, free for children under 7. Open: Oct 16–Mar 30 daily 10 a.m.–4 p.m.; Apr 1–Oct 15 daily 9 a.m.–6 p.m. (Thurs until 8 p.m.). Badenburg and Magdalenenklause closed Oct 16–Mar 30.*

Theatinerkirche (Church of the Theatines)
Altstadt

Named for the Theatines, a group of Roman Catholic clergy, this church is Munich's finest example of Italian baroque architecture. The church was begun by Italian architects in 1663 and was completed by German court architects about a century later. Fluted columns lining the center aisle support the arched ceiling of the nave. Every surface appears to be loaded with dollops of fanciful white stuccowork. The dome above the transept is decorated with an ornate gallery of large statues. Dark wooden pews and a canopied pulpit provide the only color in the all-white interior.

Theatinerstrasse 22. ☎ *089/210-6960. U-Bahn: Odeonsplatz (then a 2-minute walk south on Theatinerstrasse). Admission: Free. Open: Mon–Fri 10 a.m.–1 p.m. and 1:30–4:30 p.m.; Sat 10 a.m.–3 p.m.*

Viktualienmarkt (Produce Market)
Altstadt

Located on the square of the same name, close to Marienplatz, the Viktualienmarkt has been serving Munich residents for nearly 200 years. This is a wonderful place to stroll and sniff and take in the scene. In an area the size of a city block, you find two dozen butcher shops, five cheese sellers, a whole section of bakeries stocked with dozens of different kinds of Bavarian breads and rolls, fish sellers, wine merchants, and dozens of produce stalls. Most of the permanent stands open at 6 a.m. and stay open until 6 p.m. weekdays or until 1 p.m. Saturdays.

The Viktualienmarkt has a large beer garden. You can buy food at the market stalls to eat in the beer garden if you buy a beer, coke, water, or other beverage at the beergarden drink stand.

At the Viktualienmarkt, and in other outdoor food markets throughout Germany, remember two points: Do not touch the merchandise (doing so is against German food laws) and don't try to bargain for lower prices (prices are not negotiable).

Bounded by Prälat-Zistl-Strasse on the west, Frauen Strasse to the south, Heiliggeiststrasse on the east, and Tal on the north. U-/S-Bahn: Marienplatz (then a 5-minute walk southeast through the square).

Finding more cool things to see and do

The A-list of sights in the previous section covers only those places that you absolutely don't want to miss. But Munich has plenty more to see and do. Depending on your interests, some of the following attractions may fall onto your A-list.

✔ The **Antikensammlungen** (Museum of Antiquities), Königsplatz 1 (☎ 089/598-359; U-Bahn: Königsplatz), is an essential stop for anyone interested in ancient art. The museum's five main-floor halls house more than 650 Greek vases, from a pre-Mycenaean version carved in 3000 B.C. from a mussel shell to large Greek and Etruscan vases. The museum is open Tuesday through Sunday from 10 a.m. to 5 p.m. (until 8 p.m. on Wednesday). Admission is €3 for adults, free for children under 14, free for everyone on Sunday. A joint ticket to the Museum of Antiquities and the neighboring Glyptothek (included later in this list) is €6.

✔ Munich has many important churches in addition to those described in the preceding section. The **Asamkirche,** on Sendlinger Strasse (☎ 089/260-9357; U-/S-Bahn: Sendlinger Tor), is a remarkable rococo church built by the Asam brothers between 1733 and 1746. Multicolored marbles, gold leaf, and silver cover every square inch of this small rectangular church with rounded ends. The church is open daily from 8 a.m. to 5:30 p.m. The **Michaelskirche** (St. Michael's Church), Neuhauserstrasse 52 (☎ 089/231-7060; U-/S-Bahn: Marienplatz), a single-nave church with a barrel-vaulted ceiling completed in 1597, is the largest Renaissance church north of the Alps. The church is open Monday to Saturday from 8:30 a.m. to 7 p.m., Sunday from 6:45 a.m. to 10 p.m.

✔ Located across from the Antikensammlungen (see the first entry in this list), the **Glyptothek,** Königsplatz 3 (☎ 089/286-100; U-Bahn: Königsplatz), exhibits Germany's largest collection of ancient Greek and Roman sculpture. Here you find sixth-century B.C. *kouroi* (statues of youths), a colossal *Sleeping Satyr* from the Hellenistic period, and a haunting collection of Roman portraits. The museum is open Tuesday through Sunday from 10 a.m.–5 p.m. (until 8 p.m. on Thursday). Admission is €3 for adults, €2 for students and seniors, free for children under 14.

✔ **Olympiapark** (☎ 089/3067-2414; U-Bahn: Olympiazentrum), site of the 1972 Olympic Games, sits at the northwestern edge of Munich and is a small city unto itself. The colossal 69,000-seat stadium is covered by the largest roof in the world, made of tinted acrylic glass. **Olympiaturm** (☎ 089/3067-2750), the 960-foot- (293-meter-)

high television tower in the center of the park, is open daily from 9 a.m. to midnight. A ticket for a ride to the top costs €3.50 for adults and €2.50 for children under 15. The extraordinary view reaches all the way to the Alps.

Seeing Munich by Guided Tour

A good way to familiarize yourself with the city is to take the one-hour Höhepunkte Münchens (Highlights of Munich) bus tour. **Münchner Stadt-Rundfahrten** (☎ **089/5502-8995**) offers the tours, with commentary in English, daily at 10 a.m., 11 a.m., noon, 1 p.m., 2 p.m., 2:30 p.m., 3 p.m., and 4 p.m. Tour cost is €11 for adults, €6 for children under 14. You buy tickets on the bus and don't need to reserve in advance. The company offers many other tours, including a 2½-hour trip to Schloss Nymphenburg (Tues–Sun); cost is €18 for adults, €10 for children. All tours depart from Bahnhofplatz, in front of the Hertie department store at the main train station plaza.

Dachau: Germany's first concentration camp

In 1933, shortly after Hitler became German chancellor, Himmler ordered the first German concentration camp to be set up in Dachau, 12 miles (19 km) northwest of Munich. Between 1933 and 1945 more than 206,000 prisoners arrived (the exact number is unknown), and more than 32,000 died. The first to arrive were political prisoners (Communists and Social Democrats), followed soon after by "beggars," "antisocial elements," homosexuals, Jehovah's Witnesses, and, after 1938, growing numbers of Jews.

In 2002, parts of the **KZ-Gedenkstätte Dachau** (Dachau Concentration Camp Memorial), Alte-Roemar-Strasse 75 (☎ **08131/1741**) were redesigned to focus on the fate of the prisoners and to integrate the still-existing historic buildings into the reworked permanent exhibition. Visitors now follow the route of the prisoners, enter rooms in which citizens were stripped of all their belongings and rights, and where, after disinfecting, they were given a striped prison uniform. Inscribed boards show the rooms' original conditions and functions. Captions are in German and English.

Dachau did not have gas chambers. Prisoners died through work, hunger, disease, and mass executions by shooting. The names of many of the dead are not known, but displays showing prisoners' faces and videos of survivor interviews put a very human face on the horrific pain and suffering endured by these ordinary citizens.

To get to the camp, take S-Bahn train S2 from the Hauptbahnhof to Dachau (direction: Petershausen), and then transfer to bus 724 or 726 to the camp. The camp is open Tuesday to Sunday from 9 a.m. to 5 p.m.; admission is free.

Munich Walk Tours (☎ 0171/274-0204; Internet: www.munichwalk tours.com), conducted in English, are a great way to acquaint yourself with Munich's history and architecture. The company offers several options; the meeting point for all walks is the New Rathaus directly under the Glockenspiel on Marienplatz. No need to reserve; you pay the guide (identifiable by a yellow sign). The 2¼-hour City Walk Tour starts daily at 10:45 a.m., April through October. Hitler's Munich, lasting about 2½ hours, covers all the important facts and sites that played a role in Munich's Nazi era. The cost for both tours is €9 for adults, €8 for those under 26, free for children under 14.

Shopping for Local Treasures

Munich is the fashion capital of Germany, and when the topic is shopping, Munich ranks right up there with Paris and London. This is not a city where you're likely to find many bargains, however.

General shopping is less pricey on and around **Marienplatz** and along the main pedestrian streets **Kaufingerstrasse** and **Neuhauser Strasse.** The biggest concentration of shops selling secondhand goods is on **Westenriederstrasse.**

Sometimes called "the Bloomingdale's of Germany," **Ludwig Beck am Rathauseck,** Marienplatz 11 (☎ 089/236-910; U-/S-Bahn: Marienplatz), is Munich's best department store and a good place to shop for handmade crafts from all over Germany. **Hertie's,** Bahnhofplatz 7 (☎ 089/55120; U-Bahn: Hauptbahnhof), across from the main train station, is a good, all-purpose department store.

The best streets for elegant boutiques and specialty shops are **Briennerstrasse, Maximilianstrasse** (which also has the leading art galleries), **Maffeistrasse,** and **Theatinestrasse.** On these streets, you find branches of all the top European couturiers and Germany's and Munich's own designers: Jil Sander, Joop, Bogner, Max Dietl, and Rudolph Moshammer. Antiques devotees with deep pockets find what they want on **Ottostrasse.**

Loden-Frey, Maffeistrasse 7–9 (☎ 089/210-390; U-/S-Bahn: Marienplatz), founded in 1842, is the place for all kinds of high-quality *loden* (a waterproof wool) wear, such as coats, jackets, and hats. **Dirndl-Ecke,** Am Platzl 1/Sparkassenstrasse 10 (☎ 089/220-163; U-/S-Bahn: Marienplatz), has a large selection of high-quality Bavarian costumes, *dirndls* (a traditional German dress), folk art, and handicrafts.

Marienplatz at Christmas

Marienplatz, the main square of the inner city, is the scene of a famous *Christkindl Markt*, or Christmas Market. From late November through December the plaza overflows with stalls selling toys, tree ornaments, handicrafts, and a mouth-watering array of traditional snacks and sweets, including gingerbread, sugar-coated almonds, fruitcakes, smoked meats, and piping hot *Glühwein*, a spiced red wine.

Discovering Nightlife in Munich

There is always something going on in Munich. As southern Germany's cultural capital, Munich is renowned for its opera and symphony concerts and theater. But you can also sit back in a leafy beer garden or in a beer hall, have a beer, and enjoy the local scene. (See "The best beer gardens," earlier in this chapter.) You also find plenty of bars and dance clubs for late-night partying.

Raising the curtain on performing arts and music

Few cities in Europe can rival Munich for the sheer number of musical and theatrical events. To find out what's playing, pick up a copy of *Monatsprogramm* (€1.30) from one of the tourist offices. The best way to purchase tickets is to go directly to the venue's box office, called a *Kasse*, which is generally open during the day and an hour before the performance.

Altes Residenztheater (Cuvilliés Theater, Residenzstrasse 1 (☎ 089/2185-1940; Tram: 19), the jewel-box rococo theater in the Residenz (see "Discovering the top attractions from A to Z," earlier in this chapter), is also an important performance venue for plays and operas.

Bayerischen Staatsoper (Bavarian State Opera; ☎ 089/2185-1920) is one of the world's great opera companies. Performances of both opera and ballet take place in the National Theater, Max-Joseph-Platz 2 (Tram 19).

The famous **Münchner Philharmoniker** (Munich Philharmonic Orchestra) performs from mid-September to July in the Philharmonic Hall in the Gasteig Kulturzentrum (Cultural Center), Rosenheimerstrasse 5 (☎ 089/5481-8181; S-Bahn: Rosenheimerplatz).

Checking out bars and clubs

Cafes are quiet in the afternoon, but pick up noise and steam as the evening wears on. In a cafe you can sit with a coffee or a drink and order light meals or pastries. Nightclubs in Munich, as in the rest of the world, tend to get going around 11 p.m. or midnight.

Bars and cafes

Alter Simp, Türkenstrasse 57 (☎ **089/272-3083;** Tram: 18), is a popular cafe that doesn't really get going until after 11 p.m. The cafe is open daily from 10 a.m. to 4 a.m.

Café Extrablatt, Leopoldstrasse 7 (☎ **089/333-333;** U-Bahn: Universität), is a sprawling, smoke-filled hangout for writers, artists, and the occasional celeb. The cafe is open Monday through Thursday from 8 a.m. to midnight, Friday and Saturday from 9 a.m. to 1 a.m., and Sunday from 9 a.m. to midnight.

Havana Club, Herrnstrasse 30 (☎ **089/291-884;** S-Bahn: Isartor), is a lively singles bar fueled by rum-based cocktails. The club hours are Monday through Wednesday from 6 p.m. to 1 a.m. and Thursday through Saturday from 7 p.m. to 2 a.m.

Master's Home, Frauenstrasse 11 (☎ **089/229-909;** U-/S-Bahn: Marienplatz), is done up like an Edwardian-era London club and attracts an eclectic assortment of locals and tourists. You find a restaurant on the premises if you get hungry. The club is open nightly from 6 p.m. to 3 a.m.

Nachtcafé, Maximilianplatz 5 (☎ **089/595-900;** Tram: 49), is one of the most happening nightspots in Munich, attracting soccer stars, movie stars, writers, and waves of "ordinary" patrons to its bar, restaurant, and stage shows (which begin at 11 p.m.). The decor is updated 1950s; the music is jazz, blues, and soul. There's no cover charge. The café is open daily from 9 p.m. to 6 a.m.

Nightclubs

Set within an old factory, **Kunstpark Ost,** Grafingerstrasse 6 (☎ **089/ 4900-2730;** S-Bahn: Ostbahnhof) is Munich's newest complex of bars, restaurants, and dance clubs. You can move from venue to venue according to your interest level. All the bars are open by 8 p.m. (don't show up before then); discos start around 10:30 p.m. Cover ranges from €4 to €8.

Fast Facts: Munich

American Express

American Express, Promenadeplatz 6
(☎ 089/290-900; tram: 19), is open for mail
pickup and check cashing Monday through
Friday from 9 a.m. to 6 p.m. and Saturday
from 9:30 a.m. to 12:30 p.m.

Business Hours

See the Appendix for details.

Country Code and City Code

The city code for Munich is **089**.

Currency Exchange

You can exchange money at the currency
exchange in the Hauptbahnhof (main train
station) daily from 6 a.m. to 11:30 p.m.

Emergencies

For emergency medical aid, or for the police,
call **110**. For the fire department, call **112**.

Internet Access

Times Square Online Bistro in the
Hauptbahnhof, Bayerstrasse side (☎ 089/
5508-8000), has computer workstations, a
bistro, and bar, and is open daily from 7 a.m.
to 1 a.m.

Pharmacies

International Ludwig's Apotheke,
Neuhauserstrasse 11 (☎ 089/260-3021;
U-/S-Bahn: Marienplatz), a drugstore where
English is spoken, is open Monday to Friday

from 9 a.m. to 8 p.m. and Saturday from
9 a.m. to 4 p.m.

Post Office

The Postamt München (main post office)
is across from the Hauptbahnhof, at
Bahnhofplatz 1 (☎ 089/599-0870). The office
is open Monday to Friday from 7 a.m. to
8 p.m., Saturday from 8 a.m to 4 p.m., and
Sunday from 9 a.m. to 3 p.m.

Restrooms

You find restrooms in cafes, restaurants, and
beer halls throughout the Altstadt.

Safety

Munich, like all big cities, has its share of
crime, especially pickpocketing and purse-
and camera-snatching. Most robberies
occur in the much-frequented tourist areas,
such as Marienplatz and the Hauptbahnhof.

Transit Assistance

For information on the U-Bahn and trams,
call the public transportation authority, MVV,
at ☎ 089/4142-4344.

Web Sites

The tourist office Web site, www.
muenchen-tourist.de, is the best
site for general information. You find more
information on Munich and Bavaria at
www.bavaria.com.

Chapter 15

Bavaria: The German Alps and Fairy-Tale Castles

- -

In This Chapter

▶ Driving through the Bavarian Alps

▶ Visiting the alpine resort of Garmisch-Partenkirchen

▶ Exploring the medieval town of Füssen

▶ Discovering the fairy-tale castles of Ludwig II

- -

Although Bavaria's recorded history dates back some 1,100 years, the region didn't become a kingdom until 1806, by order of Napoleon. Bavaria remained a kingdom until 1918, when a German republic replaced the Bavarian monarchy. Brief as it was, many Bavarians still regard that royal era with nostalgia. When they speak wistfully about "the king," they mean only one: Ludwig II, the legendary "dream king" (or "mad king," depending on your interpretation) whose castles at Linderhof and Neuschwanstein draw hundreds of thousands of visitors.

Upper Bavaria *(Oberbayern),* the southernmost part of Germany, gently rises through foothills covered with verdant pastures, lake-splashed countryside, and groves of evergreens to the dramatic heights of the Alps that divide Germany and western Austria. Visitors find a great deal to enjoy in this mountainous region in addition to Ludwig's castles. At every turn, you find romantic villages, rococo churches, houses with fancifully painted facades, historic buildings, world-class ski and winter-sports resorts, and nature on a grand scale. (See the "The Bavarian Alps" map in this chapter.)

Bavarian Alps: Traveler Basics

Visiting the German Alps may sound like a daunting experience, but the mountains are actually fairly easy to get to, especially from Munich. Having a car opens up the delights of this highly picturesque region, but you can also get to the Alps by train.

Getting to the Bavarian Alps and deciding when to go

If you're driving through the Bavarian Alps, I recommend that you make **Garmisch-Partenkirchen** or **Füssen** your headquarters. From either of these towns, with a car, you can easily reach the major attractions along the Alpenstrasse in two or three days. Munich is the major driving gateway, with the **A95** Autobahn leading to Eschenlohe; from there, **E533** leads directly to Garmisch-Partenkirchen.

Although I recommend exploring the Bavarian Alps by car, mostly because of the freedom a car gives you, you can also reach Füssen, Garmisch-Partenkirchen, and Lindau by train. I include train information for each of these towns later in this chapter.

Unless you're a hard-core winter-sports enthusiast, I recommend that you explore the Bavarian Alps in spring or early autumn. In winter, mountain passes often close because of snow. In summer, visitors jam the roads, lakes, hiking trails, inns, and tourist sites.

Driving the German Alpine Road

The best way to see the Bavarian Alps is by car. The 289-mile (465-km) **Deutsche Alpenstrasse** (German Alpine Road) is one of the most scenic roads in Europe. Constructed in the 1930s, the road runs from Lindau on Lake Constance (see Chapter 16) to Berchtesgaden National Park, close to Salzburg, Austria. The winding, well-paved road passes clear, cold lakes, some 25 castles, and dozens of health resorts and historic towns nestled in the forested mountains. Along the route are world-famous sights such as the Zugspitze, Germany's highest peak, and the castles of Neuschwanstein, Hohenschwangau, and Linderhof. From east (Berchtesgaden) to west (Lindau), the Alpenstrasse follows many different roads: B305, B307, B2, B23, B17, B310, and B308. Signs posted along the way direct you to the next section. You can access more information about the Alpenstrasse (in English) on the Web at www.german-alpine-road.de.

Greetings from Bavaria

In Bavaria, people generally use the greeting *Grüss Gott* (pronounced *grease* got) instead of *Guten Morgen* (good morning) or *Guten Tag* (good day). The saying means, roughly, "God greets you." Goodbye is *für Gott* (for God; *fear* got) or *für dich* (for you; *fear* dikh).

The Bavarian Alps

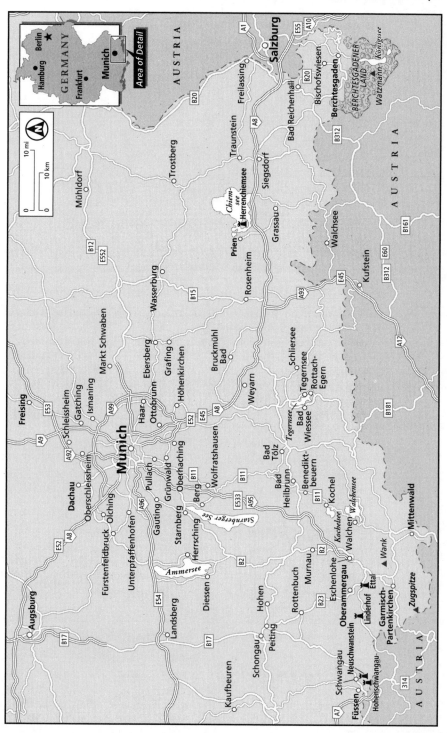

Skiing in the Alps

The skiing in the Bavarian Alps is the best in Germany. Ski slopes on the **Zugspitze,** Germany's highest peak, begin at 8,700 feet (2,650 meters). The best-known ski resort in this premiere ski area is Garmisch-Partenkirchen (see "Garmisch-Partenkirchen: Doing the Zugspitze," later in this chapter). The second great alpine skiing area in the Bavarian Alps is **Berchtesgadener Land**, an area east of Garmisch-Partenkirchen within yodeling distance of Austria. In Berchtesgadener Land, where the nearest town is Berchtesgaden, the snow conditions are good until March at Jenner, Rossfeld, Götschen, and Hochschwarzeck. For more information on skiing and ski resorts in Berchtesgaden Land, contact the local tourist information agency, Kurdirektion des Berchtesgadener Landes, Königsseestrasse 2, 83471 Berchtesgaden (☎ **08562/9670;** Internet: www.berchtesgadener-land.com).

Garmisch-Partenkirchen: Doing the Zugspitze

Located about 60 miles (97 km) southwest of Munich, the twin villages of Garmisch and Partenkirchen comprise Germany's top winter-sports resort. (See the "Garmisch-Partenkirchen" map in this chapter.) In 1936 the fourth Winter Olympics took place here, and in 1978 the towns hosted the World Alpine Ski Championships. Garmisch-Partenkirchen enjoys a stunning location at the foot of the Wetterstein range. Two giant peaks, the Alpspitze and the Waxensteine, rear up to the south of town, hiding Germany's tallest mountain, the famed **Zugspitze.**

Unfortunately, the towns have a commercial, touristy air. Yet, you still find charming details: the sound of cowbells in the meadows outside town, streets and lanes (particularly in Partenkirchen) with a quiet, village atmosphere, and country folk in traditional Bavarian dress.

Getting there

Trains run frequently from all directions to Garmisch-Partenkirchen. The trip time from Munich is 1 hour 22 minutes. For information and schedules, call **German Rail** at ☎ **01805/996-633.**

To reach Garmisch-Partenkirchen by **car,** take the **A95** Autobahn from Munich and exit at Eschenlohe. The trip takes about one hour.

Finding information

The **Tourist Information office** at Richard-Strauss-Platz 2 (☎ **08821/180-700;** Internet: www.garmisch-partenkirchen.de) is open Monday to

Garmisch-Partenkirchen

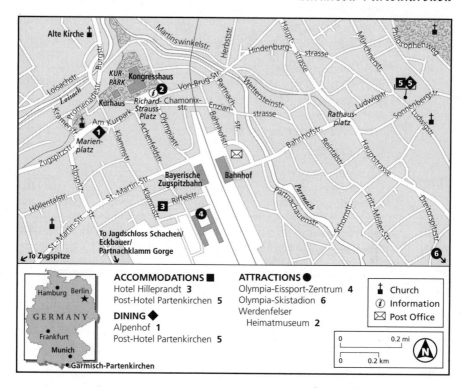

ACCOMMODATIONS ■
Hotel Hilleprandt **3**
Post-Hotel Partenkirchen **5**

DINING ◆
Alpenhof **1**
Post-Hotel Partenkirchen **5**

ATTRACTIONS ●
Olympia-Eissport-Zentrum **4**
Olympia-Skistadion **6**
Werdenfelser
  Heimatmuseum **2**

✝ Church
ⓘ Information
✉ Post Office

Saturday from 8 a.m. to 6 p.m. and Sunday and holidays from 10 a.m. to noon. The office supplies maps and details of area hikes and attractions.

Getting around Garmisch-Partenkirchen

A free municipal bus runs every 15 minutes between the *Bahnhof* (train station) and Marienplatz, Garmisch's main square. From Marienplatz, you can walk to all the centrally located hotels. The **Bayerische Zugspitzbahn** at Garmisch (☎ **08821/7970**) provides rail service to the top of the Zugspitze and other local peaks.

Staying in Garmisch-Partenkirchen

Hotel Hilleprandt
$ **Garmisch**

This chalet, with wooden balconies, a pretty garden, an outdoor terrace, and a backdrop of forest-covered mountains, is an excellent budget choice. The 13 rooms, some with a private balcony, are small but very comfortable. The tiled bathrooms have either showers or tub-shower combinations. The hotel is close to the Zugspitze Bahnhof and the Olympic Ice Stadium. Children under 6 stay free in their parents' room.

Riffelstrasse 17, 82467 Garmisch-Partenkirchen. ☎ *08821/2861. Fax: 08821/74548. Internet:* www.hotel-hilleprandt.de. *Rack rates: €74–€96 double. Rates include buffet breakfast. MC, V.*

Post-Hotel Partenkirchen
$–$$ Partenkirchen

Founded in 1492, the Post-Hotel Partenkirchen is one of the town's most prestigious hotels. Antiques and elaborately carved furnishings (the style is called "Bavarian Baroque") decorate the 59 stylish rooms. Some rooms have balconies with views of the Alps. Bathrooms are larger than average and have tub and shower combinations. This is a full-service hotel with a golf course and tennis courts.

Ludwigstrasse 49, 82467 Garmisch-Partenkirchen. ☎ *08821/93630. Fax: 08821/ 9363-2222. Internet:* www.post-hotel.de. *Rack rates: €95–€150 double. Rates include continental breakfast. AE, DC, MC, V.*

Dining in Garmisch-Partenkirchen

Alpenhof
$–$$ Garmisch BAVARIAN

Locals regard the Alpenhof as one of the finest restaurants in Garmisch. Traditional Bavarian specialties are on the menu, as well as fresh trout, grilled salmon, and ragout of venison. For dessert, try a soufflé.

Am Kurpark 10. ☎ *08821/59055. Reservations recommended. Main courses: €8–€22. MC, V. Open: Daily 11:30 a.m.–2 p.m. and 5:30–9:30 p.m. Closed 3 weeks in Nov.*

Post-Hotel Partenkirchen
$$–$$$ Partenkirchen BAVARIAN

The Post-Hotel Partenkirchen with its rustic, old-fashioned dining rooms (one called the Posthalterei and the other the Poststuberl) is always a safe bet for a good lunch or dinner. The fixed-price menus change daily. The à la carte menu usually includes specialties like calf's liver in red-pepper sauce and a *Bauernschnitzel* (country schnitzel) with bacon, eggs, pickles, and roast potatoes. In the fall, the menu includes game. A third restaurant, the Post Taverne, serves light Italian cuisine.

Ludwigstrasse 49. ☎ *08821/93630. Reservations recommended. Main courses:* €*9.50–*€*17; fixed-price menus* €*9.50–*€*24. AE, DC, MC, V. Open: Daily noon to 2 p.m. and 6–9:30 p.m.*

Exploring Garmisch-Partenkirchen

Garmisch-Partenkirchen is a center for winter sports, summer hiking, and mountain climbing. Consequently, visitors come more for outdoor activities than indoor pursuits. The best way to explore Garmisch is simply to stroll around the town and its environs, enjoying the panoramic views of the Alps and the colorful buildings that line the side streets.

Built for the 1936 Winter Olympics, the **Olympia-Eissport-Zentrum** (Olympic Ice Stadium; ☎ **08821/753-294**) in Garmisch contains three giant skating rinks with stands for 12,000 spectators. The ice rinks are open to the public daily from July until the middle of May from 10 a.m. to noon (also from 2–4 p.m. on Saturday and Sunday). Admission is €2.60 for adults, €1.50 for children 6 to 15.

On the slopes at the edge of town is the **Olympia-Skistadion** (Olympic Ski Stadium), with two ski jumps and a slalom course. Like the ice stadium, this ski facility opened in 1936 and remains an integral part of winter life in Garmisch. The World Cup Ski Jump takes place here every January 1.

If you want to learn more about the history of this region, stop in at the compact **Werdenfelser Heimatmuseum,** Ludwigstrasse 47 (☎ **08821/ 2134**), where exhibits of artifacts and folk art chronicle the last 2,000 years. You can see everything in 30 minutes. The museum is open Tuesday through Friday from 10 a.m. to 1 p.m. and 3 to 6 p.m.; Saturday, Sunday, and holiday hours are 10 a.m. to 1 p.m. Admission is €1.53 for adults, €.51 for children.

Alpine hiking is a major summertime attraction (see "Hiking around Garmisch-Partenkirchen," later in this section). People come from around the world to roam the mountain paths (called *Hohenwege,* or "high ways"), enjoy nature, and watch animals in the forest. One hiking destination, 5,628 feet (1,688 meters) above Garmisch-Partenkirchen and accessible only by foot (the climb is strenuous), is the **Jagdschloss Schachen** (☎ **08821/2996**), a hunting lodge built by Ludwig II, the "dream king," in 1871. The exterior of the lodge resembles a Swiss chalet, but the king insisted on an elaborately fanciful Moorish-style interior. The only way to see the lodge is by guided tour (in German only), given at 11 a.m. and 2 p.m. from early June to early October. Admission is €2.50 for adults, free for children under 14. You need about four hours to get there and back. The tourist office in Garmisch-Partenkirchen (see "Finding information," earlier in this section) can supply further details.

A wonderful way to spend an hour on a winter's night is in the back of a **horse-drawn sleigh.** In Garmisch, **Café Waldstein,** Königseer Fussweg 17 (☎ **08652/2427**), arranges rides. The cost is around €52 per hour per sleigh.

Ascending the Zugspitze

For a spectacular view of the Bavarian and the Tyrolean (Austrian) Alps, you can go all the way to the summit of the **Zugspitze,** Germany's tallest mountain (9,720 feet/2,960 meters). You can choose between two different ways to reach the Zugspitze from the center of Garmisch, both involving a ride on a cog railway and a cable car.

✔ The first way begins with a trip on the **Zugspitzbahn** (cog railway), which departs from the back of Garmisch's main railway station daily every hour from 8:35 a.m. to 2:35 p.m. The train travels uphill, past giant boulders and rushing streams, to the *Zugspitzplatte,* a high plateau with sweeping views. At the Zugspitzplatte, you transfer onto a cable car, the **Gletscherbahn,** for a four-minute ride uphill to the *Zugspitzgipfel* (summit), where you find extraordinary panoramas, a cafe and restaurant, a gift shop, and many alpine trails. Total travel time to the top is about 55 minutes.

✔ The second way to get to the summit of the Zugspitze is to take the **Zugspitzbahn** for a shorter trip, disembarking 9 miles (14 km) southwest of Garmisch at the lower station of the **Eibsee Sielbahn** (Eibsee Cable Car). The stop is next to an alpine lake and clearly marked. From here, the cable car carries you to the Zugspitzgipfel. The entire trip takes about 40 minutes. The Eibsee Sielbahn makes runs every half hour from 8:30 a.m. to 4:30 p.m. (5:30 p.m. in July and August).

I recommend that you purchase a round-trip ticket called a *Berg und Talfahrt* (Mountain and Valley Trip), which allows you to ascend one way and descend the other for the widest range of spectacular views. The round-trip fare is €31 for adults, €18 for children ages 5 to 15. A family ticket for two adults and one child costs €84. For more information, contact the **Bayerische Zugspitzbahn,** Olympiastrasse 27, Garmisch-Partenkirchen (☎ **08821/797-900**).

Be sure to wear warm clothing if you ascend the Zugspitze, a journey that takes at least half a day.

Hiking around Garmisch-Partenkirchen

The area around Garmisch-Partenkirchen is magnificent hiking country. The tourist office has a brochure and various information sheets outlining the best trails and their varying degrees of difficulty. All of the trails are clearly marked with signs. Most hikes take an energetic four to five hours, but some of them are shorter and easy enough for children.

One easily accessible destination is the 4,060-foot (1,240-meter) **Eckbauer** peak on the southern edge of Partenkirchen. On its lower slopes you find easy trails that can be enjoyed by first-time alpine hikers. You can also take a chairlift to the top and descend on foot in less than an hour along relatively easy forest trails. The cable car from Garmisch to the top of the Eckbauer departs year-round from the **Eckbauerbahn** (☎ 08821/7970), adjacent to the ski stadium in Garmisch. The round-trip fare is €10 for adults, €6 for children, and €23 for two adults and a child.

Another picturesque hike is through the **Partnachklamm Gorge,** a canyon with a roaring stream at the bottom and sheer cliff walls rising on both sides of the hiking trail. Take the **Graseck Seilbahn** (cable car) from its departure point at the bottom of the gorge, less than a half-mile south of Garmisch's ski stadium. The cable car operates at 20-minute intervals from 7 a.m. to 8 p.m., 11 p.m. on weekends. You get off at the first station, adjacent to the **Forsthaus Graseck** (☎ 08821/54006), a hotel where you can get a meal or drink. From the station, you descend on foot along narrow paths by the sides of the stream, sometimes passing behind waterfalls. The path crosses the gorge and returns you to the point where you entered. This is an easy and memorable adventure. You may want to wear raingear because of the mist from the waterfalls along the way. From its departure point to the Forsthaus, the three-minute cable-car ride costs €3 per person each way. The tourist office (see "Finding information," earlier in this section) can give you more information.

Discovering the local nightlife

From mid-May through September, Bavarian folk music and dancing take place every Saturday night in the **Bayernhalle,** Brauhausstrasse 19. During the same season, the **Garmisch park bandstand** hosts classical concerts Saturday through Thursday. On Friday, these concerts move to the **Partenkirchen bandstand.** Check with the local tourist office (see "Finding information," earlier in this section) for details about these programs. The twin towns also host a five-day **Johann Strauss Festival** in June.

Oberammergau: Woodcarvers and Passion Plays

An alpine village located 12 miles (20 km) north of Garmisch-Partenkirchen, Oberammergau is famed for its woodcarvers and

Hinterglas artists. You can see examples of local woodcarving on cottages and inns, and in the churchyard of the town. *Hinterglas* (behind glass) painting, an art form unique to Bavaria, Croatia, and parts of Austria, is painting done directly on glass, and in reverse. The town is worth a visit any time, but once every ten years, a crowd from all over the world converges on Oberammergau to see the **Passionspiele** (Passion Play).

Oberammergau is a stop on the Deutsche Alpenstrasse (see "Driving the German Alpine Road," earlier in this chapter), and an easy side-trip from Garmisch-Partenkirchen (see "Garmisch-Partenkirchen: Doing the Zugspitze," earlier in this chapter). Travelers also stay in Oberammergau as a base for visiting Linderhof Castle, 11 miles (17 km) south (see "Schloss Linderhof: Ludwig's Little Versailles," later in this chapter).

Getting there

Daily **trains** arrive from Munich in two hours and from Frankfurt in seven hours. For train information and schedules, call **German Rail** at ☎ **01805/996-633.** Regional **bus** service provided by **RVO Regionalverkehr Oberbayern** in Garmisch-Partenkirchen (☎ **08821/ 948-274**) also serves the town. A shuttle bus runs back and forth between Oberammergau and Garmisch-Partenkirchen daily. If you're coming by **car** from Garmisch-Partenkirchen, take E533 north and turn west onto B23 at Oberau.

Finding information

The **Verkehrs- und Reisebüro** (travel office), Eugen-Papst-Strasse 9A (☎ **08822/92310;** Internet: www.oberammergau.de), is open Monday to Friday from 8:30 a.m. to 6 p.m. and on Saturday from 8:30 a.m. to 1 p.m.

Staying and dining in Oberammergau

Hotel Alte Post, Dorfstrasse 19, 82487 Oberammergau (☎ **08822/9100;** Fax: 08822/910-100; Internet: www.altepost.ogau.de), in the heart of the village, has been around since 1612. The hotel has 60 nicely furnished rooms, all different sizes, including some with beamed ceilings. Menu specialties in the restaurant include local beef, lamb, and trout dishes. Main courses range from €10 to €15. Rack rates for a double room are €52 to €81, including buffet breakfast. The hotel and restaurant accept all major credit cards.

Exploring Oberammergau

The town is dramatically situated in a wide valley surrounded by forests, meadows, and mountains. **Berg Laber,** the mountainous mass that rises to the east of the town, is accessible via a cable car (☎ 08822/ **4770**) that operates year-round from 9 to 11:30 a.m. and 1 to 5 p.m. The 10-minute ascent costs €10 per person. To reach the top of **Berg Kolber,** to the west, you take a two-passenger chairlift (☎ 08822/4760) that operates year-round from 9 to 11:45 a.m. and 1 to 4:30 p.m. The round-trip cost is €5.10.

WellenBerg (☎ 08822/6787), the town's amazing indoor/outdoor recreation center, boasts giant open-air pools (heated, unheated, one with a wave machine), water slides, a sauna, solarium, and restaurant. Spending a couple of hours basking by (or in) a pool set in a high alpine meadow satisfies kids of all ages. A three-hour entrance ticket that includes the sauna costs €10 for adults, €7 for children. Prices are less if you use only the pools. The center is open daily.

The **Heimatmuseum** (Town Museum), Dorfstrasse 8 (☎ 08822/94136), is worth visiting to see the charming collection of 18th- to 20th-century Christmas crèches, hand-carved and painted wooden Nativity figures. The museum is open May 20 to October 15, Tuesday through Sunday, from 2 to 6 p.m.; off-season, the museum is open Saturday only from 2 to 6 p.m. Admission is €2.55 for adults, €1.55 for students, and €.50 for children under 14.

Since the 16th century Oberammergau has been known for its wood-carvers. Many of them are now trained in the village woodcarver's school. In the **Pilatushaus,** Ludwig-Thoma-Strasse (☎ 08822/1682), you can watch local carvers, *Hinterglas* painters, sculptors, and potters, as they work. The facility is open May through October Tuesday through Friday from 1:30 to 6 p.m. Admission is free.

Shopping for woodcarvings

Collectors throughout the world prize Oberammergau's woodcarvings. Most of the carvings are of religious scenes, but you also find drinking or hunting scenes. Competition is fierce for sales of these woodcarvings, many of which are made in hamlets and farmhouses throughout the region. Know before you buy that even some of the most expensive "handmade" pieces may have been carved by machine prior to being finished off by hand. If you're looking for authentic woodcarvings, the following stores are reliable:

- ✔ **Holzschnitzerei Franz Barthels,** Schnitzlergasse 4 (☎ 08822/ **6433**), sells a wide range of carvings, everything from small figures of saints for €54 to jumping jacks with movable legs for €36.

- ✔ **Tony Baur,** Dorfstrasse 27 (☎ 08822/821), has the most-sophisticated inventory of wood carvings crafted from maple, pine, and linden. Prices start around €11 and go up to €5,110.

Oberammergau's Passion Play

Actors first performed the famous **Passionspiele** (Passion Play) in Oberammergau in 1634 when the town's citizens took a vow to give thanks for being spared from the plague. Locals have performed the 5½-hour, 16-act drama depicting Christ's journey to the Cross every decade since 1680 (the last was in 2000, the next will be in 2010). The cast for this religious epic numbers in the hundreds. Actors must be natives of or have lived in the town for at least 20 years. Performances take place in the **Passionspiel Theater**, Passionswiese 1 (☎ **08822/92310**), built for the 1930 season. The text of the Passionspiel has stirred controversy for its anti-Jewish lines.

Schloss Linderhof: Ludwig's Little Versailles

A scenic drive through the Emmertal, a valley flanked by 5,000- to 6,000-foot peaks, takes you to Schloss Linderhof (☎ **08822/92030**), the most elaborate of King Ludwig II's fairy-tale palaces. Linderhof is open year-round and makes a wonderful day trip from Garmisch-Partenkirchen or Oberammergau.

Getting there

Buses run between Oberammergau and Schloss Linderhof seven times per day, beginning at 9 a.m.; the last bus leaves Linderhof at 5:35 p.m. The round-trip fare is €4.95. If you're **driving** from Oberammergau, take B23 south about 3 miles (5 km) toward Ettal, turn west at the sign for Schloss Linderhof, and then drive for 8 miles (13 km), passing the hamlet of Graswang on the way.

Exploring Schloss Linderhof

In 1869 King Ludwig II decided to redesign this former royal hunting lodge to resemble the Petit Trianon at Versailles. In the 1870s, he transformed the rustic lodge into a small, dazzling-white chateau overloaded with statues and decorations derived from many different periods and countries. Ludwig frequently stayed at Linderhof while work progressed on Neuschwanstein (see "Neuschwanstein and Hohenschwangau: Castles in the Air," later in this chapter). This is the one royal palace that he regarded as "home."

For all its ostentatiousness, Linderhof is not without charm, thanks in large part to the beauty of its natural setting in the Ammerberge range and its formal French gardens. The front of the palace faces the **Fountain of Neptune,** a large pool where a jet of water sprays high into the air from a gilded statue in its center.

Linderhof is an extremely popular tourist attraction, so arrive early or you may have a long wait. You can see the palace only by guided tour; tours in English are available at various times throughout the day. Your ticket has a specific entry time. A sign at the front of the palace tells you what group is currently being admitted. When your time arrives, feed your ticket through the electronic turnstile to gain entrance. A guide will meet your group outside the castle.

The ornate exterior is actually restrained when compared to the interior, which is a riot of rococo flashiness, glittering with gold leaf, mirrors, and crystal chandeliers. The most interesting rooms are on the second floor. Ascending a staircase of Carrara marble, you find yourself at the **West Gobelin Room,** a music room decorated with French Gobelin tapestries and carved and gilded paneling. This room leads directly into the **Hall of Mirrors,** where mirrors set in white and-gold hand-carved panels line the walls and frescoes depicting mythological scenes cover the ceiling.

The private fantasies of the self-obsessed monarch are everywhere. The **dining room** contains a "magic table," that could be lowered to the kitchen, allowing the reclusive monarch to dine without the intrusive presence of servants. The largest room in the palace is the **king's bedchamber,** overlooking the Fountain of Neptune. Like Louis XIV, the French monarch he sought to emulate, Ludwig often received visitors in his bedchamber — that's why a carved and gilded balustrade closes off his bed. He didn't sleep in this room, though. He slept in an alcove in the Hall of Mirrors.

Ludwig designed the formal **gardens** with baroque sculptures, elegant fountains, and flower beds and paths in geometrical shapes. The park contains several small, fanciful buildings, including the **Marokkanisches Haus** (Moorish Pavilion), a cast-iron pavilion walled with zinc plaques, and the **Grotte** (Grotto), inspired by the famous Blue Grotto at Capri. Built of artificial rock, with stalagmites and stalactites dividing the cavelike room into three chambers, the grotto contains an artificial lake fed by an artificial waterfall and a stage hung with a backdrop scene of the first act of Wagner's opera *Tannhäuser*. The 19th-century grotto contained the first full electrical installation in Bavaria. The original colored-light effects still illuminate the room, which could turn into a sauna bath due to under-the-floor heating. On the lake, which had artificial waves, Ludwig kept two swans and a gilded, swan-shaped boat, in which he would be rowed.

The palace and grounds are open March 23 to October 10 daily from 9 a.m. to 6 p.m. (Thursday until 8 p.m.); the Venus Grotto and Moorish

Kiosk close from October 11 to March 22, but the castle is open daily from 10 a.m. to 4 p.m. Admission in the summer is €6 for adults, €5 for seniors over 65 and students. Winter admission is €4.50 for adults, €3.50 for students and seniors. The parking fee is €2.

Füssen: Medieval Memories

Situated in foothills of the Bavarian Alps is Füssen, 74 miles (119 km) southwest of Munich. (See the "Füssen" map in this chapter.) Divided by the Lech river and located just 2½ miles (4 km) from the Austrian border, this town of 15,000 inhabitants has lovely squares and narrow, cobblestone streets flanked by medieval stone houses. Its history dates back to Roman times, when Füssen was a trading station. Tucked into the Lech valley and surrounded by 6,000- to 7,000-foot (1,800–2,100-meter) peaks, Füssen is an atmospheric place to headquarter while exploring the castles of Neuschwanstein and Hohenschwangau and other sights along the Deutsche Alpenstrasse.

Getting there

Trains from Munich (trip time 2½ hours) and Frankfurt (trip time 6–7 hours) arrive frequently throughout the day. For train information, call **German Rail** at ☎ **01805/996-633.**

By **car** from Munich, take the A7 Autobahn south. If you're driving from Garmisch-Partenkirchen, head north on B23 through Oberammergau, jog west on B472, and turn south on B17.

Finding information

Füssen Tourismus operates two tourist offices, one at Kaiser-Maximilian-Platz 1, another in the **Rathaus** (town hall), Lechhalde 3 (☎ **08362/ 93850** for both). Summer hours are Monday to Friday from 8:30 a.m. to 6 p.m. and Saturday from 9 a.m. to 2:30 p.m.; winter hours are Monday to Friday from 9 a.m. to 5 p.m. and Saturday from 10 a.m. to noon.

Staying in Füssen

Altstadt-Hotel zum Hechten
$ **Altstadt**

Owned and operated by the same family for generations, this spotless guesthouse with flower-filled flower boxes exudes an air of old-fashioned Bavarian hospitality. The 35 comfortable rooms are small to medium in size. Most of them have small shower-only bathrooms. The hotel is located directly below the castle in Füssen's *Altstadt* (Old Town).

Füssen

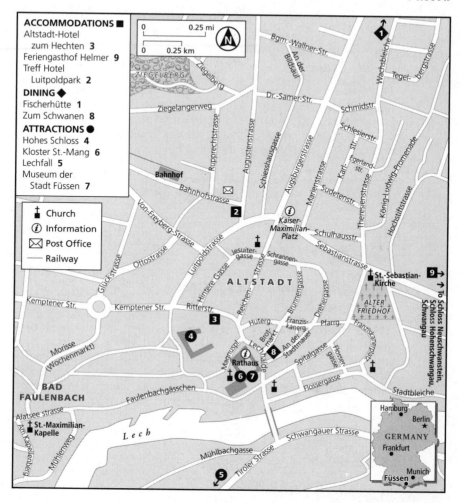

ACCOMMODATIONS ■
Altstadt-Hotel
  zum Hechten **3**
Feriengasthof Helmer **9**
Treff Hotel
  Luitpoldpark **2**
DINING ◆
Fischerhütte **1**
Zum Schwanen **8**
ATTRACTIONS ●
Hohes Schloss **4**
Kloster St.-Mang **6**
Lechfall **5**
Museum der
  Stadt Füssen **7**

✝ Church
ⓘ Information
✉ Post Office
— Railway

Ritterstrasse 6, 87629 Füssen. ☎ **08362/91600**. Fax: 08362/916-099. Internet:
www.hotel-hechten.com. Rack rates: €57 double without bathroom, €78
double with bathroom. Rates include buffet breakfast. AE, MC, V.

Feriengasthof Helmer
$ Schwangau

Located in Schwangau, a small village about 2½ miles (4 km) east of
Füssen, this traditional Bavarian guesthouse has views of the mountains
and nearby castles. The rooms are all furnished differently; some have
balconies, most have showers in the bathrooms. Stay here if you want
old-fashioned atmosphere. Kids enjoy the nearby pool and find plenty of
room to play outside.

Mitteldorf 10, 87645 Schwangau. ☎ *08362/9800. Fax: 08362/980-200. Internet:* www. hotel-helmer.de. *Rack rates: €60–€106. Rates include buffet breakfast. MC.*

Treff Hotel Luitpoldpark
$$–$$$ Altstadt

This hotel, right in the center of town, has an underground garage, a notable convenience for those with cars. The hotel frequently hosts group tours, and rooms, arranged around a central domed atrium, vary considerably in size and layout. Rooms are comfortably furnished but don't have a lot of personality; most have bathrooms with showers.

Luitpoldstrasse, 87629 Füssen. ☎ *08362/9040. Fax: 08362/904-678. Internet:* www. luitpoldpark-hotel.de. *Rack rates: €144–€184 double. Rates include buffet breakfast. AE, MC, V.*

Dining in Füssen

Fischerhütte (Fisherman's Cottage)
$$ Hopfen am See   SEAFOOD

This restaurant at the edge of a small lake 3 miles northwest of Füssen, within sight of dramatic mountain scenery, specializes in seafood from around the world. Menu offerings may include Alaskan salmon, North Atlantic lobster, French-style bouillabaisse, fresh local trout, or grilled halibut. A few meat dishes are also available. Diners can enjoy Bavarian specialties during the summer in an outdoor beer garden.

Uferstrasse 16, Hopfen am See (3 miles northwest of Füssen). ☎ *08362/91970. Reservations recommended. Main courses: €11–€23. AE, MC, V. Open: Daily 11:30 a.m.–2 p.m. and 5:30–9:30 p.m.*

Zum Schwanen
$–$$ SWABIAN/BAVARIAN

This small, old-fashioned restaurant serves a flavorful blend of Swabian and Bavarian cuisine. Specialties include homemade sausage, roast pork, lamb, and venison. Service is helpful and attentive, and portions are generous.

Brotmarkt 4. ☎ *08362/6174. Reservations recommended. Main courses: €6.50–€17. MC, V. Open: Tues–Sat 11:30 a.m.–2 p.m. and 6:30–10 p.m.*

Exploring Füssen

Füssen's main attraction is the **Hohes Schloss** (High Castle), Magnusplatz (☎ **08362/903-164**), reached by a steep lane behind the parish church. The powerful Prince-Bishops of Augsburg used the Hohes Schloss, one of the finest late-Gothic castles in Bavaria, as a summer residence. Now the castle is the home of the **Staatsgalerie,** where you find a collection of Swabian artwork from the 1400s to the 1700s. The **Rittersaal** (Knight's Hall) has an elaborately coffered ceiling. The museum is open Tuesday to Sunday April through October from 11 a.m. to 4 p.m., November through March from 2 to 4 p.m., and charges €2.50 for admission.

Immediately below the castle lies the **Kloster St.-Mang** (Monastery of St. Magnus), founded by Benedictine monks in the eighth century on the site where an Irish missionary monk named St. Magnus died in 750. In the early 18th century, Johann-Jakob Herkomer, a local architect, turned the church and monastery into a baroque gem with a strong Venetian influence. The Romansque crypt in front of the high altar contains frescoes painted around A.D. 1000 depicting St. Magnus. The **St. Anna-Kapelle** (Chapel of St. Anne) has a mural painted in 1602 depicting the macabre *Totentanz* or "dance of death."

Access to the secularized church complex is through the **Museum der Stadt Füssen** (City Museum), Lechhalde 3 (☎ **08362/903-145**), which occupies the former state apartments of the abbey and displays artifacts relating to the history and culture of the region, including a collection of locally produced violins and lutes. The museum is open Tuesday through Sunday. From April through October hours are 11 a.m. to 4 p.m., from November through March, 2 to 4 p.m. Admission is €2.50 for adults, children under 14 free. A combination ticket for the City Museum and the museum in the castle costs €3.

The Wieskirche: A masterpiece in a meadow

The **Wieskirche** (☎ **08862/501**), a pilgrimage church located in an alpine meadow (the name means "church in the meadow") a few miles north of Füssen, is one of the world's most exuberantly decorated rococo buildings. This masterpiece by Dominikus Zimmermann (1685–1766), who worked on the church with his brother from 1746 to 1754, draws visitors from all over the globe. Behind a rather sober facade, the light-flooded interior with its enormous cupola shimmers with a super-abundance of woodcarvings, gilded stucco, columns, statues, and bright frescoes.

The church is open daily from 8 a.m. to 5 p.m. (Apr–Sept until 7 p.m.). Admission is free. The church is located in Wies, 4 miles (6 km) southeast of the town of Steingaden off B17, on the Deutsche Alpenstrasse. From Füssen's train station, a bus travels to the Wieskirche twice per day Monday through Friday (weekend buses depart once a day). Departure times vary, so check the timetable at the Füssen train station or ask at the Füssen tourist office (see "Finding information," in this chapter's section on Füssen). The trip takes one hour and costs €5.10 round-trip.

The **Lechfall,** a waterfall less than a half-mile (.5 km) south of town, is a popular walk from Füssen. A pedestrian footbridge spans the falls, located where the Lech River squeezes through a rocky gorge and over a high ledge.

Neuschwanstein and Hohenschwangau: Castles in the Air

Located just 4 miles (7 km) east of Füssen, near the village of Schwangau, are two of the royal castles of Bavaria, Hohenschwangau and Neuschwanstein. Hohenschwangau, built by Maximilian II in 1836, is the less remarkable and more intimate of the two. Neuschwanstein, the most photographed building in Germany, was the fairy-tale concoction of Maximilian's son, King Ludwig II.

The royal castles of Hohenschwangau and Neuschwanstein are the most popular tourist attractions in Germany, receiving nearly a million visitors a year. Be prepared for long lines (sometimes up to three hours) in the summer, especially in August. On some days, 25,000 people visit. To save yourself time, try to arrive as soon as the castles open in the morning.

Getting there

If you're **driving** from Füssen, head east along B17. The 4-mile (7-km) drive takes about five minutes. One parking lot serves both castles. Parking costs €4. Ten **buses** a day arrive from Füssen.

Finding information and buying tickets

Information about both castles and the region in general is available in Schwangau at the **Kurverwaltung** (tourist office) in the Rathaus, Münchenerstrasse 2 (☎ 08362/81980), open Monday through Friday from 8 a.m. to 5 p.m., Saturday from 9 a.m. to noon.

A **ticket office** near the parking lot of the castles sells tickets for both Hohenschwangau and Neuschwanstein. You can see the castles only on guided tours, which last about 35 minutes each. Ask for a tour in English; these take place at various times during the day. A tour number and entry time are printed on your ticket. A digital sign informs you when your tour is ready. When the time comes, feed your ticket into the turnstile in front of the respective castle. The tour guide will meet you inside.

Ludwig II: Madman or dreamer?

For some, Ludwig II is "the mad king." For others, he is "the dream king." This strange, self-obsessed monarch has become one of the legendary figures in Bavarian history. Biographies, films, plays, and even a musical (see the " Ludwig II: The Musical" sidebar, in this chapter) have been written about him.

Born in Munich in 1845, the son of King Maximilian II and Queen Maria of Prussia, Ludwig II spent much of his youth at Hohenschwangau castle. He was only 18 years old when he was crowned king of Bavaria. Tall, handsome, and blue-eyed, Ludwig grew bored with the affairs of state and eventually became more and more obsessed with acting out his extravagant fantasies. A patron of the composer Richard Wagner, he often had Wagner's operas performed for his own solitary pleasure. At **Linderhof**, the first palace that he built (see "Schloss Linderhof: Ludwig's Little Versailles," earlier in this chapter), Ludwig went so far as to reconstruct the Venus grotto from Wagner's opera *Tannhäuser.* The most famous of his design efforts is the turreted castle of **Neuschwanstein**, perched on a crag high above the town of Schwangau. Ludwig's excesses eventually threatened to bankrupt the kingdom, and in 1886, at age 41, he was declared insane. Three days later, he was found drowned in Lake Starnberg on the outskirts of Munich, along with the physician who had declared him insane. Was he murdered or did he commit suicide? No one knows. The crypt of the Michaelskirche (St. Michael's Church) in Munich contains Ludwig's grave and those of other Wittelsbach royals.

Exploring Hohenschwangau

To reach the castle entrance, follow Alpseestrasse around to **Pindarplatz,** a picturesque viewpoint on the north bank of the Alpsee lake, and cross the avenue to the castle.

In the 12th century, Hohenschwangau was one of many castles owned by the lords of Schwangau. The castle was a 600-year-old ruin when Ludwig's father, Maximilian II, then Bavaria's crown prince, bought it in 1832. On the ruins he built the neo-Gothic castle you see today and used it as a summer holiday residence. Ludwig II spent much of his joyless childhood at Hohenschwangau with his strait-laced father and his mother, Queen Maria of Prussia.

The rooms of Hohenschwangau were designed and furnished in a ponderous "Gothic Castle" style that was fashionable in the 1830s and 1840s. Maximilian had scenes of Germanic legends painted on the walls. Swans are a recurring motif. Hohenschwangau was the capital of what was known as the *Schwangau* (Swan Country), a region where swans had always been plentiful. (You can still see swans today). The sight of the huge white birds gliding and flying around the alpine lakes fascinated both Maximilian and his son.

The **Hall of the Swan Knight,** named for the wall paintings depicting the saga of Lohengrin (a Germanic hero associated with the swan), is one of the castle's most attractive chambers. There seems little doubt that the Gothic style of the castle, with its mythical scenes of Lohengrin, the Holy Grail, and the medieval poet-singer Tannhäuser (all of whom would become subjects for operas by Richard Wagner) greatly influenced young Ludwig's imagination. Swans, knights, and solitary medieval heroes — godlike symbols of strength and purity — became recurring motifs in Ludwig's life and in Wagner's operas.

For all its overdecorated heaviness, Hohenschwangau manages to look more like an actual home than Neuschwanstein. (The former royal family still owns the castle, in fact.) The **music room** on the second floor contains copies of letters between Ludwig II and his musical idol Richard Wagner and the grand piano on which the two played duets. For many years, the extravagant dream king financed Wagner, who was first invited to Hohenschwangau by a teenaged Ludwig.

Hohenschwangau, Alpseestrasse (☎ **08362/81127**), is open daily. March 15 to October 15 hours are 8:30 a.m. to 6 p.m.; October 16 to March 14 hours are 9:30 a.m. to 4 p.m. Admission is €7 for adults and €6 for students and children 6 to 15.

Exploring Neuschwanstein

Reaching the castle entrance involves a steep ½-mile/30-minute climb from the parking lot at Hohenschwangau Castle (see the preceding section, "Exploring Hohenschwangau"). If you don't want to walk, you can take a **bus** to **Marienbrücke,** a bridge that crosses over the Pöllat Gorge at a height of 305 feet (93 meters) and offers a panoramic view of the castle dramatically perched on its crag above. The bus ride, which starts in front of the Schlosshotel Lisl near the parking lot, costs €1.80 to go up to the bridge and €1 to go back down; a round-trip ticket is €2.60. From Marienbrücke, the walk to the castle entrance includes a steep, 170-step stairway and takes ten minutes. The most picturesque way to reach Neuschwanstein is by horse-drawn **carriage.** The carriage ride, which begins at the ticket office, costs €3.50 for the trip up to the castle entrance and €1.50 for the descent. Be aware that the carriages are sometimes very crowded. Buy tickets from the bus driver or at the carriage.

Neuschwanstein, in its hard-to-reach location, is a castle built by a monarch whose architectural fantasies nearly bankrupted a country he had little interest in ruling. The structure is always referred to as a "fairy-tale" castle because it looks like an illustration out of a storybook, but its inspiration actually came from two Wagner operas:

Tannhäuser, the tale of a medieval singer who is seduced by Venus, the goddess of love, and *Lohengrin,* a knight who sought the Holy Grail. The chief set designer of the Bavarian State Opera in Munich helped with the architectural plans.

Ludwig watched the construction of his dream palace through a telescope from neighboring Hohenschwangau. Building began in 1869 and continued for some 17 years, stopping only when Ludwig died in 1886. Between 1884 and 1886, the king lived in Neuschwanstein on and off for 170 days. At Neuschwanstein he received news of his dethronement. Three days later he was dead.

Upon entering the castle, a doorway on your left leads to the king's apartments. Here you find the **study,** decorated with painted scenes from the medieval legend of Tannhäuser. Everything from curtains to chair coverings is made of silk embroidered with the gold-and-silver Bavarian coat of arms. The sumptuous ornamentation seen throughout the castle influenced *Jugendstil,* the German form of Art Nouveau.

You enter the **throne room** through a doorway at the opposite end of the entrance vestibule. This hall, designed to look like a Romanesque basilica with columns of red *porphyry* (a rock with embedded crystals) and a mosaic floor, was never completed. A stairway of white Carrara marble leads up to the golden apse where the king's throne was to stand. Paintings of Christ looking down on the 12 apostles and 6 canonized kings of Europe decorate the walls and ceiling of the throne room.

The intricate woodcarving in the **king's bedroom** took 4½ years to complete. Artisans carved wall panels to look like Gothic windows; a mural depicts the legend of the doomed lovers Tristan and Isolde. Gilded brass sconces encircle a large wooden pillar in the center of the room. The ornate bed rests on a raised platform with an elaborately carved canopy. Through the balcony window you can see the 150-foot-high (46-meter-high) waterfall in the Pöllat Gorge, with the mountains in the sdistance.

The **Sängerhalle** (Singer's Hall), decorated with marble columns and frescoes depicting the life of Parsifal, a mythical medieval knight, almost entirely takes up the fourth floor of the castle. Architects modeled the room, another architectural fantasy, after Wartburg castle in Eisenach, the site of song contests in the Middle Ages.

In September, Wagnerian and other classical music concerts take place in the Singer's Hall. For information and reservations, contact the **Verkehrsamt** (tourist office) in Schwangau (☎ **08362/81980**). Tickets go on sale in early June, and always sell out quickly.

After you leave the guided tour, you can make your way down to see the enormous **kitchens** of the castle. A 20-minute film about the life of Ludwig II is shown in an auditorium.

Located at Neuschwansteinstrasse 20 (☎ 08362/81035), the castle can be visited year-round by guided tour only. From April through September, tours depart every half-hour from 9 a.m. to 6 p.m.; October through March, from 10 a.m. to 4 p.m. Admission is €7 for adults, €6 for children and students, free for children aged 6 to 14. Neuschwanstein is closed November 1; December 24, 25, and 31; January 1; and Shrove Tuesday (the Tuesday before Ash Wednesday on the Christian calendar).

Dining near the castles

Neuschwanstein has a pleasant cafe where you can get sandwiches, desserts, and beverages. Otherwise, you encounter no lack of restaurants (or hotels) right around the parking lot near Hohenschwangau. If the weather is fine, you can eat outdoors on the terrace of **Hotel Müller,** where the restaurant serves sandwiches, herring, soup, or larger meals. Main courses go for €7.50 to €16. The restaurant also has an indoor dining room.

Ludwig II: The musical

In 2000, a musical based on the life of Ludwig II premiered in the specially built 1,400-seat **Musical Theater Neuschwanstein** on a lake within view of Neuschwanstein and Hohenschwangau castles. Called "Ludwig II — Longing for Paradise," the 2½-hour show features a large cast, a romantic score, lavish sets, and subtitles above the stage in six different languages. For tickets call ☎ 1805/583-944 in Germany or check with your travel agent. The musical is expected to run at least ten years. Ticket prices range from €50 to €160. You can get more information at the musical's Web site at www.ludwigmusical.com.

Chapter 16

The Bodensee and the Black Forest: Scenic Southwest Delights

- -

In This Chapter

▶ Enjoying the Bodensee, Germany's largest lake

▶ Discovering the island city of Lindau

▶ Exploring the Black Forest

▶ Bathing in Baden-Baden

▶ Wandering through the medieval town of Freiburg

- -

Southwestern Germany is an area rich in scenic delights. In this corner of the country, you find the Bodensee, one of the great lakes of Europe, and the legendary Black Forest. (See the "The Bodensee (Lake Constance)" map in this chapter.) Atmospheric old towns such as Freiburg share the forest setting with glamorous resorts like Baden-Baden, while towns on the lake bask in an almost Mediterranean balminess. Vineyards and fruit orchards thrive in the region's mild, sunny climate.

The Bodensee (Lake Constance)

What is the proper name, you ask: the Bodensee or Lake Constance? Both names are correct. In Germany, this 46-mile-long (74-kilometer-long) lake in the foothills of the Alps (elevation 1,300 feet/395 meters) is called the Bodensee. In Switzerland and Austria, the countries that share its 160 miles (258 kilometers) of shoreline, it's called Lake Constance.

The Bodensee is Germany's largest and Central Europe's third-largest lake. The widest point is almost 9 miles across. Visitors to the

The Bodensee (Lake Constance)

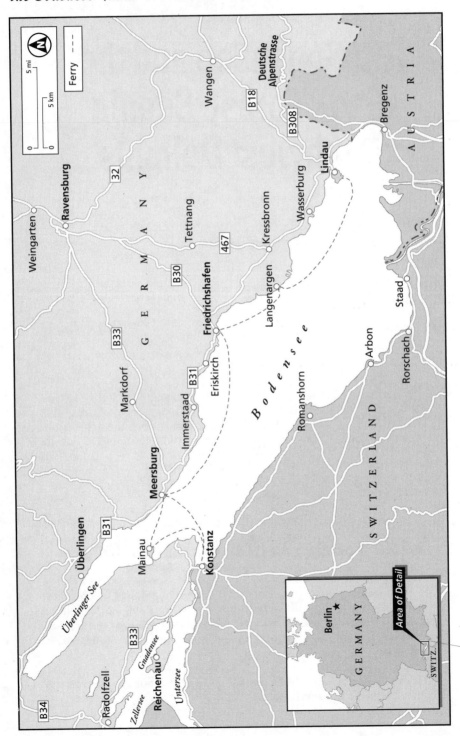

Bodensee enjoy the warm climate and stunning scenery. On the north (German) shore, vineyards slope down to crowded marinas, and charming old towns bask in the golden sun. Looking south across the lake, you see the towering, snow-capped Alps. Fierce winds from the mountains occasionally whip up the waters of the Bodensee, but for the most part the lake is placid. You even find subtropical vegetation growing in sheltered gardens. Lindau, a lovely island city on the northeastern shore, makes a good place to stay, as does the garden-island of Mainau.

Lindau: Sunny island charmer

The historic island-town of Lindau, located 111 miles (179 km) southwest of Munich at the northeastern corner of the Bodensee, marks the beginning (or end) of the Deutsche Alpenstrasse (described in Chapter 15), a scenic road that winds through the Bavarian Alps to Berchtesgaden. Many people start the drive at Lindau and travel east, but you can also start from Berchtesgaden, Garmisch-Partenkirchen, or Füssen and travel west to Lindau. (See the "Lindau" map in this chapter.)

Lindau was founded in the ninth century, and for hundreds of years the town was a center of trade among Bavaria, Italy, and Switzerland. The *Altstadt,* or old town, occupies a small island in the lake (accessible by a causeway); the newer part of Lindau spreads out to the mainland. A town of pretty, flower-bedecked squares and a harbor-side promenade, Lindau is a popular tourist destination that feels a bit like an Italian resort. A profusion of gardens gives the town a quasi-Mediterranean air. So many historic buildings line its narrow streets that the entire town is a protected landmark. Residents of neighboring Austria and Switzerland sometimes pop over to gamble in Lindau's casino.

Getting to Lindau

Lindau is one of the Bodensee's major transportation hubs. A road bridge and a causeway for walkers and trains connect the town to the mainland.

By **train,** you can get direct connections to Lindau from Munich, Basel, Prague, and Zurich. Lindau is on a major rail line, and the train station is right in the Altstadt across from the harbor. For information and train schedules call **German Rail** at ☎ **01805/996-633.**

By **car** from Munich, take the A96 Autobahn and then route B31 into Lindau. If you're driving the Deutsche Alpenstrasse from Füssen, follow B310 and B308 west, turning south on B12 (Kemptenstrasse). After you cross the causeway, park in one of the large car parks outside the Altstadt because you won't be able to drive into the historic center. Day and overnight tickets for car parks can be purchased from ticket machines.

From Lindau, you can travel by **boat** to towns in Austria and Switzerland and to Konstanz on the western side of the lake. Several ferries per day link Konstanz with Lindau, stopping at Meersburg and Mainau; the entire trip takes three hours. Check with the tourist office in Lindau or contact **Bodensee-Schiffsbetriebe,** Schützingerweg 2, Lindau (☎ 08382/ 944-416; Internet: www.vsu-online.com) and Hafenstrasse 6, Konstanz (☎ 07531/281-389).

Finding information and taking a tour

The **Tourist-Information office,** Ludwigstrasse 68 (☎ 08382/260-030; Internet: www.kindautourismus.de), across from the train station, is open Monday through Saturday from 9 a.m. to 7 p.m. and Sunday 9 a.m. to noon (Apr–Oct); winter hours are Monday through Friday 9 a.m. to noon and 2 to 5 p.m.

You can join a guided **walking tour** on Monday (in English) or Tuesday and Friday mornings (in German) at 10 a.m. from April through October. The group meets in front of the Tourist-Information office; the cost is €4.

For information on **boat trips** around the Bodensee, contact **Bodensee-Schiffsbetriebe** (☎ 08382/944-416). Their harbor-side kiosk has excursion information and timetables.

Finding an ATM

You find a 24-hour ATM at the Sparkasse Lindau-Reutin, Kemptener Strasse 50. The ATM at Volksbank Lindau-Insel, Maximilianstrasse, can be accessed from 5 a.m. to midnight.

Getting around Lindau

The charming Altstadt, the island part of Lindau, is flat and easily walkable. The Lindau Stadtbus (City Bus; ☎ 08382/704-242) provides half-hourly service to all parts of Lindau daily from early morning until 10:40 p.m. If you want a taxi, call **Taxi-Ring-Zentrale** (☎ 0800-6006-6666) or Lindauer Funk-Taxi (☎ 08382/4455).

Staying in Lindau

See also the listing for **Hotel Reutemann/Hotel Seegarten** ($–$$$) in Chapter 22.

Hotel-Garni Brugger
$ Altstadt

This welcoming 23-room hotel, located at the end of the causeway, is the best affordable choice in Lindau. The rooms are up-to-date and furnished in a functional, comfortable, modern style with lots of light. Some open onto a rear balcony. The small, tiled bathrooms have showers (two rooms have tubs and showers). Larger rooms with small sitting areas are

Lindau

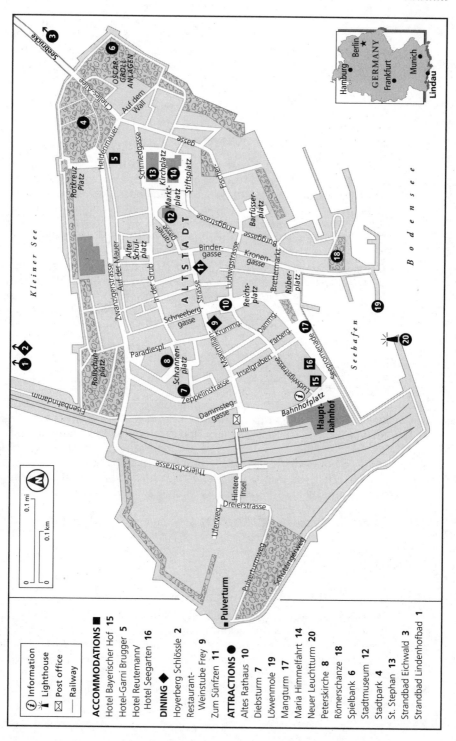

Scale: 0.1 mi / 0.1 km

N (compass)

Symbols:
- (i) Information
- Lighthouse
- Post office
- Railway

ACCOMMODATIONS ■
Hotel Bayerischer Hof **15**
Hotel-Garni Brugger **5**
Hotel Reutemann/
Hotel Seegarten **16**

DINING ◆
Hoyerberg Schlössle **2**
Restaurant-
Weinstube Frey **9**
Zum Sünfzen **11**

ATTRACTIONS ●
Altes Rathaus **10**
Diebsturm **7**
Löwenmole **19**
Mangturm **17**
Maria Himmelfahrt **14**
Neuer Leuchtturm **20**
Peterskirche **8**
Römerschanze **18**
Spielbank **6**
Stadtmuseum **12**
Stadtpark **4**
St. Stephan **13**
Strandbad Eichwald **3**
Strandbad Lindenhofbad **1**

Map labels: Seebrücke, Oscar Groll Anlagen, Auf dem Wall, Chelles-Allee, Heidenmauer, Rotkreuz Platz, Schmiedgasse, Kirchplatz, Stiftsplatz, gasse, Fischer, Kleiner See, Clamer gasse, Alter Schul-platz, Markt-platz, Linggstrasse, Burggasse, Barfüsser-platz, Zwanzigerstrasse, Auf der Mauer, In der Grub, ALTSTADT, Binder-gasse, Ludwigstrasse, Kronen-gasse, Brettermarkt, Bodensee, Schneeberg-gasse, Reichs-platz, Rüber-platz, Rollschuh-platz, Paradiespl., Schnannen-platz, Maximilian-Krumm, Damm g., Färberg., Seebafen, Eisenbahndamm, Zeppelinstrasse, Inselgraben, Ludwigstrasse, Seepromenade, Dammsteg-gasse, Bahnhofplatz, Haupt-bahnhof, Thierschstrasse, Hintere Insel, Dreierstrasse, Uferweg, Pulverturmweg, Schützingenweg, Pulverturm

Germany inset map: Hamburg, Berlin, GERMANY, Frankfurt, Munich, Lindau in an older building (a glass-roofed conservatory connects the two). The location is an easy walk from the lake and casino.

Bei der Heidenmauer 11, 88131 Lindau. ☎ *08382/93410. Fax: 08382/4133. Internet:* www.hotel-garni-brugger.de. *Rack rates: €79–€87 double. Rates include continental breakfast. AE, DC, MC, V.*

Dining in Lindau

Hoyerberg Schlössle

$$$$ Mainland CONTINENTAL

The Hoyerberg Schlüssle, located on the mainland about a 15-minute drive from the Altstadt, has few rivals on the Bodensee. You can dine inside or out, with a view of the mountains and lake. Menu offerings typically include cream of scampi soup, local perch stuffed with herbs, and saddle of venison with flour dumplings and French beans. Meals here are a memorable experience. The adjoining cafe is more informal.

Hoyerbergstrasse 64, at Lindau-Aeschach. (From the causeway, take Langenweg and Friedrichshafener Strasse northwest to Hoyerbergstrasse.) ☎ *08382/25295. Reservations required in the restaurant; not required in the cafe. Main courses: €22–€35; fixed-price menu €51. AE, DC, MC, V. Open: Restaurant Tues–Sun noon–2 p.m. and 6–10 p.m.; cafe Tues–Sat 10 a.m.–5 p.m. Closed Jan 15–Feb 28.*

Restaurant-Weinstube Frey

$ Altstadt GERMAN

The oldest *stubl* (drinking and dining room) on Maximilianstrasse, Frey's has outdoor tables on the pedestrian street and a small second-floor restaurant with a beamed ceiling and pleasantly old-fashioned ambience. You may want to sample the local Meersburger wines as you dine on chicken breast with raspberry sauce, beef stroganoff, trout baked in a potato crust, or spinach *spätzle* (a potato-based pasta) baked with cheese and ham. The restaurant can get smoky.

Maximilianstrasse 15. ☎ *08382/5278. Main courses: €7.50–€14. No credit cards. Open: Daily 11 a.m.–2:30 p.m. and 5–11:30 p.m.*

Zum Sünfzen

$–$$ Altstadt GERMAN/BAVARIAN

This old restaurant at the east end of Maximilianstrasse serves good, dependable food at reasonable prices. Dishes range from *schnitzels* (breaded veal cutlets), pepper steaks, and roast pork with homemade spätzle to filet of venison. Fresh fish from the Bodensee is a specialty.

Maximilianstrasse 1. ☎ *08382/5865. Reservations recommended. Main dishes: €9.50–€18. AE, DC, MC, V. Open: Daily 10:30 a.m.–11 p.m.*

Exploring Lindau

Lindau is best enjoyed by simply taking a couple of hours to stroll around the **Altstadt.** The town's famous harbor, completed in 1856, is the most attractive on the whole of the Bodensee. You find the harbor almost directly across from the train station. Rising from the promenade at the edge of the harbor is the 13th-century tower called the **Mangturm;** the name derives from the laundry or "mangle house" that once stood beside the tower. Flanking the harbor entrance is the 19th-century **Neuer Leuchtturm** (lighthouse) and the **Löwenmole,** a pillar with a sculpted lion (the symbol of Bavaria) looking out over the lake. You can climb up the narrow spiral staircase of the lighthouse (open daily 9:30 a.m.–5 p.m.; admission €1.60) for a panoramic vista of the Swiss and Austrian Alps across the water. At night, thousands of lights create a magical atmosphere around the harbor.

Located just north of Maximilianstrasse, Lindau's main pedestrian-only thoroughfare, the **Diebsturm** (Thieves' Tower), is the city's most famous landmark. Built around 1370 at the most westerly point of the old town wall, this round tower with projecting upper turrets and oriel (projecting) windows once served as the town jail (hence its name). The tower is not open to the public. Standing beside the Diebsturm on Schrannenplatz is Lindau's oldest building, the **Peterskirche** (St. Peter's Church; open daily 9 a.m.–5 p.m.). A rectangular building with a flat wooden ceiling and a tall, square tower, the church was built around A.D.1000. The interior walls have late-15th-century frescoes by Hans Holbein the Elder. In 1928 the church became a war memorial for the fallen soldiers of World War I.

Return to Maximilianstrasse and follow the street eastward to the **Altes Rathaus** (Old Town Hall), erected in 1422 and notable for its grandly painted façade of a princely procession. The building's stepped gables are typical of the 15th-century Gothic style, but in the 16th century the building received a Renaissance facelift. Successive eras saw the additions of other architectural styles. The interior, once used as a council hall, houses the centuries-old town library (not open to the general public).

Continuing east on Maximilianstrasse and Cramergasse brings you to the **Marktplatz** (Market Square) with a pretty, flower-bedecked fountain in the center. In a stately, 18th-century baroque town house called the Haus zum Cavazzen, you find the **Stadtmuseum** (Town Museum; ☎ 08382/944-073). The museum contains a large collection of furniture (ranging from Gothic to Art Nouveau), silverware, glassware, tin and ceramic objects, and historical toys, as well as paintings and sculptures. A special attraction is the collection of mechanical musical instruments, including barrel organs, orchestral instruments, and mechanical pianos. The museum is open April through September Tuesday to Friday from 11 a.m. to 5 p.m., Saturday from 2 to 5 p.m., and Sunday from 11 a.m. to 5 p.m. Admission is €2.50. Give yourself about a half-hour to an hour for browsing.

On the east side of Marktplatz stand side-by-side Lutheran and Catholic churches. **St. Stephan,** the Lutheran church on the left, has a barrel-vaulted ceiling and a fairly bare interior. **Maria Himmelfahrt** (Church of the Ascension), the Catholic church on the right, is full of baroque decoration and has a frescoed ceiling. The churches are generally open from 8 a.m. to 5 p.m.

Continuing east from Marktplatz on Schmiedgasse, you come to the waterside **Stadtpark** (City Park) with its modern **Spielbank** (casino).

Enjoying lakeside activities

For €9.20 you can rent a bike (*Fahrrad,* pronounced *fa*-rahd) and go cycling along the shores of the Bodensee. The bike-rental office, **Fahrrad-Station-Lindau** (☎ 08382/21261), in the train station, is open Monday through Friday from 9 a.m. to 1 p.m. and from 2 to 6 p.m., and Saturday from 9:30 a.m. to 7 p.m. **Lindenhofpark,** on the mainland, is the most scenic area for biking.

Three lakeside beaches (a beach is a *Strandbad,* pronounced *strahnd-*bod) are open in summer Monday through Friday from 10:30 a.m. to 7:30 p.m. and Saturday and Sunday from 10 a.m. to 8 p.m. The biggest beach is **Strandbad Eichwald** (☎ 08283/5539), with a grassy lakeside area and three heated swimming pools. The location is about a ½-hour walk east along Uferweg, on the mainland, or take bus 1 or 2 to Anheggerstrasse, then bus 3 to Karmelbuckel. Admission to the beach is €2.55 for adults, €1.55 for children. **Römerschanze** (☎ 08283/6830), a smaller beach popular with families, is located next to Lindau harbor in the Altstadt; this beach charges the same rates as the beach at Eichwald. The third beach, **Strandbad Lindenhofbad** (☎ 08283/6637), is located in Lindenhof park on the mainland, west of the causeway. To reach it, take bus 1 or 2 to Anheggerstrasse, then bus 4 to Alwind. Admission is €2.05 for adults and €1.30 for children.

Taking a turn at the tables

At Lindau's glitzy new **Spielbank** (*shpeel*-bank; casino), Oskar-Groll-Anlage 6 (☎ 08382/27740), you can play slot machines from noon to 2 a.m. and blackjack and roulette from 3 p.m. to 2 a.m. Admission is €2.55, and a passport is required as proof of age. Appropriate attire is a cut above casual: Men should wear a jacket and tie, and women, something dressy.

Mainau: A day trip from Lindau

The island of Mainau, famed for its subtropical gardens, makes for a pleasant day trip from Lindau. If you're driving through this part of southern Germany, you may want to stop at Mainau on your way to or from Freiburg in the Black Forest (see "Freiburg: Little Brooks and Lots of Books," later in this chapter).

Getting to Mainau

Bodensee-Schiffsbetriebe, Schützingerweg 2, Lindau (☎ 08382/944-416; Internet: www.vsu-online.com), provides daily passenger service by **boat** between Lindau, Mainau, and Konstanz, the largest city on the Bodensee. A one-way fare from Lindau to Mainau is €11. You can also drive west from Lindau to Meersburg, on the lake's north shore, and catch a **car-ferry** to Mainau. The cost is €3 for adults and €1.50 for children. Car fees range from €4.65 to €9.30, depending on the size of your car. Generally, from 8:30 a.m. to 11 p.m., two ferries per hour make the 2½-mile (4.2-km) crossing (one per hour through the night) to Konstanz; not all of them stop at Mainau, so check before boarding. Service is less frequent on Saturdays, Sundays, and holidays. Contact **Autofähre Konstanz-Meersburg** (☎ 07531/803-666) for information and schedules.

If you're **driving,** you can park and leave your car in Meersburg, hop on the ferry, and easily walk through Mainau. This is the best (and only) way to see Mainau, since cars are restricted on the island.

Visiting the island of Mainau

The semitropical island of Mainau, where palms and orange trees grow and fragrant flowers bloom year-round, lies 4 miles (6 km) north of Konstanz, in an arm of the Bodensee known as the Überlingersee. The **baroque castle** that forms the centerpiece of the island was once a residence of the Knights of the Teutonic Order. In 1853, Grand Duke Friedrich I of Baden purchased the island as a summer residence. A passionate plant lover, he laid the foundations for the **Arboretum,** the **Rose Garden,** and the Orangery, gardens that his great-grandchild, Count Lennart Bernadotte, the current owner of this 110-acre botanical wonderland, would later develop. Palms, citrus and fruit trees, orchids, azaleas, rhododendrons, tens of thousands of tulips in the spring, and roses in the summer fill the gardens. Butterflies from throughout the world flit and flutter through the **Butterfly House.** The island has a Mediterranean luxuriance that invites leisurely strolling.

The island's gardens are open daily year-round. From October 22 through March 31, hours are 9 a.m. to 6 p.m. From April 1 through October 21, hours are 7 a.m. to 10 p.m. Summer admission is €9.71 for adults, €8.18 for seniors over 65, €5.11 for students, €3.32 for children, €20 for family (parents and children up to 15). Admission during the rest of the year is €5.11 for adults, children up to age 15 free. Admission includes the gardens, the Butterfly House, the Palm House, and an exhibition on Lake Constance in the castle.

From April through mid-October, several places on the island are open daily for dining or a quick snack. The island's culinary highpoint is the **Schwedenschenke** (☎ 07531/303-156; open 11 a.m. to 11 p.m.), which features seasonal specialties such as asparagus in the spring, chanterelle mushrooms in late summer, and game dishes in the fall.

Casual dining options include the Butterfly Bistro (open 10 a.m.–8 p.m.) and the Castle Café (open 11 a.m.–6 p.m.)

For more information, call ☎ **07531/3030.** Give yourself at least two hours to explore and enjoy the island.

The Schwarzwald (Black Forest)

Travelers to the Schwarzwald (*schvahrtz*-vald), or Black Forest, come to two cities in particular: Baden-Baden, a spa resort with thermal waters and an elegant casino, and the medieval university town of Freiburg. (See the "The Schwarzwald (Black Forest)" map in this chapter.) For the Germans themselves, however, the mountainous, legend-filled forest is a favorite place to spend holidays outdoors, amidst nature. Villages with half-timbered buildings, hiking trails, and pretty spots where stressed-out city dwellers take *die Kur* (the cure) at health resorts fill the pine- and spruce-filled forest, which dominates the south-western corner of Germany. The Black Forest, about 90 miles (145 km) long and 25 miles (40 km) wide, runs parallel to the Rhine, which serves as a boundary with Switzerland to the south and France to the west. The Bodensee (Lake Constance) adjoins the forest to the east.

Visitors with limited time generally skip the area's cure and sports aspects and focus instead on the scenic pleasures of the Schwarzwald, long associated with legends, fairy tales, and cuckoo clocks.

The name "Black Forest" is a translation of the Latin *Silva Nigra,* the name given to the forest by Romans some 2,000 years ago. Why did they call it that? Because from a distance the dark green pine and fir trees look black.

You can explore the Black Forest in many ways. You can easily reach Baden-Baden and Freiburg, the two towns I recommend as overnights, by train. Having a car opens up more of the countryside. One of the most popular auto trips is from Baden-Baden to Freudenstadt on the Schwarzwald Hochstrasse (Black Forest High Road; Route B 500), which runs almost the entire length of the forest.

Baden-Baden: Hot water and gambling tables

Baden-Baden is one of the world's most famous spa resorts. The thermal springs bubbling up from beneath the town have been healing aches and pains for more than 2,000 years. The composition of the slightly radioactive mineral water is almost the same today as when the Romans built the first bath complexes here in the third century.

The Schwarzwald (Black Forest)

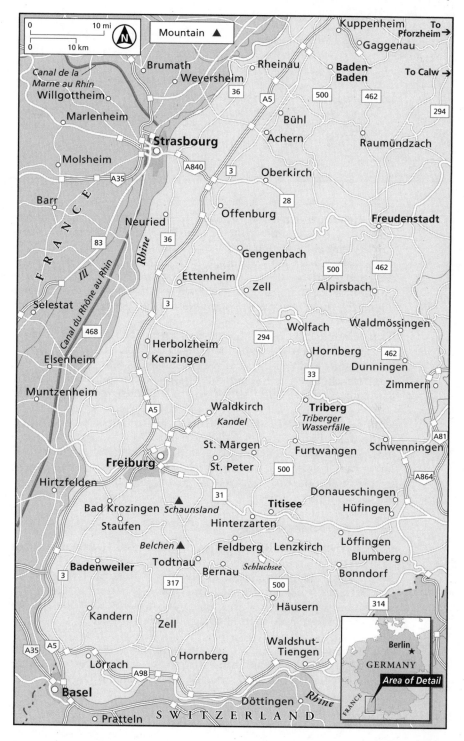

0   10 mi
0   10 km

Mountain ▲

Canal de la Marne au Rhin

Willgottheim

Marlenheim

Brumath

Weyersheim

Rheinau

Kuppenheim   To Pforzheim →

Gaggenau

36

A5

500

Baden-Baden

To Calw →

462

294

Bühl

Achern

Raumündzach

Strasbourg

Molsheim

A35

A840

3

Oberkirch

Barr

28

FRANCE

Neuried

36

Offenburg

Freudenstadt

83

Ill

Rhine

Canal du Rhône au Rhin

Gengenbach

Ettenheim

Zell

500

462

Alpirsbach

3

468

Elsenheim

Herbolzheim

Kenzingen

Selestat

294

Wolfach

Waldmössingen

Hornberg

462

Dunningen

Muntzenheim

33

Zimmern

A5

Waldkirch

Kandel

Triberg
Triberger Wasserfälle

Schwenningen

A81

Freiburg

St. Märgen

St. Peter

Furtwangen

500

A864

Hirtzfelden

31

Titisee

Donaueschingen

Hüfingen

Bad Krozingen

Schauinsland

Hinterzarten

Staufen

Belchen ▲

Feldberg

Lenzkirch

Löffingen

Blumberg

Todtnau

Schluchsee

Bonndorf

Badenweiler

Bernau

500

3

317

Häusern

314

Kandern

Zell

Waldshut-Tiengen

A35

A5

Hornberg

Lörrach

A98

Basel

Döttingen

Rhine

Prätteln

SWITZERLAND

Berlin ★

GERMANY

Area of Detail

FRANCE

From cake to sausage: Black Forest treats

Maybe you've heard of that famous thick, chocolatey cake flavored with cherry preserves and called *Schwarzwälder Kirschtorte* (Black Forest Cherry Cake). The famous cake is one of the specialties of a region that's something of a culinary crossroads. The forest's proximity to France and Switzerland has influenced the cooking you find in many Black Forest restaurants. If you want to sample other regional specialties, look for *Zwetchgentorte* (plum pastry), *Zwiebelkuchen* (onion tart), *Schwarzwald Schinken* (Black Forest smoked ham), meat and fowl dishes with creamy sauces, and wild game such as venison and boar. Most restaurants make their own *Hauswurst* (sausage) and guard the recipe.

Even the Roman emperor Caracalla traveled to this part of the Black Forest to get some relief from his arthritis. In the 19th century, European nobility and clients such as Queen Victoria and Kaiser Wilhelm I rediscovered Baden-Baden's waters, and Napoléon III gave the town a glamorous new aristocratic cachet. The personalities of the day — artists like Berlioz, Brahms, and Dostoyevsky — also helped to make Baden-Baden the most elegant and sophisticated playground in Germany.

Baden-Baden still evokes that aura of 19th-century privilege. The town has the most up-to-date spa facilities in Germany, and people still flock here to soak and be healed of various ailments and to try their luck in the famous casino. If you are not into a health regimen or interested in gambling, you may find Baden-Baden a bit boring-boring.

Located 108 miles (174 km) south of Frankfurt in the northern portion of the Black Forest, Baden-Baden attracts lots of sports and outdoor enthusiasts, who come to hike, golf, play tennis, and ride horses. The horse-racing season at nearby Iffezheim, one of *the* summer sporting events in Europe, takes place in August. (See the "Baden-Baden" map in this chapter.)

Getting to Baden-Baden

You can easily reach Baden-Baden by **train** from anywhere in Germany. Trip time from Munich is about four hours; from Frankfurt, about three hours. For train information, call **German Rail** at ☎ **01805/996-633.** The *Bahnhof* (railway station) is at Baden-Oos, about 3 miles (5 km) north of town. To get into the center of town, you take bus 201 or a taxi, always available in front of the station.

For those with a **car,** the A5 Autobahn between Basel and Frankfurt runs north–south through the entire region, and the A8 Autobahn runs east and west, connecting Baden-Baden to Munich. The drive south from Frankfurt takes about two hours; from Munich, about four hours.

Baden-Baden

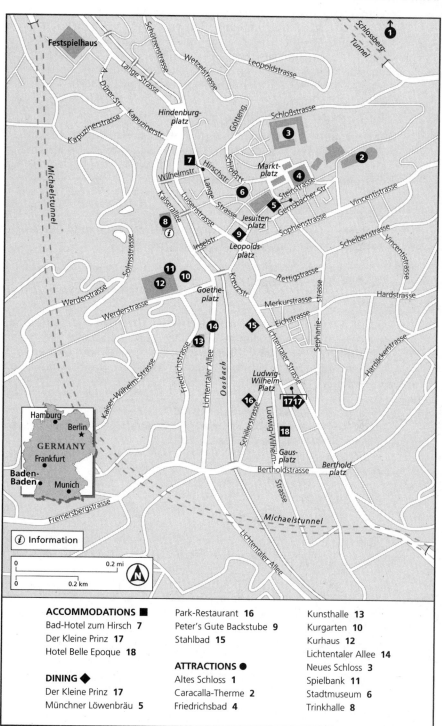

Information

0 ————— 0.2 mi
0 ————— 0.2 km

ACCOMMODATIONS ■
Bad-Hotel zum Hirsch **7**
Der Kleine Prinz **17**
Hotel Belle Epoque **18**

DINING ◆
Der Kleine Prinz **17**
Münchner Löwenbräu **5**

Park-Restaurant **16**
Peter's Gute Backstube **9**
Stahlbad **15**

ATTRACTIONS ●
Altes Schloss **1**
Caracalla-Therme **2**
Friedrichsbad **4**

Kunsthalle **13**
Kurgarten **10**
Kurhaus **12**
Lichtentaler Allee **14**
Neues Schloss **3**
Spielbank **11**
Stadtmuseum **6**
Trinkhalle **8**

Finding information

The **Tourist-Information office** in the Trinkhalle, Kaiser Allee 3
(☎ 07221/275-200), is open daily from 9 a.m. to 7 p.m. It has a complete
schedule of events and information on town and regional attractions. If
you're driving into town, you can easily access a second tourist office
outside the center, on Schwarzwaldstrasse 52 (same phone, same
hours). Both offices offer a free hotel-booking service.

Getting around Baden-Baden

Once you're in Baden-Baden, you can walk everywhere. Bus 201, which
runs at 10-minute intervals, connects the railway station to most of the
sites in town. A one-way fare is €1.80; purchase tickets from the driver
or from ticket machines at bus stops.

Staying in Baden-Baden

See also Chapter 22 for descriptions of the outstanding **Der Kleine
Prinz** ($$–$$$$) and **Hotel Belle Epoque** ($$$–$$$$).

Bad-Hotel zum Hirsch

$$–$$$

Several buildings in the heart of the Old Town were joined to make this
tranquil, old-fashioned hotel. The 59 large, old-fashioned rooms are indi-
vidually furnished with 19th-century antiques. Many of them have bal-
conies and piped-in thermal water. You find an on-site sauna and water-
cure facility.

Hirschstrasse 1, 76530 Baden-Baden. ☎ *800/223-5652 in the U.S. and Canada or
07221/9390. Fax: 07221/38148. Bus: 201. Rack rates: €135–€150 double. Rates
include buffet breakfast. AE, DC, DISC, MC, V.*

Dining in Baden-Baden

Der Kleine Prinz

$$$ **FRENCH/REGIONAL**

The restaurant in the hotel Der Kleine Prinz ("The Little Prince") is
one of the finest in the entire region, and a meal in the intimate dining
room served by the highly polished but friendly staff is a memorable
experience. Everything is homemade from the best and freshest local
ingredients, and menu offerings change daily. Try one of the tasting
menus. You might begin with assorted appetizers, move on to a salad
of fried venison with chanterelle mushrooms, follow that with cream of
zucchini soup and filet of sole with leek and truffles, have a sorbet to
cleanse your palate, and then move on to breast of duck on a
sauce of cassis, and finish with fresh strawberries with homemade ice
cream.

In the hotel Der Kleine Prinz, Lichtentaler Strasse 36. ☎ 07221/3464. Bus: 201. Main courses: €15–€28; tasting menus €52, €70. AE, DC, MC, V. Open: Daily 11:30 a.m.–2:30 p.m., 6–10:30 p.m.

Münchner Löwenbräu
$–$$ GERMAN/BAVARIAN

This restaurant serves simple, affordable, and well-prepared food in two settings: on a romantic terrace beneath linden trees or in an indoor dining room with curved, glass walls. Many kinds of German sausage are on the menu, as well as Bavarian specialties and a wide selection of cheeses. Regional devotees order pork knuckles fresh from the grill. For dessert, try the apple fritters. The restaurant also has a popular beer garden.

Gernsbacher Strasse 9 (in the Altstadt). ☎ 07221/22311. Bus: 201. Main courses: €5–€16. AE, DC, V. Open: Daily 10 a.m.–11:30 p.m.

Park-Restaurant
$$$$ INTERNATIONAL/RHINELAND

This fancy, high-priced restaurant in the glamorous Brenner's Park Hotel is one of the renowned hotel dining rooms of Europe. The emphasis is on French (Alsatian) dishes, along with regional Rhine Valley foods. Specialties include paté of quail and goose liver and roast saddle of venison or lamb with tarragon sauce. For dessert, try an ice-cream soufflé.

In Brenner's Park Hotel, Schillerstrasse 4. ☎ 07221/900-100. Bus: 201. Reservations required. Main courses: €26–€35. AE, DC, MC, V. Open: Daily 7–10:30 a.m., noon to 2 p.m., and 7:30–9:30 p.m.

Peter's Gute Backstube
$ PIZZA/LIGHT MEALS

Restaurants in Baden-Baden tend to be pricey, so it's good to know about this inexpensive cafe on busy Leopoldsplatz. Duck in here for a breakfast of eggs and ham, a slice of pizza, or a lunch-time sandwich. I also recommend stopping for a slice of afternoon *Kuchen* (cake); the coffee (all you can drink for €1.75) is very good. Pete's can't be beat for cheap, quickly served food, although the atmosphere is like a fast-food restaurant.

Sophienstrasse 10–12. ☎ 07221/392-817. Bus: 201. Breakfast €5–6.60, sandwiches €2.45. No credit cards. Open: Mon–Fri 6:30 a.m.–7 p.m., Sat 6:30 a.m.–6 p.m., Sun 8 a.m.–7 p.m.

Stahlbad
$$$–$$$$ CONTINENTAL

This elegant restaurant, with a garden terrace in the center of town, is a tranquil and charming place to dine. The atmosphere and decor, including prints, copper vessels, antique pewter plates, mugs, and engravings, evoke a tavern. Continental specialties include pepper steak and seasonal venison steak, fresh fish, and lobster thermidor. When available, the homemade fettuccine Alfredo with white truffles is worth trying.

Augustaplatz 2. ☎ 07221/24569. Bus: 201. Reservations required. Main courses €18–€30. AE, DC, MC, V. Open: Tues–Sun noon to 2 p.m. and 6–10 p.m.

Exploring Baden-Baden

When it comes to tourist destinations, Baden-Baden isn't a demanding town, with major museums and important historic sights that you must see. The pace is relaxed, and the streets are geared toward pleasurable strolls and upscale shopping. I recommend that you visit one of the bath complexes (see "Bathing in Baden-Baden," later in this chapter) and then spend a couple of hours wandering through the Altstadt.

The new **City-Bahn** (☎ 07221/991-998; Internet: www.citybahn.de) is a sightseeing train that makes stops at all of Baden-Baden's major attractions. The train runs daily from 9:30 a.m. to about 5 p.m., making stops at the Kurhaus, Lichtentaler Allee, the Caracalla Baths, and other spots. Tickets cost €4.50 for adults, €2.50 for children 5 to 15. English commentary is available on a headset.

The time-honored center of activity is **Lichtentaler Allee,** an elegant park promenade lined with rhododendrons, azaleas, roses, and ornamental trees set along the bank of the narrow Oosbach River (called the Oos; pronounced *ohs*). At the north end of the promenade are the formally landscaped grounds of the **Kurgarten** and the **neoclassical Kurhaus,** one of the town's most important buildings. Originally, the building was a "Promenade House," where the rich and prominent came to see and be seen. In the 1820s, the Kurhaus was turned into a "Conversation House," a place for more-formal gatherings and events. The site has remained the hub of Baden-Baden's social scene ever since, used for receptions and galas. The Kurhaus does not, as you may think, contain spa facilities; the right wing of the building is Baden-Baden's casino (see the next paragraph), and the left wing houses a large, lavish restaurant with a terrace overlooking the gardens with their shop-lined colonnades, concert shell, and gas lights lit and extinguished by hand every day.

Marlene Dietrich, the glamorous film star, once remarked, "The most beautiful casino in the whole world is in Baden-Baden — and I have seen them all." You can see for yourself by visiting the famous Baden-Baden **Spielbank** (Casino), Kaiserallee 1 (☎ 07221/21060), Germany's oldest casino, in operation for more than 200 years. (The Russian writer Dostoyevsky wrote *The Gambler* based on his disastrous experience at the tables here.) This is definitely not the kind of glitzy, informal, slot-machine-heaven you find in Las Vegas. The various casino rooms were designed in the style of an elegant French château. Men must wear jackets and ties; women, classy eveningwear. Guests can play French and American roulette, baccarat, blackjack, poker, and other games. Minimum bets are €5. Maximum bets are €10,000. To enter the casino, you must possess a valid passport and be at least 21 years old. The casino is open for gambling daily from 2 p.m. to 2 a.m. (until 3 a.m. Fri–Sat). Admission is €2.55 Sunday to Thursday, €5 Friday and Saturday. You find slot machines, a very recent addition, in the vaulted cellars of the Kurhaus in attractive new rooms, which also contain roulette, poker, blackjack, and bingo machines.

If you don't want to gamble, you can take a guided tour of the historic gaming rooms daily, every 30 minutes, between 9:30 a.m. and noon. (Oct–Mar 10 a.m. to noon). The tour costs €4. Arrange in advance for tours in English.

In the Kurhaus gardens you also find the **Trinkhalle** (Pump Room), Kaiserallee 3 (☎ 07221/275-200), a large hall surrounded by an open walkway built in the 1840s and decorated with frescoes depicting Black Forest legends. The building, where guests once sipped the salty, slightly radioactive waters of Baden-Baden, is now used as the main tourist office (see "Finding information," earlier in this section on Baden-Baden).

The **Kunsthalle** (State Art Gallery), Lichtentaler Allee 8a (☎ 07221/232-050), completed in 1909, showcases visiting contemporary art exhibits. The gallery is open Tuesday through Sunday from 11 a.m. to 6 p.m. (Wed until 8 p.m.). Admission is €5 for adults, €3 for students.

The **Altes Schloss** (Old Palace), a ruined castle originally called Hochbaden (High Baden), is located on a hillside above town. From the 11th to the 15th centuries, Hochbaden was the seat of the margraves of Baden. You get a nice view of the town and the Black Forest from this fortresslike structure. Admission is free.

When the margraves vacated the Old Palace, they moved to the **Neues Schloss** (New Palace), perched atop the so-called Florentine Hill north of the Old Town. The terrace offers panoramic views of Baden-Baden, as does the terrace of the cafe located above the **Orangery** (no phone; open June–Sept Wed–Sun 2–7 p.m.). The palace and its park are not open to visitors, but the former palace stables in the courtyard now house a small **Stadtmuseum** (City Museum) with historical toys and Roman and medieval archeological exhibits. The museum is open April through September, Tuesday through Sunday from 10 a.m. to 12.30 p.m. and 2 to 5 p.m.

Bathing in Baden-Baden

Getting into hot water is what Baden-Baden is all about. At the **Caracalla-Therme** (Caracalla Baths), Römerplatz 1 (☎ 07221/275-940), you decide on your own bath regimen. The slightly radioactive water, rich in sodium chloride, bubbles up from artesian wells at a temperature of about 160°F (70°C). Bathers usually begin in cooler pools, working up to the warm water. The baths also have a sauna area. You must wear bathing suits in the pools, but the scene is *au naturel* in the saunas. Medicinal treatment includes mud baths, massages, and whirlpools. The facility has a bar and a cafeteria. Admission is €11 for two hours. The baths are open daily from 8 a.m. to 10 p.m.

Friedrichsbad, Römerplatz 1 (☎ **07221/275-920**), dates back to 1877 and follows an ancient Roman-Irish bath method. The complete bath program, which takes about three hours, involves a shower, two saunas, a brush massage, thermal steam baths, and three freshwater baths ranging from warm to 60°F (15°C), followed by a 30-minute period of rest and relaxation. After experiencing the Friedrichsbad, you better understand what Mark Twain meant when he said, "Here at Baden-Baden's Friedrichsbad you lose track of time in ten minutes and track of the world in twenty." Admission is €21 for three hours without massage, €29 with soap-brush massage (3½ hours). The baths are open Monday through Saturday from 9 a.m. to 10 p.m. and Sunday from noon to 8 p.m. (last admission is two hours before closing). *Note:* Clothes may not be worn in the Friedrichsbad, and women and men share the pools.

Shopping in Baden-Baden

Sophienstrasse and **Gernsbacher Strasse,** lined with some of the most expensive boutiques in Germany, are part of a flower-flanked pedestrian zone. This is where you buy those elegant duds required to enter the casino. The women's wear available at **Escada Boutique,** Sophienstrasse 18 (☎ **07221/390-448**), is created by one of Germany's most emulated designers. Another shop, **Münchner Moden,** Lichtentalerstrasse 13 (☎ **07221/31090**), carries women's designs in loden-colored wool during autumn and winter, and offers Austrian and Bavarian silks, linens, and cottons during warmer months. The best men's store, **Herrenkommode,** Sophienstrasse 16 (☎ **07221/29292**), is a bit more international, focusing on designers Giorgio Armani and Renee Lazard.

Leather goods by Gold Pfiel and other manufacturers are sold at **Inka,** Sophienstrasse 26 (☎ **07221/23955**), where the inventory includes luggage, wallets, and handbags. Cuckoo clocks, puppets, and other locally produced items can be found at **Boulevard,** Lichtentaler Strasse 21 (☎ **07221/24495**). **Schwarzwald Bienen-Honig-Haus,** Langestrasse 38 (☎ **07221/31453**), carries beeswax- and honey-based products such as candles, cosmetics, candies, schnapps, and wine, plus many varieties of bottled honey.

Discovering the performing arts in Baden-Baden

Baden-Baden's 2,500-seat **Festspielhaus** (Festival Hall), Beim Alten Bahnhof 2 (☎ **07221/301-3101**), opened in 1998. The building is the second-largest opera and concert hall in Europe. The hall presents classical music concerts, operas, and ballets throughout the year.

Freiburg: Little Brooks and Lots of Books

With a population of about 190,000 residents (and an additional 25,000 students), Freiburg is the largest city in the Schwarzwald and considered to be its capital. Only 69 miles (111 km) southwest of Baden-Baden, this picturesque city with its medieval Altstadt, nestles in a plain below high mountain peaks. The town is called Freiburg im (in) Breisgau to distinguish it from other German and Swiss Freiburgs. Breisgau, now part of the German state of Baden-Württemberg but once part of the Roman Empire, is a historical region stretching from the Rhine to the Black Forest. (See the "Freiburg" map in this chapter.)

Although surrounded by alpine scenery, Freiburg enjoys the benefits of warm air currents that come up from the Mediterranean through Burgundy. In the summer the days can get very hot, but a cool mountain breeze called the *Höllentaler* flows down into the town like clockwork twice every night between 7 and 7:30 and 9 and 9:30 p.m., cooling things down. The Altstadt's splashing fountains and shallow, fast-flowing streams called *Bächle* (little brooks) that run alongside the streets in stone-lined channels, are ancient cooling systems. Freiburg bursts with springtime blooms while snow still covers the surrounding peaks, and in autumn, the smell of new wine fills the narrow streets even as snow is already falling on those nearby peaks.

Wine? Yes, surrounding the city are 1,600 acres of vineyards, more than you find near any other city in Germany. And wine-growing always requires celebrations. In Freiburg, on the last weekend in June, a four-day public wine-tasting festival takes place in the Münsterplatz, the square outside Freiburg's magnificent Gothic cathedral.

Festivals are a year-round part of life in Freiburg. Their pre-Lenten carnival called *Fasnet* is one of the best in Germany, with bonfires and parades. The May *Frühlingsmess* (Spring Fair) and October *Herbstmesse* (Autumn Fair) both last ten days. *Weinkost* is a long wine-tasting event in mid-August. And in June, the city hosts the two-week-long *Zeltmusik festival* (Tent Music Festival), with performances held in giant outdoor tents.

If you're traveling in the Black Forest, Freiburg makes for an atmospheric overnight (or longer) stay. Although the town was heavily damaged during World War II, including a bombing in error by the German Luftwaffe, Freiburg's medieval charm has been preserved. Wandering through its ancient streets is a pleasure at any time of year, and exploring the sights in the surrounding Schwarzwald is easy and fun. The large student presence adds a lively, youthful edge to the old city.

Getting to Freiburg

Frequent **trains** connect Freiburg to Baden-Baden and other cities throughout Germany and Europe. The train trip from Frankfurt takes about two hours; from Hamburg, about eight hours. For train information, call German Rail ☎ **01805/996-633.**

For those coming by **car,** the A5 Autobahn runs north and south through the Black Forest, providing access to Freiburg. If you're driving from the Bodensee (Lake Constance), take B31 west.

Finding information

The **Tourist Information office,** Rotteckring 14 (☎ **0761/388-1880**), is open May through October, Monday through Friday 9:30 a.m. to 8 p.m., Saturday 9:30 a.m. to 5 p.m., Sunday 10 a.m. to noon; November through April, Monday to Friday 9:30 a.m. to 6 p.m., Saturday 9:30 a.m. to 2 p.m., Sunday 10 a.m. to noon.

Getting around Freiburg

The Altstadt, where you find all the major attractions, is easily walkable. **RVF** (☎ **0761/207-280**) operates the city's bus and tram system. A one-way fare costs €1.80; a day ticket costs €4.60. **Plus-Punkt,** Salzstrasse 3 (☎ **0761/451-1500**) in the Altstadt, has schedules and information, and sells passes. The office is open Monday through Friday from 8 a.m. to 7 p.m. and Saturday from 8 a.m. to 2 p.m.

Staying in Freiburg

See also Chapter 22 for a description of **Zum Roten Bären** ($–$$), which claims to be the oldest inn in Germany,

Park Hotel Post
$–$$ Altstadt

This renovated baroque hotel with an octagonal turret is within walking distance of the rail station and major attractions. The hotel has 41 comfortable rooms with new furniture and modern conveniences but not much personality. The good-sized bathrooms have shower-tub combinations. Breakfast is the only meal served.

Eisenbahnstrasse 35–37, 79098 Freiburg (2 blocks east of the train station). ☎ *0761/ 385-480. Fax: 0761/31680. Internet:* www.park-hotel-post.de. *Rack rates: €114–€159 double. Rates include buffet breakfast. AE, MC, V.*

Rappen
$ Altstadt

The best rooms in this charming, low-key, 20-room inn have smack-dab views of Freiburg's mighty cathedral, located right outside. Rooms are

Freiburg

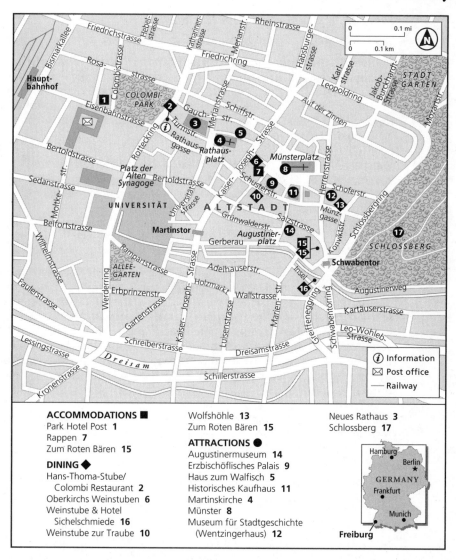

ACCOMMODATIONS ■
Park Hotel Post 1
Rappen 7
Zum Roten Bären 15

DINING ◆
Hans-Thoma-Stube/
  Colombi Restaurant 2
Oberkirchs Weinstuben 6
Weinstube & Hotel
  Sichelschmiede 16
Weinstube zur Traube 10

Wolfshöhle 13
Zum Roten Bären 15

ATTRACTIONS ●
Augustinermuseum 14
Erzbischöfliches Palais 9
Haus zum Walfisch 5
Historisches Kaufhaus 11
Martinskirche 4
Münster 8
Museum für Stadtgeschichte
  (Wentzingerhaus) 12

Neues Rathaus 3
Schlossberg 17

generally on the small side and simply but comfortably furnished. The units with private bathrooms have showers. You find plenty of activity right outside the hotel on Münsterplatz, site of a big weekday outdoor market.

Münsterplatz 13, 79098 Freiburg. ☎ **0761/31353.** *Fax: 0761/382-252. Internet:* www.hotelrappen.de. *Rack rates: €110 double with bath, €70 double without bath. Rates include buffet breakfast. AE, DC, MC, V. All trams stop just behind the hotel.*

Dining in Freiburg

Hans-Thoma-Stube/Colombi Restaurant
$$$$ **Altstadt REGIONAL/INTERNATIONAL**

Choice ingredients and masterly preparation make dining at this acclaimed restaurant in the classy Colombi Hotel a pleasure. The chef prepares a light modern cuisine, but heavier regional dishes are also on the menu. Selections change often, but may include tortellini stuffed with turkey, roast breast of duck, chanterelles over filet of venison, and fresh grilled fish. This place is dressy.

Rotteckring 16 (In the Colombi Hotel). ☎ *0761/21060. Reservations required. Main courses: €18–€25; fixed-price lunch €24–€35; fixed-price dinner €56–€62. AE, DC, MC, V. Open: Daily noon to 3 p.m. and 7–11 p.m. Tram: 10, 11, or 12.*

Oberkirchs Weinstuben
$$ **Altstadt GERMAN**

This historic wine tavern on Freiburg's busy Münsterplatz, or Cathedral Square, provides good regional cooking and comfortable rooms. You can dine in the *Weinstube* (wine tavern) with its ceiling-high ceramic stove or at a table on the square. This place serves hearty portions of good, old-fashioned food: tasty soups (bean, pea, or vegetable), meat dishes (veal schnitzel, pork filets in morel cream sauce), poultry, and seasonal dishes like pheasant. The Weinstube has 25 rooms, all with private bathrooms or showers. Doubles range from €118 to €154, including continental breakfast.

Münsterplatz 22, 79098 Freiburg. ☎ *0761/202-6868. Fax: 0761/202-6869. Reservations recommended. Main courses: €11–€22; fixed-price menus €16, €19. AE, MC, V. Open: Mon–Sat noon to 2 p.m. and 6:30–9:15 p.m. Closed Jan. Tram: 1, 4, or 5.*

Weinstube & Hotel Sichelschmiede
$$ **Altstadt REGIONAL/INTERNATIONAL**

For outdoor summer dining, this Weinstube is the most picturesque and romantic spot in Freiburg. The tavern sits on a small square flanked by a rushing *Bächle* (little brook) and horse chestnut trees. The good food arrives in extremely large portions. The chef's daily recommendation may be cream of tomato soup, a salad with smoked lox, or tagliatelle with shrimps. This is a good place to try *Zwiebel* (onion) dishes, a specialty of the region. *Zwiebelschmelze* is a spinach-and-vegetable-filled ravioli covered with sauteed onions. A simpler *Verperkarte* (late-evening menu) is available from 10 p.m. to midnight.

Insel 1. ☎ *0761/35037. Main courses: €7.50–€15. MC, V. Open: daily noon to midnight. Tram: 1.*

Weinstube zur Traube
$$–$$$ **Altstadt   FRENCH/SWABIAN**

This 600-year-old Weinstube is decorated with pewter and earthenware dishes and a 300-year-old ceramic stove. The regional cooking emphasizes fresh game, meat, and fish. If it's available, try the pike roulade with crab sauce. Ask for recommendations on local wines to accompany your meal.

Schusterstrasse 17. ☎ 0761/32190. Reservations recommended. Main courses: €18–€29; fixed-price menus €40–€60. AE, MC, V. Open: Tues–Sat noon to 3 p.m. and 6–10 p.m. Closed last 2 weeks in Aug. Tram: 10, 11, or 12.

Wolfshöhle
$$–$$$ **Altstadt   ITALIAN**

The cuisine served in this wood-paneled inn is sophisticated but fortifying. Choices typically include veal scaloppini with lemon, delicately seasoned filet of veal, well-prepared lamb dishes, and calf's liver. You may choose to begin with a hearty soup or select an appetizer such as veal with tuna, the antipasto of the day, or *carpaccio* (thinly sliced raw beef).

Konviktstrasse 8. ☎ 0761/30303. Reservations recommended. Main courses: €13–€21; fixed-price menus €23–€44. AE, DC, MC, V. Open: Summer, Mon–Sat 11 a.m. to midnight; rest of the year, Mon–Sat noon to 2 p.m. and 6 p.m. to midnight. Tram: 10, 11, or 12.

Zum Roten Bären
$$–$$$ **Altstadt   GERMAN/REGIONAL**

The "Red Bear" has one of the best kitchens in Freiburg and one of the most authentically atmospheric dining rooms. This is the place to try seasonal dishes, such as *Spargel* (white asparagus), available in May and June. The *Spargelpfannkuchen* is asparagus served with a special pancake, cooked ham, and Hollandaise sauce. A young Rivaner wine, grown on the nearby Kaiserstühl vineyards, is a light, fruity accompaniment. The menu presents a full array of wonderfully prepared dishes using local ingredients.

In the hotel Zum Roten Bären, Oberlinden 12 (just inside the Schwabentor). ☎ 0761/387-870. Main courses: €11.20–€19.80, fixed-price menus €30, €40. AE, DC, MC, V. Open: Daily 11:30 a.m.–2:30 p.m. and 6–11 p.m. Tram: 1.

Exploring Freiburg

Most of what you want to see is in the **Altstadt,** an area bounded by the Hauptbahnhof (main train station) on the west side of the inner city, the Dreisam river on the south, and a wooded hill called the Schlossberg

on the east. This is medieval Freiburg at its most appealing. Give yourself at least four hours to stroll and poke around.

All visitors eventually congregate in the **Münsterplatz** (Cathedral
Square), site of Freiburg's rose-colored **Münster** (Cathedral; ☎ **0761/
202-790;** Tram: 4, 5, or 6), one of Germany's masterpieces of Gothic
architecture. The cathedral was begun in 1200 in the Romanesque
style, but by the time the structure was completed in 1620, Gothic elements had been incorporated into the design. Its West Tower, a magnificent openwork spire atop an open octagonal belfry, is one of the most
beautiful in Germany. Gargoyles peer down from the tower's roof, one
of them with its backside turned toward the archbishop's house across
the square, supposedly a sign of the architect's contempt for the city
fathers. On your left as you enter the transept is an early 16th-century
sculpture, *Adoration of the Magi.* At the far end of the nave is a fine
13th-century statue of the Virgin. The high altar has an early 16th-
century altarpiece, *The Crowning of Mary,* by Hans Baldung Grien.
The 16th-century pulpit has carved likenesses of townspeople and
the sculptor. The cathedral contains some superb stained-glass windows; the earliest, dating from the 13th century, are in the south chancel. Admission to the cathedral is free. The building is open Monday
through Saturday from 10 a.m.–6 p.m. and Sunday 1–6 p.m.

For a wonderful view of Freiburg and the distant mountains, you can
climb to the top of the Münster's famous West Tower. From April
through October, the tower is open Monday through Saturday from
9:30 a.m. to 5 p.m., Sunday from 1 to 5 p.m.; November through March,
closed Monday.

A trio of historic buildings stands along the south side of Münsterplatz,
across from the cathedral. The mid-18th-century **Erzbischöfliches
Palais** (Archbishop's Palace) has a pale-yellow facade and an ornate
wrought-iron balcony. The oxblood-colored **Historisches Kaufhaus**
(Historical Department Store), a Gothic emporium with protruding,
pointed-roof watchtowers and a 16th-century gallery decorated with
the statues of four Habsburg emperors, is still used as the town's official reception hall. The third building to the left of the Historisches
Kaufhaus is the Baroque **Wentzingerhaus,** built in 1761 for a local
painter and sculptor and now home to the **Museum für Stadtgeschichte**
(Town History Museum; ☎ **0761/201-2515**), open Tuesday through
Sunday from 10 a.m. to 5 p.m.; admission is €2.

Chestnut trees and a fountain add to the charm of **Rathausplatz,**
another busy square just west of the cathedral. On the west side of the
square is Freiburg's **Neues Rathaus** (New Town Hall), comprised of two
highly decorated 16th-century merchants' houses connected by an
arcade. The house on the left is white with red sandstone trim, the one
on the right is red-painted stucco. The carillon at the Neues Rathaus
plays at noon. The **Martinskirche** (St. Martin's Church), across from

the Neues Rathaus, is a former Franciscan monastery that dates back to 1300; there is not much of interest inside. On the north side of the church, identifiable by its impressive Gothic doors surmounted by an oriel, a kind of protruding window, is the **Haus zum Walfisch** (House of the Whale), where the Dutch humanist Desiderius Erasmus lived from 1529 to 1531. The house is not open to the public.

East of the university you find the **Martinstor** (St. Martin's Gate), one of two surviving gates from the Middle Ages, when Freiburg was a walled city. The **Schwabentor** (Swabian Gate), the other city gate, dates from around 1200 and stands on the southeast edge of the Altstadt, near the Schlossberg. Paintings on the tower include one of St. George, the city's patron saint. The neighborhood around the Schwabentor is called the **Insel,** or Island, Quarter because rushing streams, called Bächle, surround it. The Insel is the most picturesque quarter in Freiburg, with narrow cobblestone streets and restored houses once used by fishermen and tanneries. A 14th-century Augustinian monastery with a yellow baroque front houses the **Augustinermuseum** (Augustinian Friars Museum), Augustinerplatz (☎ **0761/201-2531**), the chief attraction in the Insel Quarter. Inside you find a collection of religious art spanning more than 1,000 years. Among the treasures are some of the cathedral's original stained-glass windows, gargoyles, and medieval gold and silver plate. The museum's painting collection includes *The Snow Miracle* by Mathias Grünewald and works by Hans Baldung Grien, a pupil of Albrecht Dürer. You also find a rich collection of fine late-Gothic wooden sculpture, as well as Art Nouveau glass objects. Admission to the museum is €2 for adults, €1 for students, free for children 17 and under. The museum is open Tuesday through Sunday from 10 a.m. to 5 p.m.

From the Schwabentor a pathway climbs up the **Schlossberg,** a hill that provides good views of the cathedral. You can also ascend the Schlossberg by cable car (☎ **0761/39855**) from the Stadtgarten (City Gardens). The cable car operates June through September from 10 a.m. to 7 p.m., October through January from 11:30 a.m. to 6 p.m. The round-trip fare is €3.

The Bächle of Freiburg

To help the town stay cool in the hot summer sun, Freiburg has many lovely old fountains and a unique system of streams called *Bächle* (little brooks) that date back to the 12th century. The brooks channel water from the Dreisam River through the old university town. They were first devised to keep the city clean and to help fight fires. You can see the Bächle running alongside many Altstadt streets. According to local folklore, if you step in a Bächle, you must marry a person from Frieburg.

Driving through the Upper Black Forest

From Freiburg you can make an easy 90-mile (145-km) circuit through a scenic part of the Black Forest and be back in time for dinner. Along the way, you pass some of the forest's highest peaks and two of its most beautiful lakes.

From Freiburg, head south on Kaiser-Joseph-Strasse to Günterstal and follow the narrow, twisting road to **Schauinsland.** From the parking lot, you can climb 91 steps to an observation tower for a panoramic view toward the Feldberg, a nearby peak. The area also has easy hiking trails. Continue south to the hamlet of **Todtnau,** where you find a mile-long (1.6-km) footpath to an impressive series of waterfalls. (You need about an hour to get to the falls and back.) From Todtnau, pick up B317 west to Utzenfeld and follow the narrow road northwest to the **Belchen,** a famous mile-high peak. A new, enclosed gondola, the **Belchen Seilbahn,** Belchenstrasse 13 (☎ 07673/888-280), takes you to the peak for one of the most beautiful views in the Schwarzwald. From the grassy summit you can see the Feldberg and other nearby mountains, green hillside pastures, tile roofs in small villages, and the vast Rhine plain to the west. Give yourself about 90 minutes for the gondola ride and a stroll on the summit. The round-trip costs €5 for adults, €4 for children.

From the Belchen, backtrack to Utzenfeld and follow B317 east to Feldberg, where another enclosed gondola, the **Feldbergbahn,** ☎ 07655/8019), takes visitors to the 4,750-foot (1,450-meter) summit of a peak called **Seebuck.** The round-trip takes about an hour, and on a clear day, you can see the highest peaks of the Alps to the south. The round-trip ride costs €6 for adults, €4 for children.

Continue on B317 east and turn south on B500 to **Schluchsee,** one of the loveliest of the Black Forest lakes. From Schluchsee, head back north along B500 to **Titisee,** another popular Black Forest lake. From Titisee, you can return to Freiburg by heading west along B31.

Discovering nightlife in Freiburg

The **Konzerthaus** (Concert House) hosts a variety of events, ranging from classical music to theater to pop concerts. In June, huge tents house the annual **Zeltmusik festival** (Tent Music Festival), which emphasizes jazz but includes other musical styles as well. Summer also brings a series of chamber-music concerts to the **Historisches Kaufhaus,** in Münsterplatz, and a program of organ recitals in **Freiburg Cathedral.** Information about all venues and events, including program schedules and ticket sales, is available from the Tourist Information office (see "Finding information," earlier in this section on Freiburg).

With some 25,000 university students, the city also has a thriving bar and club scene. Two clubs in one, **Crash,** Schnewlinstrasse 3 (☎ 0761/32475; open Wed–Sat 10 p.m.–3:30 a.m.; Tram: 1, 4, or 5), serves drinks and plays background punk, house, and funk; in the basement, **Drifler's**

Club (no phone; open Thurs–Sat midnight to 4 a.m.) plays house and techno for dancers. Neither club charges a cover.

Hausbrauerei Feierling, Gerberau 46 (☎ **0761/26678;** Tram: 1 or 2), a brew-pub with a popular beer garden across the street, is open daily from 11 a.m. to midnight.

Time out: Buying a Black Forest cuckoo clock

Since 1667, when the first wooden clock was made in Waldau, clocks have been produced in the Black Forest. As early as 1840, Black Forest clocks were being shipped to China, Russia, Turkey, England, and America.

If you're looking for a traditional timepiece to take home from the Black Forest, **Triberg,** 30 miles (48 km) northeast of Freiburg on B33, is a good place to go. In addition to cuckoo clocks, shops also sell woodcarvings, music boxes, and other traditional crafts. (Please note: Triberg can be jammed with cuckoo-clock shoppers in the summer.)

You may also want to visit the **Haus der 1000 Uhren** (House of 1,000 Clocks), An der Bundesstrasse 33, Triberg-Gemmelsbach (☎ **07722/96300**), located on the B33 between Triberg and Hornberg. You can't miss the shop: A giant cuckoo clock and waterwheel are in front. Josef Weisser, a painter of clock faces, launched the business in 1824; his great-great-grandson is the current owner. The shop is open Monday through Saturday from 9 a.m. to 5 p.m. The shop ships to the United States and Canada and takes all major credit cards.

Clock watchers with time on their hands may want to drive the **Deutsche Uhrenstrasse** (German Clock Road; Internet: www.deutsche-uhrenstrasse. de). Triberg is one of the stops on this 200-mile (320-km) scenic route through the Black Forest from Villingen-Schwenningen to Bad Duerrheim. Along the way, you find all kinds of museums and sights related to clocks. One of the most interesting museums on the route is the **Deutsches Uhrenmuseum** (German Clock Museum), Robert-Gerwig-Platz 1, Furtwangen (☎ **07723/920-117**). In addition to the world's largest collection of Black Forect clocks, the museum has timepieces from all over the world and from all epochs. The museum is open daily April through October from 9 a.m. to 6 p.m., and November through March from 10 a.m. to 5 p.m. Admission is €5 for adults, €3 for students.

Part V
Western Germany

The 5th Wave   By Rich Tennant

"After visiting a Neo—Gothic church, a Neo—Gothic warehouse, and a Neo—Gothic museum, I'm ready to take out my Neo—Gothic shoe inserts and rest awhile."

In this part . . .

Western Germany, the topic of this part, includes the popular and populous Rhineland regions and many famous cities that are easy to reach and fun to explore. **Chapter 17** is all about **Cologne** (Köln in German), a lively Rhineside city famous for its spectacular Gothic cathedral. Easy day trips from Cologne include the wine-growing regions of the Rheingau and the Mosel Valley. If you're eager to ride the Rhine, I tell you about boat trips through the river's most scenic stretches. **Chapter 18** is all about **Frankfurt,** the sophisticated city with the huge international airport that is the German port of entry for many international visitors. **Chapter 19** covers two cities in western and central Germany: **Heidelberg,** the romantic town on the Neckar River, and **Nuremberg** (Nürnberg in German), with its picturesque corners and Gothic churches. From Nuremberg, I tell you how to make a side trip to **Rothenburg ob der Tauber,** Germany's most famous walled medieval city.

Chapter 17

Cologne: Wine and the Romance of the Rhine

The Rhine (spelled *Rhein* in German) is one of the world's great rivers. Some 820 miles (1,320 km) long, the river originates in southeastern Switzerland, flows through the Bodensee (Lake Constance; see Chapter 16), and forms Germany's southwestern boundary as it continues west, north, and northwest to the North Sea.

Over the centuries the Rhine has inspired many legends, the most famous being the one attached to a high rock called the Lorelei (also spelled *Loreley*) towering above the town of St. Goarshausen. Lorelei, so the story goes, was a beautiful young woman who threw herself into the Rhine in despair over a faithless lover. Transformed into a siren, she sat on the rock combing her long, blonde hair and taking out her revenge by luring fishermen and ship captains to their destruction. The Rhine is also at the musical heart of Richard Wagner's four-opera cycle *Der Ring des Nibelungen*.

For about two centuries now, the mighty Rhine has attracted visitors from around the world, who come to enjoy the romantic scenery of hilltop castles, medieval towns, and vineyard-covered slopes. The **Rhineland,** the area along the river's left, or west, bank, encompasses roughly 9,000 square miles (23,000 sq. km) and is a treasure trove for tourists. (See the "The Rhineland" map in this chapter.)

The Rhineland

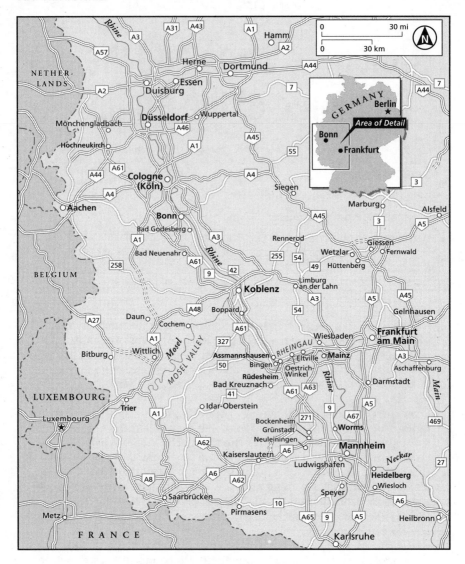

In this chapter, I give most of the coverage to **Cologne** (*Köln* in German), the Rhineland's largest and most important city. Sitting right on the river, this city makes a wonderful headquarters for exploring the Rhineland. From Cologne, you can drive into the **Rheingau,** a lovely wine-growing section of the Rhine Valley from Koblenz south to Alsace. And although not as grand and legend-filled as the Rhine, the **Mosel River Valley,** covered with meticulously tended vineyards, is also worth exploring. I cover the highlights of all these side trips later in this chapter.

Cologne: Pleasures beside the Rhine

Visitors to this lively metropolis on the Rhine, Germany's fourth-largest and oldest city, are immediately struck by Cologne's cheek-by-jowl juxtaposition of the very old with the very new. You can see Roman ruins in an underground parking garage, a dizzyingly ornate Gothic cathedral beside a modern museum complex, and a humble Romanesque church wedged in among luxury shops built in the booming 1980s. On a ten-minute walk in Cologne, you can traverse 2,000 years of history.

Cologne — spelled "Köln" in Germany and pronounced *koeln* — is far more than a city with Germany's largest cathedral, although the cathedral is, of course, what initially draws most visitors. The range of its museums, the buildings that house them, and the quality of their collections make Cologne one of the outstanding museum cities of Germany. Bursting with galleries, Cologne has become the contemporary art capital of Germany in recent years. Music, whether it's a symphony concert in the modern philharmonic hall, an opera at the highly regarded opera house, or a boisterous outdoor concert in the Rheinpark, is likewise a vital component of life here. The city is also famous as the birthplace of eau de Cologne, also called toilet water.

Cologne traces its beginnings to 38 B.C., when Roman legions set up camp here. As early as A.D. 50, the emperor Claudius gave the city municipal rights as capital of a Roman province. In addition to its substantial Roman legacy, the city boasts 12 major Romanesque churches. Older than the cathedral, the churches drew medieval pilgrims from all over Europe to "Holy Cologne," one of the most important pilgrimage cities in medieval Christendom.

The Kölner themselves are refreshingly relaxed and down-to-earth in their enjoyment of their city. Every year they welcome millions of visitors, many of whom come to attend the giant international trade fairs held in the Köln *Messe,* or trade-fair grounds. Ancient traditions are annually renewed in the city's raucous pre–Lenten Carnival (called *Fasching*), a time of masked balls, parades, and general delirium. When the weather turns warm, visitors and citizens alike stroll along the Rhine promenades and flock to outdoor taverns and restaurants to enjoy the pleasures of a *Kölsch,* Cologne's unique and delicious beer, and a substantial meal of typical Rhineland cuisine.

Getting there

Cologne is one of the major cities in western Germany, and getting there is easy by train, car, or plane.

By plane

Cologne's airport, **Konrad-Adenauer-Flughafen Köln/Bonn (☎ 02203/ 4040-0102;** Internet: www.airport-cgn.de), is located 9 miles (14 km) southeast of the city. There are direct flights from most major European cities. **Bus 170** from the airport to the Cologne Hauptbahnhof (main train station) operates from 5:40 a.m. to 11 p.m. The trip takes 20 minutes; the fare is €4.70. A **taxi** from the airport to the city center costs about €25.

By train

Cologne is a major rail hub, so reaching the city from anywhere in Germany or the rest of Europe is easy. Frequent daily trains arrive from Berlin (trip time: 5½ hours), Frankfurt (trip time: 2½ hours), and Hamburg (trip time: 4½ hours). The Cologne Hauptbahnhof is in the heart of the city, next to the cathedral. For train information and schedules, call **German Rail ☎ 01805/996-633.**

By car

Cologne is easily reached from major German cities. The **A3** Autobahn connects the city to the north and south, while the **A4** Autobahn travels east and west.

Finding information

The **Köln Tourismus Office,** Unter Fettenhennen 19 (**☎ 0221/9433;** Internet: www.koeln.de; U-Bahn: Hauptbahnhof), is located just a few steps from the cathedral. The office has city maps, a room-rental service (€3), and information on city attractions. From November through April, the office is open Monday through Saturday from 8 a.m. to 9 p.m. and Sunday 9:30 a.m. to 7 p.m.; May through October, Monday through Saturday 8 a.m. to 10:30 p.m., Sunday 9 a.m. to 10 p.m.

Getting oriented

The major sights of Cologne, including the mighty cathedral and the most important museums, are located in the **Altstadt** (Old Town), the restored and muchaltered medieval core of the city. The Altstadt spreads in a semicircle west from the Rhine to a ring road that follows the line of the 12th-century city walls (demolished, except for three gateways, in the 19th century). (See the "Cologne" map in this chapter.) The center of the Altstadt is the **Innenstadt** (Inner City), the historical heart of Cologne, where the Romans built their first walled colony.

The ring road and a greenbelt in the southwest (the location of the university) girdle **Neustadt,** the "new" part of town dating from the 19th

Cologne

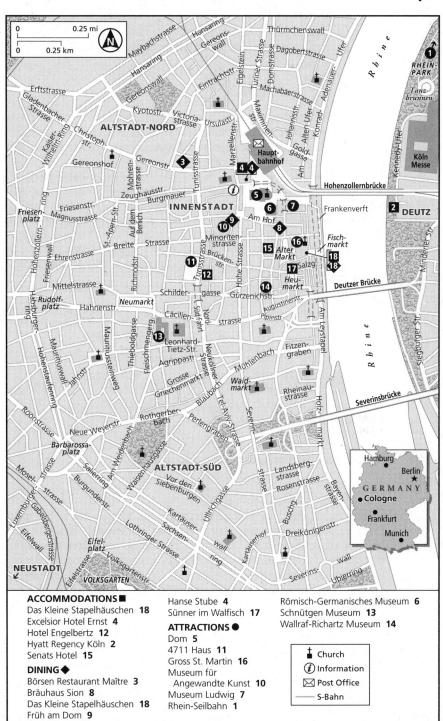

ACCOMMODATIONS ■
Das Kleine Stapelhäuschen **18**
Excelsior Hotel Ernst **4**
Hotel Engelbertz **12**
Hyatt Regency Köln **2**
Senats Hotel **15**

DINING ◆
Börsen Restaurant Maître **3**
Bräuhaus Sion **8**
Das Kleine Stapelhäuschen **18**
Früh am Dom **9**

Hanse Stube **4**
Sünner im Walfisch **17**

ATTRACTIONS ●
Dom **5**
4711 Haus **11**
Gross St. Martin **16**
Museum für
  Angewandte Kunst **10**
Museum Ludwig **7**
Rhein-Seilbahn **1**

Römisch-Germanisches Museum **6**
Schnütgen Museum **13**
Wallraf-Richartz Museum **14**

✝ Church
ⓘ Information
✉ Post Office
----- S-Bahn

century. The area across the river, on the Rhine's east bank, is called **Deutz.** Besides providing the best views of the cathedral-dominated Cologne skyline, Deutz is where you find the **Köln Messe** (trade-fair grounds) and the **Rhinepark.** The city's early industrial plants were concentrated in Deutz, and many of them are still here.

Getting around

The compact and pedestrian-friendly Altstadt, where you find the cathedral and most of the major attractions, is easily explored on foot. The city also has an excellent **bus, tram, U-Bahn** (subway)**,** and **S-Bahn** (light-rail) system. A single one-way fare within the inner city is €1.20 for adults, €1 for children. A day ticket, the **Kölner Tageskarte,** costs €5.15 and allows you to travel throughout the city's transportation network. A **Multigruppen** (family) ticket, good for up to five people traveling together, costs €7.25. Purchase tickets from the automated machines (labeled *Fahrscheine*), from bus drivers, or at the stations. Be sure to validate your ticket; validation machines are in stations and on buses. For information about public transportation, call VRS ☎ **01803/504-030.**

Taxi meters start at €1.85; the fare rises €1.20 per kilometer for rides between 6 a.m. and 10 p.m., and €1.30 per kilometer for rides between 10 p.m. and 6 a.m. To order a taxi, call ☎ **0221/2882.**

Staying in Cologne

Also see Chapter 22 for details on the Cologne's premier hotel, **Excelsior Hotel Ernst** ($$$$).

Das Kleine Stapelhäuschen
$ Altstadt

The two town houses that make up this hotel stand on a corner of a historic square, right on the Rhine in the busiest section of the Altstadt. From the wine restaurant on the ground floor (see "Dining in Cologne," later in this chapter), you climb up a curving, wooden staircase (or take the elevator) to your room. The 31 rooms are fairly basic but comfortable and not lacking in a kind of old-fashioned charm; some rooms have beamed ceilings. Ten units come with a small, tiled bathroom with shower.

Fischmarkt 1–3, 50667 Köln. ☎ *0221/257-7862. Fax: 0221/257-4232. U-Bahn: Heumarkt (then a 5-minute walk north on Buttermarkt to Fishmarkt). Rack rates: €64–€74 double without bathroom; €90–€108 double with bathroom. Rates include buffet breakfast.*

Celebrating carnival in Cologne

Cologne's Carnival, the city's "fifth season," is one of the most eagerly anticipated events in Germany. The season officially lasts from New Year's Eve to Ash Wednesday. The city buzzes with masked balls, parades, and general delirium. Natives call this citywide celebration *Fasteleer* or *Fastelovend*.

Hotel Engelbertz
$ Altstadt

This modest, family-run hotel is in a central location close to everything in the Altstadt. The hotel has 40 rooms, all with small bathrooms that have tub or shower. The decoration throughout is light, cheery, and modern.

Obenmarspforten 1–3, 50667 Köln. ☎ *0221/257-8994. Fax: 0221/257-8924. U-Bahn: Heumarkt (then a 5-minute walk west on Gürzenichstrasse, north on Hohe Strasse, and east on Obenmarspforten). Rack rates: €96 double. Rate includes breakfast. AE, MC, V.*

Hyatt Regency Köln
$$$–$$$$ Deutz

Located in Deutz, a five-minute walk across the Rhine from the train station, this modern full-service hotel features a dramatic lobby with a waterfall and a glamorous overall ambience. The 305 rooms are comfortably large and stylishly furnished. Many have views of the Rhine and the cathedral on the other side. Bathrooms have deep tubs with showers. The Hyatt has fine restaurants and a fitness center with a pool, sauna, and steam room. The staff can arrange babysitting.

Kennedy-ufer 2A, 50679 Köln-Deutz. ☎ *0180/523-1234 or 0221/828-1234. Fax: 0221/ 828-1370. Internet:* www.hyattregency.de. *U-Bahn: Hauptbahnhof (then a 5-minute walk across the bridge). Rack rates: €190–€340 double. AE, DC, MC, V.*

Senats Hotel
$–$$$$ Altstadt

This small, stylish hotel with its bright-yellow lobby is located in the heart of the Altstadt. The furnishings in the 59 rooms have a modern style. Bathrooms are on the small side but vary according to the room. The hotel has a nice ambience throughout.

Unter Goldschmied 9–17, 50667 Köln. ☎ *0221/20620. Fax: 0221/206-2200. Internet:* www.senats-hotel.de. *U-Bahn: Hauptbahnhof (then a 5-minute walk across*

Roncalliplatz and south on Unter Goldschmied). Rack rates: €110–€245. Rate includes buffet breakfast. AE, MC, V.

Dining in Cologne

Although several highly rated restaurants have established themselves here in recent years, Cologne is not a city particularly known for its gourmet dining. Rather, it's a place for conversation and drinking, generally over enormous portions of typical Rhineland fare in crowded restaurants that are *gemütlich* (a kind of cozy charm) rather than elegant.

To eat and drink as the Kölner do, visit one of the city's old tavern-restaurants (see listings for Früh am Dom and Bräuhaus Sion, later in this section). Local dishes at these and other nongourmet restaurants generally include *Halver Hahn* (a rye bread roll with Dutch cheese), *Tatar* (finely minced raw beef mixed with egg yolk, onions, and spices and served on bread or a roll), *Kölsch Kaviar* (smoked blood sausage served with raw onion rings), *Matjesfilet mit grünen Bohnen* (pickled white herring served with green butter beans and potatoes), *Hämchen* (cured pork knuckle cooked in vegetable broth), *Himmel und Äd* (apples and potatoes boiled and mashed together and served with fried blood sausage), and *Speckpfannekuchen* (pancake fried in smoked bacon fat).

Börsen Restaurant Maître

$–$$$ Altstadt CONTINENTAL/MEDITERRANEAN

This busy place, which serves Cologne's financial community, is a good spot for a weekday lunch. The location is near the stock exchange, a short walk from the cathedral. Seasonally adjusted fixed-price meals feature classic, conservative cookery made from fresh ingredients. The restaurant offers two different dining areas. In the Börsen Stube, main courses range from sausage and herring to roast duck. The Börsen Schanke, a beer restaurant, serves hearty local dishes; in summer, you can sit on its outdoor terrace beside a fountain.

Kölsch: Cologne's beer of choice

Even if you don't like beer, you'll probably like *Kölsch* (*koehlsch*), a dry, delicious, top-fermented beer that's brewed only in Cologne. Kölsch has an alcohol content of about 3%. If you go to any of the taverns in town, you can order a Kölsch from one of the blue-aproned waiters, called a *Köbes*. The waiters always serve the beer in a tall, thin glass, called a *Stangen,* which they bring to your table in a special carrier called a *Kölschkranz*. Expect to pay about €1.35 for a small glass of Kölsch on tap.

Unter Sachsenhausen 10–26. ☎ *0221/133-021. U-Bahn: Hauptbahnhof. Reservations recommended. Main courses: Börsen Stube €14–€17; Börsen Schanke €6.50–€10. AE, DC, MC, V. Open: Börsen Stube, Mon–Fri noon to 2:30 p.m.; Mon–Sat 6–11 p.m; Börsen Schanke, Mon–Fri 10 a.m.–9:30 p.m.*

Bräuhaus Sion
$$ **Altstadt**   **KÖLNER/GERMAN**

If you want a traditional local Bräuhaus where the beer is good, the wood paneling a little smoky with time and frequent polishing, and the food portions inexpensive and generous, Sion is the place. The main courses are traditional and filling Rhineland fare, such as *Riesenhämchen* (boiled pigs' knuckles) with sauerkraut, *Bockwurst* (sausage) with potato salad, or Sauerbraten (pot- or oven-roasted marinated beef) with an almond-raisin sauce.

Unter Taschenmacher 5. ☎ *0221/257-8540. U-Bahn: Heumarkt (then a 5-minute walk north along the Rhine promenade, west on Mühlengasse, and north on Unter Taschenmacher). Main courses €7.60–€15.40. No credit cards. Open: Daily 10 a.m.–11:30 p.m.*

Das Kleine Stapelhäuschen
$–$$ **Altstadt**   **GERMAN**

This popular wine restaurant (and hotel, see "Staying in Cologne," earlier in this chapter) opens onto the old fish-market square and the Rhine, just a few minutes' walk from the cathedral. Although the wine is the main reason for coming (the local Rhine wines are that special), the cuisine is also very good. You might start with escargots, marinated herring, or stuffed mushrooms. Fish main courses include roasted perch-pike on lentils with balsamic vinegar and salmon poached in Rhine wine. A Rhineland meat specialty is Sauerbraten with almonds, raisins, and potato dumplings. The menu also includes vegetarian and pasta dishes.

Fischmarkt 1–3. ☎ *0221/272-7777. U-Bahn: Heumarkt (then a 5-minute walk north on Buttermarkt to Fishmarkt). Reservations recommended. Main courses: €8–€19.40. AE, MC, V. Open: Daily noon to 11:30 p.m. Closed Dec 22–Jan 10.*

Früh am Dom
$$ **Altstadt**   **KÖLNER/GERMAN**

This is the best all-around Bräuhaus for atmosphere, economy, and hearty portions. You can eat in the upstairs or downstairs dining rooms (upstairs, on the ground floor, is better), with a different German specialty offered every day of the week. The menu is in English. A favorite dish is *Hämchen,* a Cologne specialty of smoked pork knuckle served with sauerkraut and potato purée. Other specialties include *Sauerkrautsuppe* (sauerkraut soup) and *kölsch Kaviar* (blood sausage with onion rings). Früh-Kölsch, the tavern's beer on tap, has a 1,000-year-old brewing tradition. In summer, this tavern also has a beer garden.

Am Hof 12–14. ☎ *0221/261-3211. U-Bahn: Hauptbahnhof (then a 5-minute walk south past the cathedral and across Roncalliplatz to Am Hof). Main courses: €9–€19. No credit cards. Open: 8 a.m. to midnight.*

Hanse Stube
$$$–$$$$ Altstadt   FRENCH

One of Cologne's top gourmet restaurants, Hanse Stube offers excellent cuisine and service in quiet, elegant surroundings. The menu changes daily but may include salmon with herb sour cream and avocado sherbet, cream of lemon soup with fried sweetbreads, or quail and gooseliver tart for starters. Tasty main courses include stuffed kohlrabi with truffle, iced melon risotto with shrimp skewer, and filet and liver of spring veal. For dessert, how about strawberries with cappuccino-chocolate sauce? The wine list is exemplary.

In the Excelsior Hotel Ernst, Domplatz. ☎ *0221/270-3402. U-Bahn: Hauptbahnhof (then a 2-minute walk west on Trankgasse). Reservations recommended. Main courses: €14–€30; fixed-price menus €50–€75; fixed-price business lunch €31. AE, DC, MC, V. Open: Daily noon to 2:30 p.m. and 6:30–10:30 p.m.*

Sünner im Walfisch
$–$$ Altstadt   GERMAN/FRENCH

This Brauhaus, on a narrow street set back from the Rhine, is a good choice for atmospheric dining. This step-gabled inn with a black-and-white timbered facade dates from 1626. The restaurant serves many Rhineland specialties, as well as dishes influenced by French cuisine. You might try the sole meunière or venison in season.

Salzgasse 13. ☎ *0221/257-7879. U-Bahn: Heumarkt (then a 3-minute walk west on Salzgasse). Reservations recommended. Main courses: €10–€19.50. AE, DC, MC, V. Daily 11 a.m. to midnight.*

Exploring Cologne

You find the cathedral and all the major museums in the **Innenstadt,** the roughly half-square-mile area of the original Roman colony. After a day of sightseeing, round off your visit with an evening stroll along the Rhine promenade in Deutz.

The Cologne **Welcome Card,** available from the tourist office, is good for travel on all forms of public transportation and gets you into most museums for free or at a reduced cost. A one-day card costs €9, a two-day card costs €14, and a family card good for two adults and two children costs €18.

Dom (Cathedral)

Considering how much time passed during the building of this gigantic edifice, the largest cathedral in northern Europe, it's a wonder that the Gothic facade is stylistically coherent. Over 600 years elapsed from the laying of the cornerstone in 1248 to the placement of the last *finial* (a decorative element) on the south tower in 1880. Upon completion, the Cologne cathedral was the tallest building in the world, its twin, filigreed spires rising to a height of 515 feet. Overwhelming is the simplest way to describe it.

As you enter through the central portal, the sheer size and upward surge of the interior space is awe-inspiring. The **Dreikönigschrein** (Shrine of the Three Magi), housed in a glass case at the end of the choir, is the cathedral's major treasure. The giant reliquary is a masterpiece of goldsmith work dating from the end of the 12th century. The **choir,** which can be visited only on guided tours, is the most important part of the cathedral. Consecrated in 1322, the choir contains original, richly carved oak stalls, screen paintings, and a series of statues made in the cathedral workshop between 1270 and 1290. The famous **Three Kings windows** in the *clerestory* (the area above the nave) were installed in the early 14th century. In addition to some magnificent Renaissance-era stained-glass windows in the north aisle, the cathedral really has only two other must-see treasures. The **Gero Cross,** hanging in a chapel on the north side of the choir, is a rare monumental sculpture carved in Cologne in the late 10th century and reputedly the oldest-existing large-scale crucifix in the Western world. On the south side of the choir is Stephan Lochner's altarpiece, ***Adoration of the Magi,*** created around 1445. The painting is a masterpiece of the Cologne school — Italian in format, Flemish in the precision of its execution.

The cathedral **Schatzkammer** (Treasury) is rather disappointing, and you aren't missing much if you skip it. If, on the other hand, you're in reasonably good shape, you can climb the 509 stairs of the 14th-century south tower (entry through the Portal of Saint Peter) for an inspiring view of the city and the Rhine.

You can make a circuit of the interior in about half an hour; the guided tours last one hour.

Domkloster. ☎ 0221/9258-4730. U-Bahn: Hauptbahnhof (you see the cathedral as you come out of the train station). Admission: cathedral free; treasury and tower combined €4.10 adults, €2 children and students; tower alone €1.50 adults, €.75 children and students. Open: Cathedral daily 6:30 a.m.–7:30 p.m.; tower daily 9 a.m.–5 p.m (winter until dusk); treasury daily 10 a.m.–5 p.m.; Sun and holidays

12:30–5 p.m. Tours: English-language tours Mon–Sat 10:30 a.m. and 2:30 p.m., Sun 2:30 p.m.; tour cost: €3.60 adults, €1.55 children and students.

Museum für Angewandte Kunst (Museum of Applied Art)

The treasures on display in this museum include furniture, home decor, and handicrafts from the Middle Ages to the present day. The Art Nouveau room is particularly impressive. On the ground floor and mezzanine, the exhibits, exclusively from the 20th century, include rooms and furniture by Finnish architect Alvar Aalto, German architect Mies van der Rohe, and the American designer Charles Eames, among others. Give yourself about an hour to see everything.

An der Rechtsschule. ☎ 0221/26714. U-Bahn: Hauptbahnhof (then a 5-minute walk south past the Dom on Unter Fettenhenn to An der Rechtsschule). Admission: €3.60 adults, €1.50 children 6–12. Open: Tues–Sun 11 a.m.–5 p.m.; Wed 11 a.m.–8 p.m.

Museum Ludwig

This museum dedicated to 20th-century and contemporary art opened in 1986. Exhibits represent nearly every major artist and art movement of the 20th century. The **Agfa-Foto-Historama,** a museum within the museum, is devoted to the history of photography. Give yourself at least an hour, more if you love modern art.

Bischofsgartenstrasse 1. ☎ 0221/22379. U-Bahn: Hauptbahnhof (then a 5-minute walk south past the cathedral and east on Roncalliplatz). Admission €5 adults, €2.50 children and students. Open: Tues 10 a.m.–8 p.m., Wed–Fri 10 a.m.–6 p.m., Sat–Sun 11 a.m.–6 p.m.

Rhein-Seilbahn (Rhine Cable Car)

You get the best panorama over the city of Cologne by taking the Rhein-Seilbahn, the first and only cable car in Europe designed to span a major river. In operation since 1957, the cable cars cross beside the Zoobrücke (Zoo Bridge) between the Rheinpark in Deutz and the zoo. In the enclosed gondolas, you get a great view of the cathedral and the river traffic along the Rhine. The trip takes about 15 minutes each way.

Riehler Strasse 180. ☎ 0221/762-006. U-Bahn: Zoo/Flora (then a 2-minute walk south to the departure point on the west side of the river). Open: Apr–Oct Mon–Fri 11 a.m.–6 p.m., Sat–Sun 10 a.m.–6 p.m. Admission: Round-trip ticket €5.50 adults, €3 children.

Römisch-Germanisches Museum (Roman-Germanic Museum)

Cologne's history, and the fabric of the city today, is inextricably bound with the history of Rome — a legacy that is documented in this fascinating museum. Before you enter, have a look at the section of the **Roman North Gate** preserved on Domplatz in front of the cathedral; on the right side of the museum is **Hafenstrasse,** a street, paved with its original stones, that once ran down to the Roman harbor. Portions of an original **Roman wall** still stand beneath Domplatz in the underground parking lot.

The Roman-Germanic museum was built around the magnificent **Dionysius mosaic,** produced in a Rhineland workshop in the third century and discovered in 1941 by workers digging an air-raid shelter. Towering over the mosaic, which extols the joys of good living, is the **tomb of Lucius Poblicius,** constructed around A.D. 40 for a Roman officer; it is the largest antique tomb ever found north of the Alps.

The exhibits explore themes or types: religious life, trade and industry, the cult of the dead, and so on. The museum covers the period that extends from the Stone Age to the period of Charlemagne (ninth century). On the second floor, you can see a superlative collection of Roman glassware and a world-renowned collection of Roman jewelry. On the lowest level, devoted to the daily life of the Romans, you find an ancient black-and-white mosaic floor covered with swastikas. Centuries before the symbol became ominously identified with the atrocities of the Third Reich, the swastika — probably Indian in origin — was a symbol of good luck and happiness, and was known in Latin as the *crux gamata*. You need at least an hour to browse through the entire museum.

Roncalliplatz 4. ☎ *0221/24438. U-Bahn: Hauptbahnhof (then a 3-minute walk south past the cathedral to Roncalliplatz). Admission: €3.60 adults, €2 children. Open: Tues–Sun 10 a.m.–5 p.m.*

Schnütgen Museum

The Romanesque church of St. Cäcilien (St. Cecilia, patron saint of music) houses one of Cologne's finest art collections. Try not to miss this small, splendid sampling of sacred art from the early Middle Ages to the baroque. The relics, reliquaries, crucifixes, and sculpture on display give you an idea of the artistic blessings bestowed upon "Holy Cologne." Outside, around the back, a skeleton has been spray-painted on the walled-in western portal of the church. Called simply *Tod* (Death), this oddly engaging work is by the Zürich graffiti artist Harald Nägele.

The Roman city of Colonia

By 50 B.C. Julius Caesar had extended the borders of the Roman Empire as far as the Rhine and established an alliance with the Germanic Ubii tribe on the site of present-day Cologne. The area became a military garrison with an imperial shrine and was eventually, in A.D. 50, granted rights as a Roman city called Colonia Claudia Ara Agrippinensium (CCAA). Cologne's Roman period lasted until A.D. 401, when the Roman legions were recalled from the Rhine frontier.

Cäcilienstrasse 29. ☎ 0221/23620. U-Bahn: Neumarkt (then a 5-minute walk west on Pipinstrasse, which becomes Cäcilienstrasse). Admission: €2.50 adults, €1.50 children. Open: Tues–Fri 10 a.m.–5 p.m., Sat–Sun 11 a.m.–5 p.m.

Wallraf-Richartz Museum

The Wallraf-Richartz Museum is one of the country's greatest repositories of art from the Middle Ages to the late 19th century. Opened in 1861, the museum is also one of Germany's oldest. In 2000, the museum moved to a new building designed by Cologne architect Oswald Mathias Ungers. The new museum nicely shows off the art but somehow feels like an office building from the 1950s.

On the first floor, you find an outstanding collection of paintings by the medieval Cologne school (most done between 1330 and 1550). Many of the paintings and altarpieces depict legends from the lives of martyred saints who became identified with the "Holy Cologne" of the Middle Ages — St. Ursula in particular. The Renaissance section includes works by Albrecht Dürer and Lucas Cranach. A memorable collection of 17th-century Dutch and Flemish paintings holds pride of place on the second floor. Here you find Rubens's *Self-Portrait Amidst the Circle of Friends from Mantua* and an enigmatic self-portrait by Rembrandt. In addition to important French and Spanish works, the museum boasts a rich collection of 19th-century paintings, with major pieces by the German Romantic painter Caspar David Friedrich, Gustave Courbet, Edvard Munch, Auguste Renoir, and Vincent van Gogh, among scores of others. Give yourself about two hours if you want to browse through all the galleries.

Martinstrasse 39. ☎ 0221/22372. U-Bahn: Heumarkt (then a 3-minute walk north on Unter Käster to Martinstrasse). Admission: €5.11 adults, €2.60 students and children. Open: Tues 10 a.m.–8 p.m., Wed–Fri 10 a.m.–6 p.m., Sat–Sun 11 a.m.–6 p.m.

Shopping in Cologne

The first *Füssgänger* (pedestrians-only) shopping zones in Germany originated in Cologne and present a seemingly endless and interconnected conglomeration of shops and shopping arcades.

Hohe Strasse, the main north-south street in Roman times, is now Cologne's busiest commercial drag, jammed every day except Sunday with shoppers, musicians, organ grinders, snack shops, fruit sellers, and endless stores. On Hohe Strasse and its surrounding streets, you find all the major international designer-clothing boutiques, stores selling silver, fine jewelry, and perfumeries, plus the big department stores. **Schildergasse** is where you find international men's fashions, fine leather bags and purses, and French, German, and Italian designer shoes.

> ## Cologne from Cologne: No. 4711
>
> Any kind of toilet water is now called *eau de Cologne,* or simply "cologne," but *Echt Kölnisch Wasser* (the original eau de Cologne) remains the official designation of origin for the distinctive toilet waters created in the city of Cologne. **4711 Haus,** Glockengasse 4711 (☎ **0221/925-0450;** U-Bahn: Neumarkt), sells the orange-and-lavender scented water first developed in Cologne in 1709 by Italian chemist Giovanni Maria Farina. The Mühlens family, another early producer of Kölnisch Wasser, also lived and worked in this house at number 4711. The street number eventually became the trademark name for their product. You can buy 4711 cologne in all sizes and shapes, as soap, and even as premoistened towelettes. The smallest bottle costs about €4.

A few shops worth knowing about: **H.H. Weiss,** Ehrenstrasse 159, sells antique silver and pocket watches; **Schirmbusch,** Ehrenstrasse 104, carries a huge selection of umbrellas; **Walter König's Postkartenlade,** Breite Strasse 93, stocks a large selection of art postcards and greeting cards; **Filz Gnoss,** Apostelnstrasse 21 (☎ **0221/257-0108**), sells unusually decorated and comfortable felt slippers as well as those enormous *Überpantoffeln* you slip over your shoes and slide around in when touring German palaces.

Discovering nightlife in Cologne

One of Germany's major cultural centers, Cologne offers a variety of fine arts and nightlife options. To find out what's going on in the city, pick up a copy of *Monats Vorschau* (€1.20 at newsstands). You can purchase tickets at a venue's box office *(Kasse)* or at **Köln-Ticket,** Roncalliplatz 4, next to the cathedral (☎ **0221/2801;** U-Bahn: Hauptbahnhof).

Dance clubs

E-Werk, Schanzenstrasse 28 (☎ **0221/962-790;** U-Bahn: Keupstrasse), is a combination disco–concert hall housed within a former electrical power plant. Recorded music alternates with live acts. E-Werk is open every Friday and Saturday night at 10 p.m.

Live bands and DJs play for dancers at **MTC,** Zulpicher Strasse 10 (☎ **0221/170-2764;** U-Bahn: Zulpicherplatz), open from 10 p.m. to 3 a.m. with a €4 to €10 cover.

Gay and lesbian bars

Chains, Stephansstrasse 4 (☎ **0221/238-730;** U-Bahn: Neumarkt), a gay bar in the Marienplatz area, is open from 10 p. m. to 2 or 3 a.m.

The most sophisticated rendezvous for gays and lesbians in Cologne is **Gloria,** Apostelnstrasse 11 (☎ **0221/254-433**; U-Bahn: Neumarkt), open Sunday to Thursday from 9 a.m. to 1 a.m., Friday and Saturday from 9 a.m. to 3 a.m.

Quo Vadis Pub, a good gay bar for men and women, is near Marienplatz at Pipinstrasse 7 (☎ **0221/258-1414**; U-Bahn: Heumarkt). The bar is open daily from noon to midnight during the week and from 11 a.m. to 1 a.m. on the weekend.

Jazz clubs

Klimperkasten (also known as **Papa Joe's Biersalon**), Alter Markt 50–52 (☎ **0221/258-2132**; U-Bahn: Hauptbahnhof), is a small and intimate jazz and piano bar with live music every night beginning around 8 p.m.

Papa Joe's Jazzlokal, Buttermarkt 37 (☎ **0221/257-7931**; U-Bahn: Heumarkt), is best on Sunday, when the music begins at 3:30 p.m. and lasts until 1 a.m. The club is also open for live jazz Monday to Saturday from 7 p.m. to 2 a.m. The club doesn't charge a cover.

The performing arts

The **Kölner Philharmonie** concert hall, Bischofsgartenstrasse 1 (☎ **0221/2801**; U-Bahn: Hauptbahnhof), completed in the late 1980s, is the home of two fine orchestras: the **Gürzenich Kölner Philharmoniker** and the **Westdeutscher Rundfunk Orchestra** (West German Radio Orchestra). The hall also presents pop and jazz programs. Ticket prices vary, anywhere from €8 to €125, according to the event.

Oper der Stadt Köln (Cologne Opera), Offenbachplatz (☎ **0221/2212-8400**; Internet: www.buehnenkoeln.de; U-Bahn: Neumarkt), is the Rhineland's leading opera house. Dance programs also take place here. Tickets range from €11 to €60.

The **Schauspielhaus,** Offenbachplatz (☎ **0221/8400**; U-Bahn: Neumarkt), is the site of three theaters, each with its own performances and schedules.

Taverns

Päffgen Bräuhaus, Friesenstrasse 64–66 (☎ **0221/135-461**; U-Bahn: Friesenplatz), a 110-year-old tavern, serves its Kölsch brand of beer, along with regional cuisine. Seating is available indoors and out. The tavern is open daily from 10 a.m. to midnight.

Altstadt Päffgen, Heumarkt 62 (☎ **0221/257-7765**; U-Bahn: Heumarkt), also serves the local Kölsch with German dishes. The tavern is open Tuesday to Sunday from noon to midnight.

Cruises along the Rhine

Cologne is a major embarkation point for Rhine cruises. Even if you don't have time for a long Rhine cruise, you can enjoy a trip on the river aboard one of the many local boats.

KD (Köln–Düsseldorfer Deutsche Rheinschiffahrt), Frankenwerft 15, (☎ **0221/208-8318;** Internet: www.k-d.com), offers boat tours of the Rhine from Cologne. The KD ticket booth and boarding point is right on the river, a short walk south from the cathedral.

The one-hour **Panorama Rundfahrt** (round-trip) is a pleasant way to see the stretch of Rhine immediately around Cologne. The tour departs daily at 10:30 a.m., noon, 1:45 p.m., and 6:15 p.m. The cost is €5.60. A daily **Nachmittags** (afternoon) cruise with *Kaffee und Kuchen* (coffee and cake) leaves at 3:30 p.m. and returns at 5:45 p.m.; the cost is €8.80. Prerecorded commentary in English plays on both of these sightseeing cruises.

If you want to see the most scenic stretch of the Rhine, with the legendary Lorelei rock and many hilltop castles, take one of KD's **day-long cruises between Mainz and Koblenz,** departing Mainz daily at 8:45 a.m. and 9:45 a.m. and returning at 7:20 p,m, and 8:20 p.m. The round-trip cost is €46.

For more information on Rhine river cruises, contact **Viking KD River Cruises of Europe,** represented in North America by JFO Cruise Service, 2500 Westchester Ave., Purchase, NY 10577 (☎ **800/346-6525),** or visit the company's Web site at www.rivercruises.com.

The Mosel Valley: Great Wines, Beautiful Scenery

The Mosel Valley, southwest of Cologne, is a scenic wine-growing region like the nearby Rheingau (see the "Sampling the wines of Rheingau" sidebar in this chapter). Winding through the steep slopes of the Eifel and Hunsruck hills in the German state of Rheinland-Palatinate, the Mosel Valley follows the course of the Mosel River (spelled *Moselle* in English) for more than 100 miles (160 km) between **Trier** and **Koblenz,** where the waters flow into the Rhine. (See the "The Mosel Valley" map in this chapter.)

The valley encompasses thousands of acres of vineyards, a full 10% of the national total. Its beautiful scenery, fine wine, Roman ruins, medieval castles, and riverside towns with cobbled streets and half-timbered houses make the Mosel Valley a prime area for exploration.

The Mosel Valley

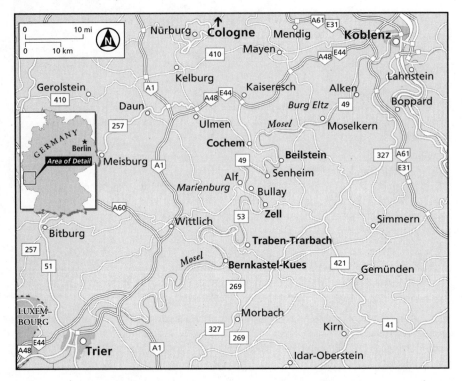

Touring the valley by boat or car

If you're headquartering in Cologne and want to enjoy a **boat cruise** down the Mosel River, the easiest way is to take a train to Koblenz. From there, a boat operated by **KD (☎ 0221/20881;** Internet: www. rivercruises.com) sails down the Mosel to Cochem, 32 miles (51 km) southwest of Koblenz. Between April 27 and October 20, boats depart daily from Koblenz at 9:45 a.m. and arrive in Cochem at 3 p.m. A return boat departs at 3:40 p.m., arriving in Koblenz at 8 p.m. The round-trip fare is €22.

The **A49** Autobahn runs between Koblenz and Trier; the prettier **A53** runs alongside the Mosel between Zell and Schweich.

Stopping in Cochem

About halfway down the Mosel River from Koblenz is Cochem, a medieval riverside town surrounded by vineyards. Cochem is a popular spot for wine tastings and festivals. The **Tourist Information office,** Endertplatz 1 (☎ 0267/60040; Internet: www.cochem.de), is open November through March Monday through Friday from 9 a.m. to 1 p.m. and 2 p.m. to 5 p.m.; April through October Monday through Thursday from 9 a.m. to 5 p.m. and Friday from 9 a.m. to 6 p.m. The office is also open Saturday from May through August (9 a.m.–5 p.m.), and Sunday in July and August (9 a.m. to noon).

If you're driving through the Mosel Valley, Cochem is your best choice for an overnight stopover between Koblenz and Trier. You can also reach Cochem by train from Trier or Koblenz.

Mosel-Wein-Woche (Mosel Wine Week), celebrating the region's wines with tasting booths and a street fair, begins the first week of June. The similar **Weinfest** takes place the last weekend of August. For information, contact the Cochem Tourist Information office.

Cochem's biggest attraction is **Reichsburg Cochem** (☎ 02671/1787), a restored 11th-century castle at the top of the hill behind the town. The castle, the most famous and photographed sight along the Mosel River, is open daily mid-March to November from 9 a.m. to 6 p.m. Admission is €4 for adults and €2 for children and students.

Sampling the wines of Rheingau

The Rhine Valley from Koblenz south to Alsace, with its almond, cherry, fig, and other fruit trees and its sheltered sunny slopes covered with vineyards, is like a northern extension of Italy. This part of the Rhineland not only turns out fine wines, but has been fundamentally formed by the culture of wine, as reflected in its economy, traditions, and festivals.

The **Rheingau wine district** follows a 27-mile (45-km) stretch of the Rhine west of Mainz and Wiesbaden, between the attractive Rhineside towns of **Biebrich** and **Bingen.** Vineyards have produced wine here since Roman times. The wind-sheltered southern slopes of the Taunus range, on the river's northern bank, get plenty of sunshine and comparatively little rain, conditions the Romans recognized as perfect for grape-growing. The Rheingau wine grapes produce a delicately fruity wine with a full aroma. Eighty percent of this wine comes from the Riesling grape, and wine fans consider Rheingau Rieslings to be among the best white wines made anywhere.

If you take a Rhine cruise between Koblenz and Mainz (see the "Cruises along the Rhine" sidebar in this chapter), you sail through this scenic wine-growing region. If you're driving, the **B42** highway runs beside the river between **Boppard** and **Eltville,** the Rheingau's unofficial capital.

Both a hotel and a wine restaurant, **Alte Thorschenke,** Brückenstrasse 3, 56812 Cochem (☎ **02671/7059;** Fax: 02671/4202), is one of the oldest and best-known establishments along the Mosel. The half-timbered structure, originally built in 1332, added a modern wing and became a hotel in 1960. A creaking wooden staircase (you can also take the elevator) leads to most of the 35 rooms. A few of the rooms have four-poster beds; all contain shower-tub combinations. Rack rates range from €85 to €120 for a double, buffet breakfast included. All major credit cards are accepted. The hotel is closed from January 5 to March 15.

For a fine meal, drive to Enterttal, 1 mile (1.6 km) northwest of Cochem, and dine at **Weissmühle im Enterttal,** Endertstrasse 1 (☎ **02671/8955**). Try the trademark dish of fresh trout stuffed with herbs, baked, and kept warm at your table with a hot stone. Main courses range from €12 to €23. Diners Club, MasterCard, and Visa are accepted. The restaurant is open daily from noon to 2 p.m. and 6 to 9 p.m.

Chapter 18

Frankfurt am Main: Apple Wine and Euros

. . . .

In This Chapter

▶ Arriving in Frankfurt

▶ Getting around the city

▶ Finding the best hotels and restaurants

▶ Strolling through the Altstadt

▶ Discovering *Apfelwein,* cabaret, and more

. . . .

*L*ocated on the River Main, and sometimes called "Mainhattan" because of its skyscraper-studded skyline, Frankfurt is Germany's fifth-largest city. Because the Frankfurt airport serves as the country's main international hub, many travelers get their first introduction to Germany in this city. (See the "Frankfurt am Main" map in this chapter.)

Frankfurt has been a major banking city since the Rothschilds opened their first bank here over 200 years ago. Today, Frankfurt is not only the financial center of Germany but of the entire European Union (EU), home of the Bundesbank, Germany's central bank, and the Central Bank of the EU. At last count, 438 banks maintained headquarters here, a fact which helps account for all those designer skyscrapers (more than in any other German city, and including the tallest building in Europe). The huge € symbol that stands on Willy-Brandt-Platz in front of the new opera house could be regarded as the city's logo.

Frankfurt definitely focuses on business. Millions of visitors descend on the city during its trade fairs in spring and autumn. The best known is the International Book Fair, the most important meeting place in the world for the acquisition and sale of book rights and translations.

Leveled during Allied bombing raids in World War II, a small portion of Frankfurt's Altstadt (Old Town) was lovingly rebuilt. But Frankfurt is first and foremost a modern, cosmopolitan city. Besides being a much-visited business center, the city is a tourist destination with fine museums and art collections, a rich cultural life, great shopping, and a lively nightlife.

Frankfurt am Main

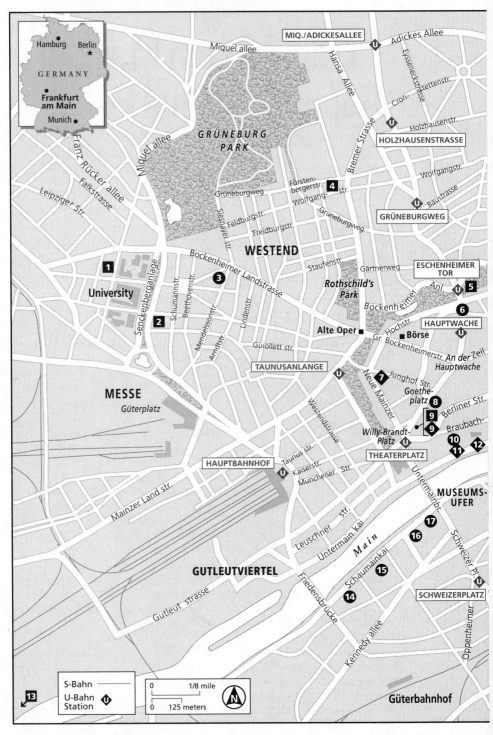

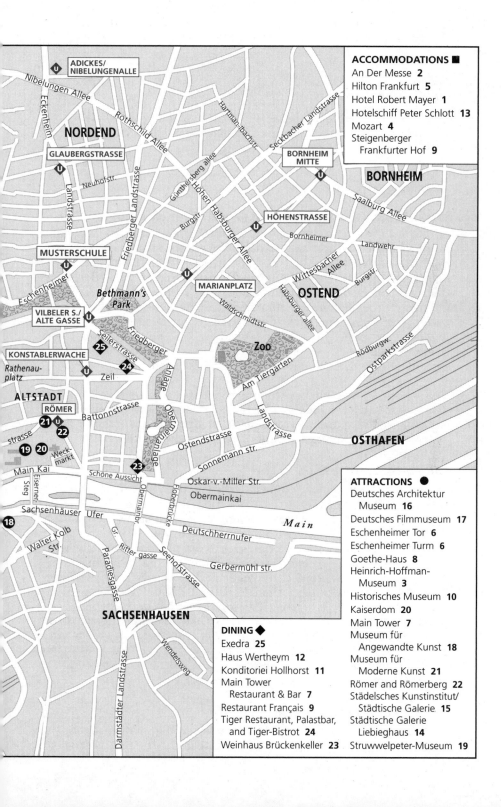

ACCOMMODATIONS ■
An Der Messe **2**
Hilton Frankfurt **5**
Hotel Robert Mayer **1**
Hotelschiff Peter Schlott **13**
Mozart **4**
Steigenberger
 Frankfurter Hof **9**

DINING ◆
Exedra **25**
Haus Wertheym **12**
Konditoriei Hollhorst **11**
Main Tower
 Restaurant & Bar **7**
Restaurant Français **9**
Tiger Restaurant, Palastbar,
 and Tiger-Bistrot **24**
Weinhaus Brückenkeller **23**

ATTRACTIONS ●
Deutsches Architektur
 Museum **16**
Deutsches Filmmuseum **17**
Eschenheimer Tor **6**
Eschenheimer Turm **6**
Goethe-Haus **8**
Heinrich-Hoffman-
 Museum **3**
Historisches Museum **10**
Kaiserdom **20**
Main Tower **7**
Museum für
 Angewandte Kunst **18**
Museum für
 Moderne Kunst **21**
Römer and Römerberg **22**
Städelsches Kunstinstitut/
 Städtische Galerie **15**
Städtische Galerie
 Liebieghaus **14**
Struwwelpeter-Museum **19**

A very strong American presence exists in this city on the Main river. Nearly 40,000 American soldiers were stationed in Frankfurt until 1990.

Getting There

All roads, rail lines, and air corridors lead to Frankfurt. If you fly into Germany from outside of Europe, chances are you'll land at the city's airport.

By plane

The city's airport, **Flughafen Frankfurt/Main** (☎ **069/6901;** Internet: www.frankfurt-airport.de), lies 7 miles (11 km) from the city center. Europe's busiest airport and Germany's major international gateway, this airport serves more than 110 countries worldwide, with direct flights from many U.S. and Canadian cities, including Atlanta, Boston, Chicago, Denver, Dallas, Detroit, Miami, Newark, New York, Philadelphia, Pittsburgh, Washington, D.C., Montreal, and Toronto. A people-mover system (called Sky Line) links the two airport terminals, in which you find many banks (Commerz Bank, Dresdner Bank, SEB Bank, and Finanz Bank) with currency exchange windows. Privately operated currency exchanges (Travelex is one) and ATMs are also there.

The airport has two railway stations and a bus terminal. The long-distance **AIRail Terminal** links the airport to cities throughout Germany and neighboring countries. Regional and local trains operate from the **Regional Station** directly below **Terminal 1.**

Taking the train into the city

The simplest method for getting into the city from the airport is by **train. S8** and **S9** trains (direction Offenbach or Hanau) to Frankfurt's city center depart about every ten minutes from the regional train station, platform 1. These two S-Bahn lines take you to Frankfurt's Hauptbahnhof (main railway station) in about ten minutes. A one-way ticket costs €4.85. Tickets are available from the RMV ticket machines (with English translations) at the regional station and at the **Deutsche Bahn (DB) Travel Center,** Terminal 1, Level 0 (☎ **069/691-844**), open daily from 6 a.m. to 11:30 p.m. (RMV are the initials of the public transportation authority.) The RMV ticket machines have special fast-selection buttons for the S-Bahn journey to Frankfurt. They are marked: *Einzelfahrt Frankfurt* (single ticket to Frankfurt) and *Tageskarte Frankfurt inkl. Flughafen* (a reduced-price one-day transportation ticket within Frankfurt, including the trip from the airport).

Hopping a bus into the city

If you want to travel to the city center by bus, you have many options from which to choose. The bus station is located in front of Terminal 1.

You find bus stops in front of Terminal 1 on the arrivals level and in front of Terminal 2 on Level 2. Some airlines offer special bus-shuttle services to Frankfurt from the airport; check when you purchase your ticket.

Catching a cab into the city

A taxi ride from the airport to the city center costs about €25 and takes about 20 minutes. Taxis are available in front of the terminals.

By train

Frankfurt's **Hauptbahnhof** is the busiest in Europe, with connections to all major German and European cities. **Touristinfo Hauptbahnhof,** opposite the main entrance (☎ **069/2123-8800**), is open Monday to Friday from 8 a.m. to 9 p.m., and Saturday and Sunday from 9 a.m. to 6 p.m. You find currency exchange windows and bank ATMs in the station. For travel information, including schedules and fares, call **Deutsche Bahn** (☎ **01805/996-633**).

By car

The A3 and A5 Autobahns intersect near Frankfurt's airport. The **A3** comes in from the Netherlands, Cologne, and Bonn and continues east and south to Würzburg, Nürnberg, and Munich. The **A5** comes from the northeast (Hannover) and continues south to Heidelberg and Basel, Switzerland. From the west, the **A60** connects with the **A66,** which leads to Frankfurt.

Finding Information After You Arrive

You find tourist information in three locations.

- ✔ **Touristinfo Hauptbahnhof,** opposite the main entrance of the train station (☎ **069/2123-8800;** Internet: www.frankfurt-tourismus.de), is open Monday to Friday from 8 a.m. to 9 p.m., Saturday and Sunday from 9 a.m. to 6 p.m. This office offers a hotel-booking service for €2.50.

- ✔ **Touristinfo Römer,** Römerberg 27 (☎ **069/2123-8800**), in the Altstadt, is open Monday to Friday from 9:30 a.m. to 5:30 p.m., Saturday and Sunday from 10 a.m. to 4 p.m.

- ✔ **Cityinfo Zeil,** Zeil 94 (same phone as above), located on Frankfurt's main shopping street, is open Monday through Friday from 10 a.m. to 6 p.m., and Saturday from 10 a.m. to 4 p.m. The small office has brochures and general information on attractions in Frankfurt.

Orienting Yourself in Frankfurt

The **Main River** divides Frankfurt. You find most of the historic sights and several museums in the **Altstadt** on the north bank. Concentrated in the **city center** around the Altstadt are hotels, restaurants, and nightlife. The Altstadt area is also referred to as the **Innenstadt,** or Inner City. The exclusive **Westend** district, west of the Altstadt, is a residential and embassy quarter. It was the only part of Frankfurt that was not destroyed during the World War II Allied bombing of the city. The huge, modern Frankfurt **Messe** (trade-fair convention center) is considered part of the Westend.

The **Hauptbahnhof** is located at the western edge of the city center. As you walk out of the station, Baselerstrasse is on your right and heads south toward the Main River. You have a choice of streets heading east to the Altstadt: Münchner Strasse leads directly into **Theaterplatz,** with its opera house; Taunusstrasse goes to three of the major Altstadt squares in the southern part of the city: **Goetheplatz, Rathenauplatz,** and the **Hauptwache.**

Museumsufer, the embankment along the river's south side, is the site of many prominent museums, some of them housed in former riverside villas. **Sachsenhausen,** a district on the south side of the river, is a popular entertainment quarter filled with Frankfurt's famous apple-wine taverns.

Getting around Frankfurt

Once you're in the Altstadt, you can easily get everywhere, including the Museumsufer on the opposite bank of the river, on foot. For longer distances, you can take the U-Bahn (subway), a tram, or a bus.

Using public transportation

A network of modern subways *(U-Bahn),* trams *(Strassenbahn),* and buses, administered by the **RMV (Rhein-Main Verkehrsverbund;** ☎ **069/19449;** Internet: www.vgf-ffm.de), links Frankfurt. All forms of public transportation can be used interchangeably at a single price based on fare zones. Tickets are good for one hour on routes going in the same direction. Purchase your tickets *(Fahrscheine)* at ticket counters or from the coin-operated machines found in U-Bahn stations and next to tram and bus stops. The ticket machines have user screens in English to guide you through the process. The city has fare zones. A one-way single ticket *(Einzelfahrkarte)* within the city center costs €1.20 for adults, €.70 for children.

Buy your ticket before you board the U-Bahn or trams in Frankfurt (on buses you can buy a ticket from the driver). If you're caught traveling without the proper ticket, you may be fined €30 on the spot.

Two special tickets help you save money on public transportation in Frankfurt:

- ✔ A **24-hour ticket** (*Tageskarte*), good for unlimited travel inside Frankfurt's central zone, costs €3.50 for adults and €2.15 for children. You can buy this ticket from the ticket machines.

- ✔ The **Frankfurt Card,** available at the city's tourist offices, allows unlimited travel anywhere within the greater Frankfurt area, transport on the airport shuttle bus, a reduction on the tourist offices' sightseeing tour (see "Seeing Frankfurt by Guided Tour"), and half-price admission to many of the city's museums. The cost is €7.50 for a one-day card and €11 for a two-day card.

Taking a taxi

To call a taxi, dial ☎ **069/230-001.** You don't have to pay a surcharge for calling a cab. You can also get a cab at one of the city's clearly designated taxi stands, or by hailing one on the street (the car's roof light will be illuminated if it's available). Taxis charge by the trip and by the carload, without extra surcharges for luggage. The initial charge is €1.95; each kilometer costs €1.25 to €1.35, depending on the time of day.

Staying in Style

During busy trade fairs, finding a room in Frankfurt can be difficult. I recommend that you book your hotel in advance. If you arrive without a room, the tourist office in the main train station can help find you a room for a €2.50 fee. You can book a room for free by calling ☎ 069/ 2123-0808 or by visiting the Web site www.frankfurt-tourismus.de.

Frankfurt is one of the two German cities (Munich is the other) with lots of air-hotel packages available from major airlines. You can save a bundle by booking one of these packages. See Chapter 6 for more information on packages to Germany.

Because Frankfurt is such a business-oriented city, hotels tend to be more expensive than elsewhere in Germany. Rates sometimes go up during the trade fairs. Many hotels offer lower weekend rates.

An Der Messe
$$–$$$$ **Westend**

This quiet, 46-room charmer is just a 5-minute walk from the train station, the banking district, and the fairgrounds. Rooms are large and stylishly furnished, many with an Asian motif. The large bathrooms have tub-and-shower combos. The hotel can arrange baby-sitting.

Westendstrasse 104, 60325 Frankfurt am Main. ☎ ***800/221-6509** in the U.S. or 069/747-979. Fax: 069/748-349. Internet:* www.hotel-an-der-messe.de. *U-Bahn: Bockenheimer Warte (then a 5-minute walk south on Senckenberganlage and east on Westendstrasse. Rack rates: € 148–€ 282 double. Rates include breakfast. AE, DC, MC, V.*

Hilton Frankfurt

$$$$ **City Center**

With a soaring 12-story atrium and vast expanses of glass, this is one of Frankfurt's newest (the facility opened in 1998) and most modern hotels. You find a sense of hip, high-design theatricality in the 342 bedrooms. Prices vary according to size, view, and degree of luxury. Rooms overlooking the hotel's central atrium are the least expensive. The hotel has a health club and a pool, a bonus for most kids. The staff can also arrange baby-sitting.

Hochstrasse 4, 60313 Frankfurt am Main. ☎ ***800/445-8667** in the U.S. or 069/1338-000. Fax: 069/1338-1338. Internet:* www.frankfurt.hilton.com. *U-Bahn: Eschenheimer Tor (then a 3-minute walk west on Hochstrasse). Rack rates: € 300–€ 400 double. AE, DC, MC, V.*

Hotel Robert Mayer

$$–$$$ **Westend**

This artfully decorated hotel is within walking distance of Frankfurt's trade-fair complex. The building dates from 1905, but the rooms were completely redone in 1994, when 11 artists were hired to lend their individual visions to each of the 11 bedrooms. One room design was inspired by Frank Lloyd Wright, another looks Italian postmodern with pop art. All the rooms are comfortable. Many restaurants are nearby.

Robert-Mayer-Strasse 44, 60486 Frankfurt am Main. ☎ ***069/970910.** Fax: 069/9709-1010. Internet:* www.art-hotel-robert-mayer.de. *U-Bahn: Bockenheimer Warte (then a 10-minute walk south of Senckenberganlage and west on Robert-Mayer-Strasse). Rack rates: € 129–€ 200 double. Rates include breakfast. AE, DC, MC, V.*

Hotelschiff Peter Schlott

$ **Höchst**

Permanently moored at the Frankfurt suburb of Höchst, this 1950s riverboat has 19 small but evocative rooms. All of them have washbasins, ten have tiny showers, but none have private toilets. Everything is cabin-size and very basic (just a cut above a hostel), and mattresses are a bit thin, but if you love boats you'll enjoy hearing the waters of the Main lapping beneath your porthole. The ship's narrow and steep staircases are not easy to navigate if you have lots of luggage or difficulties walking.

Mainberg, 65929 Frankfurt-Höchst. ☎ *069/300-4643. Fax: 069/307-671. Internet:* www.hotel-schiff-schlott.de. *S-Bahn: Höchst (then a 10-minute walk south on Königsleiter Strasse to Mainberg on the river). Rack rates: €60–€71 double without shower; €80–€85 double with shower. Rates include breakfast. AE, DC, MC, V.*

Mozart

$ Westend

Many consider this to be the best small hotel in Frankfurt. The location is a few blocks east of the Palmengarten and south of the university, right off the busy Fürstenbergerstrasse. The interior decor is completely white and pink. The 35 rooms, each with a shower-only bathroom, are small but comfortable. The breakfast room, with its crystal chandeliers and Louis XV–style chairs, looks like an 18th-century salon. The staff is polite and helpful.

Parkstrasse 17, 60322 Frankfurt am Main. ☎ *069/156-8060. Fax: 069/156-8061. E-mail:* gotthilf@hotelmozart.de. *U-Bahn: Holzhausenstrasse (then a 10-minute walk south on Landstrasse and west on Fürstenbergerstrasse to Parkstrasse). Rack rates: €84–€114 double. Rates include buffet breakfast. AE, DC, MC, V. Closed Dec 24–Jan 1.*

Dining Out

In recent years Frankfurt has become, along with Berlin and Munich, one of Germany's great dining capitals, with restaurants that offer an array of richly varied cuisines. The *Apfelwein* (*ep*-ful-vine; apple-wine) taverns in Sachsenhausen (see the sidebar "Sachsenhausen and the apple-wine taverns," later in this chapter), on the south bank of the Main, tend to serve traditional Hessian dishes such as *Rippchen mit Kraut* (pickled pork chops with sauerkraut), *Haspel* (pigs' knuckles), and *Handkäs mit Musik* (strong, smelly cheese with vinegar, oil, and chopped onions; not for the faint of heart or recommended for honeymooners). One dish unique to Frankfurt is *grüne Sosse,* a green sauce made from seven herbs and other seasonings, chopped hard-boiled eggs, and sour cream, usually served with boiled eggs, boiled beef (*Tafelspitz*), or poached fish.

Exedra

$–$$ City Center   GREEK/MACEDONIAN

Behind an ornate 19th-century facade is one of the best Greek restaurants in Frankfurt. This large and fairly plain *taverna,* with big windows overlooking the street, serves as a cafe-bar in the early mornings. All the

Frankfurter versus hot dog

In Sachsenhausen and taverns around the city, you find real Frankfurters, smoked sausages made from pork and spices. The oldest-known recipe dates from 1487. The local product has been labeled "genuine Frankfurt sausage" since about 1900 in order to distinguish it from the American hot dog (hot dogs are for sale in Frankfurt, too, but always under the name "hot dog"). Unlike the hot dog, Frankfurters are always served in pairs, and they contain no fillers.

menu offerings are reliably good. The grilled lamb with feta cheese sauce and grilled sweet peppers and the pan-fried veal with white wine and lemon sauce are both excellent.

Heiligkreuzgasse 29. ☎ 069/287-397. U-Bahn: Konstablerwache (then a 5-minute walk east on Zeil and north on Kapperfeldstrasse to Heiligkreuzegass). Reservations recommended. Main courses: €11–€19. AE, DC, MC, V. Open: Mon–Thurs 8:30 a.m.–1 a.m., Fri–Sat 8 a.m.–2 a.m, Sun 4 p.m.–1 a.m.

Haus Wertheym
$–$$ Altstadt   GERMAN/HESSIAN

This atmospheric restaurant, in a half-timbered house rebuilt after World War II, sits on a cobblestone street just west of the Römer. Wood paneling and antique accessories overload the interior, and the waiters can be brusque. The menu, which hasn't changed much in the last half-century, includes Nuremberg Bratwursts, pork *schnitzels* (breaded cutlets), *Frankfurter Hacksteak* (chopped steak), and a good *Tafelspitz* (boiled beef). Most menu items come with the restaurant's trademark green sauce.

Fahrtor 1. ☎ 069/281-432. U-Bahn: Römer (then a 3-minute walk west to Fahrtor). Reservations recommended. Main courses: €9–€13. No credit cards. Open: Wed–Mon 11 a.m.–11 p.m.

Main Tower Restaurant & Bar
$$–$$$ City Center   INTERNATIONAL

The 53rd floor of Frankfurt's second-tallest skyscraper is the setting for this starkly minimalist restaurant with views that extend for miles. The cuisine is fresh and reliable, if not particularly imaginative. Appetizers range from smoked salmon with a pesto sauce to *beef carpaccio* (raw beef thinly sliced) with eggplant. You may choose from main courses, such as chicken strips with a red Thai curry or grilled fish served on black tagliatelli with a yellow-pepper purée.

In the Landesbank Hessen-Thüringen Building, Neue Mainzer Strasse 52–58. ☎ *069/3650-4777. U-Bahn: Willy-Brandt-Platz (then a 5-minute walk north on Neue Mainzer Strasse). Reservations recommended. Main courses: €14–€20; fixed-price lunches €13–€15. AE, DC, MC, V. Open: Sun–Thurs 10 a.m.–1 a.m., Fri–Sat 10 a.m.–2 a.m.*

Restaurant Français
$$$$ **City Center   FRENCH**

This dressy, upscale restaurant (jackets and ties for men) occupies two stately blue-and-gold dining rooms in the Steigenberger Frankfurter Hof, Frankfurt's most prestigious hotel. The imaginative French cuisine is beautifully prepared and presented. Appetizers may include a goose-liver terrine with a kumquat sauce, beetroot tart with caviar, cream soup with sea urchin, or quail consommé with truffle-stuffed tortellini. For the main course, you may find saltwater crayfish served with a vegetable couscous, or suckling pig served with stuffed vegetables, caramelized garlic, and purple mustard sauce.

In the Steigenberger Frankfurter Hof, Am Kaiserplatz. ☎ *069/21502. U-Bahn: Willy-Brandt-Platz (take the Willy-Brandt-Platz exit; the hotel is a 1-minute walk north on Friedenstrasse). Reservations required. Main courses: €28–€33; fixed-price lunch €34. AE, DC, MC, V. Open: Daily noon to 2 p.m. and 6:30–10 p.m.*

Tiger Restaurant, Palastbar, and Tiger-Bistrot
$$$$ **City Center   MEDITERRANEAN/INTERNATIONAL**

Come to these three places if you want to check out "the scene" (and be seen). The gourmet Tiger Restaurant, in a basement-level dining room adjacent to the Tigerpalast, a famous cabaret theater, earned a Michelin star in 1997. High-powered politicians and celebrities come to dine on seasonal Mediterranean cuisine. Expect to find dishes such as sautéed foie gras with glazed figs and truffle sauce; a strudel of sole and scallops with spinach; lobster lasagne with leeks and shellfish sauce; and pan-seared red mullet with sautéed arugula, served with a creamy artichoke risotto. Meals in the Palastbar and the Tiger-Bistrot, which opened in 2001, are less elaborate and cheaper, with fixed-price options.

Heiligkreuzegasse 16–20. ☎ *069/9200-2250. U-Bahn: Konstablerwache (then a 5-minute walk east on Zeil and north on Kapperfeldstrasse to Heiligkreuzegasse). Reservations required. Main courses: Tiger Restaurant €20–€32; Palastbar and Tiger-Bistrot €18–€21; fixed-price menus in Palastbar and Tiger-Bistrot €25–€41. AE, MC, V. Open: Tiger Restaurant Tues–Sun 5 p.m.–2 a.m.; Palastbar Tues–Sun 5 p.m.–3 a.m.; Tiger-Bistrot Tues–Sat 5 p.m.–1 a.m.*

Weinhaus Brückenkeller
$$$ **Altstadt   GERMAN/INTERNATIONAL**

Located in the heart of the Altstadt, this leading restaurant harks back to the 19th century, both in food and tavernlike decor. A typical meal may begin with cream of sorrel soup or goose liver with green beans, followed by a tender saddle of venison or lamb. The *Tafelspitz* (boiled beef) is the best in town. For dessert, try the soufflé of strawberries with vanilla sauce. You can choose from an excellent assortment of German wines.

Schützenstrasse 6. ☎ 069/298-0070. U-Bahn: Römer (then a 10-minute walk east on Mainkai and Schöne Aussicht and north on Schützenstrasse). Reservations required. Main courses: €23–€30. AE, DC, MC, V. Open: Mon–Sat 7–11 p.m. Closed Dec 20–Jan 8.

Sightseeing in Frankfurt

You can Frankfurt's compact Altstadt and most of its Innenstadt on foot. Nearly all the main sights lie within the boundaries of the old town walls (which today form a stretch of narrow parkland around the Altstadt) or are just across the river along the **Museumsufer** (Museum Embankment).

Allow about a half-day to explore the attractions of the Altstadt, specifically the **Römerberg,** the historic core of the old city; the **Kaiserdom;** and the **Goethe House,** birthplace of Germany's greatest writer. At the northern edge of the Altstadt is the city's most important square, called **An der Hauptwache,** named for the old guardhouse *(Hauptwache)* which stands upon it. Give yourself another half or full day to visit the museums on the south bank of the river. The **Städelsches Kunstinstitut** gallery (called "the Städel" for short) is the most important of the seven museums on the Museumsufer.

Two museums are free on Wednesday: Museum für Angewandte Kunst and Museum für Moderne Kunst. Many museums are also open until 8:00 p.m. on that day.

Walking through the city

Many visitors to Frankfurt are in the city for only one day before heading off to other German destinations. If you want to see the city on foot, take advantage of the vast network of *Fussgängerzonen* (pedestrian streets) for sightseeing and shopping. For a general walking tour, start at the **Alte Oper** (U-Bahn: Alte Oper), stroll east along Grosse Bockenheimer Strasse (better known as Fressgass', or Gluttony Lane, because food stores and restaurants line the street), and continue to **An der Hauptwache,** Frankfurt's Times Square. Northwest of the Hauptwache is the **Börse,** Frankfurt's stock exchange. A block to the north of Hauptwache, at the end of Grosse Eschenheimer Strasse, stands the **Eschenheimer Turm,** a restored medieval tower, and the **Eschenheimer Tor,** a medieval gateway. Running east from An der Hauptwache is the broad **Zeil,** the busiest shopping street in Germany. South of An der Hauptwache, via

Liebfrauenstrasse and Neue Kräme, the **Römerberg** and the **Kaiserdom** form the heart of the **Altstadt.** From there, Limpurgergasse leads to the river and the iron footbridge called the **Eisener Steg,** which crosses to the **Museumsufer** along the south bank of the Main. From the footbridge and the south bank, you have the best views of Frankfurt. Further south, beyond Gartenstrasse, lies the picturesque district of **Sachsenhausen,** famed for its apple-wine taverns.

Discovering the top attractions from A to Z

Deutsches Architektur Museum (German Architecture Museum)
Museumsufer

This museum is for those with an interest in architecture or urban planning. On display is a collection of 19th- and 20th-century architectural plans and models, examples of international modern architecture, and a series of exhibits showing how human dwellings have evolved over time in different parts of the world. A pair of 19th-century villas house the museum, designed by Oswald Matthias Ungers. The museum has a very good gift shop.

Schaumainkai 43. ☎ *069/2123-8844. U-Bahn: Schweizer Platz (then a 5-minute walk north on Schweizer and west on Schaumainkai). Admission: €4 adults, €2 students and children. Open: Tues–Sun 10 a.m.–5 p.m. (Wed until 8 p.m.).*

Deutsches Filmmuseum (German Film Museum)
Museumsufer

This is one of the two top film museums in Germany (the other is in Berlin). The first-floor galleries chronicle the history of the German and European filmmaking industry with examples of moviemaking equipment and models illustrating how special effects are shot. Old German films play continuously on the second floor. If you have an interest in film, you can easily spend an hour or more here.

Schaumainkai 41. ☎ *069/2123-8830. U-Bahn: Schweizer Platz (then a 5-minute walk north on Schweizer and west on Schaumainkai). Admission: €2.50 adults, €1.30 students and children. Open: Tues, Thurs, Fri, Sun 10 a.m.–5 p.m., Wed 10 a.m.– 8 p.m., Sat 2–8 p.m.*

Goethe-Haus (Goethe House)
City Center

Johann Wolfgang von Goethe (1749–1832), Germany's greatest writer, was born in this spacious, light-filled house and lived here until 1765, when he moved to Weimar (see Chapter 13). Reconstructed after war-time damage, the ochre-colored house still manages to convey the feeling of a prosperous, tranquil homelife in bygone days. The interior decoration reflects the baroque, rococo, and neoclassical styles of the 18th century. Paintings of friends and family adorn the walls. The room where Goethe wrote is on the second floor; the room next door displays one of his most cherished childhood possessions, a puppet theater. Annexed to the house is the modern, glass-fronted **Goethe-Museum.** Of interest to Goethe specialists, the museum constains a library of books, manuscripts, graphic artworks, and paintings associated with Goethe and his works. To see the house and museum, give yourself about half an hour.

Grosser Hirschgraben 23–25. ☎ *069/138-800. U-/S-Bahn: Hauptwache (then a 5-minute walk west). Admission: €3.50 adults, €1.50 students, €1 children. Open: Apr–Sept Mon–Fri 9 a.m.–6 p.m., Sat–Sun and holidays 10 a.m.–4 p.m.; Oct–Mar Mon–Fri 9 a.m.–4 p.m., Sat–Sun and holidays 10 a.m.–4 p.m.*

Historisches Museum (Historical Museum)
Altstadt

The exhibits in this large, drab-looking museum at the south end of the Römerberg showcase the history and culture of Frankfurt from its earliest settlement to the present day. Collections include examples of gold and silver plateware and jewelry; pottery and porcelain; and paintings, lithographs, and photographs. On the first floor, have a look at the models of the Altstadt at various periods of its development (Middle Ages, end of World War II, present day). As you can see from the models, when Allied bombs fell on Frankfurt in 1944, one of Europe's largest medieval cityscapes was completely wiped out. The amount of time you spend here depends on your interest level; you can browse through in half an hour.

If you need some refueling before or after visiting the museum, stop at **Konditoriei Hollhorst** (see the sidebar "Stopping for coffee and pastry," in this chapter).

Saalgasse 19. ☎ *069/2123-5599. U-Bahn: Römer (the museum is at the west end of the square). Admission: €4 adults, €2 children 6–18. Open: Tues, Thurs–Sat 10 a.m.–5 p.m., Wed 4–8 p.m., Sun 1–5 p.m.*

Kaiserdom (Cathedral)
Altstadt

The famous dome-topped West tower of the Kaiserdom (also known as **Bartholomäus-Dom**/Cathedral of St. Bartholomew) dominates the Altstadt. The highly ornamented tower dates from the 15th century and is built of red sandstone. Construction on the cathedral began in the 13th century and went on to the 15th, but the structure wasn't entirely completed until 1877. The church gained cathedral status in the 14th century when it became the site of the election of the emperors (called *kaisers* in Germany)

Stopping for coffee and pastry

For a quick and inexpensive cup of coffee and an excellent piece of pastry, duck into **Konditoriei Hollhorst**, Fahntor 1 (☎ **069/282-769**; U-Bahn: Römer), a small bakery directly across from the Historisches Museum. A coffee and a delicious *Apfelhörnchen* (a pastry with apple filling) cost about €3. The Konditorei is open Tuesday through Saturday from 10:30 a.m. to 6 p.m. and Sunday from noon to 6 p.m.

of the Holy Roman Empire. Later, between 1562 and 1792, the kaisers were crowned here as well (previously, coronations had taken place in Aachen cathedral), so the church also became known as the Kaiserdom.

Destroyed by Allied bombs in 1944, the cathedral was rebuilt in 1953. The layout is a fairly simple Gothic hall-church with three naves and a transept. The rebuilt interior has carved **choir stalls,** dating from around the mid-14th century. In the north chancel look for the **Altar of Maria Schlaf** (Mary Sleeping), carved and painted in 1434 and showing the apostles grouped around the dying Mary. This is the church's only altar to survive the bombing. On the south side of the chancel, you can see a carved wood *triptych* (three-panel) altarpiece of Mary and two saints.

The **Dom Museum** (☎ **069/1337-6186**), in the church's 19th-century cloister, exhibits coronation robes of the imperial electors. The oldest vestments date from the 1400s. You can see everything in and around the cathedral and museum in about a half-hour.

Domplatz. ☎ *069/2970-3236. U-Bahn: Römer (then a 2-minute walk east). Admission: Church free, Dom Museum €2 adults, €1 children. Open: Church daily 9 a.m. to noon and 2–6 p.m.; Dom Museum, Tues–Fri 10 a.m.–5 p.m., Sat–Sun 11 a.m.–5 p.m.*

Main Tower
City Center

The outdoor observation deck on the 56th floor of this gleaming, cylindrical tower provides a spectacular panorama of Frankfurt and the entire region. Kids of all ages enjoy the heights and views. You find the Main Tower Restaurant & Bar on the 53rd floor (see the listing in "Dining Out," earlier in this chapter).

Landesbank Hessen-Thüringen Building, Neue Mainzer Strasse 52–58. ☎ *069/ 3650-4777. U-Bahn: Willy-Brandt-Platz (then a 5-minute walk north on Neue Mainzer Strasse). Admission: €4.50. Open: Observation platform daily 10 a.m.– 9 p.m. (until 7 p.m. in winter).*

Museum für Angewandte Kunst (Museum of Applied Arts)
Museumsufer

Two buildings — one an early-19th-century villa, the other a 1985 structure designed by architect Richard Meier — house this enormous collection of European, Asian, and Islamic objects. The museum has outstanding collections of glassware (including 15th-century Venetian pieces), German rococo furnishings, and porcelain. An overall view takes about an hour.

Schaumainkai 17. ☎ 069/2123-4037. U-Bahn: Römer (then a 5-minute walk south across the Eisener-Stieg footbridge to Schaumainkai). Admission: €5 adults, €2.50 students and children over 5; free on Wed. Open: Tues–Sun 10 a.m.–8 p.m.

Museum für Moderne Kunst (Museum of Modern Art)
Altstadt

Located one block north of the cathdral in the Altstadt, this museum opened in 1991 in a postmodern building designed by Austrian architect Hans Hollein. The massive triangular structure has projecting and receding window openings. Exhibitions include major artists since the 1950s, such as Americans Roy Liechtenstein, Claes Oldenburg, Andy Warhol, and George Segal, all from the New York School. Works by modern German artists are also on view. You can see the works in about an hour. A cafe-restaurant is on the premises.

Domstrasse 10. ☎ 069/2123-0447. U-Bahn: Römer (then a 3-minute walk east across Domplatz and north on Domstrasse). Admission: €5 adults, €2.50 students; free on Wed. Open: Tues–Sun 10 a.m.–5 p.m (Wed until 8 p.m.).

Römer and Römerberg
Altstadt

The Altstadt centers around three Gothic buildings with stepped gables, known collectively as the **Römer.** These houses, just west of the cathedral, were originally built between 1288 and 1305 and bought by the city a century later for use as the Rathaus (Town Hall). After his coronation in the Kaiserdom, a new emperor and his entourage would parade westward to the Römer for a banquet. In the **Kaisersaal** (Imperial Hall; ☎ 069/2123-4814), on the second floor of the center house, you can see romanticized images of 52 emperors sculpted in the 19th century to celebrate the thousand-year history of the Holy Roman Empire. The hall is open daily 10 a.m. to 1 p.m. and 2 to 5 p.m. Admission is €1.53.

Medieval city officials and their families watched plays and tournaments from a specially built gallery on the **Nikolaikirche** (St. Nicholas Church), the small chapel in front of the city hall. The chapel has a 35-bell carillon that plays at 9:05 a.m., 12:05 p.m., and 5:05 p.m. **Römerplatz**, the square in front of the Römer, is one of Frankfurt's most popular spots, with a series of rebuilt half-timbered buildings housing cafes and restaurants.

The elaborate facade of the Römer, with its ornate balcony and statues of emperors, overlooks the **Römerberg** (Roman Hill). As early as the Stone Age, people occupied this high ground that was later settled by the Romans. After Germanic tribes conquered the Romans, the settlement fell into ruins and was forgotten until construction workers in the 20th century stumbled across its remains.

U-Bahn: Römer.

Städelsches Kunstinstitut/Städische Galerie (Städel Art Institute/Städel Gallery)
Museumsufer

Frankfurt's most important art gallery contains a fine collection of European paintings. The first floor features French Impressionists such as Renoir and Monet, along with German painters of the 19th and 20th centuries, including Tischbein's famous *Portrait of Goethe in the Campagna in Italy*. If you're short on time, the second floor displays an outstanding collection of Flemish primitives, 17th-century Dutch artists, and 16th-century German masters such as Dürer, Grünewald, and Memling. One of the most impressive paintings is Jan van Eyck's *Madonna* (1433). A large altarpiece and an impish nude Venus represent the work

Struwwelpeter (a.k.a. Shockheaded Peter)

He's a memory now, but up until World War II, the image of Struwwelpeter, with his enormous shock of hair and Edward Scissorhands-length fingernails, was ingrained in the nightmares of every German child and many children throughout the world. Published in 1844, Struwwelpeter was the creation of Heinrich Hoffman (1809–1894), a Frankfurt physician who wrote gruesomely moralistic children's stories. Struwwelpeter's grotesque hair and fingernails were the result of his bad-boy behavior. The illustrated story became one of the most popular "children's books" in Germany and was translated into 14 languages (in England Struwwelpeter became "Shockheaded Peter").

The entertaining **Struwwelpeter-Museum,** Schirn, Römerberg, Bendergass 1 (☎ 069/281-333), displays original sketches and illustrations with copies of the book (and its classic image of Struwwelpeter) from many different countries. Admission is free; the museum, located alongside the Schirn Gallery, is open Tuesday to Sunday from 11 a.m. to 5 p.m. Struwwelpeter fans can also visit the **Heinrich-Hoffman-Museum,** Schubertstrasse 20 (☎ 069/747-969; U-Bahn: Westend), the home of Struwwelpeter's creator.

Sachsenhausen and the apple-wine taverns

Sachsenhausen, the district south of the River Main, has long been known for its taverns where *Apfelwein* (*ep*-ful-vine; apple-wine), not beer, is the special drink. At an apple-wine tavern, everyone sits together at long wooden tables and, sooner or later, the singing starts.

Apfelwein, pronounced *ebb*-el-vye, in the local dialect, is a dry, alcoholic, 12-proof apple cider. The wine is always poured from a blue-and-gray stoneware jug into glasses embossed with a diamond-shaped pattern. The first sip may pucker your whole body and convince you that you're drinking vinegar. If drinking straight Apfelwein is too much for you, try a *Sauergespritzt* (sour spritzer), a mixture of Apfelwein and plain mineral water, or a *Süssgespritzt* (sweet spritzer), Apfelwein mixed with lemonade-flavored mineral water.

Although available year-round, Apfelwein also comes in seasonal versions. *Süsser* (sweet), sold in the autumn, is the dark, cloudy product of the first pressing of the apple harvest. When the wine starts to ferment it's called *Rauscher*, which means it's darker and more acidic. You're supposed to drink Süsser and Rauscher straight, not mixed.

The Apfelwein taverns in Sachsenhausen display a pine wreath outside when a new barrel has arrived. The taverns usually serve traditional meals, and hard rolls, salted bread sticks, and pretzels for nibbling are on the tables, too. What you eat, including the snacks, goes on your tab. The following is a list of a few traditional Apfelwein taverns in Sachsenhasen; all of them are *Gartenlokale,* meaning they move their tables outside in good weather:

- ✔ **Zum Eichkatzerl,** Greieichstrasse 29 (☎ **069/617-480**), open Thursday to Tuesday from 3 p.m. to midnight.

- ✔ **Fichtekränzi,** Wallstrasse 5 (☎ **069/612-778**), open Monday to Saturday from 5 p.m. to midnight.

- ✔ **Zum Gemalten Haus,** Schweizer Strasse 67 (☎ **069/614-559**), open Wednesday to Sunday from 10 a.m. to midnight; closed mid-June to the end of July.

On Saturdays, Sundays, and holiday afternoons throughout the year, you can hop on the **"Ebbelwei-Express"** (☎ **069/2132-2425**), an old, colorfully painted trolley, and ride all through Frankfurt and over to the apple-wine taverns in Sachsenhausen. The entire route takes about an hour and costs €5 for adults and €2.50 for children up to 14. The fare includes a bottle of apple wine (or apple juice). You can buy tickets from the conductor. You can catch the trolley at Römer, Konstablerwache, or the main train station; service starts about 1:30 p.m. and ends about 5 p.m.

of Lucas Cranach. In the Department of Modern Art hang works by Francis Bacon, Dubuffet, Tapies, and Yves Klein. To get a good sense of what's on display, you need at least two hours.

Schaumainkai 63. ☎ 069/605-0980. U-Bahn: Schweizer Platz (then a 5-minute walk north on Schweizer and west on Schaumainkai). Admission: €6 adults, €5 children 9–16, €10 family ticket. Open: Tues–Sun 10 a.m.–5 p.m. (Wed until 8 p.m.).

Städtische Galerie Liebieghaus (Liebieg Sculpture Museum)
Museumsufer

Housed in a late-19th-century villa, this sculpture museum includes statuary from ancient Egypt, Greece, and Rome, and from medieval and Renaissance Europe. You can see several noteworthy pieces from antiquity. In the medieval section, look for the 11th-century carving of the *Virgin and Child* created in Trier, Tilman Riemenschneider's expressive *Madonna,* Andrea della Robbia's altarpiece of the Assumption, and the 16th-century *Black Venus with Mirror.* Give yourself about an hour to see the major works.

Schaumainkai 71. ☎ 069/2123-8617. U-Bahn: Schweizer Platz (then a 10-minute walk north on Schweizer and west on Schaumainkai). Admission: €4 adults, €2.50 seniors, students, and children. Open: Tues–Sun 10 a.m.–5 p.m. (Wed until 8 p.m.).

Seeing Frankfurt by Guided Tour

A very good way to see Frankfurt, especially if your time is limited, is by the daily, guided tour offered by the city's tourist offices. The 2½-hour bus tour, in English, picks up passengers at 2 p.m. from Touristinfo Römer (Römerberg 27, in the Altstadt; ☎ 069/2123-8800) and at 2:15 p.m. from Touristinfo Hauptbahnhof (opposite the main entrance of the train station; ☎ 069/2123-8800; Internet: www.frankfurt-tourismus.de). From April through October, an additional tour leaves from the Römer at 10 a.m. and from the train station at 10:15 a.m. The tour covers the entire city and includes a trip up to the top of the Main Tower, Frankfurt's tallest skyscraper, and a brief stop in the Historical Museum. The cost is €24 for adults, €17 for students, and €8.50 for children aged 6 to 12. Buy tickets at the tourist offices.

Shopping for Local Treasures

Frankfurt has several shopping areas. On the **Zeil,** a pedestrian zone between the Hauptwache and Konstablerwache, you find department stores, clothing shops, shoe stores, record stores — in short, just about everything. Shoppers generally pack the Zeil, reputedly the busiest shopping street in Germany. The **Hauptwache,** in the center of Frankfurt, has two shopping areas, one above and one below ground. **Schillerstrasse,** another pedestrian zone, lies between Hauptwache and Eschenheimer Turm, near the stock exchange. Walking from Schillerstrasse northeast toward Eschenheimer Tor, you pass many elegant boutiques and specialty shops. Southwest of the Hauptwache is **Goethestrasse,** with exclusive stores evocative of Paris or Milan.

Shops are generally open Monday through Friday from 9 a.m. to 6:30 p.m. and Saturday from 9 a.m. to 2 p.m. (until 4 or 6 p.m. on the first Saturday of the month).

Department stores

Hertie, Zeil 90 (☎ 069/929-050; U-Bahn: Hauptwache), a Frankfurt shopping tradition, carries clothes and shoes for every budget, has a toy department, and operates a food hall in the basement. **Kaufhof,** Zeil 116–123 (☎ 069/21910; U-Bahn: Hauptwache), Hertie's main competitor, stocks just about everything on its seven floors: porcelain, clothes, jewelry, glassware, gifts and gadgets. The top-floor restaurant has panoramic views of Frankfurt.

Gifts

Mercedes Benz Giftshop, Kaiserstrasse 19–21 (☎ 069/9735-5490; U-Bahn: Willy-Brandt-Platz), is the only store of its kind in Germany, selling jackets, vests, luggage, baseball caps, and key rings commemorating the snobby mystique of Mercedes.

Porcelain

Höchster Porzellan Manufaktur, Am Kornmarkt/Berliner Strasse 60 (☎ 069/295-299; U-Bahn: Römer), contains one of Germany's largest inventories of Höchst porcelain, called "white gold" and manufactured for the last 250 years. You can buy a beautiful white porcelain vase for as little as €18.

Discovering Nightlife in Frankfurt

For details of what's happening in Frankfurt, pick up *Journal Frankfurt* at newsstands throughout the city. *Fritz* and *Strandgut,* both free and available at the tourist office, also have listings.

To purchase tickets for major cultural events, go to the venue box office or to the **Touristinfo** office at the main train station or in the Römer. The department store **Hertie,** Zeil 90 (☎ 069/294-848; U-Bahn: Hauptwache), also has a theater ticket office.

One of the best ways to spend an evening in Frankfurt is at one of the apple-wine taverns in Sachsenhausen (see the sidebar "Sachsenhausen and the apple-wine taverns," in this chapter).

Raising the curtain on the performing arts

When the **Alte Oper** (Old Opera House), Opernplatz (☎ 069/134-0400; Internet: www.alteoper.de; U-Bahn: Alte Oper), opened in 1880, critics hailed the building as one of the most beautiful theaters in Europe. Destroyed in World War II, the Alte Oper didn't reopen until 1981. Today the theater, with its golden-red mahogany interior and superb acoustics, is the site of frequent symphonic and choral concerts, but opera is not performed here.

Oper Frankfurt/Ballet Frankfurt, Willy-Brandt-Platz (☎ 069/134-0400; Internet: www.opera-frankfurt.de; U-Bahn: Willy-Brandt-Platz), is Frankfurt's premier showcase for world-class opera and ballet. Ticket prices range from €10 to €110.

English Theater, Kaiserstrasse 52 (☎ 069/2423-1620; U-Bahn: Hauptbahnhof), presents English-language musicals, comedies, dramas, and thrillers from September to July. Tickets range from €22 to €34.

Theater der Stadt Frankfurt, Untermainanlage 11 (☎ 069/2123-7999; U-Bahn: Willy-Brandt-Platz), has three stages. One belongs to the **Frankfurt Municipal Opera,** the other two present dramas. A variety theater, **Kunstlerhaus Mouson Turm,** Waldschmidtstrasse 4 (☎ 069/4058-9520; U-/S-Bahn: Merianplatz), hosts plays, classical music concerts, and dance programs almost every night of the week. Tickets run €10 to €21.

Meeting at the cabaret

Tigerpalast, Heiligkreuzgasse 16–20 (☎ 069/289-691; U-Bahn: Konstablerwache), is the most famous cabaret in Frankfurt. Shows take place in a small theater, where guests sit at tiny tables to see about eight different acts per show. Each show lasts two hours with breaks for drinks (€10) and snacks. You don't need to know German to enjoy the show, which is excellent family-style entertainment. (The cabaret acts are not raunchy or suggestive, but more like circus entertainment.) Tickets are €45, half-price for children under 12. Three recommended restaurants are part of this cabaret (see Tiger-Restaurant, Palastbar, and Tiger-Bistrot in "Dining Out," earlier in this chapter).

Checking out bars and clubs

If you're going to paint the town red, be aware that porno movies, sex shows, sex shops, and discos teeming with prostitutes line several blocks in front of the main train station. This area can be dangerous at night, so don't come here alone. If you're looking for a night out, you find plenty of clubs, discos, bars, and cafes across the Main River in the **Sachsenhausen** district. Most gay bars and clubs are located in a small area between Bleichstrasse and Zeil.

Bars and cafes

Café Karin, Grosser Hirschgraben 28 (☎ **069/295-217;** U-Bahn: Hauptwache), is a relaxing, unpretentious cafe with art-filled walls, old wooden tables, daily newspapers, and cafe food. The cafe is open Monday to Thursday from 9 a.m. to 1 a.m., Friday and Saturday from 9 a.m. to 2 p.m., and Sunday from 10 a.m. to 7 p.m.

Café Laumer, Bockenheimer Landstrasse 67 (☎ **069/727-912;** U-Bahn: Westend), a classic German *Kaffeehaus* with a large garden, serves some of the best pastries in town. The cafe is open Monday to Saturday from 7:30 a.m. to 7 p.m., Sunday from 10 a.m. to 7 p.m.

Café-Restaurant in der Schirn (Schirn Café), Römerberg 6A (☎ **069/ 291-732;** U-Bahn: Römer), in the heart of the Altstadt, is a stylish steel, glass, and granite see-and-be-seen cafe-bar-restaurant designed by Philippe Starck. Tables spill out onto the pavement in summer. The restaurant is open Tuesday to Friday from noon to 3 p.m. and 6 to 10:30 p.m., Saturday and Sunday from noon to 10:30 p.m. The bar is open Tuesday to Sunday from noon to midnight.

Luna, Stiftstrasse 6 (☎ **069/294-774;** U-Bahn: Hauptwache), is a hip bar that's always packed with young professionals. The bartenders serve all manner of cocktails, including Grasshoppers, juleps, champagne fizzes, and tropical coladas. The bar is open Sunday to Thursday from 7 p.m. to 2 a.m., Friday and Saturday from 7 p.m. to 3 a.m.

Nightclubs

Cooky's, Am Salzhaus 4 (☎ **069/287-662;** U-Bahn: Hauptwache), plays a mix of hip-hop and house music. Cover is €6 to €8, depending on the night. Hours are Tuesday, Thursday, and Sunday from 11 p.m. to 4 a.m., Friday and Saturday from 10 p.m. to 6 a.m.

Nacht Leben, Kurt-Schumacher-Strasse 50 (☎ **069/20650;** U-Bahn: Konstablerwache), has a cafe-bar upstairs and a disco downstairs that plays hip-hop, funk, soul, and house. Cover for the disco is €4 to €10. Hours are Monday through Wednesday from 11:30 a.m. to 2 a.m, Thursday through Saturday from 11:30 a.m. to 4 a.m.

Gay and lesbian clubs

Blue Angel, Bronnerstrasse 17 (☎ **069/282-772;** U-Bahn: Konstablerwache), is a mixed dance club where the scene heats up after midnight. Cover is €5 to €8. Hours are daily from 9 p.m. to 1 a.m.

Harvey's Cafe Bar, Bornheimer Landstrasse 64 (☎ **069/497-303;** U-Bahn: Hauptwache), is a popular indoor/outdoor bistro that occasionally features live disco bands on the weekend. The bar is open daily from 10 a.m. to 1 a.m. (until 2 a.m. Friday and Saturday).

La Gata, Seehofstrasse 3 (☎ **069/614-581;** U-Bahn: Südbahnhof), the most upfront lesbian bar in Frankfurt, looks like an English pub and serves soups and snacks. The bar is open daily from 9 p.m. to 1 a.m.

Fast Facts: Frankfurt

American Express

Located at Kaiserstrasse 8 (☎ 069/21050; U-Bahn: Hauptwache), the American Express office is open Monday through Friday from 9:30 a.m. to 6 p.m., Saturday from 10 a.m. to 2:30 p.m.

ATMS

You find ATM machines all over Frankfurt — this is a banking city, after all.

Bookstores

The best English-language bookstore is British Bookshop, Börsenstrasse 17 (☎ 069/ 280-492; U-Bahn: Hauptwache). Hours are Monday through Friday from 9:30 a.m. to 7 p.m. and Saturday from 9:30 a.m. to 4 p.m.

Country Code and City Code

The country code for Germany is **49.** The city code for Frankfurt is 069.

Consulates

The U.S. Consulate is at Siesmayerstrasse 21 (☎ 069/75350; U-Bahn: Westend). The British Consulate is at Bockenheimer Landstrasse 42 (☎ 069/170-0020; U-Bahn: Bockenheimer Warte).

Currency Exchange

The Reise-Bank kiosk (☎ 069/2427-8591; U-Bahn: Hauptbahnhof) in the main train station is open daily from 7:30 a.m. to 10 p.m.

Dentists and Doctors

For an English-speaking doctor or dentist in an emergency, call ☎ 069/19292. Call ☎ 069/11500 for emergency dental service.

Emergencies

Dial ☎ **110** for the police; ☎ **112** for a fire, first aid, and ambulance.

Internet Access

CyberRyder, Tongegasse 31 (☎ 069/ 9139-6754; info@cyberyder.de; U-Bahn: Hauptwache), is open Monday through Thursday from 9 a.m. to 11 p.m., Friday and Saturday from 9 a.m. to 1 a.m., and Sunday from 2 to 11 p.m.

Pharmacies

In Germany a drugstore is an *Apotheke* (ah-po-*tay*-kuh). For information about pharmacies open near you, call (☎ 069/11500).

Post Office

The post office at the main train station (☎ 069/242-4270; U-Bahn: Hauptbahnhof) is open Monday through Friday from 6:30 a.m. to 9 p.m., Saturday from 8 a.m. to 6 p.m., and Sunday and holidays from 11 a.m. to 6 p.m.

Restrooms

You find many well-kept public facilities in central Frankfurt, especially in the Altstadt. A restroom is called a *Toilette* (toy-*let*-uh) and is often labeled WC, with either F (for *Frauen*, women) or H (for *Herren*, men).

Safety

Frankfurt is a relatively safe city, but you should stay out of the area around the main train station at night.

Web Sites

The Tourist Information office Web site, www.frankfurt-tourismus.de, is good for general information. You find more specific information at www.germany-tourism.de

Chapter 19

Heidelberg and Nuremberg: Castles and Kaisers

I devote this chapter to two special cities in central Germany. **Heidelberg,** located on the Neckar River in the state of Baden-Württemberg, is one of Germany's most romantic cities. **Nuremberg,** or Nürnberg as its known in German, is a historic and very attractive city in the state of Bavaria.

Both of these castle-crowned cities are worth visiting for a day or two. **Rothenburg ob Tauber,** a remarkable medieval walled town, can be visited as a side trip from Nuremberg.

Heidelberg: Romance on the River

Heidelberg, on the Neckar River 55 miles (88 km) south of Frankfurt, is renowned for its castle and its university. (See the "Heidelberg" map in this chapter.) According to a song from the operetta *The Student Prince,* which is set in Heidelberg, summertime in Heidelberg is a time for music and romance. Today, summer is also a time when droves of visitors from around the globe invade this beautiful city. Many Americans know Heidelberg because of the nearby U.S. Army base.

Heidelberg is one of the few German cities that was not leveled by air raids in World War II, so you can still see original buildings from the Middle Ages, Renaissance, baroque, and neoclassical eras. This architecture is certainly a major part of Heidelberg's appeal. But some of its legendary romantic allure stems from what was basically a 19th-century public-relations campaign. The looming ruins of the ancient castle, the old lanes and squares, the leafy hills and woodlands beside the Neckar,

Heidelberg

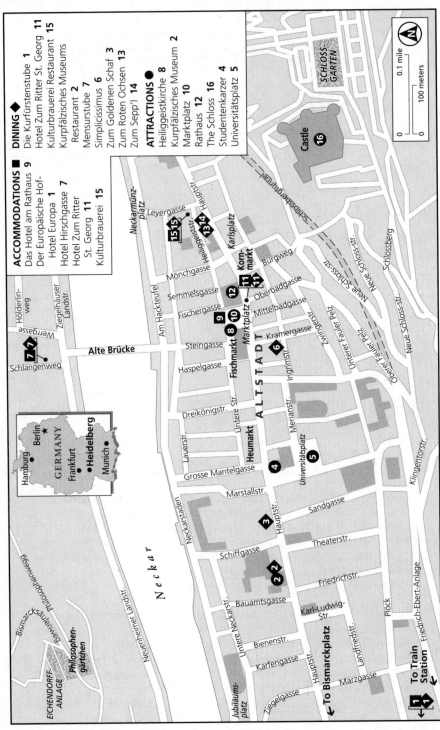

ACCOMMODATIONS ■
Das Hotel am Rathaus **9**
Der Europäische Hof-
Hotel Europa **1**
Hotel Hirschgasse **7**
Hotel Zum Ritter
St. Georg **11**
Kulturbrauerei **15**

DINING ◆
Die Kurfürstenstube **1**
Hotel Zum Ritter St. Georg **11**
Kulturbrauerei Restaurant **15**
Kurpfälzisches Museums
Restaurant **2**
Mensurstube **7**
Simplicissimus **6**
Zum Goldenen Schaf **3**
Zum Roten Ochsen **13**
Zum Sepp'l **14**

ATTRACTIONS ●
Heiliggeistkirche **8**
Kurpfälzisches Museum **2**
Marktplatz **10**
Rathaus **12**
The Schloss **16**
Studentenkarzer **4**
Universitätsplatz **5**

and the youthful student population all had great appeal to the German Romantics. The great writer Goethe and many other poets, painters, and musicians "discovered" Heidelberg in the early 19th century. They praised the town in their writings and immortalized it in their music and paintings. The town came to symbolize Old World German Romanticism at its most picturesque.

Getting there

Heidelberg is easily accessible by train from all major cities in Germany and Europe. The train trip to Heidelberg's Hauptbahnhof (main train station) is only one hour from Frankfurt and about three hours from Nuremberg. For train schedules and information, call **Deutsche Bahn** ☎ **01805/996-633.**

Finding information

Tourist-Information, Pavillon am Hauptbahnhof (☎ **06221/19433;** Internet: www.heidelberg.de), is open Monday through Saturday from 9 a.m. to 7 p.m. and Sunday from 10 a.m. to 6 p.m. (closed Sun from Nov–Mar). The office has maps and brochures. You find additional Tourist Information offices at Neckarmünzplatz (☎ **0621/13740;** open summer only 9 a.m.–6:30 p.m.), and at the Schloss (castle), Neue Schlossstrasse 54 (no phone; open summer only 10 a.m.–5 p.m.)

The **Heidelberg Card,** available for €12 from the Tourist Information office at the train station and at many hotels, provides admission to Heidelberg Castle and discounts on attractions, walking and boat tours, and unlimited use of public transportation.

Taking a guided tour

A two-hour **guided walking tour** of the city (in German) departs from the Lion's Fountain on Universitätsplatz at 10:30 a.m. daily from April through October, and on Saturdays only from November through March. Between April and October, a walking tour in English departs from the same place Thursday through Sunday at 10:30 a.m. The cost is €6 for adults, €4 for students and children. Purchase your ticket from the Tourist Information Office at the train station.

From April through October, **guided bus tours** of the city (in German and English), including the castle, depart from Universitätsplatz on Thursday and Friday at 2:30 p.m., Saturday at 10:30 a.m. and 2:30 p.m., and Sunday and holidays at 10:30 a.m.; November through March the tour takes place Saturday only at 2:30 p.m. The cost is €12 for adults, €9 for students and children. Purchase tickets at the Tourist Information Office at the train station.

From Easter through October, **Rhein-Neckar-Fahrgastschiffahrt** (☎ **06221/20181;** Internet: www.rnf-schiffahrt.de) offers daily **guided boat tours** (commentary in German and English) on the Neckar River between Heidelberg and Neckarsteinach. The round-trip tour lasts about three hours and costs €9.50 for adults, €5.50 for children. Boats depart from the landing stage near the Stadthalle, between the Theodor-Heuss-Brücke (bridge) and the Alte Brücke (Old Bridge).

Orienting yourself

Your first glimpse of "romantic old Heidelberg" as you emerge from the Hauptbahnhof on the west side of town may be disappointing. The city, like many in Germany and throughout Europe, has a modern and a historic face, and the modern one is what you encounter first. Modern Heidelberg centers around **Bismarckplatz** (streetcar lines 1 and 2 run there from the train station), an area of tall buildings and shopping plazas. The **Altstadt** (Old Town), to the east, is where you want to focus your sightseeing activities. The Altstadt is a long wedge of slate-roofed buildings along the Neckar River, beneath the Schloss.

Hauptstrasse, a wide, busy pedestrian street with narrow medieval lanes on both sides, runs from Bismarckplatz into the compact Altstadt. The main squares in the Altstadt are **Universitätsplatz,** a focal point for famed Heidelberg University; **Fischmarkt,** dominated by the Heiliggeistkirche (Church of the Holy Spirit); the **Marktplatz,** or Market Square; and the **Kornmarkt.** The Schloss crowns a hill to the south, above the Altstadt. Across the Neckar River is the **Philosophenweg** (Philosopher's Way), a popular walking trail; a zoo; and a botanical garden.

Getting around Heidelberg

Once you're in the Altstadt you can walk everywhere. However, the Altstadt is about a half-hour walk from the train station, so I recommend that you take a streetcar or bus to Bismarckplatz or Universitätsplatz to begin your explorations.

Heidelberg is crisscrossed with a network of streetcars and buses operated by the local transportation department, **HSB** (☎ **06221/513-2000**). Many bus and streetcar lines intersect at Bismarckplatz in the town center. Buses 41 and 42 travel between the railway station and Universitätsplatz, on the west side of the Altstadt. A single fare on the bus or tram costs €1.80; a 24-hour pass, valid for up to five persons traveling within a group, costs €5.35. A **Bergbahn** (funicular; ☎ **06221/ 22796**) runs from Kornmarkt, in the Altstadt, up to the castle, between 9 a.m. and 7:40 p.m. daily; the round-trip fare is €3 for adults, €2 for children and students.

Staying in Heidelberg

See also the listing for the outstanding **Der Europäische Hof-Hotel Europa** ($$$$) in Chapter 22.

Das Hotel am Rathaus

$–$$ **Altstadt**

This is one of Heidelberg's nicest affordable hotels, located right in the heart of the city on the Marktplatz. The 17 rooms are small but very pleasant, with simple modern furnishings and tiled bathrooms with showers. Some larger rooms are suitable for families. The one potential drawback: The hotel doesn't have an elevator.

Heiliggeiststrasse 1, 69117 Heidelberg. ☎ *06221/14730. Fax: 06221/147-337. Internet:* www.hotels-in-heidelberg.de. *Bus: 11 to Rathaus/Kornmarkt (then a 4-minute walk north on Oberbadgasse to Heiliggeiststrasse on the east side of Marktplatz). Rack rates: €110–€154 double. Rates include breakfast buffet. AE, DC, MC, V.*

Hotel Hirschgasse

$$$–$$$$ **North side of the river**

Nestled on the hillside of a historic lane adjoining the famous Philosophenweg on the north side of the Neckar, this historic hotel enjoys a tranquil and romantic setting. The hotel dates from 1472 and has lodged such impressive figures as Mark Twain and Bismarck. The 20 rooms are all sumptuously comfortable suites decorated with Laura Ashley fabrics, and all come equipped with shower-tub-whirlpool combinations in the bathrooms. The **Mensurstube** restaurant is one of the most historically atmospheric spots in town (see the next section, "Dining in Heidelberg"). The Altstadt is a ten-minute walk from the hotel.

Hirschgasse 3, 69100 Heidelberg. ☎ *06221/4540. Fax: 06221/454-111. Internet:* www.hirschgasse.de. *Bus: 34 (from Bismarckplatz to Hirschgasse stop). Rack rates: €195–€335 double. AE, DC, MC, V.*

Hotel Zum Ritter St. Georg

$–$$$ **Altstadt**

Located right on the Marktplatz on Hauptstrasse, the main street in the Altstadt, the Zum Ritter St. Georg is a well-preserved rarity from the German Renaissance. Built in 1592 as the home of a cloth merchant, the hotel is among Heidelberg's sightseeing attractions thanks to its highly decorated, gabled facade. The hotel doesn't have public lounges. Many of the 40 rooms are modest in size, but the beds are comfortable. Most of the rooms contain tiled bathrooms with shower-tub combinations. Although they have Romantic Altstadt views, the front rooms can also be noisy because of neighboring cafes and restaurants. The dining room specializes in venison and duck breast.

Hauptstrasse 178, 69117 Heidelberg. ☎ *06221/1350. Fax: 06221/135-230. Internet:* www.ritter-heidelberg.de. *Bus: 11 to Rathaus/Kornmarkt (then a 3-minute walk north on Oberbadgasse to Marktplatz). Rack rates:* €*105 double without bathroom,* €*155–*€*210 double with bathroom. Rates include buffet breakfast. AE, DC, MC, V.*

Kulturbrauerei
$–$$ Altstadt

This small (21 rooms), hip, brand-new hotel, just a couple of minutes' walk from the river, is connected to a microbrewery. The hotel has a cool, minimalist style. The medium-size rooms have light-colored hardwood floors and are furnished with comfortable beds and large wooden cupboards. Bathrooms are adequately roomy with tub-shower combinations (four rooms have showers only). Unfortunately, the hotel doesn't have air conditioning, and courtyard-facing rooms can be noisy in the summer, when tables are set up in the microbrewery's beer garden. If you don't stay here, you may want to dine in the on-site restaurant (see the next section, "Dining in Heidelberg").

Leyergasse 6, 69117 Heidelberg. ☎ *06221/90000. Fax: 06221/900-099. Internet:* www.heidelberger-kulturbrauerei.de. *Bus: 11 or 33 to Neckarmünzplatz (then a 3-minute walk south on Leyergasse). Rack rates:* €*116–*€*135 double. AE, MC, V.*

Dining in Heidelberg

Die Kurfürstenstube
$$$$ Altstadt   FRENCH

The best dining spot in Heidelberg is the wood-paneled Die Kurfürstenstube in the deluxe Der Europäische Hof-Hotel Europa. The menu is in English, but the cuisine is mainly French, with both fixed-price and à la carte meals. The restaurant uses only the highest-quality seasonal ingredients. Look for culinary delights such as creamed pea soup with crayfish or iced lobster and melon soup with white port, medallions of venison with glazed cherries and celery purée, roast John Dory (fish) with garlic-flavored cream sauce or roasted loin of lamb with chanterelle mushrooms and *pecorino* (cheese) gnocchi. The dessert menu is equally scrumptious, and the wine list is the most impressive in town.

In Der Europäische Hof-Hotel Europa, Friedrich-Ebert-Anlage 1. ☎ *06221/5150. Streetcar: 1 or 2 to Bismarckplatz (then a 3-minute walk south to Friedrich-Ebert-Anlage). Reservations required. Main courses:* €*25–*€*30; fixed-price menus* €*57,* €*60,* €*75. AE, DC, MC, V. Open: Daily noon to 3:30 p.m. and 6:30–11:30 p.m.*

Hotel Zum Ritter St. Georg
$$ Altstadt GERMAN/INTERNATIONAL

At this restaurant, located in one of Heidelberg's most famous Renaissance buildings, you can dine in the large Rittersaal (Knights' Hall) or the smaller Councillors' Chamber. The house specialty is saddle of venison for two (in season); locals flock here when this dish is on the menu. A good beginning might be snail soup with herbs or tomato soup with whipped cream. Other menu offerings include staples such as pork loin with sauerkraut or roast salmon in a basil-cream sauce. If you like beer, try the Dortmunder Actien-Brauerei. A children's menu includes dishes such as *Wiener Würstchen* (small "Vienna-style" sausages).

Hauptstrasse 178. ☎ *06221/1350. Bus: 11 to Rathaus/Kornmarkt (then a 3-minute walk north on Oberbadgasse to Marktplatz). Reservations recommended. Main courses €9.50–€14; fixed-price menus €19–€33. AE, DC, MC, V. Open: Daily noon to 2 p.m. and 6–10 p.m.*

Kulturbrauerei Restaurant
$ Altstadt GERMAN/REGIONAL

Part of a microbrewery and hotel complex (see the previous section, "Staying in Heidelberg"), this large, popular restaurant was formerly a dance hall. You can eat on the balcony or, in summer, in the beer garden. Come here if you're in the mood for hearty portions of traditional German food washed down by one of the homemade Scheffel's beers. You can order salads, seasonal specialties (herring, pork stomach, spareribs), dishes from the grill (Bratwursts, pork filet with mushrooms, roast fish), or vegetarian meals.

Leyergasse 6. ☎ *06221/90000. Bus: 11 or 33 to Neckarmünzplatz (then a 3-minute walk south on Leyergasse). Main courses: €9–€18. MC, V. Open: Daily 11 a.m.– 11 p.m.*

Kurpfälzisches Museums Restaurant
$$ Altstadt GERMAN/INTERNATIONAL

On a warm summer's day or evening, nothing is more enjoyable or romantic than dining in the museum's garden courtyard with its splashing fountain. The restaurant also has a pleasant dining room. Fresh fish dishes may include zander with lemon cream, swordfish with a pepper crust, or tuna fish with tomatoes, olives, and herbs. You can also get meat dishes: a good rib-eye steak, lamb with rosemary, or pork medallions in a pepper-cream sauce with homemade *Spätzle* (a potato-based pasta). For dessert, try the mocha and Grand Marnier parfait with fruit sauce.

Hauptstrasse 97. ☎ *06221/24050. Streetcar: 1 or 2 to Bismarckplatz (then a 5-minute walk east on Hauptstrasse). Reservations recommended for dinner. Main courses: €13–€20. MC, V. Open: Daily 10 a.m. to midnight.*

Mensurstube

$$–$$$ **North Bank** **GERMAN/REGIONAL**

No other place in Heidelberg captures bygone days quite like this rustic and cozy spot in the ancient Hotel Hirschgasse, where swords hang from the ceiling, while you sit at tables more than two centuries old. The limited menu wisely sticks to traditional dishes made with fresh ingredients. Potato soup is a good starter, followed by homemade noodles, oxtail, or lamb shank. The menu often includes *Rinderfilet* (filet of beef) served with bone marrow and a red-wine sauce. Almost everything is best accompanied by Pils beer on tap.

In the Hotel Hirschgasse, Hirschgasse 3. ☎ 06221/4540. Bus: 34 (from Bismarckplatz to Hirschgasse stop). Reservations recommended. Main courses €15–€20. AE, DC, MC, V. Open: Daily noon to 2 p.m. and 6–10 p.m.

Simplicissimus

$$$–$$$$ **Altstadt** **FRENCH**

This elegant gourmet restaurant in the Altstadt is known for its *cuisine moderne*. The menu changes often but may include lamb with a red wine and onion purée, fresh mushrooms in cream sauce with homemade noodles, duck breast with asparagus, or crayfish with fresh melon and herb-flavored cream sauce. Service is friendly, and the wine list is good.

Ingrimstrasse 16. ☎ 06221/183-336. Bus: 11, 12, 33, 35, or 41. Reservations required. Main courses €28–€48; fixed-price menu €35, €55. AE, MC, V. Open: Wed–Mon 6–11 p.m. Closed 2 weeks in Mar and Aug.

Zum Goldenen Schaf

$$ **Altstadt** **GERMAN/REGIONAL**

Located on Hauptstrasse, the main street in the Altstadt, this historic restaurant offers a menu emphasizing regional dishes from Swabia and the Pfalz. You may want to try the *Kringelbratwurst* (roast sausage with sauerkraut and mashed potatoes) or Swabian *Sauerbraten* (marinated beef with red cabbage and noodles). Portions are hearty and very filling, but try to save room for warm apple strudel with vanilla ice cream and whipped cream.

Hauptstrasse 115. ☎ 06221/20879. Streetcar: 1 or 2 to Bismarckplatz (then a 5-minute walk east on Hauptstrasse). Main courses: €8–€17. AE, DC, MC, V. Open: Mon–Fri noon to 1 a.m., Sat–Sun 11 a.m.–1 a.m.

Exploring Heidelberg

Heidelberg is a wonderfully pleasant town to explore, and wandering through the old lanes and squares of the Altstadt is as essential a part of any tour as visiting the tourist attractions. The town has few must-see attractions, and for many visitors there is only one: the famous Schloss that looks down on the Altstadt.

Visiting the top attraction

The Schloss (Heidelberg Castle)

Most visitors reach the huge red-sandstone castle on foot, or by taking a two-minute cable-car ride from Kornmarkt (see "Getting around Heidelberg," earlier in this chapter). Walking is the most rewarding approach because of the constantly changing views of the town and surrounding countryside. The easiest and most gradual path begins at the Klingentor; you also find a shorter, steeper path up Burgweg from Kornmarkt.

Set amidst woodlands and terraced gardens, the enormous ruins of the castle are undeniably picturesque. Even in its deteriorated state, the Schloss is one of the finest Gothic-Renaissance castles in Germany, and one of the most famous historic monuments in Europe. Plan to spend about two hours here.

Entering at the main gate, you first come upon the **Pulverturm** (Gun Tower) and a terrace with views of Heidelberg and the Neckar Valley. The **Elizabethentor** (Elizabeth's Gate), erected by Friedrich V in 1615 for his teenaged wife, Elizabeth Stuart, daughter of the English king James I, leads to the bridge crossing the former moat.

Along the north side of the courtyard stretches the **Friedrichsbau** (palace of Friedrich IV), erected 1601 to 1607 and less damaged than other parts of the castle. Its restored rooms can be seen on guided tours. The palace's terrace offers a magnificent view of Heidelberg and the Neckar Valley. At the west end of the terrace, in the 16th-century cellars of the castle, sits the **Grosse Fass** (Great Cask). This enormous wine barrel, the largest in the world, was built in 1751, and once held more than 55,000 gallons (208,000 liters) of wine.

To the east, connecting the palace of Friedrich IV to the **Ottheinrichsbau** (palace of Ottheinrich), is the shell of the **Spiegelbau** (Hall of Mirrors building), constructed in 1549. Housed within Ottheinrich's palace is the **Apothekenmuseum** (Pharmacy Museum; ☎ 06221/25880), re-creating a baroque- and rococo-era chemist's shop with utensils and laboratory equipment from the 17th and 18th centuries. The museum is open daily from 10 a.m. to 5 p.m.; your castle entrance ticket includes admission.

The **Hortus Palatinus** (Castle Gardens) were originally created in the 17th century. In the southeast corner, you find the remains of a grotto and a sandstone sculpture of Father Rhine.

The history of Heidelberg Castle

An elevated fortress rose above Heidelberg as early as 1225, but the castle as it stands today was built in two main phases. During the first phase, between about 1400 and 1544, fortifications and living quarters were constructed. The second phase, from 1549 to 1620, saw the transition from Gothic to Renaissance styles as various Prince Electors of the Palatinate added to the building. The castle was the residence of the Prince Electors for centuries until French troops sacked and destroyed it in the late 17th century. Once rebuilt, the castle was struck by lightning. In the 19th century, the ruins of the castle became a symbol for the German Romantics and a mecca for tourists from around the world.

Schlossberg. ☎ *06221/538-431. Admission: Castle grounds, free; entrance court-yard, Pharmacy Museum, and Great Cask, €2 adults, €1 children. Tours: Frequent 1-hour guided tours of the castle in English, €3 adults, €1.50 children. Audio tours: €3. Open: Daily 8 a.m.–5:30 p.m.*

Touring the Altstadt

Marktplatz (Market Square) is the main square in the Altstadt. On market days (Wed and Sat), stalls of fresh flowers, fish, vegetables, cheese, meat, and baked goods fill the square. The **Rathaus** (Town Hall), on the east side of the square, is an early-18th-century building reconstructed in 1908 following a fire.

The late-Gothic **Heiliggeistkirche** (Church of the Holy Ghost; no phone; open daily 8 a.m.–5 p.m.), built around 1400, dominates the west end of Marktplatz. For nearly 300 years, the church was the burial place of the Palatinate electors. In 1706, a wall was erected to divide the church between Roman Catholics and Protestants. The wall has since been removed and the church restored to its original plan.

The highly decorated Renaissance mansion, now the **Hotel Zum Ritter St. Georg** (see "Staying in Heidelberg," earlier in this chapter), stands on the south side of Marktplatz. A Huguenot cloth merchant who emigrated from France to Heidelberg erected the building in 1592. The hotel is named for the statue of the *Ritter* (knight) at the top.

A five-minute walk west from the Marktplatz on Hauptstasse and south one block on Grabengasse brings you to **Universitätsplatz** (University Square). On the northeastern side is the Alte Universität (Old University), a building from the 18th century, and at the south end of the square is the Neue Universität (New University), completed in 1932. Heidelberg University, founded in 1386, is the oldest in Germany.

A few steps past the Old University, you find the **Studentenkarzer** (Students' Prison), Augustinerstrasse 2 (☎ 06221/543-554), where from 1778 to 1914 generations of students were incarcerated in cramped cells for minor offenses. Graffiti and drawings, including portraits and silhouettes, cover the walls and even the ceilings. Admission is €2.50 for adults, €2 for students and children 14 and under. The prison is open April through October Tuesday through Saturday from 10 a.m. to 4 p.m., November through March Tuesday through Friday from 10 a.m. to 2 p.m.

A two-minute walk west on Hauptstrasse from Universitätsplatz brings you to the **Kurpfälzisches Museum** (Museum of the Palatinate), Hauptstrasse 97 (☎ 06221/583-402). Housed in a baroque palace, Heidelberg's most noteworthy museum contains a large collection of regional painting and sculpture from the 15th to the 19th centuries. The one masterpiece on display is Tilman Riemenschneider's 1509 wooden altarpiece showing Christ and the Apostles. You can also see an archaeological collection with a cast of the jawbone of the 600,000-year-old Heidelberg Man *(Homo heidelbergensis),* discovered in the vicinity nearly 100 years ago, and a section on the history of the Palatinate. Give yourself about 45 minutes to browse through the various exhibits. The museum restaurant (see "Dining in Heidelberg," earlier in this chapter) is a good choice for lunch or dinner. Admission to the museum is €2.50 for adults, €1.50 for students and children 17 and under. The museum is open Tuesday through Sunday from 10 a.m. to 5 p.m. (Wed until 8 p.m.).

Shopping in Heidelberg

The main shopping street is the traffic-free **Hauptstrasse.** A lively **outdoor market** is held on Wednesday and Saturday at the Marktplatz. Some noteworthy shops include:

- ✔ **Altstadt-Galerie Stefan,** UntereStrasse 18 (☎ 06221/28737), sells charming original engravings for as little as €10.

- ✔ **Black Forest Shop,** Hauptstrasse 215 (☎ 06221/619-983), near Karlsplatz, sells Hummel figurines, cuckoo clocks, and beer steins.

- ✔ **Gätschenberger,** Hauptstrasse 42 (☎ 06221/14480), is known for its array of fine linens and embroideries for bed, bathroom, and table.

- ✔ **Michael Kienscherff,** Hauptstrasse 177 (☎ 06221/24255; tram: 1 or 5), offers a wide assortment of handicrafts from all over Germany: music boxes, nativity scenes, nutcrackers, and glass and crystal ornaments.

- ✔ **Muckels Maus,** Plöck 71 (☎ 06221/23886), is the place to find beautifully handcrafted puppets, antique-looking and ultramodern dolls, and wooden blocks and figures.

Living it up after dark in Heidelberg

The large student population keeps Heidelberg humming after dark. Early evenings often start in the bars along Hauptstrasse; late nights get rolling in clubs around Marktplatz.

The performing arts

The main performance stage is **Theater der Stadt,** Friedrichstrasse 5 (☎ 06221/583-502; bus: 41 or 42), where nightly entertainment includes plays, opera, and dance productions. For five weeks beginning in late July, the **Schlossfest-Spiele** festival brings opera, classical music, jazz, and theater to venues around the area, including Heidelberg Castle. Contact ☎ 06274/58352 for tickets.

Historic taverns

Heidelberg's most famous and revered student tavern, **Zum Roten Ochsen** (Red Ox Inn), Hauptstrasse 217 (☎ 06221/20977), opened in 1703. Revelers sit at long oak tables arranged in horseshoe fashion around a pianist. As the evening progresses, the songs become louder and louder. A mug of beer costs €2.30 and up. Meals go from €10 to €18. The tavern is open April through October Monday through Saturday from 11:30 a.m. to 2 p.m. and 5 p.m. to midnight; November through March hours are 5 p.m. to midnight.

Next door is **Zum Sepp'l,** Hauptstrasse 213 (☎ 06221/23085), filled with photographs and memorabilia. The building dates from 1634. Meals cost €8 to €13. A mug of beer goes for €2.95. A pianist performs nightly. It's open Monday through Friday from 5:30 p.m. to midnight, Saturday and Sunday from noon to 2:30 p.m. and 5:30 p.m. to midnight.

Nuremberg: Renaissance and Rebirth

Nuremberg, or Nürnberg in German, is located in Bavaria, 92 miles (148 km) northwest of Munich. (See the "Nuremberg" map in this chapter.") This strikingly attractive and lively city has about half a million residents. Spending a day or more exploring its streets, churches, historic buildings, and museums is definitely worth it.

"Nourenberc," as the city was originally known, dates back to about 1050. In 300 years, the city grew from a fortress and military base in eastern Franconia (a medieval duchy of south-central Germany) to a virtually self-governing Free Imperial City *(Freie Reichsstadt).* From 1356 onward, each newly elected emperor of the Holy Roman Empire had to convene his first *Reichstag,* or meeting with the princes of the empire, in Nuremberg. The city's role as capital of the empire, and its location at the crossroads of major trade routes, made it one of the wealthiest and most important cities in medieval Germany. During the

Nuremberg

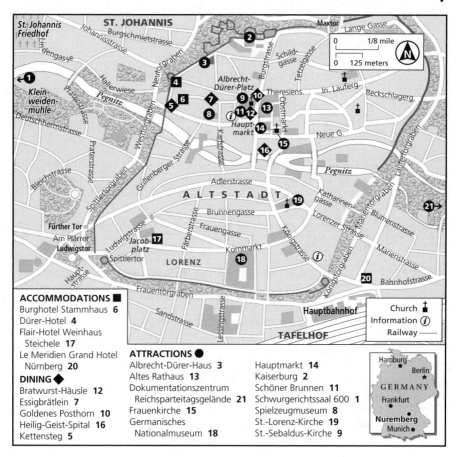

ACCOMMODATIONS ■
Burghotel Stammhaus **6**
Dürer-Hotel **4**
Flair-Hotel Weinhaus
   Steichele **17**
Le Meridien Grand Hotel
   Nürnberg **20**

DINING ◆
Bratwurst-Häusle **12**
Essigbrätlein **7**
Goldenes Posthorn **10**
Heilig-Geist-Spital **16**
Kettensteg **5**

ATTRACTIONS ●
Albrecht-Dürer-Haus **3**
Altes Rathaus **13**
Dokumentationszentrum
   Reichsparteitagsgelände **21**
Frauenkirche **15**
Germanisches
   Nationalmuseum **18**

Hauptmarkt **14**
Kaiserburg **2**
Schöner Brunnen **11**
Schwurgerichtssaal 600 **1**
Spielzeugmuseum **8**
St.-Lorenz-Kirche **19**
St.-Sebaldus-Kirche **9**

Church ✝
Information ⓘ
Railway ——

GERMANY
Hamburg
Berlin ★
Frankfurt
Nuremberg
Munich ●

15th and 16th centuries, a cultural flowering made Nuremberg the center of the German Renaissance.

But the city fell into decline until, under Hitler, Nuremberg made its second, and most infamous, mark on German history. To Hitler, the city's architecture and previous role in the Holy Roman Empire represented the quintessence of Germany. After he seized power in 1933, Hitler made Nuremberg the Nazi party's permanent convention and rally site. As a result, no other German city, with the exception of Dresden, suffered such war-time devastation. After the war, the Nazi war crimes trials were held here, convened by the International Military Tribunal.

In the postwar years, many of Nuremberg's most important buildings, including some of the finest Gothic and Renaissance churches in Germany, were restored or reconstructed in the Altstadt, the historic center. Nearly every German city has a restored Altstadt, but few have been reborn with the kind of evocative grace and charm of Nuremberg.

As you wander through the streets of this ancient capital of the Holy Roman Empire, you find reminders of Nuremberg's brightest period.

Getting there

You can easily reach Nuremberg **by train** from anywhere in Germany or Europe. Travel time from Frankfurt is about 2 hours; from Munich, 1 hour 40 minutes; from Berlin, 6 hours. For information and schedules, call **Deutsche Bahn ☎ 01805/996-633.** The city's **Hauptbahnhof** is within walking distance of all the major attractions.

For those traveling **by plane,** connections are available to Nuremberg's small airport, **Flughafen Nürnberg (☎ 0911/93700),** four miles (6 km) north of the city center, from major German and European cities.

By car from Munich, take the A9 Autobahn north; from Frankfurt, head southeast along the A3 Autobahn; from Berlin, take the A9 Autobahn south.

Finding information and taking a tour

Tourist Information, opposite the train station at Königstrasse 93 (**☎ 0911/233-6132;** Internet: www.nuernberg.de), is open Monday through Saturday from 9 a.m. to 7 p.m. An additional branch at Hauptmarkt 18 (**☎ 0911/233-6135**) is open Monday through Saturday from 9 a.m. to 6 p.m. and Sunday (May–Sept only) from 10 a.m. to 1 p.m. and 2 to 4 p.m.

A guided 2½-hour **walking tour** of the city center in English departs daily (May–Oct and Nov 30–Jan 6) at 1 p.m. from the Tourist Information office at the Hauptmarkt. The tour includes a visit to the Kaiserburg (Imperial Castle). The cost is €7.50, children under 14 free, plus admission to the castle. Buy your tickets from the Tourist Office or from the guide.

A small sightseeing "train" operated by **Nürnberger Altstadtrund-fahrten (☎ 0911/421-919)** runs through the Altstadt, passing all the major sights on a 40-minute tour with commentary in German (English translations available). The train departs from the fountain in the Hauptmarkt, in front of the tourist office, several times a day from 10:30 a.m. to 4 p.m. Cost is €4 for adults, €2 for children.

Orienting yourself

Nearly all that is of interest to the visitor is found in Nuremberg's **Altstadt,** one of the most successfully restored historic city centers in Germany. Roughly oval in shape, the entire Altstadt lies within a double wall of medieval fortifications, parts of which still remain and have rampart walks and gateway towers.

The **Hauptbahnhof** lies on the southern perimeter of the Altstadt; crowning the northern periphery is the **Kaiserburg,** the old imperial castle. The small, picturesque **Pegnitz River** bisects the Altstadt. You find historic sights both north and south of the river. To the north lies the **Hauptmarkt,** the city's main market square.

Getting around Nuremberg

Nuremberg's Altstadt is almost entirely closed to traffic. Although the Altstadt is larger than the historic centers in many other German cities, all of its sights are easily accessible on foot. In 30 minutes, you can walk from the Hauptbahnhof to the Kaiserburg through the heart of the city's medieval core and past most of the historic monuments. Walking in the Altstadt is easier than using public transportation.

Nuremberg's transportation system consists of a **U-Bahn** (subway), **trams**, and **buses.** Fares are based on zones. The easiest way to use the system is to buy a **TagesTicket** (day ticket) for €3.50 (tickets purchased on Saturday are also good all day Sunday). Buy your tickets from the machines in the U-Bahn stations. For more information, call the city's transportation authority, **VGN** at ☎ **0911/270-750.** For a **taxi,** call ☎ **0911/19410.**

Staying in Nuremberg

See also Chapter 22 for a listing of **Le Meridien Grand Hotel Nürnberg** ($$$–$$$$).

Burghotel Stammhaus
$–$$ Altstadt

This reliable, 46-room hotel provides good, solid comfort in a great Altstadt location for a reasonable price. Bedrooms are compact and nicely furnished. The functional bathrooms are tiled and come with shower units. The hotel is below the castle walls in one of the most historic parts of the old city, next to Dürer's house.

Lammsgasse 3, 90403 Nürnberg. ☎ *0911/204-414. Fax: 0911/22882. Internet:* www. altstadthotel-nuernberg.de. *Tram: Tiergärtnertor (then a 5-minute walk south on A.-Dürer-Strasse to Lammsgasse). Rack rates: €90–€170 double. Rates include continental breakfast. AE, DC, MC, V.*

Dürer-Hotel
$–$$ Altstadt

The 107-room Dürer stands beside the birthplace of its namesake, alongside the castle wall and close to all the major sightseeing attractions in the Altstadt. The ambience throughout is modern and pleasant. Medium-size rooms done in pastel colors open onto the street or a back garden. The smallish tiled baths have showers (some have tub-shower combinations). You can enjoy your breakfast, the only meal served, in a pretty room off the lobby.

Neutormauer 32, 90403 Nürnberg. ☎ *0911/208-091. Fax: 0911/223-458. Internet:* www.altstadthotels-nuernberg.de. *Tram: Tiergärtnertor (then a 5-minute walk southwest along the city wall). Rack rates: €120–€167 double; special weekend and summer rates. Rates include buffet breakfast. AE, DC, MC, V.*

Flair-Hotel Weinhaus Steichele
$–$$ Altstadt

Despite renovations in 1998, this small, charming hotel from 1860 still retains its old-fashioned allure. The location is a tranquil street near Jacobsplatz, not far from the train station. The building is a beautiful stone structure with a sloping roofline. A modern annex next door blends harmoniously with the older building. The 58 rooms, decorated in a rustic Bavarian style, each have a small shower-only bathroom. The Weinhaus is noted for its excellent kitchen and selection of wines from its own vineyards in Baden and Rheinpfalz.

Knorrstrasse 2–8, 90402 Nürnberg. ☎ *0911/202-280. Fax: 0911/221-914. U-Bahn: Weisser Turm (then a 3-minute walk south on Knorrstrasse). Rack rates: €75–€130 double. Rates include buffet breakfast. AE, DC, MC, V.*

Dining in Nuremberg

Nuremberg is in a region called Franconia, known for its hearty and relatively uncomplicated cuisine. The city is famous for its finger-size *Rostbratwürste* made of pork and various spices and then broiled on a charcoal grill. You may hear the sausage seller in an open booth on the street shouting, "*Eins, zwei, drei . . .*" (one, two, three . . .) and so on. The hungry consumer shouts back the number of Bratwursts he or she desires. The locals consider fewer than six Bratwursts a snack; people typically consume up to 14 for lunch. Your Bratwursts may come with sauerkraut or rye bread with very hot mustard. Seasonal game and fish dishes are also staples in restaurants serving Franconian fare.

Bratwurst-Häusle
$ FRANCONIAN

This is the most famous Bratwurst house in the city, located opposite the Rathaus and close to the church of St. Sebald. In winter, the open grill in the rustic, wood-paneled dining room warms you; in summer, you can dine on a leafy outdoor terrace. Come to sample original *Nürnberger Rostbratwurste* (6, 8, 10, or 12 pieces), served on pewter plates. You can also get them to go *(zum mitnehmen)*. A good beer to go with your Wursts is Lederer Pils, a beer brewed locally since 1468.

Rathausplatz 1. ☎ *0911/227-695. U-Bahn: Lorenzkirche (then a 5-minute walk north on Königsttrasse to Rathausplatz). Main courses: €5.50–€10. AE, MC, V. Open: Mon–Sat 10 a.m.–10:30 p.m.*

Essigbrätlein
$$$$ FRANCONIAN/CONTINENTAL

The city's most ancient restaurant, dating from 1550, was originally a meeting place of wine merchants. Its upscale Franconian and Continental cuisine is inventive and refreshing, with many nouvelle recipes. Look for an ever-changing menu based on seasonal availability. The traditional specialty is roast loin of beef (what the name of the restaurant means in German).

Weinmarkt 3. ☎ *0911/225-131. Bus: 36 to Hauptmarkt (then a 5-minute walk north on Winklerstrasse to Weinmarkt). Reservations required. Main courses: €17–€24; fixed-price lunch €35; fixed-price dinner €60–€75. AE, DC, MC, V. Open: Tues–Fri noon to 1:30 p.m.; Tues–Sat 7–9:30 p.m. Closed Jan 1–15 and 2 weeks in Aug (dates vary).*

Goldenes Posthorn
$$–$$$ FRANCONIAN

No other restaurant in Nuremberg can match the antique atmosphere of the Goldenes Posthorn, which claims to be in the oldest house in Germany. Among its mementos is a drinking glass reputedly used by Albrecht Dürer. The restaurant's Franconian cuisine features such old-fashioned but satisfying dishes as quail stuffed with goose liver and nuts, venison in red wine with plums, fresh carp (in winter), and Wurst with a mixture of onions and vinegar. The restaurant has a fine wine list, including vintages that date back to 1889.

Glöckleingasse 2. ☎ *0911/225-153. Bus: 36 to Burgstrasse (then a 2-minute walk south to Glöckleingasse). Reservations required. Main courses: €6.25–€19; fixed-price meals €15 lunch, €20–€38 dinner. AE, DC, MC, V. Open: Mon–Sat noon to 2:30 p.m. and 6–11:30 p.m.*

Heilig-Geist-Spital
$ FRANCONIAN

Nuremberg's largest historical wine house, in business for 650 years, overlooks the Pegnitz River and is an atmospheric spot to dine. The main dishes are typical Franconian fare, hearty and filling. Carp is a specialty, as is pork knuckle and Sauerbraten. In season, you can order leg of venison with noodles and berries. The wine list is abundant and excellent, with more than 100 vintages.

Spitalgasse 16. ☎ *0911/221-761. Bus: 46 or 47 to Spitalgasse. Main courses: €10–€14. AE, DC, MC, V. Open: Daily 11 a.m. to midnight.*

Kettensteg

$ FRANCONIAN/INTERNATIONAL

This restaurant and beer garden beside the river in a romantic corner of the Altstadt is a real scene on warm evenings, when the tables fill up fast and everyone stays late, talking and drinking and eating under the trees. The menu is limited to just a few dishes, such as penne pasta with chicken and tomato sauce, Wiener schnitzel with french fries, and Bratwursts. Vegetarians can choose from vegetable lasagne or various salads. Kettensteg is a nice place to relax and have a good time.

Maxplatz 35. ☎ *0911/221-081. Bus: 36 to Maxplatz. Main courses: €8–€11. No credit cards. Open: 11 a.m.–11 p.m.*

Exploring Nuremberg

You need at least one full day to explore the main attractions of Nuremberg, nearly all of which are found in the Altstadt. Most of the historic core is for pedestrians only, so walking is a pleasure.

Albrecht-Dürer-Haus (Albrecht Dürer House)

Albrecht Dürer, one of the great German artists of the Renaissance, lived in this house from 1509 to 1528. Built in 1420, it's the only completely preserved Gothic house left in Nuremberg. Typical of the well-to-do burghers' houses of the 15th century, the structure has a first floor of sandstone surmounted by two half-timbered stories and a gabled roof. Exhibits inside the house are devoted to Dürer's life and works. Furnishing many of the rooms are important historical pieces, original etchings and woodcuts, and copies of Dürer's paintings.

Albrecht-Dürer-Strasse 39. ☎ *0911/231-2568. Tram: Tiergärtnertor (then a 3-minute walk south on Albrecht-Dürer-Strasse). Admission: €4 adults, €2 students and children 6–15. Open: Tues–Sun 10 a.m.–5 p.m. (Thurs until 8 p.m.). Tours: Guided tours in English Sat 2 p.m.*

Germanisches Nationalmuseum (German National Museum)

Germany's largest and most important museum of German art and culture is the one must-see museum in Nuremberg. The collection covers the entire spectrum of German craftsmanship and fine arts from their beginnings to the present day. The prehistoric and early historical sections contain finds from the Stone Age and from the burial sites of the Merovingians (a Frankish dynasty ruling from about A.D. 500–750). The extensive painting and sculpture sections include works by Renaissance greats Albrecht Dürer and Veit Stoss, a sculptor and woodcarver known for his "nervous" angular forms and realism. The world's first globe, created by Martin Behaim, is on display, as is a self-portrait by Rembrandt. Everyday life in Germany through the ages is documented with domestic furnishings, folk objects, dollhouses, historic musical instruments, weapons, and the healing arts. This is an exhaustive and exhausting place, and you should give yourself at least two hours.

Kartäusergasse 1. ☎ *0911/13310. U-Bahn: Opernhaus (then a 3-minute walk north on Kartäusergasse). Admission: €4 adults, €3 children and students. Open: Tues–Sun 10 a.m.–5 p.m. (Wed until 9 p.m.).*

Hauptmarkt (Main Market Square)

The cobblestoned Hauptmarkt, just north of the Pegnitz River at the northern end of Königstrasse, is Nuremberg's geographic and symbolic heart. Filled with stalls selling fresh flowers, fruits, and vegetables, the Hauptmarkt is the most colorful square in the city. In the northwest corner stands the **Schöner Brunnen** (Beautiful Fountain), a 60-foot (18-meter) high pyramid-shaped stone fountain from 1396. The 14th-century **Frauenkirche** (Church of Our Lady; ☎ 0911/206-560; open Mon–Sat 9 a.m. to 6 p.m., Sun 12:30–6 p.m.), on the eastern edge of the square, has on its facade a gilded 16th-century mechanical clock called the *Männleinlaufen* (a hard-to-translate word meaning "little men running"); every day at noon, figures of the seven electors appear and pay homage to Emperor Karl IV. The oldest part of the **Altes Rathaus** (Old Town Hall), on Rathausplatz just off the market square, dates from 1340; a later section, completed in 1622, marks the architectural transition from Renaissance to baroque style.

Kaiserburg (Imperial Castle)

The Kaiserburg, looming above the city from its hilltop at the northern edge of the Altstadt, was the official residence of the German kings and emperors from 1050 to 1571. The oldest portion, the 11th-century **Fünfeckturm** (Pentagonal Tower), has been in ruins since fire destroyed it in 1420. Watchmen and guards used the ramparts with their parapet walks and secret passages to protect the kings and emperors, who lived in the inner core of the castle complex. Most of the buildings were constructed during the 12th century. With their heavy oak beams and painted ceilings, the great **Rittersaal** (Knights' Hall) on the ground floor and the **Kaisersaal** (Imperial Hall) on the second floor look much as they did when King Frederick III rebuilt them in the 15th century. The rooms are decorated with period Gothic furnishings.

The council of Nuremberg erected another set of buildings in the 14th and 15th centuries when its responsibilities expanded to include the protection of the emperor. The new buildings include the **Kaiserstallung** (Emperor's Stables), now a youth hostel; the massive bastions of the fortress; the **Tiefer Brunnen** (Deep Well); and the castle gardens. There is a fine view of the roofs and towers of Nuremberg from its terraces. Allot at least an hour to explore the various nooks and crannies of the castle.

The **Kaiserburg Museum** (☎ 0911/13310) contains antique weaponry, armor, and paintings, and explains the history of the castle.

Burgstrasse. ☎ 0911/225-726. Tram: Tiergärtnertor (then a 10-minute walk north following signs). Admission: €5 adults, €4 students; free for children 16 and under. Open: Apr–Sept daily 9 a.m.–6 p.m.; Oct–Mar daily 10 a.m.–4 p.m.

Spielzeugmuseum (Toy Museum)

Nuremberg is a major toy center, and toys, both hand- and machine-made, fill all three floors of this museum. Some date from medieval times. Exhibits include a large collection of dolls and old dollhouses, optical toys (such as peep shows, magic lanterns, and stereoscopes), and model railways and other miniature vehicles. Objects on the top floor illustrate the history of toys since 1945, including Barbie dolls and Lego blocks. Kids can play with toys, draw, or do crafts in a supervised playroom. You don't have to be a kid, though, to enjoy this acclaimed museum. Give yourself at least an hour, more if you have kids in tow.

Karlstrasse 13–15. ☎ 0911/231-3164. Bus: 36 to Hauptmarkt (then a 3-minute walk west on Augustinerstrasse and north on Karlstrasse). Admission: €4 adults, €2 students and children. Open: Tues–Sun 10 a.m.–5 p.m. (Wed until 9 p.m.).

St.-Lorenz-Kirche (Church of St. Lawrence)

The largest and most beautiful Gothic church in Nuremberg rises above Lorenzerplatz. The St.-Lorenze-Kirche was begun in 1270 and took more than 200 years to complete. Twin towers flank the west portal with its sculptures depicting the theme of redemption, from Adam and Eve through the Last Judgment. Inside, soaring pillars adorned with expressive Gothic sculptures line the nave, and a magnificent stained-glass rosette window glows above the organ at the west end. The church contains two more remarkable works: *The Angelic Salutation* (1519), carved in linden wood by Veit Stoss, hangs over the entrance to the choir, and, to the left of the altar, a stone tabernacle by Adam Krafft (1496) presents likenesses of the sculptor and two apprentices.

Lorenzer Platz 10. ☎ 0911/209-287. U-Bahn: Lorenzkirche (the church is on the square as you exit). Admission: Free. Open: Mon–Sat 9 a.m.–5 p.m., Sun 1–4 p.m.

St.-Sebaldus-Kirche

Consecrated in 1273, this church dedicated to Nuremberg's patron saint represents the stylistic transition from late Romanesque to early Gothic styles. The nave and west choir are Romanesque; the larger east choir, consecrated in 1379, is Gothic. Between the two east pillars is a 16th-century crucifixion group dominated by a life-size crucifix by Veit Stoss.

Sebalderplatz. ☎ 0911/214-2516. U-Bahn: Lorenzkirche (the church is on the square as you exit the station). Admission: Free. Open: Mar–May daily 9:30 a.m.–6 p.m.; June–Oct daily 9:30 a.m.–8 p.m.; Nov–Feb daily 9 a.m.–4 p.m.

Judgment at Nuremberg

If you're interested in a famous landmark of World War II, visit the **Schwurgerichtssaal 600** (International Military Tribunal), Fürther Strasse 110 (☎ 0911/231-5421; U-Bahn: Bärenschanze), where the Nuremberg Trials took place. Here, in room 600, a specially remodeled courtroom, 21 of the surviving leaders of the Third Reich stood trial in November 1945 for crimes against humanity. Afterward, ten were hanged. The building still serves as a courthouse, so tours (in German only) are available only on Saturday and Sunday from 1 to 4 p.m. Admission is €2.

In November 2001, the huge Congress Hall designed by Hitler's architect, Albert Speer, reopened as the new **Dokumentationszentrum Reichsparteitagsgelände** (Documentation Center Nazi Party Rally Grounds). A glass corridor now pierces Speer's Congress Hall, which is larger than the Colosseum in Rome. The corridor houses an exhibition that chronicles the ruthless misuse of power under National Socialism. The center is open Tuesday through Sunday 10 a.m. to 5 p.m.; the €5 admission includes an audio guide. To reach the center, take bus 5 to Luitpoldhain.

Shopping in Nuremberg

Located across from the railway station, the **Handwerkerhof** (Craftsmen's Courtyard; U-Bahn: Hauptbahnhof) is an enclave of half-timbered shops and stalls where artisans create and sell a wide range of handicrafts (along with touristy souvenirs). The shops are open weekdays (and Sun in Dec) from 10 a.m. to 6:30 p.m., and Saturday from 10 a.m. to 4 p.m.

Hofman, Rathausplatz 7 (☎ **0911/204-848;** Bus: 36), sells painted tin figures of soldiers and Christmas decorations. **Steiff Galerie,** Kaiserstrasse 1–9 (☎ **0911/235-5075;** U-Bahn: Lorenzerkirche), has classic and collectible Steiff bears for €89 to €139.

From Advent Sunday to December 24, Nuremberg's Hauptmarkt becomes the setting for the **Christkindlmarkt,** the oldest Christmas fair in Germany, held here for some 400 years. The Christmas fair transforms Hauptmarkt into a small town of wood-and-cloth stalls selling tree ornaments, handicrafts, candies, fruitcakes, *Lebkuchen* (see the sidebar "Love that Lebkuchen"), tinsel, and *Glühwein* (hot red wine spiced with cloves and cinnamon). There are daily performances by singers and musicians, and theater, dance, and puppet groups. The square is especially beautiful at night, when all the surrounding buildings are floodlit.

Living it up after dark in Nuremberg

The **Städtische Bühnen** (State Theaters), Richard-Wagner-Platz 2–10 (☎ **0911/231-3808;** U-Bahn: Opernhaus), is a theater complex offering

Love that Lebkuchen

Lebkuchen (*layb*-koo-kin) is to Nuremberg what marzipan is to Lübeck. The city's been the capital of Lebkuchen since the early 15th century. These delicious honey-and-spice cakes evolved into their round shape in Nuremberg. While jealously guarding their recipes, many places make and sell Lebkuchen in several different forms. **Lebkuchen Frauenholz,** Bergstrasse 1 (☎ **0911/243-464;** U-Bahn: Lorenz-kirche), sells Lebkuchen packed in containers that look like half-timbered German houses. Many consider **Lebkuchen Schmidt,** Zollhausstrasse 30 (☎ **0911/896-6555;** Internet: www.lebkuchen-schmidt.com), to be the best Lebkuchen store in Nuremberg. Lebkuchen makes a great, inexpensive gift.

productions of drama (in the Schauspielhaus) and opera (in the Opernhaus). Tickets range from €8 to €50.

An artists' hangout, **Triebhaus,** Karl-Griolenberger-Strasse 28 (☎ **0911/ 223-041;** U-Bahn: Weisser Turm), opens early for big breakfasts (served all day) that run from €3.30 to €14.50 and offers soup, salad, and sandwich specials from €3.50 to €6.50 until 10:30 p.m. The cafe is open Monday through Friday from 8 a.m. to 1 a.m. and Saturday and Sunday from 9 a.m. to 1 a.m.

Café Ruhestörung, Tetzelgasse 21 (☎ **0911/221-921;** U-Bahn: Lorenz-kirche), has a pleasant patio where you can order a drink or a sandwich. The cafe is open Monday through Friday from 7:30 a.m. to 1 a.m. and Saturday and Sunday from 9:30 a.m. to 1 a.m.

A Side Trip: Rothenburg ob der Tauber

Rothenburg, a completely intact, walled medieval city located above the Tauber River about 55 miles (90 km) west of Nuremberg, comes as something of a revelation to many visitors. After seeing so many German cities that were partially or completely destroyed in World War II, and rebuilt afterward, the ancient streets of Rothenburg seem like something lifted out of a fairy tale. (See the "Rothenburg ob der Tauber" map in this chapter.)

Rothenburg has been a major tourist attraction since mass tourism began some 90 years ago. Yes, you may encounter hordes of tourists, especially in the summer months and on weekends, but don't let that deter you from visiting this remarkable town seemingly untouched by the passage of time.

Rothenburg ob der Tauber

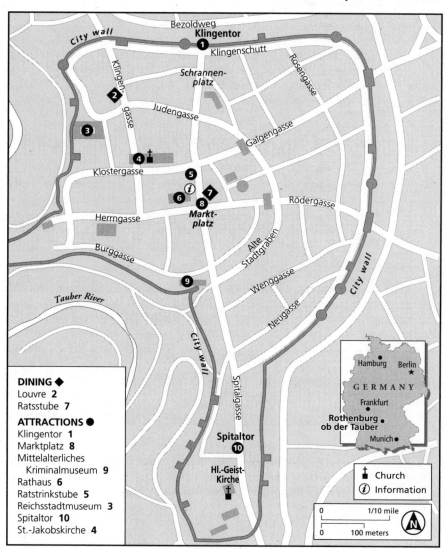

DINING ◆
Louvre **2**
Ratsstube **7**
ATTRACTIONS ●
Klingentor **1**
Marktplatz **8**
Mittelalterliches
  Kriminalmuseum **9**
Rathaus **6**
Ratstrinkstube **5**
Reichsstadtmuseum **3**
Spitaltor **10**
St.-Jakobskirche **4**

✝■ Church
ⓘ Information

Getting there

You can reach Rothenburg **by train** from Nuremberg, Heidelberg, or Stuttgart, but you need to transfer trains at Würzburg or Ansbach and again at Steinach. For information, call **Deutsche Bahn** (☎ 01805/996-633). If you come **by car** from Nuremberg, take the A6 west and the A7 north.

Finding information

Tourist Information, Marktplatz (☎ **09861/40492**; Internet: www.
rothenburg.de), is open November through April Monday through
Friday from 9 a.m. to noon and 1 to 5 p.m. and Saturday from 10 a.m.
to 1 p.m.; May through October hours are Monday through Friday from
9 a.m. to 6 p.m. and Saturday from 10 a.m. to 3 p.m. The office can help
you find a hotel room and offers general information on the city.

Dining in Rothenburg ob der Tauber

Louvre, Klingengasse 15 (☎ **09861/87809**), the town's only Michelin-
starred restaurant, is a stylish place to dine (call ahead for a reservation). Come here for *Neuer Küche* (new cuisine), not traditional dishes.
Appetizers may include goose-liver terrine with huckleberries and
white port or consommé of crayfish with ravioli. Fresh fish is nearly
always on the menu. Main courses range from €10 to €23. The restaurant is open daily for dinner only, 6 to 11 p.m.

The **Ratsstube,** Marktplatz 6 (☎ **09861/92411**), right on the bustling
market square, has a tavernlike interior and is a favorite of those who
prefer hearty Franconian cooking (including Sauerbraten and venison)
without a lot of fuss and bother. American-style breakfasts are also
available. Main courses range from €9 to €18. The restaurant is open
Monday through Saturday from 9 a.m. to 11 p.m., and on Sunday from
noon to 6 p.m. (closed Jan–Mar). MasterCard and Visa are accepted.

Exploring Rothenburg ob der Tauber

Medieval walls encircle the entire town. For an excellent visual introduction, take a half-hour walk on the town ramparts from the massive
16th-century **Spitaltor** (a medieval tower-gate at the end of the
Spitalgasse) to the **Klingentor** (another tower-gate). Then just stroll
around and soak up the atmosphere in one of Europe's best-preserved
medieval cities. As you're walking, look for a Rothenburg specialty
called *Schneeballen* (snowballs), crisp, round pastries covered with
powdered sugar. You can buy them in bakeries all over town.

At the center of Rothenburg is the **Marktplatz.** Flanking the square to
the west is the **Rathaus** (☎ **09861/40492**; open Mon–Fri 8 a.m.–6 p.m.),
which consists of a 13th-century Gothic section and a newer Renaissance
structure with a 165-foot (50-meter) tower. From the tower's top, you get a
great view of the town below (admission €1 adults, €.50 children; open
Apr–Oct 9:30 a.m.–12:30 p.m. and 1–5 p.m.). Adjacent to the Rathaus is
the **Ratstrinkstube** (Councillors' Tavern), an old inn with three clocks on
its gabled facade. Windows on either side of the lowest clock open several times a day (11 a.m., noon, and 1, 2, 3, 9, and 10 p.m.) to reveal the
figures of General Tilly and Herr Nusch, chief protagonists in the drinking

bout that saved Rothenburg (for the whole story, see information on the Reichstadtsmuseum, later in this section).

South of the Rathaus, a 14th-century hospital with Rothenburg's only 18th-century baroque facade houses the macabre-minded **Mittelalterliches Kriminalmuseum** (Medieval Justice Museum), Burggasse 3 (☎ 09861/5359). Medieval crime and punishment are the subjects of the museum's four floors. On display are chastity belts, shame masks, a shame flute for bad musicians, a dunking basket, and an Iron Maiden. Admission is €3 adults, €1.50 for children under 13. The museum is open April through October daily from 9:30 a.m. to 6 p.m.; November and January through February daily from 2 to 4 p.m.; December and March daily from 10 a.m. to 4 p.m.

The Gothic **St.-Jakobskirche** (Church of St. James), Klostergasse 15 (☎ 09861/700-620), is worth visiting to see the Heiliges-Blut-Altar (Altar of the Holy Blood), a masterpiece created by the famous Würzburg sculptor Tilman Riemenschneider (around 1460–1531). The fine painted-glass windows in the church choir date from the late-Gothic period. Admission is €1.50 adults, €.50 children. The church is open April through October Monday through Friday from 10 a.m. to 5:30 p.m., Sunday from 7:30 a.m. to 5:30 p.m.; December daily from 10 a.m. to 5 p.m.; November and January through March daily from 10 a.m. to noon and 2 to 4 p.m.

Just north of the Jakobskirche is the **Reichsstadtmuseum** (City Museum), Klosterhof 5 (☎ 09861/939-043), housed in a 700-year-old Dominican nunnery. You can visit the amazingly well-preserved cloisters and also the convent hall, kitchen, and apothecary. The museum collection includes an enormous tankard that holds 3½ liters (more than 6 pints). In 1631, during the Thirty Years' War, General Tilly, commander of the armies of the Catholic League, captured the Protestant city of Rothenburg. He said he would spare the town from destruction if one of the town burghers could down the huge tankard full of wine in one draught. Former mayor Nusch accepted the challenge and succeeded, thus saving Rothenburg (it took Nusch three days to sleep off the hangover). Admission to the museum is €3 for adults, €1.50 for children and students. The museum is open April through October daily from 10 a.m. to 5 p.m.; November through March daily from 1 to 4 p.m.

Shopping in Rothenburg ob der Tauber

Kunstwerke Friese, Grüner Markt (☎ 09861/7166), specializes in cuckoo clocks and carries Hummel figurines, pewter beer steins, music boxes, and dolls. Every day is Christmas at **Käthe Wohlfahrt's Weinachtsdoft** (Christmas Village), Herrngasse 1 (☎ 09861/4090), a Christmas-related emporium filled with shops carrying thousands upon thousands of handmade Christmas ornaments.

Part VI
Northern Germany

The 5th Wave   By Rich Tennant

"Douglas, I'd like to talk to you about the souvenirs you brought back from our trip to Germany."

In this part . . .

Northern Germany, bordering the Baltic and the North seas, is the focus of this part. In **Chapter 20,** I tell you all about **Hamburg,** the region's largest city and greatest port. From Hamburg you can make an easy side trip to beautiful **Lübeck,** with so many historic buildings that UNESCO recognizes the city as a World Heritage Site. Both of these cities were members of the powerful Hanseatic League that ruled the seas and dominated trade in northern Europe for hundreds of years.

Chapter 20

Hamburg and Lübeck: Hanseatic Cities of the North

- -

In This Chapter

▶ Discovering the port city of Hamburg

▶ Touring the harbor by boat

▶ Exploring medieval Lübeck

- -

*T*his chapter covers two cities with a long history of seafaring, trade, and commerce. In medieval times, Hamburg and Lübeck were important members of the Hanseatic League, the most powerful commercial network in Europe. Hansa cities formed trade affiliations that linked northern Germany to the eastern Baltic regions and Scandinavia. In fact, Hamburg and Lübeck still retain the term *Hansestadt* (Hanseatic City) in their official titles.

Hamburg, with its busy harbor, is one of the most colorful and cosmopolitan of all German cities. In this wealthy city, the country's second-largest metropolis, you find artistic and cultural attractions and an entertainment scene that goes around-the-clock. Hamburg makes a good base for exploring other cities in the north.

Lübeck, with its medieval walls, church spires, and cobblestone lanes, is one of the most picturesque and atmospheric cities in the north. This former capital of the Hanseatic League is an easy day trip from Hamburg, but its charms may beguile you to stay longer.

Don't expect warm, sunny weather in northern Germany at any time of the year. If you are traveling in the north, even in the summer, an umbrella, raincoat, and sweater will probably come in handy.

Hamburg: Germany's Gateway to the World

Hamburg, located on the Elbe River about 62 miles (100 km) from the North Sea, has a flat, watery landscape that spreads out over 294 square miles. (See the "Hamburg" map in this chapter.) The terrain is characteristic of northern Germany: low, windswept, often gray and misty but also densely green and filled with marshlands and lakes. A sense of the vast northern seas permeates the city.

Everyone carries away a different impression of this bustling, prosperous city, which is also one of Germany's 16 federal states. Some find Hamburg to be a bit smug, even haughty, a city of "high culture" and elegance. For others, Hamburg is sin-city incarnate, land of the lurid Reeperbahn, a street where sex is sold over and not under the counter. Hamburg has a huge, bustling, horn-blaring port and sedate late-19th-century neighborhoods. Although much of the city was destroyed during World War II, you find historic buildings standing side by side with steel-and-glass structures. Because of the Elbe and two enormous inner-city lakes, you're as much aware of water here as land — Hamburg has more bridges than Venice and Amsterdam combined.

Intriguing Hamburg is worth a day or two of your time. If you want to explore northern Germany, this city makes a good headquarters. With its strongly international flair, Germans often call it the "gateway to the world."

Getting there

Hamburg is the largest city in northern Germany and easy to reach by train, plane, and car.

By plane

Five miles (8 km) north of the city center is Hamburg's airport, **Flughafen Hamburg-Fuhlsbüttel,** Paul-Baumer-Platz 1–3 (☎ **040/50750**). Most major European cities have direct flights to Hamburg. The terminal contains an array of easily identified banks with currency-exchange windows, and other independent currency-exchange services and ATMs.

The easiest way to get into the city is by the **Airport Express bus,** which stops in front of Terminals 1 and 4. The bus runs every 15 to 20 minutes (5 a.m.–9:20 p.m.) to the city's Hauptbahnhof (main train station); the journey takes about 25 minutes. The one-way fare is €4.35 for adults and €2.05 for children under 12. A **taxi** from the airport to the city costs about €17 and takes about 30 minutes, depending on traffic. Taxi stands are in front of all the terminals.

By train

Hamburg has two major rail stations. Most trains arrive at the centrally located **Hamburg Hauptbahnhof,** Hachmannplatz 10 (☎ **040/3918-3046**), and then make a second stop at **Hamburg-Altona** (☎ **040/3918-2387**), in the western part of the city. An S-Bahn line connects the two stations. Hamburg has train connections with all major German and European cities. From Berlin, the trip time is 2½ hours. For train information, call **Deutsche Bahn** (German Rail) at ☎ **01805/996-633.**

By car

The **A1** Autobahn reaches Hamburg from the south and west, the **A7** from the north and south, the **A23** from the northwest, and the **A24** from the east. _A word to the wise:_ Park your car and use public transportation in this busy city.

Finding information

Tourismus-Zentrale Hamburg operates the **Tourist-Information** office (☎ **040/3005-1201**) in the main train station near the main Kirchenallee entrance. The office is open daily from 7 a.m. to 11 p.m. and can book a hotel room for you for a €4 fee. In the harbor area, you find **Tourist Information** (☎ **040/3005-1200**) at St. Pauli Landungsbrücken between Piers 4 and 5. This office is open daily from 8 a.m. to 8 p.m.

Taking a bus tour

A guided bus tour is the best way to get a feel for Hamburg and its various neighborhoods and special areas. Daily tours on double-decker buses operated by **Hamburger Stadtrundfahrten** (☎ **040/430-3481**) leave from the main train station (Hauptbahnhof), Kirchenallee entrance. The 90-minute Top Tour departs every 30 minutes beginning at 9:30 a.m. (tours at 11 a.m. and 3 p.m. only in winter). Cost is €12 for adults, €6 for children up to 14. The Gala Tour lasts 2 hours and 30 minutes and includes towns along the Elbe River; daily departures at 10 a.m. and 2 p.m. Cost is €18 for adults, €8.75 for children. From April through October, a three-hour Night Tour on Friday and Saturday includes a visit to some clubs in the St. Pauli district. Cost, including two drinks, is €30. Tickets for all tours are available on the bus. All tours have live commentary in English.

Orienting yourself

The Hauptbahnhof is located on the eastern fringe of **central Hamburg,** the city's commercial and shopping district. Central Hamburg surrounds the **Alster,** a lake rimmed by Hamburg's most significant buildings. Two bridges, the Lombardsbrücke and the Kennedybrücke, divide

Hamburg

ACCOMMODATIONS ■
Aussen Alster **28**
Hamburg Marriott **14**
Hotel Hafen Hamburg **6**
Hotel Prem **29**
Hotel Side **13**
Kempinski Hotel Atlantic
  Hamburg **26**
Park Hyatt Hamburg **22**
Pension Schmidt **25**
Wedina **27**

DINING ◆
Alten Rathaus **16**
Apples Restaurant **22**
Cremon **17**
Die Rösterei **23**
Eisenstein **3**
Fischküche **18**
Le Paquebot **21**
Ratsweinkeller Hamburg **19**
Voltaire **2**

ATTRACTIONS ●
Alster lake **30**
Erotic Art Museum **4**
Hafen **5**
Hamburger Kunsthalle **24**
Museum für Hamburgische
  Geschichte **8**
Rathaus **15**
St. Jacobikirche **20**
St. Michaelis **7**
Tierpark Hagenbeck **1**
Wallringpark
  Alter Botanischer Garten **12**
  Grosse Wallanlagen **9**
  Kleine Wallanlagen **10**
  Planten und Blomen **11**

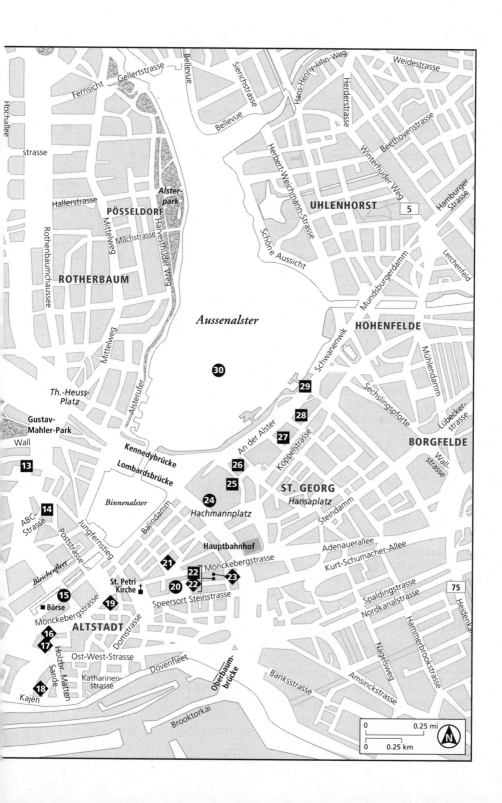

the Alster into the **Binnenalster** (Inner Alster) and the larger
Aussenalster (Outer Alster). **Pösseldorf,** northwest of Aussenalster,
is a tree-filled residential district with many fine 19th-century villas
and *Jugendstil* (Art Nouveau) buildings.

Flanking the Binnenalster on the south is the **Jungfernstieg,** Hamburg's
most vital artery and shopping district. Two canals, **Alsterfleet** and
Bleichenfleet, run south from Binnenalster, channeling the Alster to
the Elbe. Many of Hamburg's finest hotels and restaurants cluster
around the Binnenalster and the Rathaus (City Hall), a short distance
to the south.

The **Port (***Hafen***) of Hamburg,** the world's seventh-largest harbor,
stretches for nearly 25 miles (40 km) along the Elbe River, south of
Central Hamburg and the Alster. The **St. Pauli** district, the old sailor's
quarter that became the center of Hamburg nightlife, is located northwest of the river. The **Reeperbahn,** a famous neon-lit boulevard with
cafes, sex shows, bars, discos, and music halls, bisects St. Pauli.

The western district of **Altona,** formerly a city in its own right, now
integrated into Greater Hamburg, is the scene of Hamburg's famous
Fischmarkt (fish market), which takes place at dawn every Sunday.
The Altona neighborhood is a great place to explore or have dinner.

Getting around Hamburg

Hamburg is not a compact city and can't be easily covered on foot. To
see everything of interest, you have to depend on public transportation or taxis. **Hamburger Verkehrsverbund (HVV),** Steinstrasse 12
(☎ 040/19449), operates the **U-Bahn** (subway), **S-Bahn** (light rail),
A-Bahn (commuter rail), buses, and harbor ferries.

The Hamburg **Welcome Card** is good for travel on all public transport,
admission to 11 Hamburg museums, and a discount on city tours,
guided tours of the port, and lake cruises. A one-day card costs €6.80
for adults, €13 for a group ticket (*Gruppenkarte,* good for two or more
people traveling together). A three-day card costs €14 for adults, €23
for a group ticket. You can buy the card at the Tourist Information
offices (see "Finding information," earlier in this chapter).

The U-Bahn (subway) and buses

Hamburg's **U-Bahn** serves the entire central area and connects with the
S-Bahn light-rail trains in the suburbs. The U-Bahn is the fastest means
of getting around, but **buses** offer a good alternative and let you see
more of the city. The fare is the same for both U-Bahn and bus and
depends on how far you travel.

A **single one-way fare** for both U-Bahn and bus costs between €1.30
and €2.55, depending on the distance. Buy your ticket from the bus

driver or from the automatic vending machines at U-Bahn stations and bus stops. A **Tageskarte** (day ticket) for unlimited use of public transportation costs €4.25 for adults and €7.05 for a family (up to five people traveling together).

Taxis

For a taxi, call ☎ **040/441-011** or 040/666-666. Taxi meters begin at €1.55 and rise from €1.30 to €1.55 per kilometer, depending on the time of day.

Staying in Hamburg

Hamburg is an expensive city with plenty of first-class hotels and a limited number of budget accommodations, especially in the center of the city. If you arrive without a room, Hamburg's **Tourist Information** office (Internet: www.hamburg-tourismus.de) in the main train station can help you find accommodations. The office charges a €4 fee per reservation. You can also call the tourist office's special **hotel hotline,** open daily from 8 a.m. to 8 p.m., at ☎ **040/300-51300.** You also find hotel-booking desks at the airport.

See also Chapter 22 for details on the **Kempinski Hotel Atlantic Hamburg** ($$$$).

Aussen Alster
$$ Central Hamburg

This small, stylish hotel in a late-19th-century building sits on a quiet residential street near the Aussenalster lake. The 27 medium-size rooms are minimalist in terms of decor but very comfortable and meticulously maintained. The bathrooms are small with shower-tub combinations. You find an on-site sauna and solarium. The hotel can arrange baby-sitting.

Schmilinskystrasse 11, 20099 Hamburg. ☎ *040/241-557. Fax: 040/280-3231. U-Bahn: Hauptbahnhof (then a 5-minute walk east on Steindamm and west on Stiftstrasse, which becomes Schmilinskystrasse). Rack rates: €129–€155 double. Rates include buffet breakfast. AE, DC, MC, V.*

Hamburg Marriott
$$–$$$$ Central Hamburg

This large, traditionally styled hotel is near the Hanse Viertel, a fashionable area filled with boutiques, wine bars, shops, and restaurants. Geared toward business travelers, this hotel features an array of business-oriented in-room amenities. The 227 rooms are priced according to size and degree of luxury. The well-done bathrooms have shower-tub combinations. The hotel has a fitness center with pool and sauna. The hotel can arrange baby-sitting.

ABC Strasse 52, 20354 Hamburg. ☎ *800/228-9290 in the U.S. or 040/35050. Fax: 040/ 3505-1777. Internet:* www.marriott-hotels.com. *U-Bahn: Gänsemarkt (then a 3-minute walk south on ABC Strasse). Rack rates: €159–€245 double. Rates include breakfast. AE, DC, MC, V.*

Hotel Hafen Hamburg
$–$$ St. Pauli/Harbor area

This Hamburg landmark, originally built in the mid-19th century as a home for sailors, offers rooms with panoramic views of the river and harbor. The building was restored and converted into a hotel in 1979, and today consists of three adjacent buildings with a total of 255 rooms. The rooms vary in size, but most are large with updated modern furnishings; all have well-equipped bathrooms with a shower-tub combination. The third and fourth floors are nonsmoking. The neighboring ship-shaped **Hotel Residenz,** the Hafen's modern sister hotel, was built in 1995.

Seewartenstrasse 9, 20459 Hamburg. ☎ *040/311-130. Fax: 040/3111-3755. Internet:* www.hotel-hamburg.de. *U-/S-Bahn: Landungsbrücken (then a 7-minute walk north through the small park outside the station to Seewartenstrasse). Rack rates: Hafen €90–€125 double, Residenz €110–€165. Breakfast €12. AE, DC, MC, V.*

Hotel Prem
$–$$$ Central Hamburg

Called the "white house on the Alster," the facade of this centrally located mansion-hotel overlooks the Aussenalster, and the rear faces a quiet garden. Each of the 53 rooms is individually decorated, some with French antiques, others with a contemporary flair. Although not large, rooms are comfortable; if you want quiet, ask for a room facing the garden. Half the bathrooms are well-equipped with big mirrors, marble tubs, and showers; the rest have shower stalls only.

An der Alster 9, 20099 Hamburg. ☎ *040/2483-4040. Fax: 040/280-3851. Internet:* www. hotel-prem.de. *U-Bahn: Lohmülen Strasse (then a 5-minute walk northwest on Bülaustrasse to An der Alster). Rack rates: €115–€200 double. Breakfast €15. AE, DC, MC, V.*

Hotel Side
$$$–$$$$ Central Hamburg

Hamburg's newest hotel, which opened in the spring of 2001, takes high design to new heights. A stark white and steel high-tech minimalism is offset by dramatic, glowing colors and contemporary furniture placed as carefully as sculptures. Built around a central atrium, the 178 good-size rooms are quiet and comfortable. The luxurious bathrooms have a tub-shower combination. A terrace on the eighth floor opens onto panoramic views of Hamburg. Amenities include a health club with pool. You may find a bit of attitude, but staying here is definitely a worthwhile experience.

Drehbahn 49, 20354 Hamburg. ☎ *40/309-990. Fax: 40/3099-9399. Internet:* www. side-hamburg.de. *U-Bahn: Gänsemarkt (then a 3-minute walk north on Dammtorstrasse and west on Drehbahn). Rack rates: €180–€280. Breakfast €18. AE, DC, MC, V.*

Park Hyatt Hamburg
$$–$$$$ Central Hamburg

One of the most beautifully designed hotels in Hamburg, the Hyatt occupies a former trading house from 1912 that was transformed into a hotel in 1998. Lots of wood and warm-toned fabrics adorn the 252 spacious rooms. The large bathrooms have a separate area for Japanese-style soaking tubs. This is a full-service hotel with every amenity you can imagine, the largest pool in Hamburg, and a fine-dining restaurant called **Apples** (see "Dining in Hamburg," later in this chapter).

Bugenhagenstrasse 8, 20095 Hamburg. ☎ *040/3332-1234. Fax: 40/3332-1235. Internet:* www.hamburg.hyatt.de. *U-Bahn: Hauptbahnhof (then a 5-minute walk west across Steintor Wall to Bugenhagenstrasse). Rack rates: €170–€250 double. Breakfast €22. Special weekend and summer rates. AE, DC, MC, V.*

Pension Schmidt
$ Central Hamburg

This small, traditional, 17-room pension sits right across the street from the superdeluxe Kempinski Hotel Atlantic Hamburg (see Chapter 22) and costs a fraction of the price. You won't find anything fancy here. But the double rooms are of a decent size and have an old-fashioned comfort of their own. The rooms have private bathrooms with showers. Breakfast costs extra, but you can eat in your room.

Holzdamm 14, 20099 Hamburg. ☎ *040/280-83-90. Fax: 040/243-705. Internet:* www. t-online.de/home/Pension-Schmidt. *U-Bahn: Hauptbahnhof (then a 5-minute walk north on Holzdamm). Rack rates: €55 double without bathroom; €65 double with bathroom. Breakfast €6. AE, DC, V.*

Wedina
$ Central Hamburg

This recently remodeled hotel is in three different buildings painted three different colors (red, blue, and yellow). Most of the 42 rooms open onto a small, Tuscan-style garden. They range in size from small to medium and are individually decorated with modern furnishings. The smallish bathrooms have a shower-tub combination. The hotel does not have an elevator, and to reach rooms on the third floor, you have to climb 55 steps.

Gurlittstrasse 23, 20099 Hamburg. ☎ *040/243-011. Fax: 040/280-3894. E-mail:* wedina@aol.com. *U-Bahn: Hauptbahnhof (then a 5-minute walk north along Koppel Strasse to Gurlittstrasse). Rack rates: €105–€140 double. Rates include buffet breakfast. AE, DC, MC, V.*

Dining in Hamburg

It shouldn't come as any surprise that most of Hamburg's traditional cuisine comes from the sea. On the menus of the city's many fish restaurants you usually find lobster, shrimp, turbot, plaice, salmon, sole, fresh oysters, and eel (*Aalsuppe,* or eel soup, is a famous Hamburg dish). Traditional meat dishes include *Stubenküchen* (hamburger steak), and *Labskaus* — made with beer, onions, corned beef, potatoes, herring, and pickle — is a hearty, protein-packed dish that sailors and dockworkers order. Pancakes (*Pfannkuchen)* with cranberries or other fruit toppings are popular. *Rote Grütze,* a local dessert specialty, is a compote of red fruits served with vanilla ice cream or cream.

Alten Rathaus

$–$$ Altstadt   NORTH GERMAN

This restaurant occupies a mid–19th-century building in the most historic part of the Altstadt. A good lunch spot, Alten Rathaus offers different specials every day of the week. Popular staples include homemade *Sauerfleisch* (stewed, marinated meat in aspic), a fish dish of zander and salmon in a mustard sauce, and herring filets with potatoes. You can also get *Labskaus,* turkey steak, or simple pasta dishes.

Börsenbrücke 10. ☎ *040/3751-8908. U-Bahn: Rathaus (then a 5-minute walk southwest on Johannis-Mönckebergstrasse to Börsenbrücke). Main courses: Lunch €5.10–€10, dinner €14–€18. No credit cards. Open: Year-round Mon–Fri 11:30 a.m.–3 p.m., and Sept–Mar 6–10 p.m.*

Apples Restaurant

$$$–$$$$ Central Hamburg   INTERNATIONAL

Centered around an open kitchen and wood-fired oven, Apples is the showcase restaurant of the Park Hyatt Hamburg. The menu, which changes according to seasonal availability, features fresh, organically grown produce. Appetizers may include wok-fried squid with spring vegetables and black bean sauce or asparagus with black truffle vinaigrette. As a main course, you may find grilled lobster, chargrilled turbot and peppers, rack of lamb, or oven-roasted duck. Fresh specials of the day are also available. Come here for an elegant evening out.

In the Park Hyatt Hamburg, Bugenhagenstrasse 8. ☎ *040/3332-1234. U-Bahn: Hauptbahnhof (then a 5-minute walk west across Steintor Wall to Bugenhagenstrasse). Reservations required. Main courses: €19–€31. AE, DC, MC, V. Open: 6:30 a.m.–2:30 p.m. and 6–11 p.m.*

Cremon

$ Harbor area   NORTH GERMAN

If you want to eat lunch with the locals, with a minimum of fuss, this bar-restaurant is a good place to try. From the below-street-level location, you can see the Nikolaifleet canal from the windows. The restaurant serves four or five hot dishes of fish and meat buffet-style at lunchtime; a cold buffet is available in the evening. Typical offerings include goulash with noodles, salmon, jacket potatoes with sour cream and crab or other fillings, and the Cremonteller, a platter with crab, meat, cheese, and bread and butter.

Cremons 33–34. ☎ *040/362-190. U-Bahn: Baumwall (then a 10-minute walk east on Kajen and north on Cremons). Main courses: €4–€6 per dish. MC, V. Open: Daily 11 a.m.–11 p.m.*

Die Rösterei
$ Central Hamburg   LIGHT MEALS/BREAKFAST/DESSERTS

Located in the shopping arcade attached to the Park Hyatt hotel, this casual cafe is a good place to stop for breakfast, a light lunch, or afternoon coffee. For breakfast, you can order eggs, sausages and cold cuts, and croissants. Luncheon offerings usually include chicken and fish dishes plus daily specials and several different salads. The cafe roasts its own coffee beans, so you can get a cappuccino with your afternoon *Kuchen* (cake). You can eat on the balcony overlooking the shops or in the wood-paneled dining room.

Mönckebergstrasse 7. ☎ *040/3039-3735. U-Bahn: Mönckebergstrasse (then a 2-minute walk east on Mönckebergstrasse). Breakfast €3.50–€8.70, main courses €9–€11. No credit cards. Open: Mon–Sat 9 a.m.–9 p.m., Sun 10 a.m.–9 p.m.*

Eisenstein
$$–$$$ Altona   INTERNATIONAL

The menu in this hip Altona restaurant, housed in a former tram station, includes specialties from Thailand, Japan (including sushi and sashimi), southern France, and Italy, as well as fresh, traditional versions of North German cuisine, particularly fresh Atlantic fish. Popular offerings include breast of duck with caramelized cherries, homemade pastas, and saltimbocca.

Friedensallee 9. ☎ *040/3904-606. S-Bahn: Altona (then a 10-minute walk west on Hauptstrasse and northwest on Bahrenstrasse, which becomes Friedensallee). Reservations recommended. Main courses: €13–€18; fixed-price lunch €13, fixed-price dinner €25. No credit cards. Open: Daily noon to 3 p.m. and 6 p.m. to midnight.*

Fischküche
$$ Harbor area   SEAFOOD

This pleasant fish restaurant in a modern building has a bright dining room and outdoor tables. The food is robust, and the service is no-nonsense. The menu changes all the time, depending on the catch of the day. Choices may include different kinds of clear or creamy fish soup, herring filets on black bread with onions, a mixed fish platter, flounder with spaghetti and lemon-butter sauce, or codfish with potatoes and onion.

Kajen 12. ☎ *040/365-631. U-Bahn: Baumwall (then a 3-minute walk west to Kajen). Reservations recommended. Main courses: €8–€32. AE, DC, MC, V. Open: Mon–Fri noon to 3 p.m. and 6–11 p.m.*

Le Paquebot
$$ Central Hamburg   INTERNATIONAL

In warm weather, you can sit outside on the square and enjoy a good meal at this quietly stylish restaurant and bar. (Indoor dining is available year-round.) For starters, you might try the avocado salad with herring or some crostini. Main courses typically include offerings such as cannelloni stuffed with mushrooms and ricotta, salmon filet, and breast of chicken with basil and mushrooms. The young wait staff usually speak English.

Gerhart-Hauptmann-Platz 70. ☎ *040/326-519. U-Bahn: Mönckebergstrasse (then a 2-minute walk across Gerhart-Hauptmann-Platz). Main courses: €12–€16. AE, MC, V. Open: Daily 11 a.m.–11 p.m.*

Ratsweinkeller Hamburg
$$ Central Hamburg   HAMBURG/INTERNATIONAL

In business since 1896, the Ratsweinkeller Hamburg has high, vaulted ceilings, wood-paneled columns, and large stained-glass windows. Don't bother with appetizers; the main courses are more than enough. Try the halibut steak in curry sauce, the fresh sole, or the Hamburg crab soup. Or, step up to the herring buffet featuring many different condiments and sauces. If you don't like fish, you can choose from other dishes such as chicken breast in a green rice crust or turkey curry.

Grosse Johannisstrasse 2. ☎ *040/364-153. U-Bahn: Rathaus (then a 3-minute walk south on Grosse Johannisstrasse). Reservations recommended. Main courses: €13–€20; fixed-price menus €13–€24. AE, DC, MC, V. Open: Mon–Sat 11 a.m.–10:30 p.m., Sun 11 a.m.–4 p.m. Closed holidays.*

Voltaire
$$ Altona   INTERNATIONAL

This pleasant, reasonably priced restaurant is across from Eisenstein (see the listing earlier in this section) in the popular Altona area. The dining room is a high-ceilinged brick-walled room with big windows and a bistrolike atmosphere. The menu borrows from French, Italian, and German cuisine, with coq au vin and spaghetti with mushroom sauce available every day. You also find many different salad choices. Meat and fish dishes typically include entrecôte with mustard sauce, rabbit with sweet-and-sour sauce, wild duck with plum sauce, scampi, and herring. Voltaire also has a good wine list and live jazz on most evenings.

Friedensalle 14–16. ☎ 040/397-004. S-Bahn: Altona (then a 10-minute walk west on Hauptstrasse and north on Bahrenstrasse, which becomes Friedensallee). Main courses: €9–€13. No credit cards. Open: Daily 6 p.m.–1 a.m.

Exploring Hamburg

Surprisingly enough, Hamburg is not a city with many world-class cultural attractions. Sightseeing usually centers around the giant harbor and the picturesque Alster lake.

Alster lake

Sailboats, excursion ferries, windsurfers, and canoes ply the waters of this lake that forms the watery heart of central Hamburg. Dividing the Alster is the **Binnenalster,** a smaller, inner lake with canals running south to the Elbe, and the **Aussenalster,** a larger body of water ringed by fine villas. Damming the meandering Alster River created the lake in 1235. Walking paths and parkland surround the 4 miles (7 km) of shoreline. **Alsterpark,** which covers 175 acres on the northwest banks, features beautiful trees, flower gardens, and panoramic views of the Hamburg skyline.

U-Bahn: Hallerstrasse (then a 10-minute walk east on Hallerstrasse to the park).

Hafen (Harbor)

Hamburg is probably most famous for its busy harbor, one of the largest in the world. Its official history dates back to 1189, when the emperor Friedrich Barbarossa issued an edict granting free-trading privileges to Hamburg. The city still commemorates the event every year in early May with three days of huge harborside celebrations, including a windjammer parade, fireworks, and hundreds of booths.

Seeing the Alster by boat

You can tour both inner *(Binnen)* and outer *(Ausser)* Alster by boat. **ATG-Alster-Touristik,** Am Anleger Jungfernstieg (☎ 040/357-4240), offers daily 50-minute trips that depart about every half-hour, April through September, from 10 a.m. to 6 p.m.; from November through March, tours depart daily at 10:30 a.m., noon, and 1:30 and 3 p.m. The ships leave from the Jungfernstieg quayside (U-Bahn: Jungfernstieg). The cost for the tour is €9 for adults and €4.50 for children under 16. A brochure and cassettes with a description of the tour in English are available at no additional cost. The same company offers boat tours of Hamburg's canals and along the Elbe.

The harbor is an open tidal port, in which the North Sea tides influence the water level of the Elbe River. Just southeast of Hamburg, where the Elbe splits into two arms, there is a giant network of quays, warehouses, and drydocks.

Tourist activity centers around the **St.-Pauli-Landungsbrücken,** a long, floating landing stage where you can embark on boat tours of the harbor. Docked just east of the landing stage at Pier 1 is the **Rickmer Rickmers** (☎ **040/319-5959**), a 19th-century clipper ship, now a museum of maritime history. This former East Indies windjammer is open daily from 10 a.m. to 5:30 p.m. Admission is €3 for adults, €2.50 for children ages 4 to 12.

The best way to see the port and all its activity is by taking a **guided harbor tour.** Excursion boats operated by **HADAG** (☎ **040/311-7070**) leave from St. Pauli Landungsbrücken, Piers 1 through 9. Tours depart from April through October daily every hour from 10 a.m. to 5:30 p.m.; from November through March Saturday and Sunday only at 11 a.m., 12:30, 2, and 3:30 p.m. From March through November, an English-language tour departs daily from Pier 1 at noon. The 75-minute trip costs €9 for adults, €5 for children.

U-Bahn: St.-Pauli-Landungsbrücken (the harbor is right across the street).

Hamburger Kunsthalle (Fine Arts Museum)

Northern Germany's leading art museum displays outstanding works from the medieval era to the present day. The museum has an outstanding collection of 19th-century German Romantic paintings, including works by Philipp Otto Runge and Caspar David Friedrich. You can also see dazzling works by German impressionists Max Liebermann and Lovis Corinth, and late-19th/early-20th-century artists Edvard Munch, Leon Kirchner, Otto Dix, Max Beckmann, Paul Kandinsky, and Paul Klee. The new **Galerie der Gegenwart** (Contemporary Gallery) wing displays art since 1960. Allow yourself at least two hours to see everything on view.

Glockengiesserwall 1. ☎ *040/2854-2612. U-Bahn: Hauptbahnhof (exit at Hauptbahnhof Nord, then a 2-minute walk north on An der Kunsthalle). Admission: €7.50 adults, €4 children. Open: Tues–Sun 10 a.m.–6 p.m. (Thurs until 9 p.m.).*

Museum für Hamburgische Geschichte (Hamburg History Museum)

This museum provides a portrait of Hamburg from the 8th through the 20th centuries. Scale models show the changing face of the port, and reconstructed period rooms — from the hall of a 17th-century merchant's house to an air-raid shelter from World War II — illustrate the different eras in Hamburg's history. Give yourself about an hour to browse through the exhibits.

Tracing your German ancestry

The **Museum für Hamburgische Geschichte** (see the listing in this chapter) is especially worth a visit if you have German ancestors and want to do genealogical research. The museum's office of historic emigration contains passenger lists of all the people who shipped out of Hamburg from the 1850s to about 1930. On record are hundreds of thousands of emigrants' names including the names of the cities and towns in which they originated. To use the service, you should bring records with you that indicate the approximate date that your ancestors left Germany.

Holstenwall 24. ☎ *040/4284-12360. U-Bahn: St. Pauli (then a 2-minute walk east across Millentordamm). Admission: €7.50 adults, €1.50 children. Open: Mon 1–5 p.m., Tues–Sun 10 a.m.–6 p.m.*

Rathaus (Town Hall)

Hamburg's Rathaus, built in the late 19th century on a foundation of oak pilings, is the largest of the old buildings in the Altstadt. You can visit the interior of this Renaissance-style structure with its 647-rooms on a guided tour. The Rathaus's 160-foot (49-meter) clock tower overlooks Rathausmarkt and the **Alsterfleet,** the city's largest canal. The **Alsterarkaden,** across the canal, is an arched passageway with upscale clothing shops, jewelry stores, and boutiques. You can combine a visit to the Rathaus with a stop at the 16th-century **Börse** (Stock Exchange), Adolphsplatz 1 (☎ **040/361-3020**), which stands back-to-back with the Rathaus. Guides conduct free tours of the Börse on Tuesday and Thursday at 11 a.m. and noon. Tours of the Rathaus and the Börse last about 30 to 45 minutes.

Rathausplatz. ☎ *040/4283-12063. U-Bahn: Rathaus. Admission: Rathaus tour €1 adults, €.50 children. Tours (in English): Mon–Thurs hourly 10:15 a.m.–3:15 p.m., Fri–Sun 10:15 a.m.–1 p.m.*

St. Jacobikirche (St. James's Church)

World War II bombings almost completely destroyed the 13th-century Gothic Jacobikirche. The rebuilt church contains several medieval altars, pictures, and sculptures, as well as one of Hamburg's musical treasures, a baroque organ built in 1693 by Arp Schnitger, a master craftsman whose instruments were played by Johann Sebastian Bach. The 60-register organ at St. Jame's is one of only two surviving Schnitger organs in Germany.

Jakobikirchhof 22, entrance on Steinstrasse. ☎ *040/327-744. U-Bahn: Mönckebergstrasse (then a 2-minute walk south to Jakobikirchhof). Admission: Free. Open: Mon–Sat 10 a.m.–5 p.m., Sun 10 a.m. to noon.*

St. Michaelis (St. Michael's Church)

Constructed of brick, like so many other buildings in Hamburg, St. Michael's, completed in 1762, is one of the finest baroque churches in northern Germany. The tower, with its hammered-copper roof, is a famous Hamburg landmark and the principal reason to visit. Take the elevator or climb the 449 steps to enjoy the sweeping view from the top. The crypt, one of the largest in Europe, contains the tomb of composer Carl Philipp Emanuel Bach. Give yourself about 15 minutes to visit the church and tower. One block to the south of the church are the **Krameramtswohnungen,** Hamburg's last remaining 17th-century brick and timber almshouses, which have been made into art galleries.

Krayenkamp 4C, Michaeliskirchplatz. ☎ 040/3767-8100. S-Bahn: Stadthausbrücke (then a 10-minute walk west on Michaelisstrasse). Admission: Church free; tower €2.50 adults, €1.25 children. Open: Daily Apr–Sept 9 a.m.–6 p.m., Oct–Mar 10 a.m.–5 p.m.

Tierpark Hagenbeck (Zoo)

Founded in 1848, Hamburg's zoo is home to about 2,500 animals. This zoo in the northwest suburbs offers sea-lion and dolphin shows, elephant and camel rides, a train ride through a fairyland, and a spacious children's playground. A restaurant serves fixed-price meals for €9.50 to €14 from 11:30 a.m. to closing.

Hagenbeckallee at Steilingen. ☎ 040/540-0010. U-Bahn: Hagenbeck's Tierpark. Admission: €12 adults, €8.50 children 7–16, children under 6 free. Open: Spring–fall daily 9 a.m.–6 p.m.; winter daily 9 a.m.–5 p.m.

Wallringpark

Four beautifully maintained parks and gardens comprise this greenbelt area west of the Altstadt and Alster lake. **Planten und Blomen** (Plants and Flowers), laid out in 1936, contains the largest Japanese garden in Europe, with rock gardens, flowering plants, miniature trees, and winding pathways. The **Alter Botanischer Garten** (Old Botanical Garden), south of Planten and Blomen, is known for its rare plant specimens and greenhouses filled with tropical flora. The **Kleine** (small) and **Grosse** (large) **Wallanlagen** parks contain many recreational facilities, including a roller-skating rink, playgrounds, restaurants, and an ice-skating rink in winter. A miniature railway connects all four parks.

U-Bahn: Dammtor (the station is at the southeastern corner of the park).

Shopping in Hamburg

Hamburg is a big shopping city, but don't expect to find many bargains, or any kind of local specialty or handicraft. Stores are generally open Monday through Friday from 9 a.m. to 6:30 p.m. (some until 8 p.m. on

---

The famous Hamburg Fischmarkt

The Hamburg **Fischmarkt (fish market),** between Hexenberg and Grosse Elbstrasse (U-Bahn: Landungsbrücken), takes place every Sunday from 5 a.m. in summer or from 7 a.m. the rest of the year. Besides fish, you can buy flowers, fruit, vegetables, plants, and pets at this traditional market, in existence since 1703. The nearby taverns are open to serve Fischmarkt visitors and vendors.

Thursday) and on Saturday from 9 a.m. to 2 p.m. (until 4 or 6 p.m. on *langer Samstag,* the first Saturday of the month).

From the Hauptbahnhof, two major shopping streets fan out in a south-westerly direction toward the Rathaus: the pedestrian-only **Spitaler-strasse** and **Mönckebergstrasse.** These streets contain some of the city's less expensive stores. Two of the city's oldest and most prestigious shopping streets, **Grosse Bleichen** and **Neuer Wall,** run parallel to the canals, connected transversely by **Jungfernstieg** and **Ufer Strasse** on the Binnenalster.

Karstadt, Mönckebergstrasse 16 (☎ **040/30940**), is part of a department-store chain that carries many of the same brands and items as the other leading department stores. Less expensive is **Kaufhof,** Mönckebergstrasse 3 (☎ **040/333-070**), which offers better deals on merchandise markdowns. **Alsterhaus,** Jungfernstieg 22 (☎ **040/359-011**), carries more-fashionable merchandise.

Living it up after dark in Hamburg

To find out what's happening in Hamburg, pick up a copy of *Hamburger Vorschau* for €1.20. Published once a month, the magazine is available at tourist offices, hotels, and newsstands. You can obtain tickets at venue box offices, at tourist offices, or through the service **Theaterkasse Central,** Gerhart-Hauptmann-Platz 48, Landesbank-Galerie (☎ **040/337-124;** U-Bahn: Mönckebergstrasse).

The performing arts

Hamburgische Staatsoper (Hamburg State Opera), Dammtorstrasse 28 (☎ **040/351-721;** S-Bahn: Dammtor), one of the world's leading opera houses, is the home of the **Hamburg State Opera** and the **Hamburg Ballet.** Ticket prices range from €5 to €77. The ticket office is at Grosstheaterstrasse 34.

The **Musikhalle,** Johannes-Brahms-Platz (☎ **040/346-920;** U-Bahn: Messehallen), hosts concerts by the **Hamburg Symphony,** the **Hamburg Philharmonic,** and the **NDR Symphony,** as well as choirs, chamber orchestras, and guest artists. Ticket prices vary from program to program.

Hamburg has dozens of theaters, but you need to understand German in order to enjoy the productions. One exception is the **English Theatre of Hamburg,** Lerchenfeld 14 (☎ **040/227-7089;** U-Bahn: Mundsburg), the only English-speaking theater in the northern part of Germany. Tickets range from €12 to €25.

The club, bar, and music scenes

Hamburg is famous for its nightlife. The following list gives a small sampling of bars, beer halls, nightclubs, dance clubs, and live-music venues.

- ✔ **After Shave,** Spielbudenplatz 7 (☎ **040/319-3215;** S-Bahn: Reeperbahn), a dance club for 20 to 30 year olds, features funk, soul, jazz, and fusion. The club is open from 11 p.m. to 4 a.m. Thursday, to 5 a.m. Friday, and to 6 a.m. Saturday. Cover is €5 to €8.

- ✔ **Bayrisch Zell,** Reeperbahn 10 (☎ **040/314-281;** S-Bahn: Reeperbahn), a giant beer hall, is one of the most popular places in the St. Pauli district, attracting singles and couples young and old. If someone catches your fancy, you can call him or her from the phone on your table. The food is good, too, with meals ranging from €5 to €12. The hall is open daily from 7 p.m. to 3 a.m.

- ✔ **Club Grosse Freiheit,** Grosse Freiheit 36 (☎ **040/317-7711;** S-Bahn: Reeperbahn), in St. Pauli, is where the Beatles performed in their earliest days. Today this cultural institution is a free-for-all venue with acts that change nightly. Cover is €4.50 to €22.

- ✔ **Cotton Club,** Alter Steinweg 10 (☎ **040/343-878;** S-Bahn: Stadthausbrücke), the oldest and best established of the Hamburg jazz clubs, features jazz and Dixieland bands from throughout Europe and the U.S. The club is open year-round Monday through Saturday from 8 p.m. to midnight; from September to April, it's also open Sunday nights from 11 p.m. to 3 a.m. Cover charge is €4 to €15, depending on the band.

- ✔ **Dennis' Swing Club,** Papenhuderstrasse 25 (☎ **040/229-9192;** U-Bahn: Hamburgerstrasse), features some of the finest jazz talent in the city in a bilingual German-English format. The club is open Tuesday to Sunday from 8:30 p.m. to 2 a.m. Cover is €5 to €8.

Gay and lesbian clubs

Hamburg, like Berlin, is one of the major gay centers of Europe, with a dense concentration of gay shops, bars, and cafes along **Lange Reihe** just northeast of the train station (U-Bahn: Hauptbahnhof). The free magazine ***Dorn Rosa,*** distributed at most gay and lesbian bars, lists the city's many gay and lesbian clubs, restaurants, bars, and events.

St. Pauli and the Reeperbahn: For adults only

Commercialized sex is a major tourist attraction in Hamburg. The place where it all hangs out is the St. Pauli district, just west of the center, along a half-mile thoroughfare called the **Reeperbahn** (pronounced *ray*-per-bahn; S-Bahn: Reeperbahn). The name literally translates as "rope street" and refers to the nautical rope produced there during the 18th and 19th centuries. By the mid-1800s, St. Pauli, close to Hamburg's great harbor, had become a hangout for sailors and prostitutes, who set up shop with the legal sanction of municipal authorities. Many of the prostitutes who work there today are licensed and must submit to a medical examination every two weeks.

St. Pauli is a place to visit at night. The area is not exclusively devoted to sex, and you do find all kinds of theaters (mostly for musicals and comedies), cabarets, bars, discos, and restaurants (although I wouldn't recommend dining in this area). The district's sex-related bars and theaters are up and running by 8 p.m. Between midnight and 5 a.m., thousands of "working girls" strut their stuff along the Reeperbahn and through St. Pauli's streets. The most famous street besides the Reeperbahn itself is **Herbertstrasse,** where bordellos line both sides of the street, and the women display themselves behind plate-glass windows. Herbertstrasse is only open to men over the age of 18; metal gates block each end of the street. Please note that women are not welcome on Herbertstrasse, and may even be doused with a bucket of water if they enter.

Grosse Freiheit, a street whose name appropriately translates as "Great Freedom," is known for its erotic theaters. Municipal regulations forbid prostitution, or overt solicitation, inside erotic theaters. The district also contains the **Erotic Art Museum,** Nobistor 10A (☎ **040/3178-4126**), at the corner of Reeperbahn and Groose Freiheit. Open to those over 16, the museum presents its displays and changing exhibits in a way that's both academic and titillating. The museum is open Sunday through Thursday from 10 a.m. to midnight, Friday and Saturday from 10 a.m. to 2 a.m.; admission is €7.50.

Lübeck: In a (Hanseatic) League of Its Own

Seven Gothic church spires rise above the picturesque town of Lübeck, located 41 miles (66 km) northeast of Hamburg in the state of Schleswig-Holstein. (See the "Lübeck" map in this chapter.) Along the ancient streets of its Altstadt, you find more buildings from the 13th to the 15th centuries than in any other city in northern Germany. Most of the buildings, including the churches, are fine examples of the red-brick

Lübeck

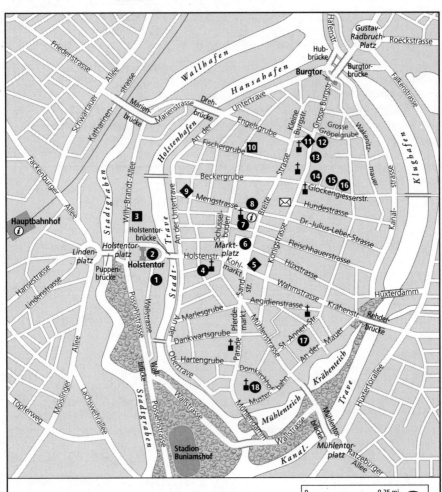

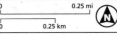

Lübeck's Nobel sons

Lübeck has had several famous sons, notably Thomas Mann and Willy Brandt. As a young man, Brandt (1913–1992), who later became West German chancellor and won the Nobel Peace Prize in 1971, opposed the Nazis so vehemently that he had to flee on a boat to Norway. The writer Thomas Mann (1875–1955) used his home-town of Lübeck as the setting for his novel *Buddenbrooks,* which catapulted the 27-year-old author to international fame in 1902. In 1929, Mann won the Nobel Prize for literature.

architecture so characteristic of northern Germany. The city's architectural heritage is so rich that UNESCO placed Lübeck on its World Heritage list of international monuments.

From the 13th century on, Lübeck was the capital of the Hanseatic League, the powerful association of merchants that controlled trade along the Baltic as far as Russia. The town still retains the name *Hansestadt Lübeck.*

Lübeck makes a rewarding day trip from Hamburg, less than an hour away by train, but its charms may beguile you to stay overnight. With its enormous churches, high-gabled houses, massive gates, and historic buildings at every turn, Lübeck is a delightful city to explore.

Getting there

By train, you can reach Lübeck from anywhere in Germany or Europe. Dozens of trains arrive daily from Hamburg, only 40 minutes away. For train schedules and information, call **German Rail** (☎ 01805/996-633).

By boat, you can take a passenger or car ferry service between Denmark (the port of Rødbyhaven) and Lübeck (the port of Puttgarden). **Scand-Lines** (☎ 04371/865-161; Internet: www.scandlines.com) offers daily departures. **TT Saga Line** (☎ 04502/80181; Internet: www.ttline.de) operates between the German port of Travemünde and the Swedish port of Trelleborg.

By car, you can reach Lübeck via the **A1** Autobahn north and south.

Finding information

In the train station, **Touristinformation Hauptbahnhof** (☎ 0451/864-675) is open Monday through Saturday from 9 a.m. until 1 p.m. and 3 to 6 p.m. The **Lübeck und Travemünde Tourist Service,** Breite Strasse 62

Special events in Lübeck

The **Schleswig-Holstein Music Festival,** one of the best music festivals in Germany, occurs in Lübeck (which has a famed music school) with performances from early July until the end of August every year. For more information, contact ☎ **0800/7463-2002;** Internet: www.shmf.de. A **Christmas market** featuring hand-made wares from all over northwestern Germany takes place during the three weeks preceding Christmas.

(☎ **01805/882-233,** €.24 per minute; Internet: www.luebeck-tourism us.de), behind the Rathaus, is open January through May and October through November, Monday through Friday from 9:30 a.m. to 6 p.m. and Saturday from 10 a.m. to 3 p.m.; June through September and December, hours are Monday through Friday from 9:30 a.m. to 7 p.m., Saturday from 10 a.m. to 3 p.m., and Sunday from 10 a.m. to 2 p.m. This office can help you with hotel reservations.

Orienting yourself

The Trave and Wakenitz rivers and other waterways encircle Lübeck's **Altstadt,** an oval-shaped island a little over a mile long and less than a mile wide. Eight bridges connect the old town with greater Lübeck on the "mainland." Only about 12,000 residents (out of about 225,000) live on the island.

The **Hauptbahnhof** sits on the mainland on the west side of the Altstadt. Nearby, in the Altstadt, is the **Holstentor,** a fortified, turreted gate that is one of the town's principle landmarks. The historic **Rathaus, Markt** (market square), and **Marienkirche** (Church of St. Mary) are the principal sights in the center of the Altstadt. **Breite Strasse,** the main pedestrian shopping street, runs past these sights to the east. **Königstrasse,** another important street, is a block east of Breite Strasse. At the northern end of Königstrasse is the **Heiligen-Geist-Hospital,** a 15th-century almshouse, and a few blocks north of it is the **Burgtor** gate. The **Dom** (cathedral) stands at the island's southern tip.

Getting around Lübeck

The Altstadt and all the major attractions can be reached on foot from the train station. You can also take Bus 5, 6, 7, 11, 14, or 16 from the train station into the Altstadt. The fare is €1.80.

A fun and relaxing way to see Lübeck is by water. Excursion boats operated by **MAAK-Linie** (☎ **0451/706-3859;** Internet: www.maak-linie. de) leave from docks on the Trave River just north of the Holstentor. In summer, departures are hourly between 10 a.m. and 6 p.m. (between

11 a.m. and 4 p.m. the rest of the year). The trip (commentary in German only) lasts one hour and encircles the entire Altstadt. Cost is €7 for adults, €5.50 for seniors, and €3 for children.

Staying in Lübeck

Klassik Altstadt Hotel
$ Altstadt

If you want to stay in a smaller, older hotel in the Altstadt, this is a good choice. The 28, individually decorated rooms, all named for famous Lübeckers, have a pleasant, traditional style. Most of the bathrooms have showers, a few have tubs.

Fischergrube 52, 23552 Lübeck. ☎ *0451/702980. Fax: 0451/73778. Internet:* www. klassik-altstadt-hotel.de. *Rack rates: €105 double. Rates include buffet breakfast. AE, MC, V.*

Radisson SAS Senator Hotel Lübeck
$$–$$$ Altstadt

If you want a modern, full-service hotel, the Radisson is the best place to stay. A pedestrian bridge connects the hotel from its riverside location to the Altstadt. The 231 medium-size rooms are attractively furnished. Bathrooms have shower-tub combinations. Amenities include an on-site health club with pool, sauna, and steam rooms, and a computer in the lobby that allows you to check your e-mail. Children up to age 12 stay for free in their parents' room.

Willy-Brandt-Allee 6, 23554 Lübeck. ☎ *800/333-3333 in the U.S. or 0451/1420. Fax: 0451/142-2222. Internet:* www.senatorhotel.de. *Rack rates: €140–€180. AE, MC, V.*

Dining in Lübeck

Historischer Weinkeller
$$–$$$ Altstadt

The Historischer Weinkeller, located beneath the 13th-century Heiligen-Geist-Hospital (see the next section, "Walking through Lübeck"), is an excellent and atmospheric restaurant with an international menu. You can choose from several different fixed-priced menus. You may begin with smoked Norwegian salmon, goose-liver pâté, or a fish-based soup. Entrees range from filet of cod with sauerkraut and poached haddock in a mustard sauce to meat dishes and vegetarian choices.

Koberg 8. ☎ *0451/76234. Fixed-price menu €25–€38. AE, MC, V. Open: Daily noon to midnight.*

The sweet side of Lübeck

Lübeck is the world capital of marzipan, a sweet almond paste. According to legend, Lübeckers ran out of flour during a long siege and started grinding almonds to make bread. They were so pleased with the sweet results that they've been making marzipan ever since. To sample Lübeck's famous marzipan, stop in at **Cafe Niederegger,** Breitestrasse 98 (☎ **0451/53010**), located right across from the main entrance to the Rathaus since 1806. On the ground floor, you can purchase bars and boxes of marzipan to take away (an excellent gift idea), or you can go upstairs to the pleasant cafe for dessert and coffee. Niederegger's is open daily from 9 a.m. to 6 p.m.

Schabbelhaus
$$–$$$ **Altstadt**

Occupying two elegant town houses on a lovely medieval street, Schabbelhaus serves North German and Italian cuisine. The atmospheric dining room overlooks a small garden. Try the crab soup, if available, followed by fresh fish from the Baltic Sea. You can also get pasta dishes such as tagliatelle with fresh mushrooms or with salmon and lemon. The service is attentive, and the wine list is excellent.

Mengstrasse 48–52. ☎ *0451/72011. Main courses: €9–€20; fixed-price lunch €16–€19. AE, MC, V. Open: Mon–Sat noon to 2:30 p.m. and 6–11 p.m.*

Walking through Lübeck

Concentrate your sightseeing in Lübeck's remarkable **Altstadt,** surrounded by the Trave River and its canals. About one-fifth of the Altstadt was destroyed in a 1942 bombing, but approximately 1,000 medieval buildings still stand within a 2-square-mile (5-sq.-km) area around the Marktplatz. Builders used brick as the predominant material for houses, churches, shops, and guild halls. The city mandated the use of brick after fires in the 13th century destroyed many wooden structures.

What follows is a **walking tour** of the Altstadt that begins at the train station. The entire walk, with stops at museums, takes about four to five hours.

1. From the train station, cross the **Puppenbrücke** (Dolls' Bridge) and head east into the Altstadt. The bridge got its irreverent name from the seven statues of classical gods and goddesses that stand on its stone railings.

2. Once you enter the Altstadt, directly in front of you is the 15th-century **Holstentor** (Holsten Gate), once the main town entrance.

The **Museum Holstentor** (☎ 0451/122-4129), a small local history museum housed within the gate, contains a model of Lübeck as the town appeared in the mid-17th century, models of Hanseatic *Kogge* (cogs, or single-sail vessels), and medieval torture instruments. The museum is open Tuesday through Sunday from 10 a.m. to 5 p.m. in summer and until 4 p.m. in winter. Admission is €3 for adults, €.50 for students and children under 18. You can see everything inside 30 minutes.

3. Just south, across the street from the Holstentor, stand the **Salzspeicher** (Salt Lofts), a group of six gabled Renaissance buildings; the oldest dates from 1579, the newest from 1745. Merchants stored salt (considered "white gold") from nearby Lüneburg in these buildings before shipping it to Scandinavia where the salt was used to preserve fish.

4. Continuing a few blocks east on Holstenstrasse, you reach Lübeck's **Rathaus,** Rathausplatz (☎ 0451/122-1005), one of the oldest and most beautiful in Germany. The Rathaus was rebuilt several times since the first foundation stone was laid in 1230. The present building, topped by slender turrets, is a mixture of Gothic and Renaissance styles. Black glazed-brick *courses* (horizontal lines) and round panels emblazoned with coats of arms adorn the red-brick walls. The building sits on brick arcades that allow easy access to the main entrance on Breite Strasse. You can see the interior on a guided tour (in German) Monday through Friday at 11 a.m., noon, and 3 p.m.; the cost is €2.60 for adults and €.50 for children and students.

5. The Rathaus stands on the north and east sides of the **Marktplatz,** a large square filled with meat, fruit, and vegetable stalls every Monday and Thursday. In December the Markt is the site of Lübeck's Christmas Market.

6. Towering above the Markt and the Rathaus is one of Northern Germany's most outstanding examples of the brick Gothic style, the twin-towered **Marienkirche** (St. Mary's Church), Schüsselbuden 13 (☎ 0451/397-700). The Marienkirche served as a model for many other churches built in the Baltic region. Its central nave, 120 feet high, has the highest brick vaulting in the world. During the World War II bombing attack the tower bells crashed down into the church and embedded themselves in the stone floor. They are still there, left as a reminder and warning of the horrors of war. Organ concerts take place during the summer and fall, carrying on a tradition established by St. Mary's best-known organist and composer, Dietrich Buxtehude (1637–1707).

7. If you're a fan of the great German writer Thomas Mann, whose works include *Death in Venice, The Magic Mountain,* and *Buddenbrooks,* plan to spend at least half an hour at **Buddenbrookhaus,** Mengstrasse 4 (☎ 0451/122-4192), just north of the

Marienkirche. This big, solid stone house with a gabled roof belonged to Mann's grandparents and was the model for the family home Mann wrote about in *Buddenbrooks.* Inside, you find a comprehensive collection of photographs, letters, and documents chronicling Mann's life, and that of his family, from birth to death. Mann's brother, Heinrich Mann (1871–1950), was the author of *Professor Unrat,* the source of the movie *The Blue Angel.* On the second floor are period rooms and artifacts. The house is open daily from 10 a.m. to 5 p.m.; admission is €5 for adults, €2.50 for students.

8. An outstanding collection of German Romantic and German Impressionist paintings is on view at **Museen Behnhaus/ Drägerhaus,** Königstrasse 9–11 (☎ **0451/122-4148**), a few blocks north of the Rathaus. The museum, formed from two 18th-century town houses, also displays major 20th-century artists such as Leon Kirchner, Max Beckmann, and Ernst Barlach, and has exhibits relating to the city's cultural life in the 18th and 19th centuries. The museum is open Tuesday through Sunday from 10 a.m. to 5 p.m. (until 4 p.m. Oct–Mar). Admission is €3 for adults, €.50 for students and children 6 to 18.

9. On Glockengiesserstrasse, just to the south of the Museen Behnhaus/Drägerhaus, are two ancient almshouses worth seeing. The **Füchtingshof** at no. 23 was built in the 17th century for the widows of seamen and merchants. Step through the ornamented baroque portal and you enter a tranquil courtyard with houses still occupied by widows. The **Glandorps-Gang,** at no. 41, and the **Glandorps-Hof,** at nos. 49–51, are the city's oldest almshouses, dating from 1612 and built for the widows of merchants and craftsmen.

10. A short distance to the north stands the **Heiligen-Geist-Hospital** (Hospital of the Holy Spirit), Am Koburg (☎ **0451/122-2040**). This building, with its belfry and four turreted spires, is one of the oldest social-welfare institutions in Europe, and one of the most important monumental buildings of the Middle Ages. Philanthropic local citizens founded the hospital in 1230. In the early-19th century, when the building was converted to a shelter for elderly men and women, 130 tiny wooden cabins without ceilings were built within its enormous main hall. The cabins remain intact, and you can poke your head inside them (no admission charge).

11. On the south side of town, you find Lübeck's **Dom,** Mühlendamm 2–6 (☎ **0451/74704**). Construction on this massive edifice began in 1173. The church was destroyed in World War II and later rebuilt. Except for its size, the church itself isn't that interesting. The building is open daily from 10 a.m. to 6 p.m.

12. Two blocks northeast of the Dom, you find the **St.-Annen-Museum,** St.-Annen-Strasse 15 (☎ **0451/122-4137**). Housed in a 16th-century Augustinian convent which was later used as an almshouse and a

prison, the museum has a noteworthy collection of medieval and Renaissance altarpieces, including a work by Hans Memling. You can see everything in about half an hour. The museum is open Tuesday through Sunday from 10 a.m. to 5 p.m. Admission is €3 for adults, €.50 for students and children 6 to 18.

13. To round off your tour of Lübeck, head over to the 750-year-old **Petrikirche** (St. Peter's Church), Schmiedestrasse (☎ **0451/397-330**), and take the elevator up to the top of its tower for a memorable view of Lübeck and its port. The church is open daily from 9 a.m. to 7 p.m. Admission is €3 for adults, €1.50 for students and children.

Part VII
The Part of Tens

The 5th Wave   By Rich Tennant

In this part . . .

This part is full of extra-special hints, helpers, and recommendations. First off, in **Chapter 21,** I give you ten German lessons, providing useful words and phrases in ten different categories. Then, in **Chapter 22,** I give you my list of ten personally recommended hotels — so if you want to travel really well in Germany and you have deep pockets, you know right where to go. In **Chapter 23,** I help you to focus your sightseeing by giving you quick summaries of what I regard as the ten best museums in Germany.

Chapter 21

Ten *(Zehn)* German Lessons

· ·

In This Chapter

▶ Getting to know the basics: Days, numbers, time, and more

▶ Traveling from place to place: Directions and transportation

▶ Finding the fun: Entertainment and attractions

· ·

Maybe you're going to take some German lessons or listen to a German tape before you fly off to Deutschland. But maybe you're not — in which case, this chapter is especially for you. This chapter presents ten basic categories — from travel to entertainment — and gives you a few basic words or phrases (and their pronunciations) in each one. Turn to this handy glossary if you're wondering how to say something *auf Deutsch* (owf *doytsch;* in German). For food and restaurant words, see the Cheat Sheet in the front of the book.

Bear in mind that you encounter different regional pronunciations and dialects throughout Germany.

Basic Words and Phrases

Yes = Ja (yaw). **No** = Nein (nine). **Please** = Bitte (*bit*-tuh). **Thank you** = Danke (*donk*-uh). **Good morning** = Guten morgen (*goo*-ten *mor*-gun). **Good evening** = Guten abend (*goo*-ten *ah*-bent). **How are you?** = Wie geht es dir (vee *gate* ess dear)? **How much does it cost?** = Wie kostet es (vee *cost*-tet ess)? **Women** = Damen (*dom*-in). **Married woman** = Frau (frow). **Girl or unmarried woman** = Fräulein (*froy*-line). **Men** = Herren (*hair*-en). **Man** = Herr (hair). **Boy** = Knabe (kuh-*nob*-buh). **Parents** = Eltern (*el*-turn). **Children** = Kinder (*kin*-dur). **Family** = Familie (fuh-*me*-lee-uh).

Accommodations

Do you have a room available? = Haben Sie ein Zimmer frei (*hob*-ben zee ein *tsim*-mer fry)? **Hotel** = Hotel (ho-*tel*). **Guesthouse** = Gasthof (*gahst*-hofe) or Gasthaus (*gahst*-house). **B&B** = Pension (pen-see-*own*).

Room = Zimmer (*tsim*-mer). **Room number** = Zimmer nummer (*tsim*-mer noomer). **Double room** = Doppelzimmer (*dop*-pel-tsim-mer). **Single room** = Einzelzimmer (*ine*-zul-tsim-mer). **Bed** = Bett (bet). **Double bed** = Doppelbett (*dop*-pel-bett). **Single bed** = Einzelbett (*ine*-zul-bett). **Bathtub** = Bad (bod). **Shower** = Dusche (*doo*-sha). **Toilet** = Toilette (toy-*let*-tuh). **Stairs** = Treppe (*trep*-puh). **Elevator** = Fahrstuhl (*far*-shtool). **Towel** = Handtuch (*hond*-tuke). **Pillow** = Kopfkissen (*kopf*-kis-sen). **Soap** = Seife (*sigh*-fuh). **Water** = Wasser (*vahs*-ser). **Hot** = heiss (hise). **Cold** = kalt (kahlt). **Breakfast** = Frühstück (*froo*-shtook). **Breakfast buffet** = Frühstücksbuffet (*froo*-shtooks-boo-fay).

Colors

Black = Schwarz (shvartz). **Blue** = blau (blau). **Green** = grün (groon). **Orange** = orange (oh-*rahnj*-ah). **Pink** = rosa (*ro*-sa). **Purple** = purpur (pur-*pur*). **Red** = rot (rote). **Yellow** = gelb (gelb). **White** = weiss (vise).

Days of the Week

Monday = Montag (*moan*-tog). **Tuesday** = Dienstag (*deens*-tog). **Wednesday** = Mittwoch (*mitt*-voch). **Thursday** = Donnerstag (*doe*-ners-tog). **Friday** = Freitag (*fry*-tog). **Saturday** = Samstag (*zoms*-tog) or Sonnabend (*sone*-uh-bent). **Sunday** = Sonntag (*zone*-tog).

Directions

Street = Strasse (*shraw*-suh) or Weg (vegg). **Where is . . . ?** = Wo ist . . . (*voe ist . . .*)? **Left** = links (lynx). **Right** = rechts (rexts). **Straight ahead** = geradeaus (guh-*rod*-duh-owse). **East** = Ost (oast). **West** = West (vest). **North** = Nord (nord). **South** = Süd (sued). **Meter** = Meter (*may*-ter). **Kilometer** = Kilometer (*kill*-oh-may-ter). **Open** = offnen (*ofe*-nin). **Closed** = geschlossen (*ger*-shlosn).

Entertainment and Attractions

Ticket = Karte (*car*-tuh). **Box office** = Kasse (*kah*-suh). **Evening box office** (usually open 1 hour before performance) = Abendkasse (*ah*-bent-kah-suh). **Opening hours** = Öffnüngszeiten (*ohff*-noongs-sight-en). **Closed** = geschlossen (guh-*schloss*-en). **Museum** = Museum (moo-*zay*-ume). **Opera** = Oper (*oh*-per). **Concert** = Konzert (cone-*sert*). **Theater** (building) = Schauspielhaus (*shau*-shpeel-house). **Movies/cinema** = Kino (*keen*-oh). **Do you have tickets for this evening?** = Haben Sie Karten für heute abend (hob-ben zee *car*-ten fear hoy-tuh *ah*-bent)?

Numbers

1 = eins (einz). **2** = zwei (zvy). **3** = drei (dry). **4** = vier (fear). **5** = fünf (fihnf). **6** = sechs (zex). **7** = sieben (*zee*-ben). **8** = acht (okt). **9** = neun (noyn). **10** = zehn (tzane).

11 = elf (elf). **12** = zwölf (tzwelf). **13** = dreizehn (*dry*-tsane). **14** = vierzehn (*fear*-tsane). **15** = fünfzehn (*foonf*-tsane). **16** = sechszehn (*zek*-tsane). **17** = siebzehn (*tseeb*-tsane). **18** = achtzehn (*ok*-tsane). **19** = neunzehn (*noine*-tsane). **20** = zwanzig (*tswan*-tsig).

30 = dreizig (*dry*-tsig). **40** = vierzig (*fear*-tsig). **50** = fünfzig (*foonf*-tsig). **60** = sechszig (*zek*-tsig). **70** = siebzig (*zeeb*-tsig). **80** = achtzig (*ok*-tsig). **90** = neunzig (*noine*-tsig). **100** = hundert (*whon*-dert).

Seasons and Elements

Spring = Frühling (*froo*-ling). **Summer** = Sommer (*zoam*-er). **Autumn** = Herbst (erbst). **Winter** = Winter (*vin*-ter). **Rain** = Regen (*ray*-gun). **Snow** = Schnee (schnay). **Sun** = Sonne (*zone*-uh).

Time

Time = Zeit (zite). **What time is it?** = Welche Zeit ist es (vell-tcha *zite* ist es)? **Clock/watch** = Uhr (uer). **Hour** = Stunde (*shtoon*-duh). **Minute** = Minute (min-*ooh*-tuh). **Morning** = Morgen (*mor*-gun). **Afternoon** = Nachmittag (*nock*-mit-tog). **Evening** = Abend (*ah*-bent). **Midnight** = Mitternacht (*mit*-ter-knockt). **Day** = Tag (tog). **Night** = Nacht (knocked). **Early** = Früh (fhree). **Late** = Spät (shpate).

Transportation

Ticket = Fahrkarte (*far*-car-tuh). **One-way ticket** = Einzelfahrkarte (*ine*-sell-far-car-tuh). **Round trip** = Hin und züruck (hin und zoo-*rook*). **Reservation** = Resevierung (res-uh-*veer*-oong). **Seat** = Platz (plotz). **Arrival** = Ankunft (*on*-koonft). **Departure** = Abfahrt (*ob*-fart). **Transfer** = umsteigen (*oom*-shty-gun). **Get in/all aboard** = einsteigen (*ine*-shty-gun). **Get out** = aussteigen (*owsh*-shty-gun). **Window** = Fenster (*fen*-ster). **Door** = Tür (tooer). **Train** = Bahn (bon). **Train station** = Bahnhof (*bon*-hofe). **Main train station** = Hauptbahnhof (*howpt*-bon-hofe). **Track** = Gleis (glice). **Train car** = Wagen (*vog*-gin). **Restaurant car** = Speisewagen (*shpeye*-suh-vog-gin). **Airplane** = Flugmaschine (*floog*-ma-sheen-uh). **Airport** = Flughafen (*floog*-hof-fen). **Streetcar** = Strassenbahn (*shtraw*-sen-bon). **Bus** = Bus (boose) or Autobus (*ow*-to-boos). **Car** = Auto (*ought*-toe) or Wagen (*vog*-gen).

Warning Signs

This extra section alerts you to words and phrases that you may hear or read while traveling.

Achtung! = Attention! **Vorsicht!** = Careful! **Vorsicht Stufe!** = Careful, stairs! **Vorsicht frisch gebohnert!** = Careful, freshly waxed floor! **Nicht hinauslehnen!** = Don't lean out! **Bitte nichts behühren!** = Please don't touch! **Nicht gestattet!** = Not allowed! **Nicht hinauslehnen!** = Don't lean against! **Nicht aus dem Gras betreten!** = Don't walk on the grass!

Chapter 22

Ten of the Best German Hotels

- -

In This Chapter

▶ Discovering Germany's finest hotels

▶ Finding extra-special comfort and personal service

▶ Combining atmospheric ambience with delectable dining

- -

*E*very hotel I recommend in this guidebook is a good one, and you can stay at any one of them in comfort. However, for those who want to stay at Germany's *finest* hotels, I compiled a list of my favorites in this chapter. Each one of these places offers something extra in terms of service, comfort, and aesthetic. At these hotels you find the highest standards of German hotel-keeping — and those standards are very high indeed.

Der Europäische Hof-Hotel Europa, Heidelberg

The impeccable, family-run Der Europäische Hof-Hotel Europa ($$$$; ☎ 800/223-4541 in the U.S. and Canada, or 06221/5150; Internet: www. europaeischerhof.com) is the best hotel in Heidelberg and the only five-star hotel in the Rhine-Neckar region. Built in 1865 and carefully expanded over the decades, the property has a kind of glamorous elegance that few hotels can match. The large, traditionally furnished rooms have luxuriously appointed bathrooms. The new pool and sauna area is beautifully designed. The hotel's restaurant, **Die Kurfürstenstube,** is the top gourmet restaurant in Heidelberg. Those in charge have thoughtfully taken care of every detail in this service-oriented hotel. See Chapter 19 for a map showing the hotel's location.

Der Kleine Prinz, Baden-Baden

In 2002, the readers of *Condé Nast Traveler* voted the family-owned and -operated Der Kleine Prinz ($$–$$$$; ☎ 07221/346-600; Internet: www. derkleineprinz.de) the best hotel in Germany. Named for the children's book character created by Antoine de Saint-Exupery, Der Kleine

Prinz (The Little Prince) resides in two turn-of-the-century mansions. Each of the large, high-ceilinged rooms is furnished differently, with hand-chosen furniture and accessories. Der Kleine Prinz is one of only two hotels in Baden-Baden to have air conditioning. Personalized service is the hotel's strong point. The rates include a superlative breakfast buffet and afternoon high tea. Free Internet use is another amenity. The owners recently opened their second property, the **Hotel Belle Epoque** ($$$–$$$$; ☎ **07221/300-660;** Internet: www.hotel-belle-epoque. de), just a block away. The same impeccably high standards prevail in this small, sumptuous hotel created from a villa built in 1870. See Chapter 16 for a map showing the hotels' locations.

Excelsior Hotel Ernst, Cologne

Walk out of the train station in Cologne and you stare up, mesmerized, at the enormous cathedral, one of the architectural wonders of Europe. You can see the cathedral from some of the rooms in the grand Excelsior Hotel Ernst ($$$$; ☎ **0221/2701;** Internet: www.excelsior hotelernst.de), founded in 1863. The exterior looks a bit unassuming, but the lobby and public areas are gleaming and elegant with marble floors and beautiful finishes. Guest rooms are spacious and beautifully appointed, with very large and fully equipped bathrooms. The hotel's fitness center has a whirlpool and steam room, and guests have access to a business center with computers and high-speed Internet service. The **Hanse Stube** restaurant is one of Cologne's top gourmet restaurants. Hotel Excelsior Ernst really stands out for its incredibly friendly and helpful staff. They make you feel most welcome, without a hint of snobbery. See Chapter 17 for a map with the hotel's location.

Hotel Brandenburger Hof, Berlin

The beautifully appointed, 86-room Hotel Brandenburger Hof ($$$$; ☎ **030/214-050;** Internet: www.brandenburger-hof.com) offers superior service, an on-site spa, and one of the top restaurants in Berlin. Centrally located in western Berlin, the hotel is close to the Ku-Damm and the main train station, Bahnhof Zoologischer Garten. Guest rooms in this turn-of-the-century building are unusually large for Berlin and furnished in an elegant Bauhaus style. Bathrooms have wood and granite finishes. You can enjoy the sumptuous breakfast buffet, included in the price of the room, in a glass-walled conservatory built around a Japanese garden. The hotel's gourmet restaurant, **Die Quadriga** (named for the four-horse chariot atop the Brandenburg Gate), earned a Michelin star. See Chapter 11 for a map showing the hotel's location.

Hotel Reutemann/Hotel Seegarten, Lindau

One of the nicest places to stay on the Bodensee is the upscale lake-side Hotel Reutemann/Hotel Seegarten ($–$$$; ☎ 08382/9150; Internet: www.bayerischerhof-lindau.de), two connected buildings with 64 rooms between them, located right on the harbor promenade. The Reutemann has large rooms and bathrooms with showers and big tubs. The Seegarten has flower-filled balconies and spacious rooms, some with lake views The decor is modern in both. Even more luxurious is the adjacent **Hotel Bayerischer Hof**, part of the same management. All three buildings share a lakefront garden with sunbathing areas, outdoor pool, fitness center, and sauna. The room rate includes a lovely breakfast buffet. Children under 10 stay free and babysitting can be arranged. You can drive to these hotels and park in the underground garage. See Chapter 16 for a map with the hotels' location.

Kempinski Hotel Atlantic Hamburg

Movie stars, politicians, and royalty stay at Kempinski Hotel Atlantic Hamburg ($$$$; ☎ 800/426-3135; Internet: www.kempinski.atlantic.de) — with good reason because the hotel is the finest in northern Germany. Situated across from the Alster lake, this hotel was one of the few buildings to escape wartime destruction. Age is a real asset for this grande dame because hotels nowadays simply don't have rooms (or hallways) as generously proportioned as the ones here, with high ceilings and spacious bathrooms. Everything is posh but comfortable. Amenities include an on-site pool and sauna and beautiful public spaces. You can even make a grand entrance down the staircase into the lobby. See Chapter 20 for a map with the hotel's location.

Kempinski Hotel Vier Jahreszeiten München

Along chic Maximilianstrasse, tucked beneath a porte cochere, you find the entrance of the grand Kempinski Hotel Vier Jahreszeiten München ($$$$; ☎ 800/426-3135 in the U.S. or 089/21250; Internet: www.kempinski.com). Founded in 1858, the Vier Jahreszeiten (Four Seasons) exudes a subdued, old-fashioned self-assurance in keeping with its history as the hotel of choice for royalty and celebs. The large rooms are richly appointed and technologically up-to-date. Bathrooms are roomy. Amenities include an on-site health club with pool. The hotel is just a few minutes' walk from the Residenz and the National Theater. See Chapter 14 for a map with the hotel's location.

Le Meridien Grand Hotel Nürnberg

At one time, you could find hotels like Le Meridien Grand Hotel Nürnberg ($$$–$$$$; ☎ 800/543-4300 in the U.S. or 0911/23220; Internet: www.grand-hotel.de) all over Europe. They were always the largest and most glamorous places to stay. Built before World War I, this grand hotel escaped destruction in World War II and consequently still retains much of its unique Art Nouveau atmosphere and detailing. Le Meridien recently acquired the hotel and has spruced up the property even more. The guest rooms, the largest in Nuremberg (some with an entrance vestibule), have roomy, marble-clad bathrooms. See Chapter 19 for a map showing this hotel's location.

Sorat Art'otel Berlin

So-called Art hotels are springing up all over Germany, but the Sorat Art'otel Berlin ($$–$$$$; ☎ 030/884-470; Internet: www.sorat-otels.com) was the first and deserves special mention for that reason. Designed by artist Wolf Vostell, the Sorat features a modern European design aesthetic in its public spaces, art installations set into the corridors, and original artwork in all 133 rooms. The rooms aren't particularly large, but they're all comfortable and well designed. The filling breakfast buffet, included in the room rate, is served in a large, light-filled room with contemporary furniture. The convenient location is close to the Ku-Damm. See Chapter 11 for a map that includes the hotel.

Zum Roten Bären, Freiburg

Zum Roten Bären ($–$$; ☎ 0761/387-870; Internet: www.roten-baeren.de), which means "At the Red Bear," is the oldest inn in Germany, with a pretty painted facade and a list of innkeepers that goes back to the 14th century. Zum Roten Bären is not a luxury hotel but rather a wonderfully atmospheric and unpretentious inn with only 25 rooms. Rooms in the older section have more charm; those in the modern wing have little balconies overlooking leafy gardens and red-tiled rooftops. The hotel restaurant is the best in Freiburg for traditional Black Forest fare and regional wines from the nearby Kaiserstühl vineyards. Standing just outside the hotel is one of Freiburg's medieval gateways, and the surrounding neighborhood is wonderfully picturesque. See Chapter 16 for a map showing the hotel's location.

Chapter 23

Ten Great German Museums

Germany is full of museums — more museums on every subject, in fact, than you could ever hope to visit. In this chapter, I assemble a list of my top recommendations. You often need to know German to enjoy the text-heavy exhibits in many German museums, but displays in these places let you enjoy art and objects without language barriers. You find addresses, opening times, and admission prices in the cited chapters.

I also include two museums in Stuttgart, a city that I don't cover in this book because of space restrictions. Stuttgart, a famous car-manufacturing center, is the cultural capital of Baden-Württemberg in southwest Germany and contains several fine museums. The city is an easy day trip from Heidelberg (see Chapter 19).

Albertinum, Dresden

Over the centuries, German rulers accrued vast collections of art treasures. Today these collections form the basis of museums throughout Germany. One of the greatest is the Albertinum in Dresden, which holds the dazzling cache assembled by Albert, a Saxon king, between 1884 and 1887. The legendary **Grünes Gewölbe** (Green Vaults), named for the wall color, contain 18th-century treasures, including rococo chests, ivory carvings, gold jewelry, bronze statuettes, intricately designed mirrors, and priceless porcelain. The **Gemäldegalerie Neue Meister** (New Masters Gallery), which takes up two floors of the Albertinum, concentrates on works by German artists, starting with the great 19th-century Romantic artist Caspar David Friedrich, and going up to the brilliant Expressionist works of Dresden-born Otto Dix (1891–1969). See Chapter 13.

Alte Pinakothek, Munich

Masterpieces by the greatest European artists of the 14th through the 18th centuries are on display in this magnificent museum. The paintings were collected over the centuries by Bavaria's ruling family, the Wittelsbachs, and first put on public display in 1836. You can see works by famous 15th-century Flemish and German artists Rogier van der Weyden, Hans Memling, Lucas Cranach the Elder, and the Brueghel family. Seek out the self-portrait by Germany's greatest artist of the Renaissance, Albrecht Dürer, who lived and worked in Nuremberg. Dürer was the first artist to paint a self-portrait; he did three, and this museum has one of the most striking, painted when Dürer was 28 years old. Works by the 15th- and 16th-century Italian painters Botticelli, Raphael, and Leonardo da Vinci hang in the galleries, and you can see more Rubens than in any other museum in Europe. See Chapter 14.

Deutsches Museum, Munich

You won't find any paintings or porcelain in this massive museum of science and technology. You can see the first electric locomotive (1879), the first electric dynamo (1866), the first automobile (1886), the first diesel engine (1897), and the laboratory bench at which the atom was first split (1938). The Automobile department contains a shining collection of luxury Daimlers, Opels, and Bugattis. The Aeronautics section displays a biplane flown by the Wright brothers in 1908 and the first airliner (1919). See Chapter 14.

Gemäldegalerie, Berlin

Berlin's famous painting gallery moved to this new building in 1998. Inside, you encounter one of Germany's greatest collections of European painting, including outstanding examples of medieval German and Dutch art and Italian masterpieces by Raphael, Bronzino, Veronese, Titian, Tintoretto, and Giorgione. The collection of 17th-century Dutch painting includes one of the largest collections of Rembrandts. See Chapter 12.

Germanisches Nationalmuseum, Nuremberg

The collections in this enormous museum present an extraordinary compendium of German art and culture through the centuries. The painting section showcases works by the great Renaissance painter Albrecht Dürer, who lived and worked in Nuremberg, and Hans Holbein, whose painting of Martin Luther is one of the highlights of the collection. The sculpture collection contains superlative pieces by Veit Stoss and Tilman Riemenschneider, artists known for their expressive realism. The world's oldest surviving globe, created in 1493, is on display. The collection of musical instruments is amazing — but so is almost everything in this varied and wide-ranging museum. Domestic furnishings, folk objects, clothes, interiors, and dollhouses document everyday life in Germany through the ages. See Chapter 19.

Jüdisches Museum, Berlin

American architect Daniel Libeskind designed the Jewish Museum, Berlin's newest and most talked about museum. The building is a piece of architectural art as important as the museum's collections. Inside, Libeskind created "psychological spaces" which evoke an uneasy sense of imbalance, imprisonment, and loss as you walk through them. The collections celebrate all aspects of Jewish life in Germany throughout the centuries, following a chronological pathway that is periodically interrupted by the powerful memorial spaces. See Chapter 12.

Mercedes-Benz-Museum, Stuttgart

This highly enjoyable museum, a must for anyone who has an interest in cars, vintage or otherwise, honors the invention of the motorcar by Carl Benz and Gottlieb Daimler. On display in chronological order are nearly 75 historical vehicles, including the first motorcycle (built in 1885) and the first Mercedes (1902). The vehicles from the 1930s are especially splendid. The racecars date from 1899 onwards, and include the Blitzen-Benz, the Silver Arrow, the Sauber Mercedes, and the 300 SL Gullwing. (The museum glosses over the war years, during which Mercedes-Benz built tanks and trucks for the Third Reich.) Give yourself at least 90 minutes. A free, English audio guide is available.

Mercedesstrasse 137, Stuttgart-Cannstatt. ☎ 0711/172-2578. S-Bahn: line 1 to Gottlieb-Daimler-Stadion, then follow signs to DaimlerChrysler, Werk (Plant) Untertürkheim Tor (Gate) 1 (about a 10-minute walk); from there, a free shuttle bus takes you to the museum. Admission: Free. Open: Tues–Sun 9 a.m.–5 p.m.

Pergamon Museum, Berlin

This giant old museum is the best reason to visit Museum Island in eastern Berlin. Created in 1930, the museum looks rather cold and forbidding, but an amazing collection of ancient Greek, Roman, and Babylonian buildings fills the space. What everyone goes to this museum to see is the Pergamon Altar, part of the enormous Temple of Zeus and Athena excavated in Pergamon, Turkey, and brought to Berlin in the 19th century. The temple, dating from 180 to 160 B.C., was considered one of the wonders of the ancient world. Other major architectural treasures include the two-storied Market Gate of Miletus, a Roman building facade from around A.D. 165; the Processional Way of Babylon with the Ishtar Gate, dating from 580 B.C.; and the throne room of Nebuchadnezzar. See Chapter 12.

Staatsgalerie, Stuttgart

Stuttgart's finest art museum exhibits works spanning some 550 years. Highlights among the oldest works include Giovanni Bellini's *The Mourning of Christ,* Hans Memlings's *Bathsheba at her Bath,* and Rembrandt's *St. Paul in Prison.* The **Neues Staatgalerie** (New State Gallery), designed by the British architect James Stirling and completed in 1984, is an icon of postmodern architecture. Here you find the 19th- and 20th-century collection, with works by the German Expressionists Ernst Kirchner, Ernst Barlach, and Max Beckmann, as well as representatives of the Bauhaus school and Blue Rider group, such as Paul Klee and Lyonel Feininger. You also find famous examples of European art from the late-19th and early-20th centuries, including works by Modigliani, Picasso, and Monet. Art lovers will want to spend a couple of hours here.

Konrad-Adenauer-Strasse 30–32. ☎ **0711/212-4050.** U-Bahn: Staatsgalerie. Admission: €4.50 for adults, free for children 13 and under; free on Wed. Open: Tues–Sun 10 a.m.–6 p.m. (Thurs until 9 p.m.).

Zwinger, Dresden

The Zwinger is a magnificent baroque palace housing a stunning collection of museums, the most important being the **Gemäldegalerie Alte Meister** (Old Masters Gallery), one of the best galleries of European painting in the world. You can see Raphael's famous *Sistine Madonna* and my personal favorite, Giorgione's *Sleeping Venus.* But take your pick: Well-known works by Titian, Correggio, Vermeer, Dürer, Rubens, and Rembrandt adorn the walls. Noteworthy too are a series of detailed townscapes of Dresden painted in the mid-18th century, so true-to-life that they were used as reference works during the post–World War II reconstruction of the city. Other museums in the Zwinger include the **Porzellansammlung** (Porcelain Collection), with Japanese, Chinese, and Meissen porcelain from the 18th and 19th centuries, and the intriguing **Mathematische-Physikalischer Salon** (Salon of Mathematics and Physics), which displays clocks and scientific instruments of the 16th to 19th centuries. See Chapter 13.

Appendix

Quick Concierge

● ●

American Express

You find American Express offices through-out Germany, including in Berlin, Bremen, Cologne, Dresden, Frankfurt am Main, Hamburg, Heidelberg, Leipzig, Munich, Nuremberg, and Stuttgart. Access addresses for American Express offices in Germany at www.americanexpress.com.

ATMs

In German cities, you can easily find 24-hour ATMs in airports, train stations, and outside banks. You can get cash 24 hours a day using your bank card or an international credit card. *Cirrus* (☎ 800/424-7787; Internet: www.mastercard.com) and *Plus* (☎ 800/843-7587; Internet: www.visa.com/atms) are the most popular networks; check the back of your ATM card to see which network your bank belongs to. The networks' toll-free numbers and Web sites give you locations of ATMs where you can withdraw money in Germany.

Business Hours

Most banks are open Monday through Friday from 8:30 a.m. to 1 p.m. and 2:30 to 4 p.m. (to 5:30 p.m. on Thursday). Money exchanges at airports and border-crossing points are generally open daily from 6 a.m. to 10 p.m. Exchanges at border railroad stations stay open for arrivals of all international trains.

Most businesses are open Monday through Friday from 9 a.m. to 5 p.m. and on Saturday from 9 a.m. to 1 p.m. Store hours can vary from town to town, but shops are generally open Monday through Friday from 9 or 10 a.m. to 6 or 6:30 p.m. (to 8:30 p.m. on Thursday). Saturday hours are generally from 9 a.m. to 1 or 2 p.m., except on the first Saturday of the month, when stores may remain open until 4 p.m. Bakeries and florist shops are sometimes open on Sunday mornings. On the four Saturdays prior to Christmas, shops throughout Germany are open until 6 p.m.

Credit Cards

You can use American Express, Diners Club, MasterCard, and Visa throughout Germany. Smaller pensions (B&Bs) and restaurants may not accept credit cards. If your credit card is lost or stolen, you can call the following numbers in Germany: American Express ☎ 954/503-8850 (collect); Diners Club ☎ 702/797-5532 (collect); MasterCard ☎ 0800/819-1040 (toll-free); Visa ☎ 0800/811-8440 (toll-free) or 417/581-9994 (collect).

Currency Exchange

You find currency exchanges, called *bureaux de change* or *Geldwechsel,* in airports, railway stations, post offices, and many banks. Currency exchange is discussed in Chapter 9.

Customs

Entering Germany: You can bring in gifts duty-free up to a total value of €175. The following items are permitted into Germany duty-free from non-EU (European Union) countries: 200 cigarettes; 1 liter of liquor above 44 proof, or 2 liters of liquor less than 44 proof, or 2 liters of wine; 50 grams of perfume and 0.25 liters of eau de cologne; 500 grams of coffee; and 100 grams of tea.

Returning to Australia: The duty-free allowance in Australia is A$400 or, for those under 18, A$200. Citizens can bring in 250 cigarettes or 250 grams of loose tobacco, and 1.125 liters of alcohol. For more information, contact Australian Customs Services, GPO Box 8, Sydney NSW 2001 (☎ 02/6275-6666 in Australia), or go to www.customs.gov.au.

Returning to Canada: For a clear summary of Canadian rules, write for the booklet "I Declare," issued by the Canada Customs and Revenue Agency (☎ 800/461-9999 in Canada; Internet: www.ccra-adrc.gc.ca). Canada allows its citizens a C$750 duty-free exemption, which includes 200 cigarettes, 2.2 pounds of tobacco, 1.5 liters of liquor, and 50 cigars. In addition, you can mail gifts to Canada from abroad at the rate of C$60 a day, provided that gifts are unsolicited and don't contain alcohol or tobacco (write on the package "Unsolicited gift, under $60 value"). *Note:* The C$750 exemption can only be used once a year and only after an absence of seven days.

Returning to New Zealand: The duty-free allowance for New Zealand is NZ$700. Citizens over 17 can bring in 200 cigarettes, or 50 cigars, or 250 grams of tobacco (or a mixture of all three if their combined weight doesn't exceed 250 grams) plus 4.5 liters of wine and beer, or 1.125 liters of liquor. Most questions are answered in a free pamphlet, available at New Zealand consulates and Customs offices, called "New Zealand Customs Guide for Travellers, Notice no. 4." For more information, contact New Zealand Customs, 50 Anzac Ave., P.O. Box 29, Auckland (☎ 09/359-6655; Internet: www.customs.govt.nz).

Returning to the United Kingdom and Ireland: Citizens of the United Kingdom and Ireland who are returning from a European Union (EU) country go through a separate Customs exit (called the "Blue Exit") especially for EU travelers. In essence, there is no limit on what you can bring back from an EU country, as long as the items are for personal use (this includes gifts), and you have already paid the necessary duty and tax. However, customs law sets out guidance levels of 3,200 cigarettes, 200 cigars, 3 kilogram smoking tobacco, 10 liters of spirits, 90 liters of wine (of this not more than 60 liters can be sparkling wine), and 110 liters of beer. If you bring in more than these levels, you may be asked to prove that the goods are for your own use. For more information, contact HM Customs & Excise, Passenger Enquiry Point, 2nd Floor Wayfarer House, Great South West Road, Feltham, Middlesex, TW14 8NP (☎ 0181/910-3744: Internet: www.open.gov.uk).

Returning to the United States: Returning U.S. citizens can bring back $800 worth of merchandise duty-free. A flat rate of 10% duty is levied on the next $1,000 worth of purchases. You cannot bring fresh foodstuffs into the United States, only tinned foods and packaged foods. You can mail gifts back to people in the United States duty-free if the value of the entire gift package does not exceed $200. For more information, contact the U.S. Customs Service, 1300 Pennsylvania Ave., NW, Washington, DC 20229 (☎ 877/287-8867), and request the free pamphlet "Know Before You Go," also available on the Web at www.customs.ustreas.gov.

Drugstores

Pharmaceuticals are sold at a pharmacy, called an *Apotheke.* For cosmetics, go to a *Drogerie.* German pharmacies are open regular business hours. They take turns staying open nights, on Sunday, and on holidays, and each *Apotheke* posts a list of those that are open off-hours.

Electricity

The electricity is 230 volts (50 Hz). For any U.S. appliances, you need a transformer and a plug with two round prongs for German sockets.

Embassies

All embassies and consulates are located in Berlin, Germany's capital.

Australia: The embassy is at Friedrich-strasse 200 (☎ 030/880-0880; U-Bahn: Uhlandstrasse), open Monday through Friday from 9 a.m. to noon.

Canada: The embassy is at Friedrichstrasse 95 (☎ 030/203-120; U-Bahn: Friedrich-strasse), open Monday through Friday from 9 a.m. to noon.

Ireland: The embassy is at Friedrichstrasse 200 (☎ 030/220-720; U-Bahn: Uhlandstrasse), open Monday through Friday from 9:30 a.m. to noon and 2:30 to 3:45 p.m.

New Zealand: The embassy is at Friedrich-strasse 60 (☎ 030/206-210; U-Bahn: Friedrichstrasse), open Monday through Friday from 9 a.m. to 1 p.m. and 2 to 5:30 p.m.

South Africa: The embassy is at Friedrich-strasse 60 (☎ 030/220-730; U-Bahn: Friedrichstrasse), open Monday through Friday from 9 a.m. to noon.

United Kingdom: The embassy is at Under den Linden 32–34 (☎ 030/201-840; U-Bahn: Under den Linden), open Monday through Friday from 9 a.m. to 4 p.m.

United States: The embassy is at Clayallee 170 (☎ 030/832-9233; U-Bahn: Dahlem-Dorf), open Monday through Friday from 8:30 a.m. to noon.

Emergencies

Throughout Germany the emergency number for police is ☎ **110;** for fire or to call an ambulance, dial ☎ **112.**

Holidays

See Chapter 2 for a list of public holidays in Germany.

Information

See "Where to Get More Information," later in this Appendix, to find out where to get visitor information before you leave home.

Internet Access and Cybercafes

You find cybercafes in all of the larger cities in Germany; for locations, ask at the local tourist office or your hotel.

Liquor Laws

Officially, you must be 18 to consume any kind of alcoholic beverage in Germany. Bars and cafes may request proof of age. Local authorities treat drinking while driving as a very serious offense.

Medical Assistance

Most major hotels have a physician on staff or on call. If you can't get hold of a doctor and the situation is life-threatening, dial the emergency service, ☎ **112,** which is open day and night. Medical and hospital services aren't free, so be sure that you have appropriate insurance coverage before you travel. See Chapter 9 for more information on general medical matters in Germany.

Newspapers/Magazines

In Germany, you find daily editions of the *International Herald Tribune* and an international edition of *USA Today.* Many newstands carry *Time* magazine.

Police

The German word for police is Polizei (po-lit-*sigh*). Throughout the country, dial ☎ **110** for emergencies.

Post Offices

The words *Deutsche Post* identify a post office. Post offices are open from 8 a.m. to 6 p.m. Monday through Friday, 8 a.m. to noon on Saturday. In larger cities, the post office in the main train station may be open longer hours. Street mailboxes are yellow. To find international rates and services from Germany, check out the Web site for Deutsche Post, www.deutschepost.de.

Restrooms

Use the word *Toilette* (twah-*leh*-teh). Women's toilets are usually marked with an "F" for *Frauen,* and men's toilets with an "H" for *Herren.* Toilets in train stations sometimes require a €.20 coin to enter. Many toilets have attendants who expect a small tip (never more than €.50); the attendant in a men's toilet may be female.

Safety

Germany is generally a safe country in which to travel, with the usual caveats to use common sense and be aware of your surroundings. At night, avoid areas around the large railway stations in Frankfurt, Munich, Berlin, and Hamburg.

Taxes

Germany imposes a *Mehrwertsteuer,* or value-added tax (VAT), of 16 percent on most goods and services. The prices of restaurants and hotels include VAT. Stores that display a "Tax Free Shopping" sticker can issue you a Global Refund Cheque at the time of purchase. See Chapter 9 for details on how to obtain your refund.

Telephone

The country code for Germany is **49.** To call Germany from the U.S., dial the international access code 011, then 49, then the city code, then the regular phone number, which may have from 4 to 9 digits. *The phone numbers listed in this book are to be used within Germany; when calling from abroad, omit the initial 0 in the city code.*

Local and long-distance calls may be placed from post offices and coin-operated public telephone booths. The unit charge is €.15. Most phones in Germany now require a Telefonkarte (telephone card), available at post offices and newsstands in increments

of €5, €10, and €20. Telephone calls made through hotel switchboards cost significantly more than the regular charge at a pay phone or post office. To make an international call from a public phone, look for a phone marked "Inlands und Auslandsgespräche"; most have instructions in English.

To call the United States or Canada from Germany, dial 01, followed by the country code (1), then the area code, and then the number. Alternatively, you can dial the various telecommunication companies in the States for cheaper rates. From Germany, the access numbers are ☎ 0800/225-5288 for AT&T and ☎ 0800/888-8000 for MCI.

Time Zone

Germany operates on central European time (CET), which means that the country is six hours ahead of eastern standard time (EST) in the United States and one hour ahead of Greenwich mean time (GMT). Summer daylight saving time begins in April and ends in September — there's a slight difference in the dates from year to year — so there may be a period in early spring and in the fall when there's a seven-hour difference between EST and CET. Always check if you're traveling during these periods, especially if you need to catch a plane.

Tipping

If a restaurant bill says *Bedienung,* it means a service charge has already been added, so just round yours up to the nearest euro. If not, add 5 to 10 percent, depending on your satisfaction. Round up to the nearest euro for taxis. Bellhops get €1 per bag, as does the doorperson at a hotel, restaurant, or nightclub. Room cleaning staffs get small tips in Germany, as do concierges who perform special favors such as obtaining theater or opera tickets. Tip hairdressers or barbers 5 to 10 percent.

Water

Tap water is safe to drink in all German towns and cities, but bottled drinking water is a way of life. Restaurants do not freely offer water with your meal. You order *Sprudelwasser* (*shprew*-dil-vos-er; water with gas) or *Still* (shtill; noncarbonated water).

Weights and Measures

Germany uses the metric system. Heights are given in centimeters (cm) and meters (m), distances in kilometers (km), and weights in grams (g) or kilograms (kg). Temperature is measured in degrees Celsius (0°C = 32°F). To translate Celsius into Fahrenheit, multiply the number by 1.8 and add 32.

Toll-Free Numbers and Web Sites

Major airlines serving Germany

Aer Lingus
☎ 800/474-7424
☎ 01/886-8888 (Ireland)
www.aerlingus.com

American Airlines
☎ 800/443-7300
www.aa.com

British Airways
☎ 800/247-9297
☎ 0345/222-111 (U.K.)
www.british-airways.com

British Midland
☎ 0345/554-554 (U.K.)
www.flybmi.com

Continental Airlines
☎ 800/231-0856
www.continental.com

Delta Air Lines
☎ 800/241-4141
www.delta.com

Lufthansa
☎ 800/645-3880
www.lufthansa-usa.com

Northwest Airlines
☎ 800/225-2525
www.nwa.com

Qantas
☎ 800/227-4500
☎ 008/112-121 (Australia)
www.qantas.com

United Airlines
☎ 800/538-2929
www.united.com

Major car-rental agencies operating in Germany

Alamo
☎ 800/462-5266
☎ 0800/272-200 (U.K)
www.alamo.com

Auto Europe
☎ 800/223-5555
☎ 207/842-2222 (Australia)
☎ 0800/169-6417 (U.K.)
www.autoeurope.com

Avis
☎ 800/331-1212
☎ 136-333 (Australia)
☎ 0870/606-0100 (U.K.)
www.avis.com

Budget
☎ 800/527-0700
☎ 800/472-3325 (Europe)
www.budget.com

Hertz
☎ 800/654-3001
☎ 800/263-0600 (Canada)
☎ 01805/333-535 (Germany)
www.hertz.com

National
☎ 800/CAR-RENT
☎ 800/227-3876 (Europe and Australia)
☎ 0990/565-656 (U.K.)
www.nationalcar.com

Rail Europe
☎ 888/382-RAIL
☎ 800/361-RAIL (Canada)
www.raileurope.com

Major hotel chains in Germany

Best Western Hotels
☎ 800-WESTERN (ask for "International")
www.bestwestern.com

Hilton International
☎ 800/HILTONS
www.hilton.com

Hyatt
☎ 800/233-1234
www.hyatt.com

Inter-Continental Hotels & Resorts
☎ 800/327-0200
www.intercontinental.com

Kempinski Hotels & Resorts
☎ 800/426-3135
www.kempinski.com

Le Meridien Hotels & Resorts
☎ 800/225-5843
www.meridien.com

Radisson SAS Hotels & Resorts
☎ 800/333-3333
www.radissonsas.com

Sheraton
☎ 800/325-3535
www.sheraton.com

Steigenberger Hotels & Resorts
☎ 800/223-5652
www.steigenberger.de

Where to Get More Information

For more information on Germany, you can call or visit the following German National Tourist Board offices:

✔ **In Germany:** The **German National Tourist Board** headquarters is at Beethovenstrasse 69, 60325 Frankfurt am Main (☎ **069/2123-8800**). The general Web site is www.germany-tourism.de.

✔ **In Australia:** C/o German-Australian Chamber of Industry and Commerce, P.O. Box A980, Sydney South NSW 1235 (☎ **02/9267-8148;** Fax: 02/9267-9035).

✔ **In Canada:** 175 Bloor St. E., Suite 604, Toronto, ON M4W 3R8 (☎ **877/315-6237** or 416/968-1570; Fax: 416/968-1986).

✔ **In South Africa:** C/o Lufthansa German Airlines, P.O. Box 10883, Johannesburg 2000, South Africa (☎ **011/646-1615;** Fax: 011/484-2750).

✔ **In the United Kingdom:** P.O. Box 2695, London W1A 3TN (☎ **020/7317-0908;** Fax: 020/7495-6129).

✔ **In the United States:** 122 E. 42nd St., 52nd Floor, New York, NY 10168-0072 (☎ **212/661-7200;** Fax: 212/661-7174); 401 North Michigan Avenue, Suite 2525, Chicago, IL 60611-4212 (☎ **312/644-0723;** Fax: 312/644-0724); and P.O. Box 641009, Los Angeles, CA 90064 (☎ **310/234-0250;** Fax: 310/474-1604).

Contacting regional tourist boards

For specific information on a particular region, contact regional tourist boards or check their Web sites. *Note:* The Web sites of some regional offices may be in German only.

Northern Germany

✔ Hamburg: **Tourismus Zentrale Hamburg,** Steinstrasse 7, 20095 Hamburg (☎ **040/3005-1300;** Internet: www.hamburg-tourism.de).

✔ Schleswig-Holstein: **Tourismusverband Schleswig-Holstein,** Niemannsweg 31, 24105 Kiel (☎ **0431/56000;** Internet: www.sht.de).

Eastern Germany

✔ Brandenburg: **MB Tourismus Marketing Brandenburg,** Am Neuen Markt 1, 14476 Potsdam (☎ **0331/200-4747;** Internet: www.reiseland-brandenburg.de).

✔ Thuringia: **Service Center Thüringen Tourismus,** Weimarische Strasse 45, 99099 Erfurt (☎ **0361/37420;** Internet: www.thueringen-tourismus.de).

✔ Saxony: **Tourismus Marketing Gesellschaft Sachsen,** Bautzner Strasse 45–47, 01067 Dresden (☎ **0351/491-700;** Internet: www.sachsen-tour.de).

Southern Germany

✔ Bavaria: **Bayern Tourismus Marketing,** Leopoldstrasse 146, 80804 München (☎ **089/212-3970;** Internet: www.btl.de).

✔ Bodensee (Lake Constance): **Internationale Bodensee-Tourismus,** Insel Mainau, 78465 Konstanz (☎ **07531/90940;** Internet: www.bodensee-tourismus.de).

Western and central Germany

✔ Baden-Württemberg: **Tourismus-Marketing Baden-Württemberg,** Esslinger Strasse 8, 70182 Stuttgart (☎ **0711/238-580;** Internet: www.tourismus-baden-wuerttemberg.de).

✔ North Rhine-Westphalia: **Tourismusverband Nordrhein-Westfalen,** Emil-Hoffman-Strasse 1a, 50996 Köln (☎ **02236/967-255;** Internet: www.tourismusverband.nrw.de).

✔ Rhineland-Palatinate: **Rheinland-Pfalz Tourismus,** Löhrstrasse 103–105, 56068 Koblenz (☎ **0261/915-200;** Internet: www.rlp-info.de).

Surfing the Net

Throughout this guide, I mention various Web sites. In this section, I point you toward the best of them.

Tourist info on all of Germany

For general information on all of Germany, try these sites for starters:

✔ www.germany-tourism.de: The Web page for the German National Tourist Board in Germany offers useful information on all aspects of German life, travel, and culture.

✔ www.visits-to-germany.com: This is another useful version of the German National Tourist Board's general Web site.

✔ www.yahoo.com: Type in "Germany" and Yahoo's search engine will call up their Germany Destination Guide with the latest news, a photo gallery, and special offers.

General info on specific cities

The following tourist information center Web sites provide directories of hotels, restaurants, attractions, and events in specific cities through-out Germany (not all sites have information in English):

✔ **Aachen:** www.aachen-tourist.de

✔ **Baden-Baden:** www.baden-baden.com

✔ **Berlin:** www.berlin.de

- ✔ **Bremen:** www.bremen-tourism.de
- ✔ **Cologne:** www.koeln.de
- ✔ **Dresden:** www.dresden.de
- ✔ **Frankfurt:** www.frankfurt-tourismus.de
- ✔ **Freiburg im Breisgau:** www.freiburg.de
- ✔ **Füssen:** www.fuessen.de
- ✔ **Garmisch-Partenkirchen:** www.garmisch-partenkirchen.de
- ✔ **Hamburg:** www.hamburg-tourism.de
- ✔ **Heidelberg:** www.cvb-heidelberg.de
- ✔ **Leipzig:** www.leipzig.de
- ✔ **Lindau:** www.lindau-tourismus.de
- ✔ **Lübeck:** www.luebeck-tourismus.de
- ✔ **Munich:** www.munich.de
- ✔ **Nuremberg:** www.nuernberg.de
- ✔ **Rothenburg ob der Tauber:** www.rothenburg.de
- ✔ **Stuttgart:** www.stuttgart-tourist.de
- ✔ **Weimar:** www.weimar.de
- ✔ **Wittenberg:** www.wittenberg.de

Making Dollars and Sense of It

Expense	Daily cost	x	Number of days	=	Total
Airfare					
Local transportation					
Car rental					
Lodging (with tax)					
Parking					
Breakfast					
Lunch					
Dinner					
Snacks					
Entertainment					
Babysitting					
Attractions					
Gifts & souvenirs					
Tips					
Other					
Grand Total					

Fare Game: Choosing an Airline

When looking for the best airfare, you should cover all your bases — 1) consult a trusted travel agent; 2) contact the airline directly, via the airline's toll-free number and/or Web site; 3) check out one of the travel-planning Web sites, such as www.frommers.com.

Travel Agency_____ Phone_____
    Agent's Name_____ Quoted fare_____

Airline 1_____ Quoted fare_____
    Toll-free number/Internet_____

Airline 2_____ Quoted fare_____
    Toll-free number/Internet_____

Web site 1_____ Quoted fare_____

Web site 2_____ Quoted fare_____

Departure Schedule & Flight Information

Airline_____ Flight #_____ Confirmation #_____

Departs_____ Date_____ Time_____ a.m./p.m.

Arrives_____ Date_____ Time_____ a.m./p.m.

Connecting Flight (if any)

Amount of time between flights_____ hours/mins

Airline_____ Flight #_____ Confirmation #_____

Departs_____ Date_____ Time_____ a.m./p.m.

Arrives_____ Date_____ Time_____ a.m./p.m.

Return Trip Schedule & Flight Information

Airline_____ Flight #_____ Confirmation #_____

Departs_____ Date_____ Time_____ a.m./p.m.

Arrives_____ Date_____ Time_____ a.m./p.m.

Connecting Flight (if any)

Amount of time between flights_____ hours/mins

Airline_____ Flight #_____ Confirmation #_____

Departs_____ Date_____ Time_____ a.m./p.m.

Arrives_____ Date_____ Time_____ a.m./p.m.

Sweet Dreams: Choosing Your Hotel

Make a list of all the hotels where you'd like to stay and then check online and call the local and toll-free numbers to get the best price. You should also check with a travel agent, who may be able to get you a better rate.

Hotel & page	Location	Internet	Tel. (local)	Tel. (Toll-free)	Quoted rate

Hotel Checklist

Here's a checklist of things to inquire about when booking your room, depending on your needs and preferences.

- ❏ Smoking/smoke-free room
- ❏ Noise (if you prefer a quiet room, ask about proximity to elevator, bar/restaurant, pool, meeting facilities, renovations, and street)
- ❏ View
- ❏ Facilities for children (crib, roll-away cot, babysitting services)
- ❏ Facilities for travelers with disabilities
- ❏ Number and size of bed(s) (king, queen, double/full-size)
- ❏ Is breakfast included? (buffet, continental, or sit-down?)
- ❏ In-room amenities (hair dryer, iron/board, minibar, etc.)
- ❏ Other_____

Places to Go, People to See, Things to Do

Enter the attractions you would most like to see and decide how they'll fit into your schedule. Next, use the "Going My Way" worksheets that follow to sketch out your itinerary.

Attraction/activity	Page	Amount of time you expect to spend there	Best day and time to go

Going "My" Way

Day 1

Hotel_____ Tel._____

Morning_____

_____

Lunch_____ Tel._____

Afternoon_____

_____

Dinner_____ Tel._____

Evening_____

_____

Day 2

Hotel_____ Tel._____

Morning_____

_____

Lunch_____ Tel._____

Afternoon_____

_____

Dinner_____ Tel._____

Evening_____

_____

Day 3

Hotel_____ Tel._____

Morning_____

_____

Lunch_____ Tel._____

Afternoon_____

_____

Dinner_____ Tel._____

Evening_____

_____

Going "My" Way

Day 4

Hotel _____ Tel. _____

Morning _____

_____

Lunch _____ Tel. _____

Afternoon _____

_____

Dinner _____ Tel. _____

Evening _____

_____

Day 5

Hotel _____ Tel. _____

Morning _____

_____

Lunch _____ Tel. _____

Afternoon _____

_____

Dinner _____ Tel. _____

Evening _____

_____

Day 6

Hotel _____ Tel. _____

Morning _____

_____

Lunch _____ Tel. _____

Afternoon _____

_____

Dinner _____ Tel. _____

Evening _____

_____

Index

• B •

• *E* •

• O •

• *T* •

● *V* ●

Dedication

This book is dedicated to Henry Bair, who introduced me to Berlin and the rest of Germany.

Author's Acknowledgments

I would like to thank RailEurope and Richard Rheindorf and Sandra Tharas of the German National Tourist Office in New York for their assistance. Special thanks also go to Gary Larson, Stephen Brewer, Jerry Baab, and Lutz Otto in Berlin, Jörg Trobitius in Munich, and my editor, Lisa Torrance Duffy.

Publisher's Acknowledgments

We're proud of this book; please send us your comments through our Dummies online registration form located at www.dummies.com/register/.

Some of the people who helped bring this book to market include the following:

Editorial

Editors: Lisa Torrance Duffy, Senior Editor; Mary Goodwin, Project Editor

Cartographer: Elizabeth Puhl

Editorial Manager: Michelle Hacker

Editorial Assistant: Elizabeth Rea

Senior Photo Editor: Richard Fox

Front Cover Photo: Neuschwanstein Castle, Bavaria, © Doug Armand/ Getty Images

Back Cover Photo: Oktoberfest, Munich, © Ulli Seer/Getty Images

Cartoons: Rich Tennant, www.the5thwave.com

Production

Project Coordinator: Regina Snyder

Layout and Graphics: Carrie Foster, Joyce Haughey, LeAndra Johnson, Stephanie D. Jumper, Michael Kruzil, Kristin McMullan, Jacque Schneider, Julie Trippetti, Jeremey Unger

Proofreaders: Tyler Connoley, David Faust, Susan Moritz, Charles Spencer, TECHBOOKS Production Services

Indexer: TECHBOOKS Production Services

Publishing and Editorial for Consumer Dummies

Diane Graves Steele, Vice President and Publisher, Consumer Dummies

Joyce Pepple, Acquisitions Director, Consumer Dummies

Kristin A. Cocks, Product Development Director, Consumer Dummies

Michael Spring, Vice President and Publisher, Travel

Brice Gosnell, Publishing Director, Travel

Suzanne Jannetta, Editorial Director, Travel

Publishing for Technology Dummies

Andy Cummings, Vice President and Publisher, Dummies Technology/General User

Composition Services

Gerry Fahey, Vice President of Production Services

Debbie Stailey, Director of Composition Services

Contents at a Glance